MW01108199

The Student's Blackstone

You are holding a reproduction of an original work that is in the public domain in the United States of America, and possibly other countries.You may freely copy and distribute this work as no entity (individual or corporate) has a copyright on the body of the work.This book may contain prior copyright references, and library stamps (as most of these works were scanned from library copies).These have been scanned and retained as part of the historical artifact.

This book may have occasional imperfections such as missing or blurred pages, poor pictures, errant marks, etc. that were either part of the original artifact, or were introduced by the scanning process. We believe this work is culturally important, and despite the imperfections, have elected to bring it back into print as part of our continuing commitment to the preservation of printed works worldwide. We appreciate your understanding of the imperfections in the preservation process, and hope you enjoy this valuable book.

THE STUDENT'S BLACKSTONE.

COMMENTARIES

ON

THE LAWS OF ENGLAND.

In Four Books.

By SIR WILLIAM BLACKSTONE, Knt.,
ONE OF THE JUSTICES OF THE COURT OF COMMON PLEAS.

ABRIDGED

AND

ADAPTED TO THE PRESENT STATE OF THE LAW,

By ROBERT MALCOLM KERR, LL.D.
BARRISTER-AT-LAW.

LONDON:
JOHN MURRAY, ALBEMARLE STREET.
1865.

LONDON : PRINTED BY WILLIAM CLOWES AND SONS, STAMFORD STREET
AND CHARING CROSS.

PREFACE.

"THE STUDENT'S BLACKSTONE," as hitherto published, contained those portions only of the Commentaries which relate to the British Constitution and the Rights of Persons. It comprised the first volume of Sir William Blackstone's great work, and a few passages from the third and fourth volumes, inserted in order that the compilation might be complete in itself.

The present work is, as the title-page imports, an abridgment of the whole Commentaries of Blackstone, with such alterations as the legislative changes of the last century have made necessary. The reader ought, therefore, to find in the following pages an outline of the whole law of England, however concisely it may be stated. Of the success of the Editor in accomplishing his task, those for whose hands the book is intended will be best able to judge.

TEMPLE, *October*, 1865.

CONTENTS.

INTRODUCTION.

THE LAWS OF ENGLAND.

BOOK THE FIRST.—OF THE RIGHTS OF PERSONS.

Book the Third.—OF PRIVATE WRONGS.

CHAPTER I.

OF THE REDRESS OF PRIVATE WRONGS.

CHAPTER II.

OF THE PUBLIC COURTS OF COMMON LAW AND EQUITY.

CHAPTER III.

OF COURTS OF A SPECIAL JURISDICTION.

CHAPTER IV.

OF THE COGNIZANCE OF PRIVATE WRONGS.

CHAPTER V.

OF WRONGS, AND THEIR REMEDIES, RESPECTING THE RIGHTS OF PERSONS.

Injuries affecting personal security:—Injuries to life—Injuries affecting limbs or body; threats, assault, battery, &c.—Injuries affecting

CHAPTER VI.

OF INJURIES TO PERSONAL PROPERTY.

CHAPTER VII.

OF INJURIES TO REAL PROPERTY; AND, FIRST, OF DISPOSSESSION, OR OUSTER.

CHAPTER VIII.

OF INJURIES TO REAL PROPERTY.

CHAPTER IX.

ON INJURIES PROCEEDING FROM, OR AFFECTING THE CROWN.

CHAPTER X.

OF THE PURSUIT OF REMEDIES BY ACTION.

CHAPTER XVI.

OF EXECUTION.

PAGE

CHAPTER XVII.

OF THE JURISDICTION OF THE COURTS OF EQUITY.

CHAPTER XVIII.

OF THE PROCEEDINGS IN COURTS OF EQUITY.

BOOK THE FOURTH.—OF PUBLIC WRONGS.

CHAPTER I.

OF THE NATURE OF CRIMES; AND THEIR PUNISHMENT.

CHAPTER II.

OF THE PERSONS CAPABLE OF COMMITTING CRIMES.

CONTENTS.

CHAPTER XXVIII.

OF JUDGMENT AND ITS CONSEQUENCES.

CHAPTER XXIX.

ON REVERSAL OF JUDGMENT.

CHAPTER XXX.

OF EXECUTION.

APPENDIX.

INTRODUCTION.

SECTION I.

OF LAWS IN GENERAL.

Definition of law—Law of nature—Law of nations—Municipal law—Regular forms of government—The British Constitution—Duty of the supreme power to make laws—The several parts of every law.

LAW, in its general and comprehensive sense, signifies a rule of action; and is applied indiscriminately to all kinds of action, whether animate or inanimate, rational or irrational. Thus we say, the laws of motion, of gravitation, of optics, or mechanics, as well as the laws of nature and of nations. And it is that rule of action which is prescribed by some superior, and which the inferior is bound to obey.

This is the general signification of law; and in those creatures that have neither the power to think nor to will, such laws must be invariably obeyed, so long as the creature itself subsists, for its existence depends on that obedience. But laws, in their more confined sense, and in which it is our present business to consider them, denote the rules, not of action in general, but of *human* action or conduct; that is, the precepts by which man, the noblest of all sublunary beings, a creature endowed with both reason and free-will, is commanded to make use of those faculties in the general regulation of his behaviour.

Man, considered as a creature, must necessarily be subject to the laws of his Creator, for he is entirely a dependent being. A being, independent of any other, has no rule to pursue, but such as he prescribes to himself; but a state of dependence will inevitably oblige the inferior to take the will of him on whom he depends, as the rule of his conduct. And consequently, as man depends absolutely upon his Maker for everything, it is necessary that he should in all points conform to his Maker's will.

This will of his Maker is called the *law of nature*. For as God, when he created matter, and endued it with a principle of mobility, established certain laws for the perpetual direction of that motion;

B

so, when he created man, and endued him with free-will to conduct himself in all parts of life, he laid down certain rules, whereby that free-will is regulated and restrained, and gave him also the faculty of reason to discover the purport of those laws. These rules are the eternal, immutable laws of good and evil, to which the Creator himself in all his dispensations conforms; and which he has enabled human reason to discover, so far as they are necessary for the conduct of human actions. For he has so intimately connected, so inseparably interwoven, the laws of eternal justice with the happiness of each individual, that the latter cannot be obtained but by observing the former: and if the former be punctually obeyed, it cannot but induce the latter. This rule of obedience may thus be reduced to one paternal precept, "that man should pursue his own true and substantial happiness." This is the foundation of what we call ethics or natural law; which, being coeval with mankind, is superior in obligation to any other. It is binding over all the globe, in all countries, and at all times: no human laws are of any validity, if contrary to its precepts; and such of them as are valid derive all their force and all their authority, mediately or immediately, from this original.

If man were to live in a state of nature, unconnected with other individuals, there would be no occasion for any other rules than those prescribed by the law of nature. Neither could any other possibly exist: for a law always supposes some superior who is to make it; and in a state of nature we are all equal, without any superior but Him who is the author of our being. But man was formed for society; and is neither capable of living alone, nor indeed has the courage to do it. However, as it is impossible for the whole race of mankind to be united in one great society, they must necessarily divide into many; and form separate states, commonwealths, and nations, entirely independent of each other, and yet liable to a mutual intercourse. Hence arises a second kind of law to regulate this mutual intercourse, called the *law of nations;* which, as none of these states will acknowledge a superiority in the other, cannot be dictated by any; but depends entirely upon the rules of natural law, or upon mutual agreements between these several communities: in the construction of which we have no other rule to resort to but the law of nature; being the only one to which all communities are equally subject and therefore the civil law very justly observes, that *quod naturalis ratio inter omnes homines constituit, vocatur jus gentium.*

Thus much I think it necessary to premise concerning the law of nature, and the law of nations, before treating of the principal subject of this section, *municipal law;* that is, the rule by which particular districts, communities, or nations are governed; and which is usually defined to be "a rule of civil conduct prescribed by the "supreme power in a state, commanding what is right, and prohibit-"ing what is wrong."

It is a *rule*: not a transient, sudden order from a superior, to or concerning a particular person; but something permanent, uniform, and universal. An act of the legislature to attaint Titius of high treason, does not enter into the idea of a municipal law: it is spent upon Titius only, and is rather a sentence than a law. But an act to declare that the crime of Titius shall henceforth be deemed high treason, has permanency, uniformity, and universality, and therefore is properly a *rule*.

It is also called a *rule*, to distinguish it from *advice* or *counsel*, which we are at liberty to follow or not, as we see proper: our obedience to the *law* depends not upon *our approbation*, but upon the *maker's will*. It is also called a *rule*, to distinguish it from a *compact* or *agreement*, for a compact is a promise proceeding *from* us, law is a command directed *to* us.

Municipal law is also "a rule *of civil conduct*." The law of nature is the rule of our *moral* conduct. Municipal law regards man as a citizen, and bound to other duties towards his neighbour than those prescribed by the law of nature: duties, which he has engaged in by enjoying the benefits of the common union; and which amount to no more, than that he do contribute, on his part, to the subsistence and peace of the society.

It is likewise "a rule *prescribed*." Because a bare resolution, confined in the breast of the legislator, without manifesting itself by some external sign, can never be properly a law. It is requisite that this resolution be notified to those who are to obey it. All laws should be therefore made to commence *in futuro*, and be notified before their commencement; which is implied in the term "*prescribed*."

But, further: municipal law is "a rule of civil conduct prescribed *by the supreme power in a state*;" it being obviously requisite to the very essence of a law, that it be made by the supreme power, the person or body in whom the sovereignty of the state is lodged.

This may justify a short inquiry concerning the nature of society and civil government, the only true and natural foundations of which are the wants and fears of individuals. For though society may not have had its formal beginning from any convention of individuals, actuated by their wants and their fears; yet it is the *sense* of their weakness and imperfection that *keeps* mankind together, that demonstrates the necessity of this union, and is, therefore, the solid and natural foundation, as well as the cement, of civil society. This is what we mean by the original contract of society; that the whole shall protect all its parts, and that every part shall pay obedience to the will of the whole; without which submission of all, it is impossible that protection can be certainly extended to any.

When civil society is once formed, government at the same time results, of course, as necessary to preserve and to keep that society in order: for unless some superior be constituted, whose commands and decisions all the members are bound to obey, they would still remain as in a state of nature, without any judge upon earth to define their several rights, and redress their several wrongs.

In what manner, however, the several forms of government we now see in the world at first actually began, it is not my business or intention to discuss. By what right soever they subsist, there is and must be in all of them a supreme, irresistible, absolute, uncontrolled authority, in which the *jura summa imperii*, or the rights of sovereignty, reside. And this authority is placed in those hands, wherein (according to the opinion of the founders of such respective states, either expressly given, or collected from their tacit approbation) the qualities requisite for supremacy, wisdom, goodness, and power, are most likely to be found.

Political writers will not allow more than three regular forms of government; the first, when the sovereign power is lodged in an aggregate assembly, consisting of all the free members of a community, which is called a *democracy*; the second, when it is lodged in a council, composed of select members, and then it is styled an *aristocracy*; the last, when it is intrusted in the hands of a single person, and then it takes the name of a *monarchy*. By the sovereign power is meant the making of laws; for wherever that power resides, all others must conform to, and be directed by it, whatever appearance the outward form of the government may be. For the legislature may at any time alter that form, and put the execution of the laws into whatever hands it pleases; and all the other powers of the state must obey the legislature, or else the constitution is at an end.

In a democracy, public virtue, or goodness of intention, is more likely to be found than either of the other qualities of government. In aristocracies there is more wisdom to be found than in the other frames of government; but there is less honesty than in a republic, and less strength than in a monarchy. A monarchy is, indeed, the most powerful of any; for the legislative and executive powers are united in the hand of the prince, subject to the imminent danger of his employing that strength to improvident or oppressive purposes.

These three species of government have, all of them, their several perfections and imperfections. Democracies are usually the best calculated to direct the end of the law; aristocracies to invent the means by which that end shall be obtained; and monarchies to carry those means into execution.

The British constitution is supposed to combine the advantages of each. For the executive power being lodged in a single person, has all the advantages of strength and despatch that are to be found in the most absolute monarchy: and the legislature is intrusted to three distinct powers, entirely independent of each other; first, the crown; secondly, the lords spiritual and temporal, which is an aristocratic assembly of persons selected for their piety, their birth, their wisdom, their valour, or their property; and thirdly, the house of commons, chosen by the people from among themselves, which makes it a kind of democracy. This aggregate body composes the British parliament, wherein is lodged the sovereignty of the British constitution; that is to say, the right to make laws, or in the words of our definition, *to prescribe the rule of civil action.*

Thus far as to the *right* of the supreme power to make laws; but further, it is its *duty* likewise. For since the respective members are bound to conform themselves to the will of the whole body or state, it is expedient that they receive directions from the state declaratory of that its will. But as it is impossible to give injunctions to every particular man, relative to each particular action, it is incumbent on the state to establish general rules for the perpetual information and direction of all persons in all points, whether of positive or negative duty. And this, in order that every man may know what to look upon as his own, what as another's; what absolute and what relative duties are required at his hands; what degree he retains of his natural liberty; what he has given up as the price of the benefits of society; and after what manner he is to use and exercise those rights which the state assigns him, in order to secure the public tranquillity.

From what has been advanced, the truth of the former branch of our definition is (I trust) sufficiently evident; that "*municipal law* " *is a rule of civil conduct prescribed by the supreme power in a state.*" I proceed now to the latter branch of it; that it is a rule so prescribed, "*commanding what is right, and prohibiting what is wrong.*"

Now, in order to do this completely, it is first of all necessary that the boundaries of right and wrong be established and ascertained by law. And when this is once done, it will follow of course that it is likewise the business of the law, considered as a rule of civil conduct, to enforce these rights, and to restrain or redress these wrongs. It remains, therefore, only to consider in what manner the law is said to ascertain the boundaries of right and wrong; and the methods which it takes to command the one and prohibit the other.

For this purpose every law may be said to consist of several parts: one, *declaratory*; whereby the rights to be observed, and the wrongs to be eschewed, are clearly defined and laid down: another, *directory*; whereby the subject is instructed and enjoined to observe those rights, and to abstain from the commission of those wrongs: a third, *remedial*; whereby a method is pointed out to recover a man's private rights, or redress his private wrongs: to which may be added a fourth, usually termed the *sanction*, or *vindicatory* branch of the law; whereby it is signified what evil or penalty shall be incurred by such as commit any public wrongs, and transgress or neglect their duty.

The first of these, the *declaratory* part of the municipal law, depends upon the wisdom and will of the legislator. Natural rights, such as are life and liberty, need not the aid of human laws to be more effectually invested in every man than they are; neither do they receive any additional strength when declared by the municipal laws to be inviolable. On the other hand, no legislature has power to abridge or destroy them, unless the owner shall himself commit some act that amounts to a forfeiture. Neither do natural *duties* (such as the maintenance of children and the like) receive any sanction from being also declared to be duties by the law of the land. The case is the same as to crimes that are forbidden by the superior law, and styled *mala in se*, such as murder; which contract no additional turpitude from being declared unlawful by the inferior legislature. But with regard to things in themselves indifferent, the case is entirely altered. These become right or wrong, according as the legislator sees proper, for promoting the welfare of the society, and more effectually carrying on the purposes of civil life. Thus our common law has declared, that the goods of the wife do instantly upon marriage become the property of the husband; and our statute law has declared all monopolies a public offence: yet that right and this offence have no foundation in nature; but are merely created by the law, for the purposes of civil society. And so, as to injuries or crimes, it must be left to our own legislature to decide in what cases the seizing of another's cattle shall amount to a trespass or a theft; and where it shall be a justifiable action, as when a landlord takes them by way of distress for rent.

The *directory* part of a law stands much upon the same footing; the declaration being usually collected from the direction. Thus the law that says, "thou shalt not steal," implies a declaration that stealing is a crime.

The *remedial* part of the law is a necessary consequence of it; for in vain would rights be declared if there were no method of asserting them, when wrongfully withheld or invaded. This is what we mean properly, when we speak of the protection of the law. When, for instance, the *declaratory* part of the law has said, "that the field " or inheritance, which belonged to Titius's father, is vested by his " death in Titius ;" and the *directory* part has "forbidden any one " to enter on another's property, without the leave of the owner :" if Gaius, after this, will presume to take possession of the land, the *remedial* part of the law will then interpose its office; will make Gaius restore the possession to Titius, and also pay him damages for the invasion.

With regard to the *sanction* of laws, or the evil that may attend the breach of public duties, it is observed, that human legislators have for the most part chosen to make the sanction of their laws *vindicatory* rather than *remuneratory*, or to consist rather in punishments than in rewards. The dread of evil is a much more forcible principle of human action than the prospect of good; for which reason the law seldom, if ever, proposes any privilege or gift to such as obey it; but constantly comes armed with a penalty denounced against transgressors.

I have now gone through the definition of a municipal law: and have shown that it is a " rule—of civil conduct—prescribed—by the "supreme power in a state—commanding what is right, and pro- " hibiting what is wrong." I proceed now to consider the origin and nature of the laws of England.

SECTION II.

OF THE LAWS OF ENGLAND.

Early laws traditional—Alfred's Dom-boe—Laws of Edward the Confessor —Unwritten or common law—Particular customs—Peculiar laws—Civil and canon law—Written or statute law.

THE municipal law of England may with sufficient propriety be divided into two kinds: the *lex non scripta*, the unwritten or common law; and the *lex scripta*, the written or statute law.

The *lex non scripta*, or unwritten law, includes not only *general customs*, or the common law properly so called; but also the *particular customs* of certain parts of the kingdom; and likewise those *particular laws*, that are by custom observed only in certain courts and jurisdictions.

When I call these parts of our law *leges non scriptæ*, I would not be understood as if all those laws were at present merely *oral*, or communicated from former ages to the present solely by word of mouth. It is true indeed that, in the profound ignorance of letters which formerly overspread the whole western world, all laws were entirely traditional, for this plain reason, because the nations among which they prevailed had but little idea of writing. But with us, at present, the monuments and evidences of our legal customs are contained in the records of the several courts of justice, in books of reports and judicial decisions, and in the treatises of learned sages of the profession, preserved and handed down to us from the times of highest antiquity. I, therefore, style these parts of our law *leges non scriptæ*, because their original institution and authority are not set down in writing, as acts of parliament are, but they receive their binding power, and the force of laws, by long and immemorial usage, and by their universal reception throughout the kingdom.

Our ancient lawyers insist that these customs are as old as the primitive Britons, and continued down, through the several mutations of governments and inhabitants, to the present time, unchanged and unadulterated. This may be the case as to some; but this assertion must be understood with many grains of allowance; and ought only to signify, as the truth seems to be, that there never was any formal exchange of one system of laws for another: though the Romans, the Picts, the Saxons, the Danes, and the Normans, who successively occupied parts of England, must have insensibly introduced and incorporated many of their own customs with those that were before established; thereby in all probability improving the texture and wisdom of the whole by the accumulated wisdom of divers particular countries.

And indeed our early historians all positively assure us, that our body of laws is of this compounded nature. For they tell us, that in the time of Alfred the local customs of the several provinces of the kingdom were grown so various, that he found it expedient to compile for general use his *dome-book*, or *liber judicialis;* which is said to have been extant so late as the reign of King Edward IV., but is now unfortunately lost. But the irruption and establishment of the Danes in England, which followed soon after, introduced new customs, and caused this code of Alfred to fall into disuse; or at least to be mixed with other laws. So that about the beginning of the eleventh century, there were three principal systems of laws prevailing in different districts. 1. The *Mercen-Lage*, or Mercian laws, which were observed in many of the midland counties, and those bordering on the principality of Wales, the retreat of the ancient Britons. 2. The *West-Saxen-Lage*, or laws of the West Saxons, which obtained in the counties to the south and west of the island, from Kent to Devonshire. 3. The *Dane-Lage*, or Danish law, the very name of which speaks its origin and composition.

Out of these, Edward the Confessor extracted one uniform law or digest of laws, to be observed throughout the whole kingdom; which seems to have been no more than a new edition, or fresh promulgation of Alfred's dome-book, with such additions and improvements as the experience of a century and a half had suggested. These however are the laws which our historians so often mention as the laws of Edward the Confessor; which our ancestors struggled so hardly to maintain under the first princes of the Norman line; and which subsequent princes so frequently promised to keep and restore, as the most popular act they could do, when pressed by foreign emergencies or domestic discontents. They are the laws which gave rise to that collection of maxims and customs which is now known as the common law; a name either given to it, in contradistinction to other laws, as the statute law, the civil law, the law merchant, and the like; or more probably, as a law common to all the realm, the *jus commune* or *folk-right*.

This unwritten or common law is properly distinguishable into three kinds: 1. General customs; which are the universal rule of the whole kingdom, and form the common law, in its stricter signification. 2. Particular customs; which for the most part affect only the inhabitants of particular districts. 3. Certain particular laws; which by custom are adopted by particular courts.

I. As to general customs, or the common law, properly so called; this is that law by which proceedings in the ordinary courts of justice are directed. For example, that the eldest son alone is heir to his ancestor;—that property may be acquired and transferred by writing;—that a deed is of no validity unless sealed and delivered;—that wills shall be construed favourably, and deeds strictly;—that money lent upon bond is recoverable by action of debt;—that breaking the public peace is an offence, and punishable by fine and imprisonment;—all these are doctrines that are not set down in any written statute or ordinance, but depend merely upon immemorial usage, that is, upon common law, for their support.

But here a very natural question arises: how are these customs or maxims to be known, and by whom is their validity to be determined? The answer is, by the judges in the several courts of justice. They are the depositaries of the laws; the living oracles, who must decide in all cases of doubt, and who are bound by an oath to decide according to the law of the land. These judicial decisions are the most authoritative evidence that can be given of the existence of such a custom as shall form a part of the common law. The judgment itself, and all the proceedings previous thereto, are carefully preserved, under the name of *records*, in public repositories set apart for that particular purpose; and to them recourse is had, when any critical question arises in the determination of which former precedents may give light or assistance. For it is an established rule to abide by former precedents, where the same points come again in litigation; as well to keep the scale of justice even and steady; as also because the law in that case being solemnly determined, what before was uncertain, and perhaps indifferent, is now become a permanent rule, which it is not in the breast of any subsequent judge to alter or vary from, according to his private sentiments; he being sworn to determine, not according to his own private judgment, but according to the known laws and customs of the land; not delegated to pronounce a new law, but to maintain and expound the old one.

The decisions, therefore, of courts are held in the highest regard, and are not only preserved as authentic records in the several courts, but are handed out to public view in the numerous volumes of Reports which furnish the lawyer's library. Of these, a regular series, from the reign of Edward II. to that of Henry VIII., were taken by the prothonotaries of the court, and published *annually*, whence they are known as the Year-Books. But the most valuable are those published by Lord Chief Justice Coke, whose other writings, indeed, the Institutes, as he is pleased to call them, are so highly esteemed, that they are generally cited without the author's name.

II. The second branch of the unwritten laws of England are particular customs, or laws which affect only the inhabitants of particular districts.

These particular customs, or some of them, are without doubt the remains of that multitude of local customs out of which the common law, as it now stands, was collected at first by the Saxon kings. But for reasons that have been now long forgotten, particular counties, cities, towns, manors, and lordships, were very early indulged with the privilege of abiding by their own customs, in contradistinction to the rest of the nation at large; which privilege is confirmed to them by several acts of parliament.

Such is the custom of *gavelkind* in Kent and some other parts of the kingdom, which ordains, among other things, that not the eldest son only of the father shall succeed to his inheritance, but all the sons alike: and that, though the ancestor be attainted and hanged, yet the heir shall succeed to his estate, without any escheat to the lord. Such is the custom that prevails in divers ancient boroughs, and therefore called *borough-english*, that the youngest son shall inherit the estate, in preference to all his elder brothers. Such is the custom in other boroughs that a widow shall be entitled, for her dower, to all her husband's lands; whereas at the common law she shall be endowed of one third part only. Such also are the special and particular customs of manors, of which every one has more or less, and which bind all the copyhold and customary tenants that hold of the same manors. Such likewise is the custom of holding divers inferior courts, with power of trying causes in cities and trading towns; the right of holding which, when no royal grant can be shown, depends entirely upon immemorial and established usage. Such, lastly, are many particular customs within the city of London, with regard to trade, apprentices, widows, orphans, and a variety of other matters. All these are contrary to the general law of the land, and are good only by special usage; though the customs of London are also confirmed by act of parliament.

To this head may most properly be referred a particular system of customs used only among one set of the queen's subjects, called the custom of merchants, or *lex mercatoria :* which, however different from the general rules of the common law, is yet engrafted into it, and made a part of it; being allowed, for the benefit of trade, to be of the utmost validity in all commercial transactions: for it is a maxim of law, that " *cuilibet in sua arte credendum est.*"

III. The third branch of the *leges non scriptæ* are those peculiar laws which by custom are adopted and used only in certain peculiar courts and jurisdictions. And by these I understand the civil and canon laws.

It may seem a little improper at first view to rank these laws under the head of *leges non scriptæ*, or unwritten laws, seeing they are set forth by authority in the Pandects, the Code, and the Institutes, in the decrees of councils and the decretals of popes. But I do this, because it is most plain, that it is not on account of their being *written* laws that either the canon law, or the civil law, have any obligation within this kingdom : neither do their force and efficacy depend upon their own intrinsic authority ; which is the case of our written laws, or acts of parliament. They bind not the subjects of England, because their materials were collected from popes or emperors ; were digested by Justinian, or declared to be authentic by Gregory. These considerations give them no authority here : all the strength that either the papal or imperial laws have obtained in this realm is only because they have been received by immemorial usage in some particular cases ; and then they form a branch of the *leges non scriptæ*, or customary laws. If they are in some other cases introduced by consent of parliament, they owe their validity to the *lex scripta*, or statute law.

By the *civil law* is generally understood the municipal law of the Roman Empire, as comprised in the institutes, the digest, and the code of the Emperor Justinian, and the *novellæ*, or new constitutions of himself and some of his successors.   These form the body of Roman law, or *Corpus Juris Civilis.* The *canon law* is a body of Roman ecclesiastical law, relative to such matters as that church either has, or pretends to have, the proper jurisdiction over, compiled from the opinions of the ancient Latin fathers, the decrees of general councils, and the decretal epistles and bulls of the holy see. All these together form the *Corpus Juris Canonici*, or body of the Roman canon law.

Besides these pontifical collections, there is also a kind of national canon law, composed of *legatine* and *provincial* constitutions, and adapted only to the exigencies of this church and kingdom.   The *legatine* constitutions were enacted in national synods, held under Otho and Othobon, legates from Gregory IX. and Clement IV. in the reign of Henry III.   The *provincial* constitutions are principally the decrees of provincial synods, held under divers archbishops of Canterbury, from Langton in the reign of Henry III. to Chichele in the reign of Henry V.; and adopted by the province of York in the reign of Henry VI.   At the dawn of the Reformation, it was enacted in parliament that a review should be had of the canon law; and, till such review should be made, all canons, ordinances, and synodals provincial, being then already made, were to be used and executed. As no such review has yet been perfected, upon this statute now depends the authority of the canon law in England.

There are four species of courts, in which the civil and canon laws are used.   1. The courts of the archbishops and bishops, and their officers, usually called, courts christian, or the ecclesiastical courts. 2. The military courts, which are now entirely disused.   3. The courts of admiralty.   4. The courts of the two universities.   In all, their reception in general, and the different degrees of that reception, are grounded entirely upon custom.   For,

1. The courts of common law have the superintendence over these courts; to keep them within their jurisdictions, to determine wherein they exceed them, and to restrain and prohibit such excess.

2. The common law has reserved to itself the exposition of all such acts of parliament as concern either the extent of these courts, or the matters depending before them.   And,

3. An appeal lies from all of them to the crown, in the last resort; the jurisdiction exercised by them being in theory derived from the Crown of England, and not from any foreign potentate, or intrinsic authority of their own.

And, from these three strong marks and ensigns of superiority, it appears beyond a doubt, that the civil and canon laws are only sub-ordinate, *leges sub graviori lege,* and by no means a distinct inde-pendent species of laws, but only inferior branches of the unwritten laws of England.

The *leges scriptæ,* the written laws of the kingdom, are statutes, acts, or edicts, made by the sovereign, by and with the advice and consent of the lords spiritual and temporal, and commons, in parlia-ment assembled.   The oldest of these now extant, and printed in our statute books, is the famous *Magna Charta,* as confirmed in parlia-ment 9 Henry III.: though doubtless there were many acts before that time, the records of which are now lost, and the determinations of them perhaps at present currently received for the maxims of the old common law.   And these statutes are either *general* or *special, public* or *private.*   A general or public act is a universal rule, that regards the whole community: and of this the courts of law are bound to take notice judicially and *ex officio.*   Special or private acts are rather exceptions than rules, being those which only operate upon particular persons, and private concerns: and of these the judges are not bound to take notice, unless they be formally shown and pleaded.*

Statutes also are said to be either *declaratory* or *remedial.*   Decla-ratory, where the old custom of the kingdom is fallen into disuse, or become disputable; in which case parliament has sometimes thought proper to declare what the common law is and ever has been.   Thus the statute of Treasons does not make any new species of treason; but only, for the benefit of the subject, declares those several kinds of offences which before were treason at the common law.   Remedial statutes are those which are made to supply defects in the common law itself, either by enlarging the law where it was too narrow, or by restraining it where it was too lax.   Hence another division of remedial acts of parlia-ment into *enlarging* and *restraining* statutes.   To instance again in the case of treason.   Clipping the coin was an offence not sufficiently guarded against by the common law: therefore it was at one time thought expedient to make it high treason, so that this was an *enlarg-ing* statute.   At common law spiritual corporations might lease out their estates for any term of years, till prevented by a statute of Queen Elizabeth: this was therefore a *restraining* statute.

These are the several grounds of the laws of England: over and

---

* The stat. 13 Eliz. c. 10, to prevent spiritual persons from making leases for longer terms than twenty-one years, or three lives, is a *public* act, being a rule prescribed to the whole body of spiritual persons in the nation.   An act to enable the Bishop of Chester to make a lease to A. B. for sixty years, is an exception to this rule; it concerns only the parties and the bishop's successors, and is therefore a *private* act.

above which, equity is also frequently called in to assist, to moderate, and to explain them.   What equity is will be shown hereafter.
At present I shall only add, that there are courts of equity established for the benefit of the subject; to detect latent frauds and
concealments, which the process of the courts of law is not adapted
to reach ; to enforce the execution of such matters of trust and confidence as are binding in conscience, though not cognizable in a court
of law; to deliver from such dangers as are owing to misfortune or
oversight; and to give a more specific relief, and one more adapted
to the circumstances of the case, than can always be obtained by the
generality of the rules of the positive or common law.

THE LAWS OF ENGLAND.

BOOK THE FIRST.

OF THE RIGHTS OF PERSONS.

CHAPTER I.

OF THE ABSOLUTE RIGHTS OF INDIVIDUALS.

The English liberties—Right of personal security—Right of personal liberty—Right of property—Securities for the enjoyment of these rights.

THE objects of the laws of England are so very numerous and extensive, that in order to consider them with any tolerable ease and perspicuity, it will be necessary to distribute them methodically, under proper and distinct heads; avoiding as much as possible divisions too large and comprehensive on the one hand, and too trifling and minute on the other; both of which are equally productive of confusion.

Now, as municipal law is a rule of civil conduct, commanding what is right, and prohibiting what is wrong; it follows, that the primary and principal objects of the law are RIGHTS and WRONGS. In the prosecution therefore of these commentaries, I shall follow this very simple and obvious division; and shall in the first place consider the *rights* that are commanded, and secondly the *wrongs* that are forbidden by the laws of England.

Rights are, however, liable to another subdivision; being either, first, those which concern and are annexed to the persons of men, and are then called *jura personarum*, or the *rights of persons;* or they are, secondly, such as man may acquire over external objects or things unconnected with his person, which are styled *jura rerum*, or the *rights of things*. Wrongs also are divisible into, first, *private wrongs*, which, being an infringement merely of particulars rights, concern individuals merely, and are called civil injuries; and secondly, *public wrongs*, which being a breach of general and public rights, affect the whole community, and are called crimes and misdemeanors.

The object of the laws of England falling into this fourfold division, the present commentaries will therefore consist of the four following parts :—1. *The rights of persons;* with the means whereby such rights may be either acquired or lost. 2. *The rights of things;* with the means also of acquiring and losing them. 3. *Private wrongs,* or civil injuries; with the means of redressing them by law. 4. *Public wrongs,* or crimes and misdemeanors; with the means of prevention and punishment.

We are now, first, to consider the *rights of persons;* which are of two sorts; first, such as are due *from* every citizen, and are usually called civil *duties;* and, secondly, such as belong to him, which is the more popular acceptation of *rights* or *jura.* But both may be comprised in this latter division; for, as all social duties are of a relative nature, at the same time that they are due *from* one man, or set of men, they must also be due *to* another.

Persons also are divided by the law into either natural persons or artificial. Natural persons are such as nature formed us; artificial are such as are created and devised by human laws for the purposes of society and government, which are called corporations or bodies politic.

 The rights of persons considered in their natural capacities are also of two sorts, absolute and relative. Absolute, which are such as appertain and belong to particular men, merely as individuals or single persons : relative, which are incident to them as members of society, and standing in various relations to each other. The first, that is, absolute rights, will be the subject of the present chapter.

By the absolute *rights* of individuals, we mean such as would belong to their persons merely in a state of nature, and which every man is entitled to enjoy, whether out of society or in it. But with regard to the absolute *duties,* which man is bound to perform, considered as a mere individual, it is not to be expected that any human municipal law should at all explain or enforce them; for the end and intent of such laws being only to regulate the behaviour of mankind, as they are members of society, and stand in various relations to each other, they have consequently no concern with any other but social or relative duties. Let a man, therefore, be ever so abandoned in his principles, or vicious in his practice, provided he keeps his wickedness to himself, and does not offend against the rules of public decency, he is out of the reach of human laws. But if he makes his vices public, though they be such as seem principally to affect himself (as drunkenness, or the like), they then become, by the bad example they set, of pernicious effects to society; and therefore it is then the business of human laws to correct them. Here the circumstance of publication is what alters the nature of the case. *Public* sobriety is a relative duty, and therefore enjoined by our laws ; *private* sobriety is an absolute duty, which, whether it be performed or not, human tribunals can never know ; and therefore they can never enforce it by any civil sanction. But with respect to *rights*, the case is different. Human laws define and enforce as well those rights which belong to a man considered as an individual, as those which belong to him considered as related to others.

The absolute rights of man are usually summed up in one general appellation, and denominated the *natural liberty* of mankind. This natural liberty consists properly in a power of acting as one thinks fit, without any restraint or control, unless by the law of nature. But every man, when he enters into society, gives up a part of his natural liberty as the price of so valuable a purchase; and in consideration of receiving the advantages of mutual commerce, obliges himself to conform to those laws which the community has thought proper to establish. And this species of legal obedience is infinitely more desirable than that savage liberty which is sacrificed to obtain it. For no man that considers a moment would wish to retain the uncontrolled power of doing whatever he pleases : the consequence of which is, that every other man would also have the same power; and then there would be no security to individuals in any of the enjoyments of life. Political, therefore, or *civil liberty*, which is that of a member of society, is no other than natural liberty so far restrained by human laws (and no further) as is necessary and expedient for the general advantage of the public. Hence we may collect that the law, which restrains a man from doing mischief to his fellow-citizens, though it diminishes the natural, increases the civil liberty of mankind; but that every causeless restraint of the will of the subject, is a degree of tyranny : nay, that even laws themselves, if they constrain our conduct in matters of mere indifference, without any good end in view, are regulations destructive of liberty : whereas, if any public advantage can arise from observing such precepts, the control of our private inclinations, in one or two particular points, will conduce to preserve our general freedom in others of more importance, by supporting that state of society, which alone canse cure our independence. So that laws, when prudently framed, are by no means subversive, but rather introductive of liberty ; for where there is no law there is no freedom. But then, on the other hand, that constitution or frame of government, that system of laws is alone calculated to maintain civil liberty which leaves the subject entire master of his own conduct, except in those points wherein the public good requires some direction or restraint.

The absolute rights of every Englishman (which, in a political sense, are usually called their liberties), are coeval with our form of government. At some times we have seen them depressed by tyrannical princes; at others so luxuriant as even to tend to anarchy, a worse state than tyranny itself, as any government is better than none at all.   But the vigour of our free constitution has always delivered the nation from these embarrassments: and, as soon as the convulsions consequent on the struggle have been over, the balance of our rights and liberties has settled to its proper level; and their fundamental articles have been from time to time asserted in parliament, as often as they were thought to be in danger.

First, by the Great Charter of Liberties, which was obtained from King John, and afterwards, with some alterations, confirmed in parliament by Henry III., his son.   Afterwards by the *Confirmatio Cartarum*, whereby the Great Charter is directed to be allowed as the common law; and all judgments contrary to it are declared void.   Next, by a multitude of subsequent corroborating statutes, from the first Edward to Henry IV.   Then, after a long interval, by the Petition of Right; a parliamentary declaration of the liberties of the people, assented to by King Charles I. in the beginning of his reign.   Which was followed by the *Habeas Corpus* Act, passed under Charles II.   To these succeeded the Bill of Rights, or declaration delivered by the lords and commons to the Prince and Princess of Orange; and afterwards enacted in parliament when they ˙became king and queen.   Lastly, these liberties were again asserted at the commencement of the last century, in the Act of Settlement, the statute declaring them to be "the birthright of "the people of England," according to the ancient doctrine of the common law.

Thus much for the *declaration* of our rights and privileges.   The rights themselves consist in a number of private immunities; which are indeed no other, than either that *residuum* of natural liberty, which is not required by the laws of society to be sacrificed to public convenience; or else those civil privileges, which society has engaged to provide, in lieu of the natural liberties so given up by individuals.   And these may be reduced to three principal or primary articles; the right of *personal security*, the right of *personal liberty*, and the right of *private property*: because, as there is no other known method of compulsion, or of abridging man's natural free-will, but by an infringement or diminution of one or other of these important rights, the preservation of these, inviolate, may justly be said to include the preservation of our civil immunities in their largest and most extensive sense.

I. The right of personal security consists in a person's legal and uninterrupted enjoyment of his life, his limbs, his body, his health, and his reputation.

1. Life is a right inherent by nature in every individual; and it

begins in contemplation of law as soon as an infant is able to stir
in the mother's womb.   For if a woman is quick with child, and by
a potion or otherwise, kills it in her womb; or, if any one beat her,
whereby the child dies in her body, and she is delivered of a dead child ;
this is a heinous misdemeanor.   An infant in *ventre sa mere* is also
supposed in law to be born for many purposes.   It is capable of
having a legacy ; it may have a guardian assigned to it ; and an
estate may be limited to its use, as if it were then actually born.
And in this point the civil law agrees with ours.

2. A man's limbs enable him to protect himself from external injuries in a state of nature.   To these therefore he has a natural,
inherent right ; and they cannot be wantonly destroyed or disabled
without a manifest breach of civil liberty.   And both the life and
limbs of a man are of such high value, in the estimation of the law
of England, that it pardons even homicide if committed *se defendendo*, or in order to preserve them.   For whatever is done by a
man, to save either life or member, is looked upon as done by the
highest necessity and compulsion.   Therefore if a man through fear
of death or personal injury, which is called in law *duress*, is prevailed upon to execute a deed, or do any other legal act; these,
though accompanied with all other the requisitite solemnities, may
be afterwards avoided, if forced upon him by a well-grounded apprehension of losing his life, or even his limbs, in case of his non-compliance.   And the law not only regards life and member, and protects
every man in the enjoyment of them, but also furnishes him with
everything necessary for their support.   For there is no man so indigent or wretched, but he may demand a supply sufficient for all
the necessaries of life from the more opulent part of the community,
by means of the several statutes enacted for the relief of the poor,
of which in their proper places.

These rights, of life and member, can only be determined by the
death of the person ; which was formerly accounted to be either a
civil or natural death.   The civil death commenced, if any man was
banished or abjured the realm, or entered into religion; that is,
became a monk ; in which cases he was absolutely dead in law, and
his next heir should have his estate; for which reason leases, and
other conveyances for life, were usually made to have and to hold
for the term of one's *natural* life.   And this natural life cannot legally
be disposed of or destroyed by any individual, neither by the person
himself, nor by any other of his fellow creatures, merely upon their
own authority ; but it may be forfeited for the breach of those laws
of society which are enforced by the sanction of capital punishments, though the law of England now very seldom inflicts any
punishment extending to life, unless upon the highest necessity.

3. Besides his limbs, the rest of his person is also entitled, by the same natural right, to security from the corporal insults of menaces, assaults, beating, and wounding.

4. The preservation of a man's health from such practices as may prejudice or annoy it; and,

5. The security of his reputation or good name from the arts of detraction and slander, are rights to which every man is entitled, by reason and natural justice; since without these it is impossible to have the perfect enjoyment of any other advantage or right. But these three last articles it will suffice to have barely mentioned among the rights of persons, referring the more minute discussion of their several branches to our third book, which treats of the infringement of these rights, under the head of personal wrongs.

II. Next to personal security, the law of England regards, asserts, and preserves the personal liberty of individuals. Concerning which we may make the same observations as upon the preceding article; that it is a right strictly natural; that the laws of England have never abridged it without sufficient cause; and that in this kingdom it cannot ever be abridged at the mere discretion of the magistrate, without the explicit permission of the laws.

Of great importance to the public is the preservation of this personal liberty; for if once it were left in the power of any, the highest, magistrate to imprison arbitrarily whomsoever he or his officers thought proper, there would soon be an end of all other rights and immunities. The confinement of the person, in any wise, is in law an imprisonment. So that the keeping a man against his will in a private house, arresting or forcibly detaining him in the street, is an imprisonment. And the law so much discourages unlawful confinement, that if a man is under *duress of imprisonment*, until he seals a bond or the like, he may allege this duress, and avoid the extorted bond. To make imprisonment lawful, it must either be by process from the courts of judicature, or by warrant from some legal officer having authority to commit to prison; which warrant must be in writing, under the hand and seal of the magistrate, and express the causes of the commitment, in order to be examined into, if necessary, upon a *habeas corpus* (of which we shall treat in the third book of these commentaries). For if there be no cause expressed in the warrant, the gaoler is not even bound to detain the prisoner.

A natural and regular consequence of this personal liberty is, that every Englishman may claim a right to abide in his own country so long as he pleases; and not to be driven from it unless by the sentence of the law. For exile, or transportation, are punishments unknown to the common law; and whenever the latter is inflicted, it is by the express direction of some modern act of parliament.

And the law is in this respect so liberally construed for the benefit of the subject, that, though *within* the realm the sovereign may command the service of all his liegemen, yet he cannot send any man *out of* the realm, even upon the public service; excepting sailors and soldiers, the nature of whose employment implies an exception: he cannot even constitute a man lord lieutenant of Ireland against his will, nor make him a foreign ambassador. For this might in reality be no more than an honourable exile.

III. The third absolute right, inherent in every Englishman, is that of property: which consists in the free use, enjoyment, and disposal of all his acquisitions, without any control or diminution, save only by the laws of the land, which are extremely watchful in ascertaining and protecting this right. So great indeed is the regard of the law for private property, that it will not authorize the least violation of it; no, not even for the general good of the whole community. If a new road, for instance, were to be made through the grounds of a private person, it might perhaps be extensively beneficial to the public; but the law permits no man, or set of men, to do this without the consent of the owner. All that the law does, is to oblige the owner to alienate his possessions for a reasonable price; and even this is an exertion of power which the legislature, or those to whom it commits this its exercise, ought to indulge with caution.

Nor is this the only instance in which the law of the land has postponed even public necessity to the rights of private property. For no subject of England can be constrained to pay any taxes, even for the defence of the realm, or the support of government, but such as are imposed by his own consent, or that of his representatives in parliament. This is enacted expressly by the *Confirmatio Cartarum*, and in numerous acts of parliament since passed, the last of these (1 W. & M. st. 2, c. 2), declaring that levying money for or to the use of the crown, by pretence of prerogative, without grant of parliaiament, or for longer time, or in other manner, than the same is or shall be granted, is illegal.

We have thus taken a short view of the principal absolute rights which appertain to every Englishman. But in vain would these rights be declared by the dead letter of the laws, if the constitution had not established certain other auxiliary subordinate rights of the subject, which serve to protect the three great and primary rights. of personal security, personal liberty, and private property. These are,

1. The constitution, powers, and privileges of parliament, of which I shall treat at large in the ensuing chapter.

2. The limitation of the royal prerogative, by bounds so certain and notorious, that it is impossible the sovereign should either

mistake or legally exceed them without the consent of the people. Of this also I shall treat in its proper place.

3. A third subordinate right is that of applying to the courts of justice for redress of injuries. Since the law is in England the supreme arbiter of every man's life, liberty, and property, courts of justice must at all times be open to the subject, and the law be duly administered therein, according to the emphatic words of *Magna Charta*, spoken in the person of the king, who in judgment of law is ever present and repeating them in all his courts; *nulli vendemus, nulli negabimus, aut differemus rectum vel justitiam:* and therefore every subject, "for injury done to him, *in bonis, in terris, vel* "*persona*, by any other subject, be he ecclesiastical or temporal, "without any exception, may take his remedy by the course of the "law, and have justice and right for the injury done to him, freely "without sale, fully without any denial, and speedily without "delay."

4. If there should happen any uncommon injury, or infringement of the rights before mentioned, which the ordinary course of law is too defective to reach, there still remains a fourth subordinate right, appertaining to every individual, namely, the right of petitioning the sovereign, or either house of parliament, for the redress of grievances. Care only must be taken, lest, under the pretence of petitioning, the subject be guilty of any riot or tumult; for under these regulations it is declared by the statute 1 W. & M. st. 2, c. 2, that the subject has a right to petition; and that all commitments and prosecutions for such petitioning are illegal.

5. The fifth and last auxiliary right of the subject, that I shall at present mention, is that of having arms for their defence, which is also declared by the same statute, and is indeed a public allowance of the natural right of resistance and self-preservation, when the laws are found insufficient to restrain the violence of oppression.

In these several articles consist the rights, or, as they are frequently termed, the liberties of Englishmen. So long as these remain inviolate, the subject is perfectly free; for every species of oppression must act in opposition to one or other of these rights, having no other object upon which it can possibly be employed. To preserve these from violation, it is necessary that the constitution of parliament be supported in its full vigour; and limits, certainly known, be set to the royal prerogative. And lastly, to vindicate these rights, when attacked, the subjects of England are entitled, in the first place, to the regular administration of justice; next, to the right of petitioning the sovereign and parliament for redress of grievances; and, lastly, to the right of having and using arms for self-preservation and defence.

CHAPTER II.

OF THE PARLIAMENT.

Origin of parliament—Manner and time of assembling—Its constituent parts —Its laws and customs—Its privileges—Laws and customs of the Lords —of the Commons.: Money bills — Qualifications of electors, and of members—Proceedings at elections—Method of making laws—Adjourn-ment—Prorogation—Dissolution.

WE are next to treat of the rights and duties of persons, as members of society. These relations are either public or private: we will first consider those that are public.

The most universal public relation, by which men are connected together, is that of government, namely, as governors and governed, or, in other words, as magistrates and people. Of magistrates some also are *supreme*, in whom the sovereign power of the state resides; others are *subordinate*, deriving all their authority from the supreme magistrate, and accountable to him for their conduct.

In all tyrannical governments the supreme magistracy, or the right both of *making* and of *enforcing* the laws, is vested in one and the same man, or one and the same body of men; and wherever these two powers are united together, there can be no public liberty. In England this supreme power is divided into two branches; the one legislative, to wit, the parliament; the other executive, consisting of the sovereign alone. In this chapter we shall consider the British parliament; in which the legislative power is vested by our consti-tution.

The origin of parliament is one of those matters which lie so far hidden in the dark ages of antiquity, that the tracing of it out is a thing equally difficult and uncertain. The word *parliament* itself is of modern date; derived from the French, and signifying an assembly that met and conferred together. It was first applied to general assemblies of the states under Louis VII. in France, about the middle of the twelfth century. But it is certain that, long before the introduction of the Norman language into England, all matters of importance were debated and settled in the great council of the realm; which was called sometimes *micel-synoth* or great council, or *micel-gemote* or great meeting, and more frequently *witena-gemote* or the meeting of wise men. We have instances of this meeting so early as the reign of Ina king of the West Saxons, Offa king of the Mercians, and Ethelbert king of Kent, in the several realms of the heptarchy. And, after their union, King Alfred ordained that these councils should meet twice in the year; and there is no doubt but that similar great councils were occasionally held under the first

princes of the Norman line.   Parliaments, or general councils, are
thus coeval with the kingdom itself.   How they were composed is
another question, which has been matter of great dispute among our
learned antiquaries; and particularly, whether the commons were
summoned at all; or if summoned, at what period they began to
form a distinct assembly.   But it is not my intention here to enter
into controversies of this sort.   I proceed therefore to inquire wherein
consists this constitution of parliament, as it now stands, and has
stood for the space of at least five hundred years.   And in the prosecution of this inquiry, I shall consider, first, the manner and time of
its assembling; secondly, its constituent parts; thirdly, the laws and
customs relating to parliament, considered as one aggregate body;
fourthly and fifthly, the laws and customs relating to each house
separately and distinctly taken; sixthly, the method of proceeding,
and of making statutes, in both houses; and lastly, the manner of
the parliament's adjournment, prorogation, and dissolution.

I. The parliament is regularly to be summoned by the sovereign's
writ, for it is a branch of the royal prerogative, that no parliament
can be convened by its own authority, or by the authority of any,
except the sovereign alone.   And this prerogative is founded upon
very good reason.   For, supposing it had a right to meet spontaneously, it is impossible to conceive that all the members and each of the
houses, would agree unanimously upon the proper time and place of
meeting, and if half of the members met, and half absented themselves, who shall determine which is really the legislative body, the
part assembled, or that which stays away?   It is therefore necessary
that the parliament should be called together at a determinate time
and place: and highly becoming its dignity, that it should be called
together by none but one of its own constituent parts; and of the
three constituents parts, this office can only appertain to the sovereign; as this is a single person, whose will may be uniform and
steady; and the only branch of the legislature that has a separate
existence, and is capable of performing any act at a time when no
parliament is in being.   The sovereign only, then, can convoke a
parliament.   And this by the ancient statutes of the realm he is
bound to do every year, or oftener, if need be.   Not that he is, or ever
was, obliged by these statutes to call a *new* parliament every year;
but only to permit a parliament to sit annually for the redress of
grievances, and despatch of business, *if need be*; a necessity which
now cannot but arise annually, since the supplies are voted only for
one year at a time, and the Mutiny Acts are passed for one year
only.

II. The constituent parts of a parliament are, the sovereign sitting
there in his political capacity, and the three estates of the realm;

the lords spiritual, the lords temporal, and the commons. And the
sovereign and these three estates together, form the great corporation or body politic of the kingdom, of which the crown is said to be
caput, principium et finis. For upon their coming together, the
sovereign meets them, either in person or by representatives: without which there can be no beginning of a parliament; and the crown
also has alone the power of dissolving them.

It is highly necessary for preserving the balance of the constitution, that the executive power should be a branch, though not the
whole, of the legislative. The total union of them would be productive of tyranny; the total disjunction of them would in the end
produce the same effects, by causing that union against which it
seems to provide. The legislative would soon become tyrannical, by
making continual encroachments, and gradually assuming to itself
the rights of the executive power. To hinder, therefore, any such
encroachments, the sovereign is a necessary part of the parliament:
and, as this is the reason of his being so, very properly, therefore,
the share of the legislation, which the constitution has placed in the
crown, consists in the power of *rejecting* rather than *resolving*; this
being sufficient to answer the end proposed. The crown cannot begin
of itself any alterations in the present established law; but it may
approve or disapprove of the alterations suggested and consented to
by the two houses. The legislative, therefore, cannot abridge the
executive power of any rights which it now has by law, without its
own consent; since the law must perpetually stand as it now does,
unless all the powers will agree to alter it. Herein, indeed, consists
the excellence of the English government, that all the parts of it
form a mutual check upon each other. In the legislature, the people
are a check upon the nobility, and the nobility a check upon the
people, by the mutual privilege of rejecting what the other has
resolved: while the sovereign is a check upon both, which preserves
the executive power from encroachments. And this very executive
power is again checked and kept within due bounds by the two houses,
through the privilege they have of inquiring into, impeaching, and
punishing the conduct (not, indeed, of the sovereign, which would
destroy his constitutional independence; but, what is more beneficial
to the public) of his evil and pernicious councillors. Thus every
branch of our civil polity supports and is supported, regulates and is
regulated, by the rest: for the two houses naturally drawing in two
directions of opposite interest, and the prerogative in another still different from them both, they mutually keep each other from exceeding their proper limits; while the whole is prevented from separation,
and artificially connected together by the mixed nature of the crown,
which is a part of the legislative, and the sole executive magistrate.

Let us now consider these constituent parts of the parliament, each in a separate view. The royal person and its attributes will be the subject of the next, and many subsequent chapters.

The next in order are the spiritual lords. These consist of the Archbishops of Canterbury and York, the Bishops of London, Durham, and Winchester, and twenty-three other bishops of dioceses in England, according to their priority in consecration; and four lords spiritual from Ireland, who sit in parliament by rotation. But though these lords spiritual are in the eye of the law a distinct estate from the lords temporal, and are so distinguished in most of our acts of parliament, yet in practice they are usually blended together under the one name of *the lords;* they intermix in their votes; and the majority of such intermixture binds both estates.

The *lords temporal* consist of all the peers of the realm, by whatever title of nobility distinguished. Some of these sit by descent, as do all ancient peers; some by creation, as do all new-made ones; others, since the union with Scotland, by election, which is the case with the sixteen peers who represent the body of the Scots nobility for the parliament for which they are elected; and, since the union with Ireland, with the twenty-eight representative peers, who are elected for life, to represent the Irish nobility. The number of *lords temporal* is thus indefinite, for it may be increased at will by the power of the crown, by the creation of peers of the United Kingdom.

The commons consist of all such men of property in the kingdom, as have not seats in the House of Lords; every one of whom has a voice in parliament, either personally or by his representatives. In a free state, every man who is supposed a free agent, ought to be in some measure his own governor; and, therefore, a branch, at least, of the legislative power should reside in the whole body of the people. And this power, when the territories of the state are small, and its citizens easily known, should be exercised by the people in their collective capacity, as was wisely ordained in the petty republics of Greece, and the first rudiments of the Roman state. But this will be highly inconvenient when the public territory is extended to any considerable degree, and the number of citizens is increased. In so large a state as ours, it is, therefore, very wisely contrived, that the people should do that by their representatives, which it is impracticable to perform in person; representatives, chosen by a number of separate districts, where all the voters are, or easily may be, distinguished. The counties are therefore represented by knights elected by the proprietors and occupiers of land; and the cities and boroughs are represented by citizens and burgesses, chosen by the mercantile part, or supposed trading interest of the nation. But every member serves for the whole realm. For the end of his coming thither is not particular, but general: not barely to advantage his constituents, but the *common* wealth; and therefore he is not bound to consult with, or take the advice of, his constituents upon any particular point, unless he himself thinks it proper or prudent so to do.

III. We are next to examine the laws and customs relating to parliament, considered as one aggregate body.

The power and jurisdiction of parliament is so transcendent that it cannot be confined either for causes or persons within any bounds. It has sovereign and uncontrollable authority in the making, abrogating, repealing, reviving, and expounding of laws, concerning matters of all possible denominations, ecclesiastical or temporal, civil, military, maritime, or criminal: this being the place where that absolute despotic power, which must in all governments reside somewhere, is entrusted by the constitution. All mischiefs and grievances, operations and remedies, that transcend the ordinary course of the laws, are within the reach of this extraordinary tribunal. It can regulate or new model the succession to the crown; it can alter the established religion; it can change and create afresh even the constitution of the kingdom and of parliaments themselves; it can, in short, do everything that is not naturally impossible; and, therefore, some have not scrupled to call its power, by a figure rather too bold, the omnipotence of parliament.

In order to prevent the mischiefs that might arise, by placing this extensive authority in hands that are either incapable, or else improper, to manage it, it is provided by the custom and law of parliament, that no one shall sit or vote in either house, unless he be *twenty-one years of age*; and by several statutes, that no member be permitted to sit or vote in the House of Commons (except for the choosing of a speaker), till he has taken the oath of allegiance. *Aliens* are likewise incapable of being members of either house of parliament. And there are not only these standing incapacities; but if any person is made a peer by the crown, or elected to serve in the House of Commons by the people, yet may the respective houses upon complaint of any crime in such person, and proof thereof, adjudge him disabled and incapable to sit as a member; and this by the law and custom of parliament. For, as every court of justice has laws and customs for its direction, some the civil and canon, some the common law, others their own peculiar laws and customs, so the high court of parliament has also its own peculiar law, called the *lex et consuetudo parliamenti*; a law which has its origin from this one maxim, "that whatever matter arises concern-

" ing either house of parliament, ought to be examined, discussed,
" and adjudged in that house to which it relates, and not elsewhere."
Hence, for instance, the lords will not suffer the commons to interfere in settling the election of a peer of Scotland; the commons will
not allow the lords to judge of the election of a burgess; nor will
either house permit the subordinate courts of law to examine the
merits of either case. But the maxims upon which they proceed,
together with the method of proceeding, rest 'entirely in the breast
of the parliament itself; and are not defined and ascertained by any
particular stated laws.

The *privilege* of parliament is likewise very large and indefinite.
It was principally established in order to protect its members not
only from being molested by their fellow-subjects, but also more
especially from being oppressed by the power of the crown. If,
therefore, all the privileges of parliament were set down and ascertained, and no privilege to be allowed but what was so defined and
determined, it were easy for the executive power to devise some new
case, not within the line of privilege, and under pretence thereof to
harass any refractory member and violate the freedom of parliament.
The dignity and independence of the two houses are therefore in
great measure preserved by keeping their privileges indefinite. Some,
however, of the more notorious privileges of the members of either
house are, privilege of speech and of person. As to the first, privilege of speech, it is declared by the statute 1 W. & M., st. 2, c. 2, as
one of the liberties of the people, " that the freedom of speech, and
" debates, and proceedings in parliament, ought not to be impeached
" or questioned in any court or place out of parliament." Their
privilege of person is as ancient as Edward the Confessor, and
included formerly not only privilege from illegal violence, but also
from legal arrests, and seizures by process from the courts of law.
And still to assault by violence a member of either house is a high
contempt of parliament, and is there punishable with the utmost
severity. Neither can any member of either house be arrested
and taken into custody, unless for some indictable offence, without a
breach of the privilege of parliament.

But all other privileges which derogate from the common law in
matters of civil right are now at an end, save only as to the freedom
of the member's person; which in a peer (by the privilege of peerage) is for ever sacred and inviolable; and in a commoner (by
privilege of parliament) for forty days after every prorogation, and
forty days before the next appointed meeting: which is now in effect
as long as the parliament subsists, it seldom being prorogued for
more than fourscore days at a time.

These are the general heads of the laws and customs relating to parliament, considered as one aggregate body. We will next proceed to

IV. The laws and customs relating to the *House of Lords in particular*. These, if we exclude their judicial capacity, which will be more properly treated of in the third and fourth books of these Commentaries, will take up but little of our time.

One very ancient privilege, now obsolete, is that declared by the charter of the forest; viz., that every lord spiritual or temporal summoned to parliament, and passing through the royal forests, may, both in going and returning, kill one or two of the deer without warrant; in view of the forester if he be present, or on blowing a horn if he be absent; that he may not seem to take the royal venison by stealth. In the next place they have a right to be attended, and constantly are, by the judges of the courts of Queen's Bench and Common Pleas, and the barons of the Exchequer; as likewise by the Queen's serjeants; for their advice in points of law, and for the greater dignity of their proceedings. The secretaries of state, with the attorney and solicitor-general, were also used to attend the House of Peers, and have to this day (together with the judges, &c.), their regular writs of summons; but whenever of late years they have been members of the House of Commons, their attendance here has fallen into disuse.

Another privilege is, that every peer, by licence from the sovereign, may make any other lord of parliament his proxy, to vote for him in his absence. A privilege which a member of the other house can by no means have, as he is himself but a proxy for a multitude of other people.

Each peer has also a right, by leave of the house, when a vote passes contrary to his sentiments, to enter his dissent on the journals of the house, with the reasons for such dissent; which is usually styled his protest.

All bills likewise, that may in their consequences any way affect the right of the peerage, are by the custom of parliament to have their first rise and beginning in the House of Peers, and to suffer no changes or amendments in the House of Commons.

V. The peculiar laws and customs of the House of Commons relate principally to the raising of taxes, and the elections of members to serve in parliament.

First, with regard to taxes: it is the ancient indisputable privilege and right of the House of Commons, that all grants of subsidies or parliamentary aids do begin in their house, and are first bestowed by them; although their grants are not effectual until they have the assent of the other branches of the legislature. The lords being a permanent hereditary body, created at pleasure by the sovereign, are

supposed more liable to be influenced by the crown, and when once
influenced to continue so, than the commons, who are a temporary
elective body, freely nominated by the people. It would therefore
be extremely dangerous to give the lords any power of framing new
taxes for the subject: it is sufficient that they have a power of rejecting, if they think the commons too lavish or improvident in their
grants. But so reasonably jealous are the commons of this valuable
privilege, that herein they will not suffer the other house to exert
any power but that of rejecting; they will not permit the least
alteration or amendment to be made by the lords to the mode of
taxing the people by a money bill; under which appellation are
included all bills by which money is directed to be raised upon the
subject, for any purpose or in any shape whatsoever; either for the
exigencies of government, and collected from the kingdom in general,
as the property-tax; or for private benefit, and collected in any
particular district, as by turnpikes, parish rates, and the like.

Next with regard to the elections of knights, citizens, and burgesses; we may observe that herein consists the exercise of the
democratic part of our constitution: for in a democracy there can be
no exercise of sovereignty but by suffrage, which is the declaration
of the people's will. In all democracies therefore it is of the utmost
importance to regulate by whom, and in what manner, the suffrages
are to be given. In England, where the people do not debate in a
collective body, but by representation, the exercise of this sovereignty
consists in the choice of representatives. The laws have therefore
guarded against abuse of this power, by many provisions, which may
be reduced to these three points: 1. The qualifications of the electors. 2. The qualifications of the elected. 3. The proceedings at
elections.

1. As to the qualifications of the electors. The true reason of
requiring any qualification, with regard to property, in voters, is to
exclude such persons as are in so mean a situation that they are
esteemed to have no will of their own. If these persons had votes,
they would be tempted to dispose of them under some undue
influence or other. This would give a great, an artful, or a
wealthy man, a larger share in elections than is consistent with
general liberty. If it were probable that every man would give his
vote freely and without influence of any kind, then, upon the true
theory and general principles of liberty, every member of the community, however poor, should have a vote in electing those delegates,
to whose charge is committed the disposal of his property, his
liberty, and his life. But since that can hardly be expected in persons of indigent fortunes, or such as are under the immediate dominion of others, all popular states have been obliged to establish

certain qualifications; whereby some are excluded from voting, in order to set other individuals, whose wills may be supposed independent, more thoroughly upon a level with each other. In this way it is supposed that such only are entirely excluded as can have no will of their own, and that there is hardly a free agent to be found, who is not entitled to a vote in some place or other in the kingdom. Be that as it may, wealth, or property, is by no means disregarded in elections; for though the richest man has only one vote at one place, yet if his property be at all diffused, he has probably a right to vote at more places than one, and therefore has many representatives.

But to return to our qualifications; and first those of electors for knights of the shire. By statute 8 Hen. VI. c. 7, and subsequent acts, the knights of the shire are to be chosen by people whereof every man shall have freehold to the value of forty shillings by the year within the county; which is to be clear of all charges and deductions except parliamentary and parochial taxes. The knights of shires are the representatives of the landed interest: and their electors must therefore have estates within the county represented; and these estates must have been freehold; because beneficial leases were not in use at the making of these statutes, and copyholders were then little better than villeins, absolutely dependent upon their lords: and this freehold must have been of forty shillings annual value, because that sum would then, with proper industry, have furnished all the necessaries of life, and rendered the freeholder, if he pleased, an independent man. This forty shilling freehold continued to be the sole qualification of a county elector long after leasehold property had become of great value and importance, and copyhold tenure as unobjectionable for all practical purposes as freehold. For the owners of these two kinds of property were only admitted to the franchise in 1832, when a great change was made, not only in the qualifications of electors, but also in the distribution of seats. This was effected by the 2 Will. IV. c. 45, usually called the Reform Act; under which statute the electors of knights of the shire may now be said to consist of four classes, *freeholders, copyholders, leaseholders,* and *occupiers* of land within the county.

1. A freehold of forty shillings annual value is still the distinguishing qualification of a county elector.

2. The owner of an estate for life is not qualified as an elector unless it be of the value of ten pounds above all charges; a new qualification, and one of the chief features of the Reform Act, which may thus be said to have conferred the franchise generally on all *owners* of property of the annual value of ten pounds.

3. Leaseholders for any term created originally for a period of not less than sixty years, of the value of ten pounds; or for any term

created originally for a period of not less than twenty years, of the value of fifty pounds, were also for the first time admitted to the franchise in 1832. Finally,

4. Occupiers as tenants under one landlord, of property for which they pay a rent of not less than fifty pounds, became entitled to vote in the counties.

As for the electors of citizens or burgesses, these are supposed to be the mercantile part or trading interest of this kingdom. But as trade is of a fluctuating nature, and seldom long fixed in a place, it was formerly left to the crown to summon, *pro re natâ*, the most flourishing towns to send representatives to parliament. So that as towns increased in trade, and grew populous, they were admitted to a share in the legislature. But the misfortune was, that the deserted boroughs continued to be summoned, as well as those to whom their trade and inhabitants were transferred; except a few which petitioned to be eased of the expense, then usual, of maintaining their members: four shillings a day being allowed for a knight of the shire, and two shillings for a citizen or burgess; which was the rate of wages established in the reign of Edward III. The universities were not empowered to send burgesses to parliament, till King James I. indulged them with the permanent privilege to send constantly two of their own body, to serve for those students, who, though useful members of the community, were neither concerned in the landed nor the trading interest; and to protect in the legislature the rights of the republic of letters.

The right to vote in boroughs is still various, depending entirely on the several charters, customs, and constitutions of the respective places. But the Reform Act introduced something like uniformity; for while it preserved many then existing rights, it conferred the franchise on a new class of electors, whose rights were made to depend on the occupation of property. Thus,

1. Every burgess or freeman possessing the right at the time is declared entitled to the franchise, but no qualification is to be obtainable by the freedom of a borough for the future.*

2. The franchise is preserved to the resident freeholders or burgage tenants in cities or towns, being counties of themselves.

3. The right of voting is for the first time conferred on every occupier of premises of the value of ten pounds, rated for the relief of the poor. This qualification was the principal feature of the Reform Act, so far as regards the borough electors; and in the new parliamentary boroughs created by the statute, such as Birmingham and Manchester, the electors consist entirely of persons thus qualified.

---

* Except in the city of London, where the liverymen continue entitled to vote in the election of the members for the city.

Formerly, the right of each elector to vote was ascertained at the time of the election, and as he tendered his vote; so that, unless prepared with evidence of his title, his vote, if objected to, might be refused altogether, the polling at one election not unfrequently extending through fourteen days of animated legal discussion, in presence of the sheriff of the county or other returning officer and his legal assessors, whose decisions might afterwards form the subject of a scrutiny, lasting for months and involving enormous expense. This method of taking votes was put an end to in 1832; and a register of electors is now made up annually, alike for the counties as for the cities and boroughs; the appearance of a person's name on this register being decisive of his right to vote; its absence equally conclusive as to his want of qualification.

These lists are annually revised by barristers, appointed for the purpose, who, after public notice, hold courts for settling the lists; at which the overseers, claimants, and objectors attend; the barrister then, on hearing the parties, adding or expunging names, and making alterations in the lists according as he finds the claims or objections to be well founded. An appeal from his decision may be allowed by him; and if allowed, is determined by the court of Common Pleas.

Next, as to the qualifications of persons to be *elected* members of the House of Commons. Some of these depend upon the law and custom of parliament, declared by the House of Commons; others upon certain statutes. And from these it appears: 1. That they must not be aliens born, or minors, idiots, lunatics, or outlaws in criminal prosecutions. 2. That they must not be any of the judges, nor of the representative peers of Ireland, nor of the commissioners in bankruptcy, police magistrates, or revising barristers; nor of the clergy, for they sit in the convocation; nor persons attainted of treason or felony, for they are unfit to sit anywhere. 3. That sheriffs of counties, and mayors of boroughs are not eligible in their respective jurisdictions, as being returning officers; but that the sheriffs of one county are eligible to be knights of another. 4. That no persons concerned in the management of any duties or taxes created since 1692, except the commissioners of the Treasury, nor any of a long list of public officials mentioned in different statutes are capable of being elected. 5. That no person holding a contract on account of the public service, is capable of being elected, or sitting as a member during the time he executes or holds such contract. 6. That no person having a pension under the crown during pleasure, or for any term of years, is capable of being elected or sitting. 7. That if any member accepts an office under the crown (except an officer in the army or navy accepting a new commission), his seat is void; but such member is capable of being re-elected. 8. That if any candidate is declared guilty of bribery, treating, or undue influence, he is incapable of being elected, or sitting in parliament for the particular place during the parliament then in existence. Subject to these standing restrictions and disqualifications, every subject of the realm is eligible of common right: though there are instances wherein persons in particular circumstances have forfeited that common right, and have been declared ineligible *for that parliament* by a vote of the House of Commons, or *for ever* by an act of the legislature.

3. The third point, regarding elections, *is the method of proceeding therein.* This is also regulated by the law of parliament, and by several statutes; all which I shall blend together, and extract out of them a summary account of the method of proceeding to elections.

As soon as the parliament is summoned, the lord chancellor, or if a vacancy happens during the sitting of parliament, the speaker sends his warrant to the clerk of the crown in chancery; who thereupon issues out writs to the proper returning officers, commanding them to elect their members. Elections of knights of the shire must be proceeded to by the sheriffs in person, not later than the twelfth, nor sooner than the sixth day after proclamation for that purpose made within two days after the receipt of the writ. Elections in cities and boroughs must be within six days after the receipt of the writ, of which day the returning officer is required to give three days' clear notice.

And, as it is essential to the very being of parliament, that elections should be absolutely free, therefore all undue influences upon the electors are illegal, and strongly prohibited. As soon therefore as the time and place of election are fixed, notice is given to the secretary-at-war, and all soldiers within two miles of the place of nomination or taking of the poll, are required to remain within their barracks. Riots likewise have been frequently determined to make an election void. By vote also of the House of Commons, to whom alone belongs the power of determining contested elections, no lord of parliament, or lord lieutenant of a county, has any right to interfere in the election of commoners; and, by statute, the lord warden of the cinque ports shall not recommend any members there. If any officer of the excise, customs, stamps, or certain other branches of the revenue, presume to intermeddle in elections, by persuading any voter, or dissuading him, he forfeits 100l. and is disabled to hold any office.

Thus are the electors of one branch of the legislature secured from any undue influence from either of the other two, and from all external violence and compulsion. But the greatest danger is that in which themselves co-operate, by the infamous practice of bribery and corruption ; to prevent which various statutes have been passed from time to time; by which bribery and the using of undue influence are made misdemeanours; candidates offending are disqualified from sitting in parliament, and other guilty persons from being admitted to or continuing on the register of electors.

Undue influence being thus (I wish the depravity of mankind would permit me to say, effectually) guarded against, the election is to be proceeded to on the day appointed ; the sheriff or other returning officer first taking an oath against bribery, and for the due execution of his office. The election in the first instance is determined, after the nomination of the candidates, by a show of hands ; but if a poll be demanded, the proceedings are for that purpose adjourned, in the case of county elections, until the next day but two after the day of nomination, and in the case of cities and boroughs until the following day.

In all elections, except in the universities, only one day is allowed for recording the votes, this limitation of the time for polling being found in practice very conducive to the purity of elections. In the universities, on account of the distance many of the electors may have to travel, the polling may continue for five days. If, however, the proceedings at any election are interrupted or obstructed by riot or open violence, the returning officer may adjourn the nomination or the taking of the poll at any particular place until the following day, and so on from time to time until the interruption has ceased.

At the polling, the only duty of the returning officer now is to inquire for whom the elector votes, such vote being then recorded by the poll-clerks in the poll-books. In county elections, after the close of the poll, the books are sealed and delivered to the sheriff, who on the next day but one opens them, casts up the number of votes, and declaring the state of the poll, makes proclamation of the member or members chosen. In borough elections the returning officer may declare the final state of the poll, either on its close or on the following day.

The election being closed, the returning officer returns the writ, with the names of the persons elected, to the clerk of the crown in chancery, the members returned by him being the sitting members, until the House of Commons, upon petition, shall adjudge the return to be false or illegal. The form and manner of proceeding upon such petition are now regulated by the statute 11 & 12 Vict. c. 98, under the provisions of which a select committee of five members is appointed and sworn to inquire into the allegations of the petition, and report the decision to the house. And this abstract of the proceedings at elections of knights, citizens, and burgesses, concludes our inquiries into the laws and customs more peculiarly relative to the House of Commons.

VI. I proceed then, sixthly, to the method of making laws; which is much the same in both houses: and I shall touch it very briefly, beginning in the House of Commons. But, first, I must premise, that for despatch of business each house of parliament has its *speaker*. The speaker of the House of Lords is the lord chancellor, or keeper of the sovereign's great seal, or any other appointed by royal commission: and if none be so appointed, the House of Lords may elect. The speaker of the House of Commons is chosen by the house; but must be approved by the sovereign. In each house the act of the majority binds the whole; and this majority is declared by votes openly and publicly given.

To bring a bill into the house, if the relief sought by it is of a private nature, it is first necessary to prefer a petition; which must be presented by a member, and usually sets forth the grievance desired to be remedied. This petition (when founded on facts that may be in their nature disputed) is referred to a committee of members, who examine the matter alleged, and accordingly report it to the house; and then (or otherwise, upon the mere petition) leave is given to bring in the bill. In public matters the bill is brought in upon motion made to the house, without any petition at all.

The persons directed to bring in the bill present it in a competent time to the house, drawn out and printed, with a multitude of italics, where anything occurs that is dubious, or necessary to be settled by the parliament itself (such especially as the precise dates of times, the nature and quantities of penalties, or of any sums of money to be raised), which italics are theoretically blanks, or void spaces, being indeed only the skeleton of the bill. In the House of Lords, if the bill begins there, it is (when of a private nature) referred to two of the judges, to examine and report the state of the facts alleged, to see that all necessary parties consent, and to settle all points of technical propriety. This is read a first time, and at a convenient distance a second time; and after each reading the speaker opens to the house the substance of the bill, and puts the question whether it shall proceed any further. The introduction of the bill may be originally opposed, as the bill itself may at either of the readings: and, if the opposition succeeds, the bill must be dropped for that session; as it must also, if opposed with success in any of the subsequent stages.

After the second reading it is committed, that is, referred to a

committee, which is either selected by the house in matters of small
importance, or else, upon a bill of consequence, the house resolves
itself into a committee of the whole house: to form which, the
speaker quits the chair (another member being appointed chairman),
and may sit and debate as a private member. In these committees
the bill is debated clause by clause, amendments made, the blanks
filled up, and sometimes the bill entirely new-modelled. After it
has gone through the committee, the chairman reports it to the
house with such amendments as the committee have made; and
then the house reconsiders the whole bill again, and the question is
put upon every clause and amendment. When the house has agreed
or disagreed to the amendments of the committee, and sometimes
added new amendments of its own, the bill is then in due course
read a third time, and amendments are sometimes then made to it,
and new clauses added. The speaker then again opens the contents,
and holding it up in his hands, puts the question, whether the bill
shall pass? If this is agreed to, the title to it is then settled; after
which one of the members is directed to carry it to the lords, and
desire their concurrence; who, attended by several more, carries it to
the bar of the House of Peers, and there delivers it to their speaker,
who comes down from his woolsack to receive it.

It there passes through the same forms, and, if rejected, no more
notice is taken, but it passes *sub silentio*, to prevent unbecoming
altercations. But if it is agreed to, the lords send a message (upon
matters of high dignity and importance, by two of the judges), that
they have agreed to the same: and the bill remains with the lords
if they have made no amendment to it. But if any amendments are
made, such amendments are sent down with the bill, to receive the
concurrence of the commons. If the commons disagree to the
amendments, a conference usually follows between members de-
puted from each house; who, for the most part, settle and adjust
the difference: but, if both houses remain inflexible, the bill is
dropped. If the commons agree to the amendments, the bill is sent
back to the lords by one of the members, with a message to acquaint
them therewith. The same forms are observed, *mutatis mutandis*,
when the bill begins in the House of Lords. And when both houses
have done with any bill, it always is deposited in the House of
Peers, to wait the royal assent; except in the case of a bill of supply,
which, after receiving the concurrence of the lords, is sent back to
the House of Commons.

The royal assent may be given in two ways: 1. In person; when
the sovereign comes to the House of Peers, and sending for the commons to the bar, the titles of all the bills that have passed both
houses are read; and the royal answer is declared by the clerk of

the parliament. If the sovereign consents to a public bill, the clerk usually declares, " *le roy* (or *la reine*) *le veut*, the king (or the queen) " wills it so to be ;" if to a private bill, " *soit fait comme il est desiré*, " be it as it is desired." If the sovereign refuses his assent, it is in the gentle language of " *le roy s'avisera*, the king will advise upon " it." When a bill of supply is passed, it is carried up and presented to the king by the speaker of the House of Commons ; and the royal assent is thus expressed, " *le roy remercie ses loyal subjects, accepte* ' *leur benevolence, et aussi le veut*, the king thanks his loyal subjects, ' accepts their benevolence, and wills it so to be." The crown may give its assent to bills by letters patent or commission under its great seal, which are notified to both houses assembled together in the House of Lords. And, when the bill has received the royal assent in either of these ways, it is then, and not before, a statute or act of parliament.

This statute is placed among the records of the kingdom, there needing no formal promulgation to give it the force of a law, because every man in England is, in judgment of law, party to making an act of parliament, being present thereat by his representatives. And a statute thus made is the exercise of the highest authority that this kingdom acknowledges upon earth. It has power to bind every subject in the land, and the dominions thereunto belonging; nay, even the sovereign himself, if particularly named therein. And it cannot be altered, amended, dispensed with, suspended, or repealed, but in the same forms and by the same authority of parliament.

VII. There remains only, in the seventh and last place, to add a word or two concerning the manner in which parliaments may be adjourned, prorogued, or dissolved.

An *adjournment* is no more than a continuance of the session from one day to another, as the word itself signifies : and this is done by the authority of each house separately every day ; and sometimes for a fortnight or a month together, as at Christmas or Easter, or upon other particular occasions. But the adjournment of one house is no adjournment of the other. A *prorogation* is the continuance of the parliament from one session to another, as an adjournment is the continuation of the session from day to day. This is done by the royal authority, expressed either by the lord chancellor in the presence of the sovereign, or by commission from the crown, or frequently by proclamation. Both houses are necessarily prorogued at the same time, it being a prorogation not of the House of Lords, or Commons, but of the parliament.

A *dissolution* is the civil death of the parliament ; and this may be effected three ways : 1. By the sovereign's will, expressed either in person or by representation. For, as the crown has the sole right of convening the parliament, so also it is a branch of the royal prerogative, that he may prorogue the parliament for a time, or put a final period to its existence. If nothing had a right to prorogue or dissolve a parliament but itself, it might happen to become perpetual. It is, therefore, extremely necessary that the crown should be empowered to regulate the duration of these assemblies, under the limitations which the English constitution has prescribed: so that, on the one hand, they may frequently and regularly come together for the despatch of business, and redress of grievances; and may not, on the other, even with the consent of the crown, be continued to an inconvenient or unconstitutional length.

2. A parliament may be *dissolved* by the demise of the crown. This dissolution formerly happened immediately upon the death of the reigning sovereign; for he being considered in law as the head of the parliament, that failing, the whole body was held to be extinct. But calling a new parliament immediately on the inauguration of the successor being found inconvenient, and dangers being apprehended from having no parliament in being in case of a disputed succession, it is provided by several statutes that the parliament in being shall continue for six months after the death of any king or queen, unless sooner prorogued or dissolved by the successor.

3. Lastly, a parliament may be dissolved or expire by length of time. For if either the legislative body were perpetual; or might last for the life of the prince who convened them, as formerly; and were so to be supplied, by occasionally filling the vacancies with new representatives; in these cases, if it were once corrupted, the evil would be past all remedy: but when different bodies succeed each other, if the people see cause to disapprove of the present, they may rectify its faults in the next. As our constitution now stands the parliament must expire, or die a natural death, at the end of every seventh year, if not sooner dissolved by the royal prerogative.

CHAPTER III.

OF THE SOVEREIGN AND HIS TITLE.

The crown hereditary—Title defeasible by act of parliament—Historical view of the succession—Revolution of 1688—The Act of Settlement.

THE supreme executive power of these kingdoms is vested by our laws in a single person, the king or queen; for it matters not to which sex the crown descends: but the person entitled to it, whether male or female, is immediately invested with all the ensigns, rights, and prerogatives of sovereign power. This power being thus vested in a single person, it became necessary to the freedom and peace of the state, that a rule should be laid down, to mark out with precision *who* is that single person, to whom are committed the care and protection of the community; and to whom, in return, the allegiance of every individual is due; and our constitution accordingly has not left us in the dark upon this material occasion.

The grand fundamental maxim upon which the *jus coronæ*, or right of succession to the throne of these kingdoms, depends, I take to be this: " that the crown is, by common law and constitutional " custom, hereditary; and this in a manner peculiar to itself; but " that the right of inheritance may from time to time be changed or " limited by act of parliament; under which limitations the crown " still continues hereditary."

1. First, it is in general *hereditary*, or descendible to the next heir, on the death or demise of the last proprietor. Yet while I assert an hereditary, I by no means intend a *jure divino* title to the throne. Such a title may have subsisted under the theocratic establishments of the children of Israel in Palestine, but it never yet subsisted in any other country. So that the hereditary right which the laws of England acknowledge, owes its origin to the founders of our constitution, and to them only. They might, if they had thought proper, have made it an elective monarchy; but they rather chose to establish originally a succession by inheritance. This has been acquiesced in by general consent; and ripened by degrees into common law: the very same title that every private man has to his own estate. Lands are not naturally descendible any more than thrones; but the law has thought proper, for the benefit and peace of the public, to establish hereditary succession in the one as well as the other.

2. But, secondly, as to the particular mode of inheritance, it in

general corresponds with the feudal path of descents, chalked out by
the law in succession to landed estates. Like estates, the crown will
descend lineally to the issue of the reigning monarch, as it did from
King John to Richard II., through a regular pedigree of six lineal
generations. As in common descents, the preference of males to
females, and the right of primogeniture among the males, are strictly
adhered to. Thus Edward V. succeeded to the crown in preference
to Richard his younger brother, and Elizabeth his elder sister. Like
lands or tenements, the crown, on failure of the male line, descends,
to the issue female. Thus Mary I. succeeded to Edward VI., and
the line of Margaret Queen of Scots, the daughter of Henry VII.,
succeeded on failure of the line of Henry VIII., his son. But among
the females, the crown descends by right of primogeniture to the
eldest daughter only and her issue; and not, as in common inheritances, to all the daughters at once; the evident necessity of a sole
succession to the throne having occasioned the royal law of descents
to depart from the common law in this respect; and therefore Queen
Mary, on the death of her brother, succeeded to the crown alone,
and not in partnership with her sister Elizabeth. Again, the doctrine
of representation prevails in the descent of the crown, as it does in
other inheritances; whereby the lineal descendants of any person
deceased stand in the same place as their ancestor, if living, would
have done. Thus Richard II. succeeded his grandfather Edward III.,
in right of his father the Black Prince, to the exclusion of all his
uncles, his grandfather's younger children. Lastly, on failure of
lineal descendants, the crown goes to the next collateral relations of
the late king; provided they are lineally descended from the blood-
royal, that is from the royal stock which originally acquired the
crown. Thus Henry I. succeeded to William II., John to Richard I.,
and James I. to Elizabeth, being all derived from the Conqueror,
who was then the only regal stock.

3. The doctrine of *hereditary* right does by no means imply an
indefeasible right to the throne. It is unquestionably in the breast
of the supreme legislative authority of this kingdom to defeat this
hereditary right; and, by particular limitations and provisions, to
exclude the immediate heir, and vest the inheritance in any one else.

4. But, fourthly, however the crown may be limited or transferred, it still retains its descendible quality, and becomes hereditary
in the wearer of it. And hence the king is said never to die, in his
political capacity; though, in common with other men, he is subject
to mortality in his natural: because immediately upon the natural
death of Henry, William, or Edward, the sovereign survives in his
successor. For the right of the crown vests, *eo instanti*, upon his
heir; either the *hæres natus*, if the course of descent remains unim-

peached, or the *hæres factus*, if the inheritance be under any particular settlement. So that there can be no *interregnum*; but the right of sovereignty is fully invested in the successor by the very descent of the crown. And therefore, however acquired, it becomes in him absolutely hereditary, unless by the rules of the limitation it is otherwise ordered and determined.

In these four points consists, as I take it, the constitutional notion of hereditary right to the throne; which will be still further elucidated, and made clear beyond all dispute, from a short historical view of the succession to the crown, the doctrines of our ancient lawyers, and the several acts of parliament that have from time to time been made, to create, to declare, to confirm, to limit, or to bar the hereditary title to the throne.

King Egbert, about the year 800, found himself in possession of the throne of the West Saxons by a long and undisturbed descent from his ancestors of above three hundred years. How his ancestors acquired their title, whether by force, by fraud, by contract, or by election, it matters not much to inquire; his right must be supposed indisputably good, because we know no better.

From Egbert to the death of Edmund Ironside, a period of above two hundred years, the crown descended regularly through a succession of fifteen princes, without any deviation or interruption: save only that the sons of King Ethelwolf succeeded to each other in the kingdom, without regard to the children of the elder branches, according to the rule of succession prescribed by their father, and confirmed by the witena-gemote, in the heat of the Danish invasions: and also that King Edred, the uncle of Edwy, mounted the throne for about nine years, in the right of his nephew, a minor, the times being very troublesome and dangerous. But this was with a view to preserve, and not to destroy, the succession; and accordingly Edwy succeeded him.

King Edmund Ironside was obliged, by the hostile irruption of the Danes, at first to divide his kingdom with Canute, King of Denmark; and Canute, after his death, seized the whole of it, Edmund's son being driven into foreign countries. Here the succession was suspended by actual force, and a new family introduced upon the throne: in whom, however, this new-acquired throne continued hereditary for three reigns; when, upon the death of Hardicanute, the ancient Saxon line was restored in the person of Edward the Confessor.

He was not, indeed, the true heir to the crown, being the younger brother of Edmund Ironside, who had a son Edward, surnamed (from his exile) the Outlaw, still living. But this son was then in Hun-

gary : and, the English having just shaken off the Danish yoke, it
was necessary that somebody on the spot should mount the throne;
and the Confessor was the next of the royal line then in England.
On his decease without issue, Harold I. usurped the throne; and
almost at the same instant came on the northern invasion : the right
to the crown being all the time in Edgar Atheling, the son of
Edward the Outlaw, and grandson of Edmund Ironside.

William the Norman claimed the crown by virtue of a pretended
grant from the Confessor; a grant which, if real, was in itself utterly
invalid; because it was made, as Harold well observed in his reply
to William's demand, " *absque generali senatus et populi conventu et*
" *edicto*;" which also very plainly implies, that it then was generally
understood that the king, with consent of the general council, might
dispose of the crown, and change the line of succession.

His conquest was, like that of Canute before, a forcible transfer of
the crown of England into a new family; but, the crown being so
transferred, all the inherent properties of the crown were with it
transferred also. For, the victory obtained at Hastings not being a
victory over the nation collectively, but only over the person of
Harold, the only right that the Conqueror could pretend to acquire
thereby, was the right to possess the crown of England, not to alter
the nature of the government. And, therefore, as the English laws
still remained in force, he must necessarily take the crown subject
to those laws, and with all its inherent properties; the first and
principal of which was its descendibility.

Accordingly, it descended from him to his sons William II. and
Henry I. Robert, his eldest son, was no doubt kept out of possession
by the arts and violence of his brethren : who perhaps might proceed upon a notion that he was already provided for as Duke of
Normandy by his father's will.   But, as he died without issue,
Henry at last had a good title to the throne, whatever he might have
at first.

Stephen of Blois, who succeeded him, was indeed the grandson of
the Conqueror, by Adelicia, his daughter, and claimed the throne by
a feeble kind of hereditary right : not as being the nearest of the
male line, but as the nearest male of the blood royal, excepting his
elder brother Theobald, who was Earl of Blois, and therefore seems
to have waived, as he certainly never insisted on, so troublesome and
precarious a claim. The real right was in the Empress Matilda,
daughter of Henry I.; the rule of succession being that the daughter
of a son shall be preferred to the son of a daughter. So that Stephen
was little better than a usurper; and therefore, he rather chose to
rely on a title by election, while the empress did not fail to assert

her hereditary right by the sword; which dispute was attended
with various success, and ended at last in the compromise made at
Wallingford, that Stephen should keep the crown, but that Henry,
the son of Maud, should succeed him, as he afterwards accordingly
did.

Henry, the second of that name, was (next after Matilda) the
undoubted heir of the Conqueror;* and from him the crown descended to his eldest son, Richard I., who dying childless, the right
vested in his nephew Arthur, the son of Geoffrey his next brother:
but John, the youngest son of King Henry, seized the throne; claiming, as appears from his charters, the crown by hereditary right:
that is to say, he was next of kin to the deceased king, being his
surviving brother: whereas Arthur was removed one degree further,
being his brother's son, though by right of representation he
stood in the place of his father Geoffrey.   And however flimsy
this title, and those of William Rufus and Stephen of Blois, may
appear at this distance to us, after the law of descents has now been
settled for so many centuries, they were sufficient to puzzle the understanding of our ancestors.   However, on the death of Arthur and
his sister Eleanor without issue, a clear and indisputable title vested
in Henry III., the son of John: and from him to Richard II.,
a succession of six generations, the crown descended in the true
hereditary line.

Upon Richard's resignation, he having no children, the right
reverted to the issue of his grandfather, Edward III. That king
had many children, besides his eldest, Edward the Black Prince,
the father of Richard II.: but, to avoid confusion, I shall only
mention three: William, his second son, who died without issue;
Lionel, Duke of Clarence, his third son; and John of Gaunt, Duke
of Lancaster, his fourth. By the rules of succession, therefore, the
posterity of Lionel, Duke of Clarence, were entitled to the throne
upon the resignation of King Richard. But Henry, Duke of Lancaster, the son of John of Gaunt, having then a large army in the
kingdom, the pretence of raising which was to recover his patrimony
from the king, and to redress the grievances of the subject, it was

* He had also another connexion in blood, which endeared him still further
to the English. He was lineally descended from Edmund Ironside, the last of
the Saxon race of hereditary kings. For Edward the Outlaw, son of Edmund
Ironside, had (besides Edgar Atheling, who died without issue) a daughter
Margaret, who was married to Malcolm, King of Scotland; and in her the
Saxon hereditary right resided. She had several children, and among the rest
Matilda, wife of Henry I., who by him had the Empress Matilda, the mother
of Henry II. Upon which account the Saxon line is frequently said to have
been restored in his person: though, in reality, that right subsisted in the sons
of Queen Margaret; King Henry's best title being as heir to the Conqueror.

impossible for any other title to be asserted with any safety; and
he became king under the title of Henry IV.   But though the
people unjustly assisted Henry IV. in his usurpation of the crown,
yet he was not admitted thereto, until he had declared that he
claimed, not as a conqueror but as a successor, descended by right
line of the royal blood; as appears from the rolls of parliament in
those times.

However, as in Edward III.'s time we find the parliament approv-
ing and affirming the law of the crown, so in the reign of Henry IV.,
they actually exerted their right of new-settling the succession by
the statute 7 Hen. IV. c. 2, enacting "that the inheritance of the
" crown and realms of England and France, and all other the king's
" dominions, shall be *set and remain* in the person of our sovereign
" lord the king, and in the heirs of his body issuing;" which serves
to show that it was then generally understood that the king and
parliament had a right to regulate the succession to the crown.

The crown now descended regularly from Henry IV. to his son
and grandson, Henry V. and VI.; in the latter of whose reigns the
house of York asserted their dormant title; and at last established
it in the person of Edward IV.   At his accession to the throne, after
a breach of the succession that continued for three descents, and
above threescore years, the distinction of a king *de jure* and a king
de facto began to be first taken; in order to indemnify such as had
submitted to the late establishment, and to provide for the peace of
the kingdom by confirming all honours conferred and all acts done,
by those who were now called the usurpers, not tending to the disherison of the rightful heir.

Edward IV. left two sons and a daughter; the eldest of which
sons, king Edward V., enjoyed the regal dignity for a very short time,
and was then deposed by Richard, who usurped the royal dignity;
having previously insinuated to the populace a suspicion of bastardy
in the children of Edward IV., to make a show of some hereditary
title; after which he is believed to have murdered his two nephews,
upon whose death the right of the crown devolved to their sister
Elizabeth.

The tyrannical reign of King Richard III. gave occasion to Henry
Earl of Richmond to assert his title to the crown; a title the most
remote and unaccountable that was ever set up, and which nothing
could have given success to, but the universal detestation of Richard.
For, besides that he claimed under a descent from John of Gaunt,
whose title was now exploded, the claim (such as it was) was through
John Earl of Somerset, a bastard son, begotten by John of Gaunt
upon Catherine Swinford.   Notwithstanding all this, immediately
after the battle of Bosworth Field, he assumed the regal dignity;
and his possession was established by parliament, holden the first

year of his reign. In the act for which purpose, the parliament seems to have copied the caution of their predecessors in the reign of Henry IV.; and therefore carefully avoided any recognition of Henry VII.'s right, which indeed was none at all; and the king would not have it by way of new law or ordinance, whereby a right might seem to be created and conferred upon him; and therefore a middle way was rather chosen, by way of *establishment*, and that under covert and indifferent words, "that the inheritance of the " crown should *rest, remain*, and *abide* in King Henry VII. and the " heirs of his body :" thereby providing for the future, and at the same time acknowledging his present possession; but not determining either way, whether that possession was *de jure* or *de facto* merely. However, he soon after married Elizabeth of York, the undoubted heiress of the Conqueror, and thereby gained by much his best title to the crown. Whereupon the act made in his favour was so much disregarded, that it never was printed in our statute books.

Henry VIII., the issue of this marriage, succeeded to the crown by clear indisputable hereditary right, and transmitted it to his three children in successive order. But in his reign we at several times find the parliament busy in regulating the succession to the kingdom. The crown was finally limited to Prince Edward by name, after that to the Lady Mary, and then to the Lady Elizabeth, and the heirs of their respective bodies; which succession took effect accordingly, being indeed no other than the usual course of the law, with regard to the descent of the crown.

. Upon Queen Mary's marriage with Philip of Spain, the hereditary right to the crown was again asserted and declared in parliament; and on Queen Elizabeth's accession, her right is recognised in still stronger terms than her sister's.

On the death of Queen Elizabeth, without issue, the line of Henry VIII. became extinct. It therefore became necessary to recur to the other issue of Henry VII. by Elizabeth of York his queen; whose eldest daughter Margaret having married James IV. king of Scotland, King James the Sixth of Scotland, and of England the First, was the lineal descendant from that alliance. So that in his person, as clearly as in Henry VIII., centred all the claims of different competitors, from the Conquest downwards, he being indisputably the lineal heir of the Conqueror. And, what is still more remarkable, in his person also centred the right of the Saxon monarchs which had been suspended from the Conquest till his accession. For Margaret, the sister of Edgar Atheling, the daughter of Edward the Outlaw, and grand-daughter of King Edmund Ironside, was the person in whom the hereditary right of the Saxon kings, supposing it not abolished by the Conquest, resided. She married Malcolm king of Scotland, by whom she had several sons; and the royal family of Scotland from that time downwards were the offspring of Malcolm and Margaret. Of this royal family King James I. was the direct lineal heir, and therefore united in his person every possible claim by hereditary right to the English as well as Scottish throne, being the heir both of Egbert and William the Conqueror.

And it is no wonder that a prince of more learning than wisdom, who could deduce an hereditary title for more than eight hundred years, should easily be taught by the flatterers of the times to believe there was something divine in this right, and that the finger of Providence was visible in its preservation. Whereas, though a wise institution, it was clearly a human institution; and the right inherent in him no natural, but a positive right. And in this and no other light was it taken by the English parliament.

But, wild and absurd as the doctrine of divine right most undoubtedly is, it is still more astonishing, that when so many human hereditary rights had centred in this king, his son and heir Charles I. should be told that he was an elective prince; elected by his people, and therefore accountable to them for his conduct. The confusion which followed will be a standing argument in favour of hereditary and constitutional monarchy to future ages. Soon after the death of the Protector, a parliamentary convention restored the regal heir, and solemnly acknowledged that immediately upon the decease of King Charles, " the imperial crown of these realms did by " inherent birthright, and lawful and undoubted succession, descend " and come to his most excellent majesty Charles II., as being " lineally, justly, and lawfully, next heir of the blood royal of this " realm; and thereunto they most humbly and faithfully did submit " and oblige themselves, their heirs, and posterity for ever."

Thus I think it clearly appears, that the crown of England has ever been a hereditary crown; though subject to limitations by parliament. The remainder of this chapter will consist principally of those instances not already referred to, wherein the parliament has exercised the right of altering and limiting the succession.

The first instance, in point of time, is the famous bill of exclusion, which in the latter end of the reign of King Charles II. passed the House of Commons, but was rejected by the lords; the king having also declared beforehand, that he never would be brought to consent to it. And from this transaction we may collect two things: 1. That the crown was universally acknowledged to be hereditary; and the inheritance indefeasible unless by parliament: else it had been needless to prefer such a bill. 2. That the parliament had a power to have defeated the inheritance: else such a bill had been ineffectual. However, as the bill took no effect, James II. succeeded to the throne, and might have enjoyed it during the remainder of his life, but for the Revolution in 1688.

The true principle upon which that memorable event proceeded, was an entirely new case in politics, which had never before happened in our history. It was not a defeasance of the right of succession, and a new limitation of the crown, by the king and both houses of parliament; it was the act of the nation alone, upon a conviction that there was no king in being. For in a full assembly of the lords and commons, met in a convention upon the supposition of this vacancy, both houses came to the resolution that the throne was vacant. Thus ended at once the old line of succession. The facts appealed to, the king's endeavour to subvert the constitution by breaking the original contract, his violation of the fundamental laws, and his withdrawing himself out of the kingdom, were evident and notorious; and the consequences drawn from these facts, it belonged to our ancestors to determine, they alone having most indisputably a competent jurisdiction to decide this great and important question.

This single postulatum, the vacancy of the throne, being once established, the rest that was then done followed almost of course. For, if the throne be at any time vacant, the right of disposing of this vacancy seems naturally to result to the lords and commons, the trustees and representatives of the nation. For there are no other hands in which it can so properly be intrusted; and there is a necessity of its being intrusted somewhere, else the whole frame of government must be dissolved and perish. The lords and commons having therefore determined this main fundamental article, that there was a vacancy of the throne, they proceeded to fill up that vacancy in such a manner as they judged the most proper.

Upon the principles before established, the convention might no doubt have vested the regal dignity in a family entirely new, and strangers to the royal blood, but they were too well acquainted with the benefits of hereditary succession, and the influence which it has by custom over the minds of the people, to depart any further from the ancient line than temporary necessity required. They therefore settled the crown, first on King William and Queen Mary, King James's eldest daughter, for their joint lives: then on the survivor of them, and then on the issue of Queen Mary: upon failure of such issue, it was limited to the Princess Anne, King James's second daughter, and her issue; and lastly, on failure of that, to the issue of King William, who was the grandson of Charles I, and nephew as well as son-in-law of King James II., being the son of Mary his eldest sister. This settlement included all the Protestant posterity of King Charles I., except such other issue as King

James might at any time have, which was totally omitted, through fear of a popish succession. And this order of succession took effect accordingly. These three princes therefore, King William, Queen Mary, and Queen Anne, did not take the crown by hereditary right or *descent*, but by way of donation or *purchase*, as the lawyers call it; by which they mean any method of acquiring an estate otherwise than by descent.

Towards the end of King William's reign, when all hopes of any surviving issue from any of these princes died with the Duke of Gloucester, the king and parliament thought it necessary again to exert their power of limiting and appointing the succession, in order to prevent another vacancy of the throne, which must have ensued upon their deaths, as no further provision was made at the Revolution, than for the issue of Queen Mary, Queen Anne, and King William. The parliament had previously excluded from the crown every person who should be reconciled to, or hold communion with, the see of Rome. To act therefore consistently with themselves, and at the same time pay as much regard to the old hereditary line as their former resolutions would admit, they turned their eyes on the Princess Sophia, electress and Duchess Dowager of Hanover, the youngest daughter of Elizabeth Queen of Bohemia, daughter of James I., nearest of the ancient blood royal who was not incapacitated by professing the popish religion. On her therefore, and the heirs of her body, being Protestants, the remainder of the crown, expectant on the death of King William and Queen Anne, without issue, was settled; and at the same time it was enacted that whosoever should hereafter come to the possession of the crown should join in the communion of the Church of England as by law established.

This is the last limitation of the crown that has been made by parliament. The Princess Sophia dying before Queen Anne, the inheritance thus limited descended on her son and heir George I., and having on the death of the queen taken effect in his person, from him it descended to George II.; and from him to his grandson and heir, George III. From him again it descended to his eldest son, George IV., who dying without issue was succeeded by William IV., the third son of George III.; the second son Frederick Augustus, Duke of York, having previously died without issue. On the death of William IV., the inheritance descended to the only child of Edward Duke of Kent, the fourth son of George III., our present sovereign Queen Victoria.

Hence it is easy to collect, that the title to the crown is at present hereditary, though not quite so absolutely hereditary as it formerly was. The descent was formerly absolute, and the crown went to

D

the next heir without any restriction; but now, upon the new settlement, the inheritance is conditional, being limited to such heirs only of the body of the Princess Sophia as are Protestant members of the Church of England, and are married to none but Protestants. And in this due medium consists, I apprehend, the true constitutional notion of the right of succession to the imperial crown of these kingdoms. It was the duty of an expounder of our laws to lay this constitution before the student in its true and genuine light: it is the duty of every good Englishman to understand and to defend it.

CHAPTER IV.

OF THE ROYAL FAMILY.

The Queen Consort—Dowager—The Prince of Wales.

THE first and most considerable branch of the royal family, regarded by the laws of England (supposing the sovereign to be a king) is the *queen*.

The queen is either *regent*, *consort*, or *dowager*. The queen *regent*, or *sovereign*, holds the crown in her own right; and has the same powers, prerogatives, and duties as a king. The queen *consort* is the wife of the reigning king; and she is participant of divers prerogatives above other women.

She is a public person, distinct from the king. She may purchase and convey lands, and do other acts of ownership, without the concurrence of her lord. She is also capable of taking a grant from the king, which no other wife is from her husband. She has separate courts and offices distinct from the king's, not only in matters of ceremony, but even of law; and her attorney and solicitor general are entitled to a place within the bar. She may sue and be sued alone, and may have a separate property in goods as well as lands, and has a right to dispose of them by will.

She has also some pecuniary advantages, which form her distinct revenue. This before and after the conquest consisted in certain rents out of the demesne lands of the crown, which were frequently appropriated to particular purposes: as to buy wool for her Majesty's use, to purchase oil for her lamps, or to furnish her attire from head to foot.

Another ancient perquisite belonging to the queen consort, mentioned by all our old writers, and therefore only worthy of notice, is this: that on the taking of a whale on the coasts, which is a royal fish, it shall be divided between the king and queen; the head only being the king's property, and the tail of it the queen's. *"De stur-*"gione observetur, quod rex illum habebit integrum: de balena vero "sufficit si rex habeat caput, et regina caudam."* The reason of this whimsical division was to furnish the queen's wardrobe with whale-bone, a reason more whimsical than the division itself.

But further: though the queen is in all respects a subject, yet, in point of the security of her life and person, she is put on the same footing with the king. It is equally treason to compass or imagine the death of our lady the king's companion, as of the king himself: and to violate, or defile the queen consort, amounts to the same high crime; as well in the person committing the fact, as in the queen herself, if consenting. If, however, the queen be accused of any species of treason, she shall (whether consort or dowager) be tried by the peers of parliament, as queen Ann Boleyn was in 28 Henry VIII.

The husband of a queen regnant is her subject; and may be guilty of high treason against her: but in the instance of conjugal infidelity, he is, for obvious reasons, not subjected to the same penal restrictions.

A queen *dowager* is the widow of the king, and as such enjoys most of the privileges belonging to her as queen consort. But it is not high treason to conspire her death, or to violate her chastity, be-cause the succession to the crown is not thereby endangered. Yet still, no man can marry a queen dowager without special licence from the sovereign, on pain of forfeiting his lands and goods; and a queen dowager, when married again to a subject, does not lose her regal dignity as peeresses dowager (when commoners by birth) do their peerage, when they marry commoners.

The Prince of Wales, or heir apparent to the crown, and also his royal consort, and the princess royal, or eldest daughter of the king, are likewise peculiarly regarded by the laws. To compass the death of the former, or to violate the chastity of either of the latter, are as much high treason as to conspire the death of the king, or violate the chastity of the queen. The heir apparent to the crown is usually made Prince of Wales and Earl of Chester, by special creation and investiture; but being the king's eldest son, he is by inheritance Duke of Cornwall, without any new creation.

The rest of the royal family may be considered in two different lights, according to the different senses in which the term *royal family* is used. The larger sense includes all those who are by any possibility inheritable to the crown; which, since the Act of Settlement, means the Protestant issue of the Princess Sophia. The more confined sense includes only those who are in a certain degree of propinquity to the reigning prince, and to whom, therefore, the law pays an extraordinary regard and respect.

Their education while minors, and the approbation of their marriages, when grown up, belongs of right to the king; a rule applying to the grandchildren as well as children of the sovereign. Indeed, no descendant of King George II. (other than the issue of princesses married into foreign families) is capable of contracting matrimony, without the previous consent of the sovereign signified under the great seal; and any marriage contracted without such consent is void. But as this consent might be arbitrarily withheld, any of the said descendants who is above the age of twenty-five, may, after twelve months' notice to the privy council, contract marriage without the consent of the crown, unless both houses of parliament shall, before the expiration of the year, expressly declare their disapprobation of such intended marriage.

CHAPTER V.

OF THE ROYAL COUNCILS.

Parliament—The Peers—The Privy Council—Its executive and legislative duties—The Judicial Committee.

To assist the sovereign in the discharge of his duties, the maintenance of his dignity, and the exertion of his prerogative, the law has assigned him a diversity of councils to advise with.

1. The first of these is the high court of parliament, whereof we have already treated at large.

2. Secondly, the peers of the realm are by their birth hereditary counsellors of the crown. They are created for two reasons: 1. *Ad consulendum;* 2. *Ad defendendum, regem:* on which account the law gives them certain great and high privileges; such as freedom from arrest, &c., even when no parliament is sitting; because it intends that they are always assisting the sovereign with their counsel for the commonwealth, or keeping the realm in safety by their prowess and valour.

Instances of conventions of the peers, to advise the crown, have been in former times very frequent, though now fallen into disuse by reason of the more regular meetings of parliament. Indeed, the formal method of convoking them had been so long left off, that when Charles I., in 1640, issued writs to call a great council of the peers to meet at York, the Earl of Clarendon mentions it as a new invention, not before heard of. Besides this general meeting, it is usually looked upon to be the right of each particular peer to demand an audience, and to lay before the king such matters as he shall judge of importance to the public weal. And therefore, in the reign of Edward II., it was made an article of impeachment against the two Spencers, for which they were banished, that they would not suffer the great men of the realm to speak with the king, or to come near him.

3. But the principal council belonging to the sovereign is the privy council, generally called by way of eminence, *The Council*; a noble, honourable, and reverend assembly of the sovereign and such as he wills to be of his privy council, for the sovereign's will is the sole constituent of a privy councillor, and this also regulates their number, which is indefinite. This assembly is presided over by the lord president of the council, who has precedence next after the lord chancellor and lord treasurer.

The *duty* of a privy councillor appears from the oath of office, which consists of seven articles: 1. To advise the king according to the best of his cunning and discretion. 2. To advise for the king's honour and good of the public, without partiality through affection, love, meed, doubt, or dread. 3. To keep the king's counsel secret. 4. To avoid corruption. 5. To help and strengthen the execution of what shall be there resolved. 6. To withstand all persons who would attempt the contrary. And lastly, in general, 7. To observe, keep, and do all that a good and true councillor ought to do to his sovereign lord.

The *office* of a privy councillor is now confined to advising the sovereign in the discharge of those *executive, legislative,* and *judicial* duties which the constitution has reposed in him. The former have, since the accession of Queen Anne, been entrusted to responsible ministers; and it has consequently become the settled practice to summon to the meetings of the council those members of it only, who, for the time being, hold the reins of government, or, in other words, are the ministers of the crown.

The *legislative* functions which remain in the privy council are now solely exercised with reference to the colonies and other dependencies of the crown, over which the authority of the sovereign in council is more or less extensive. In the Channel Islands it is said to be absolute; but in modern times the legislation for these islands has generally been by act of parliament. Laws and ordinances are, however, made in the privy council for those colonies and settlements which do not possess representative assemblies; and the legislative acts of most of the other dependencies of the crown are therein approved or disallowed.

In admiralty causes, which arise out of the jurisdiction of this kingdom, and in matters of lunacy or idiocy, which are a special flower of the prerogative, an appeal lies to the sovereign in council; and from all the dominions of the crown, excepting Great Britain and Ireland, an *appellate* jurisdiction (in the last resort) is vested in the same tribunal. This *judicial* authority is vested in the judicial committee of the privy council, who hear the allegations and proofs, and make their report to the sovereign, by whom the judgment is finally given.

The *power* of the privy council is to inquire into all offences against the government, and to commit the offenders for trial. But their jurisdiction herein is only to inquire, and not to punish: and persons committed by them are entitled to their *habeas corpus* as much as if committed by an ordinary justice of the peace.

The dissolution of the privy council depends upon the royal pleasure; and he may, whenever he thinks proper, discharge any particular member, or the whole of it, and appoint another. By the common law also it was dissolved *ipso facto* by the demise of the sovereign; but to prevent the inconvenience of having no council in being at the accession of a new prince, the privy council is enabled by statute to continue for six months after the demise of the crown, unless sooner determined by the successor.

CHAPTER VI.

OF THE SOVEREIGN'S DUTY.

To govern according to law; to execute judgment in mercy; and to maintain the established religion.

I PROCEED next to the duties incumbent on the sovereign by our constitution; the most important of which is to govern his people according to law. "The king," says Bracton, who wrote under Henry III., "ought not to be subject to man, but to God, and to the "law; for the law maketh the king. Let the king therefore render "to the law, what the law has vested in him with regard to others; "dominion and power: for he is not truly king, where will and "pleasure rules, and not the law." And again, "the king also hath "a superior, namely, God, and also the law, by which he was made a

" king." For " the laws of England (12 & 13 Will. III., c. 2) are
" the birthright of the people thereof; and all the kings and queens
" who shall ascend the throne of this realm ought to administer the
" government of the same according to the said laws."

The terms of what is sometimes called the *original contract* between king and people, are contained in the coronation oath, administered by one of the prelates, to every king or queen who succeeds
to the crown of these realms, in the following terms:—

" Will you solemnly promise and swear to govern the people of
this kingdom of England, and the dominions thereto belonging,
according to the statutes in parliament agreed on, and the laws and
customs of the same ? *The king or queen shall say:* I solemnly
promise so to do. *Archbishop or bishop:* Will you to your power
cause law and justice, in mercy, to be executed in all your judgments? *King or queen:* I will. *Archbishop or bishop:* Will you
to the utmost of your power maintain the laws of God, the true
profession of the gospel, and the Protestant reformed religion established by the law? And will you preserve unto the bishops and
clergy of this realm, and to the churches committed to their charge,
all such rights and privileges as by law do or shall appertain unto
them, or any of them ? *King or queen:* All this I promise to do.
*After this, the king or queen, laying his or her hand upon the
Holy Gospels, shall say:* The things which I have here before promised I will perform and keep: So help me God: *and then shall
kiss the book.*"

This is the form of the coronation oath, as it is now prescribed by
our laws. But in what form soever it be conceived, this is most indisputably a fundamental and original express contract; though doubtless the duty of protection is impliedly as much incumbent on the
sovereign before coronation as after: in the same manner as allegiance to the sovereign becomes the duty of the subject immediately
on the descent of the crown, before he has taken the oath of allegiance, or whether he ever takes it all. This reciprocal duty of the
subject will be considered in its proper place. At present we are
only to observe, that in the sovereign's part of this original contract
are expressed all the duties that a monarch can owe to his people:
viz., to govern according to law; to execute judgment in mercy; and
to maintain the established religion.

CHAPTER VII.

OF THE ROYAL PREROGATIVE.

Sovereignty—Cannot be sued—Perfection, the king can do no wrong—Perpetuity, the king never dies—Prerogative to send and receive ambassadors—To make peace and war—As generalissimo—As the fountain of justice—And of honour—And as head of the church.

ONE of the principal bulwarks of civil liberty, is the limitation of the sovereign's prerogative by bounds so certain and notorious, that it is impossible he should ever exceed them, without the consent of the people, on the one hand; or without, on the other, a violation of the original contract, which subsists between the prince and the subject. It will now be our business to consider this prerogative minutely, to demonstrate its necessity in general, and to mark out in the most important instances its particular extent and restrictions: from which considerations this conclusion will evidently follow, that the powers which are vested in the crown by the laws of England are necessary for the support of society, and do not intrench any further on our *natural* liberties, than is expedient for the maintenance of our *civil.*

By the word *prerogative*, then, we usually understand that special pre-eminence which the crown has, over and above all other persons, and out of the ordinary course of the common law,. in right of the regal dignity. It signifies, in its etymology, something that is required or demanded before, or in preference to, all others; And hence it follows, that it can only be applied to those rights and capacities which the sovereign enjoys alone, in contradistinction to others, and not to those which he enjoys in common with any of his subjects.

Prerogatives are either *direct* or *incidental.* The *direct* are such positive parts of the royal authority, as spring from the sovereign's political person; as, the right of sending ambassadors, of creating peers, and of making war or peace. But such prerogatives as are *incidental* always bear a relation to something else, distinct from the person of the sovereign, and are indeed only exceptions, in favour of the crown, to those general rules that are established for the rest of the community; such as, that the sovereign can never be a joint-tenant; and that his debt shall be preferred before a debt to any of his subjects. These will better be understood when we come to consider the rules themselves to which they are exceptions. And therefore we will at present only dwell upon the sovereign's direct prerogatives.

These direct prerogatives may again be divided into three kinds: being such as regard, first, the royal *character*; secondly, the royal *authority*; and, lastly, the royal *income*. In the present chapter we shall only consider the two first of these divisions, which relate to the sovereign's political *character* and *authority*; or, in other words, his *dignity* and regal *power*; to which last the name of prerogative is frequently narrowed and confined. The other division, which forms the royal *revenue*, will require a distinct examination.

First, then, of the *royal dignity*. Under every monarchical establishment, it is necessary to distinguish the prince from his subjects, not only by the outward pomp and decorations of majesty, but also by ascribing to him certain qualities, as inherent in his royal capacity, distinct from and superior to those of any other individual in the nation. The law therefore ascribes to the king, in his high political character, certain attributes of a great and tran-scendant nature, by which the people are led to pay him that respect which may enable him with greater ease to carry on the business of government.

1. And, first, the law ascribes to the king the *attribute* of *sovereignty* or pre-eminence. He is said to have *imperial* dignity; and in charters before the Conquest is frequently styled *basileus* and *imperator*, the titles respectively assumed by the emperors of the East and West. His realm is said to be an *empire*, and his crown *imperial*. Hence it is, that no suit or action can be brought against the sovereign, even in civil matters, because no court can have jurisdiction over him. Who, says Finch, shall command the king? Hence it is, likewise, that the person of the sovereign is sacred, even though the measures pursued in his reign be completely tyran-nical and arbitrary: for no jurisdiction upon earth has power to try him in a criminal way; much less to condemn him to punish-ment.

Are then, it may be asked, the subjects of England totally desti-tute of remedy, in case the crown should invade their rights, either by private injuries, or public oppressions? To this we may answer, that the law has provided a remedy in both cases.

And, first, as to *private injuries*: if any person has, in point of property, a just demand upon the crown, he must petition him in one of his courts of law, where his judges will administer right as a matter of grace, though not upon compulsion. For the end of such action is not to *compel* the prince to observe the contract, but to *persuade* him. And, as to personal wrongs, it is well observed by Locke, "the harm which the sovereign can do in his own person not " being likely to happen often, nor to extend itself far; nor being " able, by his single strength, to subvert the laws, nor oppress the

" body of the people (should any prince have so much weakness and
" ill-nature as to endeavour to do it), the inconveniency, therefore,
" of some particular mischiefs, that may happen sometimes when
" a heady prince comes to the throne, are well recompensed by
" the peace of the public and security of the government, in the
" person of the chief magistrate being thus set out of the reach
" of danger."

Next as to cases of ordinary *public oppression,* where the vitals of
the constitution are not attacked, the law has also assigned a remedy.
For, as a sovereign cannot misuse his power without the advice of
evil counsellors, and the assistance of wicked ministers, these men
may be examined and punished. The constitution has therefore
provided, by means of indictments and parliamentary impeachments,
that no man shall dare to assist the crown in contradiction to the
laws of the land.

2. Besides the *attribute* of sovereignty, the law also ascribes to the
king, in his political capacity, absolute *perfection.* The king can do
no wrong. Which maxim is not to be understood as if everything
transacted by the government was of course just and lawful, but
means only two things. First, that whatever is exceptionable in the
conduct of public affairs is not to be imputed to the sovereign, nor is
he answerable for it personally to his people. And, secondly, it
means that the prerogative of the crown extends not to do any
injury; it is created for the benefit of the people, and therefore cannot be exerted to their prejudice.

The sovereign, moreover, is not only incapable of *doing* wrong, but
even of *thinking* wrong; he can never mean to do an improper
thing: in him is no folly or weakness. And therefore, if the crown
should be induced to grant any privilege to a subject contrary to
reason, or prejudicial to the commonwealth, or a private person, the
law will not suppose the sovereign to have meant either an unwise
or an injurious action, but declares that he was deceived in his
grant; and thereupon such grant is rendered void, merely upon the
foundation of fraud and deception, either by or upon those agents
whom the crown has thought proper to employ.

In further pursuance of this principle, the law also determines
that on the part of the sovereign, there can be no negligence, or
laches, and therefore no delay will bar his right. *Nullum tempus
occurrit regi* has been the standing maxim upon all occasions: for
the law intends that the king is always busied for the public good,
and therefore has not leisure to assert his right within the times
limited to subjects. In the king also can be no stain or corruption
of blood; for if the heir to the crown were attainted of treason or
felony, and afterwards the crown should descend to him, this would

purge the attainder *ipso facto*. Neither can the king in judgment
of law, as king, ever be a minor or under age; and therefore his
royal grants and assents to acts of parliament are good, though he
has not, in his natural capacity, attained the legal age of twenty-one.
But it has been usually thought prudent when the heir-apparent has
been very young, to appoint a guardian, or regent for a limited time:
the very necessity of such extraordinary provision being sufficient
to demonstrate the truth of that maxim of the common law, that in
the king is no minority; and therefore he has no legal guardian.

3. A third *attribute* of the sovereign is his *perpetuity*. The king
never dies.   Henry, Edward, or George may die; but the king
survives them all.   For, immediately upon the decease of the reigning prince in his natural capacity, his kingship by act of law is
vested at once in his heir; who is, *eo instanti*, king to all intents
and purposes.   And so tender is the law of supposing even a possibility of his death, that his natural dissolution is generally called his
demise; an expression which signifies merely a transfer of property;
for when we say the demise of the crown, we mean only that, in
consequence of the disunion of the king's natural body from his
body politic, the kingdom is transferred or demised to his successor;
and so the royal dignity remains perpetual.

We are next to consider those branches of the royal prerogative
which invest the sovereign with a number of authorities and powers;
in the exercise whereof consists the executive part of government.
These prerogatives respect either this nation's intercourse with
foreign nations, or its own *domestic* government and civil polity.

With regard to foreign concerns, the sovereign is the delegate or
representative of his people.   It is impossible that the individuals of
a state in their collective capacity can transact the affairs of that
state with another community equally numerous as themselves.
In the sovereign, therefore, as in a centre, all the rays of his people
are united, and form by that union a consistency, splendour, and
power, that make him respected by foreign potentates.   What is
done by the royal authority, with regard to foreign powers, is therefore the act of the whole nation: what is done without the concurrence of the crown, is the act only of private men.

1. The sovereign, therefore, considered as the representative of his
people, has the sole power of sending ambassadors to foreign states,
and receiving ambassadors at home.

An ambassador represents the person of his sovereign; and as that
sovereign owes no subjection to any laws but those of his own
country, his envoy is not subject to the control of the private law of
that state wherein he is appointed to reside.   If he grossly offends,

or makes an ill use of his character, he may be sent home and accused before his master, who is bound either to do justice upon him, or avow himself the accomplice of his crimes. But there is great dispute among the writers on the laws of nations, whether this exemption of ambassadors extends to all crimes, as well natural as positive, or whether it only extends to such as are *mala prohibita*, and not to those that are *mala in se*, as murder. Our law seems to have formerly taken in the restriction, as well as the general exemption; holding that an ambassador is privileged by the law of nature and nations; and yet, if he commits any offence against the law of reason and nature, he shall lose his privilege. But the security of ambassadors is of more importance than the punishment of a particular crime. And few, if any, examples have happened within the last two centuries where an ambassador has been punished for any offence.

In respect to *civil* suits, all the foreign jurists agree, that neither an ambassador, nor any of his train, can be prosecuted for any debt or contract in the courts of that kingdom wherein he is sent to reside. Our law-books are silent upon this subject previous to the reign of Queen Anne; when an ambassador from Peter the Great was arrested in London for a debt of fifty pounds, which he had there contracted: Instead of relying upon his privilege, he gave bail to the action, and complained to the queen. The persons concerned in the arrest were prosecuted in the court of Queen's Bench, and convicted of the facts by the jury, the question of law, how far those facts were criminal, being reserved to be afterwards argued before the judges. In the mean time the Czar resented this affront very highly, and demanded that the sheriff of Middlesex and all others concerned should be punished with instant death. But the queen (to the amazement of that despotic court) directed her secretary to inform him, " that she " could inflict no punishment upon any, the meanest, of her subjects, " unless warranted by the law of the land; and therefore was per- " suaded that he would not insist upon impossibilities." A bill was, however, brought into parliament, and afterwards passed into a law, to prevent such outrageous insolence for the future. And a copy of this act, elegantly engrossed and illuminated, accompanied by a letter from the queen, was sent to Moscow, and accepted as a satisfaction by the Czar.

This statute, (7 Ann. c. 12,) recites the arrest which had been made, contrary to the law of nations, and in prejudice of the rights and privileges of ambassadors, &c.; and enacts, that for the future all process against the person of any ambassador shall be utterly void; but expressly provides, that no trader within the description of the bankrupt laws, who shall be in the service of any ambassador, ' shall be thereby privileged or protected; nor shall any one be punished for arresting an ambassador's servant, unless his name be registered with the secretary of state, and by him transmitted to the sheriffs of London and Middlesex.

2. It is also the prerogative of the crown to make treaties and alliances with foreign states. For it is essential to the goodness of a league, that it be made by the sovereign power; and then it is binding upon the whole community. Whatever contracts, therefore, the sovereign engages in, no other power in the kingdom can legally delay, resist, or annul. And lest this plentitude of authority should be abused, the constitution has interposed a check, by means of parliamentary impeachments, for the punishment of such ministers, as from criminal motives advise or conclude any treaty, which shall afterwards be judged to derogate from the honour and interest of the nation.

3. Upon the same principle also the sole prerogative of making war and peace is vested in the crown. For the right of making war, which by nature subsisted in every individual, is given up by all private persons that enter into society, and is vested in the sovereign power. Whatever hostilities, therefore, may be committed by private citizens, the state is not affected thereby : such unauthorized volunteers in violence, indeed, are not ranked among open enemies, but are properly treated like pirates and robbers. And the reason why a denunciation of war ought always to precede the actual commencement of hostilities, is not so much that the enemy may be put upon his guard (which is matter rather of magnanimity than right), but that it may be certainly clear that the war is not undertaken by private persons, but by the community. Wherever the right resides of beginning a war, there also must reside the right of ending it, or the power of making peace. And the same check of parliamentary impeachment, for improper or inglorious conduct, in beginning, conducting, or concluding a national war, is in general sufficient to restrain the ministers of the crown from a wanton or injurious exercise of this great prerogative.

4. But as the delay of making the war may sometimes be detrimental to individuals who have suffered by depredations from foreign potentates, our laws in some respects arm the subject with powers to impel the prerogative; by directing the ministers of the crown to issue letters of marque and reprisal upon due demand : the prerogative of granting which is plainly derived from that of making war. But the granting of letters of marque has long been disused; and the conference which met at Paris in 1856, after the close of the war with Russia, having recommended the entire abolition of

privateering, may possibly lead, ere long, to treaties by which the prerogative of the crown in issuing letters of marque will become merely matters of history.

5. Upon exactly the same reason stands the prerogative of granting safe-conducts, without which, by the law of nations, no member of one society has a right to intrude into another. Great tenderness is shown by our laws, however, not only to foreigners in distress, whose goods are cast on our shores, but with regard also to the admission of strangers who come spontaneously. For so long as their nation continues at peace with ours, and they themselves behave peaceably, they are under the protection of the laws; though liable to be sent home whenever the sovereign sees occasion. But no subject of a nation at war with us can come into the realm, travel upon the high seas, or send his goods and merchandise from one place to another, without danger of seizure, unless he has letters of safe-conduct, for which passports are now usually substituted and allowed to be of equal validity.

These are the principal prerogatives of the crown respecting this nation's intercourse with *foreign* nations; in all of which he is considered as the representative of his people. But in *domestic* affairs he is considered in a great variety of characters, and from thence there arises an abundant number of other prerogatives.

1. First, he is a constituent part of the supreme legislative power; and, as such, has the prerogative of rejecting such provisions in parliament, as he judges improper to be passed.

2. The sovereign is *generalissimo*, or the first in the military command, within the kingdom ; and in this capacity he has the sole power of raising and regulating fleets and armies. This prerogative was disputed and claimed by the long parliament of Charles I.; but, upon the restoration, was solemnly declared to be in the king alone.

It extends naturally to the erecting, as well as manning and governing of forts and other places of strength; whence formerly all lands were subject to a tax, for building of castles wherever the king thought proper. This was one of the three things, from contributing to the performance of which no lands were exempted : and therefore called by our Saxon ancestors the *trinoda necessitas: sc. pontis reparatio, arcis constructio, et expeditio contra hostem.* But in modern times parliament having provided the means of making defensive works, has practically obtained the control of their construction.

It is partly upon the same, and partly upon a fiscal foundation, to secure his marine revenue, that the sovereign has the prerogative of

appointing *ports* and *havens*, or such places only for persons and merchandise to pass into and out of the realm, as he in his wisdom sees
proper. By the feudal law all navigable rivers and havens were
computed among the *regalia*; and ,in England it has always been
holden, that the sovereign is lord of the whole shore, and particularly
is the guardian of the ports and havens, which are the inlets and
gates of the realm. These legal ports were undoubtedly at first
assigned by the crown; since to each of them a court of portmote is
incident, the jurisdiction of which must flow from the royal authority.
But as the king had not the power of resumption, or of confining the
limits of a port when once established, any person had a right to
load or discharge his merchandise in any part of the haven; whereby
the revenue of the customs was much diminished, by fraudulent
landings in obscure and private corners. This occasioned those
statutes which enable the crown to ascertain the limits of all ports,
and to assign proper *wharfs* and *quays* in each port, for the exclusive
landing and loading of merchandise; a power which has since been
transferred to the commissioners of the Treasury, who in certain
cases must consult the Admiralty.

The erection of beacons, lighthouses, and sea-marks, is also a
branch of the royal prerogative: whereof the first was anciently
used in order to alarm the country, in case of the approach of an
enemy; and all of them are signally useful in guiding and preserving vessels at sea by night as well as by day. The superintendence
and management of all lighthouses, buoys, and beacons, is now vested
in the Trinity-house.

To this branch of the prerogative may also be referred the power
vested in the sovereign of licensing the importation of utensils of
war, and of prohibiting the exportation of military and naval stores,
and likewise the right of confining his subjects to stay within the
realm, or of recalling them when beyond the seas. By the common
law, every man may go out of the realm for whatever cause he
pleases; but, because that every man ought of right to defend the
realm, the sovereign at his pleasure may command him by his writ,
that he go not beyond the seas, or out of the realm, without license;
and, if he do the contrary, he shall be punished for disobeying the
sovereign's command.   At present everybody has, or at least assumes,
the liberty of going abroad when he pleases. But if the sovereign, by
the writ of *ne exeat regno*, thinks proper to prohibit him from so
doing, and the subject disobeys, it is a high contempt of the royal
prerogative, and is punishable by fine and imprisonment.*

* This writ was at first employed to prevent the clergy from going to
Rome; it was afterwards extended to laymen concerting measures against the
state; and has at length become a part of the ordinary process of the Court
of Chancery, in order to get bail from any person who is about to go abroad.

3. Another capacity, in which the sovereign is considered in domestic affairs, is as the *fountain of justice* and general conservator of the peace of the kingdom. The original power of judicature is lodged in the society at large; but as it would be impracticable to render justice to every individual, by the people in their collective capacity, every nation has committed that power to certain select magistrates; and in England this authority has immemorially been exercised by the sovereign or his substitutes, the judges, to whom, by the long and uniform usage of many ages, our sovereigns have delegated their whole judicial power. They, in their several courts, are the depositaries of the fundamental laws of the kingdom, and have therein a known and stated jurisdiction, regulated by certain and established rules, which the crown itself cannot now alter but by act of parliament.

In prosecutions for offences, the sovereign appears in another capacity, that of *prosecutor*. All offences are theoretically against either his peace, or crown and dignity. For though they generally seem to be rather offences against the kingdom than the crown, yet, as the public has delegated all its powers, with regard to the execution of the laws, to one visible magistrate, all affronts to that power are offences against him to whom they are so delegated. He is therefore the proper person to prosecute for all public offences, being the person injured in the eye of the law. And hence also arises another branch of the prerogative, that of *pardoning* offences; for it is reasonable that he only who is injured should have the power of forgiving.

Another consequence of this prerogative is the legal *ubiquity* of the sovereign. In law he is present in all his courts, though he cannot personally distribute justice. And from this ubiquity it follows, that the crown can never be nonsuit; for a nonsuit is the desertion of the suit or action by the non-appearance of the plaintiff in court.

From the same origin, of the sovereign being the fountain of justice, we may also deduce the prerogative of issuing proclamations; which have a binding force only when they are grounded upon the laws of the realm. For though the making of laws is the work of the legislative branch of the sovereign power, yet the manner, time, and circumstances of putting those laws in execution are frequently left to the discretion of the executive magistrate.

---

so as to withdraw his person or property from the jurisdiction of the court. The legality of this application of the writ was settled in the time of King Charles II., and its use soon became so fully established, that the granting of it has long been considered a matter of right.

4. The sovereign is likewise the *fountain of honour, of office,* and *of privilege ;* the constitution entrusting him with the sole power of conferring dignities and honours, in confidence that he will bestow them upon none but such as deserve them. And therefore all degrees of nobility, of knighthood, and other titles, are received by immediate grant from the crown : either expressed in writing, by writs or letters patent, as in the creation of peers and baronets; or by corporeal investiture, as in the creation of a simple knight. He has also the prerogative of conferring privileges upon private persons, such as granting precedence to any of his subjects, or converting aliens into denizens. He also can erect corporations, whereby a number of private persons are united together, and enjoy many powers and immunities in their political capacity, which they were utterly incapable of in their natural. Of these I shall speak more at large in a subsequent chapter.

5. Another light, in which the laws of England consider the sovereign with regard to domestic concerns, is as the *arbiter of commerce,* that is, domestic commerce only. It would lead me into too large a field, if I were to attempt to enter upon the nature of foreign trade, its privileges, regulations, and restrictions ; and would also be quite beside the purpose of these commentaries, which are confined to the laws of England. The affairs of commerce generally are regulated by a law of their own, called the law merchant, or *lex mercatoria,* which all nations agree in and take notice of. And in particular it is held to be part of the law of England, which decides the cause of merchants by the general rules which obtain in all commercial countries ; and that often even in matters relating to domestic trade, as for instance with regard to the drawing, the acceptance, and transfer of inland bills of exchange.

To this branch of the prerogative may be referred the important functions now exercised by the Board of Trade, which is specially charged to superintend all government measures brought before parliament relating to trade and commerce ; and has several duties to perform, some of them of a ministerial and others of a judicial character. It has the general superintendence of all matters relating to merchant ships and seamen ; lays down rules as to the examination and qualification of applicants for the posts of masters and mates of foreign-going as well as of home-trade passenger-ships; grants licenses to persons to engage or supply seamen or apprentices; inquires into and adjudicates on claims for wages; investigates cases of alleged incompetency and misconduct on the part of masters of sea-going vessels, and appoints officers to report on the condition and efficiency of steam-vessels and their machinery. It exercises a supervision over railways and railway companies, not only with respect to their original formation, but also as to their subsequent working; inquires into the circumstances of accidents, and provides if need be, for the greater safety of the public.

The board, through the medium of its registrar, is charged with the registration of all joint-stock companies. A similar duty with respect to copyright in designs is imposed on it; and under its immediate control are placed all the schools of design now established in the large towns of the kingdom. One of its departments is charged with the collection and publication of tables, containing information with respect to the revenue, trade, commerce, wealth, population, and other statistics of the realm; and another department collects and prepares the tables of the prices of corn which regulate the rent-charges now paid in lieu of tithes.

Subject to these general observations, to the prerogative, so far as it relates to mere domestic commerce, fall the following articles:

First, the establishment of *public marts*, or places of buying and selling; such as markets and fairs, with the tolls thereunto belonging. These can only be set up by virtue of the grant of the crown, or by long and immemorial usage and prescription, which presupposes such a grant.

Secondly, the regulation of *weights and measures*; but this has so frequently formed the subject of parliamentary enactment that it can no longer with propriety be referred to the prerogative.

Thirdly, as money is the medium of commerce, it is said to be the royal prerogative, as the arbiter of domestic commerce, to give it authority, or make it current. But considering the frequent interference of parliament with reference to it, the *regulation of the coinage* cannot now, I apprehend, be referred simply to the prerogative.

6. The sovereign is, lastly, considered by the laws of England as the head and supreme governor of the national church.

To enter into the reasons upon which this prerogative is founded, is matter rather of divinity than of law. I shall therefore only observe, that it is in virtue of this authority that the crown convenes, prorogues, restrains, regulates, and dissolves all ecclesiastical synods or convocations;—nominates to vacant bishoprics, and certain other ecclesiastical preferments; and is the *dernier resort* in all ecclesiastical causes, an appeal lying ultimately to him from the sentence of every ecclesiastical judge. In the sovereign in council is also vested the power of giving effect to any scheme or recommendation of the Ecclesiastical Commissioners.

CHAPTER VIII.

OF THE ROYAL REVENUE.

I. *Ordinary;* as custody of temporalities of bishops—First-fruits and tenths—Wine licenses—Mines—Treasure trove—Estrays—Forfeitures and Escheats—II. *Extraordinary;* as land-tax—Malt-tax—Property and income-tax—Customs—Excise—Post-office—Stamp duties—Succession duties—Inhabited house duty—Assessed taxes—Duty upon offices and pensions.

HAVING considered those branches of the *prerogative* which contribute to the royal dignity and constitute the executive power of the government, we proceed now to examine the *fiscal* prerogatives of the sovereign, or such as regard his *revenue;* that portion which each subject contributes of his property in order to secure the remainder.

This is either *ordinary* or *extraordinary.* The *ordinary* revenue is such as has either subsisted time out of mind in the crown, or else has been granted by parliament by way of purchase or exchange for such of the sovereign's inherent hereditary revenues as were found inconvenient to the subject. Not that the crown is at present in possession of the whole of this revenue. Much (nay the greatest part) of it is at this day in the hands of subjects, to whom it has been granted out; so that I must be obliged to recount, as part of the royal revenue, what lords of manors and other subjects look upon to be their own absolute inherent rights; because they have been vested in them and their ancestors for ages, though in reality originally derived from the grants of our ancient princes.

I. The first of the ordinary revenues of the crown, which I shall take notice of, is *the custody of the temporalities of bishops,* by which are meant all the lay revenues, lands, and tenements which belong to an archbishop's or bishop's see; and which, upon the vacancy of the bishopric, are immediately the right of the sovereign, as a consequence of his prerogative in church matters.

This revenue, formerly very considerable, is now almost reduced to nothing: for as soon as the new bishop is consecrated and confirmed, he usually receives restitution of his temporalities entire and untouched.

II. The sovereign is entitled to a corody, out of every bishopric; that is, to send one of his chaplains to be maintained by the bishop, or to have a pension allowed him till the bishop promotes him to a benefice. This, which was also in the nature of an acknowledgment to the king, as founder of the see, is now fallen into total disuse.

III. The sovereign is entitled to all the *tithes arising in extra-parochial places*: though it may be doubted how far this article, as well as the last, can be reckoned part of his revenue: since a corody supports only his chaplains, and these extra-parochial tithes are held under an implied trust, that he will distribute them for the good of the clergy in general.

IV. The next branch consists in the *first-fruits and tenths* of all spiritual preferments in the kingdom. The first-fruits, *primatæ* or *annates*, were the first year's whole profits of the spiritual prefer-ment; the tenths, or *decimæ*, were the tenth part of the annual profit of each living, which was originally claimed by the pope, under that precept of the Levitical law, which directs, that the Levites " should offer the tenth part of their tithes as a heave-offering " to the Lord, and give it to Aaron the *high* priest." But this claim of the holy see met with a vigorous resistance from parliament; and a variety of acts were passed to restrain it, particularly 6 Hen. IV. c. 1, which calls it a horrible mischief, and damnable custom. But the popish clergy still kept it on foot; and, as they thus ex-pressed their willingness to contribute so much to the head of the church, it was thought proper (when the king was declared to be so) to annex this revenue to the crown: and so it remained till Queen Anne restored to the church what had been thus indirectly taken from it; not by remitting the tenths and first-fruits entirely, but by applying these superfluities of the larger benefices to make up the de-ficiencies of the smaller. This is usually called *Queen Anne's Bounty.*

V. The next branch of the ordinary revenue of the sovereign consists in the *rents and profits of the demesne lands of the crown.* These demesne lands were anciently very extensive, comprising divers manors, honours, and lordships. But at present they are contracted within a very narrow compass, having been almost en-tirely granted away to private subjects; and the management of them is vested in the Commissioners of Woods, Forests, and Land Revenues. The parks and places to which the public has access, are managed by the Commissioners of Her Majesty's Works and Public Buildings.

VI. Hither might have been referred the advantages arising from the *profits of military tenures*, to which most lands in the kingdom were subject, till the statute 12 Car. II. c. 24, in great measure abolished them all. Hither also might have been referred the prorogative of *purveyance* and *pre-emption:* a right of buying up provisions for the royal household, at an appraised valuation, in pre-ference to all others : and also of impressing the carriages and horses of the subject, to do the sovereign's business, in the conveyance of

timber, baggage, and the like, however inconvenient to the proprietor, upon paying him a settled price. Having fallen into disuse
during the suspension of monarchy, King Charles at his restoration
consented to resign entirely these branches of revenue; and parliament, in recompense, settled on the crown the hereditary excise of
fifteen pence *per* barrel on all beer and ale sold in the kingdom, and
a proportionable sum for certain other liquors.

VII. A seventh branch of revenue arises from *wine licenses*.
These were first settled on the crown by 12 Car. II. c. 25, to make
up for the loss sustained in the abolition of the military tenures.
Abolished in the reign of George II., these licenses have been recently
revived as a source of revenue by the statute 23 Vict. c. 27.

VIII. An eighth branch of the ordinary revenue consists in the
profits arising from the *royal forests;* which consist principally in
amercements or fines levied for offences against the forest laws. But
as few, if any, courts for levying amercements have been held since
1632, this branch of revenue is practically abolished.

IX. The *profits* arising from the *ordinary courts of justice* make
a ninth branch of the royal revenue. These consist in fines imposed
upon offenders, and in fees payable in a variety of legal matters. As
none of these can be done without the intervention of the sovereign,
or his officers, the law allows him certain profits, as a recompense
for his trouble. These, in process of time, were almost all granted
out to private persons; so that, though our law proceedings are still
loaded with their payment, very little of them is now returned into
the Exchequer.*

X. A tenth branch of the royal revenue, the right to *mines*, has
its origin from the sovereign's prerogative of coinage, in order to
supply him with materials. By the common law, if gold or silver
be found in mines of base metal, the whole, according to the opinion
of some, belonged to the crown; though others held that it only did
so if the quantity of gold or silver was of greater value than the
quantity of base metal. This is now immaterial, as the king can
only have the ore on paying for the same a price fixed by statute.

XI. A branch of the sovereign's ordinary revenue, said to be
grounded on the consideration of his guarding and protecting the
seas from pirates and robbers, is the right to *royal fish*, viz., whale
and sturgeon; which, when either thrown ashore, or caught near
the coast, are the property of the crown.

* The Earl of Ellenborough has 7700*l.* per annum, as compensation for his
office of chief clerk of the Court of Queen's Bench.

XII. Another maritime revenue, and founded upon the same reason, is that of *shipwrecks*. Wreck, by the common law, was where any ship was lost at sea, and the goods or cargo were thrown upon the land; these goods belonged to the king: for by the loss of the ship all property was gone out of the original owner. But this was undoubtedly adding sorrow to sorrow, and was consonant neither to reason nor humanity. Wherefore by various statutes numerous exceptions were made to prevent goods being treated as wreck; and now if any live thing escape, or if proof even can be made of the property, the goods shall not be forfeited. And the sheriff is bound to keep them a year and a day; though, if of a perishable nature, he may sell them, and the money shall be as in their stead.

XIII. To the sovereign belongs also *treasure-trove*, which is, where any money, or coin, gold, silver, plate, or bullion, is found hidden *in* the earth, or other private place, the owner thereof being unknown. If it be found in the sea, or *upon* the earth, it does not belong to the king, but the finder, if no owner appears.

XIV. Waifs, *bona waivata*, are goods stolen, and waived or thrown away by the thief in his flight, which are given to the crown as a punishment upon the owner for not pursuing the felon and taking his goods from him. If, therefore, any party robbed do immediately follow and apprehend the thief (which is called making *fresh suit*), or convict him afterwards, he shall have his goods again; for if the party robbed can seize them first, the crown shall never have them.

XV. *Estrays* are such valuable animals as are found wandering in any manor or lordship, and no man knows the owner, in which case the law gives them to the sovereign as the general owner, in recompense for the damage which they may have done therein: and they now most commonly belong to the lord of the manor by special grant from the crown.

XVI. The next branch of the ordinary revenue of the crown consists in *forfeitures of lands and goods* for offences; the nature of which will be more properly recited when we treat of crimes and misdemeanors.

XVII. Another branch of the ordinary revenue of the crown arises from *escheats* of lands, which happen upon the defect of heirs to succeed to the inheritance; whereupon they in general revert to and vest in the sovereign, who is, in the eye of the law, the original proprietor of all the lands of the kingdom.

XVIII. The last branch of the sovereign's ordinary revenue consists in the *custody of idiots and lunatics*.

A lunatic, or *non compos mentis*, is one who has had understanding, but by disease, grief, or other accident, has lost the use of his reason, under which name are comprised all those who are judged by the Court of Chancery incapable of conducting their own affairs. To these, as well as idiots, the sovereign is guardian, being a kind of a trustee for them, to protect their property, and to account to them for all profits received, if they recover, or after their decease to their representatives. The exercise of this prerogative is now committed by special authority from the sovereign to the Lord Chancellor, to whose court are attached the masters and inspectors in lunacy. The care of the lunatic, with a suitable allowance for his maintenance, is usually given to some friend, who is then called his committee ; the next heir being seldom permitted to be the committee of the person, though generally made the manager or committee of the estate, it being clearly his interest by good management to keep it in condition. He is accountable however to the *non compos* himself, if he recovers, or otherwise to his administrators.

This may suffice for a short view of the sovereign's *ordinary* revenue, or the proper patrimony of the crown; which was very large formerly, and capable of being increased to a magnitude truly formidable. But, fortunately for the subject, this hereditary revenue, by improvident management, is sunk almost to nothing; and in order to supply the deficiency, we are obliged to have recourse to new methods of raising money, unknown to our early ancestors ; which methods constitute the *extraordinary* revenue of the crown. These are usually called by the synonymous names of aids, subsidies, and supplies, and are granted by the commons in parliament; who, when they have voted a supply to the crown, and settled the *quantum* of that supply, usually resolve themselves into what is called a *committee of ways and means*, to consider the ways and means of raising the supply so voted. The resolutions of this committee, when approved by a vote of the house, are in general esteemed final and conclusive. For, though the supply cannot be actually raised till directed by an act of parliament, yet no monied man will scruple to advance any amount to the government, on the credit of a bare vote of the House of Commons, though no law be yet passed to establish it.

The taxes which are raised upon the subject were formerly either annual or perpetual. The usual annual taxes were formerly those upon land and malt.

I. The *land-tax*, in its modern shape, superseded (at least until a recent period) all the former methods of rating either property or persons in respect of their property, whether by tenths or fifteenths, subsidies on lands, hidages, scutages, or tallages.

Tenths and fifteenths were temporary aids issuing out of personal property, and were formerly the real tenth or fifteenth part of all the movables belonging to the subject. Originally the amount was uncertain, but was reduced to a certainty in the eighth year of Edward III., when new taxations were made of every township, borough, and city in the kingdom, and recorded in the Exchequer. So that when, afterwards, the commons granted the crown a fifteenth, every parish in England immediately knew their proportion of it.

Scutages were derived from the military tenures; when every tenant of a knight's fee was bound to attend the king for forty days in every year. This personal attendance growing troublesome, the tenants compounded for it, by first sending others in their stead, and in process of time by making, in lieu of it, a pecuniary satisfaction, which at last came to be levied by assessment, at so much for every knight's fee, under the name of scutages.

Of the same nature with scutages were hidage upon lands not held by military tenure, and talliage upon cities and boroughs. But they all gradually fell into disuse upon the introduction, about the time of Richard II. and Henry IV., of subsidies, which were a tax, not immediately imposed upon property, but upon persons in respect of their reputed estates.

The grant of scutages, talliages, or subsidies did not extend to spiritual preferments; those being usually taxed by the clergy in convocation. While this continued, convocations sat as frequently as parliaments: but the last subsidies, thus given by the clergy, were in 15 Car. II., since which another method of taxation has generally prevailed, which takes in the clergy as well as the laity.

In the beginning of the civil wars between Charles I. and his parliament, the latter introduced the practice of laying weekly and monthly assessments upon the several counties of the kingdom, to be levied by a pound-rate on lands and personal estates; and from this time forwards we hear no more of subsidies, but occasional assessments were granted as the national emergencies required, which were called a land-tax, and finally made perpetual by the statute 38 Geo. III. c. 60, and fixed at 4s. in the pound; but subject to redemption by the owner of the property charged buying so much stock in the government funds as yields a dividend exceeding by a tenth part the amount of the land-tax.

II. The other tax is the malt-tax, a sum raised, ever since 1697, by a duty on malt, formerly of 6d. but now of 2s. 7d. in the bushel, and made perpetual by the statute 3 Geo. IV. c. 18.

III. Another tax of comparatively recent introduction, and which, although at present imposed only for a limited period, may not improbably become perpetual in point of fact, is the *property and income tax*. A tax of this kind was imposed in 1797, and continued until 1802, and was again revived in 1803, and continued until 1816. The present tax originated in 1842, and has been continued by subsequent acts.

The taxes which, although varied in amount, have always been perpetual in their nature, are :

I. *The customs;* or the duties paid by the merchant, at the quay, upon all imported as well as exported commodities, by the authority of parliament. Into the history of these subsidies I cannot at present enter. The tendency of modern legislation has been to make trade as free as it possibly can be made, consistently with the raising of the necessary revenue; and the result of numerous recent statutes has therefore been to reduce to a very small number indeed the articles on which duties are now levied.

II. Directly opposite in its nature to this is the *excise duty*, which is an inland imposition, paid sometimes upon the consumption of the commodity, or frequently upon the retail sale, which is the last stage before the consumption. Its original establishment was by the parliament in 1643; but the royalists at Oxford soon followed the example of their brethren at Westminster; both sides protesting that it should be continued no longer than to the end of the war, and then be utterly abolished; but afterwards, when the nation had been accustomed to it, it was continued, and remains with us to the present day. Although, from its first origin to the present time, its very name has been odious to the people of England, it has nevertheless been imposed from time to time on every conceivable article of consumption, to support the enormous expenses occasioned by our wars on the continent; and though the variety of articles subjected to this tax has been of late years greatly reduced, it is still levied on a sufficient number to preserve its original unpopularity.

III. Another branch of the revenue is levied with greater cheerfulness—the *post-office*, or duty for the carriage of letters. As we have assigned the origin of the excise to the parliament of 1643, so it is but justice to observe that this useful invention owes its first legislative establishment to the same assembly. The conveyance of letters for fixed rules was at first farmed; but in 1657, a regular post-office was erected, upon nearly the same model as has been ever since adopted. The rates of conveying letters were altered from time to time, and some further regulations added by subsequent statutes, and penalties were enacted to confine the carriage of letters to the

E

public office only, whose high charges, however, led, as might have been expected, to numerous petty frauds and evasions. Finally, in 1840, the existing system of a uniform rate was established; facilities have since been given for the transmission of printed periodical publications and other works; the money-order office has been constituted, and savings banks established in connection with the post-office.

IV. A fourth branch of the perpetual revenue consists in the *stamp duties*, which are a tax imposed upon all parchment and paper whereon private instruments of almost any nature whatsoever are written; and on probates of wills and letters of administration, and also on various licenses, as marriage licenses, and licenses to practise and exercise various callings, such as that of an attorney; and on admissions to offices and degrees. This is also a tax which, though in some instances it may be heavily felt, by greatly increasing the expense of all mercantile as well as legal proceedings, yet (if moderately imposed) is of service to the public in general, by authenticating instruments, and rendering it much more difficult than formerly to forge deeds of any standing.

V. A fifth, and very important branch of the revenue, consists in the duties charged on the succession to real and personal property, *the legacy and succession duties.*

The legacy duty is payable by every person who succeeds, whether he takes under a will or as next of kin, to personal property; and varies in amount according to the consanguinity of the next of kin, or the absence of any relationship between the legatee and the testator. The succession duty is imposed on every succession to property, according to the value and the relationship of the parties to the person from whom the property comes.

VI. A sixth branch is the *duty upon houses.* Mention is made in Domesday Book of fumage or fuage, vulgarly called smoke farthings; which were paid by custom to the king for every chimney in the house. But the first parliamentary establishment of this tax was by statute 13 & 14 Car. II., c. 10, whereby an hereditary revenue of 2s. for every hearth was granted to the king for ever. Upon the Revolution, hearth-money was declared to be "not only a great "oppression to the poorer sort, but a badge of slavery upon the "whole people;" "and therefore to erect a lasting monument of their majesties' goodness, hearth-money was abolished." This monument of goodness remains among us to this day: but the prospect of it was somewhat darkened, when in six years afterwards a tax was laid upon all houses, and a tax also upon all windows, if they exceeded nine, in such house. These rates were varied, and extended, until, in the reign of Will. IV., the house tax was abolished, the duties on windows remaining. Finally, the duties on windows were abolished; but in lieu thereof, a tax was imposed not on hearths, but on what amounts to the same thing, on inhabited houses.

VII. The seventh branch of the extraordinary perpetual revenue is a duty for every male servant, except such as are employed in husbandry, trade, or manufactures. Under this head are comprised the duties payable on private carriages, horses and dogs, hair-powder, armorial bearings, and on game certificates.

VIII. The eighth and last branch of the extraordinary perpetual revenue is the *duty upon offices* and *pensions;* consisting in an annual payment out of all salaries, fees, and perquisites of offices and pensions payable by the crown, exceeding the value of 100*l.* per annum.

The respective produces of the several taxes before mentioned were originally separate and distinct funds; but since the union with Ireland, as for a short time before, have formed *the consolidated fund;* pledged, in the first place, for the payment of the interest of the *national debt.* In 1786, when the revenue of the kingdom was first consolidated, the sum of one million was directed to be annually set apart towards the extinction of the debt. That done, the surplus may be applied in reduction of the capital. But before any part of the revenue can be thus used, it stands mortgaged by parliament to raise an annual sum for the maintenance of the royal household and the *civil list.*

The expenses formerly defrayed by the civil list were those that in any shape relate to civil government; as the expenses of the royal household; the revenues allotted to the judges; all salaries to officers of state, and every of the sovereign's servants; the appointments to foreign ambassadors; the maintenance of the royal family; the sovereign's private expenses, or privy purse; and other very numerous outgoings, as secret service money, pensions, and other bounties. But in the reign of William IV. various payments previously charged on the civil list, as the salaries of the officers of state, of the judges, and diplomatic pensions and salaries, were made directly chargeable on the consolidated fund; in consequence of which a sum of 500,000*l.* a year at present suffices for the maintenance of the royal family, and for the payment of such other sums as are still charged on the civil list. Of the whole revenue, it may be stated shortly, that one moiety is required for the interest of the national debt; and that the greater portion of the residue is applied to the maintenance of the army and navy.

This finishes our inquiries into the fiscal prerogatives of the sovereign; or his revenue, both ordinary and extraordinary. We have therefore now chalked out all the principal outlines of this vast title of the law, the supreme executive magistrate, considered in his several capacities and points of view; we now turn to those subordinate officers to whom the administration of public affairs is more immediately entrusted.

CHAPTER IX.

OF SUBORDINATE MAGISTRATES.

The sheriff—The coroner—Justices of the peace—The constable—The police force—The highway surveyor—Overseers and guardians of the poor—The Poor Law Board.

In a former chapter we distinguished magistrates into two kinds: supreme, or those in whom the sovereign power of the state resides; and subordinate, or those who act in an inferior or secondary sphere. We now proceed to inquire into the rights and duties of the principal subordinate magistrates.

And herein we are not to investigate the powers and duties of the great officers of state; because I do not know that they are in that capacity in any considerable degree the object of our laws, or have any very important share of magistracy conferred upon them. Neither shall I here treat of the office of the lord chancellor, or the other judges; because they will find a more proper place in the third part of these commentaries. But the magistrates and officers, whose rights and duties it will be proper in this chapter to consider, are such as are generally in use, and have a jurisdiction and authority dispersedly throughout the kingdom, which are principally sheriffs, coroners, justices of the peace, constables, surveyors of highways, and overseers and guardians of the poor.

I. The sheriff is an officer of great antiquity, his name being derived from two Saxon words—scire gerefa, the reeve, bailiff, or officer of the shire. He is called in Latin *vice-comes*, as being the deputy of the earl or *comes*; to whom the custody of the shire is said to have been committed at the first division of this kingdom into counties. But the earls, in process of time, were delivered of that burden, and the labour was laid on the sheriff; the king committing *custodian comitatus* to the sheriff, and him alone.

Sheriffs were originally chosen by the inhabitants of the several

counties.* But these popular elections growing tumultuous, were
put an end to, and under various statutes the sheriffs are now
assigned by the chancellor, treasurer, and the judges, who meet for
that purpose on the morrow of St. Martin, in the exchequer.   The
judges then and there propose three persons, to be reported to the
sovereign, who afterwards appoints one of them to be sheriff, which
ceremony is called *pricking* the sheriffs.

Some of our writers have affirmed, that the king, by his prerogative, may name whom he pleases to be sheriff, whether chosen by
the judges or no; and although one case, in the reign of Queen
Elizabeth, is the only authority in our books for this position, the
practice of naming what are called pocket-sheriffs, by the crown,
has continued to the present time; but this has only occurred *occasionally*, as on the death of a sheriff during his year of office.

Sheriffs can continue in their office no longer than one year: but
till a new sheriff be named, his office cannot be determined, unless
by his own death, or the demise of the crown.

It is of the utmost importance to have the sheriff appointed according to law, when we consider his functions, either as a judge,
as the keeper of the peace, as a ministerial officer of the superior
courts, or as the bailiff of the sovereign.

In his judicial capacity he presides on writs of inquiry to assess
damages in undefended suits; and in assessing the compensation to
be paid to the owners for lands taken for making railways and other
public works. He likewise decides the elections of knights of the
shire, of coroners, and of verderors of the forest.

As keeper of the peace, he is the first man in the county, and
superior in rank to any nobleman therein during his office. He may
apprehend all persons who break the peace; he is bound to pursue,
and take all traitors, murderers, felons, and other misdoers; he is
also to defend his county against any of the queen's enemies; and
for any of these purposes may command the *posse comitatus*—all the
people of his county—to attend him; and this summons every
person above fifteen years old, and under the degree of a peer, is
bound to attend upon warning, under pain of fine and imprisonment.

In his ministerial capacity, the sheriff is bound to execute all
process issuing from the superior courts of justice. When the cause
comes to trial, he must summon and return the jury; when it is
determined, he must see the judgment of the court carried into execution. In criminal matters, he also has power to arrest and imprison;
he returns the jury; he has the custody of the delinquent; and he
executes the sentence of the court, though it extend to death itself.

* In some counties the sheriffs were hereditary; and the corporation of
London still has the shrievalty of Middlesex vested in it by charter.

As the bailiff of the sovereign, it is his business to preserve the rights of the crown within his bailiwick, for so his county is frequently called in the writs; a word introduced by the princes of the Norman line, whose territory was formerly divided into bailiwicks. He must seize all lands devolved to the crown by attainder or escheat, levy all fines and forfeitures, and seize all waifs, wrecks, estrays, and the like, unless they be granted to some subject.

To execute these various offices, the sheriff has under him many inferior officers: an *under-sheriff*, who usually performs all the more important duties of the office, a very few only excepted where the personal presence of the high-sheriff is necessary; *bailiffs* to summon juries, attend the judges and justices at the assizes and quarter sessions, and execute writs, the sheriff being answerable for their misdemeanors; and *gaolers*, whose business it is to keep safely all such persons as are committed to them by lawful warrant.

II. The coroner's is also a very ancient office, so called *coronator*, because he has principally to do with pleas of the crown. And in this light the chief justice of the queen's bench is the principal coroner in the kingdom, and may exercise the jurisdiction of a coroner in any part of the realm. The coroner is chosen by the freeholders of the county. In boroughs which have a court of quarter sessions, the town council appoints and pays the coroner for the borough. In other boroughs the coroner of the county has jurisdiction. He is chosen for life; but may be removed, either by being made sheriff, which is an office incompatible with the other, or for cause, such as extortion, neglect, inability, or misbehaviour in office. His office and power are also, like those of the sheriff, either judicial or ministerial, but principally judicial. This consists, first, in inquiring, when any person is slain, or dies suddenly, or in prison, concerning the manner of his death. And this must be "*super* "*visum corporis:*" for, if the body be not found, the coroner cannot sit. His inquiry is made by a jury of twelve at least; and he may require the attendance of medical witnesses or assessors, and order a *post mortem* examination of the body. If any person be found guilty by this inquest of murder or other homicide, he is to commit him to prison for further trial. Another branch of his office is to inquire concerning shipwrecks and treasure trove; for the holding of all which inquests he may appoint a fit and proper person to act as his deputy.

The ministerial office of the coroner is only as the sheriff's substitute. For when just exception can be taken to the sheriff, the process must then be awarded to the coroner.

III. The next species of subordinate magistrates are justices of the peace, the principal of whom is the *custos rotolorum*, or keeper of the records of the county.

The sovereign is the principal conservator of the peace within all his dominions; and may give authority to any other to see the peace kept, and to punish such as break it; hence it is usually called the queen's peace. The coroner is a conservator of the peace within his own county, as is also the sheriff. Constables, tything-men, and the like, are also conservators of the peace within their own jurisdictions; and may apprehend all breakers of the peace and commit them, till they find sureties for their keeping it. But the principal conservators of the peace are the justices nominated by commission under the great seal, which appoints them all, jointly and separately, to keep the peace, and any two or more of them to inquire of and determine felonies and other misdemeanors : in which number some particular justices, or one of them, are directed to be always included, and no business to be done without their presence, the persons so named being usually called justices of the *quorum*.

The number of justices for each county is now unlimited; they ought to be of the best reputation, and most worthy men in the county, and must have in real property 100*l.* per annum clear of all deductions, or a reversion or remainder with reserved rents amounting to 300*l.* per annum.

As the office of these justices is conferred by the crown, so it subsists only during the pleasure of the sovereign, and is determinable, 1. By the demise of the crown; that is, in six months after. 2. By express writ under the great seal, discharging any particular person from being any longer justice. 3. By superseding the commission by writ of *supersedeas*. 4. By a new commission, which discharges all the former justices not included therein. 5. By accession to the office of sheriff or coroner.

The power, office, and duty of a justice depend on his commission, and on the several statutes which have created objects of his jurisdiction. His commission, first, empowers him singly to conserve the peace. It also empowers any two or more to hear and determine felonies and other offences; which is the ground of their jurisdiction at sessions. And as to the powers given to them by the several statutes, which have heaped upon them such an infinite variety of business, that few care to undertake, and fewer understand, the office; they are such, that the country is greatly obliged to any worthy magistrate, that without sinister views of his own will engage in this troublesome service. And therefore, if a justice makes any undesigned slip, great indulgence is shown to him in the courts of law; for he cannot be sued for any oversight, without notice beforehand; so as to have an opportunity of making amends.

· IV. The office of *constable* is one of considerable antiquity. They were ordained by the statute of Winchester to be appointed at the court-leets of the franchise or hundred over which they preside, or, in default of that, by the justices, for the better keeping of the peace. They were called afterwards *high* constables, to distinguish them from the *petty* constables, instituted in the reign of Edward III. These latter have two offices : one ancient, the other modern. Their ancient office is that of head-borough, tithing-man, or borsholder ; an office as ancient as the time of King Alfred ; their more modern office is that of constable merely, to assist the high constable. They are chosen by the justices at a petty sessions holden yearly for that purpose.

The general duty of all constables, both high and petty, as well as of the other officers, is to keep the peace in their several districts ; and to that purpose they are armed with very large powers, of the extent of which, considering what manner of men are for the most part put into these offices, it is perhaps very well that they are generally kept in ignorance.

The justices may swear-in *special* constables if disturbances exist or are apprehended; and any one of the secretaries of state may order persons to be so sworn in, though exempt by law from so serving.

These ancient officers have, however, been almost entirely super-seded by the modern *police force* now established throughout the kingdom ; the justices having now power to appoint a chief constable, and such chief constable to appoint other constables ; the whole, when sworn in, having all the powers, privileges, and duties which any constable duly appointed has within his constablewick.

V. The office of surveyor of the highway dates from the reign of Queen Mary. Every parish is bound of common right to keep its high-roads in repair ; unless, by tenure of lands or otherwise, this care is consigned to some particular person. From this burden no man was exempt by our ancient laws, whatever other immunities he might enjoy : this being part of the *trinoda necessitas* to which every man's estate was subject ; viz., *expeditio contra hostem, arcium constructio, et pontium reparatio.* The surveyors were originally appointed by the constable and churchwardens of the parish ; and, till recently, were chosen annually by the inhabitants, or if the inhabitants omitted to elect, by the justices. But parishes may now be united by the justices into a district, for which a *highway board* is elected, consisting of resident justices and *way-wardens* chosen by each parish, by whom the district surveyor is appointed. His duty is to put in execution the laws for the repairs of the public highways; his powers for this purpose being very extensive. The expense is paid by a rate levied in the same manner and on the same persons and property as the rates for the relief of the poor.

VI. The last of the subordinate officers or magistrates I have to mention here, are the overseers and guardians of the poor.

The poor of England, till the time of Henry VIII., subsisted entirely upon private benevolence, and the charity of well-disposed Christians. The monasteries were, in particular, their principal resource; and among other bad effects which attended these institutions, it was not perhaps one of the least that they supported and fed a very numerous and very idle poor, whose sustenance depended upon what was daily distributed in alms at the gates of the religious houses. But, upon their dissolution, the inconvenience of thus encouraging the poor in habits of indolence and beggary was quickly felt; and several statutes were made in the reign of King Henry VIII. and his children, for providing for the poor and impotent, which, the preambles to some of them recite, had of late years greatly increased. These poor were principally of two sorts: sick and impotent, and therefore unable to work; idle and sturdy, and therefore able, but not willing to exercise any honest employment. After many other fruitless experiments, by statute 43 Eliz. c. 2, overseers of the poor were directed to be appointed in every parish.

They are appointed by the justices, and their duties are to raise competent sums for the necessary relief of the impotent, old, blind, and such other poor as are not able to work; and secondly, to provide work for such as are able, and cannot otherwise get employment. And for these joint purposes they are empowered to make and levy rates upon the several inhabitants of the parish.

One defect in this measure was confining the management of the poor to small parochial districts, which are frequently incapable of furnishing proper work, or providing an able director. However, the laborious poor were then at liberty to seek employment wherever it was to be had; none being obliged to reside in the places of their settlement but such as were unable or unwilling to work, and those places of settlement being only such where they were *born*, or had made their *abode*.

After the Restoration a very different plan was adopted, which rendered the employment of the poor more difficult, by authorising the subdivision of parishes; greatly increased their number, by confining them all to their respective districts; gave birth to the intricacy of our poor laws, by multiplying and rendering more easy the methods of gaining settlements; and, in consequence, created an infinity of expensive lawsuits between contending neighbourhoods concerning those settlements and removals.

A remedy was attempted by 22 Geo. III. c. 83 (*Gilbert's Act*), enabling parishes to unite with others, in order to provide poor-houses for the reception of paupers, and directing the appointment of visitors and guardians for each parish; who were authorized to contract for supplying the poor with diet and clothing, or, as it was termed, *farming the poor*. This act is in operation in a very few places.

By other statutes restrictions were imposed on the obtaining of settlements, which gave rise to more litigation between parishes; and further facilities were given for the erection of workhouses. But the gravest abuses nevertheless pervaded the whole administration of these laws. The philanthropic but erroneous views of the local authorities led in many cases to a profuse and indiscriminate expenditure; and from this there resulted a marked demoralization of the labouring classes of the district. The amount annually expended in the relief of the poor became, in consequence, such a serious burden on the rest of the community, that it was found necessary not only to reconstruct the machinery for its distribution, but to revise the principles of our previous legislation.

This was effected in 1834 by the Poor Law Amendment Act. Commissioners were appointed, and the administration of relief to the poor was made subject to their direction and control. They were authorized to unite adjacent parishes into one *Union*; the administration of relief being then vested in a *board of guardians*, elected by the ratepayers, of which the justices of the peace acting for the county were *ex officio* members. *Relieving officers* were appointed to superintend and assist in the administration of the relief and employment of the destitute poor; and the overseers left to collect the poor rates, and keep the accounts.

The practice, which had long obtained and been found to be productive of much evil, of giving out-door relief to the able-bodied poor, unless under special circumstances and in cases of emergency, was at the same time put an end to; the law of settlement was simplified and improved, if such a phrase may be applied to a system thoroughly vicious in principle; and provision was made for the more equitable assessment of property and the collection of the poor-rates; for compelling putative fathers to maintain their illegitimate children; for the proper election of guardians; the care of pauper lunatics; and the regulation of schools.

The powers of the commissioners were in the mean time continued down to the year 1847, when all their powers and duties were transferred to certain *ex officio* commissioners and to one commissioner appointed by the crown, who act under the designation of *The Poor Law Board*.

Several acts have been subsequently passed, however, relating to other branches of the poor laws, leaving the laws relating to the relief of the poor in such a state of complexity, as to render their speedy consolidation a work rather of necessity than of mere convenience. The most recent legislation on this subject happily tends to the breaking up of that exclusive parochial system which has so long fostered and preserved the laws of settlement, the most mischievous, in the eyes of political economists, that have ever appeared in the statute rolls of the empire.

CHAPTER X.

OF THE PEOPLE, WHETHER ALIENS, DENIZENS, OR NATIVES.

Allegiance, natural or local—Who are aliens—Denizens—Naturalization.

HAVING treated of persons as they stand in the public relations of *magistrates*, I now proceed to consider such persons as fall under the denomination of the *people*; the first and most obvious division of whom is into aliens and natural-born subjects. Natural-born subjects are such as are born within the dominions of the crown of England; that is, within the legiance, or allegiance of the queen: and aliens, such as are born out of it. Allegiance is the tie or *ligamen*, which binds the subject to the sovereign, in return for that protection which the sovereign affords the subject; the oath of allegiance, which must have been taken by every subject when required, and as it was administered for upwards of six hundred years, containing a promise " to be true and faithful to the king and his heirs, and " truth and faith to bear of life and limb and terrene honour, and " not to know or hear of any ill or damage intended him, without " defending him therefrom." But, at the Revolution, the terms of this oath being thought to favour too much the notion of non-resistance, another form was introduced, which is more general; the subject only promising " that he will be faithful and bear *true* alle-" giance to the king," without mentioning " his heirs," or specifying in the least wherein that allegiance consists. The oath of supremacy was principally calculated as a renunciation of the pope's pretended authority ; and the oath of abjuration, introduced in the reign of King William, very amply supplied the loose and general texture of the oath of allegiance. For these several declarations, however, has now been substituted one single oath, which recognises the right of

the sovereign,—abjures any obedience or allegiance to any other
person,—and declares that no foreign prince, prelate, or potentate
has or ought to have any jurisdiction or authority, ecclesiastical or
spiritual, within the realm.   This oath may be tendered by two
justices of the peace to any person whom they shall suspect of dis-
affection; and to all persons above the age of twelve years, whether
natives, denizens, or aliens, either in the court-leet of the manor, or
in the sheriff's tourn, which is the court-leet of the county.   The
tolerant spirit of modern legislation has also provided particular
forms of oaths for Roman Catholics and Jews; has permitted affirma-
tions to be made by persons who object to take an oath; and has
otherwise greatly relieved the queen's subjects generally from the
penalties and disabilities consequent on the neglect or refusal to take
the oaths.

But besides these express engagements, the law also holds that
there is an implied, original, and virtual allegiance, owing from every
subject to his sovereign, antecedently to any express promise; and
although the subject never swore any faith or allegiance in form.
For as the king, by the very descent of the crown, is fully invested
with all the rights, and bound to all the duties of sovereignty, before
his coronation; so the subject is bound to his prince by an intrinsic
allegiance, before the superinduction of those outward bonds of oath,
homage, and fealty.

Allegiance is consequently distinguished into two species, the one
natural, the other local; the former being also perpetual, the latter
temporary.   *Natural allegiance* is such as is due from all men born
within the sovereign's dominions immediately upon their birth; it
cannot be forfeited, cancelled, or altered by any change of time, place,
or circumstance, nor by anything but the united concurrence of the
legislature.

Local allegiance is such as is due from an alien, or stranger born,
for so long time as he continues within the queen's dominions and
protection; and it ceases the instant such stranger transfers himself from this kingdom to another.   For as the prince affords his
protection to an alien only during his residence in this realm, the
allegiance of an alien is confined to the duration of his residence, and
to the dominions of the empire.

Allegiance then, natural or local, is the duty of all the queen's subjects, whose rights are also distinguishable by the same criterions of
time and locality.   Natural-born subjects have, as we have seen
already, a great variety of rights, which they acquire by being born
within the queen's legiance; aliens possess also certain rights, though

much more circumscribed, being acquired only by residence here, and lost whenever they remove.

An alien born may purchase lands or other estates; but not for his own use: for the crown is thereupon entitled to them. If an alien could acquire a permanent property in lands, he must owe an allegiance, equally permanent with that property, to the crown of England; which would be inconsistent with that which he owes to his own natural liege lord. Yet an alien may, at common law, acquire a property in goods, money, and other personal estate, or may hire a house for his habitation: for personal estate is of a transitory and movable nature. This indulgence to strangers is, indeed, necessary for the advancement of trade; for aliens may trade as freely as other people; and an alien may bring an action concerning personal property, and may make a will, and dispose of his personal estate. I speak of alien friends only, or such whose countries are in peace with ours; for alien enemies have no rights, no privileges, unless by the special favour of the crown, or express legislative enactment, during the time of war.

When I say that an alien is one who is born out of the sovereign's dominions, or allegiance, this also must be understood with some restrictions. The children of ambassadors born abroad are natural subjects; and by several modern statutes all children whose *fathers* (or *grandfathers* by the father's side) were natural-born subjects, are now deemed to be natural-born subjects themselves, to all intents and purposes.*

The children of aliens, born here in England, are, generally speaking, natural-born subjects, and entitled to all the privileges of such. A denizen is an alien born, but who has obtained *ex donatione legis* letters-patent to make him an English subject. He may take lands by purchase or devise, which an alien may not; but he cannot take by inheritance: for his parent, being an alien, had no inheritable blood, and therefore could convey none to the son.

Naturalization, properly so called, cannot be performed but by act of parliament: for by this an alien is put in exactly the same state as if he had been born in the king's legiance; except only that he is incapable, as well as a denizen, of being a member of the privy-council or of parliament. The legislature has recently, however, authorized the Home Secretary to grant to alien friends, resident in this country, a certificate of naturalization; which, being enrolled in chancery, confers on the grantee, on his taking an oath of

---

* The children born abroad of a *mother*, who is a natural-born subject, are capable of taking any real or personal estate by devise, purchase, or succession; and any alien woman who marries a British subject is *de facto* naturalized.

allegiance and fidelity, all the rights and capacities of a natural-born British subject, except always that of being a member of the privy council or of either house of parliament, or such other rights or capacities as may be specially excepted in the certificate.

CHAPTER XI.

OF THE CLERGY.

Archbishops and bishops—Dean and chapter—Archdeacons—Rural deans—Parsons and vicars—Curates—Churchwardens—Parish clerks and sextons.

THE people, whether aliens, denizens, or natural-born subjects, are divisible into two kinds; the clergy and the laity: the former will be the subject of the following chapter.

This body of men, being set apart from the rest of the people, in order to attend the more closely to the services of Almighty God, have thereupon large privileges allowed them by our municipal laws. A clergyman cannot be compelled to serve on a jury, nor to appear at a court-leet or view of frank-pledge; which almost every other person is obliged to do. Neither can he be chosen to any temporal office; as bailiff, reeve, constable, or the like, in regard of his own continual attendance on the sacred function. During his attendance on divine service he is privileged from arrest in civil suits, and the infraction of this privilege is an indictable misdemeanour. But as they have their privileges, so also they have their disabilities, on account of their spiritual avocations. Clergymen are incapable of sitting in the House of Commons, or of being councillors or aldermen in boroughs. They are not allowed to farm more than eighty acres, nor to be a partner in any trade or dealing for profit, unless it be carried on by the other partners. No spiritual person can be a director or managing partner; but he may carry on the business of a schoolmaster, or be a director or partner in any benefit or insurance society. He may buy or sell to the extent incidental to his occupation of land, but cannot do so in person or at a public market.

In the frame and constitution of ecclesiastical polity there are divers ranks and degrees, which I shall consider in their respective order.

I. An archbishop or bishop is elected by the chapter of his cathedral church, by virtue of a licence from the crown. Election was, in very early times, the usual mode of elevation to the episcopal chair throughout all Christendom ; and this was promiscuously performed by the laity as well as the clergy ; the king reserving the right of confirming the election, and granting investiture of the temporalities.   Hence the right of appointing to bishoprics is said to have been in the crown of England, even in Saxon times : because the rights of confirmation and investiture were in effect a right of complete donation.   The popes, however, in due course, excepted to the method of granting these investitures, which was by the king delivering to the prelate a ring, and pastoral staff or crosier : pretending that this was an attempt to confer spiritual jurisdiction : and long and eager were the contests thus occasioned.   At length, the Emperor Henry V. agreed to confer investitures *per sceptrum* and not *per annulum et baculum* ; and when the kings of England and France consented also to alter the form and receive only homage from the bishops for their temporalities, the court of Rome found it prudent to suspend its other pretensions.   King John was no doubt prevailed upon to give up, to all the monasteries and cathedrals in the kingdom, the free right of electing their prelates, whether abbots or bishops : reserving only to the crown the custody of the temporalities during the vacancy.   But the ancient right of nomination was, in effect, restored to the crown by the statute 25 Hen. VIII. c. 20 ; which enacts that, at every future avoidance of a bishopric, the king may send the dean and chapter his usual licence, or *congé d'élire*, to proceed to election ; which is always to be accompanied with a letter missive from the king, containing the name of the person whom he would have them elect: disobedience to which recommendation involves the penalties of a *præmunire*.

An archbishop is the chief of the clergy in a whole province ; and has the inspection of the bishops of that province, as well as of the inferior clergy.   In his own diocese, he exercises episcopal jurisdiction ; as in his province he exercises archiepiscopal.   As archbishop he, upon receipt of the sovereign's writ, calls the bishops and clergy of his province to meet in convocation ; and to him all appeals are made from inferior jurisdictions within his province.   During the vacancy of any see in his province, he is guardian of the spiritualities thereof, as the crown is of the temporalities ; and he executes all ecclesiastical jurisdiction therein.   If an archiepiscopal see be vacant, the dean and chapter are the spiritual guardians, ever since the office of prior of Canterbury was abolished at the Reformation.   The archbishop is entitled to present by lapse to all the ecclesiastical livings in the disposal of his diocesan bishops, if not filled within six months ; and he has a customary prerogative, like the royal corody, when a bishop is consecrated by him, to name a clerk or chaplain of his own to be provided for by such suffragan bishop. The archbishop of Canterbury has also, by statute 25 Hen. VIII. c. 21, the power of granting dispensations in any case, not contrary to the Holy Scriptures and the law of God, where the pope used formerly to grant them; which is the foundation of his granting special licences to marry at any place or time; and on this also is founded the right he exercises of conferring degrees, in prejudice of the universities.

The power and authority of a bishop, besides the administration of certain ordinances peculiar to that order, consist principally in inspecting the manners of the people and clergy, and punishing them in order to reformation, by ecclesiastical censures, and in the case of the clergy, by suspension and deposition. To this purpose he has several courts under him, and may visit at pleasure every part of his diocese. His chancellor is appointed to hold his courts for him, and to assist him in matters of ecclesiastical law; who, as well as all other ecclesiastical officers, if lay or married, must be a doctor of the civil law, so created in some university.

It is also the business of a bishop to institute, and to direct induction to all ecclesiastical livings in his diocese, to execute writs of sequestration of the profits of benefices issued by the superior courts, and to license in the first instance, and, if necessary, withdraw (subject to appeal to the archbishop) the license, and regulate the stipends of curates.

Archbishoprics and bishoprics may become void by death, deprivation for any very gross and notorious crime, and also by resignation. All resignations must be made to some superior; therefore a bishop must resign to his metropolitan; but the archbishop can resign to none but the king himself.

II. A dean and chapter are the council of the bishop, to assist him with their advice in affairs of religion, and also in the temporal concerns of his see. When the rest of the clergy were settled in the several parishes of each diocese, these were reserved for the celebration of divine service in the bishop's own cathedral; and the chief of them, who presided over the rest, obtained the name of *decanus* or dean, being probably at first appointed to superintend *ten* canons or prebendaries. All deans were formerly elected by the chapter, in the same manner as bishops, but are now appointed directly by the sovereign by letters-patent. The chapter, consisting of canons or prebendaries, are sometimes appointed by the crown, sometimes by the bishop, and sometimes elected by each other.

Deaneries and prebends may become void, like a bishopric, by death, by deprivation, or by resignation to either the crown or the

bishop. Also I may here mention once for all, that if a dean, prebendary, or other spiritual person, be made a bishop, all the preferments of which he was before possessed are void; and the crown
may present to them in the right of the prerogative royal.

III. An archdeacon has an ecclesiastical jurisdiction, immediately
subordinate to the bishop, throughout the whole of his diocese, or in
some particular part of it. He is usually appointed by the bishop
himself; and has a kind of episcopal authority, originally derived
from the bishop, but now independent and distinct from his. He
therefore visits the clergy; and has his separate court for punishment of offenders by spiritual censures, and for hearing all other
causes of ecclesiastical cognizance.

IV. The rural deans are very ancient officers of the church, but
almost grown out of use. They seem to have been deputies of the
bishop, the better to inspect the conduct of the parochial clergy, to
inquire into and report dilapidations, and to examine the candidates
for confirmation, and to have been armed, in minuter matters, with
an inferior degree of judicial and coercive authority.

V. The next, and indeed the most numerous, order of men, in the
system of ecclesiastical polity, are the parsons and vicars of churches.
A parson, *persona ecclesiæ*, is one that has full possession of all the
rights of a parochial church. He is called parson, *persona*, because
by his person the church, which is an invisible body, is represented:
and he is in himself a body corporate, in order to protect and defend
the rights of the church by a perpetual succession. A parson has,
during his life, the freehold in himself of the parsonage-house, the
glebe, the tithes, and other dues. But these are sometimes *appropriated;* that is to say, the benefice is perpetually annexed to some
spiritual corporation, either sole or aggregate, being the patron of
the living; a contrivance which seems to have sprung from the
policy of the monastic orders, who have never been deficient in
subtle inventions for the increase of their own power and emoluments. At the first establishment of parochial clergy, the tithes of
of the parish were distributed in a fourfold division; one for the use
of the bishop, another for maintaining the fabric of the church, a
third for the poor, and the fourth to provide for the incumbent.
When the sees of the bishops became otherwise amply endowed,
they were prohibited from demanding their usual share of these
tithes, and the division was into three parts only. And hence it was
inferred by the monasteries, that a small part was sufficient for the
officiating priest; and that the remainder might well be applied to
the use of their own fraternities (the endowment of which was construed to be a work of the most exalted piety), subject to the burden

of repairing the church, and providing for its constant supply. And therefore they begged and bought, for masses and obits, and sometimes even for money, all the advowsons within their reach, and then appropriated the benefices to the use of their own corporation. The tithes and the glebe they kept in their own hands, without presenting any clerk, they themselves undertaking to provide for the service of the church.

Thus were most, if not all, of the appropriations at present existing originally made; being annexed to bishoprics, prebends, religious houses, nay, even to nunneries and certain military orders, all of which were spiritual corporations. At the dissolution of the monasteries in the reign of Henry VIII., the appropriations of the several parsonages, which belonged to those respective religious houses, were given to the king. And from this root have sprung all the lay appropriations or secular parsonages which we now see in the kingdom; they having been afterwards granted out from time to time by the crown.

These appropriating corporations, or religious houses, were wont to depute one of their own body to perform divine service in those parishes of which the society was thus the parson. This officiating minister was in reality no more than a curate, deputy, or vicegerent of the appropriator, and, therefore, called *vicarius* or *vicar*. His stipend was at the discretion of the appropriator; who was compelled from time to time, by various statutes, to make a proper provision for him; which endowment has usually been by a portion of the glebe belonging to the parsonage, and a particular share of the tithes which the appropriator found it most troublesome to collect, and which is therefore generally called privy or small tithes. But no particular rule having been observed, some vicarages are more liberally, and some more scantily, endowed: and hence, the tithes of many things, as wood in particular, are in some parishes rectorial, and in some vicarial rights. The distinction, therefore, of a parson and vicar is this:—the parson has for the most part the whole right to all the ecclesiastical dues in his parish; but a vicar has generally an appropriator over him, entitled to the best part of his profits, to whom he is in effect *perpetual curate*, with a standing salary.

The method of becoming a parson or vicar is much the same. To both there are four requisites necessary: holy orders, presentation, institution, and induction. The method of conferring the holy orders of deacon and priest is foreign to the purpose of these commentaries, except so far that no person can be admitted a deacon before twenty-three, or a priest before twenty-four years of age, as required by the canons of 1603, which in this point are enforced by the statute 44 Geo. III. c. 43.

When a person has been admitted to holy orders, he may be presented to a parsonage or vicarage; that is, the patron, to whom the advowson belongs, may offer his clerk to the bishop to be instituted. The bishop may refuse him upon many accounts, as, if the patron is excommunicated, and remains in contempt forty days, or if the clerk be unfit: which unfitness is of several kinds. First, with regard to his person; as, if he be under age, or unfit to discharge the pastoral office for want of learning; of which last the bishop is sole judge. If the bishop admits the patron's presentation, the clerk so admitted is next to be instituted by him; which is a kind of investiture of the spiritual part of the benefice: for by institution the care of the souls of the parish is committed to the charge of the clerk. When the bishop is also the patron, and *confers* the living, the presentation and institution are one and the same act, and are called a *collation* to a benefice. And by institution or collation the church is full, so that there can be no fresh presentation till another vacancy. Upon institution, also, the clerk may enter on the parsonage-house and glebe, and take the tithes; but he cannot grant or let them, or bring an action for them, till induction.

Induction is performed by a mandate from the bishop to the archdeacon, and is done by giving the clerk corporal possession of the church, as by holding the ring of the door, tolling a bell, or the like: and is a form required by law, with intent to give all the parishioners due notice, and sufficient certainty of their new minister, to whom their tithes are to be paid. And when a clerk is thus presented, instituted, and inducted into a rectory, he is then, and not before, in full and complete possession, and is called in law *persona impersonata*, or parson imparsonee.

The rights of a parson or vicar, in his tithes and ecclesiastical dues, fall more properly under the second book of these commentaries: and as to his duties, they are principally of ecclesiastical cognizance; those only excepted which are laid upon him by statute. And those are indeed so numerous, that with the exception of *residence*, to which it is enough to allude, I must refer to such authors as have compiled treatises expressly upon this subject.

A parson or vicar may cease to be so, 1, by death; 2, by cession, in taking another benefice; 3, by consecration; for, as was mentioned before, when a clerk is promoted to a bishopric, all his other preferments are void the instant that he is consecrated; 4, by resignation, accepted by the ordinary; 5, by deprivation, for fit and sufficient causes allowed by the law, which it is unnecessary here to enumerate.

' Besides *parsons* and *vicars*, properly so called, there are numerous ministers of the church who have many of the rights, and are subject to most of the disabilities, of the beneficed clergy. These are the incumbents of districts, constituted parishes by special acts of parliament, or formed from time to time by virtue of the powers conferred on the Church Building Commissioners, appointed by 58 Geo. III. c. 45, all of whom are subject to the visitation and correction of the bishop.

VI. A curate is the lowest degree in the church; being in the same state that a vicar was formerly, an officiating temporary minister. There are what are called *perpetual* curacies, where all the tithes are appropriated, and no vicarage endowed, but instead thereof, such perpetual curate is appointed by the appropriator. And with regard to ordinary curates, they are the objects of several statutes, which ordain, that they shall be paid such stipend as the bishop thinks reasonable, he alone also having authority to grant, and, subject to appeal to the metropolitan, withdraw their licenses.

Thus much of the clergy, properly so called. There are also certain inferior ecclesiastical officers of whom the common law takes notice, viz. :

VII. Churchwardens, who are the guardians of the church, and representatives of the body of the parish, being sometimes appointed by the minister, sometimes by the parish, sometimes by both together, as custom directs. As to the church, churchyard, &c., they have no sort of interest therein; but if any damage is done thereto, the parson only or vicar shall have the action. Lands, however, given for the benefit of the parish, the churchwardens and overseers hold in the nature of a body corporate. Their office also is to repair the church, and make rates for that purpose. They are empowered to keep all persons orderly while in church, and formerly they were to levy a shilling forfeiture on all such as did not repair to church on Sundays and holidays.

VIII. Parish clerks and sextons are also regarded by the common law as persons who have freeholds in their offices; and therefore, though they may be punished, yet they cannot be deprived by ecclesiastical censures.

CHAPTER XII.

OF THE CIVIL, MILITARY, AND MARITIME STATES.

I. Civil: Duke—Marquis — Earl — Viscount—Baron — Knight—Esquire —
Gentleman—Yeoman. II. Military: Militia—Army—Articles of War—
Yeomanry—Volunteers. III. Maritime: Navy—Articles of the Navy.

THE lay part of the community, or such of the people as are not
comprehended under the denomination of clergy, may be divided
into three distinct states, the civil, the military, and the maritime.

I. The civil state consists of the nobility and the commonalty.
Of the nobility, I have before sufficiently spoken : we are here to
consider them according to their several titles of honour; and those
now in use are dukes, marquises, earls, viscounts, and barons.

A *duke*, though he be with us, in respect of his title of nobility,
inferior in point of antiquity to many others, yet is superior to all of
them in rank; his being the first title of dignity after the royal
family.

A *marquis, marchio*, is the next degree of nobility. His office
formerly was to guard the frontiers of the kingdom, which were
called the marches: such as, in particular, were the marches of
Wales and Scotland, while each continued to be an enemy's country;
but the title has long been a mere ensign of honour.

An *earl* is a title of nobility so ancient that its origin cannot
clearly be traced out. Among the Saxons they are called *ealdormen*,
signifying *senior* or *senator* as among the Romans; and also *schiremen*,
because they had the civil government of a shire. On the irruption
of the Danes, they changed the name to *eorles*, and in Latin were
called *comites*, from being the king's attendants. After the Conquest
they were called *counts* or *countees*, from the French; but did not
long retain that name, though their shires are called counties to this
day; and the name has long been a mere title, they having now
nothing to do with the government of the county.

The name of *vice-comes* or *viscount* was afterwards made use of
as an arbitrary title of honour by Henry VI., when he created John
Beaumont a peer, by the name of Viscount Beaumont, which was the
first instance of the kind.

A *baron's* is the most general and universal title of nobility; for originally every one of the peers of superior rank had also a barony annexed to his other titles. The origin of baronies has occasioned great inquiries among our English antiquaries, but the most probable opinion seems to be, that they were the same with our present lords of manors, to which the name of court baron (which is the lord's court, and incident to every manor) gives some countenance. Originally all lords of manors, or barons, had seats in parliament, till about the reign of John the conflux of them became so troublesome that the king was obliged to divide them, and summon only the greater barons in person, leaving the small ones to sit by representation in another house; which gave rise to the separation of the two houses of parliament. By degrees the title came to be confined to the greater barons, or lords of parliament only; and there were no other barons among the peerage but such as were summoned, by writ, in respect of the tenure of their lands or baronies, till Richard II. first made it a mere title of honour, by conferring it on divers persons by his letters-patent.

The right of peerage seems to have been originally territorial, and, when the land was alienated, the dignity passed with it as appendant. Thus the bishops still sit in the House of Lords in right of succession to certain ancient baronies annexed, or supposed to be annexed, to their episcopal lands. But when alienations grew to be frequent, the dignity of peerage was confined to the lineage of the party ennobled; and instead of territorial, became, and has long been, exclusively personal. Peers are created either by writ or by patent. The creation by writ is a summons to attend the House of Peers, by the title which the sovereign is pleased to confer: that by patent is a royal grant of any degree of peerage.

Exclusive of their capacity as hereditary councillors of the crown, a nobleman, in cases of treason and felony, shall be tried by his peers. This privilege does not extend to bishops, who, though lords of parliament, sit there by virtue of the baronies which they hold *jure ecclesiæ*, and are not ennobled in blood, and consequently not peers with the nobility. Peeresses, either in their own right or by marriage, are by statute entitled to be tried before the same judicature as peers of the realm. If a woman, noble in her own right, marries a commoner, she still remains noble, and shall be tried by her peers; but if she be only noble by marriage, then by a second marriage with a commoner she loses her dignity; for as by marriage it is gained, by marriage it is also lost. A peer or peeress cannot be arrested in civil cases. A peer sitting in judgment gives not his verdict upon oath, but upon his honour: he answers also to bills in chancery upon his honour, and not upon his oath; but when he is examined as a witness either in civil or criminal cases, he must be sworn. A peer cannot lose his nobility but by death or attainder, and he cannot be degraded but by act of *parliament.*

The commonalty, like the nobility, are divided into several degrees; and as the lords, though different in rank, yet all of them are peers in respect of their nobility, so the commoners, though some are greatly superior to others, yet all are in law peers, in respect of their want of nobility.

The first name of dignity, next beneath a peer, was anciently that of *vidames, vice-domini,* or *valvasors;* but they are now quite out of use, and our legal antiquaries are not agreed upon even their origin or office.

Now, therefore, the first personal dignity after the nobility is a *knight* of the order of St. George, or *of the Garter;* first instituted by Edward III. A.D. 1348. Next follows a *knight banneret,* who must have been created by the king in person, in the field, under the royal banner, in time of open war. Else he ranks after *baronets,* who are the next order, which title is a dignity of inheritance, created by letters-patent, and usually descendible to the issue male. It was first instituted by King James I., A.D. 1611, and sold at a fixed price, in order to raise a sum for the reduction of the province of Ulster in Ireland; for which reason all baronets have the arms of Ulster superadded to their family coat. Next follow *knights of the Bath;* an order instituted by King Henry IV., and revived by King George I. in 1725. The last of these inferior nobility are *knights bachelors,* the most ancient, though the lowest, order of knighthood amongst us; for we have an instance of King Alfred's conferring this order on his son Athelstan. Formerly every one who held a knight's fee (which amounted to 20*l.* per annum) was obliged to be knighted, or pay a fine for his non-compliance. The exertion of this prerogative as an expedient to raise money in the reign of Charles I., gave great offence, and it was consequently abolished by the statute 16 Car. I. c. 16; and this kind of knighthood has, since that time, fallen into great disregard.

These are all the names of *dignity* in this kingdom, esquires and gentlemen being only names of *worship.* But before these last the heralds rank all colonels, serjeants-at-law, and doctors in the three learned professions. Esquires and gentlemen are confounded together by Sir Edward Coke, who observes, that every esquire is a gentleman, and a gentleman is defined to be one *qui arma gerit,* who bears coat armour, the grant of which adds gentility to a man's family. But it is indeed a matter somewhat unsettled, and now of no importance whatever, what constitutes the distinction, or who is a real *esquire.* A *yeoman* is he that hath free land of forty shillings by the year; who was anciently thereby qualified to serve on juries, vote for knights of the shire, and do any other act, where the law requires one that is *probus et legalis homo*. And the rest of the commonalty are in law defined as *tradesmen*, *artificers*, and *labourers*.

II. The military state includes the whole of the soldiery, or such persons as are peculiarly appointed among the rest of the people for the safeguard and defence of the realm.

It seems universally agreed that King Alfred first settled a national militia in this kingdom, and by his prudent discipline made all the subjects of his dominion soldiers; but we are unfortunately left in the dark as to the particulars of this his so-celebrated regulation. Upon the Norman Conquest the feudal law was introduced in all its rigour, and in consequence thereof all the lands in the kingdom were divided into what were called knights' fees, in number above sixty thousand; and for every knight's fee a knight or soldier, *miles*, was bound to attend the king in his wars for forty days in a year; in which space of time, before war was reduced to a science, the campaign was generally finished, and a kingdom either conquered or victorious. This personal service in process of time degenerated into pecuniary commutations or aids, and at last all military tenures were abolished at the Restoration.

In the meantime, the assize of arms, enacted 27 Hen. II., and afterwards the statute of Winchester, under Edward I., obliged every man, according to his estate and degree, to provide a determinate quantity of such arms as were then in use, in order to keep the peace. These weapons were changed by the statute 4 & 5 Ph. & M. c. 2, into others of more modern service; before which, however, in the reign of Henry VIII., lieutenants had been introduced, as standing representatives of the crown, to keep the counties in military order.

In this state things continued till the repeal of the statutes of armour, in the reign of James I.; after which, when Charles I. issued commissions of lieutenancy, and exerted other military powers, it became a question in the Long Parliament, how far the power of the militia did inherently reside in the crown. This question became at length the immediate cause of the rupture between the king and parliament, the two houses not only denying this prerogative of the crown, but also seizing into their own hands the entire power of the militia. Soon after the Restoration, however, when the military tenures were abolished, it was thought proper to recognise the right of the crown to govern and command them, and to put the whole into a more regular method of military subordination; and the order by which the militia now stands by law is principally built upon the statutes which were then passed. The general scheme is to discipline a certain number of the inhabitants of every county, chosen by ballot; but the militia force has generally been sufficiently supplied with volunteers, without having recourse to that compulsory process, which is accordingly annually suspended by parliament. The militia are not compellable to march out of their counties, unless in case of invasion or actual rebellion within the realm, nor in any case compellable to march out of the kingdom. And, therefore, during the war with Russia an act of parliament was necessary to enable the queen to accept the services of the militia out of the realm. They are to be exercised at stated times: and when in actual service, are subject to the *Mutiny Act* and *articles of war*. This is the constitutional security provided by our laws for protecting the realm against foreign or domestic violence.

When the nation was engaged in war, more veteran troops and more regular discipline were esteemed to be necessary than could be expected from a mere militia. And therefore at such times, for the raising armies, more rigorous methods were put in use; but these are to be looked upon only as temporary excrescences bred out of the distemper of the state, and not as any part of the permanent and perpetual laws of the kingdom. For martial law, which is built upon no settled principles, but is entirely arbitrary in its decisions, is in truth and reality no law, but something indulged rather than allowed as a law. The necessity of order and discipline in an army is the only thing which can give it countenance; and therefore it ought not to be permitted in time of peace, when the queen's courts are open for all persons to receive justice according to the laws of the land. But, as the fashion of keeping standing armies has long universally prevailed over Europe, it has also for many years past been annually judged necessary by our legislature to maintain a standing body of troops, under the command of the crown; who are however *ipso facto* disbanded at the expiration of every year, unless continued by parliament.

To keep this body of troops in order, an annual act of parliament likewise passes, which commences with the important recital, " that " the raising or keeping a standing army in time of peace, unless it " be with the consent of parliament, is against law;" but that it is adjudged necessary that a body of forces should be continued for the safety of the kingdom, the defence of the possessions of the crown, and the preservation of the balance of power in Europe. This statute confers power on the sovereign to make " articles of war for " the better government of the forces;" with the limitation that no person shall by such articles be subject to suffer any punishment extending to life or limb, or be kept in penal servitude, except for crimes which are expressly made punishable in this way, by the

F

statute itself. It also authorizes the calling together of *courts martial*; prescribes their procedure; specifies the offences of which they may take cognizance, and the punishments they may inflict; and makes minute regulations as to the enlistment of recruits, the billeting of troops and the supply of carriages, the enactments of the Petition of Right being suspended in that respect.

Besides the militia and regular army, numerous corps of yeomanry and volunteers were organized during the war with France. Several of the former are still annually mustered for a short period for the purpose of exercise and drill; but they are few in number when compared with the rifle and artillery volunteers, which have recently sprung into existence, and whose organization is also regulated by recent statutes.

And thus much for the military state, as acknowledged by the laws of England.

III. The *maritime* state is nearly related to the former. The royal navy of England has ever been its greatest defence and ornament; it is its ancient and natural strength; the floating bulwark of the island; an army, from which, however strong and powerful, no danger can ever be apprehended to liberty: and accordingly it has been assiduously cultivated, even from the earliest ages.

The flourishing condition of our marine was long attributed to the provisions of the statutes called the Navigation Acts, the sole object of which was to confine the whole foreign and coasting trade of the country to British vessels. This theory is now exploded; and it would, therefore, be an idle task to trace their various provisions. Let us see then simply how our navy is regulated by law.

The power of impressing sea-faring men for the sea service by royal commission has been a matter of dispute, and was ever submitted to with great reluctance; but it seems to be part of the common law, and its legality cannot now be doubted. The voluntary enlistment of seamen is now, however, so effectually encouraged, that the navy is manned without any recourse to the revolting system of kidnapping which was formerly resorted to. Advantages in point of wages are given to seamen, to induce them to enter the service, or the reserve volunteer force; and every foreign seaman who during war serves two years, is *ipso facto* naturalized.

The discipline of the royal fleet is directed by certain express rules, articles, and orders, first enacted by the authority of parliament soon after the Restoration, and revised only a few years ago. In these *articles of the navy* almost every possible offence is set down, and the punishment thereof annexed; in which respect the seamen have much the advantage over their brethren in the land service; whose articles of war are not enacted by parliament, but framed from time to time at the pleasure of the crown.

The marine forces are subject to the discipline of the navy while on board ship; but are regulated, while on shore, by an annual Marine Mutiny Act, containing a similar recital, and corresponding provisions to those contained in the annual act applicable to the army.

CHAPTER XIII.

OF THE PEOPLE IN THEIR PRIVATE RELATIONS.

I. Master and servant—Domestics—Apprentices — Labourers—Artificers— Seamen—Factors and brokers—Wages—Truck Act——II. Husband and wife—Contract of marriage—How made—How dissolved—Its legal consequences——III. Parent and child—Legitimate children—Their rights and duties—Bastards——IV. Guardian and ward—Several kinds of guardians —Jurisdiction of Court of Chancery—Incidents of infancy.

HAVING thus commented on the rights and duties of persons as standing in the *public* relations of magistrates and people, the method I have marked out now leads me to consider their rights and duties in *private* economical relations.

The three great relations in private life are, 1. That of *master and servant*; 2. That of *husband and wife*; and 3. That of *parent and child*. . But since the parents may be snatched away by death before they have completed their duty to their children, the law has therefore provided a fourth relation, 4. That of *guardian and ward*.

· I. Of *master and servant*. Pure and proper slavery does not, nay cannot, subsist in England. A slave, the instant he lands in England, or puts his foot on the deck of a British man-of-war, becomes a freeman; that is, the law will protect him in the enjoyment of his person and his property. But the law recognises and enforces that contract whereby one freeman surrenders to another for a certain time his natural right of free action, by becoming his servant.

1. The first sort of servants acknowledged by the laws of England, are *menial servants*; so called from being *intra mœnia*, or domestics. The contract between them and their masters, if the hiring be general, the law construes to be for a year; upon a principle of natural equity that the servant shall serve, and the master maintain him, throughout all the revolutions of the respective seasons. But the contract may be made for any larger or smaller term; and is by custom determinable by a month's notice, or what is an equivalent in the case of the servant, a month's wages.

A servant may be dismissed without notice for a reasonable cause, such as moral misconduct, wilful disobedience to a lawful order, or neglect of duty; and in such cases he is not entitled to any wages from the day he is discharged, except those then due. But if wrongfully discharged, he is entitled to wages up to the end of the current period of his service. If, on the other hand, a servant who is to be paid quarterly, or yearly, or at any other fixed time, improperly leave his service, or is guilty of such misconduct as to justify his discharge during the currency of any such period, he is not entitled to wages for any part thereof, even to the day he quits.

Another species of servants are called *apprentices* (from *apprendre*, to learn), and are usually bound for a term of years, to serve their masters, and be maintained and instructed by them; this being usually done to persons of trade, in order to learn their art and mystery. Differences between them may, in certain cases, be settled by two justices; the master being bound to maintain and instruct, and the apprentice being compellable to serve.

A third species of servants are *labourers*, who are only hired by the day or the week, and do not live *intra mœnia*, as part of the family; concerning whom many statutes have at various times been passed, on principles of legislation which have long been abandoned alike in theory and in practice. Certain artificers may still, if they absent themselves from their service before the contract is completed, or do not enter on the service, be apprehended and dealt with summarily, by fine and imprisonment.

There are other statutes affecting persons who are engaged in particular occupations, but who cannot be said to form a distinct species of servants from those now under consideration. Thus the labour of children in factories is regulated by statute; the employment of women and girls is prohibited in mines, and that of boys under twelve made conditional on their having previously received a certain amount of education.

Merchant seamen are, from the increase of commerce and the consequent number of persons employed in this service, entitled to be classed as a distinct species of servants, whose contracts and conduct are in a great measure regulated by the recent acts of parliament relating to merchant shipping.

There is yet a fifth species of servants, if they may be so called, being rather in a superior, a ministerial, capacity; such as *stewards*, *factors*, and *bailiffs:* whom however the law considers as servants, *pro tempore*, with regard to such of their acts as affect their master's or employer's property. Which leads me to consider the manner in which this relation, of service, affects either the master or servant.

By apprenticeship, a person gains a settlement in that parish wherein he last served forty days ; and persons serving seven years as apprentices to any trade formerly had also an exclusive right to exercise that trade in any part of England. But these exclusive rights of trading have been abolished. By service, however, all servants and labourers become entitled to wages; which must be paid in money, payment in goods or otherwise than in current coin being prohibited by the Truck Act. And the law, in some respects, places this right to wages very high. Thus in the payment of the debts of a testator or intestate they rank before specialty debts; and by the Bankrupt laws the wages of the clerks or servants, labourers or workmen of the bankrupt, may be paid in full. It remains but to notice one important incident to the relationship of master and servant, viz., that the latter cannot in general recover damages from his master for a mere non-feazance on his part, nor for the negligence of a fellow-servant in the course of his employment; for he is, as it were, rowing in the same boat with them, and is supposed on entering the service to agree to incur any danger attaching to his position.

Let us now see how strangers may be affected by this relation of master and servant. And, first, the master may *maintain*, that is, assist his servant in any action against a stranger ; whereas, in general, it is an offence against public justice to encourage suits, by helping to bear the expense of them, and is called in law maintenance. A master likewise may justify an assault in defence of his servant, and a servant in defence of his master. And if any person retain my servant, for which the servant departeth from me, and goeth to serve the other, I may have an action against both the new master and the servant, or either of them ; but if the new master did not know that he was my servant, no action lies; unless he afterwards refuse to restore him upon information and demand.

The master is answerable for the act of his servant, if done by his command, either expressly given or implied: *nam, qui facit per alium, facit per se.* Therefore, if the servant commit a trespass by the command of his master, the master shall be guilty of it, though the servant is not thereby excused ; for he is only to obey his master in matters that are honest and lawful. If an innkeeper's servants rob his guests, the master is bound to restitution, for he must take care to provide honest servants ; and whatever a servant is permitted to do in the usual course of his business, is equivalent to a general command. If I pay money to a banker's servant, the banker is answerable for it; if I pay it to a clergyman's or a physician's servant, whose usual business it is not to receive money for his master, and he embezzles it, I must pay it over again. A wife, a friend, a relation, that usually transacts business for a man, are *quoad hoc* his servants; and the principal must answer for their conduct: for the law implies, that they act under a general command. If I usually deal with a tradesman by myself, or constantly pay him ready money, I am not answerable for what my servant takes upon trust, for here is no implied order to the tradesman to trust my servant; but if I usually send him upon trust, or sometimes on trust and sometimes with ready money, I am answerable for all he takes up; for the tradesman cannot possibly distinguish when he comes by my order, and when upon his own authority.

If a servant, again, by his negligence does any damage to a stranger, the master shall answer for his neglect. If a smith's servant lames a horse while he is shoeing him, an action lies against the master, and not against the servant; but in these cases the damage must be done while he is actually employed in the master's service, otherwise the servant shall answer for his own misbehaviour. In all the cases here put, the master may be a loser by the trust reposed in a servant, but never can be a gainer; he may be answerable for his servant's misbehaviour, but never can shelter himself by laying the blame on his agent. The reason of this is, that the wrong done by the servant is looked upon in law as the wrong of the master himself; and it is a standing maxim, that no man shall be allowed to take any advantage of his own wrong.

II. The second private relation of persons is that of *husband and wife;* arising from marriage, which our law regards in no other light than as a civil contract. The *holiness* of the matrimonial state is left entirely to the ecclesiastical law; the temporal courts not having jurisdiction to consider unlawful marriage as a sin, but merely as a civil inconvenience. Taking it, therefore, in a civil light, the law allows it to be valid where the parties were *willing* to contract, *able* to contract, and *did* contract, in the form required by law.

Consensus non concubitus faciat nuptias, the maxim of the civil law, is therefore adopted by the common law in these cases; which further considers all persons able to contract who do not labour under some particular disabilities and incapacities.

These *disabilities* were formerly considered as either canonical or civil. Consanguinity, or relationship by blood; affinity, or relationship by marriage; and corporeal infirmity were *canonical* disabilities, making the marriage voidable, but not *ipso facto* void, until sentence of nullity had been obtained. The last of these is now, however, the only *canonical* disability on which marriages, otherwise regular, can be declared void. The others have by statute been declared civil disabilities, which make the contract void *ab initio,* and not merely voidable.

Besides consanguinity and affinity, which, as already observed, we now class as *civil* disabilities, there are three others of a like nature; the *first* of which is a prior marriage, or having another husband or wife living; in which case, besides the penalties consequent upon it as a felony, the second marriage is to all intents and purposes void. The *second* is want of age, which is sufficient to avoid all other contracts, on account of the imbecility of judgment in the parties contracting: *à fortiori*, therefore, it ought to avoid this, the most important contract of any. Therefore, if a boy under fourteen, or a girl under twelve years of age, marries, this marriage is imperfect; and when either of them comes to the age of consent, they may declare the marriage void, without any divorce, or the sentence of any court. But it is nevertheless so far a marriage that, if at the age of consent they agree to continue together, they need not be married again. The *third* incapacity is want of reason; without a competent share of which, as no other, so neither can the matrimonial contract be valid.

The want of consent of parents or guardians, where either party is a minor, is treated by our law books as a civil disability; but to this it can scarcely be said to amount. The consent required by law is that of the father, or if he be dead, of the guardian; or if there be no guardian, of the mother; or if there be no mother, then of any guardian appointed by the Court of Chancery. But the marriage of a minor without the requisite consent is, nevertheless, valid; the provisions of the statute in this respect being only *directory*. It may be attended with a penalty, however; for if the marriage was solemnized by means of the false oath or fraudulent procurement of one of the parties, the party so offending is liable to forfeit all the property which would otherwise accrue from the marriage.

Finally, to constitute a valid marriage, the parties must not only be willing and able to contract, but actually must contract themselves in due form of law. Any contract made, *per verba de præsenti*, or in words of the present tense, and in case of cohabitation *per verba de futuro* also, was before the time of George II. so far a valid marriage, that the parties might be compelled in the spiritual courts to celebrate it *in facie ecclesiæ*.* But these verbal contracts are now of no force to compel a future marriage; their only operation being to give the party who is willing to perform his promise a right of civil action against the one who refuses to do so. And until the reign of William IV., no marriage was valid that was not celebrated in some parish church or public chapel, unless by dispensation from the

* In the time of the grand rebellion, all marriages were performed by the justices of the peace; and these marriages were declared valid, without any fresh solemnization, by statute 12 Car. II. c. 33.

Archbishop of Canterbury, after publication of banns, or by license from the spiritual judge; and it was essential to its validity that it should be performed by a person in orders.

The statute 6 & 7 William IV. c. 35, was passed for the relief of those who scrupled at joining in the services of the Established Church; and was the result of a long and arduous struggle, carried on for many years in and out of parliament; the bitterness of which, the question being polemical, has not yet wholly subsided. It provides for places of religious worship being registered for the solemnization of marriage; and permits of this contract being entered into before a registrar of marriages, without any religious sanction whatever; so that it is no longer essential to the validity of a marriage, either that it should be solemnized in a church, or be performed by a person in holy orders. But whether solemnized in church, celebrated in a place of worship, or entered into before the registrar, a marriage must in all cases be preceded and accompanied by certain circumstances of publicity, or be entered into in virtue of a license, which is obtainable only on oath being made that there is no legal impediment.

Marriages are dissolved by death or divorce. There are two kinds of divorce, the one for the canonical impediment before referred to, existing *before* the marriage, not supervenient, or arising *afterwards*; the other for *adultery*, committed *after* the marriage. In divorces on the ground of corporal infirmity the marriage is declared null, unlawful *ab initio;* and the issue of such marriage are bastards. In cases of divorce for a cause arising after marriage, no such result takes place, for in that case the marriage was just and lawful *ab initio.*

The canon law deems so highly of the nuptial tie, that it will not allow it to be unloosed for any cause whatsoever, that arises after the union is made; and with us, adultery was consequently only a cause of separation from bed and board; for which the best reason that could be given was, that if divorces were allowed to depend upon a matter within the power of either of the parties, they would probably be extremely frequent.

The inadequacy of this redress gave rise to the practice of dissolving marriages by special acts of parliament, or *privilegia*, a remedy that was, from its very nature, within the reach only of the wealthier classes. Its cost became, in time, a subject of natural and just complaint by those to whom redress was in this way denied; and the *Court for Divorce and Matrimonial Causes* was ultimately constituted to grant divorces as a right, not as a *privilegium.*

Lastly, what are the legal consequences of marriage, or its dissolution?

By marriage, the husband and wife are one person in law; the legal existence of the woman is incorporated and consolidated into that of the husband; under whose protection, and *cover*, she performs everything; and is therefore called in our law-French a *feme-covert, fœmina viro co-operta*; and her condition during her marriage is called her *coverture*. Upon this principle depend almost all the legal rights, duties, and disabilities, that either of them acquire by the marriage. For this reason, a man cannot grant anything to his wife, or enter into a covenant with her, for this would be to suppose her separate existence; and therefore it is also generally true, that all compacts made between husband and wife, when single, are voided by the intermarriage. A woman indeed may be attorney for her husband; for that implies no separation from, but is rather a representation of her lord. And a husband may also bequeath anything to his wife by will; for that cannot take effect till the coverture is determined by his death. The husband is bound to provide his wife with necessaries by law, as much as himself; and if she contracts debts for them, he is obliged to pay them, unless he supplies her with necessaries himself; but for anything besides necessaries, he is not chargeable, unless the wife had authority express or implied to contract for him. Also if a wife elopes, or lives with another man, the husband is not chargeable even for necessaries; and if the person who furnishes the wife with goods, is sufficiently apprised that she has no authority to pledge her husband's credit, he is not responsible. If the wife be indebted before marriage, the husband is bound afterwards to pay the debt; for he has adopted her and her circumstances together. If the wife be injured in her person or her property, she can bring no action for redress without her husband's concurrence, and in his name as well as her own; neither can she be sued, without making the husband a defendant. There are indeed cases where the wife shall sue and be sued as a *feme sole*, as, 1. Where the husband is banished, for then he is dead in law. 2. Where the wife has obtained a judicial separation; and 3. Where the wife, having been deserted, has obtained an order of justices for the protection from her husband and his creditors of the fruits of her own industry. So in the court for divorce and matrimonial causes, a woman may sue and be sued without her husband; and in our courts of equity, a married woman may, by her next friend, sue and be sued in respect of contracts relating to her separate estate.

In criminal prosecutions the wife may be indicted and punished separately; for the union is only a civil union; but husband and wife cannot give evidence for or against each other, unless the offence is against the person of the wife, for then this rule does not apply.

· There are some instances in which, for obvious reasons, the wife is separately considered; as inferior to the husband, and acting by his compulsion. Then all deeds executed, and acts done by her during her coverture, are void, except deeds properly acknowledged; in which case she must be solely and secretly examined, to learn if her act be voluntary. She cannot by will devise lands to her husband, unless under special circumstances; for at the time of making it she is supposed to be under his coercion. And in some felonies and other inferior crimes, committed by her through constraint of her husband, the law excuses her; but this extends not to treason or murder.

The husband also, by the old law, might give his wife moderate correction. In the polite reign of Charles II., this power of correction began to be doubted; and a wife may now have security of the peace against her husband, or, in return, a husband against his wife. Yet the lower rank of people, who were always fond of the old common law, still claim, and exert their ancient privilege; and the courts of law will still permit a husband to restrain a wife of her liberty, in case of any gross misbehaviour.

These are the chief legal effects of marriage during the coverture; upon which we may observe, that even the disabilities which the wife lies under, are for the most part intended for her protection and benefit. So great a favourite is the female sex of the laws of England.

III. The next, and the most universal relation in nature, is immediately derived from the preceding, being that between parent and child.

Children are of two sorts; legitimate, and spurious or bastards; each of which we shall consider in their order; and, first, of legitimate children.

1. A legitimate child is he that is born in lawful wedlock, or within a competent time afterwards; and to him the parents owe maintenance, protection, and education.

The duty of parents to provide for the *maintenance* of their children is a principle of natural law, which the municipal laws of all well-regulated states have taken care to enforce. The manner in which this obligation shall be performed with us is pointed out by the statutes 43 Eliz. c. 2, and 5 Geo. I. c. 8., the result of which, combined with the decisions of our courts on this subject, is that no person is bound to provide a maintenance for his issue, unless where the children are impotent and unable to work, either through infancy, disease, or accident, and then is only obliged to find them with necessaries, the penalty on refusal being no more than 20s. a month. And our law makes no provision to prevent the disinheriting of children by will, leaving every man's property in his own disposal, upon a principle of liberty in this as well as every other action.

From the duty of maintenance we may easily pass to that of *protection*, which is also a natural duty, but rather permitted than enjoined by any municipal laws; nature, in this respect, working so strongly as to need rather a check than a spur. A parent may maintain his children in their lawsuits without being guilty of maintenance; and he may also justify an assault and battery in defence of their persons.

The last duty of parents to their children is that of giving them an *education* suitable to their station in life; a duty pointed out by reason, and of far the greatest importance of any. Yet the municipal laws of most countries seem to be defective in this point, by not constraining the parent to bestow a proper education upon his children; and our interference is limited to annual grants by parliament for promoting the education of the children of the poor, under the control of the *Committee of Privy Council for Education*. The rich are left at their own option, whether they will breed up their children to be ornaments or disgraces to their family.

The *power* of a parent over his children is derived from the former consideration, their duty to him. He may lawfully correct his child, being under age, in a reasonable manner; and this power he may delegate, during his life, to the tutor or schoolmaster, who is then *in loco parentis*, and has such a portion of the power of the parent committed to his charge, viz., that of restraint and correction, as may be necessary to answer the purposes for which he is employed. The parents' consent or concurrence to the marriage of the child while under age is also still required, although the want of such consent does not of itself render the marriage invalid. A father has no other power over his son's *estate* than as his trustee or guardian; he may indeed have the benefit of his children's labour while they live with him, and are maintained by him; but this is no more than he is entitled to from his apprentices or servants; and the legal power of a father entirely ceases at the age of twenty-one, for the children are then enfranchised by arriving at years of discretion, when the power of the father, or other guardian, is supposed to give place to the empire of reason.

During the father's life, the mother, as such, is entitled to no power, but only to reverence and respect; and until recently, indeed, might have been excluded by the father from all access to her children. But the Court of Chancery may direct that a mother shall have access to her children; and if such children are within the age of *seven* years, that they be delivered to her until they attain that age.

The *duties* of children to their parents arise from a principle of natural justice and retribution. For to those who gave us existence we naturally owe subjection and obedience during our minority, and honour and reverence ever after. This tie of nature the law does not hold to be dissolved by any misbehaviour of the parent; and therefore a child is equally justifiable in defending the person, or maintaining the suit, of a bad parent as a good one ; and is equally compellable to maintain and provide for a wicked and unnatural progenitor, as for one who has shown the greatest tenderness and parental affection.

2. We must in this place consider, in a few words, the case of illegitimate children, or bastards ; who are such as are not only begotten, but born, out of lawful matrimony, for all children born before matrimony are bastards by law ; and so it is of all children born so long after the death of the husband that by the usual course of gestation they could not be begotten by him. But this being a matter of some uncertainty, the law is not exact as to a few days. Children born during wedlock may indeed, in some circumstances, be bastards. As if the husband be out of the kingdom of England, or, as the law somewhat loosely phrases it, *extra quatuor maria*, for above nine months, so that no access to his wife can be presumed, her issue during that period shall be bastards. So in case of divorce on the ground of corporeal imbecility, all the issue born during the coverture are bastards, because the marriage was unlawful and null from the beginning.

The only duty of parents to their bastard children which our law recognises, is that of maintenance, which may be directed by two justices, and enforced by distress and imprisonment.

The rights of a bastard are very few, being only such as he can *acquire*, for he can *inherit* nothing, being looked upon as the son of nobody, and sometimes called *filius nullius*, sometimes *filius populi*. Yet he may gain a surname by reputation, though he has none by inheritance. He cannot be heir to any one, neither can he have heirs, but of his own body ; for he has no ancestor from whom any inheritable blood can be derived. A bastard was also, in strictness, incapable of holy orders; and though that were dispensed with, yet he was utterly disqualified from holding any dignity in the church ; but this doctrine seems now obsolete ; and in most other respects there is no distinction between a bastard and another man.

IV. The only general private relation now remaining to be discussed, is that of *guardian and ward*, which bears a very near resemblance to the last, and is plainly derived out of it ; the guardian being only a temporary parent, that is, for so long a time as the ward is an infant, or under age.

Of the several species of guardians, the first are guardians *by nature;* viz., the father and (in some cases) the mother of the child. This guardianship is a mere personal right in the father or other ancestor to the custody of the *person* of the infant, until he or she attains twenty-one years of age. For if an estate be left to an infant, the father is by common law the guardian, and must account to his child for the profits. There are also guardians *for nurture,* which are the father, or, if he be dead, the mother, till the infant attains the age of fourteen years; a guardianship which, like that by nature, has no reference to the infant's property, but relates merely to his person.

Next are guardians *in socage* (an appellation which will be explained in the second book of these commentaries), called guardians *by the common law;* for when the minor is entitled to lands, the guardianship, by the common law, devolves upon his next of kin, to whom the inheritance cannot possibly descend. For the law judges it improper to trust the person of an infant in his hands who may by possibility become heir to him, that there may be no temptation, nor even suspicion of temptation, for him to abuse his trust. These guardians in socage, like those for nurture, continue only till the minor is fourteen years of age, for then, in both cases, he is presumed to have discretion, so far as to choose his own guardian.

For this he may do, unless a *testamentary guardian* be appointed by the father, by virtue of the statute 12 Car. II. c. 24.

The guardian so chosen, hence called *by election,* seems, however, to have no power beyond giving a consent to the ward's marriage; and the infant's election in no case supersedes the jurisdiction of the Court of Chancery. For the lord chancellor is, by right derived from the crown, the general and supreme guardian of all the infants in the kingdom; and will appoint a suitable guardian for an infant, where there is no other, or no other who will or can act. These guardians are treated as officers of the court, and are held responsible accordingly.

The Court of Chancery will also remove a guardian, however appointed, whenever sufficient cause can be shown for so doing. Its jurisdiction extends to the care of the person of the infant, so far as is necessary for his protection and education, and to the care of his property, for its management and preservation, and proper application for his maintenance. Upon the former ground the court will interfere with the ordinary rights of parents, as guardians by nature or by nurture; for when a father is guilty of gross cruelty to his children, or is in constant habits of drunkenness, or professes irreligious principles, or his domestic associations are such as tend to the corruption of his children, the court will deprive him of the custody of the infants, appointing at the same time a suitable person to act as guardian, and superintend their education. This interference may be obtained on the petition of the infant himself, or of any of his friends or relatives; nay, a mere stranger may at any time set the machinery of the court in motion, the infant then becoming a ward in chancery, and under the special protection of the court. No act can then be done affecting the minor's person or property, unless under its direction, every act done without such direction being considered a contempt, exposing the offender to be attached and imprisoned. Thus it is a contempt to withdraw the person of the infant from the proper custody, or to marry the infant without the approbation of the court. For the court usually gives express directions how to exercise the powers which it has conferred; prescribes the residence, and settles a scheme for the education of the infant; and regulates, if necessary, his choice of a profession or trade; approves or prohibits the minor's marriage; and performs all the other duties of guardians by nature or for nurture.

A guardian *ad litem*, or, as he is in general termed, a *prochein amy*, or next friend, is one who is appointed by the court to prosecute the suit, or manage the defence of an infant. He has no authority over the infant's person or property, but is responsible for the costs of the suit.

There are also special guardians, such as guardians in *gavelkind*, whose authority does not cease till the infant attains fifteen years of age, and guardians by the *custom* of London and other places; but they are particular exceptions, and do not fall under the general law.

The power and reciprocal duty of a guardian and ward are the same, *pro tempore*, as that of a father and child; and therefore I shall not repeat them, but shall only add, that the guardian, when the ward comes of age, is bound to give him an account of all that he has transacted on his behalf, and must answer for all losses by his wilful default or negligence.

Let us next consider the ward or person within age, for whose assistance these guardians are constituted by law. The ages of male and female are different for different purposes. A male at *twelve* years old may take the oath of allegiance; at *fourteen* may consent or disagree to marriage, may choose his guardian, may be an executor, although he cannot act until of age, and at *twenty-one* is at his own disposal, and may alien and devise his lands, goods, and chattels. A female, also, at *seven* years of age, may be betrothed or given in marriage; at *nine* is entitled to dower; at *twelve* is at years of maturity, and may consent or disagree to marriage; at *fourteen* may choose a guardian; at *seventeen* may be executrix, and at *twenty-one* may dispose of herself and her lands. So that full age in male or female is twenty-one years, which age is completed on the day preceding the anniversary of a person's birth, who till that time is an infant, and so styled in law.

Infants have various privileges, and various disabilities; but their very disabilities are privileges, in order to secure them from hurting themselves by their own improvident acts. An infant cannot be sued but under the protection, and joining the name, of his guardian, for he is to defend him against all attacks as well by law as otherwise; but he may sue either by his guardian, or, as we have already seen, by his *prochein amy*, or alone for wages in the county courts. In criminal cases, an infant of the age of *fourteen* years may be capitally punished; but under the age of *seven* he cannot. The period between *seven* and *fourteen* is subject to much uncertainty; for the infant shall, generally speaking, be judged *primâ facie* innocent: yet if he was *doli capax*, and could discern between good and evil at the time of the offence committed, he may be convicted, and undergo judgment and execution of death, though he has not attained to years of puberty or discretion.

With regard to estates and civil property an infant has many privileges, which will be better understood when we come to treat more particularly of those matters; but this may be said in general, that an infant shall lose nothing by non-claim, or neglect of demanding his right, nor shall any other *laches* or negligence be imputed to an infant, except in some very particular cases.

CHAPTER XIV.

I.—OF CORPORATIONS.

I. Corporations in general—Aggregate or sole—Ecclesiastical or lay—Civil or eleemosynary—How created—Their powers, privileges, and disabilities—How visited and how dissolved.

HITHERTO of persons in their natural capacities; but, as all personal rights die with the person, and as the necessary form of investing a series of individuals, one after another, with the same rights, would be very inconvenient, if not impracticable, it has been found necessary, when it is for the advantage of the public to have any particular rights kept on foot and continued, to constitute artificial persons, who may maintain a perpetual succession, and enjoy a kind of legal immortality, which are called bodies politic, bodies corporate *corpora corporata*, or corporations. To show the advantages of such institutions, let us consider the case of a college founded *ad studendum et orandum.* If this was a mere voluntary assembly, the individuals which compose it might indeed read, pray, study, and perform scholastic exercises together, so long as they could agree to do so; but they could neither frame nor receive any rules of conduct; none, at least, which would have any binding force, for want of a coercive power to create a sufficient obligation. Neither could they retain any privileges or immunities; for if such privileges were attacked, which of all this unconnected assembly would have the right or ability to defend them? And, when they were dispersed by death or otherwise, how should they transfer these advantages to another set of students, equally unconnected as themselves? So with regard to holding estates or other property, they could only continue the property to other persons, for the same purposes, by endless conveyances from one to the other, as often as the hands were changed.

But when united into a corporation, they and their successors are then considered as one person in law: they have one will, collected from the sense of the majority: this one will may establish rules for the regulation of the whole body, or statutes may be prescribed to it at its creation; the privileges and immunities, the estates and possessions of the corporation, when once vested in them, will be for ever vested without any new conveyance to new successors; for all the individual members that have existed from the foundation to the present time, or that shall ever hereafter exist, are but one person in law, a person that never dies; in like manner as the river Thames is still the same river, though the parts which compose it are changing every instant.

The honour of inventing these political constitutions is ascribed to the Romans; they were afterwards much considered by the civil law, in which they were called *universitates*, as forming one whole out of many individuals; or *collegia*, from being gathered together; and they were adopted also by the canon law, for the maintenance of ecclesiastical discipline. From them our spiritual corporations are derived, and the law of England now recognises several sorts of them.

Thus corporations are said to be *aggregate*, or such as consist of many persons united in one society; of which kind are the mayor and commonalty of a city, the head and fellows of a college, the dean and chapter of a cathedral. Corporations *sole* consist of one person only and his successors, in some particular station, who are incorporated by law, in order to give them some legal capacities and advantages, particularly that of perpetuity, which in their natural persons they could not have had. In this sense the sovereign is a sole corporation; so is a bishop; so are some deans, and prebendaries, distinct from their several chapters, and so is every parson and vicar. For the parson, *quatenus* parson, never dies, any more than the sovereign. All the original rights of the parsonage being thus preserved entire to the successor, the present incumbent, and his predecessor who lived seven centuries ago, are in law one and the same person, and what was given to the one was given to the other also.

Corporations are also *ecclesiastical* and *lay*. Ecclesiastical corporations are where the members that compose it are entirely spiritual persons; such as bishops, parsons, and vicars, which are sole corporations; and deans and chapters, which are bodies aggregate. Lay corporations, again, are either *civil* or *eleemosynary*. The civil are such as are erected for a variety of temporal purposes. The sovereign, for instance, is made a corporation to prevent the possibility of an *interregnum*; other lay corporations are erected for the good government of a town, and some for the better carrying on of divers special purposes; as the Colleges of Physicians in London, for the improvement of the medical science; the Royal Society for the advancement of natural knowledge; and the Society of Antiquaries for promoting the study of antiquities. The eleemosynary sort are such as are constituted for the perpetual distribution of the free alms, or bounty, of the founder of them, to such persons as he has directed. Of this kind are all hospitals for the maintenance of the poor, sick, and impotent: and all colleges, both *in* our universities, and *out* of them.

These are the several species of corporations known to our law. Of some of them, which possess peculiar qualities, and of others which have not all the usual incidents of a corporation, I shall treat separately; and with this view shall consider:—First, corporations *in general*; Secondly, *municipal* corporations; and Thirdly, *trading* corporations.

1. Corporations, by the civil law, seem to have been created by the mere act and voluntary association of their members: provided such convention was not contrary to law, for then it was *illicitum collegium*.

With us in England, the consent of the crown is absolutely necessary to the erection of any corporation, either impliedly or expressly given. The sovereign's implied consent is to be found in corporations which exist at *common law*, to which our former kings are supposed to have given their concurrence; of which sort are the sovereign himself, all bishops, parsons, vicars, and some others. Another method of implication, whereby the consent of the crown is presumed, is as to all corporations by *prescription*, such as the

City of London, and many others; which have existed as corporations, time whereof the memory of man runneth not to the contrary. The methods by which the consent of the crown is expressly given, are either by act of parliament or charter. It is observable, however, that till of late years most of those statutes, which have been usually cited as having created corporations, either confirmed such as had been before created by the sovereign; as in the case of the College of Physicians erected by Henry VIII., whose charter was afterwards confirmed in parliament; or they enabled the sovereign to erect a corporation *in futuro* with such and such powers: as is the case of the Bank of England.

But in recent times corporations have been usually created by act of parliament; many powers being usually required by our modern corporations, such as the right to levy tolls and purchase land compulsorily, which the crown cannot, and which parliament alone can confer.

And parliament, we may add, not only can erect but may remodel any existing corporations, in any manner it may see fit. This, in fact, was done by the Municipal Corporations Reform Act; by which the constitution, privileges, powers, capacities and incapacities of most of these bodies, which previously were almost as various in character as the bodies themselves were in number, were assimilated to each other in all respects.

When a corporation is erected, a *name* must be given to it; and by that name alone it must sue and be sued, and do all legal acts. When so formed and named, it acquires many powers, rights, capacities and incapacities, which we are next to consider. As, 1. To have perpetual *succession,* which is the very end of its incorporation. 2. To sue or be sued, and do all other acts as natural persons may. 3. To purchase lands, and hold them, for the benefit of themselves and their successors. 4. To have a common seal. For a corporation being an invisible body, acts and speaks only by its common seal. 5. To make by-laws or private statutes for the better government of the corporation. These five powers are inseparably incident to every corporation, at least to every corporation *aggregate:* for two of them are very unnecessary to a corporation *sole;* viz. to have a corporate seal to testify his sole assent, and to make statutes for the regulation of his own conduct.

There are also certain privileges and disabilities that attend an aggregate corporation. Thus, it must always appear by attorney; for it cannot appear in person, being invisible, and existing only in intendment of law. It may take goods and chattels for the benefit of existing members and their successors, which a sole corporation cannot do; but it cannot do any acts, or even receive a grant, during the vacancy of the headship, except only appointing another head, for a corporation is incomplete without a head.

It is also incident to every corporation to have a capacity to purchase lands for themselves and successors; and this is regularly true at the common law. But they are excepted out of the statute of wills: so that no devise of lands to a corporation by will is good: except for charitable uses, by statute 43 Eliz. c. 4: which exception is again greatly narrowed by the statute 9 Geo. II. c. 36. And their privilege of purchasing from a living grantor is much abridged by a variety of statutes, which are generally called the *statutes of mortmain:* the more particular exposition of which I shall defer till the next book of these commentaries, when we shall consider the nature and tenures of estates.

I proceed, therefore, to inquire how corporations may be *visited;* for being composed of individuals subject to human frailties, they are liable, as well as private persons, to deviate from the end of their institution.

With regard to all ecclesiastical corporations, the ordinary is their visitor, so constituted by the canon law, and from thence derived to us. The pope formerly, and now the sovereign, as supreme ordinary, is the visitor of the archbishop or metropolitan; the metropolitan has the charge and coercion of all his suffragan bishops; and the bishops in their several dioceses are in ecclesiastical matters the visitors of all deans and chapters, of all parsons and vicars, and all other spiritual corporations.

With respect to all lay corporations, the founder, his heirs, or assigns, are the visitors, whether the foundation be civil or eleemosynary. And the crown being, in general, the sole founder of all civil corporations and the endower, the perficient founder, of all eleemosynary ones, the right of visitation of the former results, according to the rule laid down, to the sovereign; and of the latter to the patron or endower. The sovereign being thus visitor of all civil corporations, the law has also appointed the place wherein he shall exercise this jurisdiction, which is the court of King's Bench: where, and where only, all misbehaviours of this kind of corporations are inquired into and redressed, and all their controversies decided.

As to eleemosynary corporations, by the dotation the founder and his heirs are of common right the legal visitors, to see that such property is rightly employed, as might otherwise have descended to the visitor himself: but, if the founder has appointed any other person to be visitor, then his assignee so appointed is invested with all the founder's power. If no visitor has been appointed by the founder, the right of visitation in default of his heirs devolves upon the crown, and is exercised by the Lord Chancellor, the King's Bench having no jurisdiction over such foundations.

We come now to consider how corporations may be dissolved. Any particular member may be disfranchised, or lose his place in the corporation, by acting contrary to the laws of the society, or the laws of the land; or he may resign it by his own voluntary act. But the body politic may also itself be dissolved in several ways; as, 1. By act of parliament, which is boundless in its operations. 2. By the natural death of all its members, in case of an aggregate corporation. 3. By surrender of its franchises into the hands of the sovereign, which is a kind of sucide; and, 4. By forfeiture of its charter, through negligence or abuse of its franchises; in which case the law judges that the body politic has broken the condition upon which it was incorporated, and thereupon the incorporation is void; the regular course to obtain this judgment being an information in nature of a *quo warranto*, to inquire by what warrant the members now exercise their corporate power, having forfeited it by such and such proceedings. At common law corporations were, indeed, dissolved, in case the mayor or other head was not duly elected on the day appointed in the charter or established by prescription; but the hardship of this led to provision being made by statute for the appointment of a new officer, in case there be no election, or a void one, made upon the prescriptive or charter day.

II.—MUNICIPAL CORPORATIONS.

The Municipal Corporations Reform Act—Its objects—The freemen—The list of electors—The town-council—Its powers and duties—Stipendiary magistrates—Recorder—Local boards.

HITHERTO of corporations in general, among which might formerly have been classed all those boroughs which are now regulated by the Municipal Corporations Reform Act. That statute applies to one hundred and seventy-eight corporate towns; the remainder—including the City of London—sixty-eight in number, were not brought within its operation. London, the greatest of all, with its many wealthy trading companies, each a corporation in itself, was reserved for separate legislation; the others, being inconsiderable either in extent or population, still continue to be governed by their charters or prescriptive usages, like corporations existing at the common law. The statute also applies to those towns which have since obtained charters of incorporation; the crown being thereby expressly enabled to grant charters extending to the householders of certain populous places, the powers, privileges, and authorities conferred by the act.

The principal objects of municipal government have usually been the appointment and superintendence of the police, the administration of justice, the lighting and paving of the town, and, in a few cases, the management of the poor. The statute I refer to did not attempt to extend the number of public objects which might be placed under municipal management; it was directed solely to the improvement of the means by which the objects of the old corporations were thereafter to be attained. It, therefore, left untouched those local laws which relate merely to the objects of municipal government; but rendered the functionaries of the municipalities eligible by, and consequently directly responsible to, the persons whose interests they are appointed to protect; and created a constituency, which ought, in ordinary cases, to include all those who are interested in the proper performance of their public duties by the municipal officers.

The constituents of the old corporations were known by the name of the *freemen*; and were usually admitted by the ruling body, which was in turn elected by the freemen. The freedom was obtainable by birth, or by marriage with the daughter or widow of a freeman, or by servitude or apprenticeship; and the rights attached to it being privileges confined to few persons, were in many cases of considerable value to the possessor, especially when they conferred a title to the enjoyment of funds derivable from corporation property. The rights of the freemen *in esse* were consequently preserved by the statute; which at the same time enacted that no freedom should thenceforth be acquired by gift or purchase; and then proceeded to provide, for the reformed corporations, a constituency consisting of every person of full age, who had occupied premises within the borough for three previous years, and, being resident within seven miles, was rated to the relief of the poor. Lists of persons thus qualified to be electors are accordingly annually made up by the overseers of their respective parishes, which are corrected and published by the town-clerk, and revised by the mayor and his assessors in the same manner as the lists of parliamentary electors. But, except the right of electing their representatives in the town-council, these burgesses have none of the exclusive privileges which were formerly enjoyed by the freemen, one of which, that of exclusive trading in the borough, was expressly abolished. The mayor and aldermen, with the constituency, constitute the corporation; and collectively with the councillors form the *town-council*; to which is intrusted its whole deliberative and administrative functions. The council appoints the town-clerk, treasurer, and other executive officers; and selects from its own body a *watch committee;* which, again, appoints a sufficient number of effective men to act as constables to preserve the peace by day and night. The council may undertake the superintendence of the lighting of the borough, provided no local act exists for the purpose; and may also constitute the *local board of health* and *burial board* of the district.

In the council is vested the power, incident to all corporations, of making by-laws for the good rule and government of the borough, and the prevention and suppression of all such nuisances as are not punishable in a summary manner. It has also the control of the borough fund; which, if insufficient for municipal purposes, may be supplemented by a borough rate. The accounts of the borough rates are audited, printed, and published.

Further, the town-council may, on voting a suitable salary, have one or more *stipendiary magistrates* appointed by the crown; and on complying with certain preliminaries as to the gaol and the salary of the judge, may also obtain a separate court of quarter sessions; for which the crown appoints a *recorder*, who is the sole judge of the court.

These municipal corporations, it will be observed, possess some peculiar powers, and are subject, on the other hand, to some peculiar restrictions not applicable to corporations in general; an observation which will apply to another species of corporations, possessing many of the municipal functions usually entrusted to the town councils of boroughs. I refer to the numerous *local boards* which, by special legislation, are invested with extensive powers for the conservation of the public health; and are for that purpose enabled to provide for the effective drainage of the towns or other populous places over which their authority extends, the removal of nuisances arising within their districts, the regulation of new buildings, the construction of streets, the supply of water, and many other matters of local importance, too numerous to mention.

III.—TRADING CORPORATIONS.

The joint-stock principle—Limited liability—Registered companies—Dissolution and winding up of these associations.

I HAVE reserved for separate consideration that class of corporations which consists of individuals associated together for the purposes of trade or business, and with a view to individual profit. The system of association to which I allude, and which has received such gigantic development in modern times, is by no means of recent origin. In stitutions founded on the same principle seem to have existed among the Saxons; and soon after the Conquest, we find *gilds* of different trades established in the various sea-ports and other towns of importance in the kingdom. These fraternities generally became in course of time chartered corporations; each possessing its common hall, making by-laws for the regulation of its particular trade, and disposing of its common property: and in this position these seem to have continued till about the time of the Reformation, when they mostly became merged in the municipal corporations, the franchises of which could in many cases be enjoyed by those only who were *free* of one or other of the companies into which the community was divided. Soon after the Revolution, the principle of association began to be applied to a variety of purposes besides those of trade. Numerous projects were started, the execution of which could only be compassed by raising capital on *the joint-stock principle.* Hence arose, in the early part of the eighteenth century, the frauds and panics, which are remembered in connection with the famous *South Sea Company;* and of which we have seen the counterparts more than once in our own times. More recently the joint-stock principle has been more usefully applied in the development of our national wealth, and a large number of useful public undertakings have been carried into effect by companies so constituted, and incorporated by acts of parliament. In these undertakings, the assistance of the legislature was necessary, not so much to give a corporate existence to the association of capitalists who joined in the scheme, for this might have been obtained by a royal charter, as to enable the company to carry out the project for which it was formed, by the compulsory purchase of property necessary for the purpose, and to make by-laws binding on the public, for protecting the rights and interests of the corporation.

It would serve no useful purpose to trace here the history of trading corporations down to the present time, or the numerous modifications to which the law relating to them has been subjected. And I content myself with alluding merely to the extension to all those associations that see fit to adopt it—of the principle of *limited liability,* or the restriction of the responsibility of each member to the amount of the capital subscribed by him, which had long been conceded to companies incorporated by act of parliament. There now exist four classes of joint-stock companies, viz.:

1. Trading companies incorporated by special acts of parliament, a class including railway, dock, harbour, and canal companies, a great many insurance companies, and a vast number of other bodies engaged in every species of profitable employment.

2. Joint-stock companies established under the statute 1 Vict. c. 73, or the preceding act, 6 Geo. IV. c. 91; which enables the crown in granting charters of incorporation to limit the liabilities of the members. But very few companies of this class exist, the powers which may be conferred under these statutes not having been found to meet the exigencies of public enterprise.

3. Banking companies, which are mentioned separately, simply because they are regulated by different statutes from ordinary joint-stock associations.

4. Registered joint-stock companies, under the Joint Stock Companies Act, 1856; which enables any seven or more persons associated for any lawful purpose, by subscribing their names to a memorandum of association, and otherwise complying with the requisitions of the statute in respect of registration, to form themselves into an incorporated company, with or without limited liability.

All these corporations may be dissolved by being wound up either voluntarily or compulsorily. A voluntary winding-up may take place whenever the period, if any, fixed for the duration of the company expires; or the event, if any, occurs upon which it is to be dissolved; or whenever the company has passed a special resolution requiring its winding-up.

A company may be wound up compulsorily: by virtue of a special resolution to that effect:—whenever it does not commence business within a year of its incorporation, or suspends business for a year:—whenever the shareholders are less than seven in number:—whenever the company is unable to pay its debts:—or whenever three-fourths of the capital have been lost or become unavailable.

And thus much of corporations existing at the common law; of the municipal boroughs as now regulated by the numerous statutes applicable to them; and of joint-stock companies—the three general heads under which corporations may most conveniently be ranked.

BOOK THE SECOND.

OF THE RIGHTS OF THINGS.

CHAPTER I.

OF PROPERTY IN GENERAL.

Origin of property—Occupancy—Origin of rights of succession.

HAVING treated of the *jura personarum*, or such rights and duties as are annexed to the persons of men, the objects of our present inquiry will be the *jura rerum*, or those rights which a man may acquire in and to such external things as are unconnected with his person.   These are what the writers on natural law style the rights of dominion, or property ; concerning the nature and origin of which I shall premise a few observations.

There is nothing which so generally strikes the imagination, and engages the affections of mankind, as the right of property. And yet there are very few that will give themselves the trouble to consider its origin and foundation. We think it enough that our title is derived by the grant of the former proprietor, by descent from our ancestors, or by the last will of the dying owner ; not caring to reflect that, strictly speaking, there is 'no foundation in nature or in natural law, why a set of words upon parchment should convey the dominion of land ; why the son should have a right to exclude his fellow-creatures from a determinate spot of ground, because his father had done so before him ; or why the occupier of a particular field or of a jewel, when lying on his death-bed, and no longer able to maintain possession, should be entitled to tell the rest of the world which of them should enjoy it after him.   But, when law is to be considered, not only as a matter of practice, but also as a rational science, it cannot be improper or useless to examine more deeply the rudiments and grounds of these positive constitutions of society.

In the beginning of the world, we are informed by holy writ, the all-bountiful Creator gave to man "dominion over all the earth;

G

"and over the fish of the sea, and over the fowl of the air, and over
"every living thing that moveth upon the earth." The earth, therefore, and all things therein, are the general property of all mankind,
exclusive of other beings, from the immediate gift of the Creator.
And, while the earth continued bare of inhabitants, it is reasonable
to suppose that all was in common among them, and that every one
took from the public stock to his own use such things as his immediate necessities required. But when mankind increased in number,
craft, and ambition, it became necessary to entertain conceptions of
more permanent dominion; and to appropriate to individuals not
the immediate *use* only, but the very *substance* of the thing to be
used. Otherwise innumerable tumults must have arisen, and the
good order of the world been continually broken and disturbed,
while a variety of persons were striving who should get the first
occupation of the same thing, or disputing which of them had
actually gained it. As human life also grew more and more refined,
abundance of conveniences were devised to render it more easy,
commodious, and agreeable; as habitations for shelter and safety,
and raiment for warmth and decency. But no man would be at
the trouble to provide either, so long as he had only an usufruc-
tuary property in them, which was to cease the instant that he
quitted possession; if, as soon as he walked out of his tent, or
pulled off his garment, the next stranger who came by would have
a right to inhabit the one, and to wear the other. In the case of
habitations in particular, even the brute creation, to whom everything else was in common, maintained a kind of permanent property
in their dwellings, especially for the protection of their young; hence
a property was soon established in every man's house and homestall,
before any right to the soil itself was established.

The article of food was a more immediate call, and therefore a
more early consideration. Such as were not contented with the
spontaneous product of the earth, sought for a more solid refresh-
ment in the flesh of beasts, which they obtained by hunting. But
the frequent disappointments incident to that occupation induced
them to gather together such animals as were of a more tame and
sequacious nature; and to establish a permanent property in their
flocks and herds in order to sustain themselves in a less precarious
manner, partly by the milk of the dams, and partly by the flesh of
the young.

All this while the soil and pasture of the earth remained still in common as before, and open to every occupant: except perhaps in the
neighbourhood of towns, where the necessity of a sole and exclusive
property in lands, for the sake of agriculture, was earlier felt, and
therefore more readily complied with. Otherwise, when the multi-

tude of men and cattle had consumed every convenience on one
spot of ground, it was deemed a natural right to seize upon and
occupy such other lands as would more easily supply their necessities. This practice is still retained among those nations that have
never been formed into civil states; and upon this principle alone
was founded the right of migration, or sending colonies to find out
new habitations, when the mother-country was overcharged with
inhabitants.

As the world by degrees grew more populous, it daily became
more difficult to find out new spots to inhabit, without encroaching
upon former occupants; and, by constantly occupying the same individual spot, the fruits of the earth were consumed, and its
spontaneous produce destroyed, without any provision for a future
supply or succession. It therefore became necessary to pursue some
regular method of providing a constant subsistence; and this necessity produced, or at least promoted and encouraged, the art of agriculture. And the art of agriculture, by a regular connection and
consequence, introduced and established the idea of a more permanent property in the soil, than had hitherto been received and
adopted. It was clear that the earth would not produce her fruits
in sufficient quantities, without the assistance of tillage: but who
would be at the pains of tilling it, if another might watch an opportunity to seize upon and enjoy the product of his industry, art, and
labour? Had not therefore a separate property in lands, as well as
movables, been vested in some individuals, the world must have
continued a forest, and men have been mere animals of prey; which,
according to some philosophers, is the genuine state of nature.
Necessity thus begat property; and, in order to insure that property,
recourse was had to civil society, which brought along with it a long
train of inseparable concomitants: states, government, laws, punishments, and the public exercise of religious duties. Thus connected
together, it was found that a part only of society was sufficient to
provide, by their manual labour, for the necessary subsistence of
all; and leisure was given to others to cultivate the human mind, to
invent useful arts, and to lay the foundations of science.

The only question remaining is, how this property became actually
vested; or what it is that gave a man an exclusive right to retain
in a permanent manner that specific land, which before belonged
generally to everybody, but particularly to nobody. And, as we
before observed that occupancy gave the right to the temporary
use of the soil, so it is agreed upon all hands that occupancy gave
also the original right to the permanent property in the *substance* of
the earth itself; which excludes every one else but the owner from
the use of it.

Property, both in lands and movables, being thus originally

acquired by the first taker, it remains in him, till he does some other
act which shows an intention to abandon it; for then it becomes,
naturally speaking, *publici juris* once more, and is liable to be again
appropriated by the next occupant. But the practice of one man's
abandoning his property, and another seizing the vacant possession,
however well founded in theory, could not long subsist in fact.   It
necessarily ceased among the complicated interests and artificial
refinements of established governments.   In these it was found,
that what became inconvenient or useless to one man, was highly
convenient and useful to another; who was ready to give in exchange
for it some equivalent, that was equally desirable to the former proprietor.   Thus mutual convenience introduced commercial traffic,
and the reciprocal transfer of property by sale, grant, or conveyance;
which may be considered either as a continuance of the original
possession which the first occupant had, or as an abandoning of the
thing by the present owner, and an immediate successive occupancy
of the same by the new proprietor.

- The most universal and effectual way of abandoning property, is
by the death of the occupant; when both the actual possession and
intention of keeping possession ceasing, the property, which is founded
upon such possession and intention, ought also to cease of course.
All property must therefore cease upon death, considering men as
absolute individuals, and unconnected with civil society: and then
the next immediate occupant would acquire a right in all that the
deceased possessed.   But as, under civilized governments, such a
constitution would be productive of endless disturbances, the law of
almost every nation has either given the dying person a power of
continuing his property, by disposing of his possessions by will; or,
in case he neglects to dispose of it, the municipal law of the country
then steps in, and declares who shall be the successor, representative,
or heir of the deceased.   Hence the right of inheritance or descent
to the children and relations of the deceased, which seems to have
been allowed much earlier than the right of devising by testament,
and which we are apt to conceive at the first view has nature on its side.
Yet we often mistake for nature what is merely established by long
and inveterate custom.   For it is obvious that a man's children or
nearest relations being usually about him on his death-bed, are the
earliest witnesses of his decease, and became therefore generally the
next immediate occupants of his property, till at length, in process
of time, this frequent usage ripened into general law.   So that to
municipal and not to natural law we owe not only the right of
inheritance, but the right to test or bequeath by will.   For while
property continued only for life, as it was at first, testaments were
useless and unknown: and when it became inheritable, the inheritance was long indefeasible, and the children or heirs at law could

not be excluded by will. Till at length it was found, that so strict
a rule made heirs disobedient, defrauded creditors of their debts,
and prevented many provident fathers from dividing their estates as
the exigence of their families required, which introduced the right
of disposing of one's property, or a part of it, by will. So that the
rights of inheritance and succession are all of them creatures of the
civil and municipal laws, and accordingly are in all respects regulated by them.

But, after all, there are some few things which, notwithstanding
the general introduction and continuance of property, must still unavoidably remain in common. Such, among others, are the elements
of light, air, and water; which a man may occupy by means of his
windows, his gardens, his mills, and other conveniences; such
also are those animals which are said to be *feræ naturæ*, or of
a wild and untameable disposition; which any man may seize upon
and keep for his own use or pleasure. All these things, so long as
they remain in his possession, every man has a right to enjoy without
disturbance; but if once they escape from his custody, or he voluntarily abandons the use of them, they return to the common stock,
and any man else has an equal right to seize and enjoy them afterwards.

CHAPTER II.

OF REAL PROPERTY.

Definition of lands, tenements, and hereditaments:—Corporeal hereditaments
  or land—Incorporeal hereditaments, viz., advowsons—Tithes—Commons
  —Ways—Offices—Dignities—Franchises—Corodies—Annuities—Rents.

THE objects of property are *things*, as contradistinguished from
persons; and things are of two kinds; things *real* and things *personal*.
Things real are such as are permanent, fixed, and immovable,
which cannot be carried out of their place, as lands and tenements;
things personal are goods, money, and all other movables, which
may attend the owner's person wherever he thinks proper to go.
Things real are usually said to consist in lands, tenements, or hereditaments. *Land* comprehends all things of a permanent, substantial nature; being a word of a very extensive signification, as will
presently appear more at large. *Tenement* is a word of still greater
extent, signifying everything that may be *holden*, provided it be of a
permanent nature, whether it be of a substantial and sensible, or of

an unsubstantial ideal kind. Thus, *liberum tenementum*, frank tenement, or freehold, is applicable not only to lands and other solid objects, but also to offices, rents, commons, and the like: and as lands and houses are tenements, so is an advowson a tenement; and a franchise, an office, a right of common, a peerage, or other property of the like unsubstantial kind, are, all of them, legally speaking, tenements. But an *hereditament* is by much the largest and most comprehensive expression; for it includes not only lands and tenements, but whatsoever may be *inherited*, be it corporeal, or incorporeal, real, personal, or mixed. Thus, an heir-loom, which by custom descends to the heir, is neither land nor tenement, but a mere movable; yet, being inheritable, is comprised under the general word hereditament.

Hereditaments then, to use the largest expression, are of two kinds, corporeal and incorporeal. Corporeal consist of such as affect the senses; such as may be seen and handled: incorporeal are not the object of sensation, can neither be seen nor handled, are creatures of the mind, and exist only in contemplation.

I. Corporeal hereditaments consist wholly of substantial and permanent objects, all which may be comprehended under the general denomination of land only. For *land* comprehendeth in its legal signification any ground, soil, or earth whatsoever; as arable, meadows, pastures, woods, moors, waters, marshes, furzes, and heath. *Water* being here mentioned as land, may seem a kind of solecism; but such is the language of the law: and therefore I cannot bring an action to recover possession of a pool or other piece of water by the name of *water* only; but I must bring my action for the land that lies at the bottom, and must call it twenty acres of *land covered with water.* For water is a movable, wandering thing, and must of necessity continue common by the law of nature; but the land, which that water covers, is permanent, fixed, and immovable; and of this the law will take notice, but not of the other.

Land has also, in its legal signification, an indefinite extent, upwards as well as downwards. *Cujus est solum, ejus est usque ad cœlum*, is the maxim of the law, therefore no man may erect any building, or the like, to overhang another's land: and downwards, whatever is in a direct line between the surface of any land and the centre of the earth, belongs to the owner of the surface; as is every day's experience in the mining countries. And therefore if a man grants all his lands, he grants thereby all his mines of metal and other fossils, his woods, his waters, and his houses, as well as his fields and meadows.

II. An incorporeal hereditament is a right issuing out of a thing corporate, whether real or personal, or concerning, or annexed to, or exercisable within, the same. It is not the thing corporate itself, which may consist in lands, houses, jewels, or the like; but something collateral thereto, as a rent issuing out of those lands or houses, or an office relating to those jewels. An annuity, for instance, is an incorporeal hereditament: for though the money, which is the product of the annuity, is of a corporeal nature, yet the annuity itself, which produces that money, is a thing invisible, and cannot be delivered over from hand to hand; and these incorporeal hereditaments are principally advowsons, tithes, commons, ways, offices, dignities, franchises, corodies or pensions, annuities, and rents.

1. *Advowson* is the right of presentation to a church, or ecclesiastical benefice. For, when lords of manors first built churches on their own demesnes, and appointed the tithes of those manors to be paid to the officiating ministers, the lord, who thus built a church, and endowed it with glebe or land, had of common right a power annexed of nominating such minister as he pleased to officiate in that church of which he was the founder, endower, maintainer, or, in one word, the patron.

This instance of an advowson will completely illustrate the nature of an incorporeal hereditament. It is not itself the bodily possession of the church and its appendages, but it is a right to give some other man a title to such bodily possession. The advowson is the object of neither the sight nor the touch; and yet it perpetually exists in the mind's eye, and in contemplation of law. It cannot be delivered from man to man by any visible bodily transfer, nor can corporeal possession be had of it. If the patron takes corporeal possession of the church, the churchyard, the glebe, or the like, he intrudes on another man's property; for to these the parson has an exclusive right. The patronage can therefore be only conveyed by operation of law, viz. by writing under seal, which is evidence of an invisible mental transfer: and being so vested it lies dormant and unnoticed, till occasion calls it forth, when it produces a visible corporeal fruit, by entitling some clerk, whom the patron shall please to nominate, to enter, and receive bodily possession of the lands and tenements of the church.

2. *Tithes* are a second series of incorporeal hereditament. They are defined to be the tenth part of the increase, yearly arising and renewing from the profits of lands, the stock upon lands, and the personal industry of the inhabitants: the first being usually called *predial*, as of corn, hops, and wood: the second *mixed*, as of wool, milk, pigs, &c., natural products, nurtured in part by the care of man: the third *personal*, as of manual occupations, trades, fisheries, and the like.

I will not put the title of the clergy to tithes upon any divine right, though such a right certainly commenced, and I believe as certainly ceased, with the Jewish theocracy. Yet an honourable maintenance for the ministers of the gospel is, undoubtedly, *jure divino;* whatever the particular mode of that maintenance may be. Many municipal laws have accordingly provided a liberal maintenance for their national priests or clergy. And so do the laws of England. But at what precise time tithes were first introduced here cannot be precisely ascertained. Possibly they were contemporary with the planting of Christianity among the Saxons by Augustin, about the end of the sixth century. But the first mention of them in any written English law, is in a decree, made in a synod held A.D. 786, wherein the payment of tithes in general is strongly enjoined. The next authentic mention of them is about the year 900, in the Anglo-Saxon laws, where this payment is not only *enjoined* but a *penalty* added upon non-observance: and this law is seconded by the laws of Athelstan, about the year 930.

Upon their first introduction, every man might give them to what priests he pleased, or might pay them into the hands of the bishop, for distribution by him. But, when dioceses were divided into parishes, the tithes of each were allotted to its own particular minister; first by common consent, or the appointments of lords of manors, and afterwards by the written law of the land. The first step towards this result was taken by Innocent III., about 1200, who in an epistle to the Archbishop of Canterbury, dated from the palace of the Lateran, enjoined the payment of tithes to the parsons of the respective parishes where every man inhabited. This epistle, says Sir Edward Coke, bound not the lay subjects of this realm; but, being reasonable and just, it was allowed of, and so became *lex terræ ;* so that tithes are due, of common right, to the parson of the parish, unless there be a special exemption; which may be either by a real composition, or by custom or prescription.

A real composition was when an agreement was made between the owner of the lands, and the parson or vicar, that such lands should for the future be discharged from payment of tithes, by reason of some land or other real recompense given to the parson, in lieu and satisfaction thereof.

A discharge by custom or prescription, was where time out of mind such persons or such lands had been, either partially or totally, discharged from the payment of tithes. And this immemorial usage or prescription, was either *de modo decimandi,* or *de non decimando.* A *modus decimandi,* commonly called by the simple name of a *modus* only, was where there was by custom a particular manner of tithing allowed, different from the general law of taking tithes in kind; such as a pecuniary compensation, as twopence an acre, or a compensation in work and labour, as, that the parson should have only the twelfth cock of hay, and not the tenth, in consideration of the owner's making it for him. A prescription *de non decimando* was a claim to be entirely discharged of tithes, and to pay no compensation in lieu of them; whence have sprung all the lands which, being in lay hands, do at present claim to be tithe-free: for if a man can show his lands to have been immemorially discharged of tithes, this is a good prescription *de non decimando*.

Tithes, however, have already to a considerable extent, and will very soon indeed become mere matter of history, through the operation of the statutes, which have been passed for their commutation into rent-charges. These are payable half-yearly, and are recoverable by distress and sale, like ordinary rents.

3. *Common*, or right of common, appears from its very definition to be an incorporeal hereditament: being a profit which a man has in the land of another; as to feed his beasts, to catch fish, to dig turf, to cut wood, or the like. And hence common is chiefly of four sorts: common of pasture, of piscary, of turbary, and of estovers.

Common of pasture is a right of feeding one's beasts on another's land: for in those waste grounds, which are usually called commons, the property of the soil is generally in the lord of the manor; as in common fields it is in the particular tenants. *Common of piscary* is a liberty of fishing in another man's water; as *common of turbary* is a liberty of digging turf upon another's ground. There is also a common for digging for coals, minerals, stones, and the like. All these bear a resemblance to common of pasture in many respects; though in one point they go much further; common of pasture being only a right of feeding on the herbage and vesture of the soil, which renews annually; but common of turbary, and those aftermentioned, are a right of carrying away the very soil itself. *Common of estovers*, or *estouviers*, that is, *necessaries*, from *estoffer*, to furnish, is a liberty of taking necessary wood, for the use or furniture of a house or farm, from off another's estate. The Saxon word *bote*, is used by us as synonymous to the French *estovers*: and therefore house-bote is a sufficient allowance of wood to repair or to burn in the house; plough-bote and cart-bote are to be employed in making and repairing instruments of husbandry; and hay-bote, or hedge-bote, is wood for repairing of hays, hedges, or fences.

4. *Ways*, or the right of going over another man's ground, are a fourth species of incorporeal hereditament. I speak not here of the public highways, nor yet of common ways, leading from a village

into the fields; but of private ways, in which a particular man may have an interest and a right, though another be owner of the soil. This may be grounded on a special permission; as when the owner of the land grants to another a liberty of passing over his grounds; or may exist by prescription, as if all the inhabitants of such a hamlet, or all the owners and occupiers of such a farm, have immemorially used to cross such a ground for such a particular purpose; or may arise by operation of law, for if a man grants me a piece of ground in the middle of his field, he at the same time tacitly and impliedly gives me a way to come at it, and I may cross his land for that purpose without trespass.

5. *Offices*, which are a right to exercise a public or private employment and to take the fees and emoluments thereunto belonging, are also incorporeal hereditaments; whether public, as those of magistrates; or private, as of bailiffs, receivers, and the like; for a man may have an estate in them. Yet a *judicial* office cannot be granted in reversion; because, though the grantee may be able to perform it at the time of the grant; yet before the office falls, he may become unable and insufficient: but *ministerial* offices may be so granted; for those may be executed by deputy. But no *public* office can be sold; for the law presumes that he who buys an office will by bribery, extortion, or other unlawful means, make his purchase good, to the manifest detriment of the public.

6. *Dignities*, which have been already referred to, bear a near relation to offices, being a species of incorporeal hereditaments, wherein a man may have a property or estate.

7. *Franchises* are a seventh species. Franchise and liberty are used as synonymous terms; and their definition is a royal privilege or branch of the sovereign's prerogative, subsisting in the hands of a subject; the kinds of them are various, and almost infinite. To be a county palatine is a franchise, vested in a number of persons. It is likewise a franchise for a number of persons to be incorporated and subsist as a body politic. Other franchises are to have a manor or lordship; to have waifs, estrays, royal fish; to have a fair or market; or to have a forest, warren, or fishery, endowed with privileges of royalty.

8. *Corodies* are a right of sustenance, or to receive victual and provision for one's maintenance, in lieu of which a sum of money is sometimes substituted. These may be reckoned a species of incorporeal hereditament. To these may be added,

9. *Annuities*, which are very distinct from rent-charges, with which they are frequently confounded; for a rent-charge issues out

of lands; an annuity is a yearly sum chargeable only upon the *person* of the grantor. Finally,

10. *Rent* is an incorporeal hereditament, and signifies a compensation or acknowledgment given for the possession of some corporeal inheritance, being defined as certain profit issuing yearly out of lands and tenements corporeal. It must be a *profit;* yet there is no occasion for it to be money: for capons, corn, and other matters may be rendered by way of rent. It must issue out of *lands and tenements corporeal;* that is, from some inheritance whereunto the owner or grantee of the rent may have recourse to distrain. Therefore a rent cannot be reserved out of an advowson, a common, an office, a franchise, or the like. Rent is regularly due and payable upon the land from whence it issues, if no particular place is mentioned in the reservation. And strictly it is demandable and payable before the time of sunset of the day whereon it is reserved, though perhaps not absolutely due till midnight. And thus much of incorporeal hereditaments.

CHAPTER III.

OF THE FEUDAL SYSTEM.

Origin of feuds—Oath of fealty—Qualities of feuds—Ancient English tenures —Knight-service and its consequences—Aids—Relief—Primer seisin—Wardship—Knighthood—Marriage—Fines for alienation—Escheat—Origin of scutages—Abolition of military tenures.

IT is impossible to understand, with any degree of accuracy, either the civil constitution of this kingdom, or the laws which regulate its landed property, without some general acquaintance with the feudal law: a system universally received throughout Europe upwards of twelve centuries ago, and which Sir Henry Spelman therefore calls the law of nations in our western world. It had its origin in the military policy of the northern nations, who poured themselves over Europe at the declension of the Roman empire, and was introduced by them in their respective colonies as the most likely means to secure their new acquisitions. To that end, large districts were allotted by the conquering general to the superior officers of the army, and by them dealt out again in smaller parcels to the inferior officers and most deserving soldiers. These allotments were called *feoda,* fiefs or fees; which last appellation in the northern languages signifies a conditional reward. Rewards they evidently were; and the condition annexed to them was, that the possessor should do service faithfully to him by whom they were given; for which purpose he took the *juramentum fidelitatis*, or oath of fealty : and in case of the breach of this oath, by not performing the stipulated service, or by deserting the lord in battle, the lands were again to revert to him who granted them.

Allotments, thus acquired, naturally engaged such as accepted them to defend them; and, as they all sprang from the same right of conquest, no part could subsist independent of the whole, wherefore all givers as well as receivers were mutually bound to defend each other's possessions. But as that could not effectually be done in a tumultuous, irregular way, subordination was necessary, and every feudatory was therefore bound, when called upon by his immediate lord, to do all in his power to defend him. Such lord was likewise subordinate to, and under the command of, his immediate superior; and so upwards to the prince himself: and the several lords were also reciprocally bound in their respective gradations to protect the possessions they had given. Thus the feudal connection was established, a proper military subjection was introduced, and an army of feudatories was always ready enlisted, not only in defence of each man's own several property, but also in defence of the whole and of every part of this their newly-acquired country; the prudence of which constitution was soon sufficiently visible in the strength and spirit with which they maintained their conquests.

Scarce had these northern conquerors established themselves in their new dominions, when the wisdom of their constitutions, as well as their personal valour, alarmed all the princes of Europe; that is, of those countries which had formerly been Roman provinces, but had revolted, or were deserted by their old masters, in the general wreck of the empire. Wherefore most, if not all, of them thought it necessary to enter into a similar policy. For whereas, before, the possessions of their subjects were perfectly *allodial*, that is, wholly independent, and held of no superior at all, now they parcelled out their royal territories, or persuaded their subjects to surrender up and retake their own landed property, under the feudal obligations, of military fealty. And thus, in the compass of a very few years the feudal system extended itself over all the western world. Which alteration of landed property, in so very material a point, necessarily drew after it an alteration of laws and customs; so that the feudal laws soon drove out the Roman, which had hitherto universally obtained, but now became for many centuries lost and forgotten.

This feudal polity was not, however, received in our island, at least as part of the national constitution, till the reign of William the Norman; and even then it seems to have been introduced, not by the mere arbitrary will of the Conqueror, but gradually by the Norman barons, and at first in such forfeited lands only as they received from the crown The regard of these nobles for the law under which they had long lived, together with the king's recommendation of this policy to the English, as the best way to put themselves on a military footing, were probably the reasons that prevailed to effect its establishment here by law. For the new polity cannot be said to have been *imposed* by the Conqueror, but nationally and freely adopted by the general assembly of the whole realm, in the same manner as other nations of Europe had before adopted it, upon the same principle of self-security.

· In consequence of this change, it became a fundamental maxim and necessary principle, though in reality a mere fiction, of our English tenures, that all lands were originally granted out by the sovereign, and are therefore holden either mediately or immediately of the crown. The grantor was called the *lord*, and the grantee was styled the feudatory or *vassal*, which was only another name for the tenant or holder of the lands; though, on account of the prejudices which we have justly conceived against the doctrines that were afterwards grafted on this system, we now use the word *vassal* opprobiously. The grant itself was perfected by the ceremony of corporeal investiture, or open and notorious delivery of possession in the presence of the other vassals; who, in case of a disputed title, were afterwards called upon to decide the difference, not only according to external proofs, adduced by the parties litigant, but also by the internal testimony of their own private knowledge.

Besides an oath of *fealty*, which was the parent of our oath of allegiance, the vassal or tenant upon investiture usually did *homage* to his lord; openly and humbly kneeling, being ungirt, uncovered, and holding up his hands both together between those of the lord, who sat before him; and there professing, that " he did become his "*man*, from that day forth, of life and limb, and earthly honour:" and then he received a kiss from his lord. Which ceremony was denominated *homagium*, or *manhood*, by the feudists, from the stated form of words, *devenio vester homo*.

When the tenant had thus professed himself to be the man of his lord, the next consideration was concerning the *service*, which, in pure, proper, and original feuds, was only twofold: to follow, or do *suit* to the lord in his courts in time of peace; and in his armies or warlike retinue when necessity called him to the field. The lord was, in early times, the legislator and judge over all his feudatories; and, therefore, the vassals of the inferior lords were bound to attend their domestic courts-baron, in order, as well to answer such complaints as might be alleged against themselves, as to form a jury or homage for the trial of their fellow tenants. In like manner the barons themselves were bound to attend the king upon summons, to hear causes of greater consequence in the king's presence, and under the direction of his grand justiciary. The military branch of service consisted in attending the lords to the wars, if called upon, with such a retinue, and for such a number of days, as were stipulated at the first donation, in proportion to the quantity of the land.

At the first introduction of feuds, as they were gratuitous, so also they were precarious, and held at the *will* of the lord, who was then the sole judge whether his vassal performed his services faithfully. Then they became certain for one or more *years*, and finally began to be granted for the *life* of the feudatory. For a long time, however, they were not *hereditary*, though frequently granted, by the favour of the lord, to the children of the former possessor; till in process of time it became unusual and was therefore thought hard to reject the heir, if he were capable to perform the services; and, therefore, infants, women, and professed monks, who were incapable of bearing arms, were also incapable of succeeding to a genuine feud. But the heir, when admitted to the feud which his ancestor possessed, used generally to pay a fine or acknowledgment to the lord, in horses, arms, and the like, for such renewal of the feud, which was called a relief, because it raised up and re-established the inheritance; or, in the words of the feudal writers, "*incertam et caducam hereditatem relevabat.*" This relief was afterwards, when feuds became absolutely hereditary, continued on the death of the tenant, though the original foundation of it had ceased.

Other qualities of feuds were, that the feudatory could not alien or dispose of his feud; neither could he exchange, nor yet mortgage, nor even devise it by will, without the consent of the lord. For the reason of conferring the feud being the personal abilities of the feudatory, it was not fit he should be at liberty to transfer this gift to another who might prove less able; and as the feudal obligation was reciprocal, the feudatory being entitled to the lord's protection, the lord could not, on the other hand, transfer his seignory without consent of his vassal.

These were the principal, and very simple, qualities of the original feuds, which were all of a military nature, though the feudatories being unable to cultivate their own lands, soon found it necessary to commit part of them to inferior tenants; obliging them to such returns in service, corn, cattle, or money, as might enable the chief feudatories to attend their military duties without distraction; which returns, or *relitus*, were the origin of rents, and by these means the feudal polity was greatly extended; these inferior feudatories being under similar obligations of fealty, to do suit of court, to pay the stipulated rent-service, and to promote the welfare of their immediate lords. But this, at the same time, demolished the ancient simplicity of feuds; and an inroad being once made upon their constitution, it subjected them, in a course of time, to great varieties and innovations. Feuds began to be bought and sold, and deviations were made from the old fundamental rules of tenure and succession, which were held no longer sacred when the feuds themselves no longer continued to be purely military. Hence these tenures began now to be divided into *feoda propria et impropria*, proper and improper feuds; under the former of which divisions were comprehended such, and such only, of which we have before spoken; and under that of improper or derivative feuds were comprised all such as did not fall within the other description; such, for instance, as were originally sold to the feudatory for a price; such as were held upon less honourable services, or for rent, in lieu of military service; such as were in themselves alienable, without mutual license; and such as might descend indifferently either to males or females.

This introduces us naturally to a consideration of the *ancient English tenures*, all the particularities attending which are to be accounted for upon feudal principles, and no other; being fruits of, and deduced from, the feudal policy. For there seem to have subsisted among our ancestors four principal species of lay tenures; to which all others may be reduced; the grand criteria of which were the natures of the several services that were due to the lords from their tenants. These services, in respect of their quality, were either *free* or *base* services; in respect of their quantity and the time of exacting them, were either *certain* or *uncertain*. *Free* services were such as were not unbecoming the character of a soldier or a freeman to perform; as, to serve under his lord in the wars, to pay a sum of money, and the like. *Base* services were such as were fit only for peasants or persons of a servile rank; as to plough the lord's land, to make his hedges, or other mean employments. The *certain* services, whether free or base, were such as were stinted in quantity, and could not be exceeded on any pretence; as, to pay a stated annual rent, or to plough such a field for three days. The *uncertain* depended upon unknown contingencies; as, to do military service in person, or pay an assessment in lieu of it when called upon, or to wind a horn whenever the Scots invaded the realm, which are free services; or to do whatever the lord should command, which is a base or villein service.

From the various combinations of these services have arisen the four kinds of lay tenure which subsisted in England till the middle of the seventeenth century, and three of which subsist to this day.

1. The first, most universal, and esteemed the most honourable

species of tenure, was that by knight-service, which differed in very few points from a proper feud. To make this, a determinate quantity of land was necessary, which was called a knight's fee, the value of which, though it varied with the times, in the reigns of Edward I. and Edward II., was stated at 20*l.* per annum, and the tenant was bound to attend his lord to the wars for forty days in every year, if called upon.

But this tenure drew after it seven fruits and consequences, as inseparably incident to the tenure in chivalry: viz., aids, relief, primer seisin, wardship, marriage, fines for alienation, and escheat.

Aids, which originally were benevolences granted by the tenant to his lord, in times of difficulty, but in time grew to be considered a matter of right, were principally three : first, to ransom the lord's person, if taken prisoner; secondly, to make the lord's eldest son a knight, a matter formerly attended with great ceremony and expense; and thirdly, to marry the lord's eldest daughter, by giving her a suitable portion; for daughters' portions were in those days extremely slender, and the lords, by the nature of their tenure, could not charge their lands with this or any other incumbrance.

Relief, relevium, was the fine incident to every feudal tenure, by way of composition with the lord for taking up the estate, which had lapsed or fallen in by the death of the last tenant; and which, by an ordinance in 27 Hen. II., called the assize of arms, was fixed at 100*s.* for every knight's fee.

Primer seisin was only incident to the king's tenants *in capite*, by a right which the king had, when any of his tenants died seised of a knight's fee, to receive of the heir a year's profits of the lands. This afterwards gave a handle to the popes, who claimed to be feudal lords of the church, to claim in like manner from every clergyman in England the first year's profits of his benefice, by way of *primitiae*, or first fruits.

These two payments, relief and primer seisin, were only due if the heir was of full age; but if he was under age the lord was entitled to the *wardship* of the heir, and was called the guardian in chivalry. This consisted in having the custody of his body and lands, without any accoun. of the profits, till the age of twenty-one in males and sixteen in females. For the law supposed the heir-male unable to perform knight-service till twenty-one; but as for the female, she was supposed capable at fourteen to marry, and then her husband might perform the service.

When the heir came of full age, provided he held a knight's fee, he was to receive the order of knighthood, and was compellable to take it upon him, or else pay a fine to the king. This prerogative was exerted as an expedient for raising money by many of our best princes, but yet was the occasion of heavy murmurs when exerted by Charles I. It was accordingly abolished by statute 16 Car. I. c. 20.

But, before they came of age, the guardian had authority over his infant wards, in respect of their *marriage*, having the power of tendering him or her a suitable match, without *disparagement* or inequality; which if the infants refused, they forfeited the value of the marriage, *valorem maritagii*, to their guardian; and if the infants married themselves without the guardian's consent, they forfeited double the value, *duplicem valorem maritagii*. This seems to have been one of the greatest hardships of our ancient tenures; and one cannot read without astonishment, that such should have continued to be the condition of this country till the year 1660; which, from the extermination of these feudal oppressions, ought to be regarded as a memorable era in the history of our law and liberty.

Another attendant of tenure by knight-service was that of *fines* due to the lord for every *alienation*. This depended on the feudal connection; it not being allowed that a fendatory should substitute a new tenant in his own stead, without the consent of the lord: and, as the feudal obligation was reciprocal, the lord also could not alienate his seignory without the consent of his tenant, which consent was called an *attornment*. This restraint upon the lords soon wore away; that upon the tenants continued longer. For, when everything came in process of time to be bought and sold, the lords would not grant a license to their tenant, to alien, without a fine being paid; apprehending that, if it was reasonable for the heir to pay a fine or relief on the renovation of his paternal estate, it was much more reasonable that a stranger should make the same acknowledgment on his admission to a newly-purchased feud.

The last consequence of tenure in chivalry was *escheat*; which took place if the tenant died without heirs of his blood, or if his blood was corrupted by commission of treason or felony. In such cases the land escheated or fell back to the lord; that is, the tenure was determined by breach of the original condition of the feudal donation. In the one case, there were no heirs of the blood of the first feudatory, to which heirs alone the grant of the feud extended; in the other, the tenant, by perpetrating an atrocious crime, forfeited his feud, which he held under the implied condition that he should not be a traitor or a felon.

These were the principal qualities, fruits, and consequences of the tenure by knight-service: of which there were some other species, such as the tenure by *grand serjeanty*, *per magnum servitium*, whereby the tenant was bound, instead of serving the king *generally* in his wars, to do some special honorary service to the king in person; as to carry his banner, his sword, or the like; or to be his butler, champion, or other officer, at his coronation. Tenure by *cornage*, which was to wind a horn when the Scots or other enemies entered the land, in order to warn the king's subjects, was a species of grand serjeanty.

The personal attendance in knight-service growing inconvenient, the tenants found means of compounding for it; first, by sending others in their stead, and in process of time making a pecuniary satisfaction in lieu of it. This pecuniary satisfaction at last came to be levied by assessments, at so much for every knight's fee; and was called *scutagium*, or, in our Norman French, *escuage*. The first time this appears to have been taken was in the 5 Hen. II., for his expedition to Toulouse; but it soon came to be so universal, that personal attendance fell quite into disuse. Our kings, when they went to war, levied scutages on all the landholders of the kingdom, to defray their expenses, and to hire troops. Which prerogative being greatly abused, it became matter of national clamour; and King John was obliged to consent by his *Magna Charta*, that no scutage should be imposed without consent of parliament; and such scutages became, as we have already seen, the groundwork of all succeeding subsidies, and the land-tax of later times.

Knight-service thus degenerating into assessment, all the advantages of the feudal constitution were destroyed, and nothing but the hardships remained. Instead of forming a national militia composed of barons, knights, and gentlemen, the whole system now tended to nothing else but a wretched means of raising money to pay an army of mercenaries. The families of all our nobility and gentry groaned under the intolerable burdens which were introduced and laid upon them by the subtlety of the Norman lawyers. For, besides the scutages to which they were liable, they might be called upon for *aids*, whenever the eldest son of the lord was to be knighted or his eldest daughter married. The heir, on the death of his ancestor, was plundered of the first emoluments of his inheritance, by way of *relief* and *primer seisin*; and if a minor, he found, after he was out of *wardship*, his woods decayed, houses fallen down, stock wasted and gone, lands ploughed to be barren; and yet to reduce him still further, he had to pay half-a-year's profits as a fine for suing out his *ouster le main*, or *livery*; that is, the delivery of his lands from his guardian's hands; and also the price or value of his *marriage*, if he refused such wife as his lord and guardian had bartered for, and imposed upon him; or twice that value if he married another woman. Add to this, the untimely and expensive honour of *knighthood*, to make his poverty more completely splendid. And when by

these deductions his fortune was so shattered and ruined, that perhaps he was obliged to sell his patrimony, he had not even that poor
privilege allowed him, without paying an exorbitant fine for a *license
of alienation.*

A slavery so complicated, and so extensive as this, called aloud
for a remedy in a nation that boasted of its freedom. Palliatives
were from time to time applied by successive acts of parliament,
which assuaged some temporary grievances. King James I. consented, in consideration of a proper equivalent, to abolish them all;
receiving by way of compensation for the loss which the crown and
other lords would sustain, an annual fee-farm rent, which was to
have been settled and inseparably annexed to the crown and assured
to the inferior lords, and be payable out of every knight's fee within
their respective seignories. An expedient much better than the
hereditary exercise, which was afterwards made the principal equivalent for these concessions. For at length the military tenures, with
all their heavy appendages, were, by the statute 12 Car. II. c. 24,
destroyed at one blow; the *Court of Wards and Liveries* which was
charged with ascertaining by *inquisitio post mortem* the value and
tenure of estates and age of the wards, so as to fix the relief and
primer seisins due to the crown, was abolished; values and forfeitures
of marriages and fines for alienations were taken away, and all sorts
of tenures, with some exceptions, turned into free and common
socage; not, it is true, at the expense of the crown and inferior
lords, but, as it was proposed then and since turned out, exclusively
at the expense of the people of England

CHAPTER IV.

OF THE MODERN ENGLISH TENURES.

Grand serjeanty—Petit serjeanty—Burgage—Gavelkind—Incidents of socage
—Pure villenage—Manors—Book-land and folk-land—Copyhold—Tenancy
in *ancient demesne*—Frankalmoign.

ALTHOUGH the oppressive part of the feudal constitution was happily
done away by the statute 12 Car. II. c. 24, the tenures of socage and
frankalmoign, the honorary services of grand serjeanty, and the
tenure by copy of court-roll, were reserved; all tenures, indeed, except frankalmoign, grand serjeanty, and copyhold, were reduced to

one species of tenure, then well known and subsisting, called free and common socage.

Socage, in its most general signification, seems to denote a tenure by any certain and determinate service; being in this sense put in opposition to knight-service, where the render was precarious and uncertain. These tenures are generally considered to be relics of Saxon liberty; retained by such persons as had neither forfeited their estates to the crown, nor been obliged to exchange their tenure for the more honourable, but, at the same time, more burdensome tenure of knight-service. As, therefore, the distinguishing mark of socage is the having its renders or services ascertained, it will include all other methods of holding free lands by certain and invariable rents and duties: and, in particular, *petit serjeanty*, tenure in *burgage*, and *gavelkind*.

Grand serjeanty, we may remember, is not abolished by the statute of Charles II., but only its slavish appendages. *Petit serjeanty* bears a great resemblance to it; for as the former is a personal service, so the other is a rent or render, both tending to some purpose relative to the person of the sovereign. Thus, the Dukes of Marlborough and Wellington hold the estates granted to their ancestors for their public services, by the tenure of petit serjeanty, and by the annual render of a small flag.

Tenure in *burgage* is where the king or other person is lord of an ancient borough, in which the tenements are held by a rent certain, and is indeed only a kind of town socage; as common socage, by which other lands are holden, is usually of a rural nature.

Tenure in *gavelkind* is principally met with in Kent, and its properties are various. But the principal is, that the estate does not escheat in case of an attainder for felony; the maxim being, "the father to the bough, the son to the plough;" and that the lands descend, not to the eldest, youngest, or any one son only, but to all the sons together.

These being the several species of socage, I proceed to show this tenure also partakes strongly of a feudal nature; from a short comparison of its incidents with those of knight-service, that

1. Both were held of superior lords. 2. Both were subject to the feudal return, rent, or service of some sort or other, which arose from the supposition of an original grant from the lord to the tenant. 3. Both were, from their constitution, subject to the oath of fealty, or mutual bond of obligation between the lord and tenant. 4. The tenure in socage was subject, of common right, to aids for knighting the son and marrying the eldest daughter. 5. Relief was due upon socage tenure, as well as upon tenure in chivalry: socage relief

being one year's rent, be the same either great or small: and due
even though the heir was under age, because the lord had no wardship over him. And as the statute of Charles II., it may be added,
reserves the reliefs incident to socage tenures, wherever lands in
fee-simple are holden by a rent, relief is still due of common right
upon the death of a tenant. 6. Primer seisin was incident to the
king's socage tenants, but was, as we have seen, entirely abolished
by the statute. 7. Wardship is also incident to tenure in socage;
but of a nature different from that incident to knight-service. For
if the inheritance descends to an infant under fourteen, the wardship
of him does not, nor ever did, belong to the lord of the fee; but his
nearest relation shall be his *guardian in socage*, and have the custody
of his land and body till he arrives at the age of fourteen, at which
age this wardship ceases; and the heir may call his guardian to
account, for at this age the law supposes him capable of choosing a
guardian for himself. It was in this particular of wardship, as also
in that of marriage, that socage had so much the advantage of military tenure. But there was this disadvantage attending it: that
young heirs, being left to choose their own guardians, might make
an improvident choice. And, therefore, when almost all the lands
in the kingdom were turned into socage tenures, the statute 12
Car. II. c. 24, enacted, that it should be in the power of any father
by will to appoint a guardian, till his child should attain the age of
twenty-one. And, if no such appointment be made, the Court of
Chancery will name a guardian, to prevent an infant heir from
improvidently exposing himself to ruin. 8. Marriage, or the *valor
maritagii*, was not in socage tenure any perquisite or advantage to
the guardian, but rather the reverse. For if the guardian married
his ward under the age of fourteen, he was bound to account to the
ward for the value of the marriage, even though he took nothing for
it, unless he married him to advantage. These doctrines of wardship and marriage in socage were so diametrically opposite to those
in knight-service, and so entirely agree with those parts of King
Edward's laws, that were restored by Henry I.'s charter, as might
alone convince us that socage was of a higher origin than the
Norman Conquest. 9. *Fines* for *alienation* were, I apprehend, due
for lands holden of the king *in capite* by socage tenure, as well as in
case of tenure by knight-service. 10. *Escheats* are equally incident
to tenure in socage, as they were to tenure by knight-service.

This much for the two grand species of tenure, under which
almost all the free lands of the kingdom were holden till the Restoration in 1660, when the former was abolished and sunk into the
latter: so that lands of both sorts are now holden by the one universal tenure of *free and common socage*.

The other grand division of tenure, is that of villein socage, or *villenage*, which is either *pure* or *privileged* villenage: from whence have arisen two other species of our modern tenures.

From the tenure of pure villenage have sprung our present *copy-hold* tenures, or tenure by copy of court-roll at the will of the lord: in order to obtain a clear idea of which it will be previously necessary to take a short view of the origin of manors, which are in substance as ancient as the Saxon constitution.

A manor, *manerium, a manendo*, because the usual residence of the owner, seems to have been a district of ground, held by great personages, who kept in their own hands so much land as was necessary for the use of their families, hence called *terræ dominicales*, or *demesne* lands; the other, or *tenemental*, lands being distributed among their tenants. The latter was either *book-land* or charter-land, being held by deed for certain rents and free-services, from which have arisen most of the freehold tenants who hold of particular manors, and owe suit and service to the same; or *folk-land*, which was held by no assurance in writing, but distributed among the common folk at the pleasure of the lord, and resumed at his discretion. The residue of the manor being uncultivated was termed the lord's waste, and served for public roads, and for common of pasture to the lord and his tenants.

In early times the king's great barons granted out smaller manors to inferior persons to be holden of themselves: which still continue to be held under a superior lord, whose seignory is frequently termed an *honour*. In imitation whereof these inferior lords carved out to others still more minute estates, to be held of themselves, and were so proceeding downwards *in infinitum*, till the superior lords observed, that by this subinfeudation they lost all their feudal profits. This occasioned, first, a provision in *Magna Charta*, that no man should either give or sell his land, without reserving sufficient to answer the demands of his lord; and, afterwards, the statute *Quia Emptores*, 18 Edw. I. c. 1, which directs, that, upon all sales or feoffments of land, the feoffee shall hold the same, not of his immediate feoffor, but of the chief lord of the fee, of whom such feoffor himself held it. And hence it is clear, that all manors existing at this day must have existed as early as Edward I.

Now, with regard to the folk-land, this was a species of tenure neither strictly feudal, Norman, or Saxon; but mixed and compounded of them all: and which also, on account of the heriots that usually attend it, may seem to have something Danish in its composition. Under the Saxon government there were a sort of people in a condition of downright servitude, belonging to the lord of the soil, like the rest of the cattle or stock upon it. These seem to have

been those who held what was called the folk-land, from which they
were removable at the lord's pleasure. On the arrival of the Normans here, it seems not improbable, that they, who were strangers to
any other than a feudal state, might give some sparks of enfranchisement to such wretched persons as fell to their share, by admitting
them, as well as others, to the oath of fealty; which conferred a
right of protection, and raised the tenant to a kind of estate superior
to downright slavery, but inferior to every other condition. This
they called villenage, and the tenants villeins, probably *a villa*, because they lived chiefly in villages, which they could not leave without the lord's permission. If they ran away, or were purloined from
him, they might be recovered by action, like beasts or other chattels.
They held, indeed, small portions of land by way of sustaining themselves and families; but it was at the mere will of the lord, who
might dispossess them whenever he pleased. They might, however,
be enfranchised by manumission, which was either express or implied: express, as where a man granted to the villein a deed of
manumission: implied, as where a man bound himself in a bond
to his villein, or gave him an estate, or brought an action against
him, for this was dealing with his villein on the footing of a freeman. So that by these and other means, villeins, in process of
time, gained considerable ground on their lords; and in particular
strengthened the tenure of their estates to that degree, that they
came to have in them an interest in many places full as good, in
others better than their lords. For many lords having permitted
their villeins and children to enjoy their possessions without interruption, the common law, of which custom is the life, now gave
them a title to prescribe against their lords; and, on performance of
the same services, to hold their lands in spite of any determination
of the lord's will. For though in general they are still said to
hold their estates *at the will of the lord*, yet it is such a will as
is *agreeable to the custom of the manor*; which customs are evidenced by the rolls of the courts-baron in which they are entered,
or kept on foot by the constant immemorial usage of the several
manors in which the lands lie. And, as such tenants had nothing
to show for their estates but these customs, and admissions in pursuance of them, entered on those rolls, or the copies of such entries
witnessed by the steward, they now began to be called *tenants by
copy of court-roll*, and their tenure itself a *copyhold*, the villein
services due to the lord having been long commuted for a small
pecuniary quit rent.

The appendages of a copyhold tenure, that it has in common with
free tenures, are fealty, services, as well in rents as otherwise,
reliefs, and escheats. But, besides these, copyholds have also

heriots, wardship, and fines. Heriots (a Danish custom, of which
we shall say more hereafter) are a render of the best beast or other
chattel, as the custom may be, to the lord on the death of the
tenant. Wardship, in copyhold estates, partakes both of that in
chivalry and that in socage. Like that in chivalry, the lord is the
legal guardian, but he may assign some relation of the infant to act
in his stead; and he, like guardian in socage, is accountable for the
profits. Of fines, some are in the nature of primer seisins, due on
the death of each tenant, others are mere fines for alienation of the
lands; in some manors only one of these sorts can be demanded, in
some both, and in others neither; all depends upon the custom.

The tenure described by our ancient writers, under the name
of *privileged* villenage, is such as has been held of the kings of
England from the Conquest downwards; being no other than an
exalted species of copyhold, subsisting at this day, viz., the tenure
in *ancient demesne*. It applies to those lands or manors, which
though now perhaps granted out to private subjects, were actually
in the hands of the crown in the time of Edward the Confessor, or
William the Conqueror; and the tenants therein have some peculiar
privileges, now of little if of any value, and which it is consequently
unnecessary here to detail. It thus appears, that whatever changes
and alterations our tenures have in process of time undergone, from
the Saxon era to the 12 Car. II., all lay tenures are now in effect reduced to two species: *free* tenure in common socage, and *base* tenure
by copy of court-roll.

I say *lay* tenures, because there is one other species of tenure, reserved by the statute of Charles II., which is of a *spiritual* nature,
and called tenure in *frankalmoign, in libera eleemosyna,* or free alms;
which is that whereby a religious corporation holds lands of the donor
to them and their successors for ever. This is the tenure, by which
almost all the ancient monasteries and religious houses held their
lands; and by which the parochial clergy, and very many ecclesiastical and eleemosynary foundations, hold them at this day. It was
an old Saxon tenure; and continued under the Norman revolution,
through the great respect that was shown to religion and religious
men in ancient times. If the service be neglected, the law gives no
remedy by distress or otherwise to the lord of whom the lands are
holden; but merely a complaint to the ordinary or visitor to correct
it. So that I only mention this tenure because *frankalmoign* is excepted by name in the statute of Charles II., and therefore subsists
in many instances at this day.

CHAPTER V.

FREEHOLD ESTATES.

Definition of freehold—Tenancy in fee-simple—Heirs—Qualified fees—Conditional fees or entails—Origin of common recoveries—and of fines—Tenancy for life—Its incidents—Tenant in tail after possibility of issue extinct—Tenant by the courtesy—Tenancy in dower—Jointures.

THE next objects of our disquisitions are the nature and properties of *estates.* And to ascertain this with precision, estates may be considered in a threefold view: first, with regard to the *quantity of interest* which the tenant has in the tenement; secondly, with regard to the *time* at which the quantity of interest is to be enjoyed; and thirdly, with regard to the *number* and *connections* of the tenants.

First, the *quantity of interest* which the tenant has may be measured by its duration and extent. Thus, either his right of possession is to subsist for an uncertain period, during his own life, or the life of another man; to determine at his own decease, or to remain to his descendants after him; or it is circumscribed within a certain number of years, months, or days; or, lastly, it is infinite and unlimited, being vested in him and his representatives for ever. And this occasions the primary division of estates into such as are *freehold,* and such as are *less than freehold.* In the present chapter we shall deal with freehold estates only.

An estate of freehold, *liberum tenementum,* or frank-tenement, is defined by Britton to be " the *possession* of the soil by a freeman." Such estate, therefore, and no other, as requires actual possession of the land, is, legally speaking, *freehold :* which actual possession could by the common law only be given by livery of scisin, which is the same as the feudal investiture. As, therefore, estates of inheritance and estates for life could not by the common law be conveyed without livery of seisin, these are properly estates of freehold; and, as no other estates were conveyed with the same solemnity, therefore no others are properly freehold estates.

Estates of freehold, thus understood, are either estates *of inheritance,* or estates *not of inheritance.* The former are again divided into, 1. Inheritances *absolute* or fee-simple; and, II. Inheritances *limited,* one species of which we usually call fee-tail.

I. Tenant in fee-simple is he that hath lands, tenements, or here-

H

ditaments, to hold to him and his heirs for ever : generally absolutely and simply ; without mentioning *what* heirs, but referring that to his own pleasure, or to the disposition of the law.   This is property in its highest degree ; and the owner thereof is said to be seised *in dominico suo*, in his demesne, *as of fee*.   It is his *demesne*, or property, since it belongs to him and his heirs for ever : yet this *dominicum* is strictly not absolute, but feudal : it is his demesne, *as of fee* : that is, it is not purely and simply his own, since it is held of a superior lord, in whom the ultimate property resides.

The word " heirs " is necessary in the grant or donation, in order to make a fee or inheritance.   For, if land be given to a man for ever, or to him and his assigns for ever, this vests in him but an estate for life.   This rule is no doubt subject to one or two exceptions.   Thus it does not extend to gifts by will, or to grants in favour of corporations or to the sovereign ; but, subject to these exceptions, the general rule is, that the word " heirs " is necessary to create an estate of inheritance.

II. Limited fees, or such estates of inheritance as are clogged with conditions, are of two sorts :—1. *Qualified*, or *base* fees ; and 2. Fees *conditional*, so called at the common law ; and afterwards fees-*tail*, in consequence of the statute *De Donis*.

1. A base, or qualified, fee is such a one as has a qualification subjoined thereto, and which must be determined whenever the qualification annexed to it is at an end.   As in the case of a grant to A and his heirs, *tenants of the manor of Dale* ; in this instance, whenever the heirs of A cease to be tenants of that manor, the grant is entirely defeated.   This estate is a fee, because by possibility it may endure for ever in a man and his heirs : yet, as that duration depends upon the concurrence of collateral circumstances which qualify and debase the purity of the donation, it is therefore a qualified or base fee.

2. A conditional fee, at the common law, was a fee restrained to some particular heirs, exclusive of others : as to the heirs *of a man's body*, by which only his lineal descendants were admitted, in exclusion of collateral heirs ; or to the heirs *male of his body*, in exclusion both of collaterals, and lineal females also.   It was called a conditional fee, by reason of the condition implied in the donation, that, if the donee died without such particular heirs, the land should revert to the donor.

Now, when any condition is performed, it is thenceforth entirely gone ; and the thing to which it was before annexed, becomes wholly unconditional.   So that as soon as the grantee had any issue born, his estate was supposed to become absolute, by the performance of the condition; at least for these three purposes: 1. To enable the tenant to alien the land, and thereby to bar not only his own issue, but also the donor of his interest in the reversion. 2. To subject him to forfeit it for treason; which he could not do, till issue born, longer than for his own life; lest thereby the inheritance of the issue, and reversion of the donor, might have been defeated. 3. To empower him to charge the land with rents, commons, and certain other incumbrances, so as to bind his issue. However, if the tenant did not in fact alien the land, the course of descent was not altered; for if the issue had afterwards died, and then the tenant, or original grantee had died, without making any alienation, the land, by the terms of the donation, could descend to none but the heirs *of his body*, and therefore, in default of them, must have reverted to the donor. For which reason, in order to subject the lands to the ordinary course of descent, the donees of these conditional fee-simples took care to alien as soon as they had performed the condition by having issue; and afterwards repurchased the lands, which gave them a fee-simple absolute, that would descend to the heirs general, according to the course of the common law.

The inconveniences which attended these fettered inheritances were probably what induced the judges to give way to this subtle finesse of construction, for such it undoubtedly was, in order to shorten the duration of these conditional estates. But, on the other hand, the nobility, who were willing to perpetuate their possessions in their own families, to put a stop to this practice, procured the statute of Westminster the Second, commonly called the statute *de donis conditionalibus*, to be made; which enacted that from thenceforth the will of the donor should be observed; and that the tenements so given, to a man and the heirs of his body, should at all events go to the issue, if there were any; or, if none, should revert to the donor.

Upon the construction of this act, the judges determined that the donee had no longer a conditional fee-simple, which became absolute and at his own disposal, the instant any issue was born; but they divided the estate into two parts, leaving in the donee a new kind of particular estate, which they denominated a *fee-tail*;* and vesting in the donor the ultimate fee-simple of the land, expectant on the failure of issue; which expectant estate is what we now call a reversion.

And as the word " heirs" is necessary to create a fee, so in further limitation of the strictness of the feudal donation, the word *body*, or some other words of procreation, are necessary to make it a fee-tail,

---

* *Feodum talliatum*, from the barbarous verb *talliare*, to cut, *i.e.*, a fee from which the heirs general were cut off.

and ascertain to what heirs in particular the fee is limited. If therefore, either the words of inheritance or words of procreation be omitted, albeit the others are inserted in the grant, this will not make an estate-tail. As, if the grant be to a man and his *issue of his body*, to a man and his *children;* these are only estates for life, there being no words of inheritance. So a gift to a man, and his *heirs male* or *female*, is an estate in fee-simple, and not in fee-tail; for there are no words to ascertain the body out of which they shall issue. In last wills, however, greater indulgence is allowed, and an estate-tail may be created by a devise to a man and his *seed*, or by other irregular modes of expression.

Thus much for estates-tail: the establishment of which family law occasioned infinite difficulties and disputes. Children grew disobedient when they knew they could not be set aside: farmers were ousted of leases made by tenants-in-tail; for, if such leases had been valid, under colour of long leases the issue might have been virtually disinherited: creditors were defrauded of their debts; for, if a tenant-in-tail could have charged his estate with their payment, he might also have defeated his issue by mortgaging it for as much as it was worth. But as the nobility were fond of the statute, because it preserved their estates from forfeiture, there was little hope of procuring a repeal by the legislature; and therefore, by the connivance of an active and politic prince, a method was devised to evade it.

About two hundred years intervened between the making of the statute *De Donis*, and the application of common recoveries to this intent in the twelfth year of Edward IV., which were then declared by the judges to be a sufficient bar of an estate-tail. For though the courts had, in the reign of Edward III., hinted their opinion that a bar might be effected upon these principles, yet it never was carried into execution; till Edward IV., observing how little effect attainders for treason had on families, whose estates were protected by entails, gave his countenance to this proceeding, and suffered Taltarum's case to be brought before the court: wherein, it was in effect determined, that a common recovery suffered by tenant-in-tail should be an effectual destruction thereof. What common recoveries were, both in their nature and consequences, and why they were allowed to be a bar to the estate-tail, must be reserved to a subsequent inquiry. At present it need only be said, that they were fictitious proceedings, introduced by a kind of *pia fraus*, to elude the statute *De Donis*, which was found intolerably mischievous, and which yet one branch of the legislature would not then consent to repeal; and that these recoveries afterwards became a most common assurance of lands; and were looked upon as the legal mode of conveyance, by which the tenant-in-tail might dispose of his lands and tenements; so that no court would suffer them to be shaken, and even acts of parliament countenanced and established them.

This expedient having greatly abridged estates-tail with regard to their duration, others were soon invented to strip them of other privileges. The next that was attacked was their freedom from forfeiture for treason. For, notwithstanding the large advances made by recoveries, in the compass of about threescore years, · towards unfettering these inheritances, and thereby subjecting the lands to forfeiture, the rapacious prince then reigning, finding them frequently resettled in a similar manner to suit the convenience of families, had address enough to procure a statute, whereby all estates of inheritance, under which general words estates-tail were covertly included, are declared to be forfeited to the crown upon any conviction of high treason.

The next attack which they suffered was by the statute 32 Hen. VIII. c. 36, which declared a fine duly levied by tenant-in-tail to be a complete bar to him and his heirs, and all other persons claiming under such entail. This was agreeable to the intention of Henry VII., whose policy it was to lay the road as open as possible to the alienation of landed property, in order to weaken the overgrown power of his nobles. But as they, from the opposite reasons, were not easily brought to consent to such a provision, it was therefore couched, in his act, under covert and obscure expressions. And the judges, though willing to construe that statute as favourably as possible for defeating entailed estates, yet hesitated at giving fines so extensive a power by mere implication, when the statute *De Donis* had expressly declared, that they should *not* be a bar to estates-tail. But the statute of Henry VIII., when the doctrine of alienation was better received, avowed and established that intention.

Lastly, by a statute of the succeeding year, all estates-tail were rendered liable to be charged for payment of debts due to the king by record or special contract; as since, by the bankrupt laws, they are also subjected to be sold for the debts contracted by a bankrupt; and now are chargeable by judgment or decree of a court of law or equity in favour of creditors, to the exclusion of the issue and remainder-men to the same extent as the debtor himself might have charged them.

So much for freehold estates of inheritance. Those estates of freehold which are not of inheritance, are *for life* only. And of these some are *conventional*, or created by the acts of the parties; others *legal*, or created by operation of law.

I. Estates for life, created by deed or grant, are where a lease is made of lands or tenements to a man, to hold for the term of his own

life, or for that of any other person, or for more lives than one: in
any of which cases he is styled tenant for life; only when he holds
the estate by the life of another, he is usually called tenant *pur
auter vie*; and the *incidents* to such an estate are principally the
following:—

1. Every tenant for life, unless restrained by covenant or agreement, may take *reasonable estovers* or *botes.* For he has a right to
the full enjoyment and use of the land, and all its profits, during his
estate therein. But he is not permitted to cut down timber or do
other waste upon the premises: for the destruction of such things as
are not the temporary profits of the tenement, is not necessary for
the tenant's complete enjoyment of his estate; but tends to the permanent and lasting loss of the person entitled to the inheritance.

2. Tenant for life, or his representatives, shall not be prejudiced
by any sudden determination of his estate, because such a determination is contingent and uncertain. Therefore, if a tenant for his
own life sows the lands, and dies before harvest, his executors shall
have the *emblements,* or profits of the crop: for the estate was determined by the *act of God,* and it is a maxim in the law, that *actus
Dei nemini facit injuriam.* So it is also, if a man be tenant for the
life of another, and *cestui que vie,* or he on whose life the land is held,
dies after the corn sown, the tenant *pur auter vie* shall have the
emblements. The same is also the rule, if a life-estate be determined
by the *act of law.* But if an estate for life be determined by the
tenant's *own act,* as by forfeiture for waste committed, in these, and
similar cases, the tenants, having thus determined the estate by their
own acts, shall not be entitled to take the emblements.

3. A third incident to estates for life relates to the under-tenants,
or lessees. For they have the same, nay greater indulgences than
their lessors, the original tenants for life. The same; for the law of
estovers and emblements with regard to the tenant for life, is also
law with regard to his under-tenant, who represents him and stands
in his place: and greater; for in those cases where tenant for life
shall not have the emblements, because the estate determines by his
own act, the exception shall not reach his lessee, who is a third
person. Instead of emblements, however, the under-tenant, on the
determination of a lease or tenancy under a landlord entitled as
tenant for life or for an uncertain interest, now holds until the
expiration of the current year, paying the succeeding landlord a fair
proportion of the rent.

II. The next estate for life is of a legal kind, viz., that of tenant-
in-tail after possibility of issue extinct. This happens where one is
tenant in special tail, and a person, from whose body the issue was

to spring, dies without issue; or, having left issue, that issue becomes extinct. As, where one has an estate to him and his heirs on the body of his present wife to be begotten, and the wife dies without issue: in this case the man has an estate-tail, which cannot possibly descend to any one; and therefore the law makes use of this long periphrasis, as absolutely necessary to give an adequate idea of his estate. The tenant is here a tenant for life, but with many of the privileges of a tenant-in-tail, as not to be punishable for waste, &c.; yet, in general, the law looks upon this estate as equivalent to an estate for life only.

III. Tenant *by the courtesy of England*, is where a man marries a woman seised of an estate of inheritance, and has by her issue, born alive, which was capable of inheriting her estate. In this case he shall, on the death of his wife, hold the lands for his life, as tenant by the courtesy of England. There are four requisites to make a tenancy by the courtesy :—1. The marriage must be legal. 2. The seisin of the wife must be an actual possession of the lands, not a bare right to them. 3. The issue must be born alive. Some have had a notion that it must be heard to cry; but that is a mistake. Crying indeed is the *strongest* evidence of its being born alive; but it is not the *only* evidence. The issue also must be born during the life of the mother; for if the mother dies in labour, and the Cæsarean operation is performed, the husband in this case shall not be tenant by the courtesy: because, at the instant of the mother's death, he was clearly not entitled, as having had no issue born, but the land descended to the child, while he was yet in his mother's womb; and the estate being once so vested, shall not afterwards be taken from him. 4. Such issue must be also capable of inheriting the mother's estate. Therefore, if a woman be tenant-in-tail *male*, and has only a *daughter* born, the husband is not thereby entitled to be tenant by the courtesy; because such issue female can never inherit the estate in tail male.

IV. Tenancy in *dower* is where a widow takes a third of such lands and tenements as her husband *died* entitled to, for seisin is not here necessary, and in which her title to dower has not been previously barred. This mode of providing for a widow seems to have been unknown in the early part of our Saxon constitution; for, in the laws of King Edmund, the wife is directed to be supported wholly out of the personal estate. Afterwards, as may be seen in gavelkind tenure, the widow became entitled to an estate in one-half of the lands, provided she remained chaste and unmarried; as is usual also in copyhold dowers, or free-bench. Some have ascribed dower to the Normans, but it was first introduced into the feudal system by the Emperor Frederick II., who was contemporary with

Henry III. It is possible, therefore, that it may be with us the relic of a Danish custom: since, according to the historians of that country, dower was introduced into Denmark by Swein, the father of our Canute, out of gratitude to the Danish ladies, who sold all their jewels to ransom him when taken prisoner by the Vandals. However this be, the reason which our law gives for adopting it is a very plain and sensible one; for the sustenance of the wife, and the nurture and education of the younger children.

The person endowed must be the actual wife of the party at the time of his decease. If she be divorced *a vinculo*, she shall not be endowed; but a judicial separation does not destroy the dower. It is, however, forfeited by adultery on the part of the wife, and by the treason of the husband.

At common law a widow was endowed of all the lands, tenements, and hereditaments of which her husband was seised *at any time during* the coverture, but under certain restrictions.* And it mattered not though the husband alienated the lands during the coverture; for he alienated them liable to dower. This law was altered some years ago; and lands to which the husband is merely *entitled*, or in which his interest is merely *equitable*, have been made subject to the dower of the widow. On the other hand the title to dower does not attach upon all the lands of which the husband was at any time seised *during* the coverture; for the widow can only be endowed out of lands of or to which he *dies* seised or entitled; and the absolute disposition of lands by him during his life or by his will, defeats the widow's right; nor will she be entitled to dower out of land purchased by the husband, where, in the deed of conveyance to him, or in any deed executed by him, it is declared that she shall not be so entitled. So that whether a wife shall be endowed or not, is now entirely in the will of the husband.

Upon preconcerted marriages, and in estates of considerable consequence, tenancy in dower happens very seldom: for the claim of the wife to dower is a great clog to alienations, and otherwise inconvenient to families, so that *jointures* are now universally resorted to. And thus much of estates of freehold.

* Thus, copyhold estates are not liable to dower, being only estates at the lord's will; unless by the special custom of the manor, in which case it is usually called the widow's free-bench.

CHAPTER VI.

OF ESTATES LESS THAN FREEHOLD.

I. Estates for years—Origin of long leases—Emblements.——II. Estates at will—Notice to quit—Copyholds—Enfranchisement.——III. Estates at sufferance.

OF estates that are less than freehold, there are three sorts: 1. Estates for years; 2. Estates at will; 3. Estates by sufferance.

I. An estate for *years* is where one has the possession of lands or tenements, for some determinate period: it takes place, for example, where a man letteth lands to another for the term of a certain number of years, agreed upon between the lessor and the lessee, and the lessee enters thereon. If the lease be but for half a year or a quarter, or any less time, this lessee is respected as a tenant for years, and is styled so in some legal proceedings: a year being the shortest term which the law in this case takes notice of.

These estates were originally granted to mere farmers or husbandmen, who every year rendered some equivalent in provisions, or other rent, to the landlords; but, in order to encourage them to manure and cultivate the ground, they had afterwards a permanent interest granted them, not determinable at the will of the lord. Yet their possession was esteemed of so little consequence, that they were rather considered as the bailiffs of the lord, who were to account for the profits at a settled price, than as having any property of their own. And their interest, such as it was, vested after their deaths in their executors, who were to make up the accounts of their testator with the lord, and were entitled to the stock upon the farm.

While estates for years were thus precarious, it is no wonder that they were usually very short, like our modern leases upon rack-rent; but when by the statute 51 Hen. VIII. c. 15, the termor, that is, he who is entitled to the term of years, was protected against fictitious actions brought to evict the landlord, which common recoveries were, and his interest rendered permanent, long terms began to be frequent, and were afterwards extensively introduced, being found extremely convenient for family settlements and mortgages: continuing subject, however, to the same rules of succession, as when they were little better than tenancies at the will of the landlord.

Every estate which must expire at a period certain and prefixed,

H 3

is an estate for years. And therefore this estate is frequently called a term, *terminus*, because its duration is bounded, limited, and determined: for every such estate must have a certain beginning, and certain end. Having a certain end, this estate is inferior to any freehold; for an estate for life, even if it be *pur auter vie*, is a freehold; but an estate for a thousand years is only a chattel, and reckoned part of the personal estate. And, because no livery of seisin is necessary to a lease for years, such lessee is not said to be *seised;* nor, indeed, does the lease vest any estate in him. It gives him only a right of entry on the tenement, which right is called his *interest in the term*, or *interesse termini*: when he has actually entered, and thereby accepted the grant, the estate is then, and not before, vested in him, and he is *possessed*, not of the land, but of the term of years therein; the possession or seisin of the *land* remaining still in him who has the freehold.

Tenant for term of years has incident to his estate, unless by special agreement, the same estovers which tenant for life is entitled to. But with regard to emblements, there is this difference: that where the term depends upon a certainty, as if the tenant holds from midsummer for ten years, and in the last year he sows a crop of corn, and it is not ripe and cut before midsummer, the landlord shall have it; for the tenant knew the expiration of his term, and therefore it was his own folly to sow what he never could reap the profits of. But where the lease for years depends upon an uncertainty: as, if the term be determinable upon a life or lives, the tenant, or his executors, shall have the emblements in the same manner that a tenant for life or his executors is entitled thereto. It is different if the lease be determined by himself: as if the tenant does anything that amounts to a forfeiture: here the emblements shall go to the lessor and not to the lessee, who has determined his estate by his own default.

II. An estate at will is where lands and tenements are let by one man to another, to have and to hold at the will of the lessor; and the tenant by force of this lease obtains possession. Such estate is at the will of both parties; so that either of them may determine his will, and quit his connection with the other at his own pleasure. Yet if the tenant sows his land, and the landlord, before the corn is ripe or before it is reaped, puts him out, the tenant shall have the emblements. But it is otherwise where the tenant himself determines the will, for in this case the landlord shall have the profits of the land.

The courts of law have long leaned as much as possible against construing demises, where no certain term is mentioned, to be tenancies at will. They have rather held them to be tenancies from year to year so long as both parties please, especially where an annual rent is reserved: in which case they will not suffer either party to determine the tenancy even at the end of the year, without reasonable notice to the other, which is generally understood to be six months.

An estate held by copy of court-roll, or, as we usually call it, a *copyhold*, was, in its origin, nothing better than a mere estate at will. But this, as we have seen, has long been nothing but a name; and every copyhold tenant may have, so far as the custom of the manor warrants, any other of the estates which we have hitherto considered, or may hereafter consider, and hold them united with this customary estate at will. He may be tenant in fee-simple, in fee-tail, for life, by the courtesy, in dower, for years, at sufferance, or on condition: subject, however, to be deprived of these estates upon the concurrence of those circumstances which the will of the lord, as established by immemorial custom, has declared to be a forfeiture or determination of those interests; as in some manors the want of issue male, in others the cutting down timber, the non-payment of a fine, and the like.

In legal parlance, however, copyhold estates are still ranked among tenancies at will; though custom has established a permanent property in the copyholders, equal to that of the lord himself, in the tenements holden of the manor. And the law has provided for the determination of this mutual will, regulated by custom, in its own way; by providing that a copyhold tenure may be put an end to, by a grant from the lord of the freehold, which is called *enfranchisement*, the tenant by this means becoming seised in common socage of the lands; or by the copyhold and freehold titles becoming united in one person, whereupon *extinguishment* takes place, the copyhold interest merging in the superior estate. And as enfranchisement is now, on the application of either lord or tenant, compulsory, and obtainable on terms which, in case of dispute, are fixed by the Enclosure commissioners appointed for this purpose by statute, these tenancies at the will of the lord will in course of time cease to exist.

III. An estate at *sufferance*, is, where one comes into possession of land by lawful title, but keeps it afterwards without any title at all. As, if a man takes a lease for a year, and, after the year is expired, continues to hold the premises without any fresh lease from the owner of the estate. This estate may be destroyed whenever the true owner shall make an actual entry on the lands and oust the tenant; for before entry, he cannot maintain an action of trespass against the tenant by sufferance, as he might against a stranger: and the reason is, because the tenant being once in by a lawful title, the law will suppose him to continue upon a title equally law-ful; unless the owner of the land by some public and avowed act, such as entry is, will declare his continuance to be wrongful. By statute 2 Geo. II. c. 19, a tenant wilfully holding over after the determination of the term, and demand of possession made by the landlord, shall pay for the time he detains the lands, double their yearly *value;* and a tenant having given notice to quit not deliver-ing up the possession at the proper time, shall pay double the former *rent;* so that tenancy by sufferance, unless with the tacit consent of the owner, is almost unknown.

CHAPTER VII.

OF ESTATES UPON CONDITION.

Offices forfeited by mis-user or non-user—Mortgages—Equity of redemption—Foreclosure—Power of sale.

BESIDES these several estates, there is another species, estates *upon condition,* which I have reserved till the last, because they are more properly qualifications of other estates, than a distinct species of themselves; seeing that any quantity of interest, a fee, a freehold, or a term of years, may be an estate upon condition. These estates are either:—I. Estates upon condition *implied;* or, II. Estates upon condition *expressed;* under which last may be included—1. Estates held in *vadio, gage,* or *pledge;* 2. Estates by *statute merchant,* or *statute staple;* 3. Estates held by *elegit.*

I. Estates upon condition implied in law, are where a grant of an estate has a condition annexed to it inseparably from its essence and constitution, although no condition be expressed in words. As, if a grant be made to a man of an office, generally, without adding other words, the law tacitly annexes hereto a secret condition, that the grantee shall duly execute his office. For an office, either public or private, may be forfeited by *mis-user* or *non-user,* both of which are breaches of this implied condition: 1. By *mis-user,* or abuse; as if a judge takes a bribe, or a park-keeper kills deer without authority. 2. By *non-user,* or neglect; which in public offices, that concern the administration of justice, or the commonwealth, is of itself a direct and immediate cause of forfeiture; unless some special damage is proved to be occasioned thereby. Franchises also, being regal privileges in the hands of a subject, are held to be granted on the same condition of making a proper use of them; and therefore they may be lost and forfeited, like offices, either by abuse or by neglect.

II. An estate on condition expressed in the grant itself is where an estate is granted, with an express qualification annexed, whereby the estate granted shall either commence, be enlarged, or be defeated, upon performance or breach of such condition. And these conditions are either *precedent* or subsequent. Thus, if an estate be limited to A, upon his marriage with B, the marriage is a *precedent* condition, and till that happens, no estate is vested in A. Or, if a man grant to his lessee for years, that upon payment of a hundred marks within the term he shall have the fee, this also is a condition *precedent*, and the fee-simple passeth not till the hundred marks be paid. So, if a man grant an estate, reserving to himself a certain rent; and that if such rent be not paid, it shall be lawful for him to re-enter, and avoid the estate: in this case the grantee and his heirs have an estate upon condition *subsequent*, which is defeasible if the condition be not strictly performed.

But in all these and in similar cases, so long as the condition remains unbroken, the grantee may hold the estate. Some estates defeasible upon condition *subsequent*, require however a more peculiar notice. Such are,—

1. Estates held *in vadio*, in *gage*, or pledge; as where a man borrows of another a specific sum, *e.g.*, 200*l.*, and grants him an estate in fee, on condition that if he, the mortgagor, shall repay the mortgagee the said sum of 200*l.* on a certain day, that then the mortgagee shall reconvey the estate to the mortgagor: in this case, the land which is so put in pledge, is by law, in case of nonpayment at the time limited, for ever dead and gone from the mortgagor; and the mortgagee's estate in the lands is then no longer conditional, but absolute.

As soon as the estate is created, the mortgagee may immediately enter on the lands; but is liable to be dispossessed upon performance of the condition by payment of the mortgage-money at the day limited. And therefore the usual way is to agree that the mortgagor shall hold the land till the day assigned for payment; when, in case of failure, whereby the estate becomes absolute, the mortgagee may enter upon it and take possession, without any possibility *at law* of being afterwards evicted by the mortgagor, to whom the land is now for ever dead. But here the courts of equity interpose; and though a mortgage be forfeited, and the estate thus absolutely vested in the mortgagee, yet they consider the real value of the tenements compared with the sum borrowed. And, if the estate be of greater value than the sum lent, they will allow the mortgagor, at any time within twenty years, to redeem his estate; paying to the mortgagee his principal, interest, and expenses. This reasonable advantage is called the *Equity of Redemption*: and enables a mortgagor to call on the mortgagee, who has possession of his estate, to deliver it back and account for the rents and profits received, on payment of his whole debt and interest. On the other hand, the mortgagee may either compel the sale of the estate, in order to get the whole of his money immediately; or else call upon the mortgagor to re- deem his estate presently, or, in default thereof, to be for ever *fore- closed* from redeeming the same; that is, to lose his equity of redemption, without possibility of recall. And in modern mortgages it is accordingly usual to give the mortgagee a power of sale, which indeed is now, unless expressly excluded, incident to every mortgage, whereby he may realize his security much more con- veniently than by a foreclosure; for the courts of equity do not interfere with the exercise of such powers, the mortgagee being only bound to account for the residue of the proceeds of the sale, after paying himself principal, interest, and the expenses of the sale. Nor is it usual for mortgagees to take possession of the mortgaged estate, unless where the security is precarious or small; or where the mortgagor neglects even the payment of interest: when the mort- gagee is frequently obliged to bring an ejectment, and take the land into his own hands. But after payment or tender by the mortgagor of principal, interest, and costs, the mortgagee cannot maintain an action of ejectment; but may be compelled to re-assign his securities.

2. Estates also defeasible on condition subsequent, are those held by *statute merchant* and *statute staple*, which were securities for money; the one entered into before the chief magistrate of some trading town, pursuant to the statute of 13 Edw. I. *de mercatoribus;* the other pursuant to the statute 27 Edw. III., c. 9, before the *mayor of the staple*, that is to say, the grand mart for the principal com- modities or manufactures of the kingdom, formerly held in certain trading towns, from whence this security derived its name. Both have fallen into entire disuse.

3. An estate *by elegit* is also an estate upon condition *subsequent*, created by operation of law, for satisfaction of a debt. For after a plaintiff has obtained judgment, the sheriff will, under a writ of execution, give him possession of the defendant's lands, to be by him enjoyed, until his debt and damages are fully paid: and during the time he so holds them, he is called tenant by *elegit*. From this it would seem that the feudal restraints of alienating lands, and charging them with the debts of the owner, were softened much earlier, and much more effectually for the benefit of trade and com- merce, than for any other consideration.

CHAPTER VIII.

OF ESTATES IN POSSESSION, REMAINDER, AND REVERSION.

I. Estates in possession.——II. Estates in remainder—Executory devises.—— III. Estates in reversion—Incidents thereof—Merger.

WE are now to consider estates in another view; viz., with regard to the *time of their enjoyment*, and in this legal way they may be regarded as, 1, in *possession*, or, 2, in *expectancy* : and of expectancies there are two sorts; one created by the act of the parties, called a *remainder* ; the other by act of law, and called a *reversion*.

I. Of estates in *possession* there is little or nothing peculiar to be observed. All the estates we have hitherto spoken of are of this kind; for, in laying down general rules, we usually apply them to such estates as are then actually in the tenants' possession.

II. An estate *in remainder* may be defined to be, an estate limited to take effect and be enjoyed after another estate is determined. As if a man seised in fee-simple granteth lands to A for twenty years, and, after the determination of the said term, then to B and his heirs for ever: here A is tenant for years, remainder to B in fee. In the first place, an estate for years is created or carved out of the fee, and given to A; and the residue or remainder of it is given to B. But both these interests are in fact only one estate; the present term of years and the remainder afterwards, when added together, being equal only to one estate in fee. They are indeed different *parts*, but they constitute only one *whole* : they are carved out of one and the same inheritance: they are both created, and may both subsist, together; the one in possession, the other in expectancy.

In the creation of a remainder by deed much nicety is required; but it is not within our scope of these elementary commentaries to explain the particular subtilties and refinements into which this doctrine of remainders has, by the variety of cases which have occurred in the course of many centuries, been spun out and subdivided. I must not, however, omit, that in devises by last will, which being often drawn up when the party is *inops consilii*, are always more favoured in construction than formal deeds, which are presumed to be made with great caution, forethought, and advice, in these devises, I say, remainders may be created in some measure contrary to the first rules of law: though our lawyers will not allow such dispositions to be strictly remainders; but call them by another name, that of *executory devises*, or devises hereafter to be executed.

III. An estate in *reversion* is the residue of an estate left in the grantor, to commence in possession after the determination of some particular estate granted out by him. As, if there be a gift in tail, the reversion of the fee is, without any special reservation, vested in the donor by act of law: and so also the reversion, after an estate for life, years, or at will, continues in the lessor. For the fee-simple of all lands must abide somewhere; and if he, who was before possessed of the whole, carves out of it any smaller estate, and grants it away, whatever is not so granted remains in him. A reversion is never therefore created by deed or writing, but arises from construction of law; a remainder can never be limited, unless by either deed or devise. But both are equally transferable, when actually vested, being both estates *in præsenti*, though taking effect *in futuro*.

The usual *incidents* to reversions are said to be *fealty* and *rent*. When no rent is reserved, fealty results of course, as an incident quite inseparable; and may be demanded as a badge of tenure, or acknowledgment of superiority; being frequently the only evidence that the lands are holden at all. Where rent is reserved, it is also incident, though not inseparably so, to the reversion. The rent may be granted away, reserving the reversion; and the reversion may be granted away, reserving the rent; by *special* words: but by a *general* grant of the reversion, the rent will pass with it, as incident thereunto, though by the grant of the rent generally, the reversion will not pass.

Before we conclude the doctrine of remainders and reversions, it may be proper to observe that whenever a greater estate and a less coincide and meet in one and the same person without any intermediate estate, the less is immediately annihilated; or in the law phrase, is said to be *merged*, that is, sunk or drowned in the greater. Thus if there be tenant for years, and the reversion in fee-simple descends to or is purchased by him, the term of years is merged in the inheritance, and shall never exist any more. But they must come to one and the same person in one and the same right, thus, if the freehold be in his own right, and he has a term in right of another, *en auter droit*, there is no merger. An estate-tail, it must be recollected, is an exception to this rule: for a man may have in his own right both an estate-tail and a reversion in fee; and the estate-tail, though a less estate, shall not merge in the fee, being protected and preserved from merger by the construction, though not by the express words, of the statute *De Donis:* on which, indeed, all such estates depend for their existence.

CHAPTER IX.

OF ESTATES IN SEVERALTY, JOINT-TENANCY, COPARCENARY, AND COMMON.

1. Severalty.——II. Joint-tenancy—How created—Its properties and incidents—Survivorship.——III. Coparcenary—How created—Its incidents—How dissolved.——IV. Tenancy in common—How created—Its incidents—Partition.

Estates, considered with respect to the number and connections of their owners, whatever be their nature, and whether they be in possession or expectancy, may be held in four different ways : in severalty, in joint-tenancy, in coparcenary, or in common.

I. He that holds lands or tenements in *severalty*, or is sole tenant thereof, is he that holds them in his own right only, without any other person being joined or connected with him in point of interest, during his estate therein. This is the most usual way of holding an estate ; and there is, therefore, nothing to be remarked concerning it, since all estates are supposed to be of this sort, unless where they are expressly declared to be otherwise.

II. An estate in *joint-tenancy* is where lands or tenements are granted to two or more persons, to hold in fee-simple, fee-tail, for life, for years, or at will.

Its *creation* depends on the wording of the deed or devise by which the tenants claim title ; for this estate can only arise by purchase or grant, that is, by the act of the parties, and never by the mere act of law. Now, if an estate be given to a plurality of persons, without adding any restrictive, exclusive, or explanatory words, as to A and B . and their heirs, this makes them immediately joint-tenants in fee of the lands. For the law interprets the grant so as to make all parts of it take effect, which can only be done by creating an equal estate in them both. As, therefore, the grantor has thus united their names, the law gives them a thorough union in all other respects. For,

The *properties* of a joint estate are derived from its unity, which is fourfold: unity of *interest*, unity of *title*, unity of *time*, and the unity of *possession*.

Joint-tenants must have one and the same *interest*. One cannot be entitled to one period of duration or quantity of interest in lands, and the other to a different; one cannot be tenant for life, and the other for years; one cannot be tenant in fee, and the other in tail. They must also have an unity of *title*; their estate must be created by one and the same act. Joint-tenancy cannot arise by descent or act of law, but merely by purchase, or acquisition by the act of the party; and, unless that act be one and the same, the two tenants would have different titles; and if they had different titles, there would be no jointure. There must also be an unity of *time*; their estates must be vested at one and the same period, as well as by one and the same title. As in case of a present estate made to A and B; or a remainder in fee to A and B after a particular estate; in either case A and B are joint-tenants of this present estate, or this vested remainder. Lastly, in joint-tenancy there must be an unity of *possession*; for joint-tenants are said to be seised *per my et per tout*, by the *moiety* and by *all*: that is, they each of them have the entire possession, as well of every *parcel* as of the *whole*. They have not, one of them, a seisin of one-half or moiety, and the other of the other moiety; neither can one be exclusively seised of one acre and his companion of another, but each has an undivided moiety of the whole, and not the whole of an undivided moiety.

Upon these principles depend many other consequences and incidents to the joint-tenants' estate. Thus, if two joint-tenants let a verbal lease of their land, reserving rent to be paid to one of them, it shall enure to both, in respect of the joint reversion; and if their lessee surrenders his lease to one of them, it shall enure to both, because of the privity of their estate. In all actions relating to their joint estate, one joint-tenant cannot sue or be sued without joining the other. Neither can one joint-tenant have an action against the other for trespass, in respect of his land, for each has an equal right to enter on any part of it. Yet if any waste be done, which tends to the destruction of the inheritance, one joint-tenant may have an action of waste against the other. So the one may maintain a suit against the other for receiving more than his due share of the profits. And so one joint-tenant may maintain ejectment against the other, if he can show any *actual ouster*, as if one were to retain the whole of the rents.

From the same principle also arises another incident of joint estates, viz., *survivorship*; by which the tenancy, upon the decease of any of the joint-tenants, remains to the survivors, and at length to the last survivor, who is then entitled to the whole estate. This right is called by our ancient authors the *jus accrescendi*, because the right upon the death of one joint-tenant accumulates and increases to the survivors. But it is to be noted that there is no survivorship of a capital, or a stock in trade, among merchants and traders; for this would be ruinous to the family of the deceased partner; and it is a legal maxim, *jus accrescendi inter mercatores pro beneficio commercii locum non habet.* This *jus accrescendi* also ought to be mutual, and therefore neither the king, nor any corporation, can be a joint-tenant with a private person. For here is no mutuality; the private person has not even the remotest chance of being seised of the entirety, by benefit of survivorship, for the king and the corporation can never die.

Joint-tenancy may be destroyed without any alienation, by merely disuniting the *possession*. And, therefore, if the joint-tenants agree to part their lands, and hold them in severalty, they are no longer joint-tenants, and the right of survivorship is at once destroyed. At common law all the joint-tenants might agree to make partition of the lands, though one of them could not compel the others so to do; but a partition may now be enforced by the Court of Chancery; or effected much more easily and expeditiously through the medium of the Inclosure Commissioners. The joint-tenancy may also be destroyed by destroying the unity of *title;* as if one joint-tenant conveys his estate to a third person: here the joint-tenancy is severed, and turned into tenancy in common; for the grantee and the remaining joint-tenant hold by different titles, though, till partition made, the unity of possession continues. Joint-tenancy may also be destroyed by destroying the unity of *interest.* And therefore, if there be two joint-tenants for life, and the inheritance is purchased by or descends upon either, it is a severance of the jointure. So that when, by any act or event, different interests are created in the several parts of the estate, or they are held by different titles, or if merely the possession is separated, so that the tenants have no longer these four indispensable properties, a sameness of interest, and undivided possession, a title vesting at one and the same time, and by one and the same act or grant, the jointure is instantly dissolved; which in general it is advantageous to effect, since thereby the right of survivorship is taken away, and each may transmit his own part to his own heirs

III. An estate held in *coparcenary* is where lands of inheritance descend from the ancestor to two or more persons. It *arises* either by common law or particular custom. By common law: as where a person seised in fee-simple, or in fee-tail dies, and his next heirs are two or more females; in this case they shall all inherit, as will be more fully shown hereafter; and these coheirs are then called *coparceners*, or, for brevity, *parceners* only. Parceners by particular custom are where lands descend, as in gavelkind, to all the males in equal degree. And, in either of these cases, all the parceners put together make but one heir, and have but one estate among them.

The *properties* of parceners are in some respects like those of joint-tenants, they having the same unities of *interest, title,* and *possession.* They may sue and be sued jointly for matters relating to their own lands, and they cannot have an action of trespass against each other. But they differ from joint-tenants, in that they are excluded from maintaining an action of waste. Parceners also differ from joint-tenants in four other points:—1. They always claim by descent, whereas joint-tenants always claim by purchase. 2. There is no unity of *time* necessary; for if a man has two daughters, to whom his estate descends, and one dies before the other, the surviving daughter and the heir of the other, or, when both are dead, their two heirs, are still parceners. 3. Parceners, though they have an *unity*, have not an *entirety* of interest. They are properly entitled each to the whole of a distinct moiety, and of course there is no *jus accrescendi*, or survivorship, between them; for each part descends severally to their respective heirs, though the unity of possession continues. And as long as the lands continue in a course of descent, and united in possession, so long are the tenants therein, whether male or female, called parceners. But if the possession be once severed by partition, they are no longer parceners, but tenants in severalty; or if one parcener aliens her share, though no partition be made, then are the lands no longer held in *coparcenary*, but in *common.*

Parceners are so called because they were always obliged to make *partition*, which joint-tenants were not; and if this was not done voluntarily, it might be compulsorily, as it is now often effected, by a bill in equity. There are some things, however, in their nature impartible. The mansion-house and common of estovers shall not be divided; but the eldest sister, if she pleases, shall have them, and make the others a reasonable satisfaction in other parts of the inheritance: or, if that cannot be, then they shall have the profits of the thing by turns, and in the same manner they take an advowson.

The estate in coparcenary may be *dissolved*, either by partition, which disunites the possession; by alienation of one parcener, which disunites the title, and may disunite the interest; or by the whole at last descending to and vesting in one single person, which brings it to an estate in severalty.

IV. Tenants in *common* are such as hold by several and distinct

titles, but by unity of possession; because none knoweth his own
severalty, and therefore they all occupy promiscuously. This
tenancy, therefore, happens where there is a unity of possession
merely, but perhaps an entire disunion of interest, of title, and of
time. For if there be two tenants in common of lands, one may
hold his part in fee-simple, the other in tail, or for life; so that
there is no necessary unity of interest: one may hold by descent, the
other by purchase; or the one by purchase from A, the other by
purchase from B; so that there is no unity of title: one's estate
may have been vested fifty years, the other's but yesterday; so there
is no unity of time. The only unity there is, is that of possession;
and for this Littleton gives the true reason, because no man can
certainly tell which part is his own: otherwise even this would be
soon destroyed.

Tenancy in common may be created by the destruction of the two
other estates, joint-tenancy and coparcenary, or by special limitation
in a deed. By destruction, I mean such destruction as does not
sever the unity of possession, but only the unity of title or interest:
as, if one of the two joint-tenants in fee aliens his estate for the life
of the alienee, the alienee and the other joint-tenant are tenants in
common; for they now have several titles, the other joint-tenant by
the original grant, the alienee by the new alienation; and they also
have several interests, the former joint-tenant in fee-simple, the
alienee for his own life only. So, if one of two parceners aliens, the
alienee and the remaining parcener are tenants in common, because
they hold by different titles, the parcener by descent, the alienee by
purchase. In short, whenever an estate in joint-tenancy or coparcenary is dissolved, it is turned into a tenancy in common.

A tenancy in common may also be created by express limitation
in a deed: but here care must be taken not to insert words which
imply a joint estate; and then if lands be given to two or more, and
it be not joint-tenancy, it must be a tenancy in common. But the
law is apt in its constructions to favour joint-tenancy rather than
tenancy in common, because the services issuing from land, as rent
&c., are not divided, nor the entire services, as fealty, multiplied, by
joint-tenancy, as they must necessarily be upon a tenancy in common; and therefore it is the usual as well as the safest way, when a
tenancy in common is meant to be created, to add express words of
exclusion as well as description, and limit the estate to A and B, to
hold *as tenants in common and not as joint-tenants.*

As to the *incidents* attending a tenancy in common: tenants in
common, like joint-tenants, are compellable by bill in equity to
make partition of their lands; yet there is no survivorship between
them, as properly they take distinct moieties of the estate. The
other incidents are such as merely arise from the unity of possession,

and are therefore the same as appertain to joint-tenants merely upon that account: such as being liable to reciprocal actions of waste, and to account for the property; and if one actually turns the other out of possession, an action of ejectment will lie against him. But, as for other incidents of joint-tenants, which arise from the privity of title, or the union and entirety of interest, such as joining or being joined in actions, unless in the case where some entire or indivisible thing is to be recovered, these are not applicable to tenants in common, whose interests are distinct, and whose titles are not joint but several. It follows that tenancies in common can only be *dissolved* two ways: 1. By uniting all the interests in one tenant, which brings the whole to one severalty. 2. By making partition between the several tenants in common, which gives them all respective severalties.

And this finishes our inquiries with respect to the nature of *estates.*

CHAPTER X.

OF THE TITLE TO THINGS REAL.

Effect of possession — Right of possession — Source of title — Statute of limitations — Advowsons.

THE foregoing chapters having been principally employed in defining the *nature* of things real, in describing the *tenures* by which they may be holden, and in distinguishing the several kinds of *estate* or interest that may be had therein, I come now to consider, lastly, the *title* to things real, with the manner of acquiring and losing it.

The lowest kind of title consists in the mere *naked possession*, or actual occupation of the estate, without any apparent right to hold and continue such possession. This may happen when one man invades the possession of another, and by force or surprise turns him out of the occupation of his lands; or it may happen when, after the death of the ancestor and before the entry of the heir, or after the death of a particular tenant and before the entry of him in remainder or reversion, a stranger contrives to get possession, and keeps out him that had a right to enter. In all which cases, and many others that might be suggested, the wrongdoer has a mere *possession*, which the rightful owner may put an end to, by the appropriate legal remedies. But till some act be done by the rightful owner to assert his title, such actual possession is *primâ facie* evidence of a legal title in the possessor.

To constitute a good and perfect title something more is necessary, namely, the *right of possession*, which may reside in one man, while the actual possession is in another. For if a man be kept out of possession, though the *actual* possession be lost, yet he has still remaining in him the *right* of possession; and this right he may exert whenever he thinks proper, by turning the intruder out of that occupancy which he has so illegally gained. Yet if he omit to do so within the time fixed by law, the intruder may imperceptibly gain an actual right of possession, which is in itself perfect and complete, so that no further remedy remains.

By our old law, if a man was turned out of possession, the intruder thereby gained what was called a *mere naked* possession, and the owner still retained the *right of possession* and *right of property*. If the intruder died, and the lands descended to his son, the son gained an *apparent* right of *possession*, but the owner still retained the *actual* right both of *possession* and *property*. If he acquiesced, however, for thirty years without bringing any action to recover possession of the land, the son gained the *actual right of possession*, and the owner retained nothing but the *mere right of property*. And even this right of property failed, or at least became without remedy, unless pursued within the space of sixty years. And hence it followed that one man might have the *possession*, another the *right of possession*, and a third the *right of property*. But the law now recognises only the *possession*, and *right of possession*, ignoring altogether any *right of property*, as distinct from these symbols of ownership. To an explanation of this modern law, I shall accordingly, as much as possible, confine myself; and the student will, I think, consider me fully justified in this course, when he observes that the great change I allude to, was effected upwards of forty years ago by the statute 3 & 4 Will. IV. c. 27. This statute provides that, at the determination of the period which it limits, the *right and title* of the person, who might within that time have pursued his remedy for the recovery of his property, *shall be extinguished;* and its great feature and chief effect therefore is, to make *right* dependent on *possession*, by limiting the period within which that right can be asserted to *twenty years* from the time at which the right of the claimant first accrued.

This right is deemed to have first accrued when the person who claims the land, or some person through whom he claims, was *dispossessed*, or discontinued his possession or receipt of rent, in case he was previously in possession; but as this limitation might produce hardship in cases where the person entitled laboured under disability at the time of his right accruing, infants, women under coverture, idiots, lunatics or persons of unsound mind, and those who were abroad beyond seas, have ten years further allowed them, from the time of their ceasing to be under their several disabilities. To prevent, however, the title of an actual possessor being thereby held too long in suspense, the extreme period of *forty years* is fixed, beyond which no person, whether under disability or no, is permitted to have any remedy; so that if a right accrue to a person under disability, who continues so during the whole forty years from the time of such accruer, he is wholly barred.

As to advowsons, being a pecular species of property, a longer period is fixed, during which the right to them may be recovered; namely, either sixty years, or the duration of three successive incumbencies. But here also the extreme period of a hundred years is fixed, beyond which, although the time may have been covered by less than three incumbencies, as may very possibly happen, no remedy remains to the person claiming.

As a general rule, then, the possession of land for a period of twenty years, without payment of rent, or acknowledgment of the title of any other person, for such acknowledgment, if given in writing, converts the possession of the tenant into the possession of the person to whom the acknowledgment is given, constitutes a sure and sufficient title. And, therefore, where the overseer of a parish let a person into possession of a cottage, a part of the parish property, at the rent of 1s. 6d. a-week, to quit at a month's notice, and the tenant remained for twenty years without paying rent or making any acknowledgment, his title was held to be unassailable. In this case bare possession had, by effluxion of time, matured into a right of property, which constituted a complete title against all the world.

CHAPTER XI.

OF TITLE BY DESCENT.

Heirs apparent and presumptive.—Lineal descent—Male succession—Female succession—Succession *per stirpes*—Collateral succession—Half-blood—Canons of descent.

WE are next to consider the several manners in which *real property* may be lost and acquired; and these are, by our law, reduced to two: *descent*, where the title is vested in a man by the single operation of law; and *purchase*, where the title is vested in him by his own act or agreement.

Descent, or hereditary succession, is the title whereby a man on the death of his ancestor acquires his estate by right of representation, as his heir-at-law. An heir, therefore, is he upon whom the law casts the estate immediately on the death of the ancestor: and an estate, so descending to the heir, is in law called the inheritance. The doctrine of descent is accordingly a point of the highest importance; and is indeed the principal object of the laws of real property in England. For all the rules relating to purchases, whereby the legal course of descents is altered, perpetually refer to this settled law of inheritance, as a *datum* or first principle universally known, and upon which their subsequent limitations are to work. In order therefore, to treat a matter of this consequence the more clearly, I shall lay aside such matters as tend to breed embarrassment and confusion in our inquiries, and confine myself entirely to this one object. I shall, therefore, pass over the division of descents into those by *custom, statute,* and *common law:* for descents by *particular custom,* as in gavelkind, and borough-english, have been already touched upon; and descents by the statute *De Donis,* have also been mentioned; and will confine my remarks to the common law doctrine of descents, as modified by the statute 3 & 4 Will. IV. c. 106, which is now the law of inheritance in England.

Before, however, I proceed to an enumeration of our modern rules or canons of inheritance, I must explain that they operate upon no descent which took place previous to the first day of January, 1834. When, therefore, an heir is to be sought for a succession which opened up previously to that date, the old rules of inheritance must be consulted; and to some of these I must shortly allude, partly on that account, and partly to enable the student to understand the more readily the alterations which the legislature has thought fit to make therein.

It must first be observed, then, that by law no inheritance can vest, nor can any person be the actual complete heir of another, till the ancestor is previously dead. *Nemo est hæres viventis.* Before that time the person who is next in the line of succession is called an heir apparent, or heir presumptive. Heirs apparent are such whose right of inheritance is indefeasible, provided they outlive the ancestor; as the eldest son, who must be heir to the father whenever he happens to die. Heirs presumptive are such who, if the ancestor should die immediately, would in the present circumstances of things be his heirs; but whose right of inheritance may be defeated by the contingency of some nearer heir being born: as a brother, or nephew, whose presumptive succession may be destroyed by the birth of a child; or a daughter, whose present hopes may be hereafter cut off by the birth of a son. Nay, even if the estate has descended, by the death of the owner, to such brother, or nephew, or daughter; in the former cases, the estate shall be divested and taken away by the birth of a posthumous child; and, in the latter, it shall also be totally divested by the birth of a posthumous son.

Now, it was formerly a rule of law, that no person could be properly such an ancestor, as that an inheritance could be derived from him, unless he had had *actual seisin* of the lands, either by his own entry, or by the possession of his own or his ancestor's lessee, or by receiving rent. The law required this notoriety of possession, as evidence that the ancestor had that property in himself which was to be transmitted to his heir; and he was not accounted an ancestor, therefore, who had had only a bare right or title to enter or be otherwise seised. The *seisin* therefore of any person, thus understood, made him the root or stock, from which all future inheritance by right of blood was to be derived, *seisina facit stipitem.* The *right* was not regarded, until by the statute I have mentioned the rule was altered, and the person *last entitled* to the land was made the root of descent.

Under the old law, again, when a person died seised, the inheritance first went to his issue. Thus, if there were Geoffrey, John, and Matthew, grandfather, father, and son; and John purchased lands, and died; Matthew succeeded him as heir; but in no case whatever could the grandfather Geoffrey do so. The land could never ascend, but was rather allowed to escheat to the lord; the rule being, 1, that inheritances should lineally descend to the issue of the person who last died *actually seised, in infinitum;* but, 2, should *never lineally ascend.* So far as it is affirmative and relates to lineal descents, this rule is almost universally adopted by all nations. But the negative branch, or total exclusion of parents and all lineal ancestors from succeeding to the inheritance of their offspring, was peculiar to our own laws; and after being long and loudly censured, as absurd and derogating from the maxims of natural justice, was entirely abrogated. Two ancient rules of law have, therefore, yielded to what I venture now to call the modern canons of descent, viz. :—

I. "Descent shall be traced from the purchaser; the person last "entitled being considered to have been the purchaser, unless he be "proved to have inherited."

II. "Inheritances shall lineally descend to the issue of the purchaser."

The next three canons of descent are the same as the old rules of law, viz. :—

III. "The male issue shall be admitted before the female."

Thus sons shall be admitted before daughters; or, as our male lawgivers have somewhat uncomplaisantly expressed it, the worthiest

of blood shall be preferred; a preference entirely agreeable to the
law of succession among the Jews, and also among the states of
Greece, or at least among the Athenians; but totally unknown to
the laws of Rome, and which seems to have arisen entirely from the
feudal law.   For though our British ancestors, the Welsh, appear to
have given a preference to males, yet our Danish predecessors who
succeeded them seem to have made no distinction of sexes, but to
have admitted all the children at once to the inheritance.   This
preference may probably be a branch of that imperfect system of
feuds, which obtained here before the Conquest.   The true reason of
it must be deduced from feudal principles: for no female could ever
succeed to a proper feud, being incapable of performing those military
services, for the sake of which that system was established.   But
our law does not extend to a total exclusion of females, as the Salic
law, and others, where feuds were most strictly retained: it only
postpones them to males; for, though daughters are excluded by
sons, yet they succeed before any collateral relations; our law, like
that of the Saxon feudists before mentioned, thus steering a middle
course between the absolute rejection of females, and the putting
them on a footing with males.

IV. " Where there are two or more males, in equal degree, the
" eldest only shall inherit; but the females all together."

This right of primogeniture in males seems anciently to have only
obtained among the Jews, in whose constitution the eldest son had
a double portion of the inheritance.   The Greeks, the Romans, the
Britons, the Saxons, and even originally the feudists, divided the
lands equally; some among all the children at large, some among
the males only.   But when the emperors began to create honorary
feuds, or titles of nobility, it was found necessary, in order to preserve
their dignity, to make them impartible, and in consequence descendible to the eldest son alone; who thus began to succeed to the
whole of the lands in all military tenures: and in this condition the
feudal constitution was established by William the Conqueror.

Socage estates frequently descended to all the sons equally, so
lately as when Glanvil wrote in the reign of Henry II.; and it is
mentioned in the Mirror, as a part of our ancient constitution, that
knights' fees should descend to the eldest son, and socage fees should
be partible among the male children.   In the time of Henry III.,
however, we find by Bracton, that socage lands, in imitation of lands
in chivalry, had almost entirely fallen into the right of succession by
primogeniture, as the law now stands: except in Kent, where they
gloried in the preservation of their ancient gavelkind tenure, of which
a principal branch was the joint inheritance of all the sons; and,
except in some particular manors and townships, where their local

customs continued their descent sometimes to all, sometimes to the youngest son only, or in other more singular methods of succession.

As to the females, they are still left as they were by the ancient law: for they were all equally incapable of performing any personal service; and, therefore, one main reason of preferring the eldest ceasing, such preference would have been injurious to the rest. However, the succession by primogeniture, even among females, took place as to the inheritance of the crown. And the right of sole succession, though not of primogeniture, was also established with respect to female dignities and titles of honour. For, if a man holds an earldom to him and the heirs of his body, and dies, leaving only daughters; the eldest shall not of course be countess, but the dignity is in suspense or abeyance till the crown shall declare its pleasure; for the sovereign being the fountain of honour, may confer it on which of them he pleases.

V. " The lineal descendants, *in infinitum*, of any person deceased " shall represent their ancestor : that is, shall stand in the same place " as the person himself would have done, had he been living."

Thus, the child, grandchild, or great-grandchild, either male or female, of the eldest son, succeeds before the younger son, and so *in infinitum*. And these representatives shall take neither more nor less, but just so much as their principals would have done; which is called succession *per stirpes*, according to the roots.

This mode of representation is a necessary consequence of the double preference given by our law, first to the male issue, and next to the first-born among the males. For, if all the children of three deceased sisters were to claim the grandfather's estate, *per capita*, without any respect to the stocks from whence they sprang, and those children were partly male and partly female; then the eldest male among them would exclude not only his own brethren and sisters, but all the issue of the other two daughters; or else the law in this instance must be inconsistent with itself, and depart from the preference which it constantly gives to the males, and the first-born, among persons in equal degree. Whereas, by dividing the inheritance according to the roots, or *stirpes*, the rule of descent is kept uniform: the issue of the eldest son excludes all others, as the son himself, if living, would have done; but the issue of two daughters divide the inheritance between them, provided their mothers, if living, would have done the same : and among these several issues, or representatives of the respective roots, the same preference to males and the same right of primogeniture obtain, as would have obtained at the first among the roots themselves.

The remaining canons of descent apply to collateral succession; in respect of which the modern differ in two main respects from the ancient rules of inheritance. The first point of difference, and one that has been already touched upon, relates to the lineal succession of parents, and other ancestors; the second to the succession of relatives by the *half*, in default of those related by the *whole* blood to the person last entitled to the inheritance. It will be necessary to preface a few observations on the old rule, which still, as we have seen, affects descents that took place previously to the year 1834,—" that, " on failure of lineal descendants or issue, of the person last seised, " the inheritance shall descend to his collateral relations, being of the " blood of the first purchaser; subject to the three preceding rules."

If, then, Geoffrey Stiles purchased land, and it descended to John Stiles his son, and John died seised thereof without issue; whoever succeeded to this inheritance must have been of the blood of Geoffrey the first purchaser, he who first acquired the estate, whether the same was transferred to him by sale or by gift, or by any other method, except that of descent.

This was a rule peculiar to our laws, and those of a similar origin; for when feuds first began to be hereditary, it was made a necessary qualification of the heir, that he should be of the blood of, that is, lineally descended from, the first feudatory or purchaser. In consequence whereof, if a vassal died seised of a feud of his own acquiring, or *feudum novum*, it could not descend to any but his own offspring; no, not even to his brother, because he was not descended, nor derived his blood, from the first acquirer. But if it was *feudum antiquum*, that is, one descended to the vassal from his ancestors, then his brother, or such other collateral relation as was descended and derived his blood from the first feudatory, might succeed to such inheritance. The true feudal reason for which rule was this: that what was given to a man, for his personal service and personal merit, ought not to descend to any but the heirs of his person.

However, in process of time, when the feudal rigour was in part abated, a method was invented to let in collateral relations of the grantee, by granting him a *feudum novum* to hold *ut feudum antiquum*; that is, with all the qualities annexed of a feud derived from his ancestors; and then the collateral relations were admitted to succeed even *in infinitum*, because they might have been of the blood of, that is descended from, the first imaginary purchaser. And of this nature ultimately came to be regarded by the law all the estates in fee simple in the kingdom.

Yet, when an estate had really descended in a course of inheritance to the person last seised, the strict rule of the feudal law was still observed; and none were admitted but the heirs of those through whom the inheritance had passed. Therefore, if lands came to a man by descent from his mother, no relation of his father, as such, could ever be his heir; and, *vice versâ,* if they descended from his father no relation of his mother, as such, could ever be admitted thereto.

This, then, was one of the general principles upon which the law of collateral inheritances depended; that, upon failure of issue in the last proprietor, the estate should descend to the blood of the first purchaser; or result back to the heirs of the body of that ancestor from whom it either really has, or was supposed to have originally descended. To give full effect to which, another rule provided that " the collateral heir should be his next collateral kinsman, of the " *whole* blood;"—for if there were a much nearer kinsman of the *half* blood, a distant kinsman of the whole blood was admitted, and the other entirely excluded; nay, the estate was allowed to escheat to the lord sooner than the half blood should inherit.

This total exclusion of the half blood from the inheritance, being almost peculiar to our law, was long regarded as a strange hardship. The rule has now been altered, so that any discussion of the feudal principles on which it was founded, would seem to be almost profit-less, unless as matter of legal history, which is not the object of these commentaries.

The only other rule of the old law which has been superseded, was that which gave the preference to the *paternal* over the *maternal* line; where the lands had, in fact, descended from a female. For the relations on the father's side were admitted *in infinitum,* before those on the mother's side were admitted at all; and the relations of the father's father, before those of the father's mother; and so on.

This rule was obviously necessary, in order to carry into execution the principal canon of collateral inheritance, that every heir must be of the blood of the first purchaser. For, when such first purchaser was not to be discovered after several descents, the lawyers not only took the next relation of the whole blood, but also, considering that a preference had throughout been given to males, judged it more likely that the lands should have descended to the last tenant from his male than from his female ancestors; and, therefore, they hunted back the inheritance through the male line, imagining that this was the most probable way of continuing it in the line of the first pur-chaser. This rule, also, has been modified to some extent by the legislature; so that it now remains for me simply to add the modern canons regulating collateral descents, after premising a few words on the leading changes introduced in our law of inheritance.

Firstly, then, we have seen that in every case descent shall now be traced from the *purchaser;* who is to be *the person last entitled* to the land, unless he inherited the same :—the person *last entitled*, including the last person *who had a right thereto*, whether he did or did not obtain the possession or the receipt of the rents and profits thereof. So that the ancient maxim of our law, *seisina facit stipitem*, is entirely annulled.

Secondly, under the old law, there being no lineal ascent, a. brother or sister was considered to have inherited *immediately* from a brother or sister ; and the common ancestor need not have been named. This rule has been set aside; so that every descent from a brother or sister must now be traced through the parent; this being a necessary consequence of one of the most important alterations effected in the ancient law of inheritance, that, namely, which provides that a father or other lineal ancestor may succeed to his son or other lineal descendant.

Thirdly, the rule that in collateral inheritances the male stock shall be preferred to the female, unless where the estate had actually descended in the maternal line, remains intact, although modified in detail.

Lastly, a relation by the half blood stands in the order of inheritance, so as to be entitled to inherit, next after any relation in the same degree of the whole blood, and his issue, when the common ancestor is a male, and next after the common ancestor when the common ancestor is a female; so that the brother of the half blood, on the part of the father, inherits next after the sisters of the whole blood on the part of the father and their issue, and the brother of the half blood on the part of the mother inherits next after the mother.

These rules of the law will, I think, be found expressed in the following canons, viz. :—

VI. " On failure of issue of the purchaser, the inheritance shall " go to his nearest lineal ancestor or the issue of such ancestor, the " ancestor taking in preference to his or her issue." Thus, if the purchaser dies without issue, the father takes before the brothers or sisters of that purchaser ; and a grandfather, not before the father or the father's issue, but before the uncles or aunts or their issue.

VII. " Paternal ancestors and their descendants shall be preferred " to maternal ancestors and their descendants, male paternal ances- " tors and their descendants to female paternal ancestors and their " descendants, and male maternal ancestors and their descendants to " female maternal ancestors and their descendants, and the mother of " a more remote female ancestor on either side and her descendants " to the mother of a less remote female ancestor and her descendants."

Thus the mother of the paternal grandfather, and her issue, shall be referred to the father's mother and her issue.

VIII. " Relations of the half blood shall inherit ; those related *ex " parte paternâ*, taking next in order to the relations male and female " of the same degree of whole blood ; those related *ex parte maternâ*, " taking next in order after their mother."

Finally, it is to be observed that the *general rules* for tracing descents now laid down apply to lands both of freehold and copyhold tenure, and whether descendible according to the common law or according to the custom of gavelkind or Borough-English, or any other custom. But the peculiarities of descent which belong to gavelkind, Borough-English, and other customary tenures, are not interfered with. Thus the rule of gavelkind tenure, by which all the sons take in equal shares, remains unaltered ; but the new canon of descent, which enables a father of the purchaser to inherit in preference to the uncles, holds equally in this species of tenure,—as also the rule admitting kindred of the half blood.

CHAPTER XII.

OF TITLE BY PURCHASE, AND FIRST BY ESCHEAT.

Definition of purchase—Escheat—Distinction between forfeiture and escheat— Corruption of blood.

PURCHASE, *perquisitio,* taken in its largest and most extensive sense, is defined : the possession of lands and tenements, which a man hath by his own act or agreement, and not by descent from any of his ancestors or kindred. In its vulgar and confined acceptation it is applied only to such acquisitions of land as are obtained by way of bargain and sale, for money or some other valuable consideration. But this falls far short of the legal idea of purchase : for, if I *give* land freely to another, he is in the eye of the law a purchaser ; for he comes to the estate by his own agreement, that is, he consents to the gift. And a man who has his father's estate settled upon him in tail, before he was born, is also a purchaser ; for he takes quite another estate than the law of descents would have given him.

But if an estate be made to A for life, remainder to his right heirs in fee, his heirs shall take by descent : for it is an ancient rule of law, that wherever the ancestor takes an estate for life, the heir cannot by the same conveyance take an estate in fee by *purchase,* but only by *descent.*

What we call *purchase, perquisitio,* the feudists called *conquest, conquæstus,* or *conquisitio:* both denoting any means of acquiring an estate out of the common course of inheritance.   Hence the appellation which was given by the Norman jurists to William the Norman, signifying that he was the first of his family who acquired the crown of England, and from whom therefore all future claims by descent must be derived.   This, then, is the legal signification of the word *perquisitio,* or purchase; and in this sense it includes the five following methods of acquiring a title:—1. Escheat.   2. Occupancy.   3. Prescription.   4. Forfeiture.   5. Alienation.

Escheat, we may remember, was one of the fruits and consequences of feudal tenure; being founded upon this single principle, that the blood of the person last seised in fee-simple is, by some means or other, utterly extinct and gone: and, since none can inherit his estate but such as are of his blood and consanguinity, it follows as a regular consequence, that when such blood is extinct, the inheritance itself must fail; the land must become what the feudal writers denominate *feudum apertum,* and must result back again to the lord of the fee, by whom, or by those whose estate he has, it was given.   These escheats are frequently divided into those *propter defectum sanguinis,* and those *propter delictum tenentis:* the one sort, if the tenant dies without heirs; the other, if his blood be attainted.   But both these species may well be comprehended under the first denomination only; for he that is attainted suffers an extinction of his blood, as well as he that dies without relations.

Bastards being the sons of nobody, have no inheritable blood; and therefore, if there be no other claimant than such illegitimate children, the land shall escheat to the lord.   The civil law differs from ours in this point, and allows a bastard to succeed to an inheritance, if after its birth the mother was married to the father.   But our law, in favour of marriage, is much less indulgent to bastards. And as bastards cannot be heirs themselves, so neither can they have any heirs but those of their own bodies.   For, as all collateral kindred consists in being derived from the same common ancestor, and as a bastard has no legal ancestors, he can have no collateral kindred; and, consequently, can have no legal heirs, but such as claim by a lineal descent from himself.   And, therefore, if a bastard purchases land, and dies without issue and intestate, the land shall escheat to the lord of the fee.

Aliens, also, are incapable of taking by descent, or inheriting: for they are not allowed to have any inheritable blood in them; rather indeed upon a principle of national or civil policy, than upon reasons strictly feudal.   Though, if lands had been suffered to fall into their hands who owe no allegiance to the crown of England, the design of introducing our feuds, the defence of the kingdom, would have been defeated. Wherefore, if a man leaves no other relations but aliens, his land shall escheat to the lord. So far then as they cannot inherit, aliens are on a level with bastards; but as they are also disabled to hold by purchase they are under still greater disabilities. And, as they can neither hold by purchase nor by inheritance, it is almost superfluous to say that they can have no heirs, since they can have nothing for an heir to inherit; but so it is expressly held, because they have not in them any inheritable blood.

By attainder for treason or other felony, the blood of the person attainted was formerly held to be so corrupted, as to be rendered no longer inheritable; but this doctrine has been much modified. And here it is requisite to distinguish between *forfeiture* of lands to the crown and *escheat* to the lord. Forfeiture of lands, and of whatever else the offender possessed, was the doctrine of the old Saxon law, as a part of punishment for the offence; and being a prerogative vested in the crown, was neither superseded nor diminished by the introduction of the Norman tenures. The doctrine of escheat upon attainder is something very different; being simply this: that the blood of the tenant, by the commission of any felony, is corrupted, and the original donation of the feud is thereby determined, it being always granted to the vassal on the implied condition of *dum bene se gesserit*. Upon the demonstration of which guilt, by legal attainder, the feudal covenant and mutual bond of fealty are held to be broken, the estate instantly falls back from the offender to the lord of the fee, and the inheritable quality of his blood is extinguished for ever. In this situation the law of feudal escheat was brought into England at the Conquest; and in general superadded to the ancient law of forfeiture. In consequence of which corruption and extinction of hereditary blood, the land of all felons would immediately revest in the lord, but that the superior law of forfeiture intervenes, and intercepts it in its passage: in case of treason for ever; in case of other felony, for only a year and a day; after which time it went to the lord in a regular course of escheat, as it would have done to the heir of the felon in case the feudal tenures had never been introduced. That this is the true operation and genuine history of escheats will most evidently appear from this incident to gavelkind lands, that they are in no case subject to escheat for felony, though they are liable to forfeiture for treason. Forfeiture, too, effects only estates vested in the offender, at the time of his offence or attainder: the law of escheat pursues the matter still further. For, the blood of the tenant being utterly corrupted, it follows, not only that all that he now has shall escheat from him, but also that he shall be incapable of inheriting anything for the future. Formerly, indeed, the channel which conveyed the hereditary blood from his ancestors to him, was not only exhausted for the present, but totally dammed up for the future. So that the person attainted was not only incapable himself of inheriting, or transmitting his own property by heirship, but also obstructed the descent of lands or tenements to his posterity, in all cases where they were obliged to derive their title through him from any remoter ancestor. But the law in this respect has been altered by statute, and the descendants of a person attainted may now trace their descent *through* him after his death.

This corruption of blood, I may add, has been long looked upon as a peculiar hardship: because the oppressive parts of the feudal tenures being abolished, it seems unreasonable to reserve one of their most inequitable consequences; namely, that the children should not only be reduced to present poverty, but also be laid under future difficulties of inheritance, on account of the guilt of their ancestors. And therefore in most, if not all, of the felonies created since the reign of Henry VIII., it is declared, that they shall not extend to any corruption of blood: and no attainder for felony, except in cases of high treason, or murder, or abetting, or counselling the same, now extends to the disinheriting of any heir, nor to the prejudice of the right or title of any person other than that of the offender during his life.

Before I conclude this head of escheat, I must mention one singular instance in which lands held in fee-simple are not liable to escheat to the lord, even when their owner is no more, and has left no heirs to inherit them. And this is the case of a corporation; for if that comes by any accident to be dissolved, the donor or his heirs shall have the land again in reversion, and not the lord by escheat; which is, perhaps, the only instance where a reversion can be expectant on a grant in fee-simple absolute.

CHAPTER XIII.

OF TITLE BY OCCUPANCY.

Special occupancy—Alluvion—Dereliction.

OCCUPANCY is the taking possession of those things, which before belonged to nobody; a right, however, which, as far as it concerns real property, has been confined by the laws of England within a very narrow compass. It extended only to a single instance: namely, where a man was tenant *pur auter vie*, or had an estate granted to himself only, without mentioning his heirs, for the life of another man, and died during the life of *cestuy que vie*, or him by whose life it was holden: in this case, he that could first enter on the land might lawfully retain the possession, so long as *cestuy que vie* lived, by right of occupancy. This seems to have been recurring to first principles, and calling in the law of nature to ascertain the property of the land, when left without a legal owner. For, had the estate *pur auter vie* been granted to a man *and his heirs* during the life of *cestuy que vie*, there the heir might enter and hold possession, being called in law a *special occupant*. But the title of common occupancy is now reduced almost to nothing by two statutes, directing that the estate *pur auter vie* after payment of debts shall go in a course of distribution like a chattel interest. That of *special* occupancy, by the heir-at-law, continues to this day; such heir being held to succeed to the ancestor's estate, not by descent, but as an occupant specially appointed by the original grant. If no special occupant be named, when the estate *pur auter vie* is of a freehold or any other tenure, it shall go to the personal representative of the person that had the estate thereof by virtue of the grant, and be distributed in the same manner as the personal estate of the testator or intestate.

In some cases, where the laws of other nations give a right by occupancy, as in lands newly created, by the rising of an island in the sea or in a river, or by the alluvion or dereliction of the waters; in these instances the law of England assigns them an immediate owner. If an island arise in the *middle* of a *river*, it belongs in common to those who have lands on each side thereof; but if it be nearer to one bank than the other, it belongs only to him who is proprietor of the nearest shore: which is agreeable to, and probably copied from, the civil law. In case a new island rise in the *sea*, though the civil law gives it to the first occupant, yet ours gives it to the crown. And as to lands gained from the sea, either by *alluvion*, by the washing up of sand and earth, so as in time to make *terra firma*; or by *dereliction*, as when the sea shrinks back below the usual water-mark; in these cases the law is held to be, that if this gain be by little and little, by small and imperceptible degrees, it shall go to the owner of the land adjoining. But, if the alluvion or dereliction be sudden and considerable, in this case it belongs to the crown; for, as the sovereign is lord of the sea, and so owner of the soil while it is covered with water, it is but reasonable he should have the soil, when the water has left it dry. This law of alluvions and derelictions, with regard to *rivers*, is nearly the same in the imperial law; from whence indeed those our determinations seem to have been drawn and adopted: but we ourselves, as islanders, have applied them to *marine* increases; and have given our sovereign the prerogative he enjoys, upon the general ground that whatever has no other owner is vested by law in the crown.

CHAPTER XIV.

A THIRD method of acquiring real property by purchase is that by prescription; which means at common law when a man can show no other title to what he claims, than that he and those under whom he claims have immemorially used to enjoy it. This immemorial usage, or usage from time whereof the memory of man runneth not to the contrary, was formerly held to be when such usage had commenced not later than the beginning of the reign of Richard I. But as in most cases it was impossible to bring proof of the existence of any usage at this early date, the courts were wont to presume the fact, upon proof only of its existence for some reasonable time back, as for a period of twenty years or more; unless indeed the person contesting the usage were able to produce proof of its non-existence, at some period subsequent to the beginning of the reign of Richard I., in which case the usage necessarily fell to the ground. The proof even of a shorter continuance than for twenty years was enough to raise the presumption, if other circumstances were brought in corroboration, indicating the existence of an ancient right. But the prescription was defeated by proof that the enjoyment, at any period within legal memory, took place by virtue of a grant or license from the party interested in opposing it, or that it was without his knowledge during the time that it was exercised. To remedy the inconvenience and injustice which sometimes resulted, the legislature interfered, and by the statute 2 & 3 Will. IV. c. 71, usually called the Prescription Act, provided for all the more usual cases where property may be claimed by prescription.

Under this head it is to be observed, then, in the first place, that nothing but incorporeal hereditaments can be claimed by prescription : as a right of way, a common, &c.; for no prescription can give a title to lands, and other corporeal substances, of which more certain evidence may be had. A man cannot be said to prescribe that he and his ancestors have immemorially used to hold the castle of Arundel : for this is clearly another sort of title ; a title by corporeal seisin and inheritance, which is more permanent, and therefore more capable of proof, than that of prescription. But as to a right of way, a common, or the like, a man may be allowed to prescribe; for of these there is no corporeal seisin, the enjoyment will be frequently by intervals, and therefore the right to enjoy them can depend on nothing else but usage.

Secondly, a prescription cannot be for a thing which cannot be raised by grant. For the law allows prescription only to supply the loss of a grant, and therefore every prescription presupposes a grant to have existed. Thus, the lord of a manor cannot prescribe to raise a tax or a toll upon strangers; for as such claim could never have been good by any grant, it shall not be good by prescription.

Thirdly, what is to arise by matter of record cannot be prescribed for, but must be claimed by grant, entered on record; such as, for instance, the royal franchises of felons' goods, and the like. These, not being forfeited till the matter on which they arise is found by the inquisition of a jury, and so made a matter of record, the forfeiture itself cannot be claimed by any inferior title. But the franchises of treasure-trove, waifs, estrays, and the like, may be claimed by prescription; for they arise from private contingencies, and not from any matter of record.

Finally, by the statute I have referred to, no claim by custom, prescription, or grant to any right of common or other profit or benefit, with certain exceptions, shall, when such right shall have been enjoyed for thirty years, be defeated by showing only that such right was first enjoyed at any time prior to such period of thirty years. When the right shall have been enjoyed for sixty years, it is to be deemed indefeasible, unless it appear that it was enjoyed by some consent or agreement expressly made for the purpose by deed in writing. For claims to any way, or other easement, or to any watercourse, or the use of any water, the shorter terms of twenty and forty years are sufficient. And for claims to the use of light, an enjoyment of twenty years constitutes an indefeasible title; unless it appear that the right was enjoyed by agreement expressly made for that purpose by deed in writing.

With regard to claims to moduses in lieu of tithes, and prescriptions *de non decimando*, or total exemption from tithes, the statute 2 & 3 Will. IV. c. 100, has provided that the proof of a modus or exemption during a period of thirty years shall, except in some particular cases, be sufficient; while the proof of its existence for sixty years gives an indefeasible title, unless it be proved that the modus or exemption originated in some agreement expressly made for the purpose by deed or writing.

CHAPTER XV.

OF TITLE BY FORFEITURE.

For crime—By alienation in mortmain—Statutes of mortmain—By alienation
to an alien—By disclaimer—By lapse—By simony—By breach of condition
—By waste—By breach of custom—By bankruptcy.

FORFEITURE is a punishment annexed by law to some illegal act, or
negligence, in the owner of lands, tenements, or hereditaments;
whereby he loses all his interest therein, and they go to the party
injured, as a recompense for the wrong which either he alone, or the
public together with himself, has sustained.

Lands, tenements, and hereditaments may be forfeited in various
degrees and by various means:—1. By crime. 2. By alienation contrary to law. 3. By disclaimer. 4. By non-presentation to a benefice, when the forfeiture is denominated a *lapse*. 5. By simony.
6. By non-performance of conditions. 7. By waste. 8. By breach
of copyhold customs. 9. By bankruptcy.

I. The foundation and justice of forfeitures for *crime* will be more
properly considered in the fourth book of these commentaries.

II. Lands may be forfeited by *alienation*, or conveying them to
another, contrary to law. This is either alienation in *mortmain*, or
alienation to an *alien*; in both of which cases the forfeiture arises
from the incapacity of the alienee to take.

1. Alienation in *mortmain, in mortuâ manu*, is an alienation to
any corporation, sole or aggregate, ecclesiastical or temporal. But
these purchases having been chiefly made by religious houses, in
consequence whereof the lands became perpetually inherent in one
dead hand, this has occasioned the general appellation of mortmain
to be applied to such alienations, and the religious houses themselves
to be principally considered in framing the statutes of mortmain: in
deducing the history of which statutes, it will be curious to observe
the great address of the ecclesiastics in eluding from time to time the
laws in being, and the zeal with which successive parliaments have
pursued them through all their finesses: how new remedies were
still the parents of new evasions: till the legislature at last, though
with difficulty, has obtained a decisive victory.

By the common law any man might dispose of his lands to any

other private man at his own discretion, especially when the feudal restraints on alienation were worn away. Yet, in consequence of these it was always and is still necessary, for corporations to have a license in mortmain from the crown or parliament to enable them to purchase lands; for as the sovereign is the ultimate lord of every fee, he ought not, unless by his own consent, to lose his privilege of escheats and other feudal profits, by the vesting of lands in tenants that can never be attainted or die. It was also requisite, whenever there was a mesne or intermediate lord between the crown and the alienor, to obtain his license also, upon the same feudal principles, for the alienation of the specific land. If no such license was obtained, the sovereign or other lord might respectively enter on the land so aliened in mortmain as a forfeiture; which forfeiture necessarily accrued in the first place to the immediate lord of the fee. When, therefore, a license could not be obtained, the contrivance of the clergy seems to have been this: the tenant who meant to alienate first conveyed his lands to the religious house, and instantly took them back again, to hold as tenant to the monastery; which kind of instantaneous seisin was probably held not to occasion any forfeiture: and then, by pretext of some other forfeiture, surrender, or escheat, the society entered into those lands in right of such their newly-acquired seigniory, as immediate lords of the fee. But, when these dotations began to grow numerous, it was observed that the feudal services were every day visibly withdrawn, and that the lords were curtailed of the fruits of their seigniories; to prevent which, it was ordained by the second of King Henry III.'s great charters, that all such attempts should be void, and the land forfeited to the lord of the fee.

But, as this prohibition extended only to religious *houses*, bishops and other sole corporations were not included therein; and the aggregate ecclesiastical bodies, who, Sir Edward Coke observes, in this were to be commended, that they ever had of their counsel the best learned men that they could get, found many means to creep out of this statute, by buying in lands that were *bonâ fide* holden of themselves as lords of the fee, and thereby evading the forfeiture; or by taking long leases for years, which first introduced those extensive terms, for a thousand or more years, which are now so frequent in conveyances. This produced the statute *de religiosis*, 7 Edw. I., which provided that *no person*, religious or other whatsoever, should buy, or sell, or receive under pretence of a gift, or term of years, or any other title whatsoever, nor should, by any art or ingenuity, appropriate to himself any lands or tenements in mortmain, upon pain that the immediate lord of the fee, or, on his default for one year, the lords paramount, and in default of all of them, the king might enter thereon as a forfeiture.

This seemed to be a sufficient security against all alienations in

mortmain : but as these statutes extended only to gifts and conveyances between the parties, the religious houses now began to set up
a fictitious title to the land, which it was intended they should have,
and to bring an action to recover it against the tenant, who, by fraud
and collusion, made no defence ; and thereby judgment was given
for the religious house, which then *recovered* the land by sentence of
law upon a supposed prior title. And thus they had the honour of
inventing those fictitious adjudications of right, which, until very
recently, remained the great assurances of the kingdom, under the
name of *common recoveries.* But upon this the statute of Westminster the second, 13 Edw. I. c. 32, enacted, that in such cases a
jury shall try the true right of the demandants or plaintiffs to the
land, and if the religious house or corporation be found to have it,
they shall still recover seisin ; otherwise it should be forfeited. And
the like provision was made in case the tenants set up crosses upon
their lands, the badges of knights templars and hospitallers, in order
to protect them from the feudal demands of their lords, by virtue of
the privileges of those religious and military orders.

Yet still it was found difficult to set bounds to ecclesiastical
ingenuity; for when they were driven out of all their former holds,
they devised a new method of conveyance, by which the lands were
granted, not to themselves directly, but to nominal feoffees *to the use
of* the religious houses ; thus distinguishing between the *possession*
and the *use,* and receiving the actual profits, while the seisin of the
lands remained in the nominal feoffee, who was held by the courts of
equity, then under the direction of the clergy, to be bound in conscience to account to this *cestuy que use* for the rents and emoluments
of the estate. And it is to these inventions that we are indebted for
the introduction of uses and trusts, the foundation of modern conveyancing. But, unfortunately for the inventors themselves, they
did not long enjoy the advantage of their new device ; for the statute
15 Ric. II. c. 5, enacted, that the lands which had been so purchased
to uses should be amortised by license from the crown, or else be
sold to private persons, and that, for the future, uses should be subject to the statutes of mortmain, and forfeitable like the lands themselves. And whereas the statutes had been eluded by purchasing
large tracts of land, adjoining to churches, and consecrating them by
the name of churchyards, such subtle imagination is also declared to
be within the compass of the statutes of mortmain. And civil or
lay corporations, as well as ecclesiastical, are also declared to be
within the mischief, and of course within the remedy provided by
those salutary laws. And, lastly, as during the times of popery,
lands were frequently given to superstitious uses, though not to any
corporate bodies, or were made liable in the hands of heirs and
devisees to the charge of obits, chaunteries, and the like, which were

equally pernicious in a well-governed state as actual alienations in mortmain; therefore, at the dawn of the Reformation, the statute 23 Hen. VIII. c. 10, declares, that all future grants of lands for any of the purposes aforesaid, if granted for any longer term than twenty years, shall be void.

During all this time, it was in the power of the crown, by granting a license of mortmain, to remit the forfeiture, so far as related to its own rights, and to enable any corporation to purchase and hold any lands in perpetuity. But, as doubts were conceived at the time of the Revolution how far such license was valid, since the king had no power to dispense with the statutes of mortmain by a clause of *non obstante*, which was the usual course, though it seems to have been unnecessary ; and as, by the gradual declension of mesne seignories through the long operation of the statute of *Quia Emptores*, the rights of intermediate lords were reduced to a very small compass ; it was therefore provided by the statute 7 & 8 Will. III. c. 37, that the crown for the future at its own discretion may grant licenses to alien or take in mortmain of whomsoever the tenements may be holden.

The statute of Henry VIII. did not extend to anything but *superstitious* uses ; and therefore a man might still give lands for the maintenance of a school, an hospital, or any other *charitable* uses. But as it was apprehended that persons on their deathbeds might make improvident dispositions even for these good purposes, and so defeat the political ends of the statutes of mortmain; it is therefore enacted by the statute 9 Geo. II. c. 36, that no lands or tenements, or money to be laid out thereon, shall be given for or charged with any *charitable* uses whatsoever, unless by deed indented, executed in the presence of two witnesses, twelve calendar months before the death of the donor, and enrolled in the Court of Chancery within six months after its execution, except stocks in the public funds, which may be transferred within six months previous to the donor's death, and unless such gift be made to take effect immediately, and be without power of revocation : and that all other gifts shall be void. The two universities, their colleges, and the scholars upon the foundation of the colleges of Eton, Winchester, and Westminster, are excepted out of this act; and other statutes have created a similar exception in favour of other public institutions, as the British Museum, Greenwich Hospital, and the Foundling Hospital.

2. Secondly, alienation *to an alien* is also a cause of forfeiture to the crown of the lands so alienated ; not only on account of his incapacity to hold them, but likewise on account of his presumption in attempting, by an act of his own, to acquire any real property.

III. A forfeiture is also the result of the civil crime of *disclaimer* ;

which occurs where a tenant who holds of any lord neglects to render him the due services, and, upon an action brought to recover them, disclaims to hold of his lord.   Which disclaimer of tenure in any court of record is a forfeiture of the lands to the lord, upon reasons most apparently feudal.   Thus if a tenant sets up a title hostile to his landlord, it is a forfeiture of his term; and it is the same if he colludes with another person to do so. So if a tenant for years attorn or pay rent to a stranger, it is a forfeiture ; and no notice to quit by the real landlord is necessary, but he may treat the tenant as a trespasser and eject him.

IV. Lapse is a species of forfeiture, whereby the right of presentation to a church accrues to the ordinary by neglect of the patron to present, to the metropolitan by neglect of the ordinary, and to the crown by neglect of the metropolitan.   For, it being for the interest of religion, and the good of the public, that the church should be provided with an officiating minister, the law has, therefore, given this right of lapse, in order to quicken the patron, who might otherwise, by suffering the church to remain vacant, avoid paying his ecclesiastical dues, and frustrate the pious intentions of his ancestors.

The term, in which the title to present by lapse accrues from the one to the other successively, is six *calendar* months ; but, if the bishop be both patron and ordinary, he shall not have a double time allowed him to collate in ; for the forfeiture accrues by law whenever the negligence has continued six months in the same person.

When the benefice becomes void by death or cession, the patron is bound to take notice of the vacancy, for these are matters of equal notoriety to the patron and ordinary ; but in case of a vacancy by resignation, or deprivation, or if a clerk presented be refused for insufficiency, these being matters of which the bishop alone is presumed to be cognizant, here the law requires him to give notice thereof to the patron, otherwise he can take no advantage by way of lapse.   And, if the right of presentation be contested, no lapse shall incur till the question of right be decided.

V. By *simony*, the right of presentation to a living is forfeited and vested *pro hâc vice* in the crown.   Simony, so called from the resemblance it is said to bear to the sin of Simon Magus, is the corrupt presentation of any one to an ecclesiastical benefice for money, gift, or reward, and is by the canon law a very grievous crime.   With us, however, the law has established so many exceptions that there is no difficulty whatever in avoiding the forfeiture.

VI. The next kind of forfeiture are those by *breach* or non-performance of a *condition* annexed to the estate, either expressly, by deed, at its original creation, or impliedly, by law, from a principle of natural reason. Both which we considered at large in a former chapter.

VII. I, therefore, now proceed to another species of forfeiture, viz., by *waste*, *vastum*, a spoil or destruction in houses, gardens, trees, or other corporeal hereditaments, to the disherison of him that hath the remainder or reversion in fee-simple or fee-tail. And this waste is either *voluntary*, which is a crime of commission, as by pulling down a house, or it is *permissive*, which is a matter of omission only, as by suffering it to fall for want of necessary reparations. If a house be destroyed by tempest, lightning, or the like, which is the act of Providence, it is no waste; but, otherwise, if the house be burnt by the carelessness or negligence of the lessee; though now by the statute 14 Geo. III. c. 78, s. 86, no action will lie against a tenant for an accident of this kind. Timber is part of the inheritance, and therefore to cut down trees is waste; but underwood the tenant may cut, and he may take sufficient estovers of common right for house-bote and cart-bote. To open the lands to search for mines of metal, coal, &c., is waste, for that is a detriment to the inheritance; but if the pits or mines were open before, it is no waste for the tenant to continue digging them for his own use; for it is now become the mere annual profit of the land. These three, then, are the general heads of waste, viz., in houses, in timber, and in land; and for waste in either of these, whether voluntary or permissive, all tenants merely for life or for any less estate are punishable or liable to be impeached, unless their leases be made, as sometimes they are, without impeachment of waste, *absque impetitione vasti*: that is, with a provision or protection that no man shall *impetere*, or sue him for waste committed. Yet even here the Court of Chancery will interfere, if the tenant attempt to commit *spoil* and *destruction* upon the estate.

VIII. An eighth species of forfeiture is that of *copyhold* estates, by *breach* of the *customs* of the manor. For copyhold estates are not only liable to the same forfeitures as those which are held in socage, for treason, felony, and waste, but also to peculiar forfeitures annexed to this species of tenure; which are incurred by the breach of either the general customs of all copyholds, or the peculiar local customs of certain particular manors. But the enfranchisement of copyholds, which is now compulsory alike on lord and tenant, if either party desire it, will in the course of time do away altogether with this species of forfeiture.

IX. The ninth and last method whereby lands and tenements may become forfeited, is that of *bankruptcy*, the nature of which will be better considered in a subsequent chapter. I shall only here observe, that when any person has been properly adjudged a bank-rupt, all his lands and hereditaments become absolutely vested in the assignees, appointed on behalf of the creditors in the manner directed by law, by virtue of such appointment alone, and without any deed or conveyance. So that in this way a bankrupt loses all his real estates, without his participation or consent.

CHAPTER XVI.

OF TITLE BY ALIENATION.

Feudal restraints or alienation—Attornment—Who may alien, and to whom—
Corporations—Infants—Femes-covertes—Aliens.

THE most usual method of acquiring a title to real estates is that of alienation, or purchase in its limited sense, under which may be comprised any sale, gift, marriage settlement, devise, or other transmission of property.

This mode of taking estates is not of equal antiquity with that of taking them by descent. For, by the feudal law, a feud could not be transferred without the consent of the lord, lest thereby a feeble or suspicious tenant might have been imposed upon him to perform the feudal services. And, as he could not alien it in his lifetime, so neither could he by will defeat the succession, by devising his feud to another family. Nor, in short, could he alien the estate unless he had also obtained the consent of his own next heir. And therefore it was usual in ancient feoffments to express that the alienation was made by consent of the heirs of the feoffor. And, on the other hand, as the feudal obligation was looked upon to be reciprocal, the lord could not transfer his seigniory without the consent of his vassal; for it was esteemed unreasonable to subject a feudatory to a new superior, with whom he might have a deadly enmity, without his own approbation; or even to transfer his fealty, without his being thoroughly apprized of it, that he might know with certainty to whom his renders and services were due. This consent of the vassal was expressed by what was called *attorning*, or professing to become the tenant of the new lord; which doctrine of attornment was afterwards extended to all lessees for life or years.

By degrees this feudal severity wore off; and experience has shown, that property best answers the purposes of civil life when its transfer is totally free and unrestrained. The road was cleared in the first place by a law of Henry I., which allowed a man to sell lands which he himself had purchased. Afterwards, he seems to have been at liberty to part with all his own acquisitions, if he had previously purchased to him and his *assigns* by name. At that time he might

part with one-fourth of inheritance of his ancestors without the consent of his heir; afterwards with a moiety, by the statutes 18 Edw. I.
c. 1, and 15 Edw. III. c. 12; and finally, with the whole. By
statutes 7 Hen. VII. c. 3, and 3 Hen. VIII. c. 4, persons attending
the king in his wars were allowed to alien without license. And
lastly, fines for alienations were abolished by statute 12 Car. II. c. 24.
The power of *charging* lands with debts was introduced by the
statute of Westminster the second, 13 Edw. I. c. 18; and they are
now not only subject to be *pawned* for the debts of the owner, but
likewise to be absolutely *sold*, either for the payment of debts, or for
division among creditors under the statutes of bankruptcy. The
restraint of *devising* lands by will, except in some places by particular
custom, lasted longer, that not being totally removed till the abolition
of the military tenures. The doctrine of *attornments* continued still
later, till at last they were made no longer necessary by the statute
4 & 5 Ann. c. 16.

In examining the nature of alienation then, which is now entirely
free, let us first inquire briefly, *who* may alien, and to *whom;* and
then, more largely, *how* a man may alien, or the several modes of
conveyance.

I. Who may alien, and to whom; or, in other words, who is
capable of conveying and who of purchasing. And herein we must
consider rather the incapacity, than capacity, of the several parties;
for all persons are *primâ facie* capable both of conveying and purchasing, unless the law has laid them under any particular disabilities.

Persons, then, attainted of treason and murder are incapable of
conveying, from the time of the offence committed, provided attainder follows; for such conveyance by them may tend to defeat the
crown of the forfeiture, or the lord of his escheat. But they may
purchase for the benefit of the crown, or the lord of the fee, though
they are disabled to *hold :* the lands so purchased, if after attainder,
being subject to immediate forfeiture; if before, to escheat, as well
as forfeiture, according to the nature of the crime. In other felonies,
no attainder extends to the disinheriting of any heir nor to the prejudice of the right or title of any other person or persons than the
offender during his natural life. So, also, corporations, religious or
others, may purchase lands; yet, unless they have a license to hold
in mortmain, they cannot retain such purchase, but it shall be
forfeited to the lord of the fee. Lay corporations, other than municipal, have, in general, power to alien their lands as freely as
private owners; but municipal corporations are, by the statute
5 & 6 Will. IV. c. 76, s. 94, restrained from alienation for any term
exceeding thirty-one years. Ecclesiastical and eleemosynary corporations, both sole and aggregate, are restrained, except under

certain conditions, from alienation beyond the life of the person constituting the corporation sole, or of him who is the head of the corporation aggregate, except by way of lease for a term not exceeding twenty-one years, or three lives.

Idiots and persons of nonsane memory, infants, and persons under duress, are not totally disabled either to convey or purchase, but *sub modo* only. For their conveyances and purchases are in general voidable, but not always actually void. It has been said, that a *non compos*, though he be afterwards brought to a right mind, shall not be permitted to allege his own insanity in order to avoid his grant; for that no man shall be allowed to stultify himself, or plead his own disability; but it has been held to be clear law that a party may come forward to maintain his own past incapacity. And, clearly, the next heir, or other person interested, may, after the death of the idiot or *non compos*, take advantage of his incapacity and avoid the grant. And so, too, if he purchases under this disability, and does not afterwards, upon recovering his senses, agree to the purchase, his heir may either waive or accept the estate at his option. In like manner, an infant may waive such purchase or conveyance, when he comes to full age; or, if he does not then actually agree to it, his heirs may waive it after him. Persons, also, who purchase or convey under duress may affirm or avoid such transactions, whenever the duress has ceased. For all these are under the protection of the law, which will not suffer them to be imposed upon, through the imbecility of their present condition; so that their acts are only binding, in case they be afterwards agreed to, when such imbecility ceases.

The case of a feme-covert is somewhat different. She may *purchase* an estate without the consent of her husband, and the conveyance is good during the coverture, till he avoids it by some act declaring his dissent. And, though he does nothing to avoid it, or even if he actually consents, the feme-covert herself may, after the death of her husband, waive or disagree to the same: nay, even her heirs may waive it after her, if she dies before her husband, or if in her widowhood she does nothing to express her consent or agreement. But the *conveyance* or other contract of a feme-covert, unless it be a conveyance made under the provisions of the statute 3 & 4 Will. IV. c. 75, is absolutely void, and not merely voidable, and therefore cannot be affirmed or made good by any subsequent agreement. The Court of Chancery, however, has long recognised the power of a feme-covert to deal at her own pleasure with property vested in trustees *for her separate use*, provided the settlement itself does not restrain her from alienation; and equity also recognises her contracts relating to such property.

The case of an alien born is also peculiar. For he may purchase anything; but after purchase he could formerly *hold* nothing except a lease for years of a house for convenience of *merchandise*, in case he were an alien friend: all other purchases, when found by an inquest of office, being immediately forfeited to the crown. But alien friends are now enabled to take and hold lands for *residence* or *business* for twenty-one years; and a person born out of the kingdom whose mother is a natural-born subject, is enabled to take any estate by devise, purchase, inheritance, or succession.

II. We are next, but principally, to inquire, *how* a man may alien or convey, which will lead me to consider the several modes of conveyance. These are of four kinds:—1. By matter *in pais*, or deed, which is an assurance transacted between two or more private persons *in pais*, in the country; that is, according to the old common law, upon the very spot to be transferred. 2. By matter of *record*, or an assurance transacted only in the public courts of record, or under the authority of a public board or commission empowered by act of parliament to record its proceedings. 3. By special *custom*, obtaining in some particular places, and relating only to some particular species of property. Which three are such as take effect during the life of the party conveying or assuring. 4. The fourth takes no effect till after his death; and that is by *devise*, contained in his last will and testament. I shall treat of each in its order, and, for convenience' sake, separately in the succeeding chapters.

CHAPTER XVII.

OF ALIENATION BY DEED.

Nature of deeds—Contracting parties—Consideration—Writing—Contents of deeds—Premises—*Habendum*—*Tenendum* — *Reddendum*—Conditions — Covenants—Conclusion—Sealing and delivery of deeds—Witnesses—How deeds avoided.——*Original Conveyances*, viz.: Feoffment—Gift—Grant—Lease—Exchange—Partition.——*Derivative Deeds*, viz.: Release—Confirmation—Surrender—Assignment—Defeazance.——*Deeds under Statute of Uses:* Covenant to stand seised to uses—Bargain and sale—Lease and release—Bargain and sale at common law.——*Other Deeds:* Bonds—Recognizances—Defeazances.

In treating of deeds I shall consider, first, their general nature; and, next, the several sorts or kinds of deeds, with their respective incidents. And, in explaining the former, I shall examine, first, what a deed is; secondly, its requisites; and thirdly, how it may be avoided.

I. First, then, a deed is a writing sealed and delivered by the parties. It is sometimes called a charter, *carta*, from its materials; but most usually, when applied to the transactions of private subjects, it is called a deed, in Latin *factum*, because it is the most solemn and authentic act that a man can possibly perform, with relation to the disposal of his property; and therefore a man shall always be *estopped* by his own deed, or not permitted to aver or prove anything in contradiction to what he has once so solemnly and deliberately avowed. If a deed be made by more parties than one, there ought to be regularly as many copies of it as there are parties, and each was formerly cut or indented on the top or side, to tally or correspond with the other; which deed, so made, was called an indenture; and this name is still retained, though the practice of indenting has been abandoned. A deed made by one party only, not being indented, but *polled* or shaved quite even, is called a *deed-poll*.

II. We are next to consider the *requisites* of a deed, the *first* of which is, that there be persons able to contract and be contracted with, for the purposes intended by the deed, and also a thing or subject-matter to be contracted for. So, as in every grant there must be a grantor, a grantee, and a thing granted; in every lease a lessor, a lessee, and a thing demised.

Secondly, the deed must be founded upon good and sufficient *consideration*, not upon an illegal contract, nor upon fraud or collusion, to deceive purchasers or creditors, any of which bad considerations will vacate the deed. A deed also, or other grant, made without any consideration, is, as it were, of no effect; for it is construed to enure, or to be effectual, only to the use of the grantor himself. The consideration may be either a *good* or a *valuable* one. A good consideration is such as that of blood, or of natural love and affection, when a man grants an estate to a near relation, being founded on motives of generosity, prudence, and natural duty : a valuable consideration is such as money, marriage, or the like, which the law esteems an equivalent given for the grant, and is therefore founded on motives of justice. Deeds made upon good consideration only, are considered as merely voluntary, and are frequently set aside in favour of creditors and *bonâ fide* purchasers.

Thirdly, the deed must be *written* or *printed*, for it may be in any character or any language; but it must be upon paper or parchment. It must also have the proper stamps imposed on it by the several statutes for the increase of the public revenue, else it cannot be given in evidence. Formerly, many conveyances were made by parol, or word of mouth only, without writing; but this giving a

K

handle to a variety of frauds, the statute 29 Car. II. c. 3, usually called the Statute of Frauds, enacts, that no interest in lands, made by livery of seisin, or by parol only, except leases not exceeding three years from the making, shall be looked upon as of greater force than a lease or estate at will, unless the same be put in writing, and signed by the party granting, or his agent lawfully authorized in writing. And now by statute 8 & 9 Vict. c. 106, all the other deeds ordinarily used in conveying property must be in writing.

Fourthly, the matter written must be *legally* and *orderly* set forth; that is, there should be words sufficient to specify the agreement and bind the parties. It is not absolutely necessary in law to have all the formal parts that are usually drawn out in deeds; it is enough if there be sufficient words to declare clearly and legally the party's meaning. But the usual forms it is prudent not to depart from, without good reason or urgent necessity. These are:—

1. The *premises* used to set forth the number and names of the parties, with their additions or titles; and the recital, if any, of such deeds or matters of fact, as are necessary to explain the transaction, including the consideration upon which the deed is made. And then follows the certainty of the grantor, grantee, and thing granted.

2, 3. Next come the *habendum* and *tenendum.* The office of the *habendum* is to determine what estate or interest is granted by the deed; as, if a grant be "to A and the heirs of his body," here A has an estate-tail. The *tenendum,* "and to hold" is now only kept in by custom. It was formerly used to signify the tenure by which the estate was to be holden; but, all these being now reduced to socage, the tenure is never specified.

4. Next follow the terms of stipulation, if any, upon which the grant is made: the first of which is the *reddendum,* whereby the grantor reserves some new thing to himself out of what he had before granted, as "rendering therefore yearly the sum of ten shil- "lings or a peppercorn, or the like."

5. Another of the terms upon which a grant may be made is a *condition,* which is a clause of contingency, on the happening of which the estate granted may be defeated; as "provided always," that if the mortgagor shall pay the mortgagee 500*l.* upon such a day, the whole estate granted shall determine; and the like.

6. Next follow *covenants,* which are clauses whereby either party may stipulate for the truth of certain facts, or may bind himself to perform, or give, something to the other. Thus, the grantor may covenant that he has a right to convey, or for the grantee's quiet enjoyment, or the like; the grantee may covenant to pay his rent, or keep the premises in repair, &c. If the covenantor covenants for

himself and his *heirs*, it is then a covenant real, and descends upon the heirs, who are bound to perform it, provided they have assets by descent, but not otherwise : if he covenants also for his *executors* and *administrators*, his personal assets, as well as his real, are likewise pledged for the performance of the covenant.

7. Lastly, comes the *conclusion*, which mentions the execution and date of the deed, either expressly or by reference to some day and year before mentioned. Not but a deed is good, although it mention no date; or has a false date; or even if it has an impossible date, as the thirtieth of February; provided the real day of its being dated or given, that is delivered, can be proved. For the date which a deed bears is merely *primâ facie* evidence of the date, the true date being the day on which the deed was delivered by the grantor.

I proceed now to the *fifth* requisite for making a good deed, the *reading* of it. This is necessary, wherever any of the parties desire it ; and, if it be not done on his request, the deed is void as to him.

Sixthly, it is requisite that the party, whose deed it is, should *seal*, and now in most cases, I apprehend should *sign* it also. The use of seals is extremely ancient. We read of it among the Jews and Persians in the earliest records of history. And in the book of Jeremiah there is a very remarkable instance, not only of an attestation by seal, but also of the other usual formalities attending a Jewish purchase. In the civil law also seals were used. But in the times of our Saxon ancestors they were not much known in England. The method of the Saxons was for such as could write to subscribe their names, and, whether they could write or not, to affix the sign of the cross; which custom our illiterate vulgar do, for the most part, to this day keep up. And indeed, this inability to write, and therefore making a cross in its stead, is honestly avowed by Caedwalla, a Saxon king, at the end of one of his charters. In like manner the Normans at their first settlement in France, used the practice of sealing only, and at the Conquest brought over into this kingdom their own fashions.

This neglect of signing, and resting only upon the authenticity of seals, remained very long among us; for it was held in all our books that sealing alone was sufficient to authenticate a deed : and so the common form of attesting deeds—"*sealed* and delivered," continues to this day; notwithstanding the statute 29 Car. II., c. 3, before mentioned, revives the Saxon custom, and expressly directs the signing, in all grants of lands, and many other species of deeds ; in which, therefore, signing seems to be now as necessary as sealing.

A *seventh* requisite to a good deal is that it be *delivered*, which is also expressed in the attestation, "sealed and *delivered*." A deed

K 2

takes effect only from this delivery; for if the date be false or impossible, the delivery ascertains the time of it. A delivery may be either absolute, that is, to the grantee himself, or to a third person, to hold till some conditions be performed on the part of the grantee; in which last case it is not delivered as a *deed*, but as an *escrow*; that is, as a scroll or writing, which is not to take effect as a deed till the conditions be performed; and then it is a deed to all intents and purposes.

The *last* requisite to the validity of a deed is the *attestation*, or execution of it *in the presence of witnesses*: though this is necessary, rather for preserving the evidence, than for constituting the essence of the deed.

III. We are next to consider how a deed may be *avoided*, or rendered of no effect. And from what has been before laid down it will follow, that if a deed wants any of the essential requisites beforementioned, it is a void deed *ab initio*. It may also be avoided by matter *ex post facto*: as, 1. By rasure, interlining, or other alteration in any material part; unless a memorandum be made thereof at the time of the execution and attestation. 2. By breaking off, or defacing the seal, with the intention of avoiding the deed, and that by the party to whom the other is bound, for mere accidental defacement is of no effect. 3. By delivering it up to be cancelled. 4. By the disagreement of such, whose concurrence is necessary, in order for the deed to stand: as, the husband, where a feme-covert is concerned; an infant, or person under duress, when those disabilities are removed, and the like. 5. By the judgment or decree of a court of judicature. This was anciently the province of the court of Star Chamber. It is now the province of the courts both of law and equity, when it appears that the deed was obtained by fraud, force, or other foul practice; or is proved to be an absolute forgery. In any of these cases the deed may be voided, either in part or totally according as the cause of avoidance is more or less extensive.

Having thus explained the general nature of deeds, we are next to consider their several species, together with their respective incidents. And herein I shall only examine the particulars of those which are generally used in the alienation of *real* estates; for it would be tedious to descant upon all the instruments made use of in *personal* concerns, but which fall under our general definition of a deed. The former being principally such as serve to *convey* the property of lands and tenements from man to man, are commonly denominated *conveyances*: which are either conveyances at *common law*, or such as receive their force and efficacy by virtue of the *statute of uses*.

Of conveyances by the common law, some may be called *original*, or *primary* conveyances; which are those by means whereof the estate is created; others are *derivative,* or *secondary;* whereby the estate, originally created, is enlarged, restrained, transferred, or extinguished.

Original conveyances are the following: 1. Feoffment; 2. Gift; 3. Grant; 4. Lease; 5. Exchange; 6. Partition: *Derivative* are, 7. Release; 8. Confirmation; 9. Surrender; 10. Assignment; 11. Defeazance.

1. A feoffment, *feoffamentum,* is a substantive derived from the verb, to enfeoff, *feoffare* or *infeudare,* to give one a feud. Feoffment is therefore *donatio feudi;* and is the most ancient method of conveyance. It may be defined the gift of any corporeal hereditament to another he that so gives, being called the *feoffor;* and the person enfeoffed the *feoffee.*

This is plainly derived from, or is indeed itself the very mode of the ancient feudal donation. If, therefore, one grants by feoffment lands to another, and limits or expresses no estate, the grantee has barely an estate for life; unless the feoffor, by express provision in the creation of the estate, has given it a longer continuance as to the heirs or heir of the body of the feoffee.

But by the mere words of the deed the feoffment is by no means perfected; there remains a very material ceremony to be performed, without which the feoffee has at common law but a mere estate at will, called *livery of seisin,* this being no other than the pure feudal investiture which was held absolutely necessary to complete the donation.

Among the ancient Goths and Swedes, contracts for the sale of lands were made in the presence of witnesses, who extended the cloak of the buyer while the seller cast a clod of the land into it, in order to give possession; and a staff or wand was also delivered from the vendor to the vendee, which passed through the hands of the witnesses. With our Saxon ancestors the delivery of a turf was a necessary solemnity, to establish the conveyance of lands. And, to this day, the conveyance of our copyhold estates is usually made from the seller to the lord or his steward by delivery of a rod or verge, and then from the lord to the purchaser by re-delivery of the same, in the presence of a jury of tenants.

For many years, however, feoffments have been little used in practice. This kind of conveyance had the effect of passing a fee, i. purporting to do so, even though the feoffor had a less estate. It was sometimes used because it also destroyed contingent remainders and powers appendant; but there was this risk, that it might create a forfeiture of the grantor's estate. Hence it was called a *tortious conveyance,* while other assurances, such as bargain and sale, lease and release, were styled innocent conveyances, having no operation beyond passing such estate as the grantor had to convey. The statute 8 & 9 Vic., c. 106, however, abolished the tortious operation of feoffments ; and enacting, at the same time, that corporeal hereditaments should lie *in grant* as well as *in livery*, practically did away with livery of seisin ; and removed altogether the grounds upon which feoffments were occasionally resorted to.

2. The conveyance by *gift, donatio*, is properly applied to the creation of an estate-tail, and differs in nothing from a feoffment but in the nature of the estate passing by it.

3. Grants, *concessiones*, are the regular method by the common law of transferring the property of *incorporeal* hereditaments, or such things whereof no livery can be had. For such reasons all corporeal hereditaments, as lands and houses, were said to lie *in livery ;* and the others, as advowsons, commons, rents, reversions, &c., to lie *in grant.* These, therefore, pass merely by the delivery of the deed. And now that the immediate freehold lies *in grant,* and that a feoffment has no tortious operation, there is practically no difference whatever between these two kinds of conveyance.*

4. A lease is a conveyance of lands or tenements, usually in consideration of rent, for life, for years, or at will, but always for a *less* time than the lessor has in the premises ; for if it be for the *whole* interest, it is more properly an assignment than a lease.

Whatever restriction, by the severity of the feudal law, might in times of very high antiquity be observed with regard to leases, yet by the common law, as it has stood for many centuries, all persons seised of any estate might let leases to endure so long as their own interest lasted, but no longer. Therefore tenant in fee-simple might let leases of any duration, for he has the whole interest ; but tenant in tail, or for life, could make no leases which should bind the issue in tail or reversioner ; nor could a husband seised *jure uxoris*, make a valid lease for any longer term than the joint lives of himself and his wife, for then his interest expired. Yet some tenants for life might make leases of equal duration with those granted by tenants in fee-simple, such as parsons and vicars with consent of the patron and ordinary. So bishops and deans, and such other sole ecclesiastical corporations, might, with the concurrence and confirmation of such persons as the law requires, have granted their lands without any limitation or control. And corporations

---

* It may be mentioned here, that by the statutory *grant*, executed in the office of land registry, or endorsed on the registrar's certificate of title, and entered afterwards on the register, all the estate and interest of the grantor, whatever its nature, passes to the grantee.

aggregate might have made what estates they pleased, without the confirmation of any other person whatsoever. Whereas now, by several statutes, this power is restrained; and, where in the other cases the restraint by the common law seemed too hard, it is in some measure removed. The former statutes are called *restraining*, the latter *enabling* statutes; but into any detail of their provisions it is not my purpose to enter. The enabling statutes specify the conditions on which leases granted by tenants in tail or for life, or tenants by the courtesy or on dower, or persons seized in right of their churches, may grant leases, valid as against their successors. The *disabling* or *restraining* statutes were passed to prevent bishops, deans, and chapters, colleges, and other ecclesiastical or eleemosynary corporations, and all parsons and vicars, from making improvident leases; which they were always ready to do, in consideration of a fine or premium paid to themselves, the interests of their successors being entirely disregarded. But to ascertain in what manner and to what extent the persons I allude to are restrained, I must refer the student to the statutes themselves.

5. An *exchange* is a mutual grant of *equal* interests, the one in consideration of the other. The word "exchange" is so requisite and appropriated by law to this case, that it cannot be supplied by any other word or expressed by any circumlocution. Entry must be made on both sides; for, if either party die before entry, the exchange is void. And if either party be evicted of those lands which were taken by him in exchange, through defect of the other's title, he shall return back to the possession of his own, by virtue of the implied warranty contained in all exchanges. The inconveniences thus attending this kind of exchange have led to its entire disuse; mutual conveyances of the properties being in ordinary cases resorted to.

A better method is provided by the statute 8 & 9 Vict., c. 118, which enables the inclosure commissioners to effect exchanges on the application of the persons interested therein; the great advantage of which is, that the order of the commissioners cannot be impeached by reason of any infirmity of estate in the persons on whose application it shall be made; and that the property on each side taken in exchange, remains and enures to the same uses, trusts, intents, and purposes, and is subject to the same charges as that given in exchange.

6. A partition, is when two or more joint tenants, coparceners, or tenants in common, agree to divide the lands so held among them in severalty, each taking a distinct part. This, too, can best be effected under the authority of the inclosure commissioners.

These are the several species of *primary* or *original* conveyances. Those which remain are of the *secondary* or *derivative* sort.

7. Releases; which are a discharge or conveyance of a man's right in lands or tenements, to another that has some former estate in the lands. And these may enure either, 1. By way of *enlarging an estate*, or *enlarger l'estate:* as, if there be tenant for life, remainder to another in fee, and he in remainder releases all his right to the particular tenant and his heirs, this gives him the estate in fee. 2. By way of *passing an estate*, or *mitter l'estate:* as when one of two coparceners releases all her right to the other, this passes the fee-simple of the whole. 3. By way of *passing an estate*, or *mitter l'estate:* as if a man be disseised, and releases to his disseisor all his right; hereby the disseisor acquires a new right, which renders that lawful which before was tortious. 4. By way of *extinguishment:* as if my tenant for life makes a lease to A for life remainder to B and his heirs, and I release to A; this extinguishes my right to the reversion, and shall enure to the advantage of B's remainder as well as of A's particular estate.

8. A confirmation is nearly allied to a release, being a conveyance of an estate or right *in esse* whereby a voidable estate is made unavoidable; as if tenant for life leases for forty years, and dies during that term, here the lease for years is voidable by him in reversion; yet, if he has confirmed the estate of the lessee for years, before the death of tenant for life, it is no longer voidable but sure and unavoidable.

9. A surrender, *sursumredditio*, or rendering up, is of a nature directly opposite to a release; for, as that operates by the greater estate's descending upon the less, a surrender is the falling of a less estate into a greater. There may also be surrender *in law* by the acceptance by the tenant of a new estate inconsistent with his prior estate. Thus a new lease made to a person in possession under an old lease, and accepted by him, operates as a surrender in law of the old one; for from such acceptance the law implies his intention to yield up the estate which he had before, though he may not by express words of surrender have declared as much.

10. An *assignment* is properly a transfer, or making over to another, of the right one has in *any* estate; but it is usually applied to an estate for life or years. And it differs from a lease only in this: that by a lease one grants an interest less than his own, reserving to himself a reversion; in assignments he parts with the whole property, and the assignee stands for most purposes in the place of the assignor. The assignee is, however, not bound by all the covenants of the assignor, the general rule being that he is bound by all covenants which *run with the land*, but not by collateral covenants which do not run with the land. Covenants for quiet enjoyment, to

pay rent and taxes, to repair and leave repaired, to cultivate the lands in a particular manner, not to carry on certain trades, have all been held to be covenants running with the land.

An assignment does not discharge the original lessee or his representatives from the covenant for payment of rent, or any other, but he still remains liable to the lessor: and this, although the latter may have recognised the assignee as his tenant. The assignee, again, is only liable on the covenants so long as his ownership lasts; and if he re-assigns to another he is completely discharged, although the assignee be a pauper, and utterly unable to perform the covenants.

But if, instead of assigning, the lessee make an under-lease out of his interest, the under-lessee is not liable to the original lessee for rent or covenants, as an assignee of the whole term would have been. He cannot, however, take irrespective of the covenants in the original lease, which run with the land; for a person contracting for an under-lease is bound to inform himself of what the covenants in the original lease are, otherwise if he enter and take possession he will be bound by them.

11. A defeazance is a collateral deed, made at the same time with a feoffment or other conveyance, containing certain conditions, upon the performance of which the estate then created may be defeated or totally undone. In this manner mortgages were, in former times, usually made; the mortgagor enfeoffing the mortgagee, and he, at the same time, executing a deed of defeazance, whereby the feoffment was rendered void on repayment of the money borrowed, at a certain day; but this method of mortgaging has long been out of use.

There yet remain to be spoken of some few conveyances which have their force and operation by virtue of the *statute of uses.*

Uses and *trusts* are, in their origin, of a nature very similar, or rather exactly the same: being a confidence reposed in a another who was tenant of the land, or *terre-tenant,* that he should dispose of the land according to the intentions of *cestui que use,* or him to whose use it was granted, and suffer him to take the profits. As, if a feoffment was made to A. and his heirs, to the use of, or in trust for, B. and his heirs; here, at the common law, A. the *terre-tenant* had the legal property and possession of the land, but B. the *cestui que use* was, in conscience and equity, to have the profits and disposal of it.

This notion was transplanted into England from the civil law, about the close of the reign of Edward III., by means of the foreign ecclesiastics; who introduced it to evade the statutes of mortmain, by obtaining grants of lands, not to their religious houses directly, but to *the use of* the religious houses: which the clerical chancellors of those times held to be binding in conscience; and, therefore, compelled the execution of such trusts in the court of chancery. And, as it was most easy to obtain such grants from dying persons, a maxim was established, that though by law the lands themselves were not devisable, yet, if a testator had enfeoffed another to his own use, and so was possessed of the use only, such use was devisable by will. But we have seen how this evasion was crushed in its infancy with respect to religious houses.

Yet, the idea being once introduced, however fraudulently, it afterwards continued to be applied to a number of civil purposes; particularly as it removed the restraint on alienations by will, and permitted the owner of lands to make various designations of their profits, as prudence, or justice, or family convenience, might require. Till, at length, during our wars in France, and the commotions between the houses of York and Lancaster, uses grew almost universal; through the desire that men had of securing their estates from forfeitures; when each of the contending parties, as they became uppermost, alternately attainted the other. Wherefore, about the reign of Edward IV. the courts of equity began to reduce them to something of a regular system.

Originally, the chancery would give no relief but against the very person himself intrusted for *cestui que use*, and not against his heir or alienee. This was altered in the reign of Henry VI., with respect to the heir; and afterwards the same rule, by a parity of reason, was extended to such alienees, as had purchased without consideration, or with express notice. A purchaser for value without notice might hold the land discharged of any trust. And, if the feoffee to uses died without heir, or committed a forfeiture or married, neither the lord who entered for his escheat or forfeiture, nor the husband who retained the possession as tenant by the courtesy, nor the wife to whom dower was assigned, were liable to perform the use: because they were not parties to the trust, but came in by act of law; though doubtless their title in reason was no better than that of the heir.

On the other hand, the use itself, or interest of *cestui que use*, was learnedly refined upon with many elaborate distinctions. And, 1. It was held that nothing could be granted to a use, whereof the use is inseparable from the possession: as ways or commons, or whereof the seisin could not be instantly given. 2. A use could not be raised without a sufficient consideration. For where a man makes a feoffment to another without consideration, equity presumes that he meant it to the use of himself, unless he expressly declares it to be to the use of another, and then nothing shall be presumed contrary to his own expressions. 3. Uses were descendible according to the rules of the common law, in the case of inheritances in possession; for in this and many other respects *equitas sequitur legem*. 4. Uses might be assigned by secret deeds between the parties, or be devised by last will and testament: for, as the legal estate in the soil was not transferred by these transactions, no livery of seisin was necessary. 5. Uses did not escheat for felony or other defect of blood; for escheats, &c., are the consequences of *tenure*, and uses are *held* of nobody; but the land itself was liable to escheat, and the lord might hold it discharged of the use. 6. No wife could be endowed, or husband have his courtesy, of a use: for no trust was declared for their benefit, at the original grant of the estate. And therefore it became customary, when estates were put in use, to settle before marriage some joint estate to the use of the husband and wife for their lives, which was the origin of modern jointures. 7. A use could not be extended by writ of *elegit*, or other legal process, for the debts of *cestui que use*. For, being merely a creature of equity, the common law, which looked no further than to the person actually seised of the land, could award no process against it.

It is impracticable, upon our present plan, to pursue the doctrine of uses through all those refinements and niceties which gave rise to Lord Bacon's complaint, that this course of proceeding " was turned " to deceive many of their just and reasonable rights. A man that " had cause to sue for land, knew not against whom to bring his " action, or who was the owner of it. The wife was defrauded of " her dower; the husband of his courtesy; the lord of his wardship, " relief, heriot, and escheat; the creditor of his extent for debt; and the poor tenant of his lease." To remedy these inconveniences abundance of statutes were provided, which made the lands liable to be extended by the creditors of *cestui que use*; allowed actions for the freehold to be brought against him, if in the actual pernancy or enjoyment of the profits; made him liable to actions of waste; established his conveyances and leases made without the concurrence of his feoffees; and gave the lord the wardship of his heir, with certain other feudal perquisites.

These provisions all tended to consider *cestui que use* as the real owner of the estate; and at length that idea was carried into full effect by the statute 27 Hen. VIII. c. 10, which is usually called the *Statute of Uses*, or, in conveyances and pleadings, the statute *for transferring uses into possession*. It enacts, that "when any person " shall be *seised* of lands, &c., to the use, confidence, or trust, of any " other person or body politic, the person or corporation entitled to " the use, shall from thenceforth stand and be seised or possessed of " the land, &c., of and in the like estates as they have in the use; " and that the estate of the person so seised to uses shall be deemed " to be in him or them that have the use." The statute thus *executes* the use, as our lawyers term it; that is, it conveys the possession to the use, and transfers the use into possession; thereby making *cestui que use* complete owner of the lands and tenements, as well at law as in equity.

The statute having thus not abolished the conveyance to uses, but only annihilated the intervening estate of the feoffee, and turned the interest of *cestui que use* into a *legal* instead of an *equitable* ownership, the courts of common law had to take cognizance of uses. And, considering them now as merely a mode of conveyance, many of the rules established in equity were adopted with improvements by the judges of the common law. The same persons only were held capable of being seised to a use, the same considerations were necessary for raising it, and it could only be raised of the same hereditaments as formerly. But as the statute, the instant it was raised, converted it into an actual possession of the land, a great number of the incidents, that formerly attended it in its fiduciary state, were now at an end. The land could not escheat or be forfeited by the act or defect of the feoffee, nor be aliened to any purchaser discharged of the use, nor be liable to dower or courtesy, on account of the seisin of such feoffee; because the legal estate never rests in him for a moment, but is instantaneously transferred to *cestui que use* as soon as the use is declared. And, as the use and the land were now convertible terms, they became liable to dower, courtesy, and escheat, in consequence of the seisin of *cestui que use*, who was now become the *terre-tenant* also; and they likewise were no longer devisable by will.

The various necessities of mankind induced also the judges very soon to depart from the rigour and simplicity of the rules of the common law, and to allow a more minute and complex construction upon conveyances to uses, than upon others. Hence, the recognition of *contingent* or *springing uses, shifting uses, resulting uses,* and other details necessary to be known of the conveyancer, but which would only confuse the reader.

The first effect of this equitable train of decision in the courts of law was that the power of the court of chancery over landed property became greatly diminished. But one or two unfortunate scruples, which the judges found it impossible to get over, restored it with tenfold increase. They held, in the first place, that "no use could be limited on a use;" and, therefore, on a feoffment to A and his heirs to the use of B and his heirs, *in trust for C and his heirs,* they held that the statute executed only the first use, and that the second was a mere nullity: not adverting that the instant the first use was executed in B, he became seised to the use of C, which second use the statute might as well be permitted to execute as it did the first; and so the legal estate might be instantaneously transmitted down through a hundred uses upon uses, till finally executed in the last *cestui que use*. Again, as the statute mentions only such persons as were *seised* to the use of others, this was held not to extend to term of years or other chattel interests, whereof the termor is not *seised*, but only *possessed*; and, therefore, if a term of one thousand years be limited to A, to the use of B, the statute does not execute this use, but leaves it as at common law. And lastly, where lands are given to one and his heirs, in trust to receive and pay over the profits to another, this use is not executed by the statute; for the land must remain in the trustee to enable him to perform the trust.

Of the two more ancient distinctions the courts of equity quickly availed themselves. In the first case, it was evident that B was never intended by the parties to have any beneficial interest: and, in the second, the *cestui que use* of the term was expressly driven into the court of chancery to seek his remedy: and therefore that court determined, that though these were not *uses* which the statute could execute, yet still they were *trusts* in equity, which in conscience ought to be performed. To this the reason of mankind assented, and the doctrine of uses was revived, under the denomination of *trusts*; and thus, by this strict construction of the courts of law, a statute made upon great deliberation, and introduced in the most solemn manner, has had little other effect than to add a few words to a conveyance.

However, the courts of equity, in the exercise of this new jurisdiction, have wisely avoided in a great degree those mischiefs which made uses intolerable. They consider a *trust-estate* as equivalent to the legal ownership, governed by the same rules of property, and liable to every charge in equity, which the other is subject to in law: and, by a long series of uniform determinations, for now more than two centuries, with some assistance from the legislature, they have raised a new system of rational jurisprudence, by which trusts are made to answer in general all the beneficial ends of uses, without their inconvenience or frauds. The trust will descend, may be aliened, is liable to debts, to executions, to forfeiture, to leases and other incumbrances, nay, even to the courtesy of the husband, as if it was an estate at law.

The only service, therefore, to which the statute of uses is now consigned, is in giving efficacy to the various kinds of deeds which have supplanted those recognised by the common law, viz. :

12. The conveyance, called a *covenant to stand seised to uses*: by which a man seised of lands, covenants that he will stand seised of the same to the use of his child, wife, or kinsman; for life, in tail, or in fee. Here, the statute executes at once the estate; for the party intended to be benefited, having thus acquired the use, is thereby put at once into corporal possession of the land, without ever seeing

it, by a kind of parliamentary magic. But this conveyance can only operate, when made upon such weighty and interesting considerations as those of blood or marriage, and it is now very seldom used.

13. The conveyance called a *bargain and sale* of lands, whereby the bargainor bargains and sells the land to the bargainee, and becomes by such a bargain seised to the use of the bargainee; and then the statute of uses completes the purchase, or, as it has been well expressed, the bargain first vests the use, and then the statute vests the possession. It was foreseen that conveyances thus made would want all those benefits of notoriety which the old common law assurances were calculated to give; and in order therefore to prevent clandestine conveyances of freeholds, it was enacted by statute 27 Hen. VIII. c. 16, that such bargains and sales should not enure to pass a freehold, unless the same be made by indenture, and *enrolled* within six months in one of the courts of Westminster-hall or with the *custos rotulorum* of the county. Clandestine bargains and sales of chattel interests, or leases for years were then thought not worth regarding; on which ground, indeed, they were overlooked in framing the statute of uses, and therefore such bargains and sales are not directed to be enrolled. But how impossible it is to foresee and provide against *all* the consequences of innovations! This omission gave rise to

  14. The conveyance by *lease and release*, first invented by Serjeant Moore soon after the statute of uses, and until recently the most common of any. It was thus contrived : a lease, or rather bargain and sale, upon some pecuniary consideration, for one year, was made by the tenant of the freehold to the lessee or bargainee. Now, this, without any enrolment, made the bargainor stand seised to the use of the bargainee, and vested in the bargainee the *use* of the term for a year, and then the statute immediately annexed the *possession*. He therefore, being thus in possession, was capable of receiving a lease of the freehold and reversion, which, by law, must be made to a tenant in possession, and, accordingly, the next day, a release was granted to him. This was held to supply the place of livery of seisin, and so a conveyance by lease and release was said to amount to a feoffment. The lease for a year, on which the whole title was founded, and which was a mere form, was made unnecessary by the statute 4 & 5 Vict. c. 21 ; and a release only was thus required. But this statutory release has been in its turn superseded by the statute, which permits freeholds to be transferred without livery of seisin ; and thus, although a deed, by which a freehold estate is conveyed, may be, and still is usually, denominated a release, it is really a grant ; and might, therefore, with perfect propriety be classed under the third species of original assurances, and not among those derivative conveyances which operate under the statute of uses.

15. Deeds of *appointment or of revocation and new appointment of uses*, one of the many methods in which the doctrine of uses has been utilized for practical purposes, are founded on a power, reserved at the raising of the uses, to revoke such as were then declared; and, having assumed a great importance in modern conveyancing, require a passing notice here. It is often usual, in marriage settlements, for instance, to declare the uses, after those given to the husband and wife, to be for the children of the marriage, in such proportions and for such estates as the husband and wife, or the survivor, shall appoint; and to confer power on the husband and wife, or survivor, to revoke any appointment that may be so made. This power, thus given, is carried into effect by a deed of appointment, which itself *conveys* no estate, but merely designates the person to take the use. Thus, if land were conveyed to A, the feoffee to uses, and his heirs, to such uses as B, the purchaser, should appoint, and in default of appointment, to B in fee, here B, if he wished to sell, might, by exercising the power of appointment, exclude his wife's dower, which would have attached at once had the estate been limited to the use of him and his heirs. For the purchaser C came in under the original conveyance, and took, upon the appointment of B, the use to which A, the feoffee or releasee to uses stood seised; and which the statute executed in C, to the exclusion altogether of B, whose estate in fee, being in default only of appointment by him, never came into existence.

16. Another kind of assurance is that founded upon a power given by a will or by an act of parliament, on which, although the words of conveyance are usually " bargain and sell," the estate passes by force of the will or act of parliament, the person who executes the power, merely nominating the party to take the estate. It is therefore not strictly a conveyance, though it has the operation of vesting an estate in the appointee. This species of conveyance is termed a *bargain and sale at common law*, to distinguish it from a bargain and sale operating under the statute of uses.

17. There is another and rather anomalous class of deeds, operating as conveyances, which cannot be said to fall under any of the preceding heads, those instruments, namely, which owe their entire efficacy to the express provisions of some act of parliament. Thus, the promoters of any undertaking, who have contracted for the purchase of lands in conformity with the Lands Clauses Consolidation Act, 1845, and cannot afterwards obtain a conveyance, are enabled, after depositing the purchase-money in the Bank of England, to execute a deed-poll, containing a recital of the transaction, in effect to convey the land for themselves, upon the execution of which the estate of the party with whom the agreement was made becomes vested absolutely in the promoters of the undertaking.

Before we conclude, it will not be improper to subjoin a few remarks upon such deeds as are used not to *convey*, but to *charge* or incumber, lands, and to *discharge* them again: of which nature are, *obligations* or bonds, *recognizances*, and *defeazances* upon them both.

1. An *obligation* or bond is a deed whereby the obligor obliges himself, his heirs, executors, and administrators, to pay a certain sum of money to another at a day appointed. If this be all, the bond is called a single one, *simplex obligatio :* but there is generally a condition added, that, if the obligor does some particular act, the obligation shall be void, or else shall remain in full force: for instance, repayment of a principal sum of money borrowed of the obligee, with interest. In case this condition is not performed, the bond becomes forfeited, or absolute, at law, and charges the obligor, while living; and after his death the obligation descends upon his heir, who, on defect of personal assets, is bound to discharge it, provided he has real assets by descent as a recompense. So that it may be called, though not a *direct*, yet a *collateral*, charge upon the lands.

2. A *recognizance* is an obligation *of record*, which a man enters into before some court of record or magistrate duly authorised, with condition to do some particular act; as, to keep the peace, to pay a debt, or the like. It is in most respects like any other bond, the form of it being, "that A B doth acknowledge to owe to our lady " the queen, to the plaintiff, to C D, or the like, the sum of ten " pounds," with condition to be void on performance of the thing stipulated. This is witnessed only by the record of the court, and not by the party's seal: so that it is not in strict propriety a deed, though the effects of it are greater than a common obligation, being allowed a priority in point of payment, and binding the lands of the cognizor, from the time of enrolment on record.

Of a nature somewhat similar to a recognizance, is a judgment of one of the superior courts, which operates as a charge upon all the property of the person against whom the judgment is entered up. The mode most usually resorted to in practice, of giving a creditor a lien upon his debtor's real property, is, where an action has been commenced, by giving a *cognovit actionem* or confession of the plaintiff's right of action, or by giving a warrant of attorney to confess a judgment, which, when entered up, in pursuance either of the cognovit or warrant of attorney, becomes a charge upon the lands of the debtor. It is of no avail, however, against *bona fide* purchasers or mortgagees of the lands, or creditors having a charge thereon, unless a memorandum be registered in the office of the Common Pleas; process of execution issued thereon, and similarly registered, *before* the date of the conveyance, mortgage, or charge; and the writ put in force within three months after its registration; and the registration of the judgment itself only holds good for five years, when it must be re-registered, in order to be binding. But as between the debtor and his creditor, to whom he executes the warrant, it is a valid charge, binding the debtor's lands, and comes properly under the head of matter *in pais*, by which estates may be affected.

3. A defeazance, on a bond, or recognizance, or judgment recovered, is a condition, which, when performed, defeats or undoes it, in the same manner as a defeazance of an estate before mentioned.

These are the principal species of deeds or matter *in pais*, by which estates may be either conveyed or at least affected. As regards conveyances, there is certainly one palpable defect, the want of sufficient notoriety; so that purchasers or creditors cannot know with any absolute certainty, what the estate and the title to it in reality are, upon which they are to lay out or to lend their money. It has often, and especially of late years, been proposed to establish a general registry of deeds affecting real property; but opinions on this most important subject are much divided, and no attempt to carry any legislative measure having this object in view has yet succeeded. A land registry, as it is called, has no doubt been established; but its operations are confined to recording the state of the title and registering the future transmission only of such property as the owners choose to enter in its books.

CHAPTER XVIII.

OF ALIENATION BY MATTER OF RECORD.

Private acts of parliament—Letters patent—Fines—Common recoveries—Disentailing deeds—Vesting orders of Court of Chancery—Land registry.

ASSURANCES by *matter of record* are such as do not entirely depend on the act or consent of the parties themselves: but the sanction of a court of record is called in to preserve, and be a perpetual testimony of the transfer of the property. Of this nature are, 1. Private acts of parliament; and 2, Grants by the crown. To this class belonged those now abolished modes of assurance,—3. Fines;—4. Common recoveries; and to the same class must now be referred,—5. Vesting orders of the court of chancery; orders of the court of bankruptcy, deeds executed and awards made by public boards under the authority of acts of parliament, and conveyances of property recorded in the land registry.

I. Private *acts of parliament* have of late years become a very common mode of assurance. For it may sometimes happen, that, by the ingenuity of some, and the blunders of other practitioners, an estate is so grievously entangled, that it is out of the power of any of the courts of law or equity to relieve the owner. Or it may sometimes happen, that, by the strictness or omissions of family settlements, the tenant of the estate is abridged of some reasonable power, which cannot be given him by the courts. In these or other cases of the like kind, the transcendent power of parliament is called in, to cut the Gordian knot; and by a particular law, enacted for this very purpose, to unfetter an estate; to give its tenant reasonable powers; or to assure it to a purchaser, against the remote or latent claims of infants or disabled persons, by settling a proper equivalent in proportion to the interest so barred.

II. The *sovereign's grants* are also matter of public record. For, no freehold may be given to the king, nor derived from him, but by matter of record. And to this end a variety of offices are erected, communicating in a regular subordination one with another, through which all the grants of the crown must pass, and be transcribed and enrolled; that the same may be narrowly inspected by the officers of the crown, who will inform the sovereign if anything contained therein is improper or unlawful to be granted. These grants are contained in charters, or letters *patent*, that is, open letters, *literæ patentes*: so called because they are not sealed up, but exposed to open view, with the great seal pendant at the bottom; and are usually directed or addressed by the sovereign to all his subjects at large. And therein they differ from certain other letters of the sovereign, sealed also with the great seal, but directed to particular persons, and for particular purposes; which, therefore, not being proper for public inspection, are closed up and sealed on the outside, and are thereupon called writs *close*, *literæ clausæ*, and are recorded in the *close-rolls*, in the same manner as the others are in the *patent-rolls*.

III. A fine, which was till quite recently a very usual method of transferring an estate of freehold, was neither more nor less than an amicable agreement of a suit, actual or fictitious, by leave of the king or his justices; whereby the lands which were the subject of the action became, or were acknowledged to be, the right of one of the parties. In its origin it was founded on an actual suit, commenced at law for recovery of the possession of land or other hereditaments; and the possession thus gained by such composition was found to be so sure and effectual, that fictitious actions were introduced for the sake of obtaining the same security.

A fine was so called because it put an *end*, not only to the suit thus commenced, but also to all other suits and controversies concerning the same matter. The party to whom the land was to be conveyed or assured, commenced an action at law against the other, the foundation of which was a supposed agreement that the one should convey the lands to the other; on the breach of which agreement the action was brought. On this there was a *primer fine*, or fee due to the crown. The suit being thus commenced, then followed the *licentia concordandi*, or leave to agree the suit. For, as soon as the action was brought, the defendant, knowing himself to be in the wrong, was supposed to make overtures of peace and accommodation to the plaintiff. Who, accepting them, but having, upon suing out the writ, given pledges to prosecute his suit, which he endangered if he now deserted it without license, he therefore applied to the court for leave to make the matter up. This leave was readily granted, but for it there was also another fine due to the king, called the *king's silver*, or sometimes the *post fine*, with respect to the *primer fine* before mentioned.

Next came the *concord*, or agreement itself, after leave obtained from the court; which was usually an acknowledgment from the defendants that the lands in question were the right of the plaintiff. And from this acknowledgment, or recognition of right, the party levying the fine was called the *cognizor*, and he to whom it was levied, the *cognizee*. If there were any feme-covert among the cognizors, she was privately examined whether she did it willingly and freely, or by compulsion of her husband. By these acts all the essential parts of a fine were completed; and, if the cognizor died the next moment, still the fine might be carried on in all its remaining parts: of which the next was the *note* of the fine, or an abstract of the concord; naming the parties, the parcels of land, and the agreement, which was duly enrolled in the proper office; after which came the last part, or *foot* of the fine, or conclusion of it; which recited the parties, day, year, and place, and before whom it was acknowledged or levied. Of this there were indentures engrossed and delivered to the cognizor and the cognizee; usually beginning thus, "*hæc est finalis concordia*, this is the final agreement," and then reciting the whole proceeding at length. And thus the fine was completely levied at common law.

Various statutes regulated with great precision the mode in which all these proceedings were to be taken, and especially provided for the fine being openly read and proclaimed in court sixteen times, and for a list of all fines levied being duly published. For the *effect* of a fine duly levied was that the right of all strangers, that is, of all persons not *parties* or *privies** to the fine, whatsoever was bound, unless they made claim within *five* years after the proclamations made. Feme-coverts, infants, prisoners, persons beyond the seas, and such as were not of whole mind, had five years allowed to them and their heirs, after the death of their husbands, their attaining full

---

* *Privies* were such as could claim under the parties by right of blood or other right of representation.

age, recovering their liberty, returning into England, or being restored to their right mind.

A *common recovery* was another species of assurance, by matter of record, invented by the ecclesiastics to elude the statutes of mortmain; and afterwards encouraged by the finesse of the courts of law, in order to put an end to all fettered inheritances, and bar not only estates-tail, but also remainders and reversions expectant thereon. I was so far like a fine, that it was an action, either actual or fictitious and in it the lands were *recovered* against the tenant of the freehold; which recovery, being a supposed adjudication of the right, bound all persons, and vested an absolute fee-simple in the plaintiff. This action was not compromised like a fine, but carried on through every regular stage of proceeding to final judgment. Let us suppose David Edwards to be tenant of the freehold, and desirous to suffer a common recovery, in order to bar all entails, remainders, and reversions, and to convey the same in fee-simple to Francis Golding. To effect this, Golding brought an action against him for the lands, alleging that the defendant Edwards, here called the tenant, had no legal title to the land; but that he came into possession of it after one Hugh Hunt had turned the plaintiff out of it. Hereupon the tenant appeared, and called upon one Jacob Morland, who was supposed, at the original purchase, to have warranted the title to the tenant; and thereupon he prayed, that the said Jacob Morland might be called in to defend the title which he had so warranted. This was called the *voucher*, *vocatio*, or calling of Jacob Morland to warranty; and Morland was called the *vouchee*. Upon this, Jacob Morland, the vouchee, appeared, and defended. Whereupon Golding, the plaintiff, desired leave of the court to *imparl*, or confer with the vouchee in private, which was, as usual, allowed him. And soon afterwards Golding returned to court, but Morland, the vouchee, disappeared, or made default. Whereupon judgment was given for the plaintiff, Golding, now called the recoverer, to recover the lands in question against the tenant, Edwards, who was now the recoveree: and Edwards had judgment to recover of Jacob Morland lands of equal value, in recompense for the lands so warranted by him, and now lost by his default. This was called the recompense, or *recovery in value*. But, Jacob Morland having no lands of his own, being usually the crier of the court who, from being frequently thus vouched, was called the *common vouchee*, it is plain that Edwards had only a nominal recompense for the lands so recovered against him by Golding; which lands were now absolutely vested in the said recoverer by judgment of law, and seisin thereof was delivered by the sheriff of the county. So that this collusive recovery operated merely in the nature of a conveyance in fee-simple, from Edwards, the tenant-in-tail, to Golding, the purchaser.

The supposed recompense in value was the reason why the issue in tail and remainder were held to be barred by a common recovery. For, if the recoveree had obtained a recompense in lands from the common vouchee, which there was a possibility in contemplation of law, though a very improbable one, of his doing, these lands would have supplied the place of those so recovered from him by collusion, and would have descended to the issue in tail and in remainder; who thus sustained no actual loss by the proceedings of the tenant-in-tail; who by this fictitious proceeding might convey the lands held in tail to the recoveror, his heirs and assigns, absolutely free and discharged of all conditions and limitations in tail, and of all remainders and reversions.

To such awkward shifts were our ancestors obliged to have recourse, in order to get the better of that stubborn statute *De Donis*. The design, for which these contrivances were set on foot, was certainly laudable, the unrivetting the fetters of estates-tail, which were attended with a legion of mischiefs to the commonwealth. But, while we applaud the end, we cannot admire the means; and many expedients were accordingly suggested to get rid of these empty forms; the most obvious remedy being to vest in every tenant-in-tail of full age the same absolute fee-simple at once, which he might obtain whenever he pleased, by the collusive fiction of a common recovery.

But fines and recoveries continued to flourish in unabated exuberance until the reign of William IV.; when a strong impulse in favour of law reform was communicated to the legislature, and amongst the many acts passed at the commencement of that reign having this object in view, none has been found more successful in operation, or has obtained greater credit as a triumph of legislative skill than the Fines and Recoveries Act;* which enables every actual tenant-in-tail to dispose of the lands entailed, either for a fee-simple absolute or any less estate, as against all persons claiming either under the entail, or in remainder, or reversion, including the crown, by a simple disentailing deed; the exercise of the power thus given being subject only to certain necessary restrictions, for the preservation of existing interests. The explanation of the scheme is, however, more matter for the practising conveyancer than for the student of our laws, and need not be entered into here except on one point. I allude to one of the purposes to

* This statute was prepared by an eminent conveyancer, who stipulated, it is said, that not one word of the bill should be altered without his consent. The perfection of this piece of legislation may be, and usually is, attributed to the fact that the interference of individual legislators, almost invariably mischievous when permitted, was peremptorily excluded.

which fines were formerly applied, viz.: the passing of the estates and interests of married women, which could not, on account of the incapacity arising from coverture, have been otherwise effectually bound. This statute enables every married woman to dispose of any estate she may have, as effectually as though she were a feme sole. But her husband must concur in the deed; which must be acknowledged by her before a judge of one of the superior courts or of a county-court, or before some of the commissioners appointed for the purpose of taking such acknowledgments. On this occasion she is examined, apart from her husband, as to her knowledge of the deed, and whether she voluntarily and freely consents to it, a ceremony which was used when a married woman was cognizor in a fine; and the object of which is too obvious to call for comment.

5. Another kind of assurances which may properly be classed among those by *matter of record*, are the orders of the Court of Chancery; by which property may be transferred from one individual to another, without a resort to any of the ordinary methods of conveyance. Such, for instance, are the orders vesting property in trustees, substituted for others who have become incapacitated, as by lunacy. The same principle applies in bankruptcy, the estate of the bankrupt, other than copyholds, now vesting at once in the assignees by virtue of their appointment only.

The awards of the inclosure commissioners, commutations of tithes by the tithe commissioners, or of manorial rights by the copyhold commissioners, and the various proceedings by which the rights and claims of parties in respect of lands are transferred, confirmed or evidenced under the authority and seal of these several commissions, may also be classed among assurances by matter of record. The arrangements thus made do not depend solely on the act and consent of the parties themselves, but must be sanctioned and ratified by the commissioners; documents sealed with whose common seal are receivable in evidence without further proof, and are also conclusive as to every formality required for their validity, having been duly observed.

6. Under this head also may be placed the short conveyances in a statutory form, authorized by the statute 25 & 26 Vict., c. 53, establishing a registry of the title to landed estates of freehold tenure, and to leasehold estates on freehold lands. These conveyances can only be used to transfer estates, the titles to which have been registered; and may either be executed at the office of the registry, or endorsed on the certificate of title held by the owner of the property. The grant or conveyance must in either case be entered on the register, which thus exhibits a species of record of the transmissions of the property.

CHAPTER XIX.

OF ALIENATION BY SPECIAL CUSTOM.

Surrender—Admittance.

WE are next to consider assurances by special custom; a very narrow title, being confined to copyhold lands, and such customary estates as are holden in ancient demesne, or in manors of a similar nature; which, being of a very peculiar kind, and originally no more than tenancies in villenage, were never alienable by deed; for, as that might tend to defeat the lord of his seigniory, it is therefore a forfeiture of a copyhold. Nor are they transferrable by matter of record; but only in the court-baron of the lord, and by a proceeding called *surrender* and *admittance*.

Surrender, *sursumredditio*, is the yielding up of the estate by the tenant into the hands of the lord, for such purposes as in the surrender are expressed. As, it may be, to the use and behoof of A and his heirs; to the use of his own will; and the like. The process, in most manors, is that the tenant comes to the steward, either in court, or out of court, or else to two customary tenants of the same manor, provided there be a custom to warrant it; and there, by delivering up a rod, a glove, or other symbol, as the custom directs, resigns into the hands of the lord, by the hands and acceptance of his said steward, or of the said two tenants, all his interest and title to the estate; in trust to be again granted out by the lord, to such persons and for such uses as are named in the surrender and the custom of the manor will warrant. If the surrender be made out of court, then, at the next or some subsequent court, the jury or homage present and find it upon their oaths; which presentment is an information to the lord or his steward of what has been transacted out of court. Immediately upon such surrender, in court, or upon presentment of a surrender made out of court, the lord by his steward grants the same land again to *cestui que use*, who is sometimes called the surrenderee, to hold by the ancient rents and customary services; and thereupon admits him tenant to the copyhold, according to the form and effect of the surrender which must be exactly pursued. And this is done by delivering up to the new tenant the rod, or glove, or the like, in the name, and as the symbol, of corporal seisin of the lands and tenements. Upon which *admittance* he pays a fine to the lord according to the custom of the manor, and takes the oath of fealty.

In this manner of transferring copyhold estates, we may plainly trace the nature of the feudal institutions. The fief is inalienable without the consent of the lord. For this purpose it is surrendered into his hands. Custom, and the indulgence of the law, which favours liberty, has now given the tenant a right to name his successor. Yet, even to this day, the new tenant cannot be admitted but by composition with the lord, and paying him a fine by way of acknowledgment for the license of alienation. Add to this the plain feudal investiture, by delivering the symbol of seisin in presence of the other tenants in open court; and, to crown the whole, the oath of fealty is annexed, the very bond of feudal subjection.

This method of conveyance is so essential to the nature of a copyhold estate, that it cannot properly be transferred by any other assurance. No feoffment or grant has any operation thereupon. If I would exchange a copyhold estate with another, I cannot do it by an ordinary deed of exchange at the common law, but we must surrender to each other's use, and the lord will admit us accordingly. Formerly, indeed, if a man would devise a copyhold he must have surrendered it to the use of his last will; and therein he must have declared his intentions, and named a devisee, who would then be entitled to admission. But wills are now by statute as effectual without a previous surrender as they would have been. with one. And the lord, it is to be observed, cannot refuse to admit when a surrender is made; for if he refuse he may be compelled to do so, the surrender and admittance being now regarded merely as forms necessary to complete the investiture; for by statute 4 & 5 Vict., c. 35, *actual* presentment by the homage is not necessary, and admittance may be made at any time or place without holding any court for the purpose.

CHAPTER XX.

OF ALIENATION BY DEVISE.

Origin of wills—Introduction of uses—Statute of wills—Competency of witnesses—New wills act—Operation of wills.

THE last method of conveying real property is by *devise*, or disposition contained in a man's last will. I shall not at present, however, inquire into the nature of wills and testaments, which are more properly the instruments to convey personal estates; but only into the origin and antiquity of devising real estates by will, and the construction of the several statutes upon which that power is now founded.

It seems sufficiently clear that, before the Conquest, lands were devisable by will. But, upon the introduction of the military tenures, the restraint of devising lands naturally took place, as a branch of the feudal doctrine of non-alienation without the consent of the lord. And some have questioned whether this restraint, which we may trace even from the ancient Germans, was not founded upon truer principles of policy than the power of wantonly disinheriting the heir by will, and transferring the estate, through the dotage or caprice of the ancestor, from those of his blood to utter strangers. The ancient law of the Athenians directed that the estate of the deceased should descend to his children; or, on failure of lineal descendants, to the collateral relations; which had an admirable effect in keeping up equality, and preventing the accumulation of estates. But when Solon made a slight alteration, by permitting them, though only on failure of issue, to dispose of their lands by testament, this soon produced an excess of wealth in some, and of poverty in others; which, by a natural progression, first produced popular tumults and dissensions; and these at length ended in tyranny, and the utter extinction of liberty; which was quickly followed by a total subversion of their state and nation. On the other hand, it would now seem hard, on account of some abuses, to debar the owner of lands from distributing them after his death. And this power, if prudently managed, has with us a peculiar propriety; by preventing the very evil which resulted from Solon's institution, the too great accumulation of property: which is the natural consequence of our doctrine of succession by primogeniture, to which the Athenians were strangers. Of this accumulation the ill effects were severely felt even in the feudal times: but it should always be strongly discouraged in a commercial country, whose welfare depends on the number of moderate fortunes engaged in the extension of trade.

However this may be, we find that, by the common law of England since the Conquest, no estate, greater than for term of years, could be disposed of by testament; except only in Kent, and in some ancient burghs, and a few particular manors, where their Saxon immunities by special indulgence subsisted. And though the feudal restraint on alienation by deed vanished very early, yet this on wills continued for some centuries after; from an apprehension of infirmity and imposition on the testator *in extremis*, which made such devises suspicious.

But when ecclesiastical ingenuity had invented the doctrine of uses as a thing distinct from the land, uses began to be devised very frequently, and the devisee of the use could in chancery compel its execution. For it is observed by Gilbert, that as the popish clergy

then generally sat in the court of chancery, they considered that
men are most liberal when they can enjoy their possessions no
longer: and therefore at their death would choose to dispose of them
to those, who, according to the superstition of the times, could intercede for their happiness in another world.   But when the statute of
uses had annexed the possession to the use, these uses, being now
the very land itself, became no longer devisable : which might have
occasioned a great revolution in the law, had not the *statute of wills*
been made about five years after, viz., 32 Hen. VIII., c. 1, explained
by 34 Hen. VIII., c. 5, which enacted, that all persons seised in fee-
simple might by will in writing devise to any other *person*, except
to bodies corporate, in order to prevent the extension of gifts in
mortmain, two-thirds of their lands, tenements, and hereditaments,
held in chivalry, and the whole of those held in socage: which,
on the alteration of tenures by the statute of Charles II., amounted
to the whole of their landed property, except their copyhold tenements.

With regard to devises in general, experience soon showed how
difficult and hazardous a thing it is, even in matters of public utility,
to depart from the rules of the common law; which are so nicely
constructed and so artificially connected together, that the least
breach in any one of them disorders for a time the texture of the
whole.   Innumerable frauds and perjuries were quickly introduced
by this parliamentary method of inheritance; for so loose was the
construction made upon this act by the courts of law, that bare
notes in the handwriting of another person were allowed to be good
wills within the statute.   To remedy which, the *statute of frauds*
and perjuries, 29 Car. II., c. 3, directed, that all devises of lands and
tenements should not only be in writing, but be signed by the testator, or some other person in his presence, and by his express direction; and be subscribed, in his presence, by three or four credible
witnesses; a number which by the Wills Act, 1 Vict., c. 26, has
been reduced to two.   A similar solemnity is requisite for revoking
a devise; though the same may be also revoked by the burning,
tearing, or destroying thereof by the devisor by his direction or in
his presence and with the intention on his part to effect such revocation; as likewise by the marriage of the testator.

In the construction of the statute of Charles, it was adjudged
that the testator's name, written with his own hand, at the beginning of his will, as, "*I John Mills do make this my last will and
testament*," was a sufficient signing, without any name at the bottom; though the other were the safer way.   It was also determined,
that though the witnesses must all have seen the testator sign, or at
least acknowledge the signing, yet they might do it at different
times.   But they must all have subscribed their names as witnesses

in his presence, lest by any possibility they should mistake the instrument. But the testator's signature, made by himself or some
one in his presence, must now be at the *foot or end* of the will, and
must be made or acknowledged in the presence of two witnesses,
present at the same time, who must attest and subscribe the will
in the presence of the testator. No particular form of attestation is,
however, necessary.

Many questions were raised under the old law, as to the *competency* of the witnesses to a will. In one case, determined by the
court of King's Bench, the judges were extremely strict in regard
to the credibility, or rather the competency, of the witnesses; for
they would not allow any legatee, nor by consequence a creditor,
where the legacies and debts were charged on the real estate, to be a
competent witness to the devise, as being too deeply concerned in
interest not to wish the establishment of the will; for, if it were
established, he gained a security for his legacy or debt from the real
estate, whereas otherwise he had no claim but on the personal assets.
This determination, however, alarmed many purchasers and creditors,
and threatened to shake most of the titles in the kingdom that depended on devises by will. For, if the will was attested by a
servant to whom wages were due, by the apothecary or attorney
whose very attendance made them creditors, or by the minister of
the parish who had any demand for tithes or ecclesiastical dues,
and these are the persons most likely to be present in the testator's
last illness, and if, in such case, the testator had charged his real
estate with the payment of his debts, the whole will, and every disposition therein, so far as related to real property, were held to be
utterly void. This occasioned the statute 25 Geo. II., c. 6, which
restored the competency and credit of such *legatees;* by declaring
void all legacies given to witnesses, thereby removing all possibility
of their interest affecting their testimony. The same statute established the competency of *creditors;* by directing their testimony to
be admitted, but leaving their credit to be considered by the court
before whom such will should be contested.

The statute 1 Vict., c. 26, having repealed the act of Geo. II.,
re-enacts and extends some of its provisions. It avoids bequests,
not only to an attesting witness, but to the husband or wife of such
witness; and expressly provides that the incompetency of a witness
to prove the execution of a will, shall not render it invalid. It further enacts that any *creditor*, or the wife or husband of any creditor,
whose debt is charged upon the property devised or bequeathed by
the will, may be admitted to prove the execution thereof as an attesting witness; and that an *executor* of a will may be admitted to prove
its execution, a point on which some doubts had previously existed.

L 2

Another inconvenience was, soon after its introduction, found to attend the method of conveyance by devise; in that creditors by specialties which affected the *heir*, provided he had assets by descent, were now defrauded of their securities, not having the same remedy against the *devisee* of their debtor. This was remedied by 3 & 4 W. & M., c. 14, since repealed; but the payment of simple contract as well as specialty debts, out of the real estate of the deceased debtor, has been provided for by other statutes.

A will of lands, made under the earlier statutes, was considered by the courts of law not so much in the nature of a testament, as of a conveyance declaring the uses to which the land should be subject. And upon this notion was founded a distinction between such devises and testaments of personal chattels; the latter operating upon whatever the testator died possessed of, the former only upon such real estates as were his at the time of executing and publishing his will. No after-purchased lands therefore passed under such devise, unless, subsequent to the purchase or contract, the devisor re-published his will; but the Wills Act, 1 Vict., c. 26, has abolished this distinction; and all property of whatever kind, of or to which a man is possessed or entitled, *at the time of his death*, passes by his will; as the instrument now, with reference to the real and personal estate comprised in it, speaks and takes effect as if executed immediately before the testator's death, unless a contrary intention appears by the document itself.

And thus we have taken a transient view of a very large and diffusive subject, the doctrine of common assurances: which concludes our observations on the *title* to things real, or the means by which they may be reciprocally lost and acquired. The subject is one of very extensive use, and of as extensive variety. And yet I am afraid it has afforded the student less amusement and pleasure in the pursuit, than the matters discussed in the preceding part of these commentaries. To say the truth, the vast alterations which the doctrine of real property has undergone from the Conquest to the present time; and the multiplicity of acts of parliament which have amended, or sometimes only altered, the common law, have made the study of this branch of our national jurisprudence a little perplexed and intricate. It has been my endeavour to select such parts of it as were of the most general use, where the principles were the most simple, the reasons of them the most obvious, and the practice the least embarrassed. Yet I cannot presume that I have always been thoroughly intelligible to such of my readers as were before strangers even to the very terms of art, which I have been obliged to make use of; though, whenever those have first occurred, I have generally attempted a short explanation of their

meaning. And therefore I shall close with the words of Sir Edward
Coke : " Albeit the student shall not at any one day, do what he
" can, reach to the full meaning of all that is here laid down, yet let
" him no way discourage himself, but proceed ; for on some other
" day, in some other place," or perhaps on a second perusal of the
same, " his doubts will be probably removed."

CHAPTER XXI.

OF THINGS PERSONAL.

Chattels real—Chattels personal.

UNDER the name of things *personal* are included all sorts of things
movable, which may attend a man's person wherever he goes ; and,
therefore, being only the objects of the law while they remain
within the limits of its jurisdiction, and being also of a perishable
quality, are not esteemed of so high a nature, nor paid so much
regard to by the law, as things that are in their nature more permanent and *immovable*, as lands and houses, and the profits issuing
thereout. These, being constantly within the reach, and under the
protection of the law, were the principal favourites of our first
legislators : who took all imaginable care in ascertaining the rights,
and directing the disposition, of such property as they imagined to
be lasting ; but entertained a very low opinion of all personal estate,
which they regarded as only a transient commodity. The amount
of it, indeed, was comparatively very trifling during the scarcity of
money and the ignorance of luxurious refinements which prevailed
in the feudal ages. Hence it was, that a tax of the *fifteenth, tenth*,
or sometimes a much larger proportion, of all the movables of the
subject, was frequently laid without scruple, though now it would
justly alarm our opulent merchants and stock-holders. And hence,
likewise, may be derived the frequent forfeitures, inflicted by the
common law, of *all* a man's goods and chattels, for misbehaviours
that at present hardly seem to deserve so severe a punishment. Our
ancient law-books do not often therefore condescend to regulate this
species of property. There is not a chapter in Britton or the Mirror
that can fairly be referred to this head ; and the little that is to be
found in Glanvil, Bracton, and Fleta, seems principally borrowed
from the civilians. But since the extension of trade and commerce,
which are entirely occupied in this species of property, we have
learned to conceive different ideas of it. Our courts now regard a

man's personalty in a light quite equal to his realty: and have adopted a less technical mode of considering the one than the other; frequently drawn from the rules which they found already established by the Roman law, but principally from reason and convenience, adapted to the circumstances of the times; preserving withal a due regard to ancient usages, and a certain feudal tincture, which is still to be found in some branches of personal property.

But things personal, by our law, do not only include things *movable*, but also something more: the whole of which is comprehended under the general name of *chattels*, derived from the technical Latin *catalla*; which primarily signified only beasts of husbandry, or *cattle*, but in its secondary sense was applied to all movables in general. In the *Grand Coustumier* of Normandy, a *chattel* is described as a mere movable, but at the same time it is set in opposition to a fief or feud: so that, not only goods, but whatever was not a feud, were accounted chattels. And it is in this latter more extended, negative sense, that our law adopts it; the idea of goods, or movables only, being not sufficiently comprehensive to take in everything that the law considers as a chattel interest.

Chattels, therefore, are distributed into two kinds, chattels *real*, and chattels *personal*.

1. Chattels *real* are such as concern, or savour of, the realty; as terms for years of land, the next presentation to a church, estates by *elegit*, or the like. And these are called real chattels, as being interests issuing out of real estates: of which they have one quality, viz., immobility, which denominates them *real*; but want the other, viz., a sufficient legal indeterminate duration: and this want it is that constitutes them *chattels*. The utmost period for which they can last is fixed and determinate, so that they are not equal in the eye of the law to the lowest estate of freehold, a lease for another's life.

2. Chattels *personal* are, properly and strictly speaking, things *movable*; which may be annexed to or attendant on the person of the owner, and carried about with him from one part of the world to another. Such are animals, household stuff, money, corn, and everything else that can properly be transferred from place to place. And of this kind of chattels it is that we are principally to speak in the remainder of this book; having been unavoidably led to consider the nature of chattels real, and their incidents, in the former chapters which were employed upon real estates.

Chattel interests being thus distinguished and distributed, it will be proper to consider, first, the nature of that *property*, or dominion, to which they are liable; and, secondly, the *title* to that property, or how it may be lost and acquired.

CHAPTER XXII.

OF PROPERTY IN THINGS PERSONAL.

Property in possession— Absolute property—Qualified property—In animals-
    In things personal—Property *in action*—Damages—Partnership prô
    perty.

PROPERTY, in chattels personal, may be either in *possession;* which
is where a man has not only the right to enjoy, but has the actual
enjoyment of the thing: or else it is in *action;* where a man has
only a bare right, without any occupation or enjoyment. And of
these the former, or property in *possession,* is divided into two sorts,
an *absolute* and a *qualified* property.

I. First, then, of property in *possession absolute;* which is where
a man has, solely and exclusively, the right, and also the occupation,
of any movable chattels; so that they cannot be transferred from
him, or cease to be his, without his own act or default. Such may
be all *inanimate* things, as goods, plate, money, jewels, and the like •
such also may be all *vegetable* productions, as the fruit of a plant,
when severed from the body of it; or the whole plant itself, when
severed from the ground.

But with regard to *animals,* which have in themselves a principle
and power of motion, and can convey themselves from one part of
the world to another, there is a great difference made with respect to
their several classes, not only in our law, but in the law of nature
and of all civilized nations. They are distinguished into such as
are *domitæ,* and such as are *feræ naturæ:* some being of a *tame* and
others of a *wild* disposition. In such as are of a nature tame and
domestic, as horses, kine, sheep, poultry, and the like, a man may
have as absolute a property as in any inanimate beings; because
these continue perpetually in his occupation, and will not stray from
his house or person, unless by accident or fraudulent enticement, in
either of which cases the owner does not lose his property.

Other animals, that are not of a tame and domestic nature, are
either not the objects of property at all, or else fall under our other
division, namely, that of *qualified, limited,* or *special* property. In
discussing which subject, I shall in the first place show how this
species of property may subsist in such animals as are *feræ naturæ,*
or of a wild nature; and then, how it may subsist in any other
things, when under particular circumstances.

First, then, a man may be invested with a qualified, but not an absolute property in all creatures that are *feræ naturæ*, either *per industriam, propter impotentiam*, or *propter privilegium*.

1. A qualified property may subsist in animals *feræ naturæ, per industriam hominis:* by a man's *reclaiming* and making them tame by art, industry, and education ; or by so confining them within his own immediate power, that they cannot escape and use their natural liberty. Such are deer in a park, hares or rabbits in an enclosed warren, doves in a dovehouse, pheasants or partridges in a mew, hawks that are fed and commanded by their owner, and fish in a private pond or in trunks. These are no longer the property of a man, than while they continue in his keeping or actual possession : but if at any time they regain their natural liberty, his property instantly ceases ; unless they have *animum revertendi*, which is only to be known by their usual custom of returning.

In all these creatures, reclaimed from the wildness of their nature, the property is not absolute, but defeasible : a property that may be destroyed if they resume their ancient wildness, and are found at large. For if the pheasants escape from the mew, or the fishes from the trunk, and are seen wandering at large in their proper element, they become *feræ naturæ* again ; and are free and open to the first occupant that has ability to seize them. But while they thus continue my qualified or defeasible property, they are as much under the protection of the law, as if they were absolutely and indefeasibly mine.

2. A qualified property may also subsist with relation to animals *feræ naturæ, ratione impotentiæ*, on account of their own inability. As when hawks, herons, or other birds build in my trees, or rabbits or other creatures make their burrows in my land, and have young ones there ; I have a qualified property in those young ones till such time as they can fly or run away, and then my property expires : but, till then, it is in some cases trespass, and in others a misdemeanor for a stranger to take them away.

3. A man may, lastly, have a qualified property in animals *feræ naturæ, propter privilegium :* that is, he may have the privilege of hunting, taking, and killing game, in exclusion of other persons. The manner in which this privilege is acquired will be shown in a subsequent chapter.

The qualified property which we have hitherto considered, extends only to animals *feræ naturæ*, when either reclaimed, impotent, or privileged. Many other things may also be the objects of qualified property. It may subsist in the very elements, of fire or light, or air, and of water. A man can obviously have no absolute perma-

nent property in these, as he may in the earth and land. Yet if a
man disturbs another, and deprives him of the lawful enjoyment of
these; if one obstructs another's ancient windows, corrupts the air
of his house or garden, fouls his water, or if he diverts an ancient
water-course that used to run to the other's mill; the law will protect the party injured in his possession. But the property in them
ceases the instant they are out of possession: for then they become
again common, and every man has an equal right to appropriate
them to his own use.

These kinds of qualification in property depend upon the peculiar
circumstances of the subject-matter, which is not capable of being
under the absolute dominion of any proprietor. But property may
also be of a qualified or special nature, on account of the peculiar
circumstances of the owner, when the thing itself is very capable of
absolute ownership. As in case of *bailment*, or delivery of goods to
another person for a particular use; as to a carrier to convey to
London, to an innkeeper to secure in his inn, or the like. Here
there is no absolute property in either the bailor or the bailee, the
person delivering or him to whom it is delivered: for the bailor has
only the right, and not the immediate possession; the bailee has the
possession, and only a temporary right. But it is a qualified property in them both; and each of them is entitled to an action, in
case the goods be damaged or taken away: the bailee on account of
his immediate possession; the bailor, because the possession of the
bailee is, mediately, his possession also. And so in other cases, as of
goods pawned or distrained or taken in execution. But a servant,
who has the care of his master's goods or chattels, as a butler of
plate, a shepherd of sheep, and the like, has not any property or
possession, either absolute or qualified, but only a mere charge or
oversight.

Having thus considered the several divisions of property in *possession*, which subsists there only, where a man has both the right
and also the occupation of the thing; I proceed to take a short view
of the nature of property in *action*, or such where a man has not the
occupation, but merely a bare right to occupy the thing in question;
the possession whereof may however be recovered by an action at
law: from whence the thing so recoverable is called a thing, or
chose in action. Thus, money due on a bond is a *chose* in action;
for a property in the debt vests at the time of forfeiture mentioned
in the obligation, but there is no possession till recovered by course
of law. If a man promises, or covenants with me, to do any act,
and fails in it, whereby I suffer damage, the recompense for this
damage is a *chose* in action: for though a right to some recompense
vests in me at the time of the damage done, yet what and how large

such recompense shall be, can only be ascertained by verdict; and the possession can only be given me by legal judgment and execution. In the former of these cases, the student will observe that the property, or right of action, depends upon an *express* contract or obligation to pay a stated sum : and in the latter it depends upon an *implied* contract, that, if the covenantor does not perform the act he engaged to do, he shall pay me the damages I sustain by this breach of covenant.

Besides actions thus arising upon contracts express or implied, there is also another kind, those, namely, which arise from some wrong or injury done by one man to another, and which are therefore said to arise *ex delicto*. For any such injury the law awards a compensation to the party aggrieved. Thus for an assault on, or wrongful imprisonment of, the person, or for an injury by libel or slander to the reputation of another, the law awards such compensation as a jury shall estimate to be the damage sustained. So for a trespass on the lands, or for carrying away the goods of another, the wrongdoer must compensate the party injured, if he demand it in an action. And to such compensation the party injured is entitled the instant he receives the injury; he has at once an inchoate or incomplete right, but still a right; and such damages therefore constitute a thing to be recovered by suit, in other words a *chose in action*. The right to sue for this compensation arises, not from any previous contract by the wrongdoer that he shall refrain from committing the injury complained of; but, in the cases above supposed, from an infringement by the wrongdoer of one of the inherent rights of every member of society, the right of personal liberty or the right of property. And the suit when brought is therefore said to be an action of *tort*.

There are thus two distinct sources of property in action, namely, injuries arising from the non-fulfilment of contracts expressed or implied, that is, *ex contractu* or *quasi ex contractu*; and injuries to one's person or property arising solely from an infringement of the natural or relative rights of the individual wronged, that is, *ex delicto* or *quasi ex delicto*. Of the nature of the former, we shall discourse at large in a subsequent chapter. The latter will form the subject of our consideration in the third book of these Commentaries.

At present we have only to remark, that upon all contracts or promises, either express or implied, and the infinite variety of cases into which they are and may be spun out, the law gives an action of some sort or other to the party injured, in case of non-performance, to compel the wrongdoer to do justice to the party with whom he has contracted; and, on failure of performing the identical thing he engaged to do, to render a satisfaction equivalent to the damage sustained. But while the thing, or its equivalent, remains in suspense, and the injured party has only the right and not the occupation, it is called a *chose* in action; being a thing rather in *potentiâ* than in *esse :* though the owner may have as absolute a property in, and be as well entitled to, such things in action, as to things in possession.   Just as for all infringements of the natural or relative rights of another, the law gives redress by action against the wrongdoer by an action to recover the damage sustained; this redress, to which the party injured, as we have said, has an undoubted right the instant the injury is sustained, until recovered by verdict, constituting a *chose in action*, precisely as do the damages sustained by a breach of contract.

Finally, things personal may belong to their owners, not only in severalty, but also in joint-tenancy, and in common, as well as real estates.   They cannot indeed be vested in co-parcenary; because they do not descend from the ancestor to the heir, which is necessary to constitute co-parceners.   But if a horse, or other personal chattel, be given to two or more, absolutely, they are joint-tenants thereof; and, unless the jointure be severed, the same doctrine of survivorship shall take place as in estates of lands and tenements. And, in like manner, if the jointure be severed, as, by either of them selling his share, the vendee and the remaining part owner shall be tenants in common, without any *jus accrescendi* or survivorship. So, also, if 100*l.* be given by will to two or more, *equally to be divided* between them, this makes them tenants in common; as we have formerly seen, the same words would have done in regard to real estates.

But the stock on a farm, though occupied jointly, and also the stock used in a joint undertaking, by way of partnership in trade, shall always be considered as common and not as joint property, and there shall be no survivorship therein.   For here, " the wares " or merchandises which they have as joint-tenants or partners, " shall not survive, but shall go to the executors of him that de- " ceaseth, and this *per legem mercatoriam*, which is part of the laws " of this realm for the advancement and continuance of commerce " and trade." *Choses in action* are not, however, within the exception, and must therefore be sued for in the name of the survivor only; but equity considers the surviving partner a trustee of the share of the deceased partner, to whose executors and administrators he must account for it.

CHAPTER XXIII.

WE are next to consider the *title* to things personal, or the various means of *acquiring*, and of *losing*, such property as may be had therein. And these methods of acquisition or loss are principally twelve: 1. By occupancy. 2. By prerogative. 3. By forfeiture. 4. By custom. 5. By succession. 6. By marriage. 7. By judgment. 8. By gift or grant. 9. By contract. 10. By bankruptcy. 11. By testament. 12. By administration.

And, first, a property in chattels may be acquired by *occupancy:* the original and only primitive method of acquiring any property at all, but which has since been restrained and abridged, by the positive laws of society, in order to maintain peace and harmony among mankind. For this purpose, gifts, and contracts, testaments, legacies, and administrations, have been introduced, in order to transfer and continue that property and possession in things personal, which has once been acquired by the owner. And, where such things are found without any other owner, they for the most part belong to the sovereign by virtue of his prerogative; except in some few instances, wherein the original right of occupancy is still permitted to subsist.

1. Thus, in the first place, it has been said, that anybody may seize to his own use such goods as belong to an alien enemy. But this must, in reason and justice, be restrained to such captors as are authorized by the public authority of the state, and to such goods as are brought into this country by an alien enemy, after a declaration of war, without a safe-conduct or passport. For where a foreigner is resident in England, and afterwards a war breaks out between his country and ours, his goods are not liable to be seized. If an enemy take the goods of an Englishman, which are afterwards retaken by another subject of this kingdom, the former owner was considered to lose his property therein, and it was indefeasibly vested in the second taker, unless they were retaken the same day, and the owner before sunset put in his claim of property; which was agreeable to the law of nations, as understood in the time of Grotius, even with

regard to captures made at sea, which were held to be the property
of the captors after a possession of twenty-four hours.   More modern
authorities require, that, before the property can be changed, the
goods must have been brought into port, and have continued a night
intra præsidia, in a place of safe custody, so that all hope of recovering them be lost.   And now, in order to vest the property of a
capture in the captors, a sentence of condemnation is, by the law of
nations, deemed necessary.

2. Thus, again, whatever movables are found upon the surface of
the earth, or in the sea, and are unclaimed by any owner, are supposed to be abandoned by the last-proprietor; and, as such, are
returned into the common stock, and therefore belong, as in a state
of nature, to the first occupant, unless they fall within the description of waifs, or estrays, or wreck, or hidden treasure; for these are
vested by law in the sovereign.

3. Thus, too, the benefit of the elements, the light, the air, and
the water, can only be appropriated by occupancy.   Thus, if I have
an ancient window, overlooking my neighbour's ground, he may not
erect any blind to obstruct the light: but if I build my house close
to his wall, which darkens it, I cannot compel him to demolish his
wall: for there the first occupancy is rather in him than in me.
So, if my neighbour makes a tanyard, which renders less salubrious
the air of my house, the law will furnish me with a remedy; but,
if he is first in possession of the air, and I fix my habitation near
him, the nuisance is of my own seeking, and may continue.

4. With regard likewise to animals *feræ naturæ*, when a man has
once so seized them, they become while living his *qualified* property,
or, if dead, are *absolutely* his own: so that to steal them, or otherwise invade this property, is sometimes a criminal offence, sometimes only a civil injury.   The restrictions laid upon this right
relate principally to royal fish, as whale and sturgeon, and *game*.
But those animals, which are not expressly so reserved, are still
liable to be taken and appropriated by any one upon their own
territories; in the same manner as they might have taken even
game itself, till these civil prohibitions were issued: there being
in nature no distinction between one species of wild animals and
another, between the right of acquiring property in a hare or a
squirrel, in a partridge or a butterfly.

5. To this principle of occupancy also must be referred the method
of acquiring a special personal property in corn growing on the
ground, or other *emblements*, by any *possessor* of the land who has
sown it; which emblements are distinct from the real estate in the
land, and subject to many, though not all, the incidents attending

personal chattels. They were devisable by testament before the statute of wills; and at the death of the owner vest in his executor and not his heir; and by the statute 11 George II. c. 10, though not by the common law, they may be distrained for rent arrear.

6. The doctrine of property arising from *accession* is also grounded on the right of occupancy. By the Roman law, if any corporeal substance received afterwards an accession by natural or by artificial means, as by the growth of vegetables, the pregnancy of animals, or the conversion of wood or metal into vessels and utensils, the original owner was entitled to the property under such its state of improvement; but if the thing itself, by such operation, was changed into a different species, as by making wine, oil, or bread, out of another's grapes, olives, or wheat, it belonged to the new operator; who was only to make a satisfaction to the former proprietor for the materials which he had so converted. And these doctrines are implicitly copied and adopted by our Bracton, and have since been confirmed by many resolutions of the courts. It has even been held, that if one takes away and clothes another's wife or son, and afterwards they return home, the garments shall cease to be his property who provided them, being annexed to the person of the child or woman.

7. But in the case of *confusion* of goods, where those of two persons are so intermixed, that the several portions can be no longer distinguished, the English law partly agrees with, and partly differs from, the civil. If the intermixture be by consent, I apprehend that in both laws the proprietors have an interest in common, in proportion to their respective shares. But if one wilfully intermixes his money, corn, or hay, with that of another man, without his approbation or knowledge, or casts gold in like manner into another's melting-pot or crucible, the civil law, though it gives the sole property of the whole to him who has not interfered in the mixture, yet allows a satisfaction to the other for what he has so improvidently lost. Our law, to guard against fraud, gives the entire property, without any account, to him whose original dominion is invaded, and endeavoured to be rendered uncertain, without his own consent.

8. There is another species of property, which, being grounded on labour and invention, is more properly reducible to the head of occupancy than any other. And this is the right which an author may be supposed to have in his own original compositions : so that no other person, without his leave, may publish or make profit of the copies. The law on this subject has been placed on a very distinct footing by several recent statutes, to which I must content myself with referring the student. I may add here, however, that the *copyright* in books is for *forty-two* years, or for the life of the

author and seven years following, whichever may be the longer; and that facilities are given for its preservation, by the establishment of a public register of copyrights, at the Hall of the Stationers' Company in the City of London. The copyright of engravings and of sculpture is provided for by other statutes; while conventions for the mutual protection of such copyrights have been entered into with France, Prussia, Belgium, Spain, and other powers. Copyright has also been granted to designs for articles of manufacture for *nine months, a year, or three years*, according to the nature of the manufacture; provided they are registered in the mode provided by the different statutes.

Some of our early sovereigns assumed to themselves the right of granting to certain favoured subjects the monopoly, or sole right of selling and dealing in particular commodities. This pretended prerogative was carried to a most injurious length in the reign of queen Elizabeth, and led to the passing of the *statute of monopolies*, 21 Jac. I. c. 3; which, while declaring the illegality of such grants of exclusive trading in general, contained an exception in favour of new and original inventions in manufacture; and enacted that the declaration against monopolies should not extend to letters-patent and grants of privilege for the term of fourteen years or under, of the sole working of any manner of new manufactures within the realm, to the true and first inventor thereof, provided such manufactures were not in use by others at the time of granting the letters-patent. Upon this exception, which, to a certain extent, recognizes the royal prerogative, the modern law of patents for inventions in manufactures may be considered to rest. It has also been the subject of considerable but hitherto unsatisfactory legislation. For experience has shown that no sooner is a patent granted than every species of ingenuity is at once exerted to obtain the advantages of the invention in another way; so that the patentee has usually, from the outset, either to defend his patent from attack, or resort to an endless variety of actions, in order to assert his right against a host of depredators.

In this way only, however, does the law recognize the right of inventors to profit by their ingenuity, a right having its origin, indeed in nature, and in the principle of *occupancy* above referred to; but which, in the present artificial state of society, must be regulated by arbitrary enactment rather than by any general rules of right.

9. Ships constitute another species of personal property of very great importance, and subject to very peculiar and special laws. They have, from time immemorial, passed by *bill of sale*, or grant in writing, and not as in the case of most other chattels, by simple delivery of possession; but the statute law further imposes the

necessity of registration, in order to complete the title. Mortgages must in like manner be entered in the register; the priority of entry therein, when there are several mortgagees, and not the date of the mortgages themselves, determining absolutely the priority of right.

CHAPTER XXIV.

OF TITLE BY PREROGATIVE, FORFEITURE AND CUSTOM.

Title by prerogative—to customs—to taxes, &c.—Copyright—Game—Title by forfeiture—Title by custom—to heriots—mortuaries—heir-looms.

II. ANOTHER method of acquiring property in personal chattels is by the *royal prerogative*: whereby a right may accrue either to the crown itself, or to such as claim under the title of the crown; as by the royal grant, or by prescription, which supposes an ancient grant.

Such, in the first place, are all *tributes, taxes,* and *customs,* whether inherent in the crown, or created by authority of parliament. In these the sovereign acquires, and the subject loses, a property, the instant they become due: if paid, they are a *chose* in possession; if unpaid, a *chose* in action. And in these several methods of acquiring property by prerogative, there is this peculiar quality, that the crown cannot have a *joint* property with any person in one entire chattel; but where the titles of the crown and a subject concur, the sovereign shall have the whole: in like manner as the crown cannot, either by grant or contract, become a joint-tenant of a chattel real with another person, but by such grant or contract shall become entitled to the whole in severalty.

This doctrine has no opportunity to take place in certain other instances of title by prerogative, that remain to be mentioned; as the chattels thereby vested are originally and solely vested in the crown, without any transfer or derivative assignment, either by deed or law, from any former proprietor. Such is the acquisition of property in wreck, in treasure-trove, in waifs, in estrays, in royal fish, in swans, and the like, which are not *transferred* to the sovereign from any former owner, but are originally *inherent* in him by the rules of law, and are derived to particular subjects, as royal franchises, by his bounty.

There is also a kind of prerogative *copyright* subsisting in certain books, which is held to be vested in the crown upon different reasons.

Thus, 1. The sovereign has the right of promulgating to the people all acts of state and government. This gives him the exclusive privilege of printing all *acts of parliament, proclamations*, and *orders of council*. 2. As head of the church, he has a right to the publication of all *liturgies*, and books of *divine service*. 3. He is also said to have a right, by purchase, to the copies of such *law-books, grammars*, and other compositions, as were compiled or translated at the expense of the crown. And upon these two last principles combined, the exclusive right of printing the translation of the *Bible* is founded. However, it seems to be agreed now, that both the Bible and statutes may be printed by others than those deriving the right from the grant of the crown, provided such editions comprise *bonâ fide* notes; but with this exception, the sole right to print these works is now vested in the universities of Oxford and Cambridge, and those deriving their right from the crown.

There existed until lately another species of prerogative property, founded upon a very different principle from any that have been mentioned before; the property in *game* which, at common law, was vested in the crown alone, and thence derived to such subjects as had received the grants of a chase, a park, a free warren, or free fishery. But the statute 1 & 2 Will. IV. c. 32, has put this branch of the law upon quite a new footing; the right to kill game upon any land being now vested in the owner, or in the occupier thereof, in the absence of a reservation of the right by the landlord. All persons killing or pursuing game are required, however, to take out a yearly certificate; and dealers selling it must also obtain a yearly license, under certain penalties.

III. The third method, whereby a title to goods and chattels may be acquired and lost, is, by *forfeiture;* as a punishment for some crime or misdemeanour in the party forfeiting, and as a compensation for the offence and injury committed against him to whom they are forfeited. But that branch of the law, which is mentioned here only for the sake of regularity will be more properly considered in the fourth part of these commentaries. At present I need only mention that this forfeiture commences from the time of *conviction*, not the time of committing the fact, as in forfeitures of real property. And, therefore, a *bonâ fide* sale of goods or chattels by the offender, after the offence and before conviction, is good, though a fraudulent conveyance of them, to defeat the interest of the crown, is void by statute 13 Eliz. c. 5.

IV. A fourth method of acquiring property in things personal, or chattels, is by *custom:* whereby a right vests in some particular persons, either by the local usage of some particular place, or by the

almost general and universal usage of the kingdom. I shall here
mention three sorts of customary interests only, as these obtain
pretty generally; viz., *heriots, mortuaries,* and *heir-looms.*

1. Heriots, which were slightly touched upon in a former chapter,
are of two sorts: heriot-*service* and heriot-*custom.* The former
amount to little more than a mere rent: the latter, of which I am
now to speak, depend merely upon immemorial usage, and are a
customary tribute of goods and chattels, payable to the lord of the
fee on the decease of the owner of the land.

The first establishment, if not introduction, of compulsory heriots
into England, was by the Danes; the laws of Canute prescribing the
several *heregeates,* or heriots, which were exacted by the king on
the death of divers of his subjects, according to their respective
dignities; from the highest *eorl* down to the most inferior *thegn,* or
landholder. These, for the most part, consisted in arms, horses,
and habiliments of war; which the word itself signifies. These
were delivered up to the sovereign on the death of the vassal,
who could no longer use them, to be put into other hands for the
service and defence of the country. And upon the plan of this
Danish establishment did William the Conqueror fashion his law of
reliefs; when he ascertained the precise relief to be taken of every
tenant in chivalry, and, contrary to feudal custom and the usage of
his own duchy of Normandy, required arms and implements of war
to be paid instead of money.

The Danish compulsive heriots being thus transmuted into reliefs,
underwent the same several vicissitudes as the feudal tenures, and
in socage estates do frequently remain to this day in the shape of a
double rent, payable at the death of the tenant; the heriots which
now continue among us, and preserve that name, seeming rather to
be of Saxon parentage, and at first to have been merely discretionary.
These are now, for the most part, confined to copyhold tenures, and
perhaps are the only instance where custom has favoured the lord:
For this payment was originally a voluntary donation, or gratuitous
legacy of the tenant; perhaps in acknowledgment of his having
been raised a degree above villenage, when all his goods and chattels
were quite at the mercy of the lord; and custom, which has on the
one hand confirmed the tenant's interest in exclusion of the lord's
will, has on the other hand established this discretional piece of
gratitude into a permanent duty. A heriot may also appertain to
free land, that is held by service and suit of court; in which case it
is most commonly a copyhold enfranchised, whereupon the heriot is
still due by custom.

This heriot is sometimes the best live beast or *averium,* which the
tenant dies possessed of, sometimes the best inanimate good, under

which a jewel or piece of plate may be included : but it is always a *personal* chattel, which immediately on the death of the tenant, who was the owner of it, being ascertained by the option of the lord, becomes vested in him as his property ; and is no charge upon the lands, but merely on the goods and chattels. Heriots will, however, in course of time, cease to be exigible ; one of the statutes, for the enfranchisement of copyholds, having at last enabled either lord or tenant to compel the extinguishment of this ancient feudal burden.

2. Mortuaries are a sort of ecclesiastical heriots, being a customary gift claimed by and due to the minister in very many parishes on the death of a parishioner. They seem originally to have been, like lay heriots, only a voluntary bequest to the church ; being intended, as a kind of amends to the clergy for the personal tithes which the laity in their lifetime might have neglected or forgotten to pay. For this purpose, *after* the lord's heriot was taken out, the second-best chattel was reserved to the church as a mortuary, and is, therefore, in the laws of Canute, called soul-scot. It was anciently usual to bring the mortuary to church along with the corpse when it came to be buried ; and thence it is sometimes called a *corsepresent* : a term which bespeaks it to have been once a voluntary donation. This custom still varies in different places, not only as the mortuary to be paid, but the person to whom it is payable. In Wales a mortuary, or corse-present, was due upon the death of every clergyman to the bishop of the diocese ; till abolished by statute 12 Ann. st. 2, c. 6. And in the archdeaconry of Chester, a custom also prevailed, that the bishop, who is also archdeacon, should have, at the death of every clergyman dying therein, his best horse or mare, bridle, saddle and spurs, his best gown or cloak, hat, upper garment under his gown, and tippet, and also his best signet or ring. By statute 28 Geo. II. c. 6, this mortuary was also put an end to. The claim of the crown to many goods, on the death of all prelates in England, seems to be of the same nature. The crown, according to Sir Edward Coke, is entitled to six things : the bishop's best horse or palfrey, with his furniture ; his cloak, or gown, and tippet ; his cup and cover ; his basin and ewer ; his gold ring ; and lastly, his *muta canum*, his mew or kennel of hounds. *Mortuaries,* which are not to be confounded with *burial fees,* are now, however, almost unknown.

3. Heir-looms are such goods and personal chattels, as, contrary to the nature of chattels, go by special custom to the heir along with the inheritance, and not to the executor. The termination, *loom,* is of Saxon origin, and signifies a limb or member ; so that an heirloom is nothing else but a limb or member of the inheritance. Deer in a real authorized park, fishes in a pond, doves in a dove-house, &c., though in themselves personal chattels, are considered to be so

annexed to the inheritance, that they accompany the land wherever it vests, by either descent or purchase. For this reason also, the ancient jewels of the crown are held to be heir-looms. Charters, likewise, and deeds, court-rolls, and other evidences of the land, together with the chests in which they are contained, pass to the heir, in the nature of heir-looms, and do not go to the executor. By almost general custom, too, whatever is strongly affixed to the free-hold, and cannot be severed without damage, is become a member of the inheritance, and shall thereupon pass to the heir; such as chimney-pieces, pumps, old fixed or dormant tables, benches, and the like.

Other personal chattels there are, which also descend to the heir in the nature of heir-looms, as a monument or tombstone, in a church, or the coat-armour of his ancestor there hung up, with the pennons and other ensigns of honour, suited to his degree. In this case, albeit the freehold of the church is in the parson, and these are annexed to that freehold, yet cannot the parson or any other take them away or deface them, but if he do so is liable to an action by the heir.

Again, heir-looms, though they be mere chattels, cannot be de-vised away from the heir by will; but such a devise is void, even by a tenant in fee-simple. For, though the owner might, during his life, have sold or disposed of them, as he might of the timber of the estate, since, as the inheritance was his own, he might mangle or dismember it as he pleased; yet, they being at his death instantly vested in the heir, the devise, which is subsequent and not to take effect till *after* his death, shall be postponed to the custom, whereby they have already descended.

CHAPTER XXV.

OF TITLE BY SUCCESSION, MARRIAGE, AND JUDGMENT.

Title by succession—in corporations aggregate—and sole—Title by marriage —to wife's chattels real—chattels personal—choses in action—parapher-nalia—Title by judgment—to damages—to costs.

In the present chapter we shall take into consideration three other species of titles to goods and chattels.

V. The fifth method, therefore, of gaining a property in chattels, either personal or real, is by *succession :* which is, in strictness of law, only applicable to corporations aggregate, as dean and chapter, mayor and commonalty, master and fellows, and the like; in which one set of men may, by succeeding another set, acquire a property in all the goods, movables, and other chattels of the corporation. The true reason whereof is, because in judgment of law a corporation never dies; and, therefore, the predecessors, who lived a century ago, and their successors now in being, are one and the same body corporate. So that a gift to such a corporation, either of lands or of chattels, without naming their successors, vests an absolute property in them so long as the corporation subsists.

But, with regard to sole corporations, a considerable distinction must be made. For, if such sole corporation be the representative of a number of persons; as the master of an hospital, who is a corporation for the benefit of the poor brethren; or the dean of some ancient cathedral, who stands in the place of, and represents in his corporate capacity the chapter; such sole corporations as these have, in this respect, the same powers as corporations aggregate have, to take personal property or chattels in succession. And, therefore, a bond to such a master, or dean, and his successors, is good in law; and the successor shall have the advantage of it, for the benefit of the aggregate society, of which he is in law the representative. Whereas, in the case of sole corporations, which represent no others but themselves, as bishops, parsons, and the like, no chattel interest can regularly go in succession; and, therefore, if a lease for years be made to the Bishop of Oxford and his successors, in such case his executors or administrators, and not his successors, shall have it. For, the word *successors*, when applied to a person in his political capacity, is equivalent to the word *heirs* in his natural; and as such a lease for years, if made to John and his heirs, would not vest in his heirs but his executors; so if it be made to John Bishop of Oxford and his successors, who are the heirs of his body politic, it shall still vest in his executors and not in such his successors.

Yet, to this rule there are two exceptions. One in the case of the crown, in whom a chattel may vest by a grant of it formerly made to a preceding sovereign and his successors. The other exception is, where, by a *particular* custom, some *particular* corporations sole have acquired a power of taking *particular* chattel interests in succession. Thus, the Chamberlain of London, who is a corporation sole, may, by the custom of London, take *bonds* and *recognizances* to himself and his successors, for the benefit of the orphan's fund: but it will not follow from thence, that he has a capacity to take a *lease for years* to himself and his successors for the same purpose; for the custom extends not to that: nor that he may take a *bond* to himself and his successors, for any other purpose than the benefit of the orphan's fund; for that also is not warranted by the custom.

VI. A sixth method of acquiring property in goods and chattels is by *marriage*; whereby those chattels which belonged formerly to the wife, are vested in the husband, with the same degree of property, and with the same powers as the wife, when sole, had over them. And hence it follows, that whatever personal property belonged to the wife, before marriage, is by marriage absolutely vested in the husband. In a real estate, he only gains a title to the rents and profits during coverture: for that, depending upon feudal principles, remains entire to the wife after the death of her husband, or to her heirs, if she dies before him; unless, by the birth of a child, he becomes tenant for life by the courtesy. But, in chattel interests, the sole and absolute property vests in the husband, to be disposed of at his pleasure, if he chooses to take possession of them: for, unless he reduces them to possession, by exercising some act of ownership upon them, no property vests in him, but they shall remain to the wife, or to her representatives, after the coverture is determined.

There is, therefore, a very considerable difference in the acquisition of this species of property by the husband, according to the subject-matter, viz., whether it be a chattel *real*, or a chattel *personal*; and, of chattels personal, whether it be in *possession* or in *action* only. A *chattel real* vests in the husband, not absolutely, but *sub modo*. As, in case of a lease for years, the husband shall receive all the rents and profits of it, and may, if he pleases, sell, surrender, or dispose of it during the coverture: it is liable to execution for his debts; and, if he survives his wife, it is to all intents and purposes his own. Yet, if he has made no disposition thereof in his lifetime, and dies before his wife, he cannot dispose of it by will; for, the husband having made no alteration in the property during his life, it never was transferred from the wife; but after his death she shall remain in her ancient possession, and it shall not go to his executors. So it is also of chattels personal, or *choses in action*; as debts upon bond, contracts, and the like: these the husband may have if he pleases; that is, if he reduces them into possession by receiving or recovering them at law. For the mere *intention* on the part of the husband to reduce the wife's choses in action is not sufficient. Thus an agreement to sell a fund to which the wife is entitled is not a reduction into possession; the acts to effect this must be such as to divest the wife's property, and make that of the husband absolute; such as a judgment recovered in an action by him alone, or receipt of the money, or the decree of a court of equity for payment to him or for his use. If he dies before he has reduced them into possession, so that, at his death, they still continue *choses in action*, they shall survive to the wife; for the husband never exerted the power he had of obtaining an exclusive property in them.

Thus, in both these species of property the law is the same, in case the wife survives the husband; but in case the husband survives the wife, the law is very different with respect to *chattels real* and *choses in action*: for he shall have the *chattel real* by survivorship, but not the *chose in action*. And the reason is this: that the husband is in possession of the *chattel real* during the coverture, by a kind of joint-tenancy with his wife; which the law will not wrest out of his hands. But a *chose in action* shall not survive to him, because he never was in possession of it at all, during the coverture. Yet he still will be entitled to be her administrator; and may, in that capacity, recover such things in action as became due to her before or during the coverture. With regard to a wife's *reversionary choses in action*, these cannot from their nature be reduced into possession; and consequently could not, until lately, be assigned or affected by the husband even with the concurrence of the wife; but this rule of law has now been altered.

As to *chattels personal in possession*, which the wife has in her own right, as ready money, jewels, household goods and the like, the husband has therein an immediate and absolute property, devolved to him by the marriage, not only potentially, but in fact, which never can again revest in the wife or her representatives.

In one instance the wife may acquire a property in some of her husband's goods; which shall remain to her after his death, and not go to the executors. These are called her *paraphernalia*; a term borrowed from the civil law, to signify the apparel and ornaments of the wife, suitable to her rank and degree; and, therefore, even the jewels of a peeress, usually worn by her, have been held to be *paraphernalia*. Neither can the husband devise by his will such ornaments and jewels of his wife; though during his life he has the power to sell them or give them away. But if she continues in the use of them till his death, she shall afterwards retain them against his executors and administrators, and all other persons except creditors where there is a deficiency of assets. And her necessary apparel is protected even against the claim of creditors.

VII. A judgment, in consequence of some suit or action in a court of justice, is frequently the means of vesting the right and property of chattel interests in the prevailing party. Of this nature are:

1. Such penalties as are given, by particular statutes, to be recovered on an action *popular*; or, in other words, to be recovered by him or them that will sue for the same. Such as the penalty of 500*l.* which those persons are by several acts of parliament made liable to forfeit, that, being in particular offices or situations in life,

neglect to take the oaths to the government: which penalty is given to him or them that will sue for the same.

2. Another species of property that is acquired and lost by suit and judgment at law, is that of *damages.* Here the plaintiff has no certain demand till after verdict; but, when the jury has assessed his damages, and judgment is given thereupon, whether they amount to twenty pounds or twenty shillings, he instantly acquires, and the defendant loses at the same time, a right to that specific sum.

3. Hither also may be referred, upon the same principle, all title to *costs* and expenses of suit, which are often arbitrary, and rest entirely on the determination of the court, upon weighing all circumstances, both as to the *quantum*, and also, in the courts of equity especially, and upon motions in the courts of law, whether there shall be any costs at all. These costs, therefore, when given by the court to either party, may be looked upon as an acquisition made by the judgment of law.

CHAPTER XXVI.

OF TITLE BY GIFT, GRANT, AND CONTRACT.

Title by gift—grants—bills of sale—Title by contract—agreements—express or implied—consideration—*nudum pactum*—usual contracts—viz.,—Sale or Exchange—Bailment—Hiring and Borrowing—Interest—Insurance—Annuities—Debts—by specialty—simple contract—Bills of Exchange.

Two of the remaining methods of acquiring a title to property in things personal, are so much connected, that it will be convenient to consider them in one chapter. I allude to title by *gift* or *grant,* and by *contract:* whereof the former vests a property in *possession,* the latter a property in *action.*

VIII. Gifts or *grants,* the eighth method of transferring personal property, are thus to be distinguished from each other, that *gifts* are always gratuitous, *grants* are upon some consideration or equivalent; and they may be divided, with regard to their subject-matter, into gifts or grants of chattels *real,* and gifts or grants of chattels *personal.* Under the head of gifts or grants of chattels *real,* may be included all leases for years of land, assignments, and surrenders of those leases; and all the other methods of conveying an estate less than freehold, which has been already considered. Yet these very seldom carry the outward appearance of a gift, being usually expressed to be made in consideration of blood or natural affection, or of five or ten shillings nominally paid to the grantor; and in case of leases, always reserving a rent, though it be but a peppercorn; any of which considerations will, in the eye of the law, convert the gift, if executed, into a grant; if not executed, into a contract.

Grants or gifts of chattels *personal*, are the act of transferring the right and the possession of them; whereby one man renounces, and another man immediately acquires, all title and interest therein; which may be done either in writing, or by word of mouth accompanied by an actual delivery of possession to the donee. But this conveyance, when merely voluntary, is somewhat suspicious, and is usually construed to be fraudulent, if creditors or others become sufferers thereby. Accordingly by statute 13 Eliz. c. 5, every grant or gift of chattels, with an intent to defraud creditors or others, shall be void as against such persons to whom such fraud would be prejudicial; but, as against the grantor himself, shall stand good and effectual. And by 17 & 18 Vict. c. 36, *bills of sale*, the usual denomination of a grant of chattels personal, must be filed in the Court of Queen's Bench within twenty-one days after the making or giving them; otherwise they will, as against creditors, be null and void.

IX. A contract which usually conveys an interest merely in action is thus defined: "an agreement upon sufficient consideration to do "or not to do a particular thing."

First then it is an *agreement*, a mutual bargain or convention; and, therefore, there must at least be two contracting parties, of sufficient ability to make a contract; as where A contracts with B to pay him 100*l.*, and thereby transfers a property in such sum to B: which property is, however, not in possession, but in action merely, and recoverable by suit at law; wherefore it could not be transferred to another person by the strict rules of the ancient common law; for no *chose in action* could be assigned or granted over, because it was thought to be a great encouragement to litigiousness, if a man were allowed to make over to a stranger his right of going to law. But this nicety is now disregarded; though, in compliance with the ancient principle, the form of assigning a *chose in action* is in the nature of a declaration of trust, and an agreement to permit the assignee to make use of the name of the assignor, in order to recover the possession. And, therefore, when in common acceptation a debt or bond is said to be assigned over, it must still be sued for in the original creditor's name, the person to whom it is transferred being rather an attorney than an assignee.

This contract or agreement may be either express or implied. *Express* contracts are where the terms of the agreement are openly

M

uttered and avowed at the time of the making, as to deliver an ox, or ten loads of timber, or to pay a stated price for certain goods. *Implied* are such as reason and justice dictate, and which therefore the law presumes that every man undertakes to perform. As, if I employ a person to do any business for me, or perform any work, the law implies that I undertook, or contracted, to pay him as much as his labour deserves. If I take up wares from a tradesman without any agreement of price, the law concludes that I contracted to pay their real value. And there is also one species of implied contracts which runs through and is annexed to all other contracts, conditions, and covenants, vjz., that if I fail in my part of the agreement, I shall pay the other party such damages as he has sustained by such my neglect or refusal.

A contract may also be either *executed*, as if A agrees to change horses with B, and they do it immediately; in which case the possession and the right are transferred together: or it may be *executory*, as if they agree to change next week; here the right only vests, and their reciprocal property in each other's horse is not in possession but in action; for a contract *executed*, which differs in nothing from a grant, conveys a *chose in possession*; a contract *executory* conveys only a *chose in action*.

Secondly; a contract is an agreement upon *sufficient consideration*. The civilians hold, that, in all contracts, either express or implied, there must be something given in exchange, something that is mutual or reciprocal. This thing, which is the price or motive of the contract, we call the consideration: and it must be a thing lawful in itself, or else the contract is void. A *good* consideration, we have before seen, is that of blood or natural affection between near relations; the satisfaction accruing from which, the law esteems an equivalent for whatever benefit may move from one relation to another. Yet it may sometimes be set aside, and the contract become void, when it tends in its consequences to defraud creditors or other third persons of their just rights. But a contract for any *valuable* consideration, as for marriage, for money, for work done, or for other reciprocal contracts, can never be impeached at law; and if it be of a sufficient adequate value, is never set aside in equity: for the person contracted with has then given an equivalent in recompense, and is therefore as much an owner, or a creditor, as any other person.

A consideration of some sort or other is so absolutely necessary to the forming of a contract, that a *nudum pactum*, or agreement to do or pay anything on one side, without any compensation on the other, is totally void in law: and a man cannot be compelled to perform it. As if one man promises to give another 100*l.*, here there is nothing contracted for or given on the one side, and therefore there is nothing binding on the other. And, however a man may or may not be bound to perform it, in honour or conscience, which the municipal laws do not take upon them to decide, certainly those municipal laws will not compel the execution of what he had no visible inducement to engage for: the maxim of our law being that *ex nudo pacto non oritur actio.* But any degree of reciprocity will prevent the pact from being nude: nay, even if the thing be founded on a prior moral obligation, as a promise to pay a just debt, though barred by the statute of limitations, it is no longer *nudum pactum.*

Thirdly, a contract is an agreement, upon sufficient consideration, *to do or not to do a particular thing.* The most usual contracts, whereby the right of chattels personal may be acquired in the laws of England, are, 1. That of *sale* or *exchange.* 2. That of *bailment.* 3. That of *hiring* and *borrowing.* 4. That of *debt.*

1. Sale or *exchange* is a transmutation of property from one man to another, in consideration of some price or recompense in value: for there is no sale without a recompense; there must be *quid pro quo.* If it be a commutation of goods for goods, it is more properly an *exchange;* but, if it be a transferring of goods for money, it is called a *sale:* which is a method of exchange introduced for the convenience of mankind, by establishing a universal medium, which may be exchanged for all sorts of other property; whereas if goods were only to be exchanged for goods, by way of barter, it would be difficult to adjust the respective values, and the carriage would be intolerably cumbersome.

If a man agrees with another for goods at a certain price, he may not carry them away before he has paid for them; for it is no sale without payment, unless the contrary be expressly agreed. And therefore, if the vendor says the price of a beast is four pounds, and the vendee says he will give four pounds, the bargain is struck; and they neither of them are at liberty to be off, provided immediate possession be tendered by the other side. But if neither the money be paid, nor the goods delivered, nor tender made, nor any subsequent agreement be entered into, it is no contract, and the owner may dispose of the goods as he pleases. But if any part of the price is paid down, if it be but a penny, or any portion of the goods delivered by way of *earnest,* the property of the goods is absolutely bound by it: and the vendee may recover the goods by action, as well as the vendor may the price of them. And such regard does the law pay to earnest as an evidence of a contract, that, by the *Statute of Frauds,* 29 Car. II. c. 3, no contract for the sale of goods, to the value of 10*l.* or more, shall be valid, unless the buyer actually receives part of the goods sold, by way of earnest on his part; or unless he gives part of the price to the vendor by.

way of earnest to bind the bargain, or in part of payment; or
unless some note in writing of the bargain be made and signed
by the party, or his agent, who is to be charged with the contract.
And this enactment is, by *Lord Tenterden's Act*, 9 Geo. IV. c. 14,
extended to all contracts for the sale of goods of the value of 10*l.*
sterling, or upwards, notwithstanding the goods may be intended to be
delivered at some future time, or may not at the time of the contract be
actually made or provided, or ready for delivery, or some act may be
requisite for the making or completing thereof, or rendering the same
fit for delivery. With regard to goods under the value of 10*l.*, no
contract or agreement for the sale of them shall be valid, unless the
goods are to be delivered within one year, or unless the contract be
made in writing, and signed by the party, or his agent, who is to be
charged therewith.

As soon as the bargain is struck, the property of the goods is
transferred to the vendee, and that of the price to the vendor; but
the vendee cannot take the goods, until he tenders the price agreed
on. Yet, if he tenders the money to the vendor, and he refuses it,
the vendee may seize the goods, or have an action against the vendor
for detaining them. And by a regular sale, without delivery, the
property is so absolutely vested in the vendee, that if A sells a horse
to B for 10*l.* and B pays him earnest, or signs a note in writing of
the bargain; and afterwards, before the delivery of the horse or
money paid, the horse dies in the vendor's custody; still he is
entitled to the money, because by the contract the property was in
the vendee. But in one particular instance, where the act of transfer is not completed, the right of property transferred by the sale to
the vendee may be divested by an act of the vendor, this occurring
when the vendor exercises that right conferred on him by the Law
Merchant, which is termed the right of *stoppage in transitu.* For
where the parties deal on credit, that is, when the contract is in fact for
the immediate delivery of the goods, but for the future payment of
the money, it may sometimes happen that before the delivery has been
completed, the vendor may discover that the vendee is insolvent,
and that he will consequently be unable to perform his part of the contract, when the time arrives for so doing. And the law, therefore,
allows the vendor, if he can, to prevent the goods coming into the
possession of the vendee. For if he has not parted with the goods at
all, he may retain them; but if they have already been put into the
hands of some third party, as a carrier, for delivery, he may give
notice to such party, who thereupon becomes bound to retain them;
and after notice, should he by mistake deliver them, the vendor may
bring an action for them even against the assignees of the vendee, if
he have in the meantime become bankrupt. Nor will partial pay-

ment destroy this right, for the effect of the stoppage *in transitu* is not to rescind the contract, which cannot be done after part-payment; its operation is to create an equitable lien upon the goods, which may be retained until full payment be made, the vendee or his assigns being then entitled to the goods. This right of stoppage ceases entirely, and cannot be exercised, when the goods have come actually or constructively into the hands of the vendee; as if after the goods have been sold, they remain in the vendor's warehouse, he receiving warehouse rent for them. In such a case the vendor holds the goods as the agent of the vendee, the delivery is considered complete, and the right of stoppage *in transitu* is gone.

This right of an unpaid vendor to stop the goods cannot, however, be exercised where the goods have been consigned by a bill of lading, and that instrument has been indorsed over by the consignee. A *bill of lading* is an acknowledgment signed by the master of a ship of the receipt of goods, which he undertakes to deliver at some foreign port, to a person therein named or to his assigns, upon payment of freight and other dues. And by the custom of merchants, which is part of the *Lex Mercatoria*, this acknowledgment is transferable by indorsement, and thereby by the right of property in the goods passes to the indorsee; against whom, if he be an assignee for value, and without notice of the insolvency, the unpaid vendor cannot stop the delivery of the goods, a doctrine at variance with the general principle of our law, which does not permit any one to transfer a greater right than he has himself.

Hitherto of the transfer of property in goods by sale, where the vendor *hath* such property in himself. But property may also in some cases be transferred by sale, though the vendor *hath none at all* in the goods: for it is expedient that the buyer, by taking proper precautions, may at all events be secure of his purchase, otherwise all commerce between man and man must soon be at an end. And therefore the general rule of the law is, that all sales and contracts of anything vendible, in fairs or markets *overt*, that is, open, shall not only be good between the parties, but also be binding on all those that have any right of property therein. Market overt in the country is only held on the special days provided for particular towns by charter or prescription; but in London every day, except Sunday, is market-day. The market-place, or spot of ground set apart by custom for the sale of particular goods, is also in the country the only market overt, but in London every shop in which goods are exposed publicly to sale, is market overt, for such things only as the owner professes to trade in. But if my goods are stolen from me, and sold out of market overt, my property is not altered, and I may take them wherever I find them.

By the civil law an implied warranty was annexed to every sale, in respect to the title of the vendor: and so too, in our law, a purchaser of goods and chattels may have a satisfaction from the seller, if he sells them *as his own* and the title proves deficient, without any express warranty for that purpose. But, with regard to the goodness of the wares so purchased, the vendor is not bound to answer, unless he expressly warrants them to be sound and good, or unless he knew them to be otherwise and has used any art to disguise them, or unless they turn out to be different from what he represented to the buyer.

2. Bailment, from the French *bailler*, to deliver, is a delivery of goods in trust, upon a contract expressed or implied, that the trust shall be faithfully executed on the part of the bailee. As if cloth be delivered, or, in our legal dialect, bailed, to a tailor to make a suit of clothes, he has it upon an implied contract to render it again when made, and that in a workmanlike manner. If money or goods be delivered to a common carrier, to convey from Oxford to London, and no condition be imposed on either side, he is under a contract in law to pay or carry them to the person appointed. If goods be delivered to an innkeeper or his servants, he is bound to keep them safely, and restore them when his guest leaves the house; unless he protects himself by requiring their deposit with him, and gives a proper notice to his guest that he does so. If a man takes in a horse or other cattle to graze and depasture in his grounds, which the law calls *agistment*, he takes them upon an implied contract to return them on demand to the owner. If a pawnbroker receives plate or jewels as a pledge or security, for the repayment of money lent thereon at a day certain, he has them upon an express contract or condition to restore them, if the pledger performs his part by redeeming them in due time. If a friend delivers anything to his friend to keep for him, the receiver is bound to restore it on demand: and it was formerly held that in the meantime he was answerable for any damage or loss it might sustain, whether by accident or otherwise; unless he expressly undertook to keep it only with the same care as his own goods, and then he should not be answerable for theft or other accidents. But the law seems now to be settled, that such a general bailment will not charge the bailee with any loss, unless it happens by gross neglect, which is an evidence of fraud: but, if he undertakes specially to keep the goods safely and securely, he is bound to take the same care of them as a prudent man would take of his own.

In all these instances there is a special qualified property transferred from the bailor to the bailee, together with the possession. It is not an absolute property, because of his contract for restitution:

the bailor having still left in him the right to a *chose* in action, grounded upon such contract. And, on account of this qualified property of the bailee, he may, as well as the bailor, maintain an action against such as injure or take away these chattels. The tailor, the carrier, the innkeeper, the agisting farmer, the pawn-broker, and the general bailee, may all of them vindicate, in their own right, this their possessory interest, against any stranger or third person. For, being responsible to the bailor, if the goods are lost or damaged by his wilful default or gross negligence, or if he do not deliver up the chattels on lawful demand, it is therefore reason-able that he should have a right of action against all other persons who may have purloined or injured them, that he may always be ready to answer the call of the bailor.

Bailees have in some cases what is called a *lien* upon the goods committed to their case, which is the right of detaining some personal chattel from the owner thereof until a debt due to the person retain-ing has been satisfied. ¯A lien may be either *particular* or *general*; the former is where the claim of retainer is made upon the goods themselves, in respect of which the debt arises, a claim which the law favours. The other, or general lien, is where goods are retained in respect of a general balance of account, which is less favoured. Thus a trainer who has a horse delivered to him to train, has a lien for his charges of keep and training; and in general, when the goods are delivered to a person to be improved or altered in character, this right arises; as when cloth is delivered to a tailor to convert into clothes; or corn to a miller to be returned in the shape of flour. The right may, however, be regulated by special agreement, and then its operation will depend upon the particular terms of the contract; but in the absence of express contract, the law implies a lien wherever the usage of trade or the previous dealings of the parties give ground for such an implication. Although, as has been said, *general* liens are not favoured by law, yet in some cases they have become allowed and established by usage, as in the case of attorneys upon the title-deeds and documents of their clients; and factors, warehousemen, and others, upon goods confided to them in the ordinary course of business; all of whom have a lien for the amount of the general balance due to them in their several capacities.

3. Hiring and *borrowing* are also contracts by which a qualified property may be transferred to the hirer or borrower: in which there is only this difference, that hiring is always for a price or recompense; borrowing is merely gratuitous. But the law in both cases is the same. They are both contracts, whereby the possession and a transient property is transferred for a particular time or use, on condition to restore the goods so hired or borrowed, as soon as the

time is expired or use performed; together with the price, in case of
hiring, either expressly agreed on by the parties, or left to be
implied by law according to the value of the service.   By this
mutual contract, the hirer or borrower gains a temporary property
in the thing hired, accompanied with an implied condition to use it
with moderation and not abuse it; and the owner or lender retains
a reversionary interest in the same, and acquires a new property in
the price or reward.   Thus, if a man hires or borrows a horse for a
month, he has the possession and a qualified property therein during
that period; on the expiration of which his qualified property determines, and the owner becomes, in case of hiring, entitled also to the
price for which the horse was hired.

There is one species of this price or reward, the most usual of any,
but concerning which many good and learned men have in former
times very much perplexed themselves and other people, by raising
doubts about its legality *in foro conscientiæ*.   That is, when money
is lent on a contract to receive not only the principal sum again, but
also an increase by way of compensation for the use; which generally
is called *interest* by those who think it lawful, and *usury* by those
who do not.   For the enemies to interest in general make no distinction between that and usury, holding any increase of money to
be indefensibly usurious.   And this they ground as well on the prohibition of it by the law of Moses among the Jews, as also upon what
is said to be laid down by Aristotle, that money is naturally barren,
and to make it breed money is preposterous, and a perversion of the
end of its institution, which was only to serve the purposes of exchange, and not of increase.   Hence, the school divines have branded
the practice of taking interest, as being contrary to the divine law
both natural and revealed; and the canon law has proscribed the
taking any, the least increase for the loan of money as a mortal sin.
With us, however, the taking of interest upon moderate and conscientious terms, or what was called *legal* interest, has long been
recognised.   But until quite recently, it was considered desirable to
regulate by law the rate at which it should be taken, and interest
beyond this limit was accordingly stigmatised with the odious appellation of usury; and it is only within the last few years that parliament has carried out a principle which political economists have
preached for above a century, and permitted the rate of interest to
regulate itself according to the exigencies of the time and the nature
of things.

So long as the rate of interest was fixed by law, the hazard was
often greater than the interest allowed would compensate.   This
gave rise to the practice of 1. Bottomry, or *respondentia*. 2. Policies
of insurance. 3. Annuities upon lives.

1. *Bottomry,* which originally arose from permitting the master of a ship, in a foreign country, to hypothecate the ship in order to raise money to refit, is in the nature of a mortgage of a ship; when the owner takes up money to enable him to carry on his voyage, and pledges the keel or *bottom* of the ship, *partem pro toto,* as a security for the repayment. In which case, it is understood, that, if the ship be lost, the lender loses also his whole money; but, if it returns in safety, then he shall receive back his principal, and also the premium or interest agreed upon, however it may exceed the legal rate of interest. And this is allowed to be a valid contract in all trading nations, for the benefit of commerce, and by reason of the extraordinary hazard run by the lender. And in this case the ship and tackle, if brought home, are answerable, as well as the person of the borrower, for the money lent. But if the loan is not upon the vessel, but upon the goods and merchandise, which must necessarily be sold or exchanged in the course of the voyage, then only the borrower, personally, is bound to answer the contract; who, therefore, in this case is said to take up money at *respondentia.*

2. A policy of *insurance* is a contract between A and B, that upon A's paying a premium equivalent to the hazard run, B will indemnify or insure him against a particular event. This is founded upon the same principle as the doctrine of interest upon loans. For if I insure a ship to the Levant, and back again, at *five per cent.*; here I calculate the chance that she performs her voyage to be twenty to one against her being lost: and, if she be lost, I lose 100*l.* and get 6*l.* Now, this is much the same as if I lend the merchant, whose whole fortunes are embarked in this vessel, 100*l.* at the rate of *eight per cent.* For, by a loan, I should be immediately out of possession of my money, the inconvenience of which we may suppose equal to *three per cent.*; if, therefore, I had actually lent him 100*l.* I must have added 3*l.* on the score of inconvenience, to the 5*l.* allowed for the hazard, which together would have made 8*l.* Thus too, in a loan, if the chance of repayment depends upon the borrower's life, it is frequent, besides the usual rate of interest, for the borrower to have his life insured till the time of repayment; for which he is loaded with an additional premium, suited to his age and constitution.

3. The practice of purchasing *annuities for lives* at a certain price or premium, instead of advancing the same sum on an ordinary loan, arose usually from the inability of the borrower to give the lender a permanent security for the return of the money borrowed, at any one period of time. He therefore stipulates, in effect, to repay annually, during his life, some part of the money borrowed; together with interest for so much of the principal as annually remains unpaid, and an additional compensation for the extraordinary hazard run, of

losing that principal entirely by the contingency of the borrower's death: all which considerations, being calculated and blended together, constitute the just proportion or *quantum* of the annuity which ought to be granted. The real value of that contingency must depend on the age, constitution, situation, and conduct of the borrower; and therefore the price of such annuities cannot, without the utmost difficulty, be reduced to any general rules.

4. The last species of contracts, which I have to mention, is that of *debt*; whereby a *chose* in action or other right to a certain sum of money, is mutually acquired and lost. This may be the counterpart of, and arise from, any of the other species of contracts. As in case of a sale, where the price is not paid in ready money, the vendee becomes indebted to the vendor for the sum agreed on; and the vendor has a property in this price, as a *chose* in action, by means of this contract of debt. In bailment, if the bailee loses or detains a sum of money bailed to him for any special purpose, he becomes indebted to the bailor in the same numerical sum, upon his implied contract, that he should execute the trust reposed in him, or repay the money to the bailor. Upon hiring or borrowing, the hirer or borrower, at the same time that he acquires a property in the thing lent, may also become indebted to the lender, upon his contract to restore the money borrowed, to pay the price or premium of the loan, the hire of the horse, or the like. Any contract, in short, whereby a determinate sum of money becomes due to any person, and is not paid, but remains in action merely, is a contract of debt. And, taken in this light, it comprehends a great variety of acquisition; being usually divided into debts of *record*, debts by *specialty*, and debts by *simple* contract.

A debt of *record* is a sum of money which appears to be due by the evidence of a court of record. Thus, when any specific sum is adjudged to be due from the defendant to the plaintiff, in an action or suit at law, this is a contract of the highest nature, being established by the sentence of a court of judicature. Debts upon recognizance I have already had occasion to refer to. They are properly ranked among this first and principal class of debts, viz., debts of record; since the contract on which they are founded is witnessed by the highest kind of evidence, viz., by matter of record.

Debts by *specialty*, or special contract, are such whereby a sum of money becomes, or is acknowledged to be, due, by deed or instrument under seal. Such as, by deed of covenant, by deed of sale, by lease reserving rent, or by bond or obligation: which last I took occasion to explain in a previous chapter of the present book. These are looked upon as the next class of debts after those of record, being confirmed by special evidence, under seal.

Debts by *simple contract* are such, where the contract upon which the obligation arises is neither ascertained by matter of record, nor yet by deed or special instrument, but by mere oral evidence, the most simple of any; or by notes unsealed, which are capable of a more easy proof, and, therefore, only better than a verbal promise. It is easy to see into what a vast variety of obligations this last class may be branched out, through the numerous contracts for money, which are not only expressed by the parties, but virtually implied in law. Some of these we have already occasionally hinted at; and the rest, to avoid repetition, must be referred to those particular heads in the third book of these commentaries, where the breach of such contracts will be considered. I shall only observe at present, that, by the statute 29 Car. II. c. 3, no executor or administrator shall be charged upon any special promise to answer damages out of his own estate, and no person shall be charged upon any promise to answer for the debt or default of another, or upon any agreement in consideration of marriage, or upon any contract or sale of any real estate, or upon any agreement that is not to be performed within one year from the making; unless the agreement, or some memorandum thereof, be in writing, and signed by the party himself, or by his authority: which enactments of the Statute of Frauds are extended by 9 Geo. IV. c. 14, Lord Tenterden's Act; which provides that no action shall be maintained, whereby to charge any person upon any promise made after full age, to pay any debt contracted during infancy, or upon any ratification after full age of any promise or simple contract made during infancy, unless such promise or ratification shall be made by some writing signed by the party to be charged therewith; and that no action shall be brought, whereby to charge any person by reason of any representation given relating to the character, conduct, credit, ability, trade, or dealings of any other person, to the intent that such other person may obtain credit, money, or goods, unless such representation be made in writing, signed by the party to be charged therewith.

But there is one species of debts upon simple contract, which, being a transaction now introduced into all sorts of civil life, under the name of *paper credit*, deserves a more particular regard. These are debts by *bills of exchange*, and *promissory notes*.

A bill of *exchange* is a security, originally invented among merchants in different countries, for the more easy remittance of money from the one to the other, which has since spread itself into almost all pecuniary transactions. It is an open letter of request from one man to another, desiring him to pay a sum named therein to a third person on his account: by which means a man at the most distant part of the world may have money remitted to him from any

trading country. If A lives in Jamaica, and owes B, who lives in
England, 1000*l.*, now if C be going from England to Jamaica, he
may pay B this 1000*l.*, and take a bill of exchange drawn by B in
England upon A in Jamaica, and receive it when he comes thither.
Thus does B receive his debt, at any distance of place, by transferring it to C; who carries over his money in paper credit, without
danger of robbery or loss. In common speech such a bill is frequently called a *draft*, but a *bill of exchange* is the more legal as
well as mercantile expression. The person, however, who writes
this letter, is called in law the *drawer*, and he to whom it is written
the *drawee*; and the third person, or negotiator, to whom it is payable, whether specially named or the *bearer* generally, is called the
payee. A cheque is a bill of exchange addressed to a banker, and
payable to a person named or *the bearer*. Such a cheque is, from
the promise implied from the banking contract, binding on the
banker having assets of the drawer, without acceptance, and if he
does not pay it, he is liable to an action by the drawer.

Bills of exchange are either *foreign* or *inland*; *foreign*, when
drawn by a merchant residing abroad upon his correspondent in
England, or *vice versâ*; and *inland*, when both the drawer and the
drawee reside within the kingdom. There is not in law any manner
of difference between them, except that inland bills do not require
to be *protested*, as is the case with foreign bills. *Promissory notes*,
or notes of hand, are a plain and direct engagement in writing, to
pay a sum specified at the time therein limited to a person therein
named, or sometimes to his order, or often to the bearer at large.
These also, by the statute, 3 & 4 Ann. c. 9, are made assignable
and indorseable in like manner as bills of exchange.

The payee, we may observe, either of a bill of exchange or promissory note, has clearly a property vested in him, not indeed in
possession but in action, by the *express* contract of the drawer in
the case of a promissory note, and, in the case of a bill of exchange,
by his *implied* contract, viz., that, provided the drawee does not pay
the bill, the drawer will: for which reason it is usual, in bills of
exchange, to express that the *value* thereof has been *received* by the
drawer, in order to show the consideration upon which the implied
contract of repayment arises. And this property, so vested, may
be transferred and assigned from the payee to any other man; contrary to the general rule of the common law, that no *chose* in action
is assignable; which assignment is the life of paper credit. It may,
therefore, be of some use to mention a few of the principal incidents
attending this transfer or assignment, in order to make it regular,
and thereby to charge the drawer with the payment of the debt to
other persons than those with whom he originally contracted.

In the first place, then, the payee, or person to whom or whose *order* such bill of exchange or promissory note is payable, may, by indorsement, or writing his name *in dorso,* or on the back of it, and delivery, assign over his whole property to the bearer, or else to another person by name, either of whom is then called *the indorsee;* and he may assign the same to another, and so on *in infinitum.* And a promissory note or cheque, payable to A, or *bearer,* is negotiable without any indorsement, and payment thereof may be demanded by any bearer of it. But, in case of a bill of exchange, if it be payable at some time after sight, the payee, or the indorsee, whether it be a general or particular indorsement, is to go to the drawee, and offer his bill for acceptance, which acceptance, so as to charge the drawer with costs, must be in writing, under or on the back of the bill. If the drawee accepts the bill, which must in all cases be in writing, he then makes himself liable to pay it; this being now a contract on his side, grounded on an acknowledgment that the drawer has effects in his hands, or at least credit sufficient to warrant the payment. If the drawee refuses to accept the bill, and it be of the value of 20*l.* or upwards, and expressed to be for value received, the payee or indorsee may, and in the case of a foreign bill ought to, protest it for *non-acceptance;* which protest must be made in writing, under a copy of such bill of exchange, by some notary public; or, if no such notary be resident in the place, then by any other substantial inhabitant in the presence of two credible witnesses; and notice of such protest must immediately be given to the drawer and indorsers. An *inland bill* need not be protested ; but *notice of its non-acceptance* must be at once given.

But, in case such bill be accepted by the drawee, and after acceptance he fails or refuses to pay it within three days after it becomes due, which three days are called *days of grace,* the payee or indorsee is then, in the case of a foreign bill, to get it protested for *non-payment,* in the same manner, and by the same persons who are to protest it in case of non-acceptance, and such protest must also be notified, within fourteen days after, to the drawer. A *protest for non-payment* is not required in the case of an *inland bill;* but *notice of dishonour* must be given immediately to the drawer and indorsers, in order to preserve the holder's remedy against them. And the drawer, on such protest being produced in the case of foreign bills, or on demand in the case of inland bills, is bound to make good to the payee, or indorsee, not only the amount of the said bill, but also interest and all charges, to be computed from the time of making such protest. But if no protest be made or notified, or notice of dishonour be given, to the drawer, and any damage accrues by such neglect, it shall fall on the holder of the bill. The bill, when refused, must be demanded of the drawer as soon as conveniently may be; for though, when one draws a bill of exchange, he subjects himself to the payment, if the person on whom it is drawn refuses either to accept or pay, yet that is with this limitation, that if the bill be not paid, when due, the person to whom it is payable shall in convenient time give the drawer notice thereof, for otherwise the law will imply it paid; since it would be prejudicial to commerce, if a bill might rise up to charge the drawer at any distance of time; when in the mean time all reckonings and accounts may be adjusted between the drawer and the drawee.

If the bill be an indorsed bill, and the indorsee cannot get the drawee to discharge it, he may call upon either the drawer or the indorser, or, if the bill has been negotiated through many hands, upon any of the indorsers; for each indorser is a warrantor for the payment of the bill, which is frequently taken in payment as much, or more, upon credit of the indorser, as of the drawer. And if such indorser, so called upon, has the names of one or more indorsers prior to his own, to each of whom he is properly an indorsee, he is also at liberty to call upon any of them to make him satisfaction, and so upwards. But the first indorser has nobody to resort to but the drawer only.

What has been said of bills of exchange is applicable also to promissory notes, that are indorsed over, and negotiated from one hand to another; only that, in this case, as there is no drawee, there can be no protest for non-acceptance; or rather the law considers a promissory note in the light of a bill drawn by a man upon himself, and accepted at the time of drawing. And, in case of non-payment by the maker, the several indorses of a promissory note have the same remedy, as upon bills of exchange against the prior indorsers.

The holder of a dishonoured bill or note may bring separate actions against the acceptor, drawer, and all the indorsers at the same time. Although, however, he may obtain judgments in all the actions, yet he can recover but one satisfaction for the value of the bill; but he may sue out execution against all the rest for the costs of their respective actions. And these instruments are, for the benefit of trade and commerce, so highly favoured by the law, that a special proceeding for recovering the amount thereof, which is at once expeditious and inexpensive, has been provided, as shall be more fully explained in the third book of these commentaries.

CHAPTER XXVII.

OF TITLE BY BANKRUPTCY.

The bankrupt laws — Petition — Adjudication — Surrender — Examination — Appointment of assignees — Proof of debts — Discovery — Discharge — Winding up of joint-stock companies.

A TENTH method of transferring property, is that of *bankruptcy*; a title which was before lightly touched upon, so far as it related to the transfer of the real estate of the bankrupt. At present, I am to treat of it more minutely, as it principally relates to the disposition of chattels, in which the property of persons concerned in trade more usually consists, than in lands or tenements.

1. A bankrupt is properly defined to be "a trader who secretes "himself or does certain other acts, with intent to defeat or delay his "creditors." He was formerly considered merely in the light of a criminal or offender: and in this spirit we are told by Sir Edward Coke, that we have fetched as well the name as the wickedness of bankrupts from foreign nations. But at present the laws of bankruptcy are considered as laws calculated for the benefit of trade, and founded on the principles of humanity as well as justice; and to that end they confer some privileges, not only on the creditors, but also on the bankrupt or debtor himself. On the creditors, by compelling the bankrupt to give up all his effects to their use, without any fraudulent concealment: on the debtor, by exempting him from the rigour of the general law, whereby his person might be confined at the discretion of his creditor, though in reality he has nothing to satisfy the debt: whereas the law of bankruptcy, taking into consideration the sudden and unavoidable accidents to which men in trade are liable, has given them the liberty of their persons, and some pecuniary emoluments, upon condition they surrender up their whole estate to be divided among their creditors. The law of England, consequently, and till quite recently, allowed the benefit of the laws of bankruptcy to none but actual *traders*: justly considering, that if persons in other situations of life ran in debt without the power of payment, they should take the consequences of their own indiscretion, even though they met with sudden accidents that might reduce their fortunes.

And the position of those debtors who were not entitled to the benefit of the bankrupt laws, was, consequently, one of great hardship. For as a judgment creditor had a right to take the person of the debtor, and to cause him to be detained in prison until he satisfied the claim against him, the unhappy debtor might possibly be detained for years in hopeless confinement. This, indeed, became so common an occurrence, that special acts of parliament were passed for the liberation of these insolvents; but these statutes were only temporary in their nature, and partial in their operation; and the evil remained practically unabated until the year 1813, when the statute 53 Geo. III. c. 102, first provided permanently for the relief of insolvent prisoners. This act was followed by others, until finally the statute 1 & 2 Vict. c. 110, consolidated the law on this subject, and established a regular system, and a court for the relief of insolvent debtors.

The proceedings in these cases, brought before this tribunal, were analogous to those in a bankruptcy, with one essential point of difference; that whereas the bankrupt was relieved from all claims upon him whatever, the insolvent remained burdened with the whole amount of the debts, which his present property was unequal to discharge; and all future acquisitions which he might make were for the benefit of his creditors until they were fully paid. The result was that a *trader*, however reckless, could, as a bankrupt, be ultimately freed from all his obligations; while a *non-trader*, however unfortunate, had no effectual means of escape from the pressure of his liabilities.

The palpable injustice which in many cases resulted from this state of the law, led at last to the repeal of all the statutes passed for the relief of insolvents; and the subjection of all debtors whatever to the bankrupt laws: the sole distinction between traders and non-traders now consisting in this, that what constitutes an act of bankruptcy in the one, is not necessarily an act of bankruptcy in the other. I shall not, however, examine by what *acts* a man may become a bankrupt, but content myself with referring the reader to the several statutes on this subject, and the resolutions formed by the courts thereon.

The first proceeding in ordinary cases is the filing of the *petition for adjudication*, on which the court either adjudicates the trader to be a bankrupt, or dismisses the petition. The next proceeding, in case an adjudication is made, is the *surrender* of the bankrupt, and his *examination;* the appointment of creditors' assignees, and the *proof of debts* against the estate. The last proceeding is the application of the bankrupt for his *discharge*, and the opposition to it, if any: before or after which, periodical *audits* must be made, and *dividends* declared, until the whole of the assets are distributed.

When a petition has been filed, the court may issue a warrant for the arrest of the debtor, and for the seizure of all his property. But in ordinary cases, the court proceeds to adjudicate the trader a bankrupt, and to appoint an *official assignee* to act in the bankruptcy; whose duty it is, immediately on his appointment, to take possession of all the bankrupt's property. Of this adjudication, notice is given to the bankrupt in cases where he is not the petitioner, so that he may, if so advised, dispute its validity.

If it is then submitted to, or sustained, notice is given in the Gazette, and two public meetings of the creditors appointed for the bankrupt to surrender and conform, and for the choice of creditors' assignees.

At the first of these meetings the majority of the creditors may transfer the administration of the estate to the county court; otherwise an election must be made of assignees, in whom the estate shall be vested for the benefit of the creditors.

In the mean time, however, and immediately on the adjudication being made, the *official assignee* becomes the depository of all the bankrupt's property; and may sell or dispose of goods of a perishable nature, receive rents, interest, proceeds of sales, or other moneys which may accrue from the estate, and act generally for the benefit of the creditors under the orders of the court.

At the second of these meetings, at farthest, the bankrupt must *surrender*; or, in default of doing so, be guilty of a misdemeanor punishable by imprisonment not exceeding three years. When he does so appear, he is examined touching all matters relating to his debts and effects; and he must next also file a statement of his accounts—to the truth of which he may be required to make oath —an abstract of which must be circulated among the creditors who have proved their debts, so that they may appear and oppose his passing, if so advised.

The bankrupt, upon his examination, is bound upon pain of imprisonment not exceeding three years, formerly the penalty was death, to make a *full discovery* of all his estate and effects, as well in expectancy as in possession, and how he has disposed of the same; and is to deliver up all in his own power to the assignees, except the necessary apparel of himself, his wife, and his children.

Hitherto, everything is in favour of the creditors; and the law seems to be pretty rigid and severe against the bankrupt; but, in case he proves honest, it makes him full amends for all this rigour and severity. For, if the bankrupt has made an ingenuous discovery, and has conformed in all points to the direction of the law, the court proceeds to appoint a public meeting for the allowance of the *discharge.* And unless any of the creditors succeed in showing a good cause to the contrary, the court may then certify that the bankrupt has made a full discovery, and conformed to the law in all respects, and grant him his discharge. He is thereupon entitled to a decent and reasonable *allowance* out of his effects, for his future support and maintenance, and to put him in a way of honest industry; but this is now left entirely in the discretion of the creditors. He has, however, an indemnity granted him of being freed for ever from all debts owing by him at the time he became a bankrupt, and from all claims and demands provable under the bankruptcy, even though judgment shall have been obtained against him, and he lies in prison upon execution for such debts: and, for that, among other purposes, all proceedings in bankruptcy are entered of record, as a perpetual bar against actions to be commenced on this account: though, in general, the production of the certificate, properly allowed, is sufficient evidence of all previous proceedings. Thus, the bankrupt becomes a clear man again: and, by the assistance of his allowance and his own industry, may become a useful member of the commonwealth; which is the rather to be expected, as he cannot be entitled to these benefits, unless his failures have been owing to misfortunes, rather than to misconduct and extravagance.

By the adjudication, or rather by the act of bankruptcy followed by adjudication, all the estates and effects, debts, contracts, and choses in *action* of the bankrupt are vested in the assignees, as fully as in the bankrupt himself; and it is their duty to convert the whole into money with all convenient speed, for division among the creditors. They may pursue any *legal* method of recovering this property so vested in them, by an action at law or suit in equity, and, with the consent of the creditors, compound any debts owing to the bankrupt, and refer any matters to arbitration. The amounts realized must be distributed among the creditors at fixed periods, and the accounts of the estate also made up and audited. If any surplus remains, after paying every creditor his full debt, it shall be restored to the bankrupt; but this very rarely happens.

A debtor, unable to meet his engagements, may effect in some cases a private arrangement with his creditors, by which the publicity consequent upon the ordinary proceedings in a bankruptcy may be in some degree avoided. This may be effected either by a direct application to the court, or by an arrangement by deed effected with the creditors themselves; whereupon the debtor receives a protection certificate, which has the same effect as a discharge in bankruptcy.

The proceedings hitherto explained relate to the cases of individuals, whether traders or not, or trading solely or in partnership with others: but they comprise no provisions suitable to the case of a trading corporation or chartered company becoming unable to meet its engagements. These associations are not made bankrupt in the proper sense of the term; but are wound up, as it is called, either in the Court of Bankruptcy or Court of Chancery, the objects of the proceedings being in both cases the same—to realize the assets in the first place, and then distribute them among the creditors in the proportion of their respective debts.

CHAPTER XXVIII.

OF TITLE BY WILL AND ADMINISTRATION.

Origin of executors—of administrators—Who may make a will—Requisites of wills—Intestacy—Right to administration—Duties of executors and administrators.

THERE yet remain to be examined two other methods of acquiring personal estates, viz., by *testament* and *administration*. And these I propose to consider in one and the same view, they being in their nature so connected and blended together, as makes it impossible to treat of them distinctly, without manifest tautology and repetition.

When property came to be vested in individuals by the right of occupancy, it became necessary, for the peace of society, that this occupancy should be continued, not only in the present possessor, but in those persons to whom he should think proper to transfer it; which introduced the doctrine and practice of alienations, gifts, and contracts. But these precautions would be very imperfect, if they were confined to the life of the occupier; for upon his death all his goods would again become common, and create an infinite variety of confusion. The law has therefore given to the proprietor a right of continuing his property after his death, in such persons as he shall name; and, in defect of such appointment, has directed the goods to be vested in certain particular individuals, exclusive of all other persons. The former method of acquiring personal property we call a *testament*: the latter, an *administration*.

Testaments are of very high antiquity; and with us, indeed, the power of bequeathing is coeval with the first rudiments of the law. It did not extend originally to *all* a man's personal estate. On the contrary, in the reign of Henry II., a man's goods were to be divided into three equal parts; of which one went to his heirs, another to his wife, and the third was at his own disposal; or, if he died without a wife, he might then dispose of one moiety, and the other went to his children. And this continued to be the law at the time of *Magna Charta*, and perhaps for some time afterwards. But it has been gradually and imperceptibly altered, and the deceased may now, by will, dispose of the whole of his goods and chattels.

In case a person make no disposition of his goods, he was, and is, said to die intestate; and in such cases, it is said, that by the old law the king was entitled to seize upon his goods, as the *parens patriæ* and general trustee of the kingdom. This prerogative the king continued to exercise for some time by his own ministers of justice; and probably in the county court, where matters of all kinds were determined; and it was granted as a franchise to many lords of manors, who had till recently a prescriptive right to grant administration to their intestate tenants and suitors, in their own courts baron. Afterwards the crown, in favour of the church, invested the prelates with this branch of the prerogative; which was done, says Perkins, because it was intended by the law, that spiritual men are of better conscience than laymen, and that they had more knowledge what things would conduce to the benefit of the soul of the deceased.

The goods of the intestate being thus vested in the ordinary upon the most solemn and conscientious trust, the reverend prelates were therefore not accountable to any, but to God and themselves, for their conduct. But this trust was so grossly abused, that as early as the statute of Westm. 2, it was enacted that the ordinary should pay the debts of the intestate so far as his goods extended, in the same manner that executors were bound in case the deceased had left a will. Though the prelates were now made liable to the creditors of the intestate for their just and lawful demands, yet the *residuum*, after payment of debts, remained still in their hands, to be applied to whatever purposes the conscience of the ordinary should approve. The flagrant abuses of which power occasioned the legislature again to interpose, and therefore the statute 31 Edw. III. c. 11, took it out of their hand, and directed that, in case of intestacy, the ordinary should depute the nearest and most lawful friends of the deceased to administer his goods. This is the origin of *administrators*, who were at first only the officers of the ordinary. And though the authority of the prelates has now been transferred to the crown, to be exercised in the Court of Probate, upon this footing stands the general law of administrations at this day.

I proceed now to inquire who may, or may not, make a testament. And this law is entirely prohibitory; for every person has full power and liberty to make a will, that is not under some special prohibition by law or custom, which prohibitions are principally upon three accounts: for want of sufficient discretion; for want of sufficient liberty and free will; and on account of their criminal conduct.

1. In the first species are to be reckoned *infants*, that is, persons under twenty-one, who are incapable of making a will. Madmen, or otherwise *non compotes*, idiots or natural fools, persons grown childish by reason of old age or distemper, such as have their senses besotted with drunkenness—all these are incapable, by reason of mental disability, to make any will so long as such disability lasts.

2. Such persons, as are intestable for want of liberty or freedom of will, are by the civil law of various kinds; as prisoners, captives, and the like. But the law of England does not make such persons absolutely intestable; but only leaves it to the court to decide whether or no such persons could be supposed to have *liberum animum testandi*. A married woman is incapable of devising *lands*, and also incapable of making a testament of *chattels*, without the license of her husband. For all her personal chattels are absolutely his; and he may dispose of her chattels real, or shall have them to himself if he survives her. Yet by her husband's license she may make a testament; and the husband, upon marriage, frequently covenants with her friends to allow her that license. The queen consort is an exception to this general rule, for she may dispose of her chattels by will without the consent of her lord: and any feme-covert may make her will of goods, which are in her possession *in autre droit*, as executrix or administratrix; for these can never be the property of the husband: and if she has any pin-money or separate maintenance, it is said she may dispose of her savings thereout by testament, without the control of her husband, as she may of personal property given to her for her sole and separate use.

Testaments were formerly divided into two sorts; *written*, and *verbal* or *nuncupative*; the former were in writing, the latter depended upon oral evidence, being declared by the testator in *extremis* before a sufficient number of witnesses, and afterwards reduced to writing. A *codicil* is a supplement to a will, and to be taken as part of a testament: and this might also have been either written or nuncupative. But as *nuncupative* wills are liable to great impositions, and may occasion many perjuries, the Statute of Frauds laid them under many restrictions; and the statute 1 Vict. c. 26, finally did away with all nuncupative wills, except in the case of soldiers in actual service and mariners or seamen at sea; who may still dispose of their personal estate in this manner.

Every will, with this exception, whether of personal or real estate, must now be signed by the testator, or by some person in his presence, and by his direction, in the presence of two witnesses at least, present at the same time, who must subscribe and attest the will in the testator's presence. And no further publication besides this is required.

No testament is of any effect till after the death of the testator; and hence it follows that testaments may be avoided three ways: 1. If made by a person labouring under any of the incapacities before mentioned : 2. By making another testament of a later date : and, 3. By cancelling or revoking it. For, though I make a last will and testament irrevocable in the strongest words, yet I am at liberty to revoke it : because my own act or words cannot alter the disposition of law, so as to make that irrevocable which is in its own nature revocable. 4. Marriage, also, is by the statute I have alluded to, an express revocation of a prior will.

We are next to consider what is an executor, and what an administrator, and how they are both to be appointed.

An *executor* is he to whom another man commits by will the execution of that his last will and testament. And all persons are capable of being executors, that are capable of making wills, and many others besides; as feme-coverts, and infants. This appointment of an executor is essential to the making of a will. If the testator does not name executors, or names incapable persons, or the executors named refuse to act; in any of these cases the court grants administration *cum testamento annexo* to some other person; and then the duty of the administrator is very little different from that of an executor.

But if the deceased died wholly intestate, without making either will or executors, then general *letters of administration* must be granted to the nearest and most lawful friends of the deceased to administer his goods. And this leads us naturally to a consideration of the rules followed in tracing consanguinity, whereby the nearest and most lawful friends are ascertained.

Consanguinity is defined to be the connection or relation of persons descended from the same stock or common ancestor; and is either lineal or collateral.

Lineal consanguinity is that which subsists between persons, of whom one is descended in a direct line from the other, as between John Stiles and his father, grandfather, great-grandfather, and so upwards in the direct ascending line; or between John Stiles and his son, grandson, great-grandson, and so downwards in the direct descending line. Every generation in this lineal direct consanguinity, constitutes a different degree, reckoning either upwards or downwards; the father of John Stiles is related to him in the first degree, and so likewise is his son; his grandsire and grandson in the second; his great-grandsire and great-grandson in the third.

Collateral kinsmen are such as lineally spring from one and the same ancestor, who is the *stirps*, or root, from whence these relations are branched out. As if John Stiles has two sons, who have each a numerous issue; both these issues are lineally descended from John Stiles as their common ancestor; and they are collateral kinsmen to each other, because they are all descended from this common ancestor, and all have a portion of his blood in their veins, which denominates them *consanguineos*. And the degrees in which they are related, we compute by beginning at the common ancestor, and reckoning downwards; and in whatsoever degree the two persons, or the most remote of them, is distant from the common ancestor, that is the degree in which they are related to each other. Thus *Titius* and his brother are related in the first degree; for from the father to each of them is counted only one; *Titius* and his nephew are related in the second degree; for the nephew is two degrees removed from the common ancestor, viz., his own grandfather, the father of *Titius*.

The Court of Probate therefore in granting administration is guided by these rules: 1. It must grant administration of the goods of the wife to the husband or his representatives; and of the husband's effects, to the widow or next of kin; but it may grant it to either, or both, in its discretion. 2. Among the kindred, those are to be preferred that are the nearest in degree to the intestate; but, of persons in equal degree, the court may take which it pleases. And, therefore, 3. In the first place, the children, or, on failure of children, the parents of the deceased, are entitled to the administration; both which are indeed in the first degree; though the children are generally allowed the preference. Then follow brothers, grandfathers, uncles, or nephews, and the females of each class respectively, and lastly, cousins. 4. The half blood is admitted to the administration as well as the whole. 5. If none of the kindred take out administration, a creditor may, by custom, do it. 6. If the executor refuses, or dies intestate, the administration may be granted to the residuary legatee, in exclusion of the next of kin. 7. And, lastly, the court may, in defect of all these, commit administration to such discreet person as it approves of.

Having thus shown what is, and who may be, an executor or administrator, I proceed, lastly, to inquire into some few of the principal points of their office and duty. These in general are very much the same in both executors and administrators; excepting that an executor may do many acts before he proves the will; but an administrator may do nothing till letters of administration are issued; for the former derives his power from the will, and not from the probate, the latter owes his entirely to the appointment of the court. If a stranger takes upon him to act as executor, without any just authority, as by intermeddling with the goods of the deceased, and many other transactions, he is called in law an executor of his own wrong, *de son tort*, and is liable to all the trouble of an executorship; but merely locking up the goods, or burying the corpse of the deceased, will not amount to such an intermeddling as will charge a man as executor of his own wrong. Let us however see what are the power and duty of a rightful executor or administrator, who takes the administration of the estate on himself.

1. He must *bury* the deceased in a manner suitable to the estate which he leaves behind him; necessary funeral expenses being allowed, previous to all other debts and charges.

2. He must prove the *will* of the deceased: which is done either in *common form*, which is only upon his own oath before the court or its registrar; or *per testes*, in more solemn form of law, in case the validity of the will be disputed. In defect of any will, the person entitled to be administrator must also, at this period, *take out letters of administration* under the seal of the court; whereby an executorial power to collect and administer, that is, dispose of the goods of the deceased, is vested in him: and he must enter into a bond with sureties, faithfully to execute his trust.

3. The executor or administrator is to make an *inventory* of all the goods and chattels, whether in possession or action, of the deceased; which he is to deliver in to the court upon oath, if thereunto lawfully required.

4. He is to *collect* all the goods and chattels so inventoried. Whatever is so recovered, that is of a saleable nature and may be converted into ready money, is called *assets*, that is, sufficient, from the French *assez*, to make him chargeable to a creditor or legatee, so far as such goods and chattels extend.

5. The executor or administrator must *pay* the *debts* of the deceased; observing therein the rules of priority; otherwise, on deficiency of assets, if he pays those of a lower degree first, he must answer those of a higher out of his own estate. And, first, he may pay all funeral charges, and the expense of proving the will, and the like. Secondly, debts due to the crown on record or specialty. Thirdly, such debts are by particular statutes to be preferred to all others; as money due upon poor rates, for letters to the post-office, and some others. Fourthly, debts of record; as registered judgments and decrees in equity. Fifthly, debts due on special contracts; as

for rent, or upon bonds under seal. Lastly, debts on simple contracts, viz., upon notes unsealed, and verbal promises.

What has been stated as to the *order* in which the debts of the deceased are to be paid from the *assets*, refers only to *legal* assets, between which and *equitable* assets a distinction is to be made, the latter comprising every kind of property which comes to an executor's hands in any other than his legal capacity, and so can only be reached in equity. These are applicable in payment of all debts of whatever degree *pari passu.* And where the administration of assets falls into the hands of a court of equity, they are distributed in equal proportion, without regard to their nature or degree, except that voluntary bonds, or other special contracts without consideration, are postponed to other debts.

6. When the debts are all discharged, the *legacies* claim the next regard; which are to be paid by the executor so far as his assets will extend; but he may not give himself the preference herein, as in the case of debts.

A legacy is a bequest or gift of goods and chattels by testament, and the person to whom it was given is styled the legatee. This bequest transfers an inchoate property to the legatee; but the right is not perfect without the assent of the executor; for, if I have a *general* or *pecuniary* legacy of 100l., or a *specific* one of a piece of plate, I cannot in either case take it without the consent of the executor. For in him all the chattels are vested, and it is his business first of all to see whether there is a sufficient fund left to pay the debts of the testator; the rule of equity being, that a man must be just before he is permitted to be generous. And in case of a deficiency of assets, all the *general* legacies must abate proportionably, in order to pay the debts; but a *specific* legacy, of a piece of plate, a horse, or the like, is not to abate at all, or allow anything by way of abatement, unless there be not sufficient without it. Upon the same principle, if the legatees have been paid their legacies, they are afterwards bound to refund a rateable part, in case debts come in more than sufficient to exhaust the *residuum* after the legacies paid.

If the legatee dies before the testator, the legacy is a lost or *lapsed* legacy, and shall sink into the *residuum*, except it be a gift to a child or other issue of the testator, which does not lapse if the legatee die leaving issue which survives the testator. And if a *contingent* legacy be left to any one, as *when* he attains, or *if* he attains, the age of twenty-one, and he dies before that time, it is a lapsed legacy. But a legacy to one, *to be paid* when he attains the age of twenty-one years, is a *vested* legacy; an interest which commences *in præsenti* although it be *solvendum in futuro;* and if the legatee dies before that age, his representatives shall receive it out of the testator's per-

N

sonal estate, at the same time that it would have become payable, in case the legatee had lived.

Besides these formal legacies, contained in a man's will and testament, there is also permitted another death-bed disposition of property, which is called a donation *causâ mortis.* And that is, when a person in his last sickness, apprehending his dissolution near, delivers or causes to be delivered to another the possession of any personal goods, under which have been included bonds, and bills drawn by the deceased upon his banker, to keep in case of his decease. This gift, if the donor dies, needs not the assent of his executor: yet it shall not prevail against creditors, and is accompanied with this implied trust, that, if the donor lives, the property thereof shall revert to himself, being only given in contemplation of death, or *mortis causâ.*

7. When all the debts and particular legacies are discharged, the surplus or *residuum* must be paid to the residuary legatee, if any be appointed by the will; and if there be none, to the next of kin, who are to be investigated by the same rules of consanguinity as those who are entitled to letters of administration; of whom we have sufficiently spoken.* And this finishes our inquiry as to the different modes of acquiring personal property.

* There is only one exception to this rule, viz., where the nearest relations are a grandfather or grandmother, and brothers or sisters; although all these are related in the second degree, yet the former shall not participate with the latter; for which exception it does not appear that any good reason can be given.

BOOK THE THIRD.

OF PRIVATE WRONGS.

CHAPTER I.

OF THE REDRESS OF PRIVATE WRONGS.

I. By the act of the party injured, viz.—1. Self-defence; 2. Reception of
goods; 3. Entry on lands; 4. Abatement of nuisances; 5. Distress for
rent, &c.; what may be distrained; impounding the distress; replevin;
6. Seizing heriots; and next, by the act of both parties, viz.—1. Accord;
2. Arbitration.——II. By operation of law, viz.—1. Retainer; Remitter.
——III. By suit in court; courts of record and not of record; attorneys;
counsel.

MUNICIPAL law was defined, at the outset of these commentaries, to
be, "a rule of civil conduct commanding what is right, and pro-
" hibiting what is wrong." From hence it follows that the primary
objects of the law are the establishment of rights, and the prohibition of wrongs, which gave rise to a division of our subject under
two general heads; under the former of which, and in the second
part of this treatise, fell a consideration of the *rights* that were established, and under the latter are now to be defined the *wrongs* that
are forbidden and redressed by the laws of England.

These wrongs are divisible into two sorts; *private wrongs* and
public wrongs. The former are an infringement of the private or
civil rights belonging to individuals, considered as individuals; and
are thereupon frequently termed *civil injuries:* the latter are a
violation of public rights and duties, which affect the whole community; and are distinguished by the harsher appellation of *crimes*
and *misdemeanors.* To a consideration of the first of these species
of wrongs our attention is now to be directed.

The more effectually to accomplish the redress of private injuries,
courts of justice are instituted in every civilized society, in order to
protect the weak from the insults of the stronger, by expounding
and enforcing those laws, by which rights are defined and wrongs
prohibited. This remedy is therefore *principally* to be sought by

application to these courts of justice; that is, by civil suit or action. For which reason our chief employment now will be to consider the redress of private wrongs, by *suit* or *action* in courts. But as there are certain injuries of such a nature, that some of them furnish and others require a more speedy remedy than can be had in the ordinary forms of justice, there is allowed in those cases an extrajudicial kind of remedy; of which I shall first treat: and to that end, shall distribute the redress of private wrongs into three several species: first, that which is obtained by the *mere act* of the *parties* themselves: secondly, that which is effected by the *mere act* and operation of *law*; and, thirdly, that which arises from *suit* or *action* in courts, which consists in a conjunction of the other two, the act of the parties co-operating with the act of law.

Firstly. Of that redress which is obtained by the *mere* act of the *parties.*

This is of two sorts; viz., first, that which arises from the act of the injured party only; and, secondly, that which arises from the joint act of all the parties together.

Of the first sort is,

I. The *defence* of one's self, or the mutual and reciprocal defence of such as stand in the relations of husband and wife, parent and child, master and servant. In these cases, if the party himself, or *any* of these his relations, be forcibly attacked in his person or property, it is lawful for him to repel force by force; and the breach of the peace, which happens, is chargeable upon him only who began the affray. For the law, in this case, makes it lawful in him to do himself that immediate justice, to which he is prompted by nature, and which no prudential motives are strong enough to restrain. But care must be taken that the resistance does not exceed the bounds of mere defence and prevention; for then the defender would himself become an aggressor.

II. Recaption or *reprisal* is another species of remedy by the mere act of the party injured. This happens when any one has deprived another of his property in goods or chattels personal, or wrongfully detains one's wife, child, or servant: in which case the owner of the goods, and the husband, parent, or master, may lawfully claim and retake them, wherever he happens to find them; so it be not in a riotous manner, or attended with a breach of the peace. If, for instance, my horse is taken away, and I find him in a common, a fair, or a public inn, I may lawfully seize him to my own use; but I cannot justify breaking open a private stable, or entering on the grounds of a third person, to take him, except he be feloniously stolen; but must have recourse to an action at law.

III. As recaption is a remedy given to the party himself, for an injury to his *personal* property, so, thirdly, a remedy of the same kind for injuries to *real* property, is by *entry* on lands and tenements, when another person without any right has taken possession thereof. In this case the party entitled may make a formal entry thereon, declaring that thereby he takes possession. Should he in possession resist such entry, he is entitled to do so; and in that event, it is attended with no effect whatever: But if the person in possession acknowledges the right of the person making the entry for instance, by admitting himself to be his tenant in the premises entered upon, the possession of the tenant becomes at once the possession of the landlord; and such an entry gives the rightful owner seisin, puts into immediate possession him that hath right of entry on the estate, and thereby makes him complete owner of the property. This remedy must be pursued in a peaceable manner, and put with force; for if one turns or keeps another out of possession forcibly, this is an injury both of a civil and criminal nature. The civil is remedied by immediate restitution, which puts the ancient possessor *in statu quo;* the criminal injury, or public wrong, or breach of the peace, is punished by fine. For by statute 8 Henry VI. c. 9, upon complaint made to any justice of the peace, of a forcible entry, or a forcible detainer after a peaceable entry, he shall try the truth of the complaint, and, upon force found, shall restore the possession to the party so put out.*

IV. A fourth species of remedy by the mere act of the party injured, is the *abatement,* or removal of *nuisances.* What nuisances are we shall more conveniently inquire hereafter. At present I shall only observe, that whatsoever unlawfully annoys or does damage to another, is a nuisance, and may be abated, that is, removed by the party aggrieved, so as he commits no riot in doing so. If a house or wall is erected so near to mine that it stops my ancient light, which is a *private* nuisance, I may enter my neighbour's land, and peaceably pull it down. Or if a new gate be erected across the public highway, which is a *common* nuisance, any private individual passing that way may remove it. For injuries of this kind, which obstruct or annoy such things as are of daily convenience and use, require an immediate remedy, and cannot wait for the slow progress of the ordinary forms of justice.

V. A fifth case, in which the law allows a man to be his own

* The case of a tenant, wrongfully holding over after the expiration of his term, and forcibly dispossessed by the landlord, is not within the statute. For if it were, the justices would be compellable to restore possession to the tenant, although under his previous possession he could not have maintained an action of trespass against the landlord.

avenger or to minister redress to himself, is that of *distraining* cattle or goods for nonpayment *of rent*, or *other duties*; or, distraining another's cattle *damage-feasant*, that is, doing damage, or trespassing, upon his land.   The former intended for the benefit of landlords, to prevent tenants from secreting or withdrawing their effects to his prejudice; the latter arising from the necessity of the thing itself, as it might otherwise be impossible, at a future time, to ascertain whose cattle they were that committed the trespass or damage.

As the law of distresses is a point of great use and consequence, I shall consider it with some minuteness.

1. And, first, it is necessary to premise that a distress, *districtio*, is the taking of a personal chattel out of the possession of the wrong-doer into the custody of the party injured, to procure a satisfaction for the wrong committed, the most usual injury for which a distress may be taken being nonpayment of rent. A distress may also be taken where a man finds beasts of a stranger wandering in his grounds, *damage-feasant*; that is, doing him hurt or damage, by treading down his grass, or the like, in which case the owner of the soil may distrain them till satisfaction be made him for the injury he has thereby sustained. And for several rates or duties given and penalties inflicted by special acts of parliament for assessments made for the relief of the poor, or for parochial or district works of a public nature, remedy by distress and sale is given; for the particulars of which we must have recourse to the statutes themselves.

2. As to the things which may be distrained, or taken in distress, we may lay it down as a general rule, that all chattels personal are liable to be distrained, unless particularly exempted. It will be easier, therefore, to recount those things which are so protected, with the reason of their particular exemptions. And, 1. As everything which is distrained is presumed to be the property of the wrong-doer, it will follow that such things wherein no man can have a valuable property, as dogs, cats, rabbits, and all animals *feræ naturæ*, cannot be distrained. 2. Whatever is in the personal use or occupation of any man, is for the time privileged and protected from any distress; as an axe with which a man is cutting wood, or a horse while a man is riding him. 3. Valuable things in the way of trade shall not be liable to distress. As a horse standing in a smith's shop to be shoed, or in a common inn; or cloth at a tailor's house; or corn sent to a mill or a market; or goods intrusted to a carrier, auctioneer, or commission agent: all these being privileged for the benefit of trade. But, generally speaking, whatever goods and chattels the landlord finds upon the premises, whether they in fact belong to the tenant or a stranger, are distrainable by him for rent:

for otherwise a door would be open to infinite frauds upon the land-lord; and the stranger has *his* remedy over by action against the tenant, if by the tenant's default the chattels are distrained, so that he cannot render them when called upon.

With regard to a stranger's beasts found on the tenant's land, some distinctions are taken. If put in by consent of the owner, they are distrainable immediately afterwards: but if they were on their way to a fair or market, and had been put in only to graze for a night, they would be privileged. If, again, a stranger's cattle break the fences, and come on the land, they are distrainable imme-diately as a punishment to the owner for the wrong committed through his negligence. But if the lands were not sufficiently fenced, the landlord cannot distrain, till they have been *levant* and *couchant, levantes et cubantes*, on the land, which is held to be one night at least, as the owner may then have notice whither his cattle have strayed, and it is his own negligence not to remove them. 4. There are also other things privileged by the common law; as a man's tools and utensils of his trade, the axe of a carpenter, the books of a scholar, and the like: which are said to be privileged for the sake of the public, because the taking them away would disable the owner from serving the commonwealth in his station. But even these may be distrained, if they are not in actual use, and there is not otherwise sufficient property on the premises to satisfy the demand of the landlord. So, beasts of the plough, *averia carucæ*, and sheep are privileged from distress at common law; unless there is no other sufficient subject of distress on the premises; while dead goods, or other sort of beasts, which Bracton calls *catalla otiosa*, may be distrained. But as beasts of the plough may be taken in execu-tion for debt, so they may be for distresses by statute, which par-take of the nature of executions. 5. Nothing shall be distrained for rent, which may not be rendered again in as good plight as when it was distrained: for which reason, milk, fruit, and the like, cannot be distrained, a distress at common law being only in the nature of a pledge, to be restored when the debt is paid. So, anciently, sheaves of corn could not be distrained, but a cart loaded with corn might, as that could be safely restored. But now by statute, corn in sheaves, or loose in the straw, or hay in barns or ricks, or otherwise, may be distrained, as well as other chattels. 6. Things fixed to the freehold may not be distrained; as windows, doors, and chimney-pieces: for they savour of the realty. For this reason also corn growing could not be distrained; till a statute of George II. empowered landlords to distrain corn, grass, or other products of the earth, and to cut and gather them when ripe. 7. Lastly, things *in custodiâ legis*, as a distress taken *damage-feasant*, or goods taken in execution, cannot, though remaining on the premises, be distrained; they are already in the custody of the law.

3. Distresses were formerly looked upon in no other light than as a mere pledge or security for payment of rent, or satisfaction for damage done. And so the law still continues with regard to distresses of beasts taken *damage-feasant*, and for other causes, not altered by act of parliament. But distresses for rent-arrear being found the most effectual method of compelling payment, many laws have been made, which have much altered the common law, as laid down in our ancient writers.

In the first place, then, all distresses must be made *by day*, unless in the case of *damage-feasant;* an exception being there allowed, lest the beasts should escape before they are taken; and when a person intends to make a distress, he must, by himself or his bailiff, enter on the premises, and there distrain the goods he finds, and which are not privileged, giving notice thereof to the tenant, and stating what are the goods distrained. The landlord may not break open a house to make a distress, for that is a breach of the peace; though when in the house, he may break open an inner door. But he may, by the assistance of the peace-officer of the parish, break open in the day-time any place, whither the goods have been fraudulently removed and locked up to prevent a distress; oath being first made, in case it be a dwelling-house, of a reasonable ground to suspect that such goods are concealed therein. He ought also to distrain for the whole rent due, at once; and not for part at one time, and part at another. But if he mistakes the value of the things distrained, and so takes an insufficient distress, he may take a second distress to complete his remedy. And the distress thus taken must be proportioned to the thing distrained for, for otherwise he incurs the risk of an action for taking an excessive distress.

4. When the distress is taken, the things distrained must in the first place be carried to some pound, and there impounded by the taker. A pound, *parcus*, which signifies any enclosure, is either pound-*overt*, that is, open overhead; or pound-*covert*, that is, close. No distress of cattle can be driven out of the hundred where it is taken, unless to a pound-overt within the same shire, and within three miles of the place where it was taken. This is for the benefit of the tenants, that they may know where to find and replevy the distress; which the taker must provide with sufficient food, the value being recoverable from the owner,—or sell at the expiration of seven days. And by statute 11 Geo. II. c. 19, any person distraining for rent may turn any part of the premises, upon which a distress is taken, into a pound, *pro hâc vice*, for securing of such distress; which is also for the advantage of tenants, as a distress of household goods,

which are liable to be stolen or damaged by weather, ought to be impounded in a pound-covert, else the distrainor must answer for the consequences.

5. When impounded, the goods were formerly only in the nature of a pledge or security to compel the performance of satisfaction, the distrainor not being at liberty to work or use a distrained beast. And thus the law still continues with regard to beasts taken damage-feasant, and distresses for suit or services; which must remain impounded, till the owner makes satisfaction, or contests the right of distraining by replevying the chattels. To *replevy replegiare*, that is, to take back the pledge, is, when a person distrained upon has the distress returned into his own possession, upon giving good security to try the right of taking it in a suit of law; and, if that be determined against him, to return the cattle or goods once more into the hands of the distrainor. This is called a replevin; and it answers the same end to the distrainor as the distress itself, since the party replevying gives security to return the distress, if the right be determined against him.

6. This kind of distress, though it puts the owner to inconvenience, and is therefore a punishment to *him*, yet, if he continues obstinate, and will make no satisfaction or payment, is no remedy at all to the distrainor. But for a debt due to the crown, the distress was always saleable at common law. And so, in the several statute-distresses before referred to, the power of sale is likewise usually given to effectuate and complete the remedy. And in all cases of distress for rent, if the tenant or owner do not, within five days after the distress is taken, replevy the same with sufficient security, the distrainor may cause the same to be appraised, and sell the same towards satisfaction of the rent and charges; rendering the overplus, if any, to the owner himself. And by this means a full satisfaction may now be had for rent in arrear by the mere act of the party himself; viz., by distress, the remedy given at common law; and sale consequent thereon, which is added by act of parliament.

VI. The seizing of heriots, when due on the death of a tenant, is also another species of self-remedy; not much unlike that of taking cattle or goods in distress. But the enfranchisement of copyholds will in course of time render this often oppressive proceeding unknown.

I shall now briefly mention such remedies as arise from the *joint act of all the parties* together. And these are only two, *accord* and *arbitration.*

I. Accord is a satisfaction agreed upon between the party injuring and the party injured; which, when performed, is a bar of all actions upon this account. As if a man contract to build a house or deliver a horse, and fail in it; this is an injury for which the sufferer may have his remedy by action; but if the injured party accepts a sum of money, or other thing, as a satisfaction, this is a redress of that injury, and entirely takes away the action.

II. Arbitration is where the parties, injuring and injured, submit all matters in dispute to the judgment of two or more *arbitrators*, who are to decide the controversy; and if they do not agree, it is usual to add, that another person be called in as *umpire, imperator* or *impar*, to whose sole judgment it is then referred: or frequently there is only one arbitrator originally appointed. This decision, in any of these cases, is called an *award*. And thereby the question is as fully determined, and the right claimed transferred or settled, as it could have been by the agreement of the parties or the judgment of a court of justice.

Secondly. Of that redress which is effected by the mere operation of law. Of this there are two instances only : *retainer* and *remitter*.

I. If a person indebted to another makes his creditor his executor, or if such creditor obtains letters of administration to his debtor; in either case the law allows him to *retain* so much as will pay himself. For the executor cannot, without an apparent absurdity, commence a suit against himself as representative of the deceased, to recover that which is due to him in his own private capacity; but, having the whole personal estate in his hands, so much as is sufficient to answer his own demand is, by operation of law, applied to that particular purpose. But the executor shall not retain his own debt, in prejudice to those of a higher degree; for the law only puts him in the same situation, as if he had sued himself as executor, and recovered his debt. And an executor of his own wrong is in no case permitted to retain.

II. Remitter is where he who has the true property or *jus proprietatis* in lands, but is out of possession thereof, and cannot recover possession without an action, has the freehold cast upon him by some subsequent, and of course defective, title; in this case he is remitted, or sent back by operation of law, to his ancient and more certain title. The reason given by Littleton, why this remedy, which operates silently, and by the mere act of law, was allowed, is somewhat similar to that given in the preceding article; because otherwise he who has right would be deprived of all remedy. For as he himself is the person in possession of the freehold, there is no other person against whom he can bring an action, to establish his prior right. And for this cause the law adjudges him in by *remitter*; that is, in such plight as if he had lawfully recovered the same land by suit.

Thirdly. Of the redress of injuries by *suit in court.*

Herein the act of the parties and the act of law co-operate; the act of the parties being necessary to set the law in motion, and the process of the law being, in general, the only instrument by which the parties are enabled to procure a certain and adequate redress.

And here it will not be improper to observe, that although in the several cases of redress by the act of the parties already mentioned, the law allows an extra-judicial remedy, yet that does not exclude the ordinary course of justice. Though I may defend myself from external violence, I yet am entitled to recover damages for the assault; though I may retake my goods, if I have a fair and peaceable opportunity, this power of recaption does not debar me from my action: I may either abate a nuisance by my own authority, or call upon the law to do it for me. And with regard to accords and arbitrations, these being merely an agreement or compromise, most indisputably suppose a previous right of obtaining redress some other way; which is given up by such agreement. But as to remedies by the mere operation of law, those are indeed given, because no remedy *can* be administered by suit or action.

In all other cases it is a general and indisputable rule, that where there is a legal right there is also a legal remedy, by suit or action at law, whenever that right is invaded. And in treating of these remedies by suit in court, I shall pursue the following method: *first,* I shall consider the nature and several species of courts of justice; and, *secondly,* I shall point out in which of these courts, and in what manner, the proper remedy may be had for any private injury; or, in other words, what injuries are cognizable, and how redressed, in each respective species of courts.

First, then, of courts of justice.

A court is defined to be a place wherein justice is judicially administered. And, as the sole executive power of the laws is vested in the sovereign, it follows that all courts of justice, the medium by which the sovereign administers the laws, are derived from the crown. For, whether created by act of parliament, or letters patent, or subsisting by prescription, the consent of the crown in the two former is expressly, and in the latter impliedly, given. In all these courts the sovereign is supposed to be always present; but as that is in fact impossible, the crown is there represented by the judges, whose power is only an emanation of the royal prerogative.

For the more speedy, universal, and impartial administration of justice between subject and subject, the law has appointed a prodigious variety of courts, some with a more limited, others with a more extensive jurisdiction. These will be taken notice of in their respective places: and I shall therefore here only mention one distinction, that runs throughout them all; *viz.*, that some of them are courts of *record*, others *not of record*.

A court of record is defined to be that where the acts and judicial proceedings are enrolled or recorded: which rolls are called the records of the court, and are of such high authority, that their truth is not to be called in question. Nothing can be averred against a record, nor shall any plea, or even proof, be admitted to the contrary. And if the existence of a record be denied, it shall be tried by nothing but itself: that is, upon bare inspection whether there be any such record or no; else there will be no end of disputes. All courts of record also are the courts of the sovereign, in right of the crown and royal dignity, and no other court has authority to fine or imprison, unless it be expressly conferred by the legislature.

A court not of record is defined to be the court of a private man; whom the law will not intrust with any discretionary power over the fortune or liberty of his fellow-subjects. Such are the courts-baron incident to every manor, and such other inferior jurisdictions: where the proceedings are not enrolled or recorded; but as well their existence as their truth shall be tried and determined by a jury. But this definition is to be understood as applicable to courts not of record existing at the common law; for the court of Chancery in Equity, and the Spiritual Courts among others, are courts not of record; while the new county courts and courts of bankruptcy, which are inferior courts, are expressly constituted courts of record.

In every court there must be at least three constituent parts, the *actor, reus,* and *judex*: the *actor,* or plaintiff, who complains of an injury done; the *reus,* or defendant, who is called upon to make satisfaction for it; and the *judex,* or judicial power, which is to examine the truth of the fact, to determine the law arising upon that fact, and, if any injury appears to have been done, to ascertion, and by its officers to apply the remedy. It is also usual in the superior courts to have attorneys, and advocates or counsel, as assistants.

An attorney at law answers to the *procurator,* or proctor, of the civilians and canonists. And he is one who is put in the place or *turn* of another, to manage his matters of law. Formerly every suitor was obliged to appear in person, unless by special license under letters patent. This is still the law in criminal cases. But, it is now permitted in general, by divers statutes, whereof the first is Westm. 2, c. 10, that attorneys may be made to prosecute or defend any action in the absence of the parties. The attorneys are now

admitted to the execution of their office by the superior courts; and
are in all points officers of the courts in which they are admitted.
They are privileged, on account of their attendance there, from
serving on juries, and from being arrested on civil process, *eundo
morando et redeundo;* and they are, on the other hand, peculiarly
subject to the censure and animadversion of the judges in the exercise of their professional duties.

Of advocates, or, as we generally call them, counsel, there are
two species or degrees: barristers, and serjeants. The former are
admitted, after three years' standing, in the inns of court; and are,
in our old books, styled apprentices, *apprenticii ad legem,* having
been at that time looked upon as merely learners, and not qualified
to execute the office of an advocate till they were of considerable
standing. A barrister of seven years' standing may be called to the
degree of serjeant, a separate body at the bar, bound by a solemn oath
to do their duty to their clients: and into which order the judges of
the courts of Westminster are always admitted before they are
advanced to the bench. From both these degrees some are selected
to be her majesty's counsel learned in the law: the two principal of
whom are called her attorney and solicitor general. They must not
be employed in any cause against the crown without special license,
which, however, is never refused. Together with the serjeants, they
sit within the bar of the respective courts. All of them may take
upon them the protection and defence of any suitors, whether
plaintiff or defendant; who are therefore called their *clients,* like the
dependents upon the ancient Roman orators. Those indeed practised
gratis, for honour merely, or at most for the sake of gaining influence: and with us a counsel can maintain no action for his fees;
which are given, not as *locatio vel conductio,* but as *quiddam honora-
rium;* not as a salary or hire, but as a mere gratuity, which a
counsellor cannot demand without doing wrong to his reputation.
And, in order to encourage due freedom of speech in the lawful defence of their clients, and at the same time to give a check to the
unseemly licentiousness of prostitute and illiberal men, a few of
whom may sometimes insinuate themselves even into the most
honourable profession, it has been held that a counsel is not
answerable for any matter by him spoken, relative to the cause in
hand, and suggested in his client's instructions; although it should
reflect upon the reputation of another, and even prove absolutely
groundless: but if he mentions an untruth of his own invention, or
even upon instructions if it be impertinent to the cause in hand, he
is then liable to an action from the party injured.

CHAPTER II.

OF THE PUBLIC COURTS OF COMMON LAW AND EQUITY.

I. Court of Piepoudre—II. Court Baron—III. Hundred Court—IV. Shiremote —V. New County Court—VI. Common Pleas—VII. Queen's Bench— VIII. Exchequer—IX. Exchequer Chamber—X. Chancery — XI. Rolls— XII. Vice-Chancellor's Courts—XIII. Court of Appeal in Chancery— XIV. House of Lords—XV. Courts of *Nisi Prius.*

WE are next to consider the several species and distinctions of courts of justice, which are acknowledged and used in this kingdom. And these are, either such as are of public and general jurisdiction throughout the whole realm; or such as are only of a private or special jurisdiction in some particular parts of it. And, first, of such public courts as are courts of common law and equity.

The policy of our ancient constitution, as established by the great Alfred, was to bring justice home to every man's door, by constitut- ing as many courts as there were manors in the kingdom; wherein injuries were redressed in an expeditious manner, by the suffrage of neighbours and friends. These little courts, however, communicated with others of a larger jurisdiction, and those with others of a still greater power; ascending gradually from the lowest to the supreme courts, which were constituted to correct the errors of the inferior ones, and to determine such causes as by reason of their weight and difficulty demanded a more solemn discussion. These inferior courts still continue in our legal constitution; but as the superior courts obtained, at a very early period in our history, a concurrent original jurisdiction with them, these petty tribunals soon fell into decay, and have now fallen almost into oblivion.

I. The lowest, and at the same time the most expeditious court of justice known to the law of England, is the court of *piepoudre*;[*] so called from the dusty feet of the suitors; or, according to Sir Edward Coke, because justice is there done as speedily as dust can fall from the foot. It is now entirely obsolete.

II. The *court-baron* is a court incident to every manor in the kingdom; it is usually holden by the steward, and is of two natures; the one a customary court, appertaining entirely to the copyholders, in which their estates are transferred by surrender and admittance; the other, a court of common law, held before the tenants who owe

---

* Knight's " Once upon a Time," c. " Items of the Obsolete:" London, 1857.

service to the manor, the steward being rather the registrar than the judge. Its most important business was to determine, by writ of right, all controversies relating to the right of lands within the manor; but this writ having been abolished its jurisdiction in this respect no longer exists. The court-baron may still hold plea of any personal actions, where the debt or damage does not amount to forty shillings.

III. A *hundred-court* is only a larger court-baron, being held for a particular hundred instead of a manor. The free suitors are here also the judges, and the steward the registrar.

IV. The *Schyremote*, or ancient county court, is a court incident to the jurisdiction of the sheriff. It is not a court of record, but might, until its jurisdiction was transferred to the new county courts, hold pleas of debt or damages under the value of forty shillings: over some of which causes these inferior courts have a jurisdiction exclusive of the superior courts; for in order to sue in the latter, the plaintiff must show that the cause of action amounts to 40s. The county court might also hold plea of many real actions, when these existed. The freeholders are the judges, so far as it still exists as a court, and the sheriff is the ministerial officer. For this reason all acts of parliament were wont to be there published by the sheriff; all outlawries of absconding offenders are there proclaimed; and all popular elections which the freeholders are to make, as of coroners and knights of the shire, must be made *in pleno comitatu.*

These courts having, however, fallen into disuse, their place has been, in a great measure, supplied by the—

New County Courts, which were established by the statute 9 & 10 Vict. c. 95, in order to supply the place of a great variety of inferior tribunals, which were called Courts of Requests, or Courts of Conscience, and were intended solely for the recovery of small debts. The first was established in London in the reign of Henry VIII., and gave so much satisfaction, that divers trading towns and other districts afterwards obtained acts of parliament for establishing in them courts upon nearly the same plan as that in London. This clearly proved that the nation was sensible of the great inconvenience arising from the disuse of their ancient courts; wherein causes of small value were always decided with very little trouble and expense to the parties. But no general establishment of local tribunals took place till the new county courts were called into existence in 1847; when upwards of one hundred courts of requests were abolished. This revival of the ancient Saxon system was effected by transferring the jurisdiction of the old schyremote to the new county courts; and at the same time enabling the latter to entertain all ordinary actions where the plaintiff's claim did not exceed 20*l.* The success which attended this experiment has been so great that the jurisdiction of these courts has been repeatedly extended, and their procedure at the same time gradually improved. They may now entertain suits for the recovery of all debts and demands, where the sum sued for does not exceed 50*l.*; but have no jurisdiction as yet where *title* comes in question. And their method of proceeding partakes of the simplicity which distinguished the ancient schyremote. A suit is begun by the entry of a *plaint*, setting out the nature of the plaintiff's claim; upon which a *summons* is issued, and *served* on the defendant; who is thereby required to defend at the court to which he is summoned, or otherwise judgment may be given against him. If defence is made, the matter in dispute is, on the trial, inquired into, and disposed of summarily by the judge; who decides all questions, as well of fact as of law; unless one of the parties has demanded a jury, the appropriate tribunal to determine questions of fact. The costs of the suit are entirely in the discretion of the court; and the judgment is enforced, if necessary, by execution against the goods of the unsuccessful party. But as experience has demonstrated that this does not always afford a means of obtaining the fruits of a suit, and that the fraudulent debtor will never fail to find means to defeat a just demand, the court has power, if the unsuccessful party has no goods from which the judgment may be satisfied, but has the means of paying otherwise, to commit him to prison for a period not exceeding forty days. A judgment for more than 20*l.* may also be removed into one of the superior courts, and there enforced by its ordinary process of execution.

Quite recently an extensive jurisdiction in certain matters which have hitherto been cognizable only in courts of equity, has been conferred on the county courts; in the exercise of which they have all the powers and authorities of the high court of chancery. Thus in *administration suits*, or for the *execution of trusts*, in suits for *specific performance* of contracts, or *foreclosure of mortgages*, and in questions of *partnership*, and certain other cases which need not be detailed, the suitor may resort to the county court, if the subject matter does not exceed in amount or value the sum of five hundred pounds. The suit may, however, by an order of any one of the vice-chancellors, be removed into and further prosecuted in the court of chancery; to which an appeal may be made from the decree of the county court judge.

The procedure on what may thus be termed the *equity side* of the county court, closely resembles that provided for the trial of common law actions. The plaintiff files a *plaint*, setting forth the facts in respect of which he claims *relief* of some kind; whereupon the defendant is *summoned* to appear and *answer*. He may then *confess* the plaintiff's right to the relief he seeks, or contest his demand on the *hearing;* upon which the relief sought is either refused, or a *decretal order* of some kind made. This order may direct inquiries, or the taking of accounts, or the sale of property, or the appointment of a receiver, or the issue of an injunction, or give the plaintiff some other redress. Any ministerial duties, such as the taking of accounts, then devolve upon the registrar of the court, whose *certificate* when approved forms the foundation of the *final decree.* The judgment of the court may be enforced in the same way as the decrees of the court of chancery, by sale of the goods, seizure of the lands, or attachment of the person of the defendant.

I now proceed to describe those courts which are calculated for the administration of redress, not in any one lordship, hundred, or county only, but throughout the whole kingdom at large. Of which sort is

VI. The Court of *Common Pleas,* or, as it is frequently termed in law, the Court of *Common Bench.*

By the ancient Saxon constitution there was only one superior court of justice in the kingdom; and that court had cognizance both of civil and spiritual causes, viz., the *witenagemote,* or general council, which assembled annually or oftener, wherever the king kept his Christmas, Easter, or Whitsuntide, as well to do private justice as to consult upon public business. At the Conquest the ecclesiastical jurisdiction was diverted into another channel; and the Conqueror, fearing danger from these annual parliaments, contrived also to separate their ministerial power, as judges, from their deliberative, as counsellors to the crown. He therefore established a constant court in his own hall, thence called by Bracton, and other ancient authors, *aula regia,* or *aula regis.* This court was composed of the king's great officers of state, who were assisted by certain persons learned in the laws, called the king's justiciars or justices; and by the greater barons of parliament, all of whom had a seat in the *aula regia;* over which presided one special magistrate, called the chief justiciar, or *capitalis justiciarius totius Angliæ;* who was also the principal minister of state, the second man in the kingdom, and, by virtue of his office, guardian of the realm in the king's absence. And this officer it was, who principally determined all the vast variety of cases that arose in this extensive jurisdiction; and, from the plenitude of his power, grew at length both obnoxious to the people and dangerous to the government which employed him. ▪

This great court being bound to follow the king in all his progresses, the trial of common causes therein was found very burdensome to the subject. Wherefore King John, who dreaded also the power of the justiciar, very readily consented to that article which now forms the eleventh chapter of *Magna Charta,* and enacts that

" *communia placita non sequantur curiam regis, sed teneantur in* " *aliquo loco certo.*" This certain place was established in Westminster Hall, the place where the *aula regis* originally sat; and there it has ever since continued. And the court being thus rendered fixed and stationary, the judges became so too, and a chief, with other justices of the common pleas, was thereupon appointed; with jurisdiction to hear and determine all pleas of land, and injuries merely civil between subject and subject. Which critical establishment of this principal court of common law, at that particular juncture and that particular place, gave rise to the inns of court in its neighbourhood; and, thereby collecting together the whole body of the common lawyers, enabled the law itself to withstand the attacks of the canonists and civilians, who laboured to extirpate and destroy it.

The *aula regia* being thus stripped of so considerable a branch of its jurisdiction, and the power of the chief justiciar being also considerably curbed by many articles in the great charter, the authority of both began to decline apace under the long and troublesome reign of King Henry III. And in further pursuance of this example, the other several offices of the chief justiciar were under Edward I., who new-modelled the whole frame of our judicial polity, subdivided and broken into distinct courts of judicature. A *court of chivalry* was erected, over which the constable and mareschal presided;* as did the steward of the household over another, constituted to regulate the king's domestic servants, out of which, in the reign of Charles I., sprang *the place court*, abolished only a few years ago.† The high steward, with the barons of parliament, formed an august tribunal for the trial of delinquent peers;‡ and the barons reserved to themselves, in parliament, the right of reviewing the sentences of other courts in the last resort, from which we have now the appellate jurisdiction of the House of Lords. The distribution of common law between man and man was thrown into so provident an order, that the great judicial officers were made to form a check upon each other; the Chancery issuing all original writs, by which, until recently, all actions were commenced, to the other courts; the Common Pleas being allowed to determine all causes between private subjects; the Exchequer managing the king's revenue; and the Court of King's Bench re-

---

* After the attainder of Stafford Duke of Buckingham, under Henry VIII. this court was held before the Earl Marshal only. It has cognizance by stat. 10 Rich. II. c. 2, of contracts and other matters, touching deeds of arms and war; but has long been entirely obsolete.

† This court had jurisdiction of all personal actions arising within twelve miles of Whitehall, the *verge* of the Court or royal residence, as it is called.

‡ This court will be again mentioned in its proper place in the fourth part of these commentaries.

taining all the jurisdiction which was not cantoned out to other courts, and the sole cognizance of pleas of the crown or criminal causes. For pleas or suits are regularly divided into two sorts: *pleas of the crown*, which comprehend all crimes and misdemeanors, wherein the sovereign, on behalf of the public, is the plaintiff; and *common pleas*, which include all civil actions depending between subject and subject. The former of these were originally the proper object of the jurisdiction of the Court of King's Bench; the latter of the Court of Common Pleas, which is a court of record, and is styled by Sir Edward Coke, the lock and key of the common law; for herein only could real actions, that is, actions which concerned the right of freehold or the realty, be brought. All other, or personal, pleas between man and man are likewise here determined; though in all of them the King's Bench and Exchequer soon obtained and now have also a concurrent authority.

The judges of this court are at present five in number. From their decision there is an appeal for error in law to the justices of the Court of Queen's Bench and the Barons of the Exchequer, sitting as the Court of Exchequer Chamber.

VII. The Court of Queen's Bench, called, in the reign of a king, King's Bench, because the sovereign used formerly to sit there in person, is the supreme court of common law in the kingdom, consisting of a chief justice and five *puisné* justices, who are, by their office, the sovereign conservators of the peace, and supreme coroners of the land. This court, which is the remnant of the *aula regia*, is not fixed to any certain place, but may follow the person of the sovereign; for which reason all process issuing out of this court is returnable "*ubicunque fuerimus in Angliâ.*" It has, indeed, for some centuries past, usually sat at Westminster, being an ancient palace of the crown; but might remove with the queen to York or Exeter, if she thought proper to command it.

Its jurisdiction is very high and transcendent. It keeps all inferior jurisdictions within the bounds of their authority, and may either remove their proceedings to be determined here, or prohibit their progress below. It superintends all civil corporations in the kingdom. It commands magistrates and others to do what their duty requires in every case where there is no other specific remedy. It protects the liberty of the subject, by speedy and summary interposition. It takes cognizance both of criminal and civil causes; the former in what is called the *crown side* or *crown office*; the latter in the *plea side* of the court. The jurisdiction of the crown side it is not our present business to consider;—that will be more properly discussed hereafter. But on the plea side, or civil branch, it has an original jurisdiction in all actions of trespass or other injury alleged to be committed *vi et armis*; of actions which allege any falsity or fraud: all of which savour of a criminal nature, although the action is brought for a civil remedy; and its jurisdiction is now extended to all actions whatever.

This court is likewise a court of appeal, into which may be removed, for error in law, all determinations of the Court of Common Pleas at Lancaster and of the Court of Pleas at Durham, and of all inferior courts of record in England. Yet even this so high and honourable court is not the *dernier resort* of the subject; for if he be not satisfied with any determination here, he may appeal to the Court of Exchequer Chamber; which is not to be confounded with—

VIII. The Court of Exchequer, which I have chosen to consider here, because formerly it was both a court of law and a court of equity. It was first set up by William the Conqueror, as a part of the *aula regia*, though regulated and reduced to its present order by King Edward I.; and then intended principally to order the revenues of the crown, and to recover the king's debts and duties. This court consists of two divisions: the receipt of the exchequer, which manages the royal revenue, and with which these commentaries have no concern; and the court, or judicial part of it, which, as I have stated, was formerly subdivided into a court of equity, and a court of common law. Its jurisdiction as a court of equity has been transferred to the Court of Chancery; and it is now only a court of law and revenue, with five judges—a chief and four puisné barons—like the Courts of Queen's Bench and Common Pleas. When sitting as a court of revenue it is designated the *Court of Exchequer*; in the exercise of its other jurisdiction as the *Court of Exchequer of Pleas*; and from its judgment alike in matters of revenue as in civil causes, an appeal lies to the justices of the Queen's Bench and Common Pleas, sitting in—

IX. The Court of Exchequer Chamber; which, be it noted, has no original jurisdiction whatever, but is only a court of appeal, to correct the errors of the Queen's Bench, Common Pleas, and Exchequer. It was first erected by statute 31 Edw. III. c. 12; but has been entirely remodelled by the statute 11 Geo. IV. & 1 Will. IV. c. 70. From its judgment an appeal lies to the queen in her High Court of Parliament, or, as it is usually said, to the House of Lords.

X. The High Court of Chancery is the only remaining, and in matters of civil property by much the most important of any, of the superior and original courts of justice. It has its name of chancery, *cancellaria*, from the judge who presides here, the lord chancellor or *cancellarius*; who, Sir Edward Coke tells us, is so termed *a cancellando*, from cancelling the king's letters patent when granted contrary to law, which is the highest point of his jurisdiction. But the office and name of chancellor was certainly known to the courts of the Roman emperors : and from the Roman empire it passed to the Roman church, ever emulous of imperial state ; whence every bishop has to this day his chancellor, the principal judge of his consistory. And when the modern kingdoms of Europe were established upon the ruins of the empire, almost every state preserved its chancellor, who seems to have had the supervision of all charters, letters, and such other public instruments of the crown, as were authenticated in the most solemn manner : and therefore when seals came in use, had always the custody of the sovereign's great seal. So that the office of chancellor, or lord keeper, whose authority is exactly the same, is with us at this day created by the mere delivery of the great seal into his custody : whereby he becomes, without writ or patent, an officer of the greatest weight and power of any now subsisting in the kingdom ; and superior in point of precedency to every tempora¹ lord. He is a privy councillor by his office, and prolocutor of the House of Lords by prescription ; appoints all ·justices of the peace ; is visitor, in right of the crown, of all hospitals and colleges of royal foundation ; and patron of all livings under the value of twenty marks *per annum* in the king's books. He is the general guardian of all infants, idiots, and lunatics ; and has the general superintendence of all charitable uses in the kingdom. And all this, over and above the vast and extensive jurisdiction which he exercises in his *judicial* capacity in the Court of Chancery ; wherein, as in the Exchequer, there are two distinct tribunals : the one ordinary, being a court of common law ; the other extraordinary, being a court of equity.

. The ordinary legal court is the more ancient. Its jurisdiction is to cancel letters patent, when made against law ; and to hold plea of petitions, traverses of offices, and the like ; when the sovereign has been advised to do any act, or is put in possession of any lands or goods, in prejudice of a subject's right. On a proof of which, as the sovereign can never be supposed to do any wrong, the law questions not but he will immediately redress the injury ; and refers that conscientious task to the chancellor, the keeper of his conscience. Out of this ordinary, or legal court, also issue all original writs, all commissions of the peace, of charitable uses, sewers, and the like.

But the extraordinary court, or *court of equity*, is now become the court of the greatest judicial consequence. This distinction between law and equity, as administered in different courts, is not at present known, nor seems to have ever been known, in any other country at any time : and yet the difference of one from the other, when administered by the same tribunal, was perfectly familiar to the Romans ; the *jus prætorium* being distinct from the *leges* or

standing laws. Among the Romans, however, the power of both
centered in one and the same magistrate; who was equally intrusted
to pronounce the rule of law, and to apply it to particular cases, by
the principles of equity. But with us the application of the rules
of equity fell solely into the hands of the chancellor; for when the
courts of law, proceeding merely upon the king's original writs, and
confining themselves strictly to that bottom, gave a harsh or imperfect judgment, the application for redress used to be to the king
in person, assisted by his privy council; and they were wont to refer
the matter either to the chancellor and a select committee, or by
degrees to the chancellor only; who mitigated the severity or supplied the defects of the judgments pronounced in the courts of law,
upon weighing the circumstances of the case; and in this way
obtained by degrees the equitable jurisdiction which now occupies
so large a field in English jurisprudence. Its growth was regarded
with great jealousy by parliament. Various efforts were made from
time to time to restrain and limit the authority of the chancellor.
But the crown steadily supported it; and the invention by John de
Waltham, who was bishop of Salisbury and master of the rolls to
King Richard II., of the writ of *subpœna*, returnable in the court of
chancery only, gave great efficiency if not expansion to the jurisdiction. This process was afterwards extended to other matters wholly
determinable at the common law; so much so, that in the reigns of
Henry IV. and V., the commons were repeatedly urgent to have the
writ of *subpœna* entirely suppressed. But though Henry IV., being
then hardly warm in his throne, gave a palliating answer to their
petitions, and actually passed the statute 4 Henry IV. c. 23, whereby
judgments at law are declared irrevocable unless by attaint or writ
of error, yet his son put a negative at once upon their whole application: and in Edward IV.'s time, the process by bill and *subpœna*
was become the daily practice of the court.

It was in the time of Lord Ellesmere, A.D. 1616, that arose the
notable dispute between the courts of law and equity, set on foot by
Sir Edward Coke, then chief justice of the court of King's Bench;
whether a court of equity could give relief after or against a judgment at the common law. This contest was so warmly carried on,
that indictments were preferred against the suitors, the solicitors,
the counsel, and even a master in chancery, for having incurred a
præmunire, by questioning in a court of equity a judgment in the
court of King's Bench, obtained by gross fraud and imposition.
This matter, being brought before the king, was by him referred to
his learned counsel for their advice and opinion; who reported so
strongly in favour of the courts of equity, that his majesty gave
judgment on their behalf: but, not contented with the irrefragable

reasons and precedents produced by his counsel, for the chief justice was clearly in the wrong, he chose rather to decide the question by referring it to the plenitude of his royal prerogative. Sir Edward Coke submitted to the decision, and thereby made atonement for his error: but this struggle, together with the business of *commendams*, in which he acted a very noble part, and his controlling the commissioners of sewers, were the open and avowed causes, first of his suspension, and soon after of his removal, from his office.

Lord Bacon, who succeeded Lord Ellesmere, reduced the practice of the court into a more regular system; but did not sit long enough to effect any considerable revolution in the science itself: and few of his decrees which have reached us are of any great consequence to posterity. His successors, in the reign of Charles I., did little to improve upon his plan: and after the Restoration the seal was committed to the Earl of Clarendon, who had withdrawn from practice as a lawyer nearly twenty years; and afterwards to the Earl of Shaftesbury, who had never practised at all. But with Lord Nottingham, in 1673, a new era commenced. In the course of nine years, during which he presided in the court, he built up a system of jurisprudence and-jurisdiction upon wide and rational foundations, which served as a model for succeeding judges, and gave a new character to the court; and hence he has been emphatically called "The father of Equity." His immediate successors availed themselves very greatly of his profound learning and judgment. But a successor was still wanted, who should hold the seals for a period long enough to enable him to widen the foundation, and complete the structure, begun and planned by that illustrious man. Such a successor at length appeared in Lord Hardwicke. This great judge presided in the Court of Chancery for twenty years; and his numerous decisions evince the most thorough learning, the most exquisite skill, and the most elegant juridical analysis. Few judges have left behind them a reputation more bright and enduring; few have had so favourable an opportunity of conferring lasting benefits upon the jurisprudence of their country; and still fewer have improved it by so large, so various, and so important contributions.

XI. The Lord Chancellor has, at least from the time of Henry VIII., had the assistance of the Master of the Rolls in administering justice according to the rules of equity. This great officer, who is now the custodier of the public records of the kingdom, was formerly the chief merely of the masters in chancery, who carried out the decrees and performed the ministerial functions of that court. Cardinal Wolsey is said to have been the first chancellor who devolved on the Master of the Rolls the exercise of a considerable branch of the equity jurisdiction of the court.

XII. In the course of the present century, the business of the Court of Chancery has so much increased, that it has been found necessary to add considerably to its judicial power. In 1813 a vice-chancellor was appointed; and in 1841, two additional vice-chancellors; and a third has since been added. These judges may hear and determine all matters pending in the Chancery; but from the judgment of any of them there is an appeal either to the lord chancellor, or to—

XIII. The Court of Appeal in Chancery, constituted by the statute 14 & 15 Vic. c. 83; and consisting of two lords justices, who, with or without the lord chancellor, exercise all the jurisdiction possessed by him; and may therefore entertain suits in the first instance as well as on appeal.

From the judgment or decree of the lord chancellor, or of this court of appeal in chancery, as from the court of Exchequer Chamber, an appeal lies to—

XIV. The House of Peers, the supreme court of judicature in the kingdom, having at present *no original* jurisdiction over *causes*, but only upon appeals and writs of error, to rectify any injustice or mistake of the law, committed by the courts below. To this authority this august tribunal succeeded of course upon the dissolution of the *aula regia*. They are therefore in all causes the last resort, from whose judgment no further appeal is permitted; but every subordinate tribunal must conform to their determinations; the law reposing an entire confidence in the honour and conscience of the noble persons who compose this important assembly, that they will refer themselves exclusively to the opinions, either of those peers who have held high judicial office, or of the judges, who are summoned by writ to advise them; since upon their decision all property must finally depend.

XV. Before I conclude this chapter, I must mention another species of courts, which act as auxiliaries to the foregoing; I mean the courts of *nisi prius*.

These are composed of two or more commissioners, who are twice or oftener in every year sent all round the kingdom, except London and Middlesex where sittings at *nisi prius* are holden after every term, to try by a jury of the respective counties the truth of such matters of fact as are then under dispute in the courts of Westminster Hall. They now sit by virtue of five several authorities.

1. A commission of the *peace*. 2. A commission of *oyer* and *terminer*. 3. A commission of general *gaol-delivery*; the consideration of all which belongs properly to the subsequent part of these commentaries. The fourth commission is, 4. A commission of *assize*,

that is, to take the verdict of a peculiar species of jury, called an assize, which, by the abolition of real actions, no longer exists. The other authority is, 5. That of *nisi prius*, which is a consequence of the commission of *assize*, being annexed to it by the statute of Westm. 2, and empowers them to try all questions of fact issuing out of the courts at Westminster, that are then ripe for trial by jury. These by ancient practice were to be tried at Westminster in some Easter or Michaelmas term, by a jury returned from the county wherein the cause of action arose; *nisi prius, unless before* the day fixed for this trial at Westminster, the judges of assize came into the county in question; which, I may add, they were sure to do in the vacations preceding each Easter and Michaelmas term. From these words of the ancient writ, we derive the appellation of sittings at *nisi prius.*

These, then, are the several courts of common law and equity, which are of public and general jurisdiction throughout the king-dom; a large portion of the judicial business of the country, how-ever, is done in other courts, the nature of which will be explained in the following chapter.

CHAPTER III.

OF COURTS OF A SPECIAL JURISDICTION.

Ecclesiastical Courts, viz., Archdeacon's Court—Consistory—Court of Arches, and Judical Committee of Privy Council—Court of Probate—Court of Admiralty—Court for Divorce and Matrimonial Causes—Court of Bank-ruptcy—Courts of the Counties Palatine—of the Stannaries—of the Cities and Boroughs, and of the Universities—Forest Courts—Courts of Commis-sioners of Sewers.

BESIDES the several courts treated of in the preceding chapter, and in which all injuries are redressed that fall under the cognizance of the common law of England, or that spirit of equity which ought to be its constant attendant, there still remain some other courts of a *jurisdiction equally public and general*, which take cognizance of certain other species of injuries. These are, I. the Ecclesiastical Courts, II. the Court of Probate, and III. the Court of Admiralty.

I. The Ecclesiastical Courts date from the Conquest. In the time of our Saxon ancestors there was no distinction between the lay and the ecclesiastical jurisdiction: the county court was as much a spiritual as a temporal tribunal: the rights of the church were asserted by the same judges as the rights of the laity. For this

o

purpose the bishop of the diocese and the sheriff of the county used to sit together in the county court, and had there the cognizance of all causes, as well ecclesiastical as civil: a superior deference being paid to the bishop's opinion in spiritual matters, and to that of the lay judges in temporal.

William the Conqueror, it is generally said, to please the clergy, by whom his claims had been warmly espoused, separated the ecclesiastical courts from the civil; and prohibited any spiritual cause from being tried in the secular courts, commanding the suitors to appear before the bishop only, whose decisions were thenceforth to conform to the canon law. King Henry I. revived the union of the civil and ecclesiastical courts; but the clergy having in their synod at Westminster, 3 Hen. I., ordained that no bishop should attend the discussion of temporal causes, soon dissolved this newly-effected union. And when Stephen was brought in by the clergy, one article of the oath which they imposed upon him was, that ecclesiastical persons and ecclesiastical causes should be subject only to the bishop's jurisdiction. About that time the contest began between the laws of England and those of Rome, the temporal courts adhering to the former, and the spiritual adopting the latter as their rule of proceeding; this widened the breach between them, and made a coalition afterwards impracticable, which probably would else have been effected at the general reformation of the church.

In briefly mentioning the various species of ecclesiastical courts, I would premise one observation only, that the jurisdiction of these courts is now so very limited, that they possess little if any of that importance which formerly attached to their proceedings..

1. The *Archdeacon's* Court, then, is the most inferior court in the whole ecclesiastical polity. It is held, in the archdeacon's absence, before his official. From hence an appeal lies to

2. The *Consistory* Court, which is held in the cathedral of every bishop, for the trial of ecclesiastical causes arising within the diocese. The bishop's chancellor is the judge; and from his sentence an appeal lies to the archbishop.

3. The Court of *Arches* is the Court of Appeal of the Archbishop of Canterbury, whereof the judge is called the *Dean of the Arches;* because he anciently held his court in the church of Saint Mary *le bow, sancta Maria de arcubus.* The office of dean of the arches having been for a long time united with that of the archbishop's principal official, he now, in right of the last-mentioned office, as does also the official principal of the *Archbishop of York,* receives and determines appeals from the sentences of all inferior ecclesiastical courts within the province. From him an appeal lies to the Queen,

as supreme head of the English church, in the place of the Bishop of Rome, who formerly exercised this jurisdiction.*

I pass by such ecclesiastical courts as have only what is called a *voluntary*, and not a *contentious* jurisdiction, which merely keep an open office for granting dispensations, licences, faculties, and other remnants of the papal extortions; and proceed to

4. The great court of appeal in all ecclesiastical causes; viz., the *Judicial Committee of the Privy Council*, which has been substituted for the Court of *Delegates, judices delegati*, who were formerly appointed by commission under the Great Seal, to represent the royal person, and hear all appeals to the sovereign, made by virtue of the statute 25 Henry VIII. c. 19.

Appeals to Rome were always looked upon by the English nation, even in the times of popery, with an evil eye, as being contrary to the liberty of the subject, the honour of the crown, and the independence of the whole realm; and were first introduced in very turbulent times in the reign of Stephen, A.D. 1151, at the same period that the civil and canon laws were first imported into England. But, in a few years after, to obviate this growing practice the Constitutions made at Clarendon, 11 Hen. II., expressly declare, that appeals ought to lie from the archbishop to the king; and are not to proceed any further without special licence from the crown. But the unhappy advantage given in the reigns of John, and his son Henry III., to the encroaching power of the pope, at length riveted the custom of appealing to Rome in causes ecclesiastical so strongly, that it never could be thoroughly broken off, till the grand rupture happened in the reign of Henry VIII., when all the jurisdiction previously possessed by the pope in matters ecclesiastical was transferred to the crown. Thenceforth these appeals were heard by the court of Delegates, till the statute of Henry VIII. was in this respect repealed; and the appellate jurisdiction of the crown *in Chancery* directed to be exercised by the king *in council*, by the statute 3 & 4 Will. IV. c. 41. For that purpose the *Judicial Committee of the Privy Council*, consisting of the lord chancellor, the chief justices, and others of the judges, was constituted; but though styled a committee, it is a court of record, and has full power to punish contempts, and award costs.

These are the principal courts of ecclesiastical jurisdiction; none of which, except the Judicial Committee, are allowed to be courts of record; no more than was another much more formidable jurisdic-

* Sir William Blackstone mentions in this place the *Prerogative Court* of the Archbishop of Canterbury; which ceased to exist with the doctrine of *bona notabilia*, on which its jurisdiction was founded, on the transfer of the testamentary jurisdiction of the Ecclesiastical Courts to the Court of Probate.

tion, but now deservedly annihilated, viz., the court of *High Commission* in causes ecclesiastical, erected to vindicate the dignity and peace of the church, by reforming ecclesiastical persons, and all manner of errors, heresies, schisms, offences, and enormities. Under the shelter of which very general words, means were found to vest in the commissioners almost despotic powers of fining and imprisoning, which they exerted much beyond the degree of the offence itself, and frequently over offences by no means of spiritual cognizance. For these reasons this court was justly abolished by statute 16 Car. I. c. 11; and the attempt that was made to revive it, during the reign of James II., served only to hasten that infatuated prince's ruin.

II. The *Court of Probate* was constituted as a court of record by the statute 20 & 21 Vict. c. 77, to exercise, in the name of the Queen, "all the jurisdiction and authority in relation to the granting " or revoking probate of wills and letters of administration of the " effects of deceased persons then vested in any court or person," and by that act transferred to the crown; "with full authority to hear " and determine all questions relating to matters and causes testa- " mentary." Its principal registry is in the metropolis; but for the convenience of the suitors it has nearly as many local registries as formerly there were dioceses, the districts of the former being much the same as those of the consistory courts, whose jurisdiction has been transferred to the crown. The duties of these consistory courts were, indeed, principally *administrative*; and the functions of the local registrars of the Court of Probate are in like manner chiefly exercised in *non-contentious* cases; for in *disputed* wills or administrations the court itself must decide, unless the case be one in which the county court has jurisdiction.

III. The *Court of Admiralty* has jurisdiction to determine all maritime injuries, arising upon the seas, or in parts out of the reach of the common law. It is held before the Lord High Admiral, or his deputy, who is called the judge of the court; and from its sentences an appeal lies, in ordinary course, to the sovereign in council. It has, in time of war, the authority of a *Prize* Court, a jurisdiction secured by divers treaties with foreign nations; by which particular courts are established in all the maritime countries of Europe for the decision of this question, whether lawful prize or not: for this being a question between subjects of different states, it belongs entirely to the law of nations, and not to the municipal laws of either country, to determine it.

There yet remain certain other courts, which are, I. instituted to redress or prevent *particular wrongs*; or, II. whose jurisdiction is confined to *particular localities*; or, III. is altogether private and *special in its nature*.

I. Of the *first* species are the court for Divorce and Matrimonial Causes, and the courts of Bankruptcy.

The *Court for Divorce and Matrimonial Causes* was constituted by statute 20 & 21 Vict. c. 85, to exercise in the name of the Queen all the jurisdiction then vested in any ecclesiastical court or person in matters matrimonial; and is a court of record, the judge of the Court of Probate being the judge ordinary; with authority to hear and determine all matters arising therein, subject to an appeal to the *full court*; which consists of the judge ordinary and at least two other judges of the courts of Westminster, and in certain other cases to the House of Lords.

The Court of Bankruptcy was first established by the statute 1 & 2 Will. IV. c. 56, and consists of a principal court situated in London, and seven district courts, each of which is a court of law and equity, and has all the rights and incidents of a court of record; the procedure therein, which has been regulated by several statutes, being the same in all. In certain cases the *county courts* have all the powers and authorities of the district courts of bankruptcy. And from the judgment of either an appeal lies to the court of chancery; and thence a further appeal to the House of Lords.

The proceedings of these courts, I must add, are administrative, not contentious: they are not tribunals for the trial and determination of disputed questions either of fact or of law; their proper functions are to collect and divide the property of a bankrupt among his creditors; and their proceedings accordingly are principally those of the courts themselves or of their officers, and not of the parties severally interested in the funds, which it is the office and duty of these tribunals to distribute.

II. The *second* species of courts, or those whose jurisdiction is confined to particular localities,* are

1. The court of the *Duchy Chamber of Lancaster*, held before the chancellor of the duchy or his deputy, concerning all matter of equity relating to lands holden of the crown in right of the duchy of Lancaster; the proceedings in which are the same as on the equity side in the Court of Chancery.

2. The courts of the *Counties Palatine of Lancaster and Durham*, in which the ordinary writs, under the great seal out of Chancery, do

---

* Among this class of courts might formerly have been included the courts of the *County Palatine of Chester*, of the *Royal Franchise of Ely*, and of the *Cinque Ports*; the *Palace Court*; and the *Great Sessions* and other courts of the principality of Wales.

not run; that is, in which the ordinary writs are of no force. For as originally all *jura regalia* were granted to the lords of these counties palatine, they had, of course, the sole administration of justice, by their own judges appointed by themselves and not by the crown. It would therefore be incongruous for the sovereign to send his writ to direct the judge of another's court in what manner to administer justice between the suitors. The judges of assize, who sit therein, sit, therefore, by virtue of a special commission from the crown as owner of these several franchises, and under the seal thereof; and not by the usual commission under the great seal of England. The procedure, however, is similar to that of the superior courts of common law at Westminster. And an appeal lies to the court of Queen's Bench, as an ensign of superiority reserved to the crown at the original creation of the franchises. All prerogative writs, as those of *habeas corpus*, prohibition, *certiorari*, and *mandamus*, may issue for the same reason to all these exempt jurisdictions; because the privilege, that the king's writ runs not, must be intended between party and party, for there can be no such privilege against the king.

3. The *Stannary Court*, for the administration of justice among the tinners in Devonshire and Cornwall, is also a court of record of the same local character. So are

4. The several courts within the *city of London*, and other *cities*, *boroughs*, and corporations throughout the kingdom, held by prescription, charter, or act of parliament; and

5. The *Chancellor's courts* in the two *Universities* of England. Which two learned bodies enjoy the sole jurisdiction, in exclusion of the Queen's Courts, over all civil actions and suits whatsoever, when a scholar or privileged person is one of the parties; excepting in such cases where the right of freehold is concerned.

III. The *third* species of courts, or those whose jurisdiction is *special* in its nature are—

1. The *Forest Courts*, instituted for the government of the royal forests, and for the punishment of all injuries done to the royal deer or *venison*, to the *vert* or greenswerd, and to the *covert* in which such deer are lodged. These are the courts of *Attachments*, of *Regard*, of *Sweinmote*, and of *Justice-seat;* for an account of whose jurisdiction and procedure I must refer the student to the treatises on these subjects; only remarking here, that they will soon be, if they are not already, interesting only to the antiquary; the policy of modern legislation being to remove all traces of the ancient forests, and of the obnoxious privileges formerly attached to them.

2. A similar observation might, perhaps, be made with reference to the *Courts* of the *Commissioners of Sewers*, which are temporary

tribunals, erected by commission under the great seal, with jurisdiction to overlook the repairs of sea banks and walls, and the
cleansing of public streams, ditches, and other conduits, whereby
any waters are carried off, in the county or particular district specified
in the commission. These duties are obviously so much more of
an administrative than of a judicial nature, that in modern times
powers similar to those possessed by the courts of sewers have been
freely conferred on vestries, borough councils, and other local representative bodies, charged with the improvement and police of towns
and other populous places. And the functions of the commissioners
of sewers are thus so effectually superseded, that these courts are
not likely to be ever again called into active operation.

I have now gone through the several species of private, or special
courts, of the greatest note in the kingdom, instituted for the local
redress of private wrongs; and must, in the close of all, make one
general observation from Sir Edward Coke: that these particular
jurisdictions, derogating from the general jurisdiction of the courts
of common law, are ever strictly restrained, and cannot be extended
further than the express letter of their privileges will most explicitly
warrant.

CHAPTER IV.

OF THE COGNIZANCE OF PRIVATE WRONGS.

I. By Ecclesiastical Courts, viz. : Suits as to tithes, surplice, and other fees—
Spoliation and dilapidations—Excommunication. II. By Divorce Court,
viz.: Divorce—Separation—Alimony—Restitution of conjugal rights—
Nullity and validity of marriage—and *causa jactitationis matrimonii*.
III. By Court of Probate, viz. : Proving of wills and grant of administration. IV. By Court of Admiralty : Injuries on the high seas. V. By Courts
of Common Law : Procedendo—Mandamus—Prohibition.

WE are now to consider in which of the vast variety of courts,
mentioned in the preceding chapters, every possible injury that can
be offered to a man's person or property is certain of meeting with
redress.

The authority of the courts of special jurisdiction was remarked
as those tribunals were enumerated; we will therefore confine our
present inquiry to the cognizance of civil injuries in the courts of
general jurisdiction. And the order, in which I shall pursue this
inquiry, will be by showing—1. What injuries may be remedied in
the ecclesiastical courts. 2. What in the Court for Divorce and
Matrimonial Causes. 3. What in the Court of Probate. 4. What

in the Admiralty Courts. And, 5. What in the superior courts of common law.   I shall endeavour to point out, as I proceed, what other remedies are, in particular cases, open to the parties injured; and especially when it may be more desirable to resort to a court of equity, than to sue in a court of common law.   The special or peculiar jurisdiction and the procedure of the courts of equity I shall treat of separately.

And, with regard to the jurisdiction of the ecclesiastical courts, I must not so much consider what has been claimed to belong thereto, but what the common law permits to be so.   For these tribunals, as they subsist and are admitted in England, not by any right of their own, but upon bare sufferance and toleration from the municipal laws, must have recourse to the laws of that country wherein they are thus adopted, to be informed how far their jurisdiction extends, or what causes are permitted, and what forbidden, to be discussed or drawn in question before them.   Having premised this general caution, I proceed now to consider,

I. The injuries cognizable by the Ecclesiastical courts—such, I mean, as are offered to private persons, or individuals; which are here cognizable, not for reformation of the offender himself or party *injuring*, *pro salute animæ*, as is the case with immoralities in general, when unconnected with private injuries, but for the sake of the party *injured*, to make him a satisfaction and redress for the damage which he has sustained.   These wrongs were until quite recently treated of under three general heads—causes *pecuniary*, causes *matrimonial*, and causes *testamentary*; but the jurisdiction of the Courts Christian, in causes *matrimonial* and *testamentary*, having been transferred to other tribunals, they now take cognizance only of

Pecuniary causes, which are such as arise either from the withholding ecclesiastical dues, or the doing or neglecting some act relating to the church, whereby some damage accrues to the plaintiff; towards obtaining a satisfaction for which he is permitted to institute a suit in the spiritual court.   The principal of these is the subtraction or witholding of *tithes* from the parson or vicar, whether the former be a clergyman or a lay appropriator, where the *right* does not come into question, but only the *fact*, whether or no the tithes allowed to be due are really subtracted or withdrawn.   But it now seldom happens that tithes are sued for at all in the spiritual court; for various modern statutes have provided a summary method of proceeding before magistrates in petty sessions, except where the actual title to the tithe or the actual liability or exemption of the land is *bonâ fide* in question.   And tithes themselves will ere long be a thing of the past, those not previously commuted by agreement being now convertible into rent-charges, recoverable by distress, in the same manner as rent reserved on a lease.

Another pecuniary injury, cognizable in the spiritual courts, is the *non-payment* of other ecclesiastical *dues* to the clergy ; as pensions, mortuaries, compositions, offerings, and whatsoever falls under the denomination of *surplice fees*, for marriages or other ministerial offices of the church : all which injuries are redressed by a decree for their actual payment. For *fees* also, settled and acknowledged to be due to the officers of the ecclesiastical courts, a suit will lie therein ; but not if the *right* of the fees is at all disputable ; for then it must be decided by the common law.

Under this head of pecuniary injuries may also be reduced the several matters of spoliation, dilapidations, and neglect of repairing the church and things thereunto belonging ; for which a satisfaction may be sued for in the ecclesiastical court.

Spoliation is an injury done by one clerk or incumbent to another, in taking the fruits of his benefice without any right thereunto, but under a pretended title. It is remedied by a decree to account for the profits so taken. For *dilapidations*, which are a kind of ecclesiastical waste, either voluntary, by pulling down ; or permissive, by suffering the chancel, parsonage-house, and other buildings thereunto belonging, to decay ; an action also lies, either in the spiritual court by the canon law, or in the courts of common law ; and it may be brought by the successor against the predecessor, if living, or, if dead, then against his executors.

And as to the *neglect of reparations* of the church, churchyard, and the like, the spiritual court has undoubted cognizance thereof ; and a suit may be brought therein for non-payment of a rate made by the churchwardens for that purpose. Where, however, the amount claimed does not exceed 10*l.*, and the validity of the rate, or the liability of the person from whom it is demanded, is not disputed, the only method of proceeding is under the statute 57 Geo. III. c. 127 ; which enables two justices, on the complaint of any churchwarden, to order the payment of a church-rate by any person refusing to do so. If the validity of the rate or the liability of the person charged be disputed, the churchwardens must proceed in the ecclesiastical court.

But before I dismiss this head, it may not be improper to add a few words concerning the *method of proceeding* in these tribunals, which is almost entirely according to the practice of the civil and canon laws, or rather according to a mixture of both, corrected and new modelled by their own particular usages, and the interposition of the courts of common law. Their ordinary course of proceeding is—first, by *citation*, to call the party injuring before them. Then,

by *libel*, or by articles drawn out in a formal *allegation*, to set forth
the complainant's ground of complaint.   To this succeeds the
defendant's answer upon oath; when, if he denies or extenuates the
charge, they proceed to *proofs* either in open court, or by having
witnesses examined, and their depositions taken down in writing by
an officer of the court. If the defendant has any circumstances to
offer in his defence, he must also propound them in what is called
his *defensive allegation*, to which he is entitled in his turn to the
plaintiff's answer upon oath, and may from thence proceed to *proofs*
as well as his antagonist.   When all the pleadings and proofs are
concluded, they are referred to the consideration, not of a jury, but
of a single judge; who *takes information* by hearing advocates on
both sides, and therefore forms his *interlocutory decree or definite
sentence* at his own discretion : from which there generally lies an
appeal, in the several stages already mentioned.

But the point in which these jurisdictions are the most defective,
is that of enforcing their sentences when pronounced; for which they
have no other process but that of *excommunication* ; which is described to be twofold ; the less and the greater excommunication.
The less is an ecclesiastical censure, excluding the party from the
participation of the sacraments : the greater proceeds further, and
excludes him not only from these, but also from the company of all
Christians.   Heavy as this penalty is, considered in a serious light,
there are, notwithstanding, many obstinate or profligate men who
would despise the *brutum fulmen* of mere ecclesiastical censures,
especially when pronounced by a petty surrogate in the country,
for non-payment of fees, or costs, or for other trivial causes.   The
common law, therefore, compassionately steps in to the aid of the
ecclesiastical jurisdiction, and kindly lends a supporting hand to
an otherwise tottering authority, by giving the writ *de contumace
capiendo*, upon which the person who is contumacious may be imprisoned, until released by a writ of deliverance, or discharged from
custody in due course of law.

II. Matrimonial causes, or injuries respecting the rights of marriage, until recently a branch of the ecclesiastical jurisdiction, are
now exclusively cognizable in *the Court for Divorce and Matrimonial
Causes.*   Of these the first and principal is,

1. The suit for a *divorce*, on the ground of adultery, which is
brought either by the husband against the wife and her paramour;
or by the wife against the husband ; being maintainable by the husband in respect of the simple adultery of the wife; but not by the
wife against the husband, unless his adultery has been coupled with
desertion, without reasonable excuse, for two years, or with such
cruelty as would entitle the wife to a judicial separation, or he has

been guilty of bigamy, rape, or an unnatural offence. In the suit by a husband the wife's paramour must be joined as a co-respondent, unless the court allows the omission; for he may be condemned not only in such damages as a jury may assess in respect of the adultery, but also in the whole costs of the proceedings.

2. The suit for a *judicial separation* is also a cause thoroughly matrimonial. For if it becomes improper that the parties should live together; as through intolerable cruelty, a perpetual disease, and the like, the law allows the remedy of a *judicial separation.*

3. The next species of matrimonial cause is a consequence drawn from one of the two former, which is the suit for *alimony*, a term which signifies maintenance : which suit the wife may have against her husband, if he neglects or refuses to make her an allowance suitable to their station in life.

4. The suit for *restitution of conjugal rights* is also another species of matrimonial cause: which may be brought when either lives separate from the other without sufficient reason; in which case they will be compelled to come together again, if either party be weak enough to desire it. There yet remain three other species of matrimonial causes; viz:—

5. The *suit for nullity*, which may be brought, if sufficient cause existed previous to the marriage, such as rendered it unlawful *ab initio*, that is to say, corporal imbecility.

6. That brought for *declaring the validity* of a marriage, or the legitimacy of the offspring thereof, which may be maintained by any person whose right to be deemed a natural born subject depends on his legitimacy or on the validity of a marriage. Finally, there is,

7. The suit *causa jactitationis matrimonii ;* which may be brought when one gives out that he or she is married to the complainant, in order that he or she may be enjoined perpetual silence upon that head; the only remedy that can be given for this injury.

The interference of this court is sought by *petition*, filed in its registry ; on which a *citation* issues to the respondent, requiring him to *appear* and *answer* the matters alleged against him. To this answer, when made, the complainant *replies ;* the respondent, if need be, making further answer; the *issues* ultimately joined between the parties being next ordered for *trial*, either by the court itself or by a jury if either of the parties so require. The procedure of this court is so far, as will be seen hereafter, that of the common law ; and it has accordingly the same powers to compel the attendance of jurymen and witnesses as the courts at Westminster ; the same procedure as in those courts at *nisi prius*, and after trial in motions for *new trials* and otherwise; and the same process of execution for enforcing its orders and decrees as the High Court of Chancery.

III. The authority of the *Court of Probate* is "to hear and deter- " mine all questions relating to matters and causes testamentary," a jurisdiction which, until restored to the crown by the statute 20 & 21 Vict. c. 77, belonged to the ecclesiastical courts; being principally exercised in the *consistory courts* of the diocesan bishops, and in the *prerogative court* of the metropolitan. It is properly divisible into two branches; the probate of wills, and the granting of administrations. These, when no opposition is made, are granted merely *ex officio et debito justitiæ*, and are then the object of what is called the *voluntary,* and not the *contentious* jurisdiction. But when a *caveat* is entered against proving the will or granting administra- tion, and a suit thereupon follows to determine either the validity of the testament, or who has a right to administer; this claim and obstruction by the adverse party are an injury to the party entitled, and as such are remedied by the sentence of this court, either by establishing the will or granting the administration. The *voluntary* or *non-contentious* jurisdiction, being administrative merely, gives occupation to the registrars of this court in London and in the pro- vinces where district registrars have been established; the *conten- tious* jurisdiction is principally exercised by the court itself, the method of proceeding therein being in general accordance with the practice of the courts of common law. The party propounding a will or asserting a claim to administration is required to make the necessary averments in a *declaration,* to which his adversary puts in a *plea* or answer, whereupon *issue is joined,* and the parties proceed to the *trial* of those questions of fact on which they differ, the rules of evidence observed in the superior courts of common law being alone applicable to the determination thereof. This court has the same means of compelling the production of documents, and the attendance of jurymen and witnesses, and of obtaining the examina- tion of witnesses who are abroad, as the courts of law; and the same powers of enforcing its orders and decrees by attachment and other process of execution, as the High Court of Chancery; and from its judgment an appeal lies directly to the House of Lords.

IV. The *Admiralty Courts* have jurisdiction to determine all *maritime causes*; or such injuries, which though they are in their nature of common law cognizance, yet being committed on the high seas, out of the reach of our ordinary courts of justice, are therefore to be remedied in a peculiar court of their own. If part of any con- tract, or other cause of action, does arise upon the sea, and part upon the land, the common law excludes the Admiralty Court from its jurisdiction; for, part belonging properly to one cognizance and part to another, the common or general law takes place of the particular. Therefore, though pure maritime acquisitions, which are earned and become due on the high seas, as seamen's wages, are one proper object of the admiralty jurisdiction, even though the contract for them be made upon land; yet, in general, if there be a contract made in England, and to be executed upon the seas, as a charter-party or covenant that a ship shall sail to Jamaica, or shall be in such a latitude by such a day; or a contract made upon the sea to be performed in England, as a bond made on shipboard to pay money in London or the like; these kinds of mixed contracts belong not to the admiralty jurisdiction, but to the courts of common law. In cases of *prizes* taken in time of war, and brought into our ports, the Courts of Admiralty have an undisturbed and exclusive jurisdiction to decide according to the law of nations.

The proceedings of these courts bear much resemblance to those of the civil law, but are not entirely founded thereon, and they likewise adopt and make use of other laws, as occasion requires; such as the Rhodian laws and the laws of Oleron. The first process in these courts is frequently by arrest of the defendant's person; and they also take recognizances or stipulations of certain fidejussors in the nature of bail, and in case of default may imprison both them and their principal. And all this is supported by immemorial usage, grounded on the necessity of supporting a jurisdiction so extensive; though opposite to the usual doctrines of the common law.

V. I am next to consider such injuries as are cognizable by the courts of the common law. And herein I shall for the present only remark, that all possible injuries whatsoever that do not fall within the exclusive cognizance of the other tribunals, are for that very reason within the cognizance of the common law courts. For it is a settled principle that every right when withheld must have a remedy, and every injury its proper redress. The explanation of these numerous injuries, and their respective legal remedies, will employ our attention for many subsequent chapters. But before we conclude the present, I shall just mention two species of injuries, which will properly fall now within our immediate consideration: and which are, either when justice is delayed by an inferior court that has proper cognizance of the cause; or, when such inferior court takes upon itself to examine a cause and decide the merits without a legal remedy.

1. The first of these injuries, refusal or neglect of justice, is remedied either by writ of *procedendo*, or of *mandamus*. A writ of *procedendo ad judicium* issues out of Chancery, where judges of any subordinate court do delay the parties; for that they will not give judgment, either on the one side or on the other, when they ought

so to do. In this case a *procedendo* shall be awarded, commanding them to proceed to judgment; but without specifying any particular judgment, for that, if erroneous, may be set aside on an appeal: and upon further neglect or refusal, the judges of the inferior court may be punished for their contempt by attachment. This writ is, however, rarely resorted to, the remedy by *mandamus* being preferable.

The prerogative writ of *mandamus*, for there is a writ of this name, which is merely a writ of execution, is a command issuing in the name of the sovereign from the Queen's Bench, and directed to any person, corporation, or inferior court of judicature requiring them to do some *particular* thing therein specified, which appertains to their office and duty, and which the Queen's Bench has previously determined, or at least supposes to be consonant to right and justice. A *mandamus* lies, for instance, to compel the admission or restoration of the party applying to any office or franchise of a public nature, whether spiritual or temporal; to academical degrees; to the use of a meeting-house, &c.: for the production, inspection, or delivery of public books and papers; for the surrender of the *regalia* of a corporation; to oblige bodies corporate to affix their common seal; to compel the holding of a court; and for an infinite number of other purposes, which it is impossible to recite minutely. But at present we are more particularly to remark, that it issues to the judges of any inferior court, commanding them to do justice according to the powers of their office, whenever the same is delayed. A *mandamus* may therefore be had to the courts of the city of London, to enter up judgment; to the quarter sessions, to hear an appeal; to the spiritual courts, to swear a churchwarden, and the like. This writ is grounded on the oath of the party injured, of his own right, and the denial of justice below: whereupon a rule is usually made, directing the party complained of to show cause why a writ of *mandamus* should not issue: and, if he shows no sufficient cause, the writ itself is issued, at first in the alternative, either to do thus, or signify some reason to the contrary; to which a return, or answer, must be made at a certain day. And, if the inferior judge, or other person to whom the writ is directed, returns or signifies an insufficient reason, then there issues in the second place a *peremptory mandamus*, to do the thing absolutely: to which no other return will be admitted, but perfect obedience. If the inferior judge or other person makes no return, or fails in his obedience, he is punishable for his contempt by attachment. If, however, he returns a sufficient cause, although it should be false in fact, the court will not try the truth of the fact upon affidavits; but will for the present believe him, and proceed no further on the *mandamus*; in which case the party injured may adopt one of two courses. He may either have an action against the defendant for his false return, and, if it be found to be false by the jury, he shall in such action recover damages equivalent to the injury sustained; or he may plead to the return as if it were a defence to an ordinary action. The plaintiff, if ultimately successful in either of these courses, shall have a *peremptory* mandamus to the defendant to do his duty.

2. The other injury, which is that of encroachment of jurisdiction, or calling one *coram non judice*, to answer in a court that has no legal cognizance of the cause, is also a grievance, for which the common law has provided a remedy by the writ of *prohibition;* which is a writ issuing properly only out of the Queen's Bench, being a prerogative writ; but, for the furtherance of justice, now also out of the Chancery, Common Pleas, or Exchequer; and is directed to the judge and parties to a suit in any inferior court, commanding them to cease from the prosecution thereof, upon a suggestion, that either the cause originally, or some collateral matter arising therein, does not belong to that jurisdiction, but to the cognizance of some other court. This writ may issue, for instance, to the County Courts, if they attempt to hold plea of any matter not within their jurisdiction; or it may be directed to the Courts Christian, the University Courts, or the Courts of Admiralty, where they concern themselves with any matter not within their cognizance; as if the first should attempt to try the validity of a custom pleaded, or the latter a contract made or to be executed within this kingdom. And if either the judge or the party shall proceed after such prohibition, an attachment may be had against them, to punish them for the contempt, at the discretion of the court that awarded it; and an action will lie against them, to repair the party injured in damages.

So long as the idea continued among the clergy, that the ecclesiastical state was wholly independent of the civil, great struggles were constantly maintained between the temporal courts and the spiritual, concerning the writ of prohibition and the proper objects of it, even from the time of the Constitutions of Clarendon to the exhibition of certain articles of complaint to the king by Archbishop Bancroft in 3 Jac. I., from which, and from the answers to them, much may be collected concerning the reasons of granting and methods of proceeding in prohibition.

The mode of obtaining and following out this writ has been much simplified by modern legislation. The party, who seeks the prohibition, makes an application to the court, founded on affidavit, for a rule calling upon the party to be prohibited, and the other party interested in the question between them, to show cause why a writ of prohibition should not issue. This rule will be made *absolute* at the expiration of the time allowed for showing cause, unless cause be shown; in which case the rule is discharged, the writ issues, or the party applying for it is directed to declare in prohibition. In the latter event the party seeking the intervention of the court must set out the proceedings in the court below to which he objects, and after trial of facts disputed, or argument as to the law involved, as in the case of an ordinary action, judgment is given that the writ of prohibition do or do not issue. When issued there is no course open to the parties but obedience, which will, if necessary, be enforced by attachment.

Thus careful has the law been, in compelling the inferior courts to do ample and speedy justice; in preventing them from transgressing their due bounds; and in allowing them the undisturbed cognizance of such causes as by right properly belong to their jurisdiction.

CHAPTER V.

OF WRONGS, AND THEIR REMEDIES, RESPECTING THE RIGHTS OF PERSONS.

Injuries affecting personal security: viz., injuries to life; injuries affecting limbs or body; threats, assault, battery, &c.—Injuries affecting health: nuisances.—Injuries affecting reputation: viz., libel, slander, and malicious prosecution.—Injuries affecting *personal liberty*: false imprisonment; *Habeas corpus*, its history; action for damages.—Injuries affecting relative rights of persons;—of husband; adultery;—of parent; abduction; action for seduction;—of guardian;—of master and servant.

I COME now to consider more particularly the respective remedies obtainable in the courts of law and equity, for private wrongs of any denomination whatsoever, not exclusively appropriated to any of the former tribunals. I shall, first, define the several injuries cognizable by the courts of common law, with the remedies applicable to each particular injury, pointing out in what cases relief may be more appropriately sought in the Court of Chancery: and secondly, describe the method of pursuing and obtaining these remedies in these several courts. And in dealing with the first branch of my inquiry, I shall confine myself to such wrongs as may be committed in the mutual intercourse between subject and subject: reserving such injuries as may occur between the crown and the subject to be separately considered hereafter, as the remedy in such cases is generally of a peculiar nature.

Now, since all wrong may be considered as merely a privation of right, the plain natural remedy for every species of wrong is the

being put in possession of that right, whereof the party injured is
deprived. This may either be effected by a specific delivery or
restoration of the subject-matter in dispute to the legal owner; as
when lands or personal chattels are unjustly withheld or invaded:
or, where that is not a possible, or at least not an adequate remedy,
by making the sufferer a pecuniary satisfaction in damages: as in
case of assault, breach of contract, &c.: to which damages the party
injured has acquired an incomplete or inchoate right, the instant he
receives the injury, though such right be not fully ascertained till
these damages are assessed by the intervention of the law. The
instruments whereby this remedy is obtained, are a diversity of
suits and actions, which have always been distinguished into three
kinds; actions *personal*, *real*, and *mixed*.

Personal actions are such whereby a man claims a debt, or personal
duty, or damages in lieu thereof: and likewise, whereby a man
claims damages for some injury done to his person or property. Of
the former nature are all actions for debts; of the latter all actions
for trespasses, assaults, and the like. *Real* actions, which concern
real property only, are such whereby the plaintiff claims title to
lands. These had all, upwards of a century ago, become generally
disused, upon account of the great nicety required in their management, and the inconvenient length of their process: and with three
exceptions, *dower*, *right of dower*, and *quare impedit*, have since been
abolished. *Mixed* actions were suits partaking of the nature of the
other two, wherein some real property was demanded, and also personal damages for a wrong sustained. One form of the modern
action of ejectment, that in which a landlord recovers possession
from a tenant whose rent is in arrear, and at the same time damages
equal in amount to the arrears, may be said to partake of the nature
of a mixed action.

Under these three heads may every species of remedy by action
be comprised. But in order to apply the remedy, it is necessary to
ascertain the complaint. I proceed therefore now to enumerate the
several kinds of private wrongs which may be offered to the rights
of either a man's person or his property; recounting at the same
time the respective remedies, which are furnished for every infraction of right; and in doing so, I shall follow the same method that
was pursued with regard to the distribution of rights: for as these
are nothing else but an infringement or breach of those rights,
which we have before laid down and explained, it will follow that
this negative system, of *wrongs*, must correspond and tally with the
former positive system, of *rights*. As, therefore, all rights were
divided into those of *persons*, and those of *things*, so the same general

distribution of injuries must be made into such as affect the *rights of persons*, and such as affect the *rights of property*.

The rights of *persons* were distributed into *absolute* and *relative*: *absolute*, which were such as appertained and belonged to private men, considered merely as individuals, or single persons; and *relative*, which were incident to them as members of society, and connected to each other by various ties and relations.

And the absolute rights of each individual were defined to be the right of personal security, the right of personal liberty, and the right of private property, so that the wrongs or injuries affecting them must consequently be of a corresponding nature.

I. As to injuries which affect the *personal security* of individuals, they are either injuries against their lives, their limbs, their bodies, their health, or their reputations.

1. Injuries affecting the life of man, constitute one of the most atrocious species of crimes, and are considered in the next book of these commentaries; but, until recently, could not be made the subject of complaint in a civil suit. The wife or husband of a person who had been killed, could not recover any pecuniary compensation for his or her loss, until the law was altered by the statute 9 & 10 Vict. c. 93. But an action now lies for the benefit of the wife, husband, parent, or child of the deceased. And the jury may direct, in what proportion the damages shall be divided among those for whose benefit the suit is brought.

2, 3. Injuries affecting the limbs or bodies of individuals, I shall consider in one view. And these may be committed—1. By *threats* and menaces of bodily hurt, through fear of which a man's business is interrupted. Here the party menaced may either apply to a magistrate, to have the offender bound over in recognizances to keep the peace; or he may sue for damages in a civil action. 2. By *assault*; which is an attempt or offer to beat another, without touching him: as if one lifts up his cane, or his fist, in a threatening manner at another; or strikes at him, but misses him: this is an assault, and, though no actual suffering is proved, yet the party injured may have redress by action for damages as a compensation for the injury. 3. By *battery*: which is the unlawful beating of another. The least touching of another's person wilfully, or in anger, is a battery; for the law cannot draw the line between different degrees of violence, and therefore totally prohibits the first and lowest stage of it; every man's person being sacred, and no other having a right to meddle with it, in any the slightest manner. But battery is, in some cases, justifiable; as where one who has authority, a parent or master, gives moderate correction to his child, his scholar, or his apprentice. So also on the principle of self-defence, for if one strikes me first, or even only assaults me, I may strike in my own defence; and, if sued for it, may plead *son assault demesne*, or that it was the plaintiff's own original assault that occasioned it. So likewise in defence of my goods or possession: if a man endeavours to deprive me of them, I may justify laying hands upon him to prevent him; and in case he persists with violence, I may proceed to beat him away. Thus, too, in the exercise of an office, as that of churchwarden or beadle, a man may lay hands upon another to turn him out of church, and prevent his disturbing the congregation. And, if sued for this or the like battery, he may set forth the whole case, and plead that he laid hands upon him gently, *molliter manus imposuit*, for this purpose. On account of these causes of justification, battery is defined to be the *unlawful* beating of another; for which the remedy is as for assault, by action for damages. 4. By *wounding*; which consists in giving another some dangerous hurt, and is only an aggravated species of battery. 5. By *mayhem*; which is an injury still more atrocious, and consists in violently depriving another of the use of a member proper for his defence in fight. The same remedial action lies to recover damages for this injury, an injury which, when wilful, no motive can justify but necessary self-preservation.

The injuries affecting the person, which I have mentioned, are all in their nature direct. There are others which may, in contradistinction, be termed *consequential*, as resulting from wrongful acts or neglects. Thus, if a passenger is injured by the want of care of the driver of a coach, or a person sustains an injury owing to the negligence of a carman, the owner of the coach in the first case, the carman's master in the second, will be liable in an action for damages; for it was the duty of the owner and master in each case to employ careful servants. If, on the other hand, the driver or the carman did the injury *wilfully*, even if in the master's service, he, and not the owner or master, will be liable. Consequential injuries may also be sustained from a bull, ram, monkey, or other animal being left at large, or not properly taken care of; and the owner will in such case be liable to the party injured, provided he can be shown to have been aware of the mischievous propensities of the animal. But if the party injured have imprudently exposed himself, or by his own negligence have conduced to the accident, he cannot maintain an action.

4. Injuries affecting a man's *health* are, where by any unwholesome practices of another a man sustains any apparent damage in his vigour or constitution. As by selling him bad provisions or wine; by the exercise of a noisome trade, which infects the air in his

neighbourhood; or by the neglect or unskilful management of his physician, surgeon, or apothecary. The remedy is by action for damages; and in some cases, as in that of nuisances, the party injured may proceed by complaint to the local authorities, or by indictment.

5. Lastly; injuries affecting a man's *reputation* or good name are, first, by malicious, scandalous, and slanderous *words*, tending to his damage and derogation. As if a man maliciously and falsely utter any slander or false tale of another, which may either endanger him in law, by impeaching him of some heinous crime, as to say that a man has poisoned another, or is perjured;* or which may exclude him from society, as to charge him with having an infectious disease; or which may impair or hurt his trade or livelihood, as to call a tradesman a bankrupt, a physician a quack, or a lawyer a knave.† Words also tending to scandalize a magistrate, or person in a public trust, are reputed more highly injurious than when spoken of a private man.

With regard to *words*, however, that do not thus upon the face of them, import such defamation as will be injurious, it is necessary that the plaintiff should aver some particular damage to have happened; which is called laying his action with a *per quod*. As if I say of an agent that he is an unprincipled man, he cannot for this bring any action against me, unless he can show some special loss by it, as that it was said to a person about to employ him, but who in consequence did not do so; in which case he may bring his action against me for saying he was an unprincipled man, *per quod* he lost the profits of the intended employment. Mere scurrility, or opprobrious words, which neither in themselves import, nor are in fact attended with, any injurious effects, will not support an action. So scandals, which concern matters merely spiritual, as to call a man a heretic, will not afford ground for an action; unless any temporal damage ensues, which may be a foundation for a *per quod*. Words of heat and passion, as to call a man rogue and a rascal, if productive of no ill consequence, and not of any of the dangerous species before mentioned, are not actionable: neither are words spoken in a friendly manner, as by way of advice, admonition, or concern, with-

* It is actionable to say of a man, "he is a thief;" it is not actionable to say, "he is a thief, because he has stolen a cat," the stealing of a cat not being a felony.

† Words spoken in derogation of a peer, a judge, or other great officer of the realm, are called *scandalum magnatum*, and were formerly held to be more heinous. It was held to be *scandalum magnatum* to say of a peer, "he was no more to be valued than a dog;" words which would have been perfectly harmless if uttered of any other person.

out any tincture or circumstance of ill-will; for, in both these cases, they are not *maliciously* spoken, which is part of the definition of slander. Within which last category fall communications as to the character of servants, advice as to dealing with tradesmen, and other statements of a like nature, which constitute what are called privileged communications. These the law supposes to have been not *maliciously* spoken, a presumption which may, however, be rebutted by proof of express malice on the part of the defendant. If the defendant be able to justify, and prove the words to be true, no action will lie, even though special damage has ensued: for then it is no slander or false tale. As if I can prove the tradesman a bankrupt, the physician a quack, the lawyer a knave, this will destroy their respective actions: for though there may be damage sufficient accruing from it, yet, if the fact be true, it is *damnum absque injuriâ;* and where there is no injury, the law gives no remedy.

A second way of affecting a man's reputation is by printed or written libels, pictures, signs, and the like; which set him in an odious or ridiculous light, and thereby diminish his reputation, as by publishing of an attorney *ironically*, that he was "an honest lawyer." With regard to libels in general, there are, as in many other cases, two remedies; one by indictment, and another by action. The former is for the *public* offence; for every libel has a tendency to a breach of the peace, by provoking the person libelled to break it. This offence was formerly the same, in point of law, whether the matter contained in the libel were true or false; and the defendant, on an indictment for publishing a libel, was therefore not allowed to allege the truth of it by way of justification. But the law in this respect was altered by the statute 6 & 7 Vict. c. 96, which enables the defendant to allege the truth of the matters charged, and that it was for the public benefit that they should be published. The truth of the libel may now therefore be inquired into at the trial, but does not amount to a defence, unless the publication was for the public benefit. And if, after such a plea being maintained, the defendant is convicted, the court may, in pronouncing sentence, consider whether the guilt of the defendant is aggravated or mitigated thereby.

In the remedy by civil action, which is to repair the *party* in damages for the injury done him, the defendant might always, on the other hand, as for words *spoken*, justify the truth of the facts, and show that the plaintiff had received no injury at all. And by the statute I have just referred to, he is now enabled to give in evidence, in mitigation of damages, that he made or offered an apology before action, or as soon afterwards as he had an opportunity, in case the action was commenced before. To encourage a wholesome independence in the public press, the same statute accords to a news-paper, or other periodical publication, the further privilege. of pleading that the libel was inserted without malice, and without negligence, and that before action, or at the earliest opportunity afterwards, a full apology was inserted; or if the paper be ordinarily published at intervals exceeding one week, that an offer had been made to publish the apology in any newspaper selected by the plaintiff. With such a plea money may be paid into court by way of amends; and if the jury consider the sum sufficient, they must find their verdict for the defendant.

What was said with regard to words spoken, will also hold in every particular with regard to libels by writing or printing, and the civil actions consequent thereupon. But many words which, spoken merely, are not actionable, become so if written. Thus to say of a man that he is a swindler, unless in relation to his trade or business, is not actionable, whilst to print or write of him, that he is so, is actionable. For speaking the words "rogue" and "rascal" an action will not lie; but if these words are *written and published*, an action will lie. As to signs or pictures, it seems necessary always to show the import and application of the scandal; otherwise it cannot appear, that such libel by picture was understood to be levelled at the plaintiff.

A third way of destroying or injuring a man's reputation is by preferring a malicious indictment against him; which, under the mask of justice and public spirit, may be made the engine of private enmity. For this, however, the law has given a remedy in damages, either by an action of *conspiracy*, which cannot be brought but against two at the least; or, which is the more usual way, by a special action for a malicious prosecution.

II. We are next to consider the violation of the right of personal liberty. This is effected by the injury of false imprisonment, for which the law has not only decreed a punishment as a heinous public crime, but has also given a private reparation to the party; as well by removing the actual confinement for the present, as, after it is over, by subjecting the wongdoer to a civil action, on account of the damage sustained by the loss of time and liberty.

To constitute the injury of false imprisonment there are two points requisite; 1. The detention of the person: and, 2. The unlawfulness of such detention. Every confinement of the person is an imprisonment, whether it be in a common prison, or in a private house, or even by forcibly detaining one in the public streets. Unlawful or false imprisonment consists in such confinement or detention without sufficient authority. The remedy is of two sorts; the one *removing* the injury; the other, *making satisfaction* for it. And the means of *removing* the actual injury is by writ of *habeas corpus.* *

Of this writ, the most celebrated in the English law, there are various kinds made use of by the courts at Westminster, for removing prisoners from one court into another for the more easy administration of justice. Such is the *habeas corpus ad respondendum*, when a man has a cause of action against one who is confined by the process of some inferior court; in order to remove the prisoner, and charge him with this new action in the court above. Such is that *ad satisfaciendum*, when a prisoner has had judgment against him in an action, and the plaintiff is desirous to bring him up to some superior court to charge him with process of execution. Such also are those *ad prosequendum, testificandum, deliberandum,* &c.; which issue when it is necessary to remove a prisoner, in order to prosecute or bear testimony in any court, or to be tried in the proper jurisdiction wherein the fact was committed.

But the great and efficacious writ, in all manner of illegal confinement, is that of *habeas corpus ad subjiciendum;* directed to the person detaining another, and commanding him to produce the body of the prisoner, with the day and cause of his caption and detention, *ad faciendum, subjiciendum, et recipiendum*, to do, submit to, and receive whatsoever the judge or court awarding such writ shall consider in that behalf. This is a high prerogative writ, and therefore by the common law issuing out of the court of Queen's Bench not only in term time, but also during the vacation: for the sovereign is at all times entitled to have an account, why the liberty of any of her subjects is restrained, wherever that restraint may be inflicted. If it issues in vacation, it is usually returnable before the judge himself who awarded it, and he proceeds by himself thereon; unless the term shall intervene, and then it may be returned in court. Since the mention of the King's Bench and Common Pleas, as co-ordinate in this jurisdiction, by statute 16 Car. I. c. 10, it has been held that every subject of the kingdom is equally entitled to the benefit of the common law writ, in either of those courts, at his option, as he is now by statute 56 Geo. III. c. 100 s. 2, entitled to it in the Exchequer. It has also been settled, that the like *habeas corpus* may issue out of the Court of Chancery in vacation; although upon the famous application to Lord Nottingham by Jenks, notwithstanding the most diligent search, no precedent could be found where the chancellor had issued such a writ in vacation, and therefore his lordship refused it.

* Three other writs for this purpose, the writ of *mainprize,* the writ *de odio et atid,* and the writ *de homine replegiando,* are entirely obsolete.

It is necessary to apply for this writ by motion to the court, and to show some probable cause for its issuing; for when once granted, the person to whom it is directed can return no satisfactory excuse for not bringing up the body of the prisoner. If it issued of mere course, without showing to the court or judge some reasonable ground for awarding it, a traitor or felon under sentence of death, a soldier or mariner in the queen's service, a wife, a child, a relation, or a domestic, confined for insanity, or other prudential reasons, might obtain a temporary enlargement by suing out a *habeas corpus*, though sure to be remanded as soon as brought up to the court. But if on the other hand, a probable ground be shown, that the party is imprisoned without just cause, and therefore has a right to be delivered, the writ of *habeas corpus* is then a writ of right, which " may not be denied, but ought to be granted to every " man that is committed, or detained in prison, or otherwise " restrained, though it be by the command of the king, the privy " council, or any other."

· In the outset of these commentaries the personal liberty of the subject was shown to be a natural inherent right, which could not be forfeited unless by the commission of crime, and which ought not to be abridged without the special permission of the law; a doctrine coeval with the first rudiments of the Constitution, and established on the firmest basis by *Magna Charta*, and a long succession of statutes enacted under Edward III. Yet early in the reign of Charles I. the King's Bench, relying on some arbitrary precedents, determined that they could not upon a *habeas corpus* either bail or deliver a prisoner, though imprisoned without any cause assigned, in case he was committed by the special command of the king, or by the lords of the privy council. This drew on a parliamentary inquiry, and produced the *petition of right*, 3 Car. I., which enacts that no freeman hereafter shall be so imprisoned or detained. But when, in the following year, Selden and others were committed by the lords of the council, in pursuance of his majesty's special command, under a general charge of " notable contempts and stirring up " sedition against the king and government," the judges delayed for two terms to deliver an opinion how far such a charge was bailable. And when at length they agreed that it was, they annexed a condition of finding sureties for good behaviour, which still protracted their imprisonment; the chief justice, Sir Nicholas Hyde, at the same time declaring, " that if they were again remanded for " that cause, perhaps the court would not afterwards grant a *habeas* " *corpus*, being already made acquainted with the cause of the impri- " sonment." But this was heard with indignation and astonishment by every lawyer present; according to Selden's own account of the matter, whose resentment was not cooled at the distance of four-and-twenty years.

These pitiful evasions gave rise to the statute 16 Car. I. c. 10, s. 8, whereby it is enacted, that if any person be committed by the king, or by his privy council, he shall have granted unto him, without any delay upon any pretence whatsoever, a writ of *habeas corpus*, upon demand or motion made to the Court of King's Bench or *Common Pleas*; who shall thereupon, within three court days after the return is made, examine and determine the legality of such commitment, and do what to justice shall appertain, in delivering, bailing, or remanding such prisoner. Yet still in the case of Jenks, who in 1676 was committed by the king in council for a turbulent speech at Guildhall, new shifts were made use of to prevent his enlargement by law; and in many other cases vexatious devices were practised to detain state-prisoners in custody. But whoever will attentively consider English history, may observe, that the flagrant abuse of any power, by the crown or its ministers, has always been productive of a struggle; which either discovers the exercise of that power to be contrary to law, or, if legal, restrains it for the future. This was the case in the present instance. The oppression of an obscure individual gave birth to the famous *Habeas Corpus* Act, 31 Car. II. c. 2; which requires the chancellor or any of the judges, when applied to by, or on behalf of, any person committed for any *crime*, unless for treason or felony expressed in the warrant, or unless he is convicted or charged in execution by legal process, to award a *habeas corpus* for such prisoner returnable immediately; and upon the return to discharge the party, if bailable, upon his giving security to appear and answer to the accusation in the proper court of judicature. The statute requires the writ to be returned and the prisoner brought up, within a limited time, according to the distance, not exceeding in any case twenty days;—2, imposes a penalty on officers and keepers neglecting to make a due return;—3, enacts that no person once delivered by *habeas corpus* shall be recommitted for the same offence, on penalty of 500*l*; and provides for every person committed for treason or felony being, if he requires it, in the first week of the next term, or on the first day of the next session of *oyer* and *terminer*, indicted in that term or session, or else admitted to bail: unless the king's witnesses cannot be produced at that time; and if acquitted, or if not indicted and tried in the second term or session, that he shall be discharged from his imprisonment for such imputed offence. Finally, the lord chancellor or any judge denying the writ forfeits to the party aggrieved the sum of 500*l*.

This is the substance of that great statute, which extends only to the case of commitments for such criminal charge as can produce no inconvenience to public justice by a temporary enlargement of the

F

prisoner; all other cases of unjust imprisonment being left to the
habeas corpus at common law.   But even upon writs at the common
law it is expected by the court, agreeably to ancient precedents and
the spirit of the act of parliament, that the writ shall be immediately
obeyed, and the procedure on it has accordingly been much simplified and improved by the statute 56 Geo. III. c. 100.   So that by these
admirable regulations, judicial as well as parliamentary, the remedy
is now complete for *removing* the injury of unjust and illegal confinement; a remedy the more necessary, because the oppression
does not always arise from the ill-nature, but sometimes from the
mere inattention of government: for it frequently happens in foreign
countries, and has happened in England during temporary sus-
pensions of the statute, that persons apprehended upon suspicion
have suffered a long imprisonment, merely because they were forgotten.

The operation of the writ of *habeas corpus* is by no means confined
to the liberation of the person on whose behalf it is issued from illegal
confinement in a prison: it also extends its influence to remove every
unjust restraint of personal freedom in private life, though imposed
by a husband or a father.   When, however, a woman or children are
brought up by a *habeas corpus*, the court will only set them free from
an improper or unreasonable confinement;—it cannot and will not,
for instance, determine the validity of a marriage, or the right to the
guardianship of infants, but will leave the person whose liberty is
infringed to choose where he will go: and if there be any ground to
fear that he will be seized in returning from the court, he will be
sent home under the protection of an officer.   If a child is too young
to have any discretion of its own, the court will deliver it into the
custody of its parent, or the person who appears to be its legal
guardian.

The remedy, by way of *satisfaction*, for this injury of false imprisonment, is by an action of trespass, usually called an action of
false imprisonment: which is generally, and almost unavoidably,
accompanied with a charge of assault and battery also: and therein
the party shall recover damages for the injury he has received.

III. With regard to the third absolute right of individuals, or
that of private property, I have to observe that the enjoyment of it,
when acquired, is strictly a *personal* right.   Its nature and origin,
and the means of its acquisition or loss, were considered in the second
book of these commentaries, which related to the *rights of things*.   As
the wrongs, then, that affect those rights must be referred to the
corresponding division in the present volume, I conceive it will be
more commodious and easy to consider together, rather than in a sepa-

rate view, the injuries that may be offered to the *enjoyments*, as well as to the *rights*, of property. And therefore I shall here conclude the head of injuries affecting the *absolute* rights of individuals.

We are next to contemplate those which affect their *relative* rights: as husband and wife, parent and child, guardian and ward, master and servant.

I. Injuries that may be offered to a person, considered as a *husband*, are principally three : *abduction*, or taking away a man's wife ; *adultery*, or criminal conversation with her ; and *beating* or otherwise abusing her. 1. As to the first sort, *abduction*, or taking her away, this may either be by fraud and persuasion, or open violence : though the law in both cases supposes force and restraint, the wife having no power to consent. The law gives a remedy by action, in which the husband shall recover, not the possession of the wife, but damages for taking her away. 2. *Adultery*, or criminal conversation with a man's wife, though it is, as a public crime, left by our laws to the coercion of the spiritual courts, yet, considered as a civil injury, the law gives a species of satisfaction to the husband for it, by suit against the adulterer, wherein the damages recovered are usually very large and exemplary. But these are properly increased and diminished by circumstances ; as the rank and fortune of the plaintiff and defendant ; the relation or connection between them ; the seduction or otherwise of the wife, founded on her previous behaviour and character : and the profligacy of the husband. 3. The third injury is that of *beating* a man's wife, or otherwise ill-using her ; for which the law gives the usual remedy to recover damages.

II. The injuries that may be offered to a person considered in the relation of a *parent* is that of *abduction*, or taking away of his child. It was long a matter of doubt whether it was a civil injury or not ; but the doubt has now been set at rest, no action being maintainable by the parent, except for the value of the lost services of the child, who is regarded as a servant. It is only in the character of *master* that the suit is maintainable ; but in such an action damages may be given, not only as compensation for the lost services, but also for the wounded feelings of the parent.

III. Of a similar nature to the last is the relation of *guardian* and *ward* ; and the like action which is given to a father, the guardian also has for recovery of damages, when his ward is taken away from him. But the usual method of redressing all complaints relating to wards and guardians is by an application to the Court of Chancery, which is the supreme guardian, and has the superintendent jurisdiction of all the infants in the kingdom.

IV. To the relation between *master* and *servant,* and the rights accruing therefrom, there are two species of injuries incident. The one is, retaining a man's hired servant before his time has expired; the other is beating or confining him in such a manner that he is not able to perform his work. And for either injury the law gives him a remedy by action for the damages he has sustained, or for the value of the servant's labour. The master may also have an action against the servant for the non-performance of his agreement. In these relative injuries, notice is only taken of the wrong done to the superior of the parties related, while the loss of the inferior is totally unregarded. One reason for which may be this: that the inferior has no kind of property in the company, care, or assistance of the superior, as the superior is held to have in those of the inferior, and therefore the inferior can suffer no loss or injury. The wife cannot recover damages for beating her husband, for she has no separate interest in anything during her coverture. And so the servant, whose master is disabled, does not thereby lose his maintenance or wages. He had no property in his master; and if he receives his part of the stipulated contract he suffers no injury, and is therefore entitled to no action.

CHAPTER VI.

OF INJURIES TO PERSONAL PROPERTY.

Injuries to property *in possession;* unlawful taking—action of *replevin,* unlawful detainer—action of detinue—*trover.* Injuries to property *en action*—debt—covenant—promises—Statute of Frauds—Lord Tenterden's Act—Ordinary assumpsits—Work done—Goods sold—Money received—Money paid—Accounts stated—For non-performance of implied undertakings—Warranties.

WE are now to consider the injuries that may be offered to the rights of *personal* property; and, of these, first the rights of personal property in *possession,* and then those that are in *action* only.

I. The rights of personal property in *possession* are liable to two species of injuries: 1. The amotion or deprivation of that possession: and 2. The abuse or damage of the chattels, while the possession continues in the legal owner.

1. The former, or deprivation of possession, is also devisable into two branches: 1. the unjust and unlawful *taking* them away; and

2, the unjust *detaining* them, though the original taking might be lawful.

1. And first of an unlawful *taking*. The right of property in all external things being solely acquired by occupancy, and preserved and transferred by grants, deeds, and wills, which are a continuation of that occupancy ; it follows as a necessary consequence, that when I once have gained a rightful possession of any goods or chattels, either by a just occupancy or by a legal transfer, whoever either by fraud or force dispossesses me of them, is guilty of a transgression against the law of society, which is a kind of secondary law of nature. For there must be an end of all social commerce between man and man, unless private possessions be secured from unjust invasions : and, if an acquisition of goods by either force or fraud were allowed to be a sufficient title, all property would soon be confined to the most strong, or the most cunning : and the weak and simple-minded part of mankind, which is by far the most numerous division, could never be secure of their possessions.

The wrongful taking of goods being thus most clearly an injury, the next consideration is, what remedy the law of England has given for it. And this is, in the first place, the restitution of the goods themselves so wrongfully taken, with damages for the loss sustained by such unjust invasion : which is effected by action of *replevin*, an institution ascribed to Granvil, chief justice to King Henry II. It is chiefly resorted to in one instance of an unlawful taking, that of a wrongful distress,* but the action lies upon *any* unlawful taking whatever. This and the action of *detinue* are the only actions, in which the actual specific possession of the identical personal chattel is restored to the proper owner.

An action of replevin is founded upon a distress taken wrongfully, and without sufficient cause : being a re-delivery of the pledge, or thing taken in distress, to the owner ; upon his giving security to try the right of the distress, and to restore it, if the right be adjudged against him. These replevins, or re-deliveries of goods detained from the owner to him, were originally, and till recently, effected by the sheriff ; but are now granted by the registrar of the county court of the district, in which the distress is taken, upon security being given to him by the replevisor, 1, that he will pursue his action against

---

* In the case of a distress, the goods are from the first taking in the custody of the law, and the taking them back by force is denominated a *rescous*, for which the distrainor has a remedy in damages, either by an action for the rescue, in case they were going to the pound, or by an action for the *pound-breach*, in case they were actually impounded.

the distrainor, and, 2, that if the right be determined against him
he will return the distress again. And as the end of all distresses is
only to compel the party distrained upon to satisfy the debt or duty
owing from him, this end is as well answered by such security as by
retaining the very distress, which might frequently occasion great
inconvenience to the owner, and that the law never wantonly inflicts.
The registrar, therefore, on receiving security, is immediately to
cause the chattels taken in distress to be restored into the possession
of the party distrained upon, making use of even force, if necessary ;
the party replevying being then bound to bring in his action of replevin either in one of the superior courts or in the county court of
the district wherein the distress was taken. In the latter case the
defendant, on giving security to defend the action with effect, and to
prove that he had good ground for believing *either* that the title to
some hereditament, toll, fair, or franchise was in question, *or* that
the rent or damage in respect of which the distress was taken exceeded twenty pounds, may have the suit removed into any one of
the superior courts, by *certiorari*. Upon the action being thus removed, and in actions of *replevin*, brought at once in the superior
courts, a declaration is delivered, in which the plaintiff complains of
the trespass committed upon him by the seizure of his goods; and
the distrainor, who is now the defendant, makes *avowry* ; that is, he
avows taking the distress in his own right, or the right of his wife;
and sets forth the reason of it, as for rent arrear, damage done, or
other cause ; or else, if he justifies in another's right as his bailiff or
servant, he is said to make *cognizance ;* that is, he *acknowledges* the
taking, but insists that such taking was legal, as he acted by the
command of one who had a right to distrain. On the truth and legal
merits of either avowry or cognizance, the cause is determined. If it
be determined for the plaintiff, viz., that the distress was wrongfully
taken, he has already got his goods back into his own possession,
and shall keep them, and moreover recover damages : if the defendant prevails, by the default or nonsuit of the plaintiff, then he shall
have a writ *de retorno habendo,* whereby the goods or chattels, which
were distrained and then replevied, are returned again into his
custody, to be sold or otherwise disposed of, as if no replevin had
been made.

II. Deprivation of possession may also be by an unjust *detainer* of
another's goods, though the original *taking* was lawful. As if I lend
a man a horse, and he afterwards refuses to restore it, this injury
consists in the detaining, and not in the original taking, and the regular method for me to recover possession is by action of *detinue.*
In this action of *detinue*, it is necessary to ascertain the thing detained, in such manner as that it may be specifically known and re-

covered. Therefore it cannot be brought for money, corn, or the like: for that cannot be known from other money or corn; unless it be in a bag or sack, for then it may be distinguishably marked. In order therefore to ground an action of detinue, which is only for the *detaining*, these points are necessary: 1. That the defendant came lawfully into possession of the goods, as either by delivery to him, or finding them; 2. That the plaintiff have a property; 3. That the goods themselves be of some value; and, 4. That they be ascertained in point of identity. Upon this the jury, if they find for the plaintiff, assess the respective values of the several parcels detained, and also damages for the detention. But if the jury find that a re-delivery of the chattels is impossible, they may assess the damages only. So if the chattels have been re-delivered to the owner, after action brought, they need only assess the damages for the detention. And the judgment is likewise conditional; that the plaintiff recover the said goods, or if they cannot be had, their respective values, and also the damages for detaining them.*

There was one disadvantage which formerly attended this action, viz., that the defendant was therein permitted to *wage his law*, that is, to exculpate himself by oath, and thereby defeat the plaintiff of his remedy: which privilege was grounded on the confidence originally reposed in the bailee by the bailor, in the borrower by the lender, and the like; from whence arose a strong presumptive evidence, that in the plaintiff's own opinion the defendant was worthy of credit. For this reason the action itself was much disused, and had given place entirely to the action of trover, long before wager of of law was abolished. Since then, however, detinue has been again more frequently resorted to.

The action of trover and conversion was in its origin an action for recovery of damages against such person as had *found* another's goods, and refused to deliver them on demand, but *converted* them to his own use; from which finding and converting, it is called an action of *trover* and *conversion*. The freedom of this action from wager of law, and the less degree of certainty requisite in describing

* Formerly the defendant in an action of detinue always had it in his power to retain the chattels upon payment of the value, as assessed by the jury. The remedy at law was in this respect incomplete; and it became usual to apply to the Court of Chancery, which from a very early period interfered to compel the return of the chattels themselves; for the simple reason that the damages recovered in the action, although equal to the intrinsic value of the article detained, might be infinitely less than that at which it was estimated by the owner, and therefore by no means an adequate compensation to him for the loss. The courts of common law have now, however, the same powers as the Court of Chancery to compel the return of the chattel itself.

the goods, gave it formerly so considerable an advantage over the action of *detinue*, that actions of *trover* were at length permitted to be brought against any man, who had in his possession, by any means whatsoever, the personal goods of another, and sold them or used them without the consent of the owner, or refused to deliver them when demanded. The injury lies in the conversion: for any man may take the goods of another into his possession if he finds them; but no finder is allowed to acquire a property therein, unless the owner be for ever unknown: and therefore he must not convert them to his own use, which the law presumes him to do, if he refuses to restore them to the owner: for which reason such refusal alone is *primâ facie* sufficient evidence of a conversion. The fact of the finding, or *trover*, is therefore now totally immaterial: for if the plaintiff proves that the goods are *his* property, and that the defendant had them in his possession, it is sufficient. But a conversion must be fully proved: and then in this action the plaintiff shall recover damages, equal to the value of the thing converted, but not the thing itself, which nothing will recover but an action of *detinue* or *replevin*.

2. As to the damage that may be offered to things personal, while in the possession of the owner, as hunting a man's deer, shooting his dogs, poisoning his cattle, or in anywise taking from the value of any of his chattels, or making them in a worse condition than before, these are injuries too obvious to need explanation. The owner's remedy is by an action for damages, which ought to bear proportion to the injury which he proves that his property has sustained. We have seen that it is not material whether the damage be done by the defendant himself, or his servants by his direction; for the action will lie against the master as well as the servant. We have also seen that if a man keeps a dog or other brute animal, used to do mischief, as by worrying sheep, or the like, the owner must answer for the consequences, if he knows of such evil habit.

II. We are next to consider injuries affecting the right of things in *action* only; or such rights as are founded on and arise from *contracts*; the nature and several divisions of which were explained in the preceding volume. The violation, or non-performance, of these contracts might be extended into as great a variety of wrongs, as the rights which we then considered: but I shall now consider them in a more comprehensive view, by here making only a twofold division of contracts, viz., contracts *express*, and contracts *implied*; and pointing out the injuries that arise from the violation of each, with their respective remedies.

Express contracts include three distinct species : debts, covenants, and promises.

1. The legal acceptation of *debt* is, a sum of money due by certain and express agreement: as by a bond for a determinate sum ; a bill or note, or a rent reserved on a lease ; where the quantity is fixed and specific, and does not depend upon any subsequent valuation to settle it. The non-payment of these is an injury, for which the proper remedy is by an action of debt, to compel the performance of the contract and recover the specifical sum due. So also, if I verbally agree to pay a man a certain price for a certain parcel of goods, and fail in the performance, an action of *debt* lies against me ; for this is also a *determinate* contract : but if I agree for no settled price, I am liable not to an action of debt, but to a special action, according to the nature of my contract.

2. A covenant also, contained in a deed, to do a direct act, or to omit one, is another species of express contract, the violation or breach of which is a civil injury. As if a man covenants to be at York by such a day, or not to exercise a trade in a particular place, and is not at York at the time appointed, or carries on his trade in the place forbidden : these are direct breaches of his covenant ; and may be perhaps greatly to the disadvantage and loss of the covenantee. The remedy for this is by an action on the *covenant* : in which must be set forth with precision the covenant, the breach, and the loss which has happened thereby ; whereupon the jury will give damages in proportion to the injury sustained by the plaintiff, and occasioned by such breach of the defendant's contract. The covenant, however, must be one which the law allows ; for covenants which are in themselves unreasonable, or in restraint of trade, cannot be enforced.

No person could at common law take advantage of any covenant or condition, except such as were parties or privies thereto ; and, of course, no grantee or assignee of any reversion or rent. To remedy which, and more effectually to secure to the king's grantees the spoils of the monasteries then newly dissolved, the statute 32 Hen. VIII. c. 34, gives the assignee of a reversion the same remedies against the tenant, as the assignor himself might have had ; and makes him equally liable, on the other hand, for acts agreed to be performed by the assignor, except in the case of warranty.

3. A promise is in the nature of a verbal covenant, and wants nothing but the solemnity of writing and sealing to make it absolutely the same. If therefore it be to do any explicit act, it is an express contract, as much as any covenant ; and the breach of it is an

equal injury. The remedy is by an action on what is called the *assumpsit* or undertaking of the defendant; the failure of performing which is the wrong or injury done to the plaintiff, the damages whereof a jury are to estimate and settle. As if a builder promises, undertakes, or assumes to Caius, that he will build and cover his house within a time limited, and fails to do it; Caius has an action against the builder for this breach of his express promise, undertaking, or *assumpsit*; and shall recover a pecuniary satisfaction for the injury sustained by such a delay. So also in the case before mentioned, of a debt by simple contract, if the debtor promises to pay it and does not, this breach of promise entitles the creditor to his action on the *assumpsit*, or implied promise to pay the debt sued for. Thus likewise a promissory note, or note of hand not under seal, to pay money at a day certain, is an express *assumpsit*; and the payee at common law, or by custom and act of parliament the indorsee, may recover the value of the note in damages, if it remains unpaid.

Some agreements indeed, though never so expressly made, are deemed of so important a nature, that they ought not to rest in verbal promise only, which cannot be proved but by the memory which sometimes will induce the perjury of witnesses. To prevent which, the Statute of Frauds enacts that no verbal promise shall be sufficient to ground an action upon, but at least some note or *memorandum* of it shall be made in writing, and signed by the party to be charged therewith: 1. Where an executor or administrator promises to answer damages out of his own estate. 2. Where a man undertakes to answer for the debt, default, or miscarriage of another. 3. Where any agreement is made, upon consideration of marriage. 4. Where any contract or sale is made of lands, tenements, or hereditaments, or any interest therein. 5. And lastly, where there is any agreement that is not to be performed within a year from the making thereof. And the statute 9 Geo. IV. c. 14, Lord Tenterden's Act, further enacts that no action shall be maintained, 6. Whereby to charge any person upon any promise made after full age, to pay any debt contracted during infancy, or upon any ratification after full age of any promise or simple contract made during infancy, unless such promise or ratification shall be made by some writing signed by the party to be charged therewith. And 7, that no action shall be brought, whereby to charge any person by reason of any representation given relating to the character, conduct, credit, ability, trade, or dealings of any other person, to the intent that such other person may obtain credit, money, or goods, unless such representation be made in writing, signed by the party to be charged therewith.

From these *express* contracts the transition is easy to those that are only *implied* by law. Which are such as reason and justice dictate, and which therefore the law presumes that every man has contracted

to perform; and upon this presumption makes him answerable to
such persons as suffer by his non-performance.

Of this nature are, first, such as are necessarily implied by the
fundamental constitution of government, to which every man is a
contracting party. And thus it is that every person is bound and
has virtually agreed to pay such particular sums of money as are
charged on him by the sentence, or assessed by the interpretation of
the law. And this implied agreement it is that gives the plaintiff a
right to institute a second action, founded merely on the general contract, in order to recover such damages, or sum of money, as are
assessed by the jury and adjudged by the court to be due from the
defendant to the plaintiff in any former action. So that if he has
once obtained a judgment against another for a certain sum, and
neglects to take out execution thereupon, he may afterwards bring
an action of debt upon this judgment, and shall not be put upon the
proof of the original cause of action; but upon showing the judgment once obtained, still in full force, and yet unsatisfied, the law
immediately implies, that by the original contract of society the defendant has contracted a debt, and is bound to pay it. But such
actions are discountenanced by the courts, as being vexatious and
oppressive, and the plaintiff does not recover any costs unless the
court makes an express order that he shall do so.

On the same principle it is, of an implied original contract to submit to the rules of the community whereof we are members, that a
forfeiture imposed by the bye-laws and private ordinances of a corporation upon any that belong to the body, immediately creates a
debt in the eye of the law: for which the remedy is by action of
debt.

The same reason may with equal justice be applied to all penal
statutes, that is, such acts of parliament whereby a forfeiture is inflicted for transgressing the provisions therein enacted. The party
offending is here bound by the fundamental contract of society to
obey the direction of the legislature, and pay the forfeiture incurred
to such persons as the law requires. Thus an action may be maintained against a sheriff for the penalty imposed on him for extortion,
in levying greater fees in the execution of the process of the courts
than the law allows; or against a member of parliament for voting
without having taken the proper oaths. The usual application of
these penalties or forfeitures is either to the party aggrieved, or else
to any of the queen's subjects in general. But more usually the forfeitures created by statute are given at large to any common informer; or, in other words, to any such person or persons as will sue
for the same; and hence such actions are called *popular* actions, be-

cause they are given to the people in general. Sometimes one part is given to the crown, to the poor, or to some public use, and the other part to the informer or prosecutor: and then the suit is called a *qui tam* action, because it is brought by a person, "*qui tam pro domino rege, &c., quam pro se ipso in hâc parte sequitur.*"

A second class of implied contracts are such as do not arise from the express determination of any court, or the positive directions of any statute; but from natural reason, and the just construction of law. Which class extends to all presumptive undertakings or *assumpsits*; which though never perhaps actually made, yet constantly arise from this general implication and intendment of the courts of judicature, that every man has engaged to perform what his duty or justice requires. Thus,

1. If I employ a person to transact any business for me, or perform any work, the law implies that I undertook or promised to pay him so much as his labour deserved. And if I neglect to make him amends, he has a remedy for this injury by bringing his action upon this implied *assumpsit*; wherein he is at liberty to suggest that I promised to pay him so much as he reasonably deserved, and then to aver that his trouble was really worth such a particular sum, which the defendant has omitted to pay. But this valuation of his trouble is submitted to the determination of a jury, who will assess such a sum in damages as they think he really merited. This is called an *assumpsit* on a *quantum meruit*.

2. There is also an implied *assumpsit* on a *quantum valebat*, which is very similar to the former, being only where one takes up goods or wares of a tradesman, without expressly agreeing for the price. There the law concludes, that both parties did intentionally agree, that the real value of the goods should be paid; and an action may be brought accordingly, if the vendee refuses to pay that value. This action is usually either for "*goods bargained and sold,*" or for "*goods sold and delivered.*" The former action lies where the property in the goods has passed to the defendant, though there has been no actual delivery to him, nor any actual acceptance by him: the latter where the goods have been actually or constructively delivered, as where the latter has put it in the purchaser's power to take them, or in the case of goods parted with "on sale or return," where the purchaser has not returned them within a reasonable time.

The converse of the action for the goods bargained and sold is that by the vendee against the vendor, for his breach of contract in not delivering the goods.

3. A third species of implied *assumpsits* is when one has had and

received money belonging to another, without any valuable consideration given on the receiver's part: for the law construes this to be *money had and received* for the use of the owner only; and implies that the person so receiving promised and undertook to account for it to the true proprietor. This is a very extensive and beneficial remedy, applicable to almost every case where the defendant has received money which *ex æquo et bono* he ought to refund. It lies for money paid by mistake or on a consideration which happens to fail, or through imposition, extortion or oppression, or where any undue advantage is taken of the plaintiff's situation.

4. Where a person has laid out and expended his own money for the use of another, at his request, the law implies a promise of repayment, and an action will lie on this *assumpsit.*

5. Likewise, fifthly, upon a stated account between two merchants or other persons, the law implies that he against whom the balance appears has engaged to pay it to the other; though there be not any actual promise. And from this implication it is frequent for actions to be brought, in which the plaintiff sues for money found to be due to him from the defendant *on accounts stated between them,* the legal effect of these words being an allegation, that the plaintiff and defendant had settled their accounts together, *insimul computassent,* which gave the name to this species of *assumpsit,* and that the defendant engaged to pay the plaintiff the balance, but had since neglected to do it.

If no account has been made up, then the more technical legal remedy is by bringing an action of *account, de computo;* but it is found by experience, that the most ready and effectual way to settle these matters is by suit in a court of equity.

6. The last class of contracts, implied by reason and construction of law, arises upon this supposition, that every one who undertakes any office, employment, trust, or duty, contracts with those who employ or entrust him, to perform it with integrity, diligence, and skill. And if, by his want of either of those qualities, any injury accrues to individuals, they have therefore their remedy in damages by an action. A few instances will fully illustrate this matter. If an officer of the public is guilty of neglect of duty, or of a palpable breach of it, of non-feasance or of mis-feasance; as, if the sheriff does not execute a writ sent to him, or if he wilfully makes a false return thereof; in both these cases the party aggrieved shall have an action for damages to be assessed by a jury. If a sheriff or gaoler suffers a prisoner, who is taken upon mesne process, that is, during the pendency of a suit, to escape, he is liable to an action. So if, after judgment, a gaoler or a sheriff permits a debtor to escape, who is charged in execution, 'he

is liable to the creditor in the damages, which the creditor has thereby sustained.   An attorney that betrays the cause of his client, or being retained, neglects to appear at the trial, by which the cause miscarries, is liable to an action for a reparation to his injured client. There is also in law always an implied contract with a common innkeeper, to secure his guest's goods in his inn; with a common carrier, or bargemaster, to be answerable for the goods he carries; with a common farrier, that he shoes a horse well, without laming him; with a common tailor, or other workman, that he performs his business in a workmanlike manner; in which, if they fail, an action lies to recover damages for such breach of their general undertaking. But if I employ a person to transact any of these concerns, whose common profession and business it is not, the law implies no such *general* undertaking; but, in order to charge him with damages a *special* agreement is required.   Also, if an innkeeper, or other victualler, hangs out a sign, and opens his house for travellers, it is an implied engagement to entertain all persons who travel that way; and upon this universal *assumpsit* an action will lie against him for damages, if he without good reason refuses to admit a traveller.   If any one cheats me with false cards or dice, or by false weights and measures, or by selling me one commodity for another, an action also lies against him for damages, upon the contract which the law always implies, that every transaction is fair and honest.

In contracts *likewise* for the sale of goods in a shop, it is understood that the seller undertakes that the commodity he sells *is his own*, and if it proves otherwise, an action lies against him, to exact damages for this deceit.   But except in special circumstances, as when the vendor affirms, directly or indirectly, that the goods sold are his property, there is no implied warranty of *title* on the sale of goods.   Though, if the article be bought expressly for a particular purpose, there is an implied warranty that it shall be reasonably fit for that purpose.   Thus in contracts for provisions, it is always implied that they are wholesome; and if they be not, an action will lie.

Nor does the law in general imply any warranty by the seller as to the *quality* of goods sold by him.   The rule is *caveat emptor*, so that no liability is incurred by the seller by reason of bad quality or defects, unless there be an express warranty or fraud.   But if he that sells anything does upon the sale warrant it to be good, the law annexes a tacit contract to this warranty, that if it be not so, he shall make compensation to the buyer: else it is an injury to good faith, for which an action will lie to recover damages.   The warranty must be *upon the sale;* for if it be made *after,* and not *at* the time of the sale it is a void warranty: for it is then made without any consideration; neither does the buyer then take the goods upon the credit of the vendor. But if the vendor knew the goods to be unsound, and has used any art to disguise them, or if they are in any shape different from what he represents them to be to the buyer, this artifice shall be equivalent to an express warranty, and the vendor is answerable for their goodness. A general warranty will not extend to guard against defects that are plainly and obviously the object of one's senses, as if a horse be warranted perfect, and wants either a tail or an ear, unless the buyer in this case be blind. But if cloth is warranted to be of such a length, when it is not, there an action lies for damages; for that cannot be discerned by sight, but only by a collateral proof, the measuring it. Also if a horse is warranted sound, and he wants the sight of an eye, though this seems to be the object of one's senses, yet as the discernment of such defects is frequently matter of skill, an action lies to recover damages for this imposition.

Thus much for the non-performance of contracts express or implied; which includes every possible injury to what is by far the most considerable species of personal property; viz., that which consists in action merely, and not in possession: which finishes our inquiries into such wrongs as may be offered to *personal* property, with their several remedies by suit or action.

CHAPTER VII.

I COME now to consider the *injuries* that affect real property, which are principally six: I. Ouster; II. Trespass; III. Nuisance; IV. Waste; V. Subtraction; VI. Disturbance.

Ouster, or dispossession, is a wrong or injury that carries with it the amotion of possession; for thereby the wrong-doer gets into the actual occupation of the land or hereditament, and obliges him that has a right to seek his legal remedy, in order to regain *possession*, the importance of which, as now the sole foundation of *title*, we had occasion to remark in the second book of these commentaries.

For in every complete title to lands, there are two things necessary; the possession, and the right or property therein: or as it is
expressed in Fleta, *juris et seisinæ conjunctio.* Now if the possession
be severed from the property, if A has the *jus proprietatis,* and B by
some unlawful means has gained possession of the lands, this is an
injury to A, for which the law gives a remedy, by putting him in
possession. This it now effects in one way, applicable to every
species of dispossession. But formerly the same result was attained,
by different means applicable to the particular circumstances of the
case. Thus, if B, the wrong-doer, had obtained the possession either
by fraud or force, he had only a *bare* or *naked possession,* without any
shadow of right; A, therefore, who had both the *right* of property
and the *right* of possession, might, as he still may, put an end to his
title at once, by the summary method of *entry.* But if B the wrong-
doer had died seised of the lands, then B's heir was considered to
have advanced one step further towards a good title: he had not
only a *bare* possession, but also an apparent *jus possessionis,* or *right*
of possession; the law presuming that the possession which is transmitted from the ancestor to the heir, is a rightful possession, until
the contrary be shown; and therefore A was not allowed by mere
entry to evict the heir of B. The *descent cast,* as it was called, was
said to *toll* or defeat the right of entry, and A was driven to his
action at law to remove the possession of the heir, though his entry
alone would have dispossessed the ancestor. This was effected either
by a *writ of entry,* or an *assize,* which were thence termed *possessory*
actions; serving only to regain that possession, whereof the demandant or his ancestors had been unjustly deprived by the tenant or
possessor of the land, or those under whom he claimed. They
decided nothing with respect to the *right of property;* only restoring
the demandant to that state or situation, in which he had been, or
by law ought to have been, before the dispossession committed.

I shall not attempt here to describe the method of proceeding by
writ of entry, referring the student rather to our ancient books, in
which he will find frequent mention of the *degrees* within which
such writs were brought.*

* It was upon one of them that common recoveries were grounded; these,
we may remember, being fictitious actions brought against the tenant of the
freehold, usually called the tenant to the *præcipe,* or writ of entry, in which
by collusion the demandant recovered the plan. And I may add, that it was
by another form of this writ that a widow recovered her dower. For if no
dower were assigned to her, she got *possession of one third of the lands* under a
writ of *dower unde nihil habet.* But if she were deforced of part only of her
dower, she could not then say that *nihil habet;* and therefore might have recourse to another action, by writ of *right of dower;* which was a more general
remedy; and is, with regard to her claim, of the same nature as the grand *writ
of right* about to be mentioned in the text.

The other possessory action, or writ of assize, is said to have been invented by Glanvil, chief justice to Henry II.; in whose reign justices in eyre were appointed to go round the kingdom in order to take these assizes;* which were intended, when the county courts fell into disuse, to do justice to the people at their own doors, *i.e.*, to determine the right of possession in the proper counties, and yet by the king's judges.

In a writ of entry, the title of the tenant was *disproved* by showing the unlawful commencement of his possession ; in an assize was *proved* the title of the demandant, merely by showing his or his ancestor's possession. These two remedies were thus and in all other respects so totally alike, that a judgment in one was a bar against the other.

But the right of *possession*, which was recovered by the one or other of these possessory actions we have described above, though it carries with it a strong presumption, is not always conclusive evidence of the right of *property*, which may still subsist in another man. For as one man may have the *possession*, and another the *right of possession*, so one man may have the *right of possession*, and so not be liable to eviction, and another may have the *right of property*. This *right of property* could not formerly be otherwise asserted than by the great and final remedy of a *writ of right;* which lay *concurrently* with other real actions; and also lay *after* them, being as it were an appeal to the mere *right*, when judgment had been had as to the *possession*. If, indeed, the right of possession were lost by length of time, or by judgment against the true owner in a *possessory* action, there was no other choice : this was then the only remedy that could be had ; and it was of so forcible a nature, that it overcame all obstacles, and cleared all objections that might have arisen to cloud and obscure the title. And, after issue once joined in a writ of right, the judgment was absolutely final : so that a recovery had in this action might be pleaded in bar of any other claim or demand.

The proper writ of right lay only, however, to recover lands in fee simple, unjustly withheld from the true proprietor. There were other writs *in the nature of* a writ of right in which the fee simple was not demanded ; and in others not land, but some incorporeal

---

* The word *assize* is derived from the Latin *assideo*, to sit together: and it signifies, originally, the jury who try the cause, and sit together for that purpose. By a figure it was made to signify the court or jurisdiction, which summoned this jury together by a commission of assize, or *ad assisas capiendas* ; and hence the judicial assemblies held by the royal commission in every county to deliver the gaols, and to try causes at *nisi prius*, are termed in common speech the *assizes*.

hereditament. But they all applied to estates of freehold; and formerly, therefore, the *Ouster*, or dispossession, of which we spoke at the beginning of this chapter, as the *first* of the injuries that affect real property, was treated in our law books as either of the *freehold** or of *chattels real*: a distinction of the utmost importance, not only because the remedies for an ouster of the freehold were confined in their use to that species of property, but because those which the law afforded for recovery of the possession of *chattels real* were totally inapplicable to all estates of freehold. The modern action of *Ejectment* has come to supply the place of all these different remedies; and all real actions; with the exception of *dower, right of dower,* and *quare impedit,* of which afterwards, have accordingly been abolished. And we shall best see how this result has been obtained by examining the method in which the law remedied an ouster of *chattels real,* that is, of an estate for years.†

Ouster, then, or amotion of possession, from an *estate for years,* happens only by an ejection, or turning out, of the tenant from the occupation of the land during the continuance of his term. For this injury the law formerly provided the writ of *ejectione firmæ,* which was an action of trespass in *ejectment,* and lay where lands were let for a term of years; and afterwards the lessor, reversioner, remainder-man, or any stranger, ejected or ousted the lessee of his term. He could thereby call the defendant to answer for entering on the lands so demised to him for a term that was not yet expired, and ejecting him; and in this action he recovered back his term, or the remainder of it, with damages.

Through the disuse of real actions this proceeding became the common method of trying the title to lands, and for a long time before their final abolition, it was in practice the usual mode of doing so. It may not, therefore, be improper to delineate with some degree of minuteness its history, the manner of its process, and the

---

* Ouster of the *freehold* was effected by 1. *Abatement;* 2. *Intrusion;* 3. *Disseisin;* 4. *Discontinuance;* or 5. *Deforcement.* To the practising lawyer, a knowledge of the different circumstances which gave rise to these different species of ouster is still useful, if not necessary. But it would only weary the student to explain them at length in this place; and I therefore content myself with referring him to the text books, should he find it desirable to consult them.

† This kind of ouster also took place with regard to estates held by statute-merchant, recognizance, or *elegit,* which are ranked as chattels real, if the legal proprietor was turned out before his estate was determined, by raising the sum for which it was given him in pledge. His remedy is now the same as for a term of years, viz., by action of ejectment.

principles whereon it is grounded; the more especially that the new action of ejectment is as much a reconstruction of the procedure in this action, as a creation of a new remedy for the recovery of real property.

An action at law for the damage sustained by reason of the breach of the contract contained in his lease was anciently the only remedy which the tenant had for recovering against the lessor a term from which he had ejected his lessee, together with damages for the ouster. But if the lessee was ejected by a stranger, claiming under a title superior to that of the lessor, though the lessee might still maintain an action against the lessor, for non-performance of his contract or lease, yet he could not by any means recover the term itself. He had no other remedy against the ejector but in damages for the trespass committed in ejecting him from his farm. But when the courts of equity began to oblige the ejector to make a specific restitution of the land to the party injured, the courts of law also adopted the same method of doing complete justice: and in the prosecution of a writ of ejectment, introduced a new species of remedy, viz., a judgment to recover the term, and a writ of possession thereupon.

The better to apprehend the contrivance, whereby this end was effected, we must recollect that the remedy by ejectment was in its origin an action brought by one who had a lease for years, to repair the injury done him by dispossession. In order, therefore, to convert it into a method of trying titles to the freehold, it was first necessary that the claimant should take possession of the lands, to empower him to constitute a lessee for years, who might be capable of receiving this injury of dispossession. For it would be an offence, called in our law *maintenance*, of which in the next book of these commentaries, to convey a title to another when the grantor is not in possession of the land. When, therefore, a person who had right of entry into lands determined to acquire that possession which was wrongfully withheld by the tenant therein, he made, as by law he may, a formal entry on the premises; and being so in the possession of the soil, he there, upon the land, sealed and delivered a lease for years to some third person or lessee: and having thus given him entry, left him in possession of the premises. This lessee was to stay upon the land till the prior tenant, or he who had the previous possession, entered thereon afresh and ousted him; or till some other person, either by accident or by agreement beforehand, came upon the land, and turned him out or ejected him. For this injury the lessee was entitled to his action of ejectment against the tenant, or this *casual ejector*, whichever it was that ousted him, to recover back his term and damages. But where this action was brought against such a casual ejector as is before mentioned, and not against the very tenant in possession, the court would not suffer the tenant to lose his possession without an opportunity to defend it. Wherefore it was a standing rule, that no plaintiff should proceed in ejectment to recover lands against a casual ejector, without notice given to the tenant in possession, if any there were, and making him a defendant if he pleased. And, in order to maintain the action, the plaintiff must, in case of any defence, have made out four points before the court, viz., *title, lease, entry,* and *ouster.* First, he must have shown a good *title* in his lessor, which brought the matter of right entirely before the court; then, that the lessor, being seised or possessed by virtue of such title, had made him the *lease* for the term; thirdly, that he, the lessee or plaintiff, had *entered* or taken possession in consequence of such lease; and then, lastly, that the defendant had *ousted* or ejected him. Whereupon he had judgment to recover his term and damages, and, in consequence, had a *writ of possession,* which the sheriff was to execute by delivering him the undisturbed and peaceable possession of his term.

This was formerly the regular method of bringing an action of ejectment, in which the title of the lessor came collaterally and incidentally before the court, in order to show the injury done to the lessee by this ouster. But as much trouble and formality were found to attend the actual making of the *lease, entry,* and *ouster,* a new and more easy method of trying titles was invented, which depended entirely upon a string of legal fictions; no actual lease was made, no actual entry by the plaintiff, no actual ouster by the defendant, but all were merely ideal, for the sole purpose of trying the title. To this end in the proceedings a lease for a term of years was stated to have been made, by him who claimed title, to the plaintiff who brought the action, as by John Rogers to John Doe; it was also stated that Doe, the lessee, entered, and that the defendant, Richard Roe, who was called the *casual ejector,* ousted him : for which ouster he brought this action. As soon as this action was brought, and the complaint fully stated in the declaration, Roe, the casual ejector or defendant, sent a written notice to the tenant in possession of the lands, as George Saunders, informing him of the action brought by John Doe, and transmitting him a copy of the declaration : withal assuring him that he, Roe, the defendant, had no title at all to the premises, and should make no defence; and, therefore, advising the tenant to appear in court and defend his own title, otherwise he, the casual ejector, would suffer judgment to be had against him, and thereby the actual tenant Saunders would inevitably be turned out of possession. On receipt of this friendly caution, if the tenant in possession did not within a limited time apply to the court to be admitted a defendant in the stead of Roe, he was supposed to have no right at all, and, upon judgment being had against Roe the casual ejector, Saunders, the real tenant, was turned out of possession by the sheriff.

But if the tenant in possession applied to be made a defendant, it was allowed him upon this condition: that he entered into a rule of court to confess, at the trial of the cause, three of the four requisites for the maintenance of the plaintiff's action, viz., the *lease* of Rogers the lessor, the *entry* of Doe the plaintiff, and his *ouster* by Saunders himself, now made the defendant instead of Roe: which requisites being wholly fictitious, should the defendant put the plaintiff to prove them, he must, of course, be nonsuited for want of evidence; but by such stipulated confession of *lease, entry*, and *ouster*, the trial now stood upon the merits of the *title* only. This done, the declaration was altered by inserting the name of George Saunders instead of Richard Roe, and the cause went down to trial under the name of Doe, the plaintiff, on the demise of Rogers the lessor, against Saunders, the new defendant. And therein the lessor of the plaintiff was bound to make out a clear title, otherwise his fictitious lessee could not obtain judgment to have possession of the land for the term supposed to be granted. But if the lessor made out his title in a satisfactory manner, then judgment and a writ of possession were awarded to John Doe, the nominal plaintiff, who by this trial had proved the right of John Rogers, his supposed lessor.

But if the new defendant, after entering into the common rule, failed to appear at the trial, and to confess lease, entry, and ouster, the plaintiff, Doe, must, indeed, have been there nonsuited, for want of proving those requisites; but judgment would in the end be entered against the casual ejector Roe; for the condition on which Saunders was admitted a defendant had been broken, and therefore the plaintiff was put again in the same situation as if he never had appeared at all; the consequence of which, we have seen, was, that judgment would be entered for the plaintiff, and the sheriff, by virtue of a writ for that purpose, would turn out Saunders and deliver possession to John Doe. The same process, therefore, as would have been had, provided no conditional rule had been ever made, must have been pursued as soon as the condition was broken.

This method of recovering real property was attended however with certain objections, which, notwithstanding the constant supervision of the courts, occasionally gave rise to well-founded complaints. So long, indeed, as the other legal remedies, by writs of entry and assize, were open to the suitors, these were not much attended to; but when possession for twenty years came to be regarded as almost conclusive evidence of title, and afterwards when, by the abolition of real actions, ejectment remained the only method of trying such questions, it became necessary to apply a remedy. And accordingly,

when the procedure of the superior courts of common law was reconstructed a few years ago, advantage was taken of the opportunity; a new action for the recovery of land was created; and the old action of ejectment is now, therefore, to be numbered among the relics of the past.

The old form of suit was valuable in one respect, in that it allowed no question to be raised except that of *title.* The new procedure possesses this advantage: it is an action exclusively for recovering the possession of real property, without regard to any other question which may exist between the parties. It is now commenced by a *writ,* which is directed to the tenants in possession, describes the property, states the persons in whom the right of possession is alleged to be, and commands those to whom it is directed to appear in court, and defend their possession, or otherwise they may be turned out. When *served* on the tenant in possession, this writ has thus the same effect as the notice formerly given by the casual ejector; and it is the duty of the tenant, if he has no interest on the premises to defend, to give immediate notice of the writ to his landlord. Indeed, to prevent fraudulent recoveries of the possession, by collusion with the tenant, all tenants are obliged, on pain of forfeiting three years' rent, to give notice to their landlords, when served with an ejectment: and any landlord may by leave of the court be made a co-defendant to the action, in case the tenant himself appears to it; or, if he makes default, yet execution will be stayed, in case the landlord applies to be made a defendant. And on the same principle, not only may the landlord be admitted to defend, but any other person, such as a mortgagee, a devisee in trust, or an heir, will be allowed to do so, on showing that he is in possession of the premises, by himself or his tenants.

If no appearance be entered within the time allowed, the plaintiff obtains *judgment by default,* upon which the sheriff will deliver to him the possession of the property. For it is by the entry of an appearance only that the tenant, or the landlord, or other person admitted to defend, denies that alleged right—the parties *on appearance* being thus *at issue* on the question of *title.* The claimant has then to prove his alleged right to a jury, the question for them to determine being simply whether the statement in the writ of the title of the claimant is true or false. If, at the trial, the claimant appears and the defendant fails to do so, the former recovers without even proof of his title, the defendant being considered to have, as it were, abandoned his defence. If, on the other hand, the defendant appears, but the claimant makes default, the defendant will have judgment for his costs of suit.

The damages recovered in the old actions of ejectment, though originally their only intent, were, where the title came to be considered as the principal question, very small and inadequate; amounting commonly to one shilling, or some other trivial sum. The modern action is, as we have seen, not an action of trespass for an ouster, but exclusively to assert a claim to the possession of real property, and in it consequently no damages are recovered. In order therefore to complete the remedy, when the possession has been long detained from him that had the right to it, an action lies, after a recovery in ejectment, to recover the *mesne profits* which the tenant in possession has wrongfully received. Which action must be brought in the name of the claimant in the ejectment, in whom the jury have found the right to be, against the tenant in possession. In this case the judgment in ejectment is conclusive evidence against the defendant, for all profits which have accrued since the date alleged in the writ, as the period at which the plaintiff's right of possession accrued to him; but if the plaintiff sues for any antecedent profits, the defendant may make a new defence. Thus he may plead the statute of limitations, and by that means protect himself from the payment of all mesne profits, except those which have accrued within the previous six years.

Such is the modern way of trying the *title* to lands and tenements. It is founded on the same principle as the ancient writs of assize, being calculated to try the mere *possessory* title to an estate; and has succeeded to those real actions, as being infinitely more convenient for attaining the ends of justice.

But a writ of ejectment is not an adequate means to try the title of *all* estates. Coming in place of the former action, in which damages were sought to be recovered for a supposed ouster, it lies only for the recovery of that species of real property, on which an entry can be made, and an ouster effected. On those things, whereon an entry cannot in fact be made, no entry shall be supposed by any fiction of the parties, therefore an ejectment will not lie of an advowson, a rent, a common, or other incorporeal hereditament. Nor would it lie formerly in such cases, where the entry of him that had right was taken away by a twenty years' dispossession, or otherwise. But twenty years' dispossession may now be set up by the defendant as an answer to the claimant, and a good title against all the world. This period of limitation is, however, made subject to qualification in the case of persons under disability; for if at the time at which the right of any person first accrued, such person was under the disability of infancy, coverture, idiotcy, lunacy, unsoundness of mind, or absence beyond seas, he, or the person claiming through him, may, though twenty years have expired, bring an action, within ten years next after the person to whom the right accrued shall have ceased to be under such disability, or have died, whichever event shall first happen. But no action can be brought in such case of disability, but within forty years next after the right has accrued, although the person to whom it accrued may have remained under disability during the whole of the forty years, or although the term of ten years above mentioned shall not have expired.

The action of ejectment has, I may add, been rendered an easy and expeditious remedy to landlords whose tenants are in arrear, or who hold over after their term has expired or been determined. For every landlord who has a right of re-entry in case of non-payment of rent, when half a year's rent is due and no sufficient distress is to be had, may serve a writ of ejectment on his tenant, or fix the same upon some notorious part of the premises, which shall be valid, without any formal re-entry or previous demand of rent. And a recovery in such ejectment shall be final and conclusive, both in law and equity, unless the rent and all costs be paid or tendered within six calendar months afterwards.

And a landlord, on serving a writ of ejectment on a tenant holding over after his term has expired or been determined, may give him notice that he will be required to give bail, if ordered so to do by the court or a judge, conditioned to pay the costs and damages to be recovered in the action. If bail is thereafter ordered to be given, and the tenant fails to do so, the claimant obtains immediate judgment for recovery of possession and for his costs.

Ejectments, again, between landlord and tenant, partake somewhat of the nature of what have been already described as *mixed* actions; for in them the claimant may go on, after proving his right to recover, to give evidence of the mesne profits, and the jury shall thereupon give their verdict, both as to the title and mesne profits; so that in such cases a second action for mesne profits is unnecessary. Besides these remedies a landlord may, in cases where the rent or value of the premises does not exceed 50*l*., and no fine has been paid, proceed summarily in the county court. If the rent does not exceed 20*l*., and no fine has been paid, he may proceed before the justices in petty sessions.

CHAPTER VIII.

OF INJURIES TO REAL PROPERTY.

Trespass: when justifiable—trespass *ab initio*—costs in actions of trespass—injunction in chancery. Nuisance: to corporeal hereditaments—to incorporeal hereditaments—remedy at law and in equity. Waste: who may commit—how punished or prevented. Subtraction: as of fealty, duties, rent, &c.—remedy by distress—where premises deserted. Disturbance: of franchise—of commons—enclosure—of ways—of tenure—of patronage—action of *quare impedit*.

In the preceding chapter we have considered the chief injury to real property, an ouster or amotion of the possession. Those which remain to be discussed are such as may be offered to a man's real property without any amotion from it.

II. The second species therefore of wrongs that affect a man's lands, tenements, or hereditaments, is that of *trespass*. Trespass, in its largest and most extensive sense, signifies any transgression or offence against the law of nature, of society, or of the country in which we live; whether it relates to a man's person, or his property. Therefore beating another is a trespass; for which an action of assault and battery will lie: taking or detaining a man's goods are respectively trespasses; for which the actions of *trover and detinue* are given by the law: so also non-performance of promises or undertakings is technically a trespass, upon which the action of *assumpsit* is grounded: and, in general, any misfeasance or act of one man whereby another is injuriously treated and damnified, is a transgression or trespass in its largest sense.

But in the limited and confined sense, in which we are at present to consider it, it signifies no more than an entry on another man's ground without a lawful authority, and doing some damage, however inconsiderable, to his real property, which the law entitles a trespass *by breaking his close*. For every man's land is in the eye of the law enclosed and set apart from his neighbour's: and that either by a visible and material fence, as one field is divided from another by a hedge; or by an ideal invisible boundary, existing only in the contemplation of law, as when one man's land adjoins to another's in the same field. And every such entry or breach of a man's close carries necessarily along with it some damage or other; for if no other special loss can be assigned, yet one general damage may in

Q

any case be specified, viz., the treading down and bruising his herbage.

One must have a property, either absolute or temporary, in the soil, and actual possession, to be able to maintain an action of trespass; or, at least, it is requisite that the party have possession of the vesture and herbage, or other produce of the land. Thus if a meadow be divided annually among the parishioners by lot, then after each person's several portion is allotted, they may be respectively capable of maintaining an action for the breach of their several closes; for they have an exclusive interest therein for the time. And a man is answerable for not only his own trespass, but that of his cattle also: for, if by his negligent keeping they stray upon the land of another, and much more if he permits, or drives them on, and they there tread down his neighbour's herbage, and spoil his corn or his trees, this is a trespass, for which the owner must answer in damages; and the law gives the party injured a double remedy in this case, by permitting him to distrain the cattle thus *damage-feasant*, or doing damage, till the owner shall make him satisfaction: or else by leaving him to the common remedy *in foro contentioso*, by action.

In some cases trespass is justifiable; or rather entry on another's land or house shall not in those cases be accounted trespass: as if a man comes thither to demand or pay money, these payable; or to execute, in a legal manner, the process of the law. Also a man may justify entering into an inn or public-house, without the leave of the owner first specially asked; because when a man professes the keeping of such inn or public-house, he thereby gives a general licence to any person to enter his doors. So a commoner may justify entering to attend his cattle, commoning on another's land; and a reversioner, to see if any waste be committed on the estate, from the apparent necessity of the thing.

But in cases where a man misdemeans himself, or makes an ill use of the authority with which the law intrusts him, he shall be accounted a trespasser *ab initio*; as if one comes into a tavern and will not go out in a reasonable time, but tarries there all night contrary to the inclinations of the owner; this wrongful act shall affect and have relation back even to his first entry, and make the whole a trespass. So if a reversioner, who enters on pretence of seeing waste, breaks the house, or stays there all night; or if the commoner who comes to tend his cattle cuts down a tree; in these and similar cases the law judges that he entered for this unlawful purpose, and therefore, as the act which demonstrates such his purpose is a trespass, he shall be esteemed a trespasser *ab initio*.

A man may also justify in an action of trespass, on account of the freehold and right of entry being in himself; and this defence brings the title of the estate in question.   This is therefore one way of trying the property of estates; though it is not so usual as that by ejectment, because that gives possession of the land; whereas in the action of trespass, which is merely a personal suit, the right can be only ascertained, but no possession delivered; nothing being recovered but damages for the wrong committed.   It is, however, the proper method of trying the title to some incorporeal heredita-ments.   For as any entry on the property of another is *primâ facie* a trespass, it is for the defendant to show that such entry was lawful; that is, to prove that the apparent trespass was in truth no trespass at all, as it would not be if the defendant was only using a right of way over the plaintiff's property, or exercising a right of common.

. In order to prevent trifling and vexatious actions of trespass, as well as other personal actions, several statutes have been passed, the effect of which is, that the plaintiff, if he recovers less damages than forty shillings, is not entitled to costs, unless the judge certifies that the action was brought to try a right, or that the trespass was wilful and malicious; while the plaintiff, if he recovers less than five pounds, may by a like certificate be disentitled to costs alto-gether.   The plaintiff will in no case, however, be deprived of costs in an action for a trespass in respect of which a notice not to trespass has been previously served upon the defendant, or left at his last known abode.   For every trespass is *wilful*, where the defendant has notice, and is especially forewarned not to come on the land; as every trespass is *malicious*, though the damage may not amount to forty shillings, where the intent of the defendant plainly appears to be to harass and distress the plaintiff.

The ordinary remedy for a trespass then, is by an action at law, to recover damages for the injury sustained by the plaintiff; but in those cases in which the injury is threatened before being committed, it is advisable to resort, in the first instance, to the Court of Chancery for an injunction.   Formerly, indeed, the courts of equity were ex-tremely reluctant to interfere, even in cases of repeated trespasses; but now there is not the slightest hesitation, if the acts done or threatened to be done would be ruinous or irreparable, or impair the just enjoy-ment of the property of the plaintiff.   An injunction will be granted, for instance, when a mere trespasser digs into and works a mine, to the injury of the owner, because it operates a permanent injury to the property as a mine; or when timber is being cut down by a trespasser in collusion with the tenant; or in any case, in short, in which the party exceeds the limited rights with which he is clothed;

and the acts to be restrained are or may result in irreparable damage.

Until quite recently, however, the courts of equity could only interfere by injunction; the damages sustained by the plaintiff must have been sought for in an action. This defect in the jurisdiction of these courts has now been removed; and they may assess and award damages, with or without the assistance of a jury, but otherwise precisely as the courts of common law. Therein they afford the suitor an advantage not obtainable at law; for it is only in cases where damage has been not merely threatened but actually done, that the plaintiff may obtain from the courts of common law an injunction against the repetition or continuance of the injury complained of.

III. A third species of injuries to a man's lands and tenements is by *nuisance*, which signifies anything that works hurt, inconvenience, or damage. And nuisances are of two kinds: public or *common* nuisances, which affect the community, for which reason we must refer them to the fourth part of these commentaries; and *private* nuisances, which are the objects of our present consideration, and may be defined, anything done to the hurt or annoyance of the lands, tenements, or hereditaments of another. These therefore are such as affect either corporeal or incorporeal hereditaments.

1. First, as to *corporeal* inheritances. If a man builds a house so close to mine that his roof overhangs my roof, and throws the water off his roof upon mine, this is a nuisance, for which an action will lie. Likewise to erect a house or other building so near to mine, that it obstructs my ancient lights and windows, is a nuisance of a similar nature. But in this latter case it is necessary that the windows be *ancient*; that is, have subsisted there for twenty years at least, without interruption; otherwise there is no injury done. For he has as much right to build a new edifice upon his ground as I have upon mine; since every man may erect what he pleases upon the upright or perpendicular of his own soil, so as not to prejudice what has long been enjoyed by another, and it was my folly to build so near another's ground. Also, if a person keeps his hogs, or other noisome animals, or allows filth to accumulate on his premises, so near the house of another, that the stench incommodes him and makes the air unwholesome, this is an injurious nuisance, as it tends to deprive him of the use and benefit of his house. A like injury is, if one's neighbour sets up and exercises any offensive trade; as a tanner's, a tallow-chandler's, or the like; for though these are lawful and necessary trades, yet they should be exercised in remote places; for the rule is, "*sic utere tuo ut alienum non lædas:*" this therefore is an actionable nuisance. And on a similar principle, a constant ringing

of bells in one's immediate neighbourhood may be a nuisance. But depriving one of a mere matter of pleasure, as of a fine prospect by building a wall, or the like; this, as it abridges nothing really convenient or necessary, is no injury to the sufferer, and is therefore not an actionable nuisance.

As to nuisance to one's *lands*: if one erects a smelting-house for lead so near the land of another, that the vapour and smoke kills his corn and grass, and damages his cattle therein, this is held to be a nuisance. And by consequence it follows, that if one does any other act, in itself lawful, which yet being done in that place necessarily tends to the damage of another's property, it is a nuisance : for it is incumbent on him to find some other place to do that act, where it will be less offensive. So, also, if my neighbour ought to scour a ditch, and does not, whereby my land is overflowed, this is an actionable nuisance.

With regard to *other* corporeal hereditaments : it is a nuisance to stop or divert water that uses to run to another's meadow or mill; to corrupt or poison a water-course, by erecting a dye-house or a lime-pit, for the use of trade, in the upper part of the stream ; to pollute a pond, from which another is entitled to water his cattle ; to obstruct a drain; or in short to do any act in common property, that in its consequences must necessarily tend to the prejudice of one's neighbour. So closely does the law of England enforce that excellent rule of gospel-morality, of "doing to others, as we would they should do unto ourselves."

2. As to *incorporeal* hereditaments, the law carries itself with the same equity. If I have a way, annexed to my estate, across another's land, and he obstructs me in the use of it, either by totally stopping it or putting logs across it, or ploughing over it, it is a nuisance · for in the first case I cannot enjoy my right at all, and in the latter I cannot enjoy it so commodiously as I ought. Also, if I am entitled to hold a fair or market, and another person sets up a fair or market so near mine that he does me a prejudice, it is a nuisance to the freehold which I have in my market or fair. If a ferry is erected on a river, so near another ancient ferry as to draw away its custom, it is a nuisance to the owner of the old one. For where there is a ferry by prescription, the owner is bound to keep it always in repair and readiness, for the ease of all the queen's subjects ; it would be therefore extremely hard, if a new ferry were suffered to share his profits, which does not also share his burthen. But where the reason ceases, the law also ceases with it : therefore it is no nuisance to erect a mill so near mine as to draw away the custom, unless the miller also intercepts the water. Neither is it a nuisance to set up any trade, or a school, in a neighbourhood or rivalship with another : for by such

emulation the public are like to be gainers; and if the new mill or school occasion a damage to the old one, it is *damnum absque injuriâ.*

Let us next attend to the remedies which the law has given for this injury of nuisance. And here I must premise that the law gives no *private* remedy for anything but a *private* wrong. Therefore no *action* lies for a public or common nuisance, but an *indictment* only, or in certain cases an *information* in chancery: because the damage being common to *all* the queen's subjects, no *one* can assign his particular proportion of it; or if he could it would be extremely hard, if every subject in the kingdom were allowed to harass the offender with separate actions. Yet this rule admits of one exception; where a private person suffers some extraordinary damage, beyond the rest of the queen's subjects, by a public nuisance; in which case he shall have a private satisfaction by action. As if, by means of a ditch dug across a public way, which is a common nuisance, a man or his horse suffer any injury by falling therein; there, for this particular damage, which is not common to others, the party shall have his action. So if rubbish is improperly left on a highway, or an authorized obstruction is continued for an unreasonable time, an action lies at the suit of the party injured. But if a man has abated or removed a nuisance which offended him, as we may remember it was stated in the first chapter of this book, that the party injured has a right to do, in this case he is entitled to no action. For he had choice of two remedies; either without suit, by abating it himself, by his own mere act and authority; or by suit in which he may recover damages for the injury sustained by him;—having made his election of one remedy, he is totally precluded from the other.

The remedy is by action for damages, in which a writ of injunction against the continuance of the nuisance may be claimed; for every continuance of a nuisance is held to be a fresh one; and therefore a fresh action will lie, and very exemplary damages be given, if, after one verdict against him, the defendant has the hardiness to continue it.

And this action is the only personal remedy for a private nuisance which can be obtained in the courts of common law. The Court of Chancery has, however, long exercised a jurisdiction over both public and private nuisances, its interposition being principally confined to granting *preventive* relief. In the case of a public nuisance the chancery can often give a more complete remedy than is attainable at law; for it can interpose where the courts of law cannot, to restrain and prevent such nuisances as are threatened, as well as to abate those already existing. In regard to *private* nuisances again the courts of equity will interfere either to prevent irreparable mischief, or to afford a more complete remedy than that obtainable at law. Thus, where a party builds so near the house of another, as to darken his windows, against the clear rights of the latter, an injunction will be granted to prevent the nuisance, as well as to remedy it, if already done, although an action for damages would lie at law; for the latter can in no just sense be deemed an adequate relief in such a case.

And on the same principle the courts of equity will prevent the obstruction of water-courses, the diversion of streams from mills or the pulling down of the banks of rivers. They will grant an injunction against the erection of a new ferry, injurious to an old-established ferry; or against a voluntary religious association being disturbed in their burial-ground; they will interfere to prevent rights of property being injured, obstructed, or taken away illegally by a railway company, and will in every case preserve to persons, possessing a statutory privilege or franchise, the enjoyment of it from invasion. These courts may also, as we have seen, assess and award damages to the plaintiff, in like manner as the courts of common law.

IV. The fourth species of injury, that may be offered to one's real property, is by *waste*, or destruction in lands and tenements, which the common law expresses very significantly by the word *vastum.*

The persons who may be injured by waste, are such as have some *interest* in the estate wasted; for if a man be the absolute tenant in foe simple, without any incumbrance or charge on the premises, he may commit whatever waste his own indiscretion may prompt him to, without being impeachable, or accountable for it to any one. One species of interest, which is injured by waste, is that of a person who has a right of common in the place wasted; especially if it be common of *estovers*, or a right of cutting and carrying away wood for house-bote, plough-bote, &c. Here, if the owner of the wood demolishes it, this is an injury to the commoner, for which he can recover damages by an action for this waste and destruction of the woods, out of which his estovers were to issue.

But the most usual and important interest that is hurt by this commission of waste is that of him who has the remainder or reversion of the *inheritance*, after the particular estate for life or years in being. Here, if the particular tenant commits or suffers any waste, it is a manifest injury to him that has the inheritance, as it tends to mangle and dismember it of its most desirable incidents and ornaments, among which timber and houses may justly be reckoned the principal. To him, therefore, in remainder or reversion, to whom the *inheritance* apertains in expectancy, the law has given an adequate remedy. For he who has the remainder *for life* only, is not entitled to sue at law for waste; since his interest may never perhaps come into possession, and then he has suffered no injury.

The redress for this injury of waste is of two kinds; preventive and corrective. The former remedy is to be had in the Court of Chancery. The latter or corrective remedy is to be had in the courts of common law.

The courts of equity interfere upon the principle of preserving the property, and give relief wherever the remedies furnished by the common law can not be made to apply. There are consequently many cases where a person is dispunishable at law, in which a court of equity will interfere by injunction. Thus where there is a tenant for life, remainder for life, remainder in fee, the tenant for life will be restrained from committing waste, although if he did do so, no action would lie against him by the remainder-man for life, for he has not the inheritance: nor by the remainder-man in fee, by reason of the interposed remainder for life. So, a landlord may have an injunction to stay waste against an under-lessee; or against a tenant from year to year, after notice to quit, to restrain him from removing the crops, manure, &c.; or against a lessee, to prevent him from making material alterations in a dwelling-house, as by changing it into a shop or a warehouse. And courts of equity will also grant injunctions in cases where the aggrieved party has an equitable right only. Thus where a mortgagor or mortgagee in possession commits waste, or threatens to commit it, an injunction will be granted, although there is no remedy at law. And if a tenant for life without impeachment for waste should pull down houses, or do other waste wantonly or maliciously, a court of equity will restrain it; for in such cases the party is deemed guilty of a wanton and unconscientious abuse of his rights, ruinous to the interests of other parties.

The remedy at law is by an action for damages; but as the plaintiff herein can only recover damages for waste already committed, and prevent it for the future, the remedy is inadequate; an action is consequently rarely resorted to. The redress obtainable in equity is at once more effectual and more complete; for not only may future waste be prevented, but an account may be decreed, and compensation given for the past. And it may be added here that an action will not lie for permissive waste; whereas in equity an injunction will be granted to restrain permissive as well as voluntary waste.

V. Subtraction is the fifth species of injuries affecting real property, and happens when any person who owes any suit, duty, custom, or service to another, withdraws, or neglects to perform it.

1. Fealty, suit of court, and rent, are duties and services usually issuing and arising *ratione tenuræ*, being the conditions upon which

the ancient lords granted out their lands to their feudatories : whereby it was stipulated that they and their heirs should take the oath of fealty or fidelity to their lord, which was the feudal bond or *commune vinculum* between lord and tenant; that they should do suit, or duly attend and follow the lord's courts, and there from time to time give their assistance, by serving on juries, either to decide the property of their neighbours in the court-baron, or correct their misdemeanours in the court-leet ; and, lastly, that they should yield to the lord certain annual stated returns, in military attendance, in provisions, in arms, in matters of ornament or pleasure, in rustic employments, or prædial labours, or, which is *instar omnium*, in money, which will provide all the rest; all which are comprised under the one general name of *reditus*, return, or rent. And the subtraction or non-observance of any of these conditions, by neglecting to swear fealty, to do suit of court, or to render the rent or service reserved, is an injury to the freehold of the lord, by diminishing and depreciating the value of his seignory.

The general remedy for all these is by *distress;* and it is the only remedy at the common law for the two first of them. And we may remember that distresses should be reasonable and moderate ; but in the case of distress for fealty or suit of court, no distress can be unreasonable, immoderate, or too large : for this is the only remedy to which the party aggrieved is entitled, and therefore it ought to be such as is sufficiently compulsory ; and, be it of what value it will, there is no harm done, especially as it cannot be sold or made away with, but must be restored immediately on satisfaction made. A distress of this nature, that has no bounds with regard to its quantity, and may be repeated from time to time, until the stubborness of the party is conquered, is called a *distress infinite.*

The other remedy for subtraction of rents or services is by an action of *debt*, for the breach of this express contract, of which enough has been formerly said. This is the most usual remedy, when recourse is had to any action at all for the recovery of pecuniary rents; to which species of render almost all free services are now reduced, since the abolition of the military tenures.

There were formerly several other remedies by which the lord recovered the land itself from the tenant who withheld the services, one of which was the writ of *cessavit*, which lay when a man who held lands of a lord by rent or other services, neglected or *ceased* to perform his services for two years together : in which case, if the *cesser* or neglect continued for two years, the lord or donor and his heirs had this writ to recover the land itself. But upon tender of arrears and damages before judgment, and giving security for the future performance of the services, the tenant might retain his land. It is easy to observe that

the statutes, which enable landlords who have a right of re-entry
for non-payment of rent, to serve an ejectment on their tenants, when
half a year's rent is due, and there is no sufficient distress on the
premises, have been in some measure copied from the ancient writ of
cessavit : especially as the ejectment may be put an end to in a similar manner, by tender of the rent and costs within six months after.
And the same remedy is, in substance, adopted by statute 11 Geo. II.
c. 19, s. 16, which enacts that where any tenant at rack-rent shall
be one year's rent in arrear, and shall desert the demised premises,
leaving the same uncultivated or unoccupied, so that no sufficient
distress can be had: two justices of the peace, after notice affixed
on the premises for fourteen days without effect, may give the
landlord possession thereof, and thenceforth the lease shall be void.

2. Thus far of the remedies for subtraction of rents or other
services due by *tenure*.   There are also other services, due by ancient
custom and *prescription* only.   Such is that of doing suit to another's
mill : where the persons, resident in a particular place, by usage,
time out of mind have been accustomed to grind their corn at a
certain mill ; and afterwards any of them go to another mill, and
withdraw their suit, their *secta, a sequendo*, from the ancient mill.
This is not only a damage, but an injury to the owner ; because this
prescription might have a very reasonable foundation ; viz., upon the
erection of such mill by the ancestors of the owner for the convenience
of the inhabitants, on condition, that when erected they should
all grind their corn there only.   For this injury the owner formerly
had a writ *de sectâ ad molendinum*, commanding the defendant to do
his suit at the mill, or show good cause to the contrary.   In like
manner, and for like reasons, a man might have had a writ of *secta ad
furnum, secta ad torrale, et ad omnia alia hujusmodi*; for suit due to his
public oven or bakehouse ; or to his kiln or malthouse.   But these
special remedies for subtractions, to compel the specific performance
of services due by custom, or prescription, have been abolished; and
the only mode of redress which can now be resorted to, is the universal remedy of an action to repair the party injured in damages.   And
thus much for the injury of subtraction.

V. The sixth and last species of real injuries is that of *disturbance ;*
which is usually a wrong done to some incorporeal hereditament, by
hindering or disquieting the owners in their regular and lawful enjoyment of it.   Of this injury there are five sorts ; viz., 1. Disturbance
of *franchise* . 2. Disturbance of *common*. 3. Disturbance of *ways*.
4. Disturbance of *tenure*. 5. Disturbance of *patronage*.

1. Disturbance of *franchise* happens when a man has the franchise
of holding a court-leet, of keeping a fair, of free-warren, of seizing

estrays, or any other species of franchise whatsoever; and he is disturbed in the lawful exercise thereof. As if another, by menaces, or persuasions, prevails upon the suitors not to appear at my court; or obstructs the passage to my fair; or hunts in my free-warren; or hinders me from seizing the estray, whereby it escapes or is carried out of my liberty; in every case of this kind there is an injury done to the legal owner; his property is damnified, and the profits arising from his franchise are diminished. To remedy which, as the law has given no other writ, he is therefore entitled to sue for damages by an action.

2. Disturbance of *common* occurs where any act is done, by which the right of another to his common is incommoded or diminished. This may happen where one who has no right of common, puts his cattle into the land; and thereby robs the cattle of the commoners of their respective shares of the pasture. Or if one, who has a right of common, puts in cattle which are not commonable, as hogs and goats; which amounts to the same inconvenience. Another disturbance of common is by *surcharging* it; or putting more cattle therein than the pasture and herbage will sustain, or the party has a right to do. In this case he that surcharges does an injury to the rest of the owners, by depriving them of their respective portions, or at least contracting them into a smaller compass. The usual remedies are either by distraining so many of the beasts as are above the number allowed, or else by an action of trespass, both which may be had by the lord: or lastly, by an action for damages; in which any commoner may be plaintiff.

There is yet another disturbance of common, when the owner of the land, or other person, so encloses or otherwise obstructs it, that the commoner is precluded from enjoying the benefit to which he is by law entitled. Thus, if the lord erect a wall, hedge, or fence round the common, so as to prevent the commoner's cattle from going into it, the commoner may abate the enclosure, because it is inconsistent with the grant. And disturbance may be done, not only by erecting fences, but also by driving the cattle off the land, or by ploughing up the soil of the common. Or it may be done by erecting a warren therein, and stocking it with rabbits in such quantities, that they devour the whole herbage, and thereby destroy the common. For in such case, though the commoner may not destroy the rabbits, yet the law looks upon this as an injurious disturbance of his right, and has given him his remedy by action against the owner. There is, indeed, in this case no remedy but by action, for the commoner cannot fill up the cony-burrows, as that would be meddling with the soil, and itself a trespass.

There are cases, indeed, in which the lord may enclose and abridge the common; for which, as they are no injury to any one, so no one is entitled to any remedy. This is provided for by the statute of Merton, 20 Hen. III. c. 4, the statute Westm. 2, 13 Edw. I. c. 46, and various modern statutes. But there are many difficulties, some risk, and considerable expense in acting upon them, which has led to many enclosures being effected under private acts of parliament; the result being that ultimately, by the General Inclosure Acts, the provisions usually inserted in such *privilegia* were consolidated, and the obtaining of enclosures thereby much facilitated.

3. Disturbance of *ways* principally happens when a person who has a right to a way over another's grounds, by grant or prescription, is obstructed by enclosures, or other obstacles, or by ploughing across it; by which means he cannot enjoy his right of way, or at least cannot in so commodious a manner as he might have done. If this be a way annexed to his estate, and the obstruction is made by the tenant of the land, this brings it to another species of injury; for it is then a *nuisance*, for which an action will lie, as mentioned in a former chapter. But if the right of way, thus obstructed by the tenant, be only *in gross*, that is, annexed to a man's person and unconnected with any lands or tenements, or if the obstruction of a way belonging to a house or land is made by a stranger, it is then in either case merely a disturbance; for the obstruction of a way in gross is no detriment to any lands or tenements, and therefore does not fall under the legal notion of a nuisance, which must be laid, *ad nocumentum liberi tenementi;* and the obstruction of it by a stranger can never tend to put the *right* of way in dispute: the remedy therefore for these disturbances is the universal remedy of action to recover damages.

4. Disturbance of *tenure* consists in breaking that connection which subsists between the lord and his tenant, and to which the law pays so high a regard, that it will not suffer it to be wantonly dissolved by the act of a third person. So that if there be a tenant-at-will of any lands, and a stranger contrives to drive him away, or inveigle him to leave his tenancy, this the law very justly construes to be a wrong and injury to the lord, and gives him a reparation in damages against the offender.

5. The fifth and last species of disturbance, but by far the most considerable, is that of disturbance of *patronage;* which is a hindrance or obstruction of a patron to present his clerk to a benefice. This injury was distinguished at common law from another species of injury called *usurpation;* which is an absolute ouster or dispossession of the patron, and happens when a stranger, that has no

right, presents a clerk, and he is thereupon admitted and instituted. In which case of usurpation the patron, being thus put out of the only kind of possession of which this kind of property is capable, lost by the common law not only his turn of presenting *pro hâc vice*, but also the absolute and perpetual inheritance of the advowson; so that he could not present again upon the next avoidance, unless in the meantime he recovered his right by a real action, viz., a writ of *right of advowson*; which was a peculiar writ of right, framed for this special purpose, but in every other respect corresponding with other writs of right, and, like them, finally deciding the question of *property*. Thus stood the common law.

But bishops in ancient times, either by carelessness or collusion, frequently instituting clerks upon the presentation of usurpers, and thereby defrauding the real patrons of their right of presentation, it was in substance enacted by statute Westm. 2, that if a possessory action be brought within six months after the avoidance, the patron shall, notwithstanding such usurpation and institution, recover that very presentation, which gives back to him the seisin of the advowson. Yet still, if the true patron omitted to bring his action within six months, the seisin was gained by the usurper, and the patron, to recover it, was driven to the writ of right. To remedy which it was further enacted by statute 7 Ann. c. 18, that no usurpation shall displace the estate or interest of the patron, or turn it to a mere right; but that the true patron may present upon the next avoidance, as if no such usurpation had happened. So that the title of usurpation is now much narrowed, and the law stands upon this reasonable foundation: that if a stranger usurps my presentation, and I do not pursue my right within six months, I shall lose that turn without remedy, for the peace of the church, and as a punishment for my own negligence; but that turn is the only one I shall lose thereby. Usurpation now gains no right to the usurper, with regard to any future avoidance, but only to the present vacancy: it cannot indeed be remedied after six months are past; but during those six months it is only a species of disturbance.

Disturbers of a right of advowson may therefore be these three persons; the pseudo-patron, his clerk, and the ordinary; the pretended patron, by presenting to a church to which he has no right, and thereby making it litigious or disputable; the clerk, by demanding or obtaining institution, which tends to and promotes the same inconvenience; and the ordinary, by refusing to admit the real patron's clerk, or admitting the clerk of the pretender. These disturbances are vexatious and injurious to him who has the right: and therefore if he be not wanting to himself, the law has given him for his relief an action of *quare impedit*; in which the patron is always the plaintiff, and not the clerk. For the law supposes the injury to be offered to him only, by obstructing or refusing the admission of his nominee, and not the clerk, who has no right in him till institution, and of course can suffer no injury.

I proceed, therefore, to inquire into the nature of an action of *quare impedit ;* and shall first premise the usual proceedings previous to the bringing of the action.

Upon the vacancy of a living, the patron, we know, is bound to present within six calendar months, otherwise it will lapse to the bishop. But if the presentation be made within that time, the bishop is bound to admit and institute the clerk, if found sufficient ; unless the church be full, or there be notice of any litigation. For if any opposition be intended, it is usual for each party to enter a *caveat* with the bishop, to prevent his institution of his antagonist's clerk. An institution after a *caveat* entered is void by the ecclesiastical law ; but this the temporal courts pay no regard to, and look upon a *caveat* as a mere nullity. But if two presentations be offered to the bishop upon the same avoidance, the church is then said to become *litigious ;* and, if nothing further be done, the bishop may suspend the admission of either, and suffer a lapse to incur : yet if the patron or clerk on either side request him to award a *jus patronatús,* he is bound to do it. A *jus patronatús* is a commission from the bishop, directed usually to his chancellor and others of competent learning ; who are to summon a jury of six clergymen and six laymen, to inquire into and examine who is the rightful patron ; and if, upon such inquiry made and certificate thereof returned to the commissioners, he admits and institutes the clerk of that patron whom they return as the true one, the bishop secures himself at all events from being a disturber, whatever proceedings may be had afterwards in the temporal courts.

The clerk refused by the bishop may also have a remedy against him in the spiritual court, denominated a *duplex querela ;* which is a complaint in the nature of an appeal from the ordinary to his next immediate superior ; as from a bishop to the archbishop, or from an archbishop to the sovereign in council : and if the superior court adjudges the cause of refusal to be insufficient, it will grant institution to the appellant.

Thus far matters may go on in the mere ecclesiastical course, but in contested presentations they will seldom go so far : for, upon the first delay or refusal of the bishop to admit his clerk, the patron may bring his action of *quare impedit* against the bishop, for the temporal injury done to his property, in disturbing him in his presentation. And, if the delay arises from the bishop alone, as upon pretence of incapacity, or the like, then he only is named in the writ ; but if there be another presentation set up, then the pretended patron and his clerk are also joined in the action; or it may be brought against the patron and clerk, leaving out the bishop; or against the patron only, but it is the usual and safer way to insert all three in the writ.

Immediately on the suing out of the *quare impedit*, if the plaintiff suspects that the bishop will admit the defendant's or any other clerk, pending the suit, he may have a prohibitory writ, called a *ne admittas*, which forbids the bishop to admit any clerk whatsoever till such contention be determined; and if the bishop does, after the receipt of this writ, admit any person, even though the patron's right may have been found in a *jure patronatûs*, then the plaintiff, after he has obtained judgment in the *quare impedit*, may have an action against the bishop, to recover satisfaction in damages for the injury done him by incumbering the church with a clerk pending the suit.

. In the proceedings in a *quare impedit*, the plaintiff must set out. his title at length, and prove at least one presentation in himself, his ancestors, or those under whom he claims; for he must recover by the strength of his own right, and not by the weakness of the defendant's: and he must also show a disturbance before the action brought. Upon this the bishop and the clerk may disclaim all title: save only, the one as ordinary, to admit and institute; and the other as presentee of the patron, who is left to defend his own right. And upon failure of the plaintiff in making out his own title, the defendant is put upon the proof of his, in order to obtain judgment for himself, if needful. But if it be found that the plaintiff has the right, and has commenced his action in due time, then he shall have judgment to recover the presentation; and if the church be full by institution of any clerk, to remove him. But if the church remains still void at the end of the suit, then whichever party the presentation is found to belong to, whether plaintiff or defendant, shall have a writ directed to the bishop *ad admittendum clericum*, reciting the judgment of the court, and ordering him to admit and institute the clerk of the prevailing party; and if upon this order he does not admit him, the patron may sue the bishop for damages.

.There was formerly no limitation with regard to the time within which any actions touching advowsons were to be brought; at least none later than the times of Richard I. and Henry III. And this upon very good reason: because it may very easily happen that the title to an advowson may not come in question, nor the right have opportunity to be tried within sixty years; which is the longest period of limitation assigned by the statute of Henry VIII. A period of limitation has now, however, been established, compounded of the length of time and the number of avoidances together, by 3 & 4 Will. IV. c. 27; the limitation, which is to bar an action of *quare impedit* being that, during which three clerks in succession shall have held the benefice, all of whom shall have obtained possession thereof adversely to the right of the plaintiff, or of some person through whom he claims, provided the times of such incumbencies taken together amount to the full period of sixty years. After an adverse possession of one hundred years, although three incumbencies have not taken place, the alleged right of the claimant is completely barred.

In an action of *quare impedit*, the patron only, and not the clerk, is allowed to sue the disturber. But, by virtue of several acts of parliament, there is one species of presentation, in which a remedy, to be sued in the temporal courts, is put into the hands of the clerks presented, as well as of the owners of the advowson. I mean the presentation of such benefices as belong to Roman Catholic patrons, which are vested in the two universities. Besides the *quare impedit*, which the universities as patrons are entitled to bring, they, or their clerks, are at liberty to file a bill in equity against any person presenting to such livings, and disturbing their right of patronage, or his *cestui que trust*, or any other person whom they have cause to suspect; in order to compel a discovery of any secret trusts, for the benefit of Papists, in evasion of those laws whereby this right of advowson is vested in those learned bodies. This is a particular law, and calculated for a particular purpose : for in no instance but this does the common law permit the clerk himself to interfere in recovering a presentation, of which he is afterwards to have the advantage. But when the clerk is in full possession of the benefice, the law gives him the same possessory remedies to recover his glebe, his rents, his tithes, and other ecclesiastical dues, which it furnishes to the owners of lay property.

CHAPTER IX.

ON INJURIES PROCEEDING FROM, OR AFFECTING THE CROWN.

I. Injuries from the crown—to the person—to property—remedy by petition of right or *monstrans de droit*. II. Injuries affecting the crown—remedy by action—by inquest of office—by *scire facias*, to repeal letters patent— by information in the Exchequer—by *quo warranto*—by *mandamus*.

HAVING in the preceding chapters considered the private wrongs, that may be offered by one subject to another, all of which are redressed by the command and authority of the sovereign in his several courts of justice, I proceed now to inquire into the mode of redressing

those injuries to which the crown itself is a party; which injuries
are either where the crown is the aggressor, and which therefore cannot without a solecism admit of the same kind of remedy; or else is
the sufferer, and which then are usually remedied by peculiar forms
of process, appropriated to the royal prerogative.

I. That the king can do no wrong, is, as we have already seen, a
necessary and fundamental principle of the English constitution.
Whenever therefore it happens, that, by misinformation, or inadvertence, the crown has been induced to invade the private rights of any
of its subjects, though no action will lie against the sovereign, yet
the law has furnished the subject with a decent and respectful mode
of removing that invasion, by informing the crown of the true state
of the matter in dispute: and, as it presumes that to *know of* any
injury and to *redress* it are inseparable in the royal breast, it then
issues as of course, in the sovereign's own name, his orders to his
judges to do justice to the party aggrieved.

The distance between the sovereign and his subjects is such, that
it rarely can happen that any *personal* injury can immediately and
directly proceed from the prince to any private man; and, as it can
so seldom happen, the law in decency supposes that it never will or
can happen at all.   But injuries to the rights of *property* can scarcely
be committed by the crown without the intervention of its officers;
for whom the law in matters of right entertains no respect or delicacy,
but furnishes various methods of detecting the errors or misconduct
of those agents, by whom the sovereign has been deceived, and
induced to do a temporary injustice.

The common law methods of obtaining possession or restitution
from the crown, of either real or personal property, are, 1. By
petition de droit, or petition of right: which is said to owe its origin
to King Edward I.   2. By *monstrans de droit*, manifestation or plea
of right: both of which may be preferred or prosecuted either
in the Chancery or Exchequer.   The former is of use, where the
sovereign is in full possession of any hereditaments or chattels,
and the petitioner suggests such a right as controverts the title of
the crown, grounded on facts disclosed in the petition itself; in
which case, upon this answer being endorsed by the sovereign, *soit
droit fait al partie*, let right be done to the party, a commission
shall issue to inquire of the truth of this suggestion: after the
return of which, the attorney-general is at liberty to plead in bar;
and the merits shall be determined upon issue or demurrer, as in
suits between subject and subject.   But where the right of the party,
as well as the right of the crown, appears upon record, there the
party shall have *monstrans de droit*, which is putting in a claim of

right grounded on facts already acknowledged and established, and praying the judgment of the court, whether upon those facts the crown or the subject has the right. But as this seldom happens, and the remedy by *petition* was extremely tedious and expensive, that by *monstrans* was much enlarged and rendered almost universal, by several statutes, particularly 36 Edw. III. c. 13, and 2 & 3 Edw. VI. c. 8, which also allow inquisitions of office to be traversed or denied, wherever the right of a subject is concerned, except in a very few cases. These proceedings are had in the petty-bag office in the Court of Chancery: and, if upon either of them the right be determined against the crown, the judgment is, *quod manus domini regis amoveuntur et possessio restituatur petenti, salvo jure domini regis.* And by such judgment the crown is instantly out of possession ; so that there needs not the indecent interposition of his own officers to transfer the possession from the sovereign to the party aggrieved.

Besides the common law petition of right, in which the subject, if successful, must nevertheless defray his own costs, a similar method of obtaining redress from the crown has been recently provided by the statute 23 & 24 Vict. c. 34. A petition under this act may be prosecuted in any of the superior courts ; and, provided the fiat of the crown be obtained, may, without any commission of inquiry, be served on the solicitor to the Treasury ; who must then appear and answer it, in the name of the attorney-general, according to the ordinary course of pleading in the court in which the suit is pending. The proceedings after appearance also follow the ordinary practice of the court in suits between subject and subject ; and the effect of the judgment is the same as in petitions of right at common law ; but costs may be recovered both by and from the crown, and in the latter case are defrayed from the public treasury.

II. The method of redressing such injuries as the crown may receive from the subject are,

1. By such usual common law actions, as are consistent with the royal prerogative and dignity. But it would be tedious and difficult to run through every distinction that might be gleaned from our ancient books with regard to this matter ; nor is it in any degree necessary, as much easier and more effectual remedies are usually obtained by such prerogative modes of process, as are peculiarly confined to the crown.

2. Such is that of *inquisition* or *inquest of office*: which is an inquiry made, with the assistance of a jury, by the sovereign's officer, his sheriff, coroner, or escheator, *virtute officii* or by writ to them sent for that purpose, or by commissioners specially appointed,

concerning any matter that entitles the crown to the possession of lands or tenements, goods or chattels. These inquests were more frequent during the continuance of the military tenures: when, upon the death of every tenant of the crown, an *inquisitio post mortem* was held, in order to entitle the king to the marriage or wardship of the heir, and the relief, *primer-seisin*, or other advantages, as the circumstances of the case might justify. To superintend these inquiries, the *Court of Wards and Liveries* was instituted by statute 32 Hen. VIII. c. 46, which was abolished at the restoration of King Charles II., together with the oppressive tenures upon which it was founded.

With regard to other matters, the inquests of office still remain in force, and are taken upon proper occasions. For every jury which tries a man for treason or felony, every coroner's inquest that sits upon a *felo de se*, or one killed by chance-medley, is not only with regard to chattels, but also as to real interests, in all respects an inquest of office; and if they find the treason or felony, the sovereign is thereupon, by virtue of this *office found*, entitled to have his forfeitures. - These inquests of office were devised by law, as an authentic means to give the sovereign his right by solemn matter of record; without which he in general can neither take nor part from anything. For it is a part of the liberties of England, and greatly for the safety of the subject, that the crown may not enter upon or seize any man's possessions upon bare surmises without the intervention of a jury.

With regard to real property, if an office be found for the sovereign, it puts him in immediate possession; and he shall receive all the mesne profits from the time that his title accrued. In order to avoid the possession of the crown, acquired by the finding of such office, the subject may not only have his *petition of right*, which discloses new facts not found by the office, and his *monstrans de droit*, which relies on the facts as found: but also he may in general *traverse* or deny the matter of fact itself, and put it in a course of trial by the common law process of the Court of Chancery.

3. Where the crown has unadvisedly granted anything by letters patent, which ought not to be granted, or where the patentee has done an act that amounts to a forfeiture of the grant, the remedy to repeal the patent is by writ of *scire facias* in chancery. This may be brought either on the part of the crown, in order to resume the thing granted; or, if the grant be injurious to a subject, the sovereign is bound of right to permit him to use his royal name for repealing the patent in a *scire facias*; the proceedings on which resemble those in an ordinary action.

4. An *information* in the Exchequer is a method of recovering money or other chattels, or for obtaining satisfaction in damages for any personal wrong committed in the lands or other possessions of the crown. It differs from an information filed in the Queen's Bench, of which we shall treat in the fourth book of these commentaries; in that *this* is instituted to redress a private wrong, by which the property of the crown is affected; *that* is calculated to punish some public wrong, or heinous misdemeanour in the defendant. The most usual informations are those of *intrusion* and *debt; intrusion,* for any trespass committed on the lands of the crown; and *debt,* upon any contract for moneys due to the crown, or for any forfeiture due to the crown upon the breach of a penal statute.

An information of intrusion may also be resorted to in the case of a *purpresture* upon public property; which occurs when one encroaches, or makes that several to himself, which ought to be common to many. Informations of *debt,* I may add, are most commonly used to recover forfeitures occasioned by transgressing those laws, which are enacted for the establishment and support of the revenue; in which cases the crown now recovers and is liable to pay costs, if unsuccessful, as if the suit were between subject and subject.

5. A writ of *quo warranto* is a writ issuing from the Queen's Bench against him who claims or usurps any office, franchise, or liberty, to inquire by what authority he supports his claim, in order to determine the right. It lies also in case of non-user, or long neglect of a franchise, or misuser, or abuse of it; and commands the defendant to show by what warrant he exercises such a franchise, having never had any grant of it, or having forfeited it by neglect or abuse. In case of judgment for the defendant, he shall have an allowance of his franchise; but in case of judgment for the crown, for that the party is entitled to no such franchise, or has disused or abused it, the franchise is either seized into the sovereign's hands, to be granted out again to whomever he shall please; or, if it be not such a franchise as may subsist in the hands of the crown, there is merely judgment of *ouster,* to turn out the party who usurped it.

The judgment on a writ of *quo warranto* is final and conclusive, even against the crown. Which, together with the length of its process, probably occasioned the introduction of a simpler method of prosecution, by *information* in the nature of a *quo warranto.* This is properly a criminal method of prosecution, as well to punish the usurper by a fine for the usurpation of the franchise, as to oust him, or seize it for the crown; but has long been applied to the mere purposes of trying the civil right, seizing the franchise, or ousting the wrongful possessor; the fine being nominal only. And this method of proceeding is now applied to the decision of corporation disputes between party and party, without any intervention of the prerogative, by virtue of the statute 9 Ann. c. 20; which permits an information in nature of *quo warranto* to be brought with leave of the court, at the relation of any person desiring to prosecute the same who is then styled the *relator*, against any person usurping, intruding into, or unlawfully holding any franchise or office in any city, borough, or town corporate ; provides for its speedy determination, and directs that, if the defendant be convicted, judgment of ouster, as well as a fine, may be given against him, and that the relator shall pay or receive costs according to the event of the suit.

6. The prerogative writ of *mandamus* is also made by the statutes 9 Ann. c. 20, and 6 and 7 Vict. c. 89, s. 5, a most full and effectual remedy, in the first place, for refusal of admission where a person is entitled to an office or place in any such corporation ; and, secondly, for wrongful removal, when a person is legally possessed. These are injuries for which, though redress for the party interested may be had by action, yet as the franchises concern the public, and may affect the administration of justice, this prerogative writ also issues from the Court of Queen's Bench ; commanding, upon good cause shown to the court, the party complaining to be admitted or restored to his office.

We have now gone through the whole circle of civil injuries, and the redress which the laws of England have anxiously provided for each. In which the student cannot but observe that the main difficulty which attends their discussion arises from their great variety, which is apt at our first acquaintance to breed a confusion of ideas, and a kind of distraction in the memory: a difficulty not a little increased by the very unmethodical arrangement in which they are delivered to us by our ancient writers, and the numerous terms of art in which the language of our ancestors has obscured them, Terms of art there will unavoidably be in all sciences; the easy conception and thorough comprehension of which must depend upon frequent and familiar use ; and the more subdivided any branch of science is, the more terms must be used to express the nature of these several subdivisions, and mark out with sufficient precision the ideas they are meant to convey. But I trust that this difficulty, however great it may appear at first view, will shrink to nothing upon a nearer and more frequent approach; and indeed be rather advantageous than of any disservice, by imprinting on the student's mind a clear and distinct notion of the nature of these several remedies.

CHAPTER X.

OF THE PURSUIT OF REMEDIES BY ACTION.

The original writ—The terms—Process—Outlawry—Bill of Middlesex—
Latitat—Quo minus. Writ of summons—Endorsements thereon—Writ of
capias—Arrest—who are privileged from—bail—Service of the writ—
Appearance—Judgment by default—Affidavit of merits—Actions on bills
of exchange, &c.

HAVING pointed out in the preceding pages the *nature* and several
species of courts of justice, wherein remedies are administered for all
sorts of private wrongs; and shown to which of these courts in particular application must be made for redress, according to the distinction of injuries, I defined and explained the specific remedies by
action or suit, provided for every possible degree of wrong or injury.
I am now to examine the *manner* in which these several remedies
are *pursued* and applied. What, therefore, the student may expect
in this and the succeeding chapters, is an account of the method of
proceeding in any of the personal actions we have before spoken of,
in the superior courts of common law at Westminster. The history
of a suit which I shall attempt, will, moreover, afford a general idea
of the conduct of a cause in the courts of the counties palatine, and
in the inferior courts of common law, in cities and boroughs; all
which conform, as near as may be, to the example of the superior
tribunals. And the most natural and perspicuous way of considering the subject will be, I apprehend, to pursue it in the order
wherein the proceedings themselves follow each other, rather than to
distract and subdivide it by any more logical analysis. The general,
therefore, and orderly parts of a suit are these: 1. The writ; 2. The
pleadings; 3. The issue or demurrer; 4. The trial; 5. The judgment, and its incidents; 6. The proceedings in nature of appeals;
7. The execution.

The *original*, or original writ, was formerly the foundation of
every suit. When a person has received an injury, and thinks it
worth his while to demand a satisfaction for it, he is to consider
what redress the law has given for that injury; and thereupon is to
make application to the crown, the fountain of all justice, for that
particular specific remedy which he is entitled to pursue. To this
end he was formerly obliged to sue out, or purchase by paying the
stated fees, an *original*, or original writ, from the Court of Chancery,

which is the *officina justitiæ*, the shop or mint of justice, wherein all the sovereign's writs are framed. This original writ was a mandatory letter from the sovereign in parchment, sealed with his great seal, and directed to the sheriff of the county wherein the injury was committed or supposed so to have been, requiring him to command the wrongdoer or party accused either to do justice to the complainant, or else to appear in the Court of Common Pleas, which we may remember entertained originally all suits between subject and subject, and answer the accusation against him. The day on which the defendant was ordered to appear in court, and on which the sheriff was to bring in the writ and report how far he had obeyed it, was called the *return* of the writ, it being then returned by him to the justices at Westminster, with a statement of the manner in which he had obeyed it, this being also called his *return*. And it was always made returnable at the distance of at least fifteen days from the date or *teste*, that the defendant might have time to come up to Westminster, even from the most remote parts of the kingdom; and upon some day in one of the four *terms* in which the court sits for the despatch of business.

These terms were gradually formed from the canonical constitutions of the church; being indeed no other than those leisure seasons of the year, which were not occupied by the great festivals or fasts, or which were not liable to the general avocations of rural business. Throughout all Christendom, in very early times, the whole year was one continual term for hearing and deciding causes. For the Christian magistrates, to distinguish themselves from the heathens, who were extremely superstitious in the observation of their *dies fasti et nefasti*, went into a contrary extreme, and administered justice upon all days alike. Till at length the church interposed, and exempted certain holy seasons from being profaned by the tumult of forensic litigations. As, particularly, the time of Advent and Christmas, which gave rise to the winter vacation; the time of Lent and Easter, which created that in the spring; the time of Pentecost, which produced the third; and the long vacation, between Midsummer and Michaelmas, which was allowed for the haytime and harvest. All Sundays also, and some particular festivals, as the days of the Purification, Ascension, and some others, were included in the same prohibition.

The portions of time, that were not included within these prohibited seasons, fell naturally into a fourfold division, and from some festival day that immediately preceded their commencement, were denominated the terms of St. Hilary, of Easter, of the Holy Trinity, and of St. Michael. Their commencement and termination have been since regulated by several acts of parliament; but the courts may nevertheless appoint days after term, on which they shall sit for the despatch of business.

There were in each of these terms stated days called *days in banc, dies in banco,* on some one of which all original writs must have been made returnable, and on some of which the court sat to take *essoigns,* or excuses, for such as did not appear according to the exigency of the writ: wherefore this was usually called the *essoign day* of the term. For on every return day in the term, the person summoned had three days of grace beyond the day named in the writ, in which to make his appearance; and if he appeared on the fourth day inclusive, *quarto die post,* it was sufficient. But essoigns have long been abolished; and the sittings of the courts *in banco* are now on every day of the term, and on such days after term as may be fixed for that purpose.

The next step for carrying on the suit, after suing out the original, was called the *process;*[*] which was the method taken by the law to compel a compliance with the original writ, of which the primary step was by giving the party notice to obey it *by summons,* to appear in court at the return of the original writ. If the defendant disobeyed this verbal monition, the next process was by writ of *attachment* or *pone,* so called from the words, "*pone per vadium et* "*salvos plegios,* put by gage and safe pledges A.B. the defendant." And thereby the sheriff was commanded to attach him, by taking *gage,* that is, certain of his goods, which he should forfeit if he did not appear; or by making him find *safe pledges* or sureties who should be amerced in case of his non-appearance. If after *attachment* the defendant neglected to appear, he not only forfeited this security, but was moreover to be further compelled by writ of *distringas,* or *distress infinite;* which was a subsequent process, commanding the sheriff to distrain the defendant from time to time, and continually afterwards, by taking his goods and the profits of his lands, which were called *issues,* and which by the common law he forfeited to the crown if he did not appear. The issues might be sold, if the court should so direct, in order to defray the reasonable costs of the plaintiff.

- And here by the common law the process ended, the defendant, if he had any substance, being gradually stripped of it all by repeated distresses, till he rendered obedience to the original writ. But, in

---

[*] This was sometimes called *original* process, being founded upon the original writ; and also to distinguish it from *mesne* or intermediate process, which issues, pending the suit, upon some collateral interlocutory matter; as to summon witnesses, and the like. *Mesne* process is also sometimes put in contradistinction to *final* process, or process of *execution;* and then it signifies all such process as intervenes between the beginning and end of a suit.

cases of injury accompanied with force, the law provided also a process against the defendant's *person* in case he neglected to appear, or had no substance whereby to be attached; subjecting his body to imprisonment by the writ of *capias ad respondendum.* Whence arose a practice of commencing the suit by bringing an original writ of trespass *quare clausum fregit,* for breaking the plaintiff's close *vi et armis;* which subjected the defendant's person to be arrested by writ of *capias;* and then afterwards, by connivance of the court, the plaintiff proceeded to prosecute for any other less forcible injury. This practice ultimately became the ordinary mode of commencing an action; and in course of time it became usual in practice, to sue out the *capias* in the first instance, upon a supposed return of the sheriff; and afterwards a fictitious original was drawn up, with a proper return thereupon, in order to give the proceedings a colour of regularity. When this *capias* was delivered to the sheriff, he by his under-sheriff granted a warrant to his inferior bailiffs, to execute it on the defendant. And if the sheriff of Oxfordshire, in which county the injury we may suppose was committed and the action was laid, could not find the defendant in his jurisdiction, he returned that he was not found, *non est inventus,* in his bailiwick: whereupon another writ issued, called a *testatum capias,* directed to the sheriff of the county where the defendant was supposed to reside, as of Berkshire, reciting the former writ, and that it was *testified, testatum est,* that the defendant lurked or wandered in *his* bailiwick, wherefore he was commanded to take him, as in the former *capias.* But here also, when the action was brought in one county, and the defendant lived in another, it was usual, for saving trouble, time, and expense, to make out a *testatum capias* at the first, supposing not only an original, but also a former *capias,* to have been granted, which in fact never had been. And this fiction also soon became the settled practice.

But where a defendant absconded, and the plaintiff would proceed to an outlawry against him, an original writ must then have been sued out regularly, and after that a *capias.* And if the sheriff could not find the defendant upon the first writ of *capias,* and returned a *non est inventus,* there issued out an *alias* writ, and after that a *pluries,* to the same effect as the former. And, if a *non est inventus* was returned upon all of them, then a writ of *exigent* or *exigi facias* might be sued out, which required the sheriff to cause the defendant to be proclaimed, required, or exacted, in five county courts successively, to render himself; and if he did, then to take him as in a *capias;* but if he did not appear, and was returned *quinto exactus,* he should then be outlawed by the coroners of the county. *Outlawry* is putting a man out of the protection of the law, so that he is incapable to bring an action for redress of injuries; and it is also

                                                                        B

attended with a forfeiture of all one's goods and chattels to the crown. If after outlawry the defendant appeared publicly, he might be arrested by a writ of *capias utlagatum* and committed till the outlawry had been reversed; but this was done as a matter of course, on the defendant's entering an appearance, it being considered only as a process to compel an appearance.

Such was the first process in the court of *Common Pleas.* In the *King's Bench* a plaintiff might proceed by *original* writ, but the more usual method was by a species of process entitled a *Bill of Middlesex;* so entitled, because the court generally sat in that county. This bill was always founded on a *plaint* of trespass *quare clausum fregit,* and was a kind of *capias,* which accusation indeed it was, that gave the court of King's Bench jurisdiction in civil causes, which must have been served on the defendant, if found by the sheriff; but, if he returned "*non est inventus,*" then there issued out a writ of *latitat,* to the sheriff of another county, as Berks; which recited the bill of Middlesex and testified that the defendant, "*latitat et discurrit,*" lurked and wandered about in Berks; and therefore commanded the sheriff to take him, and have his body in court on the day of the return; but in the King's Bench, as in the Common Pleas, it ultimately became the practice to sue out a *latitat* upon a supposed, and not an actual, *bill of Middlesex.*

In the Exchequer the first process was by a writ of *quo minus,* in order to give the court a jurisdiction over pleas between party and party, in which the plaintiff was alleged to be the king's farmer or debtor, and that the defendant had done him the injury complained of, *quo minus sufficiens existit,* by which he was the less able to pay the king his rent or debt. And upon this the defendant might have been arrested as upon a *capias* from the Common Pleas.

Thus differently did the three courts set out at first, in the commencent of a suit, in order to entitle the two courts of King's Bench and Exchequer to hold plea in causes between subject and subject; which by the original constitution of Westminster Hall they were not empowered to do.

The multiplicity of these proceedings often occasioned great inconvenience in practice, and the use of different kinds of process in personal actions was therefore put an end to by the statute 2 Will. IV. c. 39. Five other forms of writs were substituted : and the names of *John Doe* and *Richard Roe,* who, I may mention here, were always the pledges of prosecution for the plaintiff, as well as the common bail for the defendant when he was arrested on the *capias,* were no longer required. The writs of summons thus provided remained in use until the procedure to compel appearance was further modified by the statute 1 & 2 Vict. c. 110, by which the practice of beginning an action by arresting the defendant was entirely abolished. These changes in procedure were confined to personal actions; real actions, of which three only remain—*dower, right of dower*, and *quare impedit*—were still to be commenced by original writ. The enactments of the statute 2 Will. IV. c. 39, have more recently, however, been entirely superseded by those of the Common Law Procedure Acts of 1852, 1854, and 1861; one uniform method of commencing an action has been provided; and a plaintiff is for the first time enabled, on the non-appearance of a defendant, to proceed at once to judgment and execution.

All actions are now commenced by a writ of summons, under the seal of the court in which the action is brought, directed to the defendant; whom it commands to cause an appearance to be entered for him at the office of the court; warning him, that in default of his so doing the plaintiff may proceed to judgment and execution. The time allowed to enter this appearance depends on circumstances. If the defendant resides *within* the jurisdiction of the court, it is *eight days*; if *beyond* the jurisdiction, such further time as is reasonably necessary in the circumstances. For the plaintiff is not allowed to obtain a judgment in default of appearance, against a defendant who is resident out of England, except by the express leave of a judge; who must above all things be satisfied that the defendant has had proper time allowed him to appear to the action.

Not less careful is the law in securing for the defendant full information as to the person who is suing him; so that he may know not only whether the plaintiff's claim is just, but also to whom to address himself for a settlement of the action, if such a course be desirable; for every writ must have indorsed on it the name and abode of the attorney actually suing it out; or if no attorney is employed, then the name and abode of the plaintiff himself. The court has thus also an opportunity of ascertaining who is responsible for any irregularity in the execution of its process; as on a writ without this indorsement, a judgment by default would be set aside; the defendant having, through the plaintiff's own negligence, been deprived of the information and opportunity of avoiding litigation which the law affords him.

It is with the same view of affording the defendant the fullest information as to the nature of the proceedings, that in those cases, in which the claim is of a specific nature or amount, as in a suit for *dower* or an action of *debt*, the plaintiff is further required to indorse on the writ the nature of his claim or the amount of his demand; so as to give the defendant an opportunity of putting an end to the action at once, by yielding the one or making payment of the other.

We have seen that on the former process by *capias*, the sheriff, by the connivance of the courts, instead of arresting the defendant, gave him notice to appear to the action; no actual arrest was required, and merely nominal bail being taken. But if the plaintiff made *affidavit* that the cause of action amounted to ten pounds or upwards, then he might arrest the defendant, and make him put in substantial sureties for his appearance, called *special bail*; the sheriff, or his officer the bailiff, being then obliged actually to take the body of the defendant, and to return the writ with a *cepi corpus* indorsed thereon. The issue of a *capias* is now allowed, however, in those cases, only in which a judge is satisfied that the plaintiff has a cause of action against the defendant to the amount of *twenty pounds* or upwards, and that there is probable cause for believing that *the defendant is about to quit England.* A writ of *capias* may then be sued out along with the writ of summons, and the defendant, when arrested, will remain in custody until he finds bail, or makes a deposit in the action.

An *arrest* must be by corporal seizing or touching the defendant's body; after which the bailiff may justify breaking open the house in which he is to take him: otherwise he has no such power, but must watch his opportunity to arrest him. For every man's house is looked upon by the law to be his castle of defence and asylum, wherein he should suffer no violence. Which principle is carried so far in the civil law, that for the most part not so much as a common citation or summons, much less an arrest, can be executed upon a man within his own walls.

The queen's chaplains and certain other officials are privileged from arrest; and the servants in ordinary of the sovereign cannot be taken unless upon leave obtained from the lord chamberlain. Ambassadors and ministers of foreign states, and their domestics, are also privileged from arrest; consuls and their servants are not, nor are the couriers or messengers of foreign ministers. Peers and peeresses are privileged, so are members of parliament during the session, and for forty days after it. The judges of the superior courts cannot be arrested; and barristers or attorneys attending any court upon business cannot be taken during their actual attendance, which includes their necessary going to, waiting in, and returning from court. Certificated bankrupts and persons having an order of protection, should not be arrested; neither can a married woman be taken; nor should an infant, who, however, is left to plead his infancy. Seamen and soldiers have certain privileges in this respect conferred by the annual Mutiny acts. Clergymen performing divine service, and not merely staying in the church with a fraudulent design, are for the time privileged from arrest; as likewise members of convocation actually attending thereon. Suitors, witnesses, and other persons, necessarily attending any courts of record upon business, are not to be arrested during their actual attendance, which includes their necessary coming and returning. And no arrest can be made in the presence of the sovereign, nor in any place where the queen's justices are actually sitting. Lastly, no arrest can be made, nor process served upon a Sunday, except for treason, felony, or breach of the peace.

When the defendant is arrested he has twenty-four hours allowed him, before going to gaol, to procure bail, to get money to deposit with the sheriff, or to apply for his discharge from custody. For when regularly arrested he must either go to prison for safe custody; deposit the amount indorsed on the *capias*, and ten pounds as costs, with the sheriff; or put in *special bail*, or security for his appearance to the action, and obedience to the judgment of the court of Bail—so called, from the French *bailler*, to deliver because the defendant is bailed, or delivered to his sureties, upon their giving security for his appearance, and is supposed to continue in their friendly custody instead of going to gaol. They usually enter into a *bail-bond*, whereby they undertake, that if the defendant be condemned in the action he shall pay the costs and condemnation, or render himself a prisoner, or that they will pay it for him: which recognizance is transmitted to the court in a slip of parchment entitled a *bail-piece*. And, if excepted to, the bail must be *perfected*; that is, they must *justify* themselves in court, or before the commissioner in the country, by swearing themselves housekeepers, and each of them to be worth the full sum for which they are bail, after payment of all their debts. The bail may be discharged at any time, by surrendering the defendant into custody, within the time allowed by law; for which purpose they are at all times entitled to a warrant to apprehend him.

But to return to the writ of summons, on which, as we have already seen, the plaintiff, in suits for a *debt* or other *liquidated demand*, must indorse his claim. It is otherwise in actions brought to recover *damages*, as therein no indorsement is required; for until the jury shall assess the amount, it is unascertained. Such damages, indeed, constitute in general the only redress which courts of law can give, as they can only redress a wrong already done, having no means of preventing an injury from being committed, of restraining a breach of contract, or prohibiting its being attempted. When, therefore, the plaintiff seeks to prevent a *threatened* injury, he must resort to the Court of Chancery: when he has already sustained a wrong, he may not only maintain an action for damages, but in the same suit obtain a prohibition of the repetition or continuance of the wrongful act complained of; an injunction for this purpose being obtainable at any stage of the cause at which it becomes necessary, provided an indorsement to that effect is made on the writ. So the plaintiff may indorse on his writ a notice that he will demand a mandamus, in order that the duty of a breach of which he complains may be performed. But this writ being practically a writ of execution, its nature, and the mode in which it is enforced, falls to be described hereafter.

The writ of summons is thus a letter missive from the sovereign, notifying the defendant that the plaintiff demands from the crown, as the fountain of justice, redress for some injury which he has sustained at his hands; and therefore commanding him to appear in one of the established courts of justice, there to abide the determination of the judges; to whom, as we have already seen, the crown has delegated its whole judicial authority. The defendant is made acquainted with the plaintiff's claim, by the *service of the writ*, which is usually effected by the delivery to him of a copy, the original being shown if it be required. And this service, be it observed, ought always, if practicable, to be *personal*, and to be made by some one who knows the defendant and can swear to his identity. For, as a general rule, there is no equivalent for personal service, except an undertaking by an attorney to appear; which undertaking will, if necessary, be enforced by attachment, every attorney being an officer of the court, and subject to its direct control. If, however, the defendant keeps out of the way, so that personal service cannot be effected, the plaintiff must then use all reasonable efforts to do so; and if he can then satisfy a judge that such efforts have been made, and either that the writ has come to the defendant's knowledge, or that he wilfully evades service of it, authority may be obtained to proceed as if personal service had been effected. The service of the writ is thus in all cases the most important step in the cause, as it is the foundation of all the future proceedings therein.

The next step ordinarily taken in a defended action is the *entry of an appearance* by the defendant; for if this be not done by him, the plaintiff may sign judgment by default, and proceed to recover the debt or damages claimed by him by the ordinary process of execution. If, however, the defendant has inadvertently neglected to appear in time, so that a judgment by default has been signed against him, he is not debarred from still disputing the justice of the plaintiff's claim; for it has long been a matter of course to let in a defendant to defend on an *affidavit of merits*. He must, however, account in some way for not having entered an appearance; he must also generally pay the costs of the application; and as he is obtaining an interference of the court on his behalf calculated to delay the plaintiff, it is generally made a condition of his being allowed to appear, that he shall plead on the same day; and in some cases he may be ordered to bring money into court.

There is a peculiar, and indeed exceptional, mode of proceeding which may be adopted by the holder of an unpaid bill of exchange or promissory note, which I have reserved for consideration in this place.   It was first given by the statute 18 & 19 Vict. c. 67; previous to which the remedy open to the holder of an unpaid bill or note was precisely the same as that of a plaintiff in any other action; the defendant being at liberty to appear and plead any number of fictitious defences, the sole effect of which was to force the plaintiff to trial, and create delay and expense. This practice became so much a reproach to the administration of justice, that the legislature thought fit to place under restriction the right even of a defendant to appear to the action. All actions on bills or notes, brought *within six months* after the same have become payable, *may* consequently be commenced by a writ, which, instead of command-ing the defendant to enter an appearance, *warns* him that unless within *twelve* days after the service he obtains leave to appear, and do appear accordingly, the plaintiff may proceed to judgment and execution. The defendant cannot then simply appear; he must, if he has a defence, apply for and obtain leave to appear; and unless he obtains such leave within the time allowed, judgment by default may be signed and execution issued, eight days afterwards. This leave may, however, be obtained as a matter of right, on the de-fendant bringing into court the sum indorsed on the writ; or upon affidavits, disclosing a *legal* or *equitable* defence. But terms may also be imposed on the defendant, as for instance, that he shall give security for the amount claimed. On the other hand, he is not fore-closed by a judge's refusal of leave to appear; for even after judg-ment the court will permit a defence to the action, if special circum-stances can be stated to justify their doing so; the object of the law being not to shut out the defendant from taking the opinion of a jury in his case; but solely to prevent actions, brought on these most important instruments of commerce, from being defended on frivolous and vexatious grounds merely to obtain delay.

Thus much for process which in general is only meant to bring the defendant into court, in order to contest the suit, and abide the determination of the law.   When, having received, as we have seen he now does, full notice of the nature of the plaintiff's claim, the de-fendant does not appear in court to dispute it, he is considered to admit the justice of the demand; and the sovereign then, by his delegates the judges, sitting in his courts of justice, awards to the plaintiff that redress to which he is by law entitled, and which by

his writ he has demanded. When the defendant appears, either in
person or by attorney, as a prisoner or out upon bail, then follow the
pleadings between the parties, which we shall consider at large in the
next chapter.

CHAPTER XI.

OF PLEADING.

Declaration—Venue—Conclusion—*Non pros*—Claim of cognizance—Security
for costs—Inspection—Interpleader—Pleas in abatement or in bar—to
the jurisdiction—to the disability of plaintiff or defendant—to the action,
either confessing or denying—Payment and Set-off—The general issue—
Special pleas—Statutes of limitation—Not guilty—Estoppel—The replication—The rejoinder, &c.—New assignment—Departure—Joinder of issue.

WHEN the defendant has appeared, both parties are theoretically *in
court ;* and the plaintiff ought now to "declare" to the judges what
is his cause of action. This is usually ascertained from the pleadings, which are the mutual altercations between the plaintiff and defendant; and which formerly were put in by their counsel *ore tenus,*
or *vivâ voce,* in court, and then minuted down by the chief clerks or
prothonotaries; whence in our old law French the pleadings are
frequently denominated the *parol.* That practice gave way in time
to the more convenient course of producing previously-prepared
written pleadings; which innovation was in its turn supplanted by
our modern system, all the pleadings in an action being now simply
interchanged between the attorneys or parties, if they appear in
person; and only solemnly entered on the records of the court,
when it becomes necessary to do so, as for the purpose of giving them
in evidence.

There is a course open to the parties, however, which may render
formal pleadings unnecessary. For as the object of all pleading is to
ascertain what is in issue between the litigants, whether they
disagree upon a matter of *fact* or on a question of *law,* there is
no reason, if they can ascertain this without pleadings, why these
should be resorted to. And they are accordingly allowed to take the
simplest mode of stating the question at issue for the decision of the
proper tribunal. For if they differ on a matter of *fact,* the truth
must be determined by a jury; if they differ as to the *law,* arising
from certain facts, the court alone shall decide between them.

But if, as is most usual, the parties cannot or do not agree that the matters in dispute betwixt them shall be decided in this way, these must be evolved by the pleadings; the first of which is the *declaration, narratio,* or *count,* anciently called the *tale* : in which the plaintiff sets forth his cause of complaint at length; with the additional circumstances of time and place, when and where the injury was committed, where these are requisite.

In *local* actions, as for damages for an actual trespass, or for waste, &c., affecting land, the plaintiff must lay his declaration, or declare his injury to have happened in the very county and place that it really did happen; but in *transitory* actions, for injuries that might have happened anywhere, as debt, detinue, slander, and the like, the plaintiff may declare in what county he pleases, and then the trial must be had in that county in which the declaration is laid. But the *venue* or *visne,* that is, the *vicinia* or neighbourhood in which the injury is declared to be done, and from which the jury is to be summoned, will always be changed on an affidavit of *special facts,* as that a fair trial cannot be had in the county where it is laid, or that the witnesses live in the county to which it is proposed to change it.

The declaration concludes with a statement of what the plaintiff claims from the defendant. In most cases it is simply a sum of money : in *detinue* it is a return of his goods, and damages for their detention ; or if they have been returned, damages only. In those cases in which he has claimed an injunction, this must be repeated in the declaration ; and so where he has indorsed a claim for a writ of mandamus. For the court can only award that which the plaintiff demands as the redress to which he is entitled.

If, however, the plaintiff neglects to deliver a declaration by the end of the term next after the defendant appears, or is guilty of other delays or defaults against the rules of law in any subsequent stage of the action, he is adjudged *not to follow* or pursue his remedy as he ought to do, and thereupon a *nonsuit* or *non prosequitur,* is entered; and he is said to be *nonpros'd.* And for thus deserting his complaint, after making a false claim or complaint, *pro falso clamore suo,* he shall pay costs to the defendant. A *discontinuance* is somewhat similar to a nonsuit; for when a plaintiff leaves a chasm in the proceedings of his cause, as by not continuing it as the law requires, the suit is discontinued, and the defendant is no longer bound to attend : but the plaintiff must begin again, by suing out a new writ. Thus if the plaintiff takes no step in the cause for *a year,* he will be out of court, and his action entirely gone.

When the plaintiff has stated his case in the declaration, it is incumbent on the defendant within a reasonable time to make his

defence by putting in a *plea;* else the plaintiff will at once recover
judgment by *default,* or *nihil dicit* of the defendant. But before
defence made, if at all, *cognizance* of the suit must be *claimed;*
which may occur when any person or body corporate has the
franchise, of *holding pleas* within a particular limited jurisdiction.
Upon this claim of cognizance, if allowed, all proceedings shall cease
in the superior court, the plaintiff being at liberty to pursue his
remedy in the special jurisdiction. As, when a scholar, or other
privileged person of the universities of Oxford or Cambridge, is
impleaded in the courts at Westminster, for any cause of action
whatsoever, unless upon a question of freehold. In these cases, the
chancellor may put in a claim of cognizance; which if made in due
time and form, and with due proof of the facts alleged, is regularly
allowed by the courts. But it must be demanded before defence is
made; for this is a submission to the jurisdiction of the superior
court, and the delay is a *laches* in the lord of the franchise.

Assuming that the plaintiff has declared, the defendant must put
in his *plea* within eight days after *notice to plead;* for if he neglect
to do so the plaintiff may sign judgment against him for his default
by *nil dicit;* unless, indeed, the defendant has obtained *time to
plead.* This may be had by the order of a judge; who will, however, put the defendant on terms, to accept a short notice of trial or
otherwise, so that the plaintiff shall not be delayed by reason of any
indulgence accorded to his adversary.

There are some other proceedings too, which may be taken by a
defendant before he puts in his plea. Thus, the defendant, if the
plaintiff resides beyond the jurisdiction of the court, may apply for
and obtain *security for costs;* he may obtain *particulars of the
plaintiff's demand,* in order that he may know the precise nature of
the claim against him; he may obtain *inspection* of the bond,
or other instrument, upon which the action is brought, or
he may *administer interrogatories* to the plaintiff, as to *facts* or
documents which are required for his defence; as indeed the plaintiff may also do in order to make out his own case. All these steps
can be taken only by order of a judge. Again, if the defendant
does not claim any interest in the money or goods for which the
plaintiff is suing, and they are claimed by some other party, he may
apply to a judge for an *Interpleader* order, whereby the third party
is called upon to appear and state his claim, and maintain or relin-
quish it, his failing to do so being for ever after a bar to his prosecuting it against the defendant. Another application which may be
made by several defendants to several different actions, is for a
consolidation rule, they undertaking to abide the event of one of
them, as in the case of several actions being brought against under-
writers on a policy of insurance. In some actions again, the

defendant may demand a *view* of the thing in question, in order to ascertain its identity and other circumstances. And in real actions the tenant may pray in *aid*, or call for assistance of another to help him to plead, because of the feebleness or imbecility of his own estate; thus a tenant for life may pray in aid of him that hath the inheritance in remainder or reversion. When any of these proceedings are resorted to, a *stay of proceedings* ought at the same time to be obtained, for on the expiration of the eight days, if no stay shall have been obtained, the defendant must put in his excuse or plea.

Pleas are of two sorts; *dilatory* pleas, and pleas *to the action*. Dilatory pleas are such as tend merely to delay or put off the suit, by questioning the propriety of the remedy, rather than by denying the injury: pleas to the action are such as dispute the very cause of suit. The former kind of plea is usually termed a *plea in abatement*, because it shows ground for *abating* the proceedings. The plea to the suit itself is called a *plea in bar*, and is the substantial answer to the action.

Pleas, of either nature, must be pleaded in an established order, so invariable, that all pleas prior in the series to the plea pleaded are held to be waived. This order is as follows :—

1. To the *jurisdiction* of the court: which is a plea in bar, alleging, that it ought not to hold plea of the injury complained of; as if a suit be brought in an inferior court of common law in respect of a cause of action that did not arise within the jurisdiction thereof.

2. To the *disability of the plaintiff*, by reason whereof he is incapable to commence the suit, as, that he is an alien enemy, outlawed or attainted of treason, or to continue it, as that some person has not been joined who ought to have been a co-plaintiff, or that some person is included as a co-plaintiff who has no right to sue. The *non-joinder* or *misjoinder* of a plaintiff, as these errors are technically called, may, however, be amended.

3. To the *disability of the defendant*, which is a plea in abatement, and can be pleaded in only one instance, that of the *non-joinder* of a defendant in an action on *contract*. For in actions of *tort* the plaintiff may always remedy a *misjoinder* of defendants, by entering a *nolle prosequi*, as to the party misjoined, otherwise at the trial he will be acquitted; while in such actions there can be no plea for *non-joinder*, the maxim of the law being, that there shall be no contribution among wrongdoers, but that each shall be liable to the party injured for the full damage he has sustained. In actions *on contract* this plea is allowed, because, although each contractor is

liable to the plaintiff for the whole damage he has sustained by reason of the breach of contract, yet is each entitled to contribution from his co-contractors. But here, also, the plaintiff is at liberty to amend his writ and declaration, and proceed with the action against all the parties.

Misnaming the defendant formerly afforded ground for a plea in abatement; so did the giving him a wrong addition, as *esquire* instead of *knight*; and the death of either party is, at common law, at once an abatement of the suit. And in actions merely personal, arising *ex delicto*, for wrongs actually done or committed by the defendant, as trespass, battery, and slander, the rule is that *actio personalis moritur cum personâ*; and it never shall be revived, either by or against the executors or other representatives. For neither the executors of the plaintiff have received, nor those of the defendant have committed, in their own personal capacity, any manner of wrong or injury. But in actions arising *ex contractu* by breach of promise and the like, where the right descends to the representatives of the plaintiff, or survives, if there be more plaintiffs than one, and those of the defendant have assets to answer the demand, though the suits indeed abate by the death of the parties, yet they may always be revived against or by the executors : being, indeed, rather actions against the property than the person, in which the executors have now the same interest that their testator had before. In the same way, on the death of the plaintiff, or his bank-ruptcy, by which, as we saw in the second book of these commentaries, his rights of action are transferred to his assignees, or in case of the marriage of a female plaintiff, or the death or marriage of a female defendant, the action may be revived by or against the party to be substituted in the suit, as the case may be. For if any of these events occur after a writ is issued, or in the course of the pleading, a suggestion may be entered on the roll, the truth of which may be tried, if it be denied, and the action proceeded with as in the ordinary course; so that no abatement of the suit now takes place if the parties choose to continue it.

4. After all these pleas comes the plea *to the action ;* that is, the *plea in bar*, or answer to the merits of the complaint. This is done by confessing or denying it.

A confession of the whole complaint is not very usual, for then the defendant would probably end the matter sooner ; or not plead at all, but suffer judgment to go by default. Yet sometimes after tender and refusal of a debt, if the creditor harasses his debtor with an action, it then becomes necessary for the defendant to acknow-ledge the debt, and plead the tender; adding that he has always been ready, *tout temps prist*, and still is ready, *uncore prist*, to discharge it : for a tender by the debtor and refusal by the creditor will in all cases discharge the costs, but not the debt itself. But frequently the defendant confesses one *part* of the complaint, and traverses or denies the rest; in order to avoid the expense of carrying that part to a formal trial, which he has no ground to litigate. A species of this sort of confession is the *payment of money into court*: which is necessary upon pleading a tender, and is itself a kind of tender to the plaintiff, by paying into the hands of the proper officer of the court as much as the defendant acknowledges to be due, together with the costs hitherto incurred, in order to prevent the expense of any further proceedings. This the defendant may do in all personal actions, except assault, false imprisonment, libel, slander, malicious arrest or prosecution, and seduction. And if after the money is paid in, the plaintiff proceeds in his suit, it is at his own peril; for if he does not prove more due than is so paid into court, he shall be nonsuited and pay the defendant costs, but he shall still have the money so paid in, for that the defendant has acknowledged to be his due. To this head may also be referred the practice of what is called a *set-off*: whereby the defendant acknowledges the justice of the plaintiff's demand on the one hand; but on the other sets up a demand of his own, to counterbalance that of the plaintiff, either in the whole or in part: as, if the plaintiff sues for ten pounds due on a note of hand, the defendant may set off nine pounds due to himself for merchandise sold to the plaintiff, and in case he *pleads* such set-off, he must pay the remaining balance into court, or plead some other plea in regard to it.

Pleas, that totally deny the cause of complaint, are either the *general* issue, or a *special* plea.

1. The *general* issue is what traverses and denies at once the whole declaration, without offering any special matter whereby to evade it. As in trespass, *non culpabilis*, not guilty; in debt upon contract, *nunquam indebitatus*, that he never was indebted; in debt on bond, *non est factum*, it is not his deed; on an *assumpsit, non assumpsit*, he made no such promise: or in an action on a warranty, that he did not warrant, or on an agreement, that he did not agree. These pleas are called the general issue, because, by importing an absolute and general denial of what is alleged in the declaration, they amount at once to an issue: by which we mean a fact affirmed on one side and denied on the other.

2. Special pleas, *in bar*, of the plaintiff's demand, are very various, according to the circumstances of the defendant's case. As in actions on contract a general release, an accord, an award made in an arbitration, conditions unperformed, payment before action, or

some other fact which precludes the plaintiff from his action. A *justification* is likewise a special plea in bar: as in actions of assault and battery, *son assault demesne*, that it was the plaintiff's own original assault; in trespass to real property, that the defendant was using his right of way, or that he entered to abate a nuisance after notice given to the plaintiff to do so; or, in an action of slander, that the plaintiff is really as bad a man as the defendant said he was.

Also a man may plead the statutes of limitation in bar: or the time limited by certain acts of parliament, beyond which no plaintiff can lay his cause of action. As in an action for money secured by a mortgage, or otherwise charged upon *land*, or for *rent* on a *lease by deed*, or on a *bond* or other *specialty*, that the claim had not accrued on plaintiff, or those under whom he claims, within *twenty years*. But this plea is very rare, for if there has been a partial payment of principal or interest, or an acknowledgment in writing, which in such cases is more than likely, then the date of the last payment or of the acknowledgment in writing, is that from which this period of twenty years runs.

It is different in actions of trespass, or for injuries to personal property, of detinue, trover, replevin, debt on simple contract, and some others. Here the action need only be brought within *six years* after the cause of action accrued; and the statute of limitations, or *actio non accrevit infra sex annos*, is accordingly by no means an unfrequent plea. The period is less in some actions of *tort*. For slander, for instance, it is two years; and in all these cases, if the party entitled to sue, or liable to be sued, labours under any disability, the time of limitation does not begin to run till that disability is removed. Thus if the person entitled to sue happens, when the cause of action accrues, to be an infant, or a feme-covert or *non compos*, he may sue within the same period allowed him according to the nature of the action, after the removal of either disability. But the disability must exist *at the time* when the cause of action accrues to or against the party under disability; for if the period of limitation has once begun to run, no subsequent disability can suspend or stop it. And a rule similar to that I have already mentioned applies also to the sexennial limitation as to debts on simple contract. These are, in legal phrase, taken *out of the statute*, by any *payment* on account of principal or interest, or by an *acknowledgment in writing*, any one of which is sufficient to raise a fresh *assumpsit* or implied promise to pay the debt itself.

I may add here, that all actions on penal statutes, where any forfeiture is to the crown alone, must be sued within *two* years; and where the forfeiture is to a subject, or to the crown and a subject, within *one* year after the offence committed; and that by various statutes, actions against judges of the county courts, justices of the peace, constables, the local authorities of districts, and other persons holding public offices, must be brought within *six*, in some cases *twelve*, in some instances *three*, months after the cause of action arose. These different periods of limitation it is not, however, necessary to specify.

The use of these statutes of limitation is to preserve the peace of the kingdom, and to prevent those innumerable perjuries which might ensue, if a man were allowed to bring an action for any injury committed at any distance of time. Upon both these accounts the law therefore holds, that *interest reipublicæ ut sit finis litium*: and upon the same principle the Athenian laws in general prohibited all actions where the injury was committed *five* years before the complaint was made.

A defendant may in some cases plead in bar that he has had no notice of action; to which, by various statutes, justices of the peace, constables, officers of the local boards, officers of the revenue, surveyors of highways, and other persons having public duties to perform, are entitled, when sued for anything done by them, in virtue or in execution or supposed execution of their office. This notice of action, which is necessary in other instances besides those I have mentioned, is required that the defendant may have an opportunity of tendering amends to the plaintiff; and it must, in general, be given one calendar month at least before the action is brought. These officials are also further privileged to plead simply "*not guilty*," adding the words, "*by statute*," in order that under this plea they may set up any special defence that they are entitled to.

An *estoppel* is likewise a special plea in bar; which happens where a man has done some act, or executed some deed, which estops or precludes him from averring anything to the contrary. As where a statement of a particular fact is made in the recital of a bond or other instrument, and a contract is made with reference to that recital, it is not, as between the parties to the instrument, competent to the party bound to deny the recital. And an *equitable defence* or such facts as would in a court of equity be a complete answer to the case of the plaintiff, and afford ground for a perpetual injunction, may also be pleaded specially; so as to constitute a good plea in bar.

When the plea of the defendant is thus put in, if it does not amount to an issue or total contradiction of the declaration, but only evades it, the plaintiff may plead again, and reply to the defendant's plea: either traversing it, that is, totally denying it; as, if on an action upon a bond the defendant pleads *solvit ad diem*, that he paid the money when due; here the plaintiff in his *replica-*

tion may totally traverse this plea, by denying that the defendant paid it: or, he may allege new matter in contradiction to the defendant's plea; or the replication may *confess and avoid* the plea, by some new matter or distinction consistent with the plaintiff's former declaration. Thus in an action for trespassing upon land whereof the plaintiff is possessed, if the defendant shows a title to the land by descent, and that therefore he had a right to enter, the plaintiff may either traverse or deny the fact of the descent; or he may confess and avoid it, by replying, that true it is that such descent happened, but that since the descent the defendant himself demised the lands to the plaintiff for a term not yet expired.

To the replication the defendant may *rejoin*, or put in an answer called a *rejoinder*. The plaintiff may answer the rejoinder by a *sur-rejoinder*; upon which the defendant may *rebut*; and the plaintiff answer him by a *sur-rebutter*. The whole of this process is denominated the *pleading*; in the several stages of which it must be carefully observed not to depart or vary from the title or defence which the party has once insisted on. For this, which is called a *departure*, might occasion endless altercation. Therefore the replication must support the declaration, and the rejoinder must support the plea, without departing out of it. As in the case of pleading no award made, in an action thereon, to which the plaintiff replies, setting forth an actual award; now the defendant cannot rejoin that he has performed this award, for such rejoinder would be an entire departure from his original plea, which alleged that no such award was made: therefore he has now no other choice but to traverse the fact of the replication, or else to demur upon the law of it.

Yet in some actions the plaintiff, who has alleged in his declaration a general wrong, may in his replication, after an evasive plea by the defendant, reduce that general wrong to a more particular certainty, by assigning the injury afresh, in such manner as clearly to ascertain and identify it, consistently with his general complaint, which is called a *new* or *novel assignment*. As if the plaintiff in an action of trespass declares on a breach of his close and pulling down his fences; and the defendant pleads that he did so as occupier of another close, the occupiers of which had a right to dig and carry away sand and marl from the close of the plaintiff, and that he knocked down the plaintiff's fences because the enclosure prevented the free exercise of this right; the plaintiff may reply, by new assignment, that he sues not only for the trespasses admitted in the plea, but for other and different trespasses, to which the plaintiff must again plead either by denying these latter trespasses, or justifying them in some other way than that already stated in his plea. If the plaintiff simply denies the plea, he puts in issue the defendant's alleged right to dig sand and marl, and that only; and if such right exists, the verdict must be for the defendant; whereas by new assigning the trespasses, he compels the defendant, if he has also joined issue on the plea, to show not only that the alleged right exists, but that he committed the trespasses in exercise of that right, and that in so doing, he did nothing but what could be justified by him in the exercise of his right.

In any stage of the pleadings, when either side advances or affirms any new matter, he is understood to *aver it to be true*. So when either side traverses or denies the facts pleaded by his antagonist, he is understood to *tender an issue*, as it is called. Thus sooner or later the parties come to a point which is affirmed on one side and denied on the other. They are then said to be *at issue*, all their debates being at last contracted into a single point, which must now be determined either in favour of the plaintiff or of the defendant.

CHAPTER XII.

OF ISSUE AND DEMURRER.

Issue in *fact* or in *law*—Demurrer—Joinder in demurrer—Plea *puis darrein continuance*—Law Latin—Argument.

ISSUE, *exitus*, being the end of all the pleadings, is the third part or stage of an action, and is either upon matter of *law*, or matter of *fact*.

An issue upon matter of law is called a *demurrer*; and it confesses the facts to be true, as stated by the opposite party; but denies that, by the law arising upon those facts, any injury is done to the plaintiff, or that the defendant has made out a legitimate excuse; according to the party which first demurs, *demoratur*, rests or abides upon the point in question. As, if the matter of the plaintiff's complaint, or declaration be insufficient in law, as by not assigning any sufficient trespass, then the defendant demurs to the declaration · if, on the other hand, the defendant's excuse or plea be invalid, as if he pleads that he committed the trespass by authority from a stranger, without making out the stranger's right; here the plaintiff may demur in law to the plea: and so on in every other part of the proceedings, where either side perceives any material objection in point of law upon which he may rest his case.

The form of such demurrer is by averring the declaration or plea, the replication or rejoinder, to be *bad in substance*, that is, insufficient in law to maintain the action or the defence; and the party demurring is thereupon understood to *pray judgment* for want of sufficient matter alleged. Upon a demurrer, the opposite party must aver his pleading to be *good in substance*, which is called a joinder in demurrer, and then the parties are at issue in point of law. Which issue in law, or demurrer, the judges of the court before which the action is brought must determine.

An issue of fact is where the fact only, and not the law, is disputed. And when he that denies or traverses the fact pleaded by his antagonist has tendered the issue, the other party may immediately *join issue*; or if affirmative matter be set out in the pleading, he may at once *take issue* thereon. Which done, the issue is said to be joined, both parties having agreed to rest the fate of the cause upon the truth of the fact in question. And this issue of fact must, generally speaking, be determined by the country, *per pais*, in Latin *per patriam*, that is, by jury.

And here it will be proper to observe, that during the whole of these proceedings, from the time of the defendant's appearance in obedience to the writ, it is necessary that both the parties be in theory kept or *continued* in court from day to day, till the final determination of the suit. For the court can determine nothing, unless in the presence of both the parties, in person or by their attorneys, or upon default of one of them, after his original appearance. Therefore it is that if in the course of pleading, either party neglects to put in his declaration, plea, replication, rejoinder, and the like, within the time allotted by the standing rules of the court, the plaintiff, if the omission be his, is said to be *nonsuit* or not to follow and pursue his complaint, and shall lose the benefit of his writ; or if the negligence be on the side of the defendant, judgment may be had against him for such his default. No entry of these continuances is indeed put upon the record; but the theory remains, and either party may accordingly agree with the other to *discontinue* the suit; a course which it is not unusual for a plaintiff to adopt when he finds he has misconceived his action, or wishes to abandon it.

Again it may sometimes happen, that after the defendant has pleaded, nay, even after joinder of issue or in demurrer, there may have arisen some new matter, which it is proper for him to plead; as that the plaintiff has given him a release, or the like: here, if the defendant takes advantage of this new matter he is permitted to plead it in what is called a plea of *puis darrein continuance*, so designated, because it is supposed to be pleaded since the last adjournment of the court, and, of course, during a continuance of the

parties in court from the one sitting to the other. For it would be
unjust to exclude him from the benefit of this new defence, which
it was not in his power to make when he pleaded the former.

This plea may be pleaded at any time before verdict, but it is in
general not allowed after a demurrer, or verdict; in the former case,
because the defendant ought to stand on the invalidity of the declaration; in the latter, because relief may be had in another way,
namely, by writ of *audita querela*, of which hereafter. And these
pleas *puis darrein continuance*, when brought to a demurrer
in law or issue of fact, shall be determined in like manner as other
pleas.

We have said, that demurrers, or questions concerning the
sufficiency of the matters alleged in the pleadings, are to be determined by the judges of the court, upon solemn argument by counsel
on both sides, and to that end a demurrer book is made up, containing all the proceedings at length, which are afterwards entered on
record; and copies thereof, called *paper-books*, are delivered to the
judges to peruse. The *record* is a history of the most material proceedings in the cause entered on a parchment roll, and continued
down to the present time; in which must be stated the writ of summons, all the pleadings, the declaration, plea, replication, rejoinder
and whatever further proceedings have been had; all entered *verbatim* on the roll, and also the issue or demurrer, and joinder
therein.

These were formerly all written, as indeed all public proceedings
were, in Norman or law French, and so continued till the reign of
Edward III., in the thirty-sixth year of whose reign it was enacted,
that for the future all pleas should be pleaded, answered, debated,
and judged in the English tongue; but be entered and enrolled in
Latin. This Latin, which continued in use for four centuries,
answers so nearly to the English, oftentimes word for word, that
it is not at all surprising it should generally be imagined to be totally
fabricated at home, with little more art of trouble, than by adding
Roman terminations to English words. Our law-Latin, is, however,
in reality a mere technical language; and, as Sir John Davis observes
of the law-French, "so very easy to be learned, that the meanest wit
" that ever came to the study of the law, doth come to understand
" it almost perfectly in ten days without a reader." It continued in
use from its first introduction, till the time of Cromwell; when,
among many other innovations in the law, the language of our
records was altered and turned into English. But at the Restoration
this novelty was no longer countenanced; and thus it continued
without any sensible inconvenience, till about the year 1730, when
it was again thought proper that the proceedings at law should be
done into English, and it was accordingly so ordered by the statute

4 Geo. II. c. 26, " That the common people might have knowledge
" and understanding of what was alleged or done for and against
" them in the process and pleadings, the judgment and entries in a
" cause." Which purpose has, I fear, not been answered : being apt
to suspect that the people are now, after many years' experience,
altogether as ignorant in matters of law as before. But to return to
our demurrer.

When the substance of the record is completed, and copies are
delivered to the judges, the matter of law upon which the demurrer
is grounded is upon solemn argument determined by the court ; and
judgment is thereupon accordingly given. As, in an action of trespass, if the defendant in his plea confesses the fact, but justifies it
causâ venationis, for that he was hunting ; and to this the plaintiff
demurs, that is, he admits the truth of the plea, but denies the justification to be legal : now, on arguing this demurrer, if the court be
of opinion that a man may not justify trespass in hunting, they will
give judgment for the plaintiff ; if they think that he may, then
judgment is given for the defendant. Thus is an issue in law, or
demurrer, disposed of.

An issue of fact takes up more form and preparation to settle it;
for here the truth of the matters alleged must be solemnly examined
and established by proper evidence in the channel prescribed by law.
To which examination, of facts, the name of *trial* is usually confined,
which will be treated of at large in the succeeding chapter.

CHAPTER XIII.

OF THE TRIAL.

TRIAL is the examination of the matter of fact in issue ; of which
there are many different species, according to the difference of the
subject, or thing to be tried. For the law so industriously endeavours
to investigate truth at any rate, that it will not confine itself to one,

or to a few, manners of trial, but varies its examination of facts according to the nature of the facts themselves; this being the one invariable principle pursued, that as well the best method of trial, as the best evidence upon that trial which the nature of the case affords, and no other, shall be admitted in our courts of justice.

The species of trials in civil cases are now six in number: by *record*; by *inspection*, or *examination*; by *certificate*; by *witnesses*; by *jury*; and by *the court*. Trials by inspection, by certificate, and by witnesses are very unusual, but as they are still recognised modes of trial, in certain cases, they fall to be described in due course.*

I. The trial by *record*, is only used in one particular instance; and that is where a matter of record is pleaded in any action, a judgment or the like; and the opposite party pleads, "*nul tiel record*," that there is no such matter of record existing. Hereupon the party pleading the record has a day given him to bring it in; and, on his failure, his antagonist shall have judgment to recover. The trial, therefore, of this issue is merely by the record; for a record or enrolment is a monument of so high a nature, and importeth in itself such absolute verity, that if it be pleaded that there is no such record, it shall not receive any trial by witness, jury, or otherwise, but only by itself. Thus titles of nobility, as whether earl or no earl, baron or no baron, shall be tried by the sovereign's writ or patent only, which is matter of record. Also in case of alien, whether alien friend or enemy, shall be tried by the league or treaty between his sovereign and ours; for every league or treaty is of record. And also, whether a manor be held in ancient demesne or not, shall be tried by the record of *domesday* in the Exchequer.

II. The trial by *inspection* or *examination* is very unusual, and indeed almost unknown. It occurs when for the greater expedition of a cause, in some point or issue being either the principal question or arising collaterally out of it, but being evidently the object of sense, the judges of the court, upon the testimony of their own senses, shall decide the point in dispute. As to set aside a recognizance entered into by an infant; here, and in other cases of the like sort, a writ shall issue to the sheriff, commanding him that he constrain the said party to appear, that it may be ascertained by the

---

* In the original work of the learned commentator, an account is introduced in this place of two species of trial, both now abolished, the trial by *wager of battle*, and that by *wager of law*. I refer to them in this note, as I have had occasion to mention the right of a defendant to *wage his law*. As matters of historical interest I shall describe them shortly in an Appendix.

view of his body by the justices whether he be of full age or not. If, however, the court has, upon inspection, any doubt of the age of the party, as may frequently be the case, it may proceed to take proofs of the fact; and, particularly, may examine the infant himself upon an oath of *voire dire*, *veritatem dicere*, that is, to make true answer to such questions as the court shall demand of him; or the court may examine his mother, his godfather, or the like. In like manner if a defendant pleads in abatement of the suit that the plaintiff is *dead*, and one appears and calls himself the plaintiff, which the defendant denies: in this case the judges shall determine by inspection and examination, whether he be the plaintiff or not. But all such points when disputed are now usually decided upon affidavits.

Also, to ascertain any circumstances relative to a particular day past, it has been tried by an inspection of the almanac by the court. Thus, upon a writ of error from an inferior court, that of Lynn, the error assigned was that the judgment was given on a Sunday, it appearing to be on 26th February, 26 Eliz., and upon inspection of the almanacs of that year, it was found that the 26th of February in that year actually fell upon a Sunday: this was held to be a sufficient trial, and that a trial by jury was not necessary, although it was an error in fact; and so the judgment was reversed. But in all these cases the judges, if they conceive a doubt, may order it to be tried by jury.

III. The trial by *certificate* is allowed in such cases, where the evidence of the person certifying is the only proper criterion of the point in dispute. For, when the fact in question lies out of the cognizance of the court, the judges must rely on the solemn averment or information of persons in such a station, as affords them the most clear and competent knowledge of the truth. As therefore such evidence, if given to a jury, must have been conclusive, the law, to save trouble and circuity, permits the fact to be determined upon such certificate merely. Thus the customs of the city of London shall be tried by the certificate of the mayor and aldermen, certified by the mouth of their recorder; and in some cases the certificate of the sheriffs of London shall be the final trial; as if the issue be, whether the defendant be a citizen of London, or a foreigner, in case of privilege pleaded to be sued only in the city courts. Of a nature somewhat similar to which is the trial of the privilege of the University, when the Chancellor claims cognizance of the cause, because one of the parties is a privileged person. In this case, the charters, confirmed by act of parliament, direct the trial of the question, whether a privileged person or no, to be determined by the certificate and notification of the Chancellor under seal, to which it is usual to add an *affidavit* of the fact. In certain matters also of ecclesiastical jurisdiction, as *excommunication* and *orders;* these shall be tried by the bishop's certificate. *Ability* of a clerk presented, *admission, institution* and *deprivation* of a clerk, shall also be tried by certificate from the ordinary or metropolitan, because of these he is the most competent judge: but *induction* shall be tried by a jury, because it is a matter of public notoriety, and is likewise the corporal investiture of the temporal profits. *Resignation* of a benefice may be tried in either way, but it seems most properly to fall within the bishop's cognizance. The trial of all customs and practice of the courts shall be by certificate from the proper officers of those courts respectively; and, what return was made on a writ by the sheriff or under-sheriff, shall be only tried by his own certificate. And thus much for those several issues, or matters of fact, which are proper to be tried by certificate.

IV. A fourth species of trial is that by *witnesses, per testes,* without the intervention of a jury, which, like that of *inspection,* is very unusual. It is not to be confounded with the usual mode of trial in the county courts, or with the trial in certain cases by the court or a judge, which we shall describe afterwards. This is the only method of trial known to the civil law, in which the judge is left to form in his own breast his sentence upon the credit of the witnesses examined, but it is very rarely used in our law. When a widow brings an action of dower, and the tenant pleads that the husband is not dead, this being looked upon as a dilatory plea, is in favour of the widow, and for greater expedition, allowed to be tried by witnesses examined before the judges; and so, says Finch, shall no other case in our law. But Sir Edward Coke mentions others: as to try the validity of a challenge to a juror; so that Finch's observation must be confined to trial of direct, and not collateral issues. And in every case Sir Edward Coke lays it down that the affirmative must be proved by two witnesses at the least.

V. The subject of our next inquiries will be the nature and method of the trial *by jury;* called also the trial *per pais,* or *by the country:* a trial that has been used time out of mind in this nation, and seems to have been coeval with the first civil government thereof. Some authors have endeavoured to trace the origin of juries up as high as the Britons themselves, the first inhabitants of our island; but certain it is that they were in use among the earliest Saxon colonies, their institution being ascribed by Bishop Nicholson to Woden himself, their great legislator and captain. Hence it is, that we may find traces of juries in the laws of all those nations which adopted the feudal system, as in Germany, France, and Italy;

who had all of them a tribunal composed of twelve good men and true, " *boni homines*," usually the vassals or tenants of the lord, being the equals or peers of the parties litigant : and, as the lord's vassals judged each other in the lord's courts, so the king's vassals, or the lords themselves, judged each other in the king's court. In England we find actual mention of them so early as the laws of king Ethelred, and that not as a new invention. Stiernhook ascribes the invention of the jury, which in the Teutonic language is denominated *nembda*, to Regner, king of Sweden and Denmark, who was contemporary with our king Egbert. Just as we are apt to impute the invention of this, and other parts of our juridical polity, to the superior genius of Alfred the Great ; to whom, on account of his having done much, it is usual to attribute everything ; and as the tradition of ancient Greece placed to the account of their own Hercules whatever achievement was performed superior to the ordinary prowess of mankind. Whereas the truth seems to be, that this tribunal was universally established among all the northern nations, and so interwoven in their very constitution, that the earliest accounts of the one give us also some traces of the other. Its establishment, however, and use in this island, of what date soever it be, though for a time greatly impaired and shaken by the introduction of the Norman trial by battle, was always so highly esteemed and valued by the people, that no conquest, no change of government, could ever prevail to abolish it. But I will not misspend the reader's time in fruitless encomiums on this method of trial, but shall proceed to the dissection and examination of it in all its parts, from whence, indeed, its highest encomium will arise ; since the more it is searched into and understood, the more it is sure to be valued. And this is a species of knowledge most absolutely necessary for every gentleman in the kingdom : as well because he may be frequently called upon to determine in this capacity the rights of others, his fellow subjects ; as because his own property, his liberty, and his life, depend upon maintaining in its legal force the constitutional trial by jury.

And here I shall pursue the same method that I set out with in explaining the nature of prosecuting actions in general, viz., by following the order and course of the proceedings themselves, as the most clear and perspicuous way of treating it.

When, therefore, an issue is joined, the court awards a *venire facias* upon the roll or record in these words. " *Therefore let a jury come, &c.* ;" which *award of the venire* is the authority to the sheriff to summon the jury, which, in all counties, except London and Middlesex, he now does on receiving a precept issued to him for that purpose by the judges of assize.

If the sheriff be not an indifferent person, as if he be a party to the suit, or be related by either blood or affinity to either of the parties, he is not then trusted to return the jury, but the precept is directed to the coroners, who in this, as in many other instances, are the substitutes of the sheriff, to execute process when he is deemed an improper person. If any exception lies to the coroners, the precept shall be directed to two clerks of the court, or two persons of the county named by the court, and sworn. And these two, who are called *elisors*, or electors, shall indifferently name the jury, and their return is final; no challenge being allowed to their array.

When the general day of trials is fixed, the plaintiff or his attorney must *bring down the record* to the assizes, and *enter it* with the proper officer, in order to its being called on in course. If it be not so entered it cannot be tried; therefore it is in the plaintiff's breast to delay any trial by not carrying down the record: unless the defendant being fearful of such neglect in the plaintiff, and willing to discharge himself from the action, will himself undertake to bring on the trial, giving proper notice to the plaintiff. Which proceeding is called the trial by *proviso*; by reason of the clause which was formerly in such case inserted in the sheriff's *venire*, viz., " *proviso*, " provided that if two writs come to your hands, that is, one from " the plaintiff and another from the defendant, you shall execute only " one of them." But the trial by *proviso* need not be resorted to by a defendant in order to get quit of the action; for if the plaintiff neglects to bring on the cause for trial within a certain period after issue has been joined, generally two terms, the defendant may give him twenty days' notice to bring the cause on for trial at the sittings or next following assizes; which, if the plaintiff neglect to do, the defendant may suggest his default on the record, and sign judgment for his own costs of suit.

In case the plaintiff intends to try the cause, he is bound to give the defendant ten days' *notice of trial*; and if the plaintiff then changes his mind, and does not *countermand* the notice four days before the trial, he is liable to pay costs to the defendant for not proceeding to trial. The defendant, however, or plaintiff, may, upon good cause shown to the court above, as upon absence or sickness of a material witness, obtain leave upon motion to defer the trial of the cause till the next assizes.

But we will now suppose all previous steps to be regularly settled, and the cause to be called on in court. The record is then handed to the judge, to peruse and observe the pleadings, and what issues the parties are to maintain and prove, while the jury is called and sworn. To this end the sheriff returns his execution of the precept issued to him to summon jurors, with the panel of jurors annexed, to the judge's officer in court. The jurors contained in the panel are either *special* or *common* jurors. *Special* juries were originally introduced in trials at bar, when the causes were of too great nicety for the discussion of ordinary freeholders; or where the sheriff was suspected of partiality, though not upon such apparent cause as to warrant an exception to him. But now if either of the parties desire it, *special* jurors are summoned upon a *notice* to that effect given to the sheriff, by the party who wishes to have his cause so tried, he paying the extraordinary expense thereby involved, unless the judge certifies that the cause required a special jury.*

The names of the jurors, being written on tickets, are put into a box or glass, and when each cause is called, twelve of these persons, whose names shall be first drawn out of the box, shall be sworn upon the jury, unless absent, challenged, or excused; or unless a previous *view* of the messuages, lands, or place in question, shall have been thought necessary by the court, in which case *six* or more of the jurors returned, to be agreed on by the parties, or named by a judge or other proper officer of the court, shall be appointed to have the matters in question shown to them by two persons named therein; and then such of the jury as have had the view, or so many of them as appear, shall be sworn on the inquest previous to any other jurors.

As the jurors appear, when called, they shall be sworn, unless *challenged* by either party. Challenges are of two sorts: challenges to the *array*, and challenges to the *polls*.

Challenges to the array are at once an exception to the whole panel, in which the jury are arrayed or set in order by the sheriff in his return; and they may be made upon account of partiality, or some default in the sheriff, or his under-officer, who arrayed the panel. And generally speaking, the same reasons that before the awarding the *venire* were sufficient to have directed it to the coroners or elisors, will be also sufficient to quash the array, when made by a person or officer of whose partiality there is any tolerable ground of suspicion. Also, though there be no personal objection against the sheriff, yet if he arrays the panel at the nomination, or under the direction of either party, this is good cause of challenge to the array.

Challenges to the polls, *in capita*, are exceptions to particular jurors, and are reduced to four heads by Sir Edward Coke: *propter honoris respectum; propter defectum; propter affectum;* and *propter delictum*.

* In London and Middlesex special jurors are *struck* in presence of the under-sheriffs; for whose benefit, in the matter of fees, a different practice prevails to that of all the other counties in England.

1. *Propter honoris respectum* ; as if a lord of parliament be impannelled on a jury, he may be challenged by either party, or he may challenge himself.

2. *Propter defectum* ; as if a juryman be an alien born, this is defect of birth. He must also be *liber et legalis homo*, therefore no man attainted of treason or felony, or convicted of any infamous crime, can, unless he has obtained a free pardon, be a juror ; and no man under outlawry or excommunication is qualified to serve on any inquest whatever. But the principal deficiency is defect of estate, sufficient to qualify him to be a juror. These qualifications are defined by 6 & 7 Geo. IV., c. 50, which also regulates the mode in which the special and common jury lists are to be made up. A juror must also be twenty-one years of age ; and if above sixty he is exempted, though not disqualified from serving.

3. Jurors may be challenged *propter affectum*, for suspicion of bias or partiality. This may be either a *principal* challenge, or *to the favour*. A *principal* challenge is such, where the cause assigned carries with it *primâ facie* evident marks of suspicion, either of malice or favour : as that a juror is of kin to either party within the ninth degree ; that he has been arbitrator on either side ; that he has an interest in the cause : that there is an action depending between him and the party ; that he has taken money for his verdict ; that he has formerly been a juror in the same cause ; that he is the party's master, servant, counsellor, steward, or attorney, or of the same society or corporation with him : all these are principal causes of challenge, which, if true, cannot be overruled, for jurors must be *omni exceptione majores*. Challenges *to the favour*, are where the party has no principal challenge, but objects only some probable circumstance of suspicion, as acquaintance and the like, the validity óf which must be left to the determination of *triors*, whose office it is to decide whether the juror be favourable or unfavourable. The triors, in case the first man called be challenged, are two indifferent persons named by the court ; and if they try one man and find him indifferent, he shall be sworn ; and then he and the two triors shall try the next, and when another is found indifferent and sworn, the two triors shall be superseded, and the two first sworn on the jury shall try the rest.

4 Challenges *propter delictum* are for some crime or misdemeanor that affects the juror's credit and renders him infamous. This was formerly the case after a conviction of treason, felony, perjury, or conspiracy ; or if for some infamous offence he had received judgment of the pillory, tumbrel or the like ; or to be branded, whipped, or stigmatized ; or if he were outlawed or excommunicated, or had been

attainted of false verdict, *præmunire*, or forgery; or, lastly, if he had proved recreant when champion in the trial by battle, and thereby had lost his *liberam legem*. But the grounds of challenge *propter delictum* are now simply those stated as grounds of challenge *propter defectum*, viz., having been convicted of treason, felony, or any infamous offence, which stain, however, a free pardon will obliterate, or being outlawed, or excommunicated, the latter being a species of outlawry in use in the ecclesiastical courts. A juror may himself be examined on oath of *voir dire, veritatum dicere*, with regard to such causes of challenge, as are not to his dishonour or discredit, but not with regard to any crime, or anything which tends to his disgrace or disadvantage.

Besides these challenges, which are exceptions against the fitness of jurors, and whereby they may be *excluded* from serving, there are also other causes to be made use of by the jurors themselves, which are matter of exemption, whereby their service is *excused*, and not *excluded*. This exemption was formerly by divers statutes, customs, and charters, and is now by the statute 6 & 7 Geo. IV. c. 50, s. 2, extended to the judges, clergymen and dissenting ministers, barristers, attorneys, officers of the courts, physicians, surgeons and apothecaries, officers in the army or navy, and the like; all of whom, if impanelled, must show their special exemption.

If by means of challenges, or other cause, a sufficient number of unexceptionable jurors do not appear at the trial, either party may pray a *tales*, in order to make up the deficiency: the judge being empowered, at the prayer of either party, to award a *tales de circumstantibus*, of persons present in court, to be joined to the other jurors to try the cause; who are liable, however, to the same challenges as the principal jurors. This is usually done till the legal number of twelve be completed; in which patriarchal and apostolical number Sir Edward Coke has discovered abundance of mystery.

When a sufficient number of persons impanelled, or *tales*-men, appear, they are then separately sworn well and truly to try the issue between the parties, and a true verdict to give according to the evidence; and hence they are denominated the jury, *jurata*, and jurors, *sc. juratores*.

The jury are now ready to hear the merits; and to fix their attention the closer to the facts which they are impanelled and sworn to try, the pleadings are opened to them by counsel on that side which holds the affirmative of the question in issue. For the issue is said to lie, and proof is always first required upon that side which affirms the matter in question. The opening counsel briefly informs them what has been transacted in the court above: the parties, the nature of the action, the declaration, the plea, replication, and other proceedings, and lastly, upon what point the issue is joined, which is there sent down to be determined.

The nature of the case, and the evidence intended to be produced, are next laid before them by counsel also on the same side; and when their evidence is gone through, and summed up if necessary, the advocate on the other side opens the adverse case, and supports it by evidence, and sums up if necessary; and then the party which began is heard by way of reply.

The nature of my present design will not permit me to enter into the numberless niceties and distinctions of what is, or is not, legal *evidence* to a jury. I shall only therefore select a few of the general heads and leading maxims, relative to this point, together with some observations on the manner of giving evidence.

And, first, evidence signifies that which demonstrates, makes clear, or ascertains the truth of the very fact or point in issue, either on the one side or on the other; and no evidence ought to be admitted to any other point. Therefore when the defendant denies his bond by the plea of *non est factum*, and the issue is, whether it be the defendant's deed or no; he cannot give a release of this bond in evidence: for that does not destroy the bond, and therefore does not prove the issue which he has chosen to rely upon, viz., that the bond has no existence.

Again, evidence in the trial by jury is of two kinds, either that which is given in proof, or that which the jury may receive by their own private knowledge. The former, or *proofs*, to which in common speech the name of evidence is usually confined, are either written, or *parol*, that is, by word of mouth. Written proofs, or evidence, are, 1. Records, and 2. Ancient deeds of thirty years' standing, which prove themselves; a rule which applies generally to deeds concerning lands, to bonds, receipts, letters, and all other ancient writings; but 3. Modern deeds, and 4. Other writings, must, in general, be verified by the *parol* evidence of witnesses.

And the one general rule that runs through all the doctrine of trials is this, that the best evidence the nature of the case will admit of shall always be required, if possible to be had; but if not possible, then the best evidence that can be had shall be allowed. For if it be found that there is any better evidence existing than is produced, the very not producing it is a presumption that it would have detected some falsehood that at present is concealed. Thus, in order to prove a lease for years, nothing else shall be admitted but the very deed of lease itself, if in being: but if that be positively proved to be burnt or destroyed, not relying on any loose negative, as that it cannot be found, or the like, then an attested copy may be produced, or *parol* evidence be given of its contents. So, no evidence of a discourse with another will be admitted, but the man himself must be produced; yet in some cases, as in proof of any general customs, or matters of common tradition or repute, the courts admit of *hearsay* evidence, or an account of what persons deceased have declared in their lifetime: but such evidence will not be received of any particular facts. So, too, books of account, or shop books, are not allowed of themselves to be given in evidence for the owner; but a servant who made the entry may have recourse to them to refresh his memory; and, if such servant, who was accustomed to make those entries, be dead, and his hand be proved, the entry made be read in evidence: for as tradesmen are often under a necessity of giving credit without any note or writing, this is therefore, when accompanied with such other collateral proofs of fairness, and regularity, the best evidence that can then be produced.

But as this kind of evidence, even thus regulated, would be much too hard upon the buyer at any long distance of time, the statute 7 Jac. I. c. 12, the penners of which seem to have imagined that the books of themselves were evidence at common law, confines this species of proof to such transactions as have happened within one year before the action brought; unless between merchant and merchant in the usual intercourse of trade. For accounts of so recent a date, if erroneous, may more easily be unravelled and adjusted.

Documents offered as proofs must in general be proved by the *parol evidence* of witnesses; but to save the expense of such proof, the party intending to produce the documents may, by a formal *notice to admit*, call on his opponent to admit them, saving all just exceptions; and if he refuses or neglects to do so, the costs of proving the documents at the trial must then be borne by him, whatever the result may be, unless the judge certify his refusal to have been reasonable. But if the documents are in the possession of his adversary, the party desiring their production at the trial may give him *notice to produce* them, and if he fails or refuses to do so, may then give *secondary evidence of their contents*, which will be admitted on proof of the service of the notice to produce.

With regard to *parol* evidence, or *witnesses*, it must first be remembered, that there is a process to bring them in by writ of *subpœna ad testificandum*: which runs into Scotland and Ireland; and which commands them, laying aside all pretences and excuses, to appear at the trial on pain of 100*l.* to be forfeited to the crown; to which the statute 5 Eliz. c. 9, has added a penalty of 10*l.* to the party aggrieved, and damages equivalent to the loss sustained by want of the evidence. But no witness, unless his reasonable expenses be tendered him, is bound to appear at all; nor, if he appears, is he

bound to give evidence till such charges are actually paid him;
except he resides within the bills of mortality, and is summoned to
give evidence within the same.   It may so happen, however, that a
witness is abroad; if so, the party requiring the evidence may, after
issue joined, apply to the court for a commission to examine him;
and so if a witness residing within the jurisdiction is so ill as to be
unable to attend and give evidence, he may be examined by a commissioner appointed by the court.   In either case the evidence of
such witnesses is taken by interrogatories or *vivâ voce*, as it may be
ordered, and is read at the trial.

All witnesses, of whatever religion or country, that have the use
of their reason, are to be received and examined, for all such are
competent witnesses; though the jury from other circumstances will
judge of their *credibility*.   The law formerly excluded not only such
persons as were *infamous*, but all who were interested in the event
of the cause: thus carefully shutting out the evidence not only of
the *parties* to the cause, but any one who had the most minute
interest in the result; for every person so circumstanced, however
insignificant his interest, was presumed incapable of resisting the
temptation to perjury; as every judge and juryman was presumed
incapable of discerning perjury committed under circumstances
especially calculated to excite suspicion.   But as it is perfectly
obvious that any witness who can throw any light upon the subject,
should be allowed to state what he knows, subject, of course, to such
observation as might be made, either as to his means of knowledge,
or his disposition to state the truth, the stringent rules of the common law have been gradually relaxed by a series of modern statutes.
And the parties to the action, and all other persons, whatever may
be their interest in the result, are now *competent* and *compellable* to
to give evidence.
No person charged with an offence is, however, competent or
compellable to give evidence against himself, nor is any person
compellable to answer any question tending to criminate himself.
A husband is not competent or compellable to give evidence for
or against his wife, or a wife competent or compellable to give evidence for or against her husband in any criminal proceeding.   And
neither husband nor wife can be witnesses in any proceeding instituted in consequence of adultery; nor the parties to the suit in any
action for breach of promise of marriage.   All rules tending to the
exclusion of evidence have thus been abrogated, except in the particular instances I have mentioned.   But no counsel, attorney, or
other person instrusted with the secrets of the cause by the party
himself shall be compelled, or allowed, if the party objects, to give
evidence of such conversation or matters of privacy as came to his

knowledge by virtue of such trust and confidence : though he may be examined as to mere matters of fact, as the execution of a deed or the like, which might have come to his knowledge without being interested in the cause.

One witness, if credible, is *sufficient* evidence to a jury of any single fact, though undoubtedly the concurrence of two or more corroborates the proof. Yet our law considers that there are many transactions to which only one person is privy; and therefore does not *always* demand the testimony of two, as the civil law universally requires.

Proof is always required, where from the nature of the case it appears it might possibly have been had. But next to *positive* proof, *circumstantial* evidence, or the doctrine of *presumptions*, must take place; for when the fact itself cannot be demonstratively evinced, that which comes nearest to the proof of the fact is the proof of such circumstances which either *necessarily*, or *usually* attend such facts; and these are called presumptions, which are only to be relied upon till the contrary be actually proved. *Violent* presumption is many times equal to full proof; for there those circumstances appear, which *necessarily* attend the fact. As if a landlord sues for rent due at Michaelmas 1864, and the tenant cannot prove the payment, but produces an acquittance for rent due at a subsequent time, in full of all demands, this is a violent presumption of his having paid the former rent, and, in the absence of explanation that the acquittance was given by mistake or obtained by fraud, is equivalent to full proof; for though the actual payment is not proved, yet the acquittance in full of all demands is proved, which could not be without such payment; and it thereby induces so forcible a presumption, that the jury will be perfectly justified in acting on it, and returning a verdict accordingly. *Probable* presumption, arising from such circumstances, as *usually* attend the fact, has also its due weight: as if, in a suit for rent due in 1864, the tenant proves the payment of the rent due in 1865; this will prevail to exonerate the tenant, unless it be clearly shown that the rent of 1864 was retained for some special reason, or that there was some fraud or mistake: for otherwise it will be presumed to have been paid before that in 1865, as it is most usual to receive first the rents of longest standing. *Light* or rash presumptions have no weight or validity at all.

. The oath administered to the witness is not only that what he deposes shall be true, but that he shall also depose the *whole* truth as to the matter in question: so that he is not to conceal any part of what he knows, whether interrogated particularly to that point or not. And all this evidence is to be given in open court, in the presence of the parties, their attorneys, the counsel, and all by-standers, and before the judge and jury ; each party having liberty to except to its competency, which exceptions are publicly stated, and by the judge are openly and publicly allowed or disallowed, in the face of the country : which must curb any secret bias or par-tiality that might arise in his own breast. And if, either in his direc-tions or decisions, he misstates the law by ignorance, inadvertence, or design, the counsel on either side may require him publicly to seal a *bill of exceptions* ; stating the point wherein he is supposed to err. This bill of exceptions is in the nature of an appeal ; examin-able, not in the court out of which the record issues for the trial at *nisi prius*, but in the next immediate superior court, upon error brought, after judgment given in the court below. But a *demurrer* to evidence shall be determined by the court, out of which the record is sent. This happens, where a record or other matter is produced in evidence, concerning the legal consequences of which there arises a doubt in law : in which case the adverse party may, if he pleases, demur to the whole evidence ; which admits the truth of every fact that has been alleged, but denies the sufficiency of them all in point of law to maintain or overthrow the issue : which draws the question of law from the cognizance of the jury, to be decided, as it ought, by the court. But neither these demurrers to evidence, nor the bills of exceptions, are at present so much in use as formerly ; since the extension of the discretionary powers of the court in granting a *new trial*, which may always be had for the mis-direction of the judge at *nisi prius*. Besides which it not unfre-quently happens that some *point* of law, on which the whole cause generally depends, is *reserved* by the judge for the consideration of the court ; in which case the court considers itself in the same situa-tion as the judge was when the point was raised, and a *nonsuit* or *verdict* is entered according to its determination, its judgment in this case being open to appeal by the party against whom it is given. It sometimes happens also that both parties, when neither feel confident of success, agree to *withdraw a juror*, which puts an end to the proceedings, leaving each party to pay his own costs ; and another not unusual proceeding at *nisi prius* is a *reference of the cause to arbitration*, which takes place generally where the question involved in the cause is matter of account, or is unfit to be litigated in open court.

This open examination of witnesses, *viva voce*, in the presence of all mankind, is much more conducive to the clearing up of truth, than the private and secret examination taken down in writing before an officer or his clerk, as is the usual practice in all courts that have borrowed their practice from the civil law ; where a witness may frequently depose that in private which he will be ashamed to testify in a public and solemn tribunal. The occasional questions of the judge, the jury, and the counsel, propounded to the witnesses on a sudden, will sift out the truth much better than a formal set of interrogatories previously penned and settled; and the confronting of adverse witnesses is also another opportunity of obtaining a clear discovery, which can never be had upon any other method of trial. Nor is the presence of the judge during the examination, a matter of small importance: for, besides the respect with which his presence will naturally inspire the witness, he is able, by use and experience, to keep the evidence from wandering from the point in issue. In short, by this method of examination, and this only, the persons who are to decide upon the evidence have an opportunity of observing the quality, age, education, understanding, behaviour, and inclinations of the witness; in which points all persons must appear alike, when their depositions are reduced to writing, and read to the judge, in the absence of those who made them; and yet as much may be frequently collected from the manner in which the evidence is delivered, as from the matter of it; one, and not the least important, of the advantages attending this way of giving testimony, *ore tenus*.

As to such evidence as the jury may have in their own consciences, by their private knowledge of facts, it was an ancient doctrine, that this had as much right to sway their judgment as the written or parol evidence which is delivered in court. And therefore it has often been held, that though no proofs were produced on either side, yet the jury might bring in a verdict. This seems to have arisen from the ancient practice in taking assizes, where the sheriff was bound to return such jurors as knew the truth of the facts. But this doctrine was gradually exploded, and is obviously quite incompatible with the grounds upon which new trials are every day awarded, viz., that the verdict was given *without*, or *contrary to*, evidence. And therefore, together with new trials, the practice seems to have been introduced, which now universally obtains, that if a juror knows anything of the matter in issue, he may be sworn as a witness, and give his evidence publicly in court.

When the evidence is gone through on both sides, the judge, in the presence of the parties, the counsel, and all others, sums up the whole to the jury; omitting all superfluous circumstances, observing wherein the main question and principal issue lies, stating what evidence has been given to support it, with such remarks as he thinks necessary for their direction, and giving them his opinion in matters of law arising upon that evidence.

The jury, after the proofs are summed up, unless the case be very clear, withdraw from the bar to consider of their verdict: and, in order to avoid intemperance and causeless delay, are to be kept without meat, drink, fire, or candle, unless by permission of the judge, till they are all unanimously agreed; a method of accelerating unanimity not wholly unknown in other constitutions of Europe, and in matters of great concern. For by the golden bull of the empire, if, after the congress was opened, the electors delayed the election of a king of the Romans for thirty days, they were to be fed only with bread and water till the same was accomplished. But if our juries eat or drink at all, or have any eatables about them, without consent of the court, and before verdict, it is fineable; and if they do so at his charge for whom they afterwards find, it will set aside the verdict. Also if they speak with either of the parties or their agents, after they have gone from the bar; or if they receive any fresh evidence in private; or if, to prevent disputes, they cast lots for whom they shall find; any of these circumstances will entirely vitiate the verdict. And it has been held, that if the jurors do not agree in their verdict before the judges are about to leave the town, though they are not to be threatened or imprisoned, the judges are not bound to wait for·them, but may carry them round the circuit from town to town in a cart.

When they are all unanimously agreed, the jury return back to the bar; and, before they deliver their verdict, the plaintiff is bound to appear in court, by himself, attorney, or counsel. The object of compelling his attendance was that he might answer the amercement to which, by the old law, he was liable, in case he failed in his suit, as a punishment for his false claim. To be *amerced*, or *a mercie*, is to be at the mercy of the court with regard to the fine to be imposed; *in misericordiâ domini regis pro falso clamore suo.* The amercement is disused, but if the plaintiff does not appear, no verdict can be given, and he is said to be *nonsuit, non sequitur clamorem suum.* Therefore it is usual for a plaintiff, when he or his counsel perceives that he has not given evidence sufficient to maintain his issue, to be voluntarily nonsuited, or withdraw himself: whereupon the crier is ordered to *call the plaintiff:* and if neither he, nor anybody for him, appears, ne is nonsuited, the jurors are discharged, the action is at an end, and the defendant shall recover his costs. The reason of this practice is, that a nonsuit is more eligible for the plaintiff, than a verdict against him: for after a nonsuit, which is only a default, he may commence the same suit again for the same cause of action; but after a verdict had, and judgment consequent thereupon, he is for ever barred from attacking the defendant upon the same ground of complaint. But in case the plaintiff appears, the jury by their foreman deliver in their verdict.

A verdict, *vere dictum*, is either *privy*, or *public*. A *privy* verdict is when the judge has left or adjourned the court: and the jury being agreed, in order to be delivered from their confinement, obtain leave to give their verdict privily to their judge out of court; which privy verdict is of no force, unless afterwards affirmed by a public verdict given openly in court. The only effectual and legal verdict, therefore, is the *public* verdict; in which they openly declare to have found the issue for the plaintiff, or for the defendant: and if for the plaintiff, they assess the damages also sustained by the plaintiff, in consequence of the injury upon which the action is brought.

Sometimes, if there arises in the case any difficult matter of law, the jury, for the sake of better information, and to avoid the danger of having their verdict disregarded, will find a *special verdict*, stating the naked facts, as they find them to be proved, and praying the advice of the court thereon; concluding conditionally, that if upon the whole matter the court shall be of opinion that the plaintiff had cause of action, they then find for the plaintiff; if otherwise, then for the defendant. This is entered at length on the record, and afterwards argued and determined in the court at Westminster, from whence the issue came to be tried.

Another method of finding a species of special verdict, is when the jury find a verdict generally for the plaintiff, but subject nevertheless to the opinion of the judge or the court above, on a *special case* stated by the counsel on both sides with regard to a matter of law; the *postea*, of which in the next chapter, being stayed in the hands of the officer of the *nisi prius*, till the question is determined, and the verdict is then entered for the plaintiff or defendant, as the case may happen. But in both these instances the jury may, if they think proper, take upon themselves to determine, at their own hazard, the complicated question of fact and law; and, without either special verdict or special case, may find a verdict absolutely either for the plaintiff or defendant.

When the jury have delivered in their verdict, and it is recorded in court, they are then discharged; and so ends the trial by jury.

VI. The last species of trial is that by the court or a judge, which may be had in certain classes of cases, where the intervention of a jury is quite unnecessary. In actions, for instance, in which the question turns on the legal effect of evidence or of undisputed facts, the presence of the jury is a useless form, for the verdict must necessarily depend entirely on the direction of the judge; while in those suits which, when brought before the jury, it is found necessary to submit to arbitration, calling a jury together merely to be discharged, can have no other effect than to bring the institution itself into contempt. Such are the cases depending on complicated questions of account, in which figures and documents must be frequently referrred to, for with these a jury is utterly unable to deal.

When the jury is dispensed with, the proceedings upon and after the trial are the same as in ordinary cases, the verdict of the judge having precisely the same effect as the verdict of a jury, except that it cannot be questioned afterwards, as being against the weight of the evidence; on which ground the verdicts of juries are not unfrequently set aside and a new trial granted.

CHAPTER XIV.

OF JUDGMENT AND ITS INCIDENTS.

The *Postea*—New trial—Arrest of judgment—Judgment *non obstante veredicto* —Repleader— *Venire de novo*—Judgments interlocutory or final—Warrant of attorney—Reference to master—Writ of inquiry—Effect of judgment as binding lands—Costs.

If the issue be an issue of fact, and upon trial it be found for either the plaintiff or defendant, or specially; or if the plaintiff makes default, or is nonsuit; or whatever, in short, is done subsequent to the joining of issue and awarding the trial, it is entered on record, and is called a *postea*. The substance of which is, that *postea, afterwards,* the said plaintiff and defendant appeared by their attorneys at the place of trial; and a jury, being sworn found such a verdict; or, that the plaintiff, after the jury sworn, made default, and did not prosecute his suit; or, as the case may happen. This is added to the roll, which is now returned to the court from which it was sent; and the history of the cause, from the time it was carried out, is thus continued by the *postea*.

Next follows the judgment of the court upon what has previously passed; both the matter of law and matter of fact being now fully weighed and adjusted. Judgment may, however, for certain causes be *suspended*, or finally *arrested:* for it cannot be entered for some days after the trial. So that if any defect of justice happened at the trial, by surprise, inadvertence, or misconduct, the party may have relief in the court above, by obtaining a new trial; or if, notwithstanding the issue of fact be regularly decided, it appears that the complaint was either not actionable in itself, or not made with

sufficient precision and accuracy, the party may supersede it by
arresting or staying the judgment.

1. Causes of *suspending* the judgment by granting a *new trial,*
are at present wholly *extrinsic,* arising from matter foreign to, or
dehors the record. Of this sort are want of notice of trial ; or any
flagrant misbehaviour of the party prevailing towards the jury,
which may have influenced their verdict ; or any gross misbehaviour
of the jury among themselves : also, if it appears by the judge's report, certified to the court, that the jury have brought in a verdict
without or contrary to evidence, so that he is reasonably dissatisfied
therewith ; or if they have given exorbitant damages ; or if the
judge himself has misdirected the jury, so that they found an unjus-
tifiable verdict ; for these, and other reasons of the like kind, it is
the practice of the court to award a *new,* or second, *trial.*

The exertion of these superintendent powers of the courts, in
setting aside the verdict of a jury and granting a new trial, is of a
date extremely ancient. I need not, however, refer to instances, for
no rule is now better understood than the maxim on which the courts
act, that where justice is not done upon one trial, the injured party
is entitled to another. A new trial is a re-hearing of the cause
before another jury ; but with as little prejudice to either party as if
it had never been heard before. No advantage is taken of the
former verdict on the one side, or the rule of court for awarding
such second trial on the other : and the subsequent verdict, though
contrary to the first, imports no tittle of blame upon the former
jury ; who, had they possessed the same lights and advantages,
would probably have altered their own opinion. The parties come
better informed, the counsel better prepared, the law is more fully
understood, the judge is more master of the subject ; and nothing
is now tried but the real merits of the case.

A sufficient ground must however be laid before the court to
satisfy them that it is necessary to justice that the cause should be
further considered. If the matter be such as did not or could not
appear to the judge who presided at *nisi prius,* it is disclosed to the
court by *affidavit :* if it arises from what passed at the trial, it is
taken from the judge's information, who usually makes a special and
minute report of the evidence. Counsel are heard on both sides to
impeach or establish the verdict, and the court give their reasons at
large why a new examination ought or ought not to be allowed.
The true import of the evidence is duly weighed, false colours are
taken off, and all points of law which arose at the trial are upon full
deliberation clearly explained and settled.

Nor do the courts lend too easy an ear to every application for a
review of the former verdict. They must be satisfied that there are

strong probable grounds to suppose that the merits have not been fairly and fully discussed, and that the decision is not agreeable to the justice and truth of the case. A new trial is not granted where the value is too inconsiderable to merit a second examination. It is not granted upon nice and formal objections, which do not go to the real merits. It is not granted in cases of strict right or *summum jus*, where the rigorous exaction of extreme legal justice is hardly reconcileable to conscience. Nor is it granted where the scales of evidence hang nearly equal: that which leans against the former verdict ought always very strongly to preponderate.

In granting such further trial, which is matter of sound discretion, the court has also an opportunity, which it seldom fails to improve, of laying the party applying under such equitable terms, as his antagonist shall desire and mutually offer to comply with : such as the admission of facts not intended to be litigated ; the production of deeds, books, and papers ; the examination of witnesses, infirm or going beyond sea ; and the like. The motion must be made within the first four days of the next succeeding term, within which term it ought to be heard and decided. This mode of proceeding has accordingly supplanted the demurrer to the evidence, and the bill of exceptions; these being now very seldom resorted to, because long experience has shown, that a motion for a second trial is the shortest, cheapest, and most effectual cure for all imperfections in the verdict, whether they arise from the mistakes of the parties themselves, of their counsel or attorneys, or even of the judge or jury.

2. Arrests of judgment arise from *intrinsic* causes, appearing upon the face of the record, as if the case laid in the declaration is not sufficient in point of law to found an action upon. For this is an invariable rule with regard to arrests of judgment upon matter of law, " that whatever is alleged in arrest of judgment must be " such matter, as would upon demurrer have been sufficient to over- " turn the action." As if, in an action for slander in calling the plaintiff a Jew, the defendant denies the words, and issue is joined thereon: now if a verdict be found for the plaintiff, that the words were actually spoken, whereby the fact is established, still the defendant may move in arrest of judgment, that to call a man a Jew is not actionable : and if the court be of that opinion, the judgment shall be arrested, and never entered for the plaintiff. But the rule will not hold *e converso*, " that everything that may be " alleged as cause of demurrer will be good in arrest of judgment ." for if a declaration or plea omits to state some particular circumstance, without proving of which, at the trial, it is impossible to support the action or defence, this omission shall be aided by a verdict.

For the verdict ascertains those facts, which before from the inaccuracy of the pleadings might be dubious ; since the law will not suppose, that a jury under the inspection of a judge would find a verdict for the plaintiff or defendant, unless he had proved those circumstances, without which his general allegation is defective. Exceptions, therefore, that are moved in arrest of judgment, must be much more material and glaring than such as will maintain a demurrer ; or, in other words, many inaccuracies and omissions, which would be fatal, if early observed, are *cured by verdict ;* and not suffered, in the last stage of a cause, to unravel the whole proceedings.

3. When the plea of the defendant is bad in law, and when, of course, its being true in point of fact is of no consequence whatever, the plaintiff may, after a verdict for the defendant, move for judgment *non obstante veredicto,* that is, that he have judgment to recover notwithstanding the verdict, which being given on a bad plea, ought to be of no avail. In this case the judgment can only be on the *confession* of the defendant, for judgment *non obstante veredicto* can obviously only be given, when the plea is in confession and avoidance ; a judgment which is always awarded on the merits, and never granted but in a very clear case, and where it is apparent that in any way of putting the case the defendant can have no merits.

4. If by the inadvertence of the pleaders the issue be joined on a fact totally immaterial or insufficient to determine the right, so that the court upon the finding cannot know for whom judgment ought to be given ; as if, in an action against an executor, he pleads that he himself, instead of the testator, made no such promise : or if, in an action of debt on bond conditioned to pay money *on* or *before* a certain day, the defendant pleads payment *on* the day, which issue, if found for the plaintiff, would be inconclusive, as the money might have been paid *before* ; in these cases the court will after verdict award a *repleader, quod partes replacitent,* unless it appears from the whole record that nothing material can possibly be pleaded in any shape whatsoever, and then a repleader would be fruitless. And whenever a repleader is granted, the pleadings must begin *de novo* at that stage of them, whether it be the plea, replication, or rejoinder, &c., wherein there appears to have been the first defect or deviation from the regular course. Whether, therefore, the plaintiff can have judgment *non obstante veredicto,* or there must be a repleader, depends on the fact of the plea containing or not a confession of a cause of action. For if a cause of action is thereby confessed, and the matter pleaded in avoidance is insufficient, the

plaintiff is entitled to judgment; but if the plea does not confess a cause of action, there must be a repleader.

5. A *venire de novo* is the old common law mode of proceeding to a second trial, and differs materially from a new trial, which, as we have already seen, is granted only for matter entirely extrinsic of the record. It is where some defect appears on the face of the record itself that a *venire de novo*, as it is called, is awarded; this term being derived from the name of the ancient jury process, which, in this instance, was awarded afresh, or *de novo*. And this differs in effect also from a new trial, for here no costs can be given, nor conditions imposed on either party, it being ordinarily awarded where the finding of the verdict is defective.

If judgment is not by some of these means arrested within four days, if the cause is tried in term, or within the first four days of the next term after the trial, if it is tried in vacation, it is then to be entered on the roll or record, although in practice this is never done, but the judgment is merely signed at the office of the court. Judgments are the sentence of the law, pronounced by the court upon the matter contained in the record, and are of four sorts. First, where the facts are confessed by the parties, and the law determined by the court, as in case of judgment upon *demurrer*: secondly, where the law is admitted by the parties, and the facts disputed, as in case of judgment on a *verdict*: thirdly, where both the fact and the law arising thereon are admitted by the defendant, which is the case of judgments by *confession* or *default*: or, lastly, where the plaintiff is convinced that either fact, or law, or both, are insufficient to support his action, and therefore abandons or withdraws his prosecution, which is the case in judgments upon a *nonsuit* or *retraxit*.

The judgment though pronounced or awarded by the judges, is not their determination or sentence, but the determination and sentence of *the law*. It is the conclusion that naturally and regularly follows from the premises of law and fact, which stands thus: against him who has rode over my corn, I may recover damages by law; but A has rode over my corn, therefore I shall recover damages against A. If the major proposition be denied, this is a demurrer in law; if the minor, it is then an issue of fact; but if both be confessed, or determined, to be right, the conclusion or judgment of the court cannot but follow. Which judgment or conclusion depends not therefore on the arbitrary caprice of the judge, but on the settled and invariable principles of justice. The judgment, in short, is the remedy prescribed by law for the redress of injuries, and the suit or action is the vehicle or means of administering it. What that remedy may be is, indeed, the result of deliberation and study to point out, and, therefore, the style of the judgment is, not that it is decreed or resolved by the court, for then the judgment might appear to be their own; but "it is considered," *consideratum est per curiam,* that the plaintiff do recover his damages, his debt, his possession, and the like; which implies that the judgment is none of their own, but the act of law pronounced and declared by the court, after due deliberation and inquiry.

All these species of judgments are either *interlocutory* or *final. Interlocutory* judgments are such as are given in the middle of a cause, upon some plea, proceeding, or default, which is only intermediate, and does not finally determine or complete the suit. Of this nature are all judgments for the plaintiff upon pleas in abatement of the suit or action; in which it is considered by the court that the defendant do answer over, *respondeat ouster;* that is, put in a more substantial plea. It is easy to observe that the judgment here given is not final, but merely interlocutory, for there are afterwards further proceedings to be had, when the defendant has put in a better answer.

But the interlocutory judgments most usually spoken of are those incomplete judgments, whereby the *right* of the plaintiff is, indeed, established, but the *quantum* of damages sustained by him is not ascertained; which is a matter that cannot ordinarily be done without the intervention of a jury. This can only happen where the plaintiff recovers; for when judgment is given for the defendant it is always complete as well as final. And this happens, in the first place, where the defendant suffers judgment to go against him by default, or *nihil dicit,* as if he puts in no plea at all to the plaintiff's declaration; by confession, as in the case of a judgment *non obstante veredicto,* or *cognovit actionem,* where he acknowledges the plaintiff's demand to be just, which is a species of judgment by default. If these, or any of them, happen in actions where the specific thing sued for is recovered, as in actions for a sum certain, the judgment is absolutely complete. And, therefore, it is very usual, in order to strengthen a creditor's security, for the debtor to execute a warrant of attorney to some attorney named by the creditor, empowering him to confess a judgment by either of the ways just now mentioned by, *nihil dicit, cognovit actionem,* or *non sum informatus,* in an action to be brought by the creditor against the debtor for the specific sum due, which judgment, when confessed, is absolutely complete and binding.

When the plaintiff's claim is not for a sum certain, but for a sum which may be ascertained merely by computation, the court will direct one of the masters to ascertain the amount by hearing the parties before it gives judgment. But where damages, properly so called, are to be recovered, a jury must be called in to assess them ; unless the defendant, to save charges, will confess the whole damages laid in the declaration, otherwise the entry of the judgment is, "that the plaintiff ought to recover his damages, (indefinitely), " but because the court know not what damages the said plaintiff " has sustained, therefore the sheriff is commanded that by the " oaths of twelve honest and lawful men he inquire into the said " damages, and return such inquisition into court. This process is called a *writ of inquiry* : in the execution of which the sheriff sits as judge, and tries by a jury, subject to nearly the same law and conditions as the trial by jury at *nisi prius*, what damages the plaintiff has really sustained ; and when their verdict is given, which must assess *some* damages, the sheriff returns the inquisition, which is entered upon the roll in manner of a *postea ;* and thereupon it is considered that the plaintiff do recover the exact sum of the damages so assessed. In like manner, when a demurrer is determined for the plaintiff upon an action wherein damages are recovered, the judgment is also incomplete, without the aid of a writ of inquiry. When a writ of injunction or mandamus has been claimed, this also will be awarded by the judgment.

When it is said that a judgment is *binding*, this means that it binds all lands, tenements, and hereditaments of which the party against whom it is recovered, or any trustee for him, is possessed at the time. But it is not of any effect, as against *bonâ fide* purchasers, or mortgagees of the judgment debtor's real estate, leaseholds included, or creditors having charges thereon, unless, *first*, a memorandum of the judgment is duly registered in the court of Common Pleas ; *secondly*, process of execution is issued thereon, and the writ registered in like manner ; and *thirdly*, the process itself put in force within three months from its registration, and the *land actually delivered* under it ; all *before* the execution of the conveyance on mortgage or creation of the charge, the Court of Chancery will then direct a sale of the debtor's interest in the estate, and the application of the proceeds in payment of the debt. The judgment debtor's *personal estate* is bound not by the *judgment* at all, but only by the delivery of the writ to the sheriff ; and, in case of his bankruptcy, its execution by their seizure and sale.

Thus much for judgments ; to which *costs* are a necessary appendage, though the common law did not allow any. The right to these, therefore, depends on several statutes ; on which, however, several exceptions have been engrafted. Thus paupers, that is, such as will swear themselves not worth five pounds, have writs *gratis*, and counsel and attorney assigned them without fee, and are excused from paying costs when plaintiffs, but shall suffer other punishment at the discretion of the judges. And it was formerly usual to give such paupers, if nonsuited, their election either to be whipped or pay the costs, though that practice is now disused. It seems, however, agreed that a pauper may recover costs, though he pays none; for the counsel and clerks are bound to give their labour to *him*, but not to his antagonist. Again, to prevent trifling and malicious actions, for words, for assault and battery, and for trespass; the plaintiff, if he recovers less than 40s., is not entitled to costs unless the judge certifies that the action was brought to try a right, besides the mere right to recover damages, or that the trespass or grievance was wilful and malicious. And in all actions for an alleged wrong, in which less than five pounds is recovered, the judge may certify to deprive the plaintiff of costs altogether. In actions upon judgments the plaintiff recovers no costs, and when he might have sued in the county court, but has resorted to a superior court, he is also, in certain circumstances, deprived of his costs, unless in either class of cases the court or a judge shall otherwise order.

After *judgment* is entered, *execution* will immediately follow, unless the party condemned thinks himself unjustly aggrieved by any of these proceedings, and then he has his remedy to reverse them by other proceedings in the nature of appeals, which we shall consider in the succeeding chapter.

CHAPTER XV.

OF PROCEEDINGS IN THE NATURE OF APPEALS.

Auditâ querelâ—Error—Bail in error—Assignment of errors—Judgment—
Writ of restitution—Error on special case—Courts of error.

If the party condemned thinks himself unjustly aggrieved, he has now two modes of questioning the propriety of the judgment by proceedings in the nature of *appeals*, viz., by writ of *auditâ querelâ*; or by bringing *error*.

I. An *auditâ querelâ* is where a defendant, against whom judgment is recovered, and who is therefore in danger of execution, or perhaps actually in execution, may be relieved upon good matter of discharge, which has happened since the judgment; as if the plaintiff has given him a general release; or if the defendant has paid the debt to the plaintiff, without procuring satisfaction to be entered on the record. In these and the like cases, wherein the defendant has good matter to plead, but has had no opportunity of pleading it, either at the beginning of the suit, or *puis darrein continuance*, which, as was shown in a former chapter, must always be before judgment, an *auditâ querelâ* lies to be relieved against the oppression of the plaintiff. It is a writ directed to the court, stating that the complaint of the defendant has been heard, *auditâ querelâ defendentis*, and then setting out the matter of the complaint, it at length enjoins the court to call the parties before them, and, having heard their allegations and proofs, to cause justice to be done between them. But the indulgence now shown by the courts in granting a summary relief upon motion, in cases of such evident oppression, has almost rendered useless the writ of *auditâ querelâ*, and driven it quite out of practice; and that the courts may not be deprived of the opportunity of giving this summary relief, this writ cannot now be sued out without a rule of court or judge's order to that effect.

II. The principal method of redress for erroneous judgments in the courts of common law at Westminster, is by alleging, or as it is called, bringing *error* in some superior court of appeal.

Error lies for some supposed mistake in the proceedings of a court of record; for to amend errors in an inferior court, not of record, a writ of *false judgment* lies. Error only lies upon matter of *law* arising upon the face of the proceedings, so that no evidence is required to substantiate or support it; there being no method of reversing an error in the determination of *facts*, but by a new trial, to correct the mistakes of the former verdict.

This proceeding is the only mode of giving effect to a *bill of exceptions*, for the judgment of the court after the trial of the issues of fact being given on the verdict of the jury irrespective altogether of the bill of exceptions, to reverse that judgment, error must be brought; in order that the whole record, to which the bill of exceptions is then attached, may be before the court of error, which has then all the materials for a proper judgment.

On the principle previously stated, that every subject when wronged is to apply to the sovereign as the fountain of justice, for that redress which the law affords him for the particular injury complained of, error was formerly brought in all cases by the party grieved suing an original writ out of chancery; which, in suits in the superior courts at Westminster, was addressed to the chief justice, and, after reciting that in the record and proceedings and also in the giving of judgment in the action, manifest error, as it was said, had intervened, it commanded the chief justice to send a transcript of the record and other proceedings under his seal to the judges of the court of Exchequer Chamber, that the same being examined by them, they might cause to be further done thereupon, what of right ought to be done. When error was brought in the House of Lords upon the judgment of the Exchequer Chamber, the writ directed the transcript and proceedings to be returned " in our " present parliament;" that the same being reviewed, " we may " further cause to be done thereupon, with the assent of the lords " spiritual and temporal in the same parliament, for correcting that " error, what of right, and according to the law and custom of " England, ought to be done." To the writ of error, the Lord Chief Justice, or in case of error brought upon the judgment of inferior courts, the judge of the court to which the writ of error was directed, made a return of a transcript as directed, and the record and proceedings were thus at once brought before the court of error for review.

A simpler and less expensive method has, however, been provided for bringing error on the judgments of the superior courts, by making it a step in the cause; the writ of error in all actions therein being dispensed with, though still necessary in certain other proceedings. The party aggrieved now delivers to one of the masters of the court, in which the judgment complained of was given, a memorandum alleging error, which being filed, the master gives the plaintiff in error a note of the receipt thereof; a copy of which, together with *a statement of the grounds of error* intended to be argued, being served on the opposite party, operates at once as a *supersedeas* of execution; which cannot issue on the original judgment, except by order of the court or a judge, until default in putting in bail—affirmance of the judgment—discontinuance by the plaintiff in error—or the proceedings being otherwise disposed of, as by judgment of *non pros.* But if there is *no statement* of the alleged error, execution may issue; any statement, however frivolous, involving, nevertheless, the necessity of obtaining leave to do so, as it is not for the party himself to decide on its frivolity.

If error be brought to reverse any judgment of an inferior court of record, where the damages are less than fifteen pounds—or, if it is brought to reverse the judgment of any superior court, he that brings it, or that is plaintiff in error, must, except in some peculiar cases, find substantial pledges of prosecution or bail; to prevent delays by frivolous pretences to appeal; and for securing payment of costs and damages, which are now payable by the vanquished party in all, except a few particular instances. Execution, there fore, against a defendant will not be stayed, unless within four days of his bringing error, he with two sureties become bound to the plaintiff below, now become the defendant in error, in double the amount awarded by the judgment, and also to pay to him all further cost and damages, if the judgment be affirmed or the proceedings in error discontinued.

The plaintiff in error next suggests on the roll that, in the proceedings in the action and the giving of judgment therein, there is error, adding thereto the defendant's denial, or *joinder in error;* after which the judgment roll is made up and carried into the court of error, which, on examining it awards the proper judgment, if the former was erroneous; unless the defendant in the mean time confesses the error by giving the plaintiff a notice to that effect, on which *judgment of reversal* may be signed. But if the defendant in error relies upon this proceeding being barred by lapse of time, or by release of error, or other matter of fact, he must give four days' written notice to the other party to assign error, which *assignment of error* is in the nature of a declaration, stating the grounds on which the plaintiff in error imputes error on the record; nothing being assignable for error that contradicts the record itself; and to this assignment the defendant in error must put in a *plea*, confessing that the judgment is erroneous, but showing that the plaintiff cannot take advantage of the error; as for instance by showing a *release of errors.* To the defendant's plea, the plaintiff *replies* or *demurs*, and the defendant again *demurs* or *rejoins*, so that ultimately an issue *of law* or *in fact* is joined, the latter being taken down for trial by the defendant in error *by proviso*, without his waiting for a default by the plaintiff, as we have seen he is obliged to do in ordinary cases.

The judgment of the court of error may be either in affirmance of the former judgment; or that it be reversed for error in law; or that the plaintiff be barred of his right to bring error, as when a plea of the statute of limitations has been found for the defendant. But the court of error may always give such judgment and award such process as the court below ought to have given, and therefore it may award a repleader, or direct a *venire de novo.*

When the judgment of the court below is affirmed, or the plaintiff in error *non pros'd*, the defendant is entitled to *damages* and *costs*, as well as to *interest* upon the sum awarded him by the court below for the time that execution has been delayed; but if the judgment of the court below is reversed, each party must pay his own costs. If, however, execution has been levied on the plaintiff in error for debt or damages, he is entitled to a *writ of restitution*, in order that he may recover all that he has thereby lost.

III. As error in law can only be brought on matter appearing on the record, it does not lie to reverse the judgment on a special case, because there nothing appears on the record. But, *unless the parties have agreed to the contrary*, an appeal, which practically amounts to the same thing, may be brought against the judgment; the proceedings for doing so being, as nearly as may be, the same as in the case of error. And the same method of proceeding by appeal may be resorted to, by either party, where, at the trial, leave has been reserved to move that a *verdict* or *nonsuit* be entered, or for a new trial; and the court either refuses or grants the application; for here, as in a special case, nothing whatever appears on the record, and, technically, *error* cannot be brought.

Error lies from the inferior courts of record in England, existing at the common law, into the Queen's Bench, which is also the court of error and appeal from the judgments of the court of pleas at Durham, the court of common pleas at Lancaster, and the mayor's court of the City of London. Each court of appeal, in their respective stages, may, upon hearing the matter of law in which the error is assigned, reverse or affirm the judgment of the inferior courts; but none of them are final, save only the House of Peers, to whose judicial decisions all other tribunals must therefore submit, and conform their own. And thus much for the reversal or affirmance of judgments at law by proceedings in the nature of appeals.

CHAPTER XVI.

OF EXECUTION.

The last step in a suit is the *execution* of the judgment, or putting the sentence of the law in force. This is performed in different manners, according to the nature of the action upon which it is founded, and of the judgment which is had or recovered.

If the plaintiff recovers in a real action or in ejectment, whereby the seisin or possession of land is awarded to him, the writ of execution is a *habere facias seisinam*, or writ of seisin, of a freehold; or a *habere facias possessionem*, or writ of possession, of a chattel interest. These are writs directed to the sheriff of the county, commanding him to give actual possession to the claimant of the land recovered: in the execution of which the sheriff may take with him the *posse comitatus*, or power of the county; and may justify breaking open doors, if the possession be not quietly delivered. But, if it ·be peaceably yielded up, the delivery of a twig, a turf, or the ring of the door, in the name of the rest, is sufficient execution of the writ.

Upon a presentation to a benefice recovered in a *quare impedit*, the execution is by a writ *de clerico admittendo;* directed, not to the sheriff, but to the bishop or archbishop, and requiring him to admit and institute the clerk of the plaintiff.

In other actions, where the judgment is that something in special be done or rendered by him against whom the judgment is given, then, in order to compel him so to do, and to see the judgment executed, a special writ of execution issues to the sheriff according to the nature of the case.

After judgment in the action brought by a replevisor, the writ of execution to obtain a return of the goods is the writ *de retorno habendo:* and, if the distress be eloigned, the defendant shall have a *capias in withernam;* but on the plaintiff's tendering the damages, the process *in withernam* shall be stayed.

In *detinue*, after judgment, the plaintiff shall have a *distringas*, to compel the defendant to deliver the goods, by repeated distresses of his chattels: or else a *scire facias* against any third person in whose hands they may happen to be, to show cause why they should not be delivered: and if the defendant still continues obstinate, then, if the judgment has been by default or on demurrer, the sheriff shall summon an inquest to ascertain the value of the goods, and the plaintiff's damages: which, being either so assessed, or by the verdict in case of an issue, shall be levied on the person or goods of the defendant. Execution may also issue for the return of the specific chattel detained, without giving the defendant the option of retaining it upon payment of the value assessed by the jury; the plaintiff being further entitled, either by the same or a separate writ of execution, to have the damages, costs, and interest recovered in the action levied on the defendant's goods. Of a similar nature is the writ of execution which may be had in actions for breach of a contract to deliver specific goods for a price in money.

Executions in actions where money only is recovered, as a debt or damages, are of five sorts: either against the body of the defendant;

T

or against his goods and chattels; or against his goods and the *profits* of his lands; or against his goods and the *possession* of his lands; or against all three, his body, lands, and goods.

1. The first of these species of execution, is by writ of *capias ad satisfaciendum*; which addition distinguishes it from the former *capias ad respondendum*, which lies to compel the defendant to give bail and enter an appearance at the beginning of a suit. It cannot be sued out against any but such as were liable to be taken upon the former *capias*, nor in actions wherein the sum recovered does not exceed twenty pounds, exclusive of the costs. The intent of it is to imprison the body of the debtor till satisfaction be made for the debt, costs, and damages; it therefore does not lie against any privileged persons, peers, or members of parliament, nor against such other persons as could not be originally held to bail. This writ is an execution of the highest nature, inasmuch as it deprives a man of his liberty, till he makes the satisfaction awarded; and therefore, when a man is once taken in execution upon this writ, no other process can be sued out against his lands or goods. It is directed to the sheriff, commanding him to take the body of the defendant and have him at Westminster on a day therein named, to make the plaintiff satisfaction for his demand.

When a defendant is once in custody upon this process, he is to be kept in *arcta et salva custodia*: and if he be afterwards seen at large, it is an *escape*; and the plaintiff may have an action thereupon against the sheriff for the value of the custody of the debtor at the moment of the escape. A rescue of a prisoner *in execution*, either going to gaol or in gaol, or a breach of prison, will not excuse the sheriff from being guilty of, and answering for the escape; for he ought to have sufficient force to keep him, since he may command the power of the county.

If the debtor when taken in execution does not make satisfaction, he must remain in prison till he does, or until he be discharged as a bankrupt; a fate from which there is now no means of escape except by payment of the debt for which he is incarcerated; as every debtor's prison must now be cleared of its prisoners at least once in every month, by an adjudication of bankruptcy against the insolvent inhabitants.

If a *capias ad satisfaciendum* is sued out, and a *non est inventus* is returned thereon, the plaintiff may sue out a writ of *scire facias* against the bail, if bail were given in the action, commanding them to show cause why the plaintiff should not have execution against them for his debt and damages: and on such writ, if they show no sufficient cause, or the defendant does not surrender himself, the plaintiff may have judgment against the bail, and take out a writ of *capias ad satisfaciendum*, or other process of execution against them.

2. The next species of execution is against the goods and chattels of the defendant ; and is called a writ of *fieri facias*, from the words in it where the sheriff is commanded, *quad fieri facias de bonis*, that he cause to be made of the goods and chattels of the defendant, the sum or debt recovered. This lies as well against privileged persons, peers, &c., as other common persons ; and against executors or administrators with regard to the goods of the deceased. The sheriff may not break open any outer doors, to execute either this or the former writ, but must enter peaceably ; and may then break open any inner door, belonging to the defendant, in order to take the goods. And he may sell the goods and chattels, even an estate for years, which is a chattel real, of the defendant, till he has raised enough to satisfy the judgment and costs : first paying the landlord of the premises, upon which the goods are found, the arrears of rent then due, not exceeding one year's rent in the whole.

If a claim be made by a third party to the goods of the person against whom the writ of *fieri facias* is issued, the sheriff may impannel a jury to try the question of property ; and according as that question is determined, surrender the goods or sell them in terms of the writ. But he now usually proceeds in such a case under the *Interpleader acts*; and obtains from a judge, at chambers, a summons directed to the execution creditor, and the party claiming the goods ; and calling upon them to appear and maintain their respective claims; which, if the claimant fail to do, his claim is barred. But if both parties appear, the judge may decide between them ; or an interpleader issue, to try the right of property, is directed ; on which the parties go to trial as in ordinary cases; or, if the question be one of law, a case may be stated for the court ; —the costs of these proceedings being exclusively in the discretion of the court, or of the judge by whom the matter is disposed of ; the decision, whether of the judge or of the court, which may be moulded to suit the circumstances of the case, not being subject to the review of a court of error.

If part only of the debt be levied on a *fieri facias*, the creditor may have a *capias ad satisfaciendum* for the residue, or may resort to the other means with which the law provides him to realise his claim.

T 2

Under the writ of *fieri facias*, goods, money, and securities only may be taken. In order to get at any stock or shares belonging to the debtor, which cannot be reached by this writ, the creditor may obtain from a judge an order, charging such property with payment of the amount for which judgment has been recovered, which operates as a *distringas*, the judgment creditor having thereupon such remedies as he would have been entitled to, if the charge had been made in his favour by the judgment debtor himself.

By neither of these methods of proceeding, however, can debts not secured by bills, bonds, or other tangible securities, be made available to the creditor. The law, therefore, allows him to attach and compel payment to himself of the debts due to his debtor; as a judge may, on his application, order all debts, owing by any third person, who is called the *garnishee*, and is allowed to dispute his indebtedness to the judgment debtor, to be attached to answer the judgment debt; and in order to discover the existence and amount thereof, may further direct the oral examination of the debtor himself. So that either by a writ of *fieri facias*, an order charging stock with the amount of the judgment, or an attachment of the debts owing to the judgment debtor, may the creditor obtain satisfaction out of the goods and chattels of his debtor.

3. A third species of execution is by writ of *levari facias*; which affects a man's goods and the *profits* of his lands, by commanding the sheriff to levy the plaintiff's debt on the lands and goods of the defendant: whereby the sheriff may seize all his goods, and receive the rents and profits of his lands, till satisfaction be made to the plaintiff. Little use is now made of this writ; the remedy by *elegit*, which takes possession of the lands themselves, being much more effectual.

But of this species is a writ of execution proper only to ecclesiastics; which is given when the sheriff, upon a common writ of execution issued, returns that the defendant is a beneficed clerk, not having any lay fee. In this case a writ goes to the bishop of the diocese, in the nature of a *levari* or *fieri facias*, to levy the debt and damages *de bonis ecclesiasticis*, which are not to be touched by lay hands: and thereupon the bishop sends out a *sequestration* of the profits of the clerk's benefice, directed to the churchwardens, to collect the same and pay them to the plaintiff, till the full sum be raised.

4. The fourth species of execution is by the writ of *elegit*, so called because it is in the choice or election of the plaintiff whether he will sue out this writ or one of the former writs of *capias* or *fieri facias*, by which the defendant's goods and chattels are

not sold, but only appraised; and all of them, except oxen and beasts of the plough, are delivered to the plaintiff, at such reasonable appraisement and price, in part of satisfaction of his debt. If the goods are not sufficient, then his lands are also delivered to the plaintiff; to hold, till out of the rents and profits thereof the debt be levied, or till the defendant's interest be expired; as till the death of the defendant, if he be tenant for life or in tail. During this period the plaintiff is called tenant by *elegit*, of whom we spoke in a former book of these commentaries. This execution, or seizing of lands by *elegit*, is of so high a nature, that after it the body of the defendant cannot be taken: but if execution can only be had of the goods, because there are no lands, and such goods are not sufficient to pay the debt, a *capias ad satisfaciendum* may then be had after the *elegit*; for such *elegit* is in this case no more in effect than a *fieri facias*. So that body and goods may be taken in execution, or land and goods; but not body and land too, upon any judgment between subject and subject in the course of the common law.

By these several writs and proceedings, the whole of the judgment debtor's property, real and personal, may be resorted to, in satisfaction of the judgment. But,

5. Upon some prosecutions given by statute, as in the case of debts acknowledged on statutes-staple, body, lands, and goods may all be taken at once in execution, to compel the payment of the debt. The process hereon is usually called an *extent* or *extendi facias*, because the sheriff is to cause the lands, &c., to be appraised to their full extended value, before he delivers them to the plaintiff, that it may be certainly known how soon the debt will be satisfied. And by the statute 33 Hen. VIII. c. 39, all obligations made to the king shall have the same force, and of consequence the same remedy to recover them, as a statute staple; though, indeed, before this statute, the king was entitled to sue out execution against the body, lands, and goods of his accountant or debtor. And his debts shall, in suing out execution, be preferred to that of every other creditor, who has not obtained judgment before the sovereign commenced his suit. The sovereign's judgment also affects all lands which his debtor has at or after the time of contracting his debt, or which any of his officers mentioned in the statute 13 Eliz. c. 4, has at or after the time of his entering on the office; so that, if such officer of the crown aliens for a valuable consideration, the land shall be liable to the sovereign's debt even in the hands of a *bonâ fide* purchaser: though the debt due to the crown was contracted by the vendor many years after the alienation. But as this rule of law might be productive of very great hardship and injustice, it is now provided by several statutes, that no judgment, statute, recognizance,

inquisition, obligation, or speciality, nor any acceptance of office within the statute 13 Eliz. c. 4, shall avail against purchasers, mortgagees, or creditors, unless and until a memorandum thereof be registered in the office of the Common Pleas; so that everybody has notice thereof, and it is his own fault if any one purchases or lends money on mortgage, without searching for judgments against the seller or mortgagor.

Hitherto of writs of execution, which put the judgment creditor in possession of the lands or goods, or of the debt, damages, or costs recovered in the action. There are two other writs of execution, which are applicable to those cases, where either the repetition or continuance of a wrongful act is to be prohibited, or the performance of a contract or duty to be enforced.

The first of these is the *Writ of Injunction*, which may issue at any time after the commencement of the action, whether before or after judgment; but can only be obtained on an application to the court or a judge. It issues to restrain the defendant from the repetition or continuance of the wrongful act or breach of contract complained of in the action, or the committal of any breach of contract or injury of a like kind, arising out of the same contract, or relating to the same property or right, and may be granted upon such terms as may seem reasonable and just. When issued, obedience will, if necessary, be enforced by attachment.

The performance again by the defendant of the contract or duty, neglect of which has formed the subject of complaint in the suit, may be compelled by a *writ of mandamus*; to which no return except that of compliance, is allowed. In case of disobedience, the writ also may be enforced by attachment, or *writ of sequestration*; or the court may direct that the act required shall be done by the plaintiff, or some other person appointed by the court, *at the expense of the defendant*; and upon its being done, the amount of the expense may be ascertained either by writ of inquiry or reference to the master, and payment thereof enforced in the ordinary way.

These are the methods which the law of England has pointed out for the execution of judgments: and when the plaintiff's demand is satisfied, either by the voluntary payment of the defendant, or by this compulsory process or otherwise, satisfaction ought to be entered on the record, that the defendant may not be liable to be hereafter harrassed a second time on the same account.

And here this part of our commentaries, which regularly treats only of redress at the common law, would naturally draw to a con-.

clusion. But, as the proceedings in the courts of equity are very
different from those at common law, and as those courts are of a
very general and extensive jurisdiction, it is in some measure a
branch of the task I have undertaken, to give the student some
general idea not only of the forms of practice adopted by those courts,
but of the matters more usually cognizable there. These will, therefore, so far as I have not already touched upon them, be the
subjects of the ensuing chapters.

CHAPTER XVII.

OF THE JURISDICTION OF THE COURTS OF EQUITY.

General nature of equity—Difference from law—Mode of proof—Mode of trial
—Mode of relief.——Matters cognizable in courts of equity. I. *Exclusive
jurisdiction*—Infants—Lunatics—Married women—Wife's equity to a settle-
ment—Charities—Bankruptcy— Trusts— Mortgages— Equity of redemp-
tion.——II. *Concurrent jurisdiction*—Injunction—Specific performance—
Discovery—Accounts—Administration of estates—Marshalling of assets—
Partnership—Fraud—Constructive frauds—Accident—Mistake—Dower—
Partition of land—Settling boundaries.——III. *Auxiliary jurisdiction*—
Restraining inequitable defences—Cancellation of deeds—Bill *quia timet*—
Bill of peace—Perpetuation of testimony—Interpleader.

BEFORE we proceed to consider the jurisdiction of the courts of
equity, it will be proper to recollect the observations which were
made in the beginning of this book on the principal tribunals of
of that kind, acknowledged by our constitution. I therein attempted
to trace, very concisely, the history, rise, and progress of the Court
of Chancery. And what was said of that court will be equally applicable to the other courts of equity. Whatever difference there may
be in the forms of practice, it arises from the different constitution
of their officers; or if they differ in anything more essential, one of
them must certainly be wrong; for truth and justice are always
uniform, and ought equally to be adopted by them all.

Let us then take a brief, but comprehensive view of the general
nature of *equity;* which in its true and genuine meaning, is the
soul and spirit if all law ; for *positive* law is construed, and *rational*
law is made by it. In this, equity is synonymous to justice; in
that, to the true sense and sound interpretation of the rule. But
the very terms of a court of *equity* and a court of *law*, as contrasted
to each other, are apt to confound and mislead us: as if the one

judged without equity, and the other was not bound by any law. Whereas every definition or illustration to be met with, which now draws a line between the two jurisdictions, by setting law and equity in opposition to each other, will be found either totally erroneous, or erroneous to a certain degree.

Thus it is said, that it is the business of a court of equity in England to abate the rigour of the common law. But no such power is contended for. Hard was the case of bond-creditors, whose debtor devised away his real estate; rigorous and unjust the rule, which put the devisee in a better condition than the heir; yet a court of equity had no power to interpose. Hard was the common law that land devised, or descending to the heir, should not be liable to the simple contract debts of the ancestor or devisor, although the money was laid out in purchasing the very land; and that the father should never immediately succeed as heir to the real estate of the son, but a court of equity could give no relief; though in both instances the artificial reason of the law, arising from feudal principles, had entirely ceased, long before these grievances were remedied by legislative enactment. In all such cases of positive law, the courts of equity, as well as the courts of law, said with Ulpian, "*hoc quidem perquam durum est, sed ita lex scripta est.*"

Again it is said, that a court of equity determines according to the spirit of the rule, and not according to the strictness of the letter; but so also does a court of law. Both, for instance, are equally bound, and equally profess, to interpret statutes according to the true intent of the legislature. In general laws all cases cannot be forseen; or if forseen, cannot be expressed: some will arise that will fall within the meaning, though not within the words of the legislator; and others, which may fall within the letter, may be contrary to his meaning, though not expressly excepted. These cases, thus out of the letter, are often said to be within the equity of an act of parliament; and so cases within the letter are frequently out of the equity. Here, by *equity*, we mean nothing but the sound interpretation of the law; though the words of the law itself may be too general, too special, or otherwise inaccurate or defective.

It has also been said, that *fraud, accident,* and *trust,* are the proper and peculiar objects of a court of equity. But every kind of *fraud* is equally cognizable in a court of law; many *accidents* are also supplied in a court of law; as, loss of deeds, wrong payments, deaths, which make it impossible to perform a condition literally, and a multitude of other contingencies; and many cannot be relieved even in a court of equity, as, if by accident, a devise be ill-executed, or a contingent remainder destroyed. A technical *trust,* indeed, created by the limitation of a second use, was forced into the courts of equity, in the manner already mentioned; and this species of trusts, extended by inference and construction, has ever since remained as a kind of *peculium* in those courts. But there are other trusts which are cognizable in a court of law, as deposits, and all manner of bailments; and especially that implied contract, so highly beneficial and useful, of having undertaken to account for money received to another's use, which is the ground of an action almost as universally remedial as a bill in equity.

Once more, it has been said that a court of equity is not bound by rules or precedents, but acts from the opinion of the judge, founded on the circumstances of every particular case. Whereas the system of our courts of equity is a laboured connected system, governed by established rules, and bound down by precedents, from which they do not depart, although the reason of some of them may, perhaps, be liable to objection. Thus the holding the penalty of a bond to be merely a security for the debt and interest, yet considering it some-times as the debt itself, so that the interest shall not exceed that penalty : the distinguishing between a mortgage at *five per cent.*, with a clause of reduction to *four*, if the interest be regularly paid, and a mortgage at *four per cent.*, with a clause of enlargement to *five*, if the payment of the interest be deferred; so that the former shall be deemed a conscientious, the latter an unrighteous, bargain ; these and other cases that might be instanced are plainly rules of positive law, supported only by the reverence that is shown, and generally very properly shown, to a series of former determinations, that the rule of property may be uniform and steady.

In short, if a court of equity in England did really act, as many writers have supposed it to do, it would rise above all law, either common or statute, and be a most arbitrary legislator in every par-ticular case. But it is not so : for the jurisprudence of our courts, both of law and equity, is founded on the same principles of justice and positive law. The rules of property, rules of evidence, and rules of interpretation in both courts are exactly the same; both ought to adopt the best, or they must cease to be courts of justice. Neither a court of equity nor of law can vary a man's will or agreement, or, in other words, make a will or agreement for him. Both courts will equitably construe, but neither pretends to control or change, a lawful stipulation or engagement.

The rules of decision are in both courts equally apposite to the subjects of which they take cognizance. Both follow the law of nations where the question is the object of that law, as in case of the privileges of ambassadors. In mercantile transactions they both follow the *law merchant*, which we have seen is part of the common

law. Where they exercise a concurrent jurisdiction, they both
follow the law of the proper *forum* : in matters originally of ecclesiastical cognizance, they both equally adopt the canon or imperial
law, according to the nature of the subject; and, if a question come
before either, which is properly the object of a foreign municipal
law, they receive information what is the rule of the country, and
decide accordingly.

Such, then, being the parity of law and reason which governs
both species of courts, wherein does their essential difference consist?
It principally consists in the different modes of administering justice
in each ; in the mode of proof, the mode of trial, and the mode of
relief.

And, first, as to the mode of *proof.* When facts, or their leading
circumstances, rest only in the knowledge of the party, a court of
equity applies itself to his conscience, and purges him upon oath with
regard to the truth of the transaction; and that being once discovered, the judgment is the same in equity as it would have been
at law.

As to the mode of *trial.* This is not by a jury, but by the court
alone, and usually by means of affidavits or written depositions, and
not the oral testimony of witnesses in open court.

It is with respect to the mode of *relief* that the courts of equity
differ most from the courts of common law. For in the former there
are not only prescribed forms of proceedings to which a party must
confine himself; but in all cases a general and unqualified judgment
only can be given for the plaintiff or for the defendant, as the case
may be, without any adaptation of it to particular circumstances.
But courts of equity are not so restrained; their forms of proceeding are flexible, and may be suited to the different circumstances of
different cases. These courts may adjust their decrees; and thereby
vary, qualify, and model the remedy so as to suit it to mutual and
adverse claims, controlling equities, and the real and substantial
rights of the parties. Nay, more, they can bring before them all
the parties interested in the subject-matter, and adjust the rights of
all, however numerous : whereas courts of common law are compelled
to limit their inquiry to the very parties in the litigation before
them, although other persons may have the deepest interest in the
event of the suit.

The chief peculiarity of the courts of equity is, however, that they
administer remedies for rights, which courts of law do not recognize
at all; or if they do recognize them, they leave them wholly to the
conscience of the parties. Thus what are technically called *trusts,*

that is, estates vested in persons upon particular trusts and confidences, are wholly without any cognizance at common law, and the abuses of such trusts and confidences are beyond the reach of any legal process. But they are cognizable in courts of equity, and here they are called *equitable estates ;* and an ample remedy is given to the *cestius que trust,* the parties beneficially interested, for any wrong and injury they may sustain, whether arising from negligence or from misconduct. There are also, as we have already seen, cases of impending irreparable injuries, or meditated mischiefs; cases of losses and injuries by mistake; cases of oppressive proceedings ; and cases of unconscionable bargains and others, in all of which courts of equity grant redress, but of which the common law has no means of taking notice.

This leads us naturally to a consideration of the matters cognizable in the courts of equity. These have hitherto been treated of by the best legal writers as either *exclusive* of, *concurrent* with, or *auxiliary* to that of the courts of common law ; the *first* head referring to those branches of jurisdiction which are the peculiar property of the Court of Chancery ; the *second* comprising those matters which are equally entertained by courts of law and equity, although the remedies afforded in each may be different; the *third,* or auxiliary jurisdiction of Chancery, being so denominated with reference to those cases in which equity lends its aid to remove impediments to the obtaining of relief in a court of law.

I. The *exclusive* jurisdiction of the courts of equity comprises the guardianship which these courts exercise over the person and property of infants and lunatics, the peculiar protection they afford to married women, the superintendence they possess over charities, their appellate jurisdiction in bankruptcy, and such matters as statutory enactments have expressly confided to their administrative care. Equitable estates and interests which owe their very being to the doctrines of equity, are necessarily the particular objects of the courts, in which those doctrines are law. And first of infants.

1. Upon the abolition of the Court of Wards, the care which the crown was bound to take as guardian of its infant tenants, was totally extinguished in every feudal view, but resulted to the crown in the Court of Chancery, together with the general protection of all other *infants* in the kingdom. When, therefore, a child has no other guardian, or the father, by his conduct, such as gross cruelty or immorality, has disqualified himself for the charge of his child, the Court of Chancery has a right to appoint one; and from all proceedings relative thereto, an appeal lies to the House of Lords.

2. As to *idiots* and *lunatics*, the crown used formerly to commit the custody of them to proper committees, in every particular case; but now, to avoid solicitations, and the very shadow of undue partiality, a warrant is issued by the sovereign, under the royal sign manual, to the chancellor to perform this office for him; a similar authority being also conferred on the lords justices of the Court of Appeal. If the chancellor or lords justices act improperly in granting such custodies, the complaint must be made to the sovereign himself in council; such complaint, when made, being examined and reported on by the judicial committee.

3. The protection which courts of equity afford to married women is principally with reference to their property. The common law doctrine which gives to a husband the possession and control of his wife's personal estate, including her *choses in action*, is not one which finds favour in equity; and the Court of Chancery had accordingly seized upon every opportunity to control and modify the rigour of this principle. The common law considers the wife as merged in the husband; equity, for many purposes, treats the husband and wife, not as one, but as two separate persons, having distinct rights and interests. And one of the most peculiar of these rights is the *equity of the wife to have a settlement of her own property.* Not that the court can restrict the legal rights with which the law clothes the husband. For when he has reduced the personal estate of his wife into possession, he may dispose of it at his pleasure without restraint or interference. But when he is obliged to seek the aid of equity in regard to the wife's property, as for instance when it is vested in *trustees* for her benefit, the court lays hold of the occasion, and upon the ground that he who seeks equity must do equity, requires the husband to make a settlement on the wife out of that or some other property, for her due maintenance and support. The court will also require a settlement on the issue of the marriage, unless the wife dissent, and then the court withholds its aid, for the equity of the children is not an equity to which they are in their own right entitled.

4. The sovereign, as *parens patriæ*, has the general superintendence of all *charities*, which he exercises by the keeper of his conscience, the chancellor. And therefore, whenever it is necessary, the attorney-general, at the relation of some informant, who is usually called the *relator*, files *ex officio* an information in the Court of Chancery to have the charity properly established. A large portion of the administrative powers of the court of equity with reference to charities has latterly, however, been conferred on *the Charity Commissioners for England and Wales*, who have authority to inquire into all charities, their nature, and administration, and the condition of

the estates and funds belonging to them; and to take or direct such proceedings as are necessary to carry out beneficially the objects of the founders.

5. By the statutes relating to *bankruptcy* an appeal lies, as we have already seen, in certain cases to the Court of Chancery, and then to the House of Lords.

6. The form of a *trust*, or second use, gives the courts of equity an exclusive jurisdiction as to the subject-matter of all settlements and devises in that form, and of all the long terms created in the present complicated mode of conveyancing. This is a very ample source of jurisdiction; but the trust is governed by very nearly the same rules as would govern the estate in a court of law, if no trustee was interposed; and, by a regular positive system established in the courts of equity, the doctrine of trusts is now reduced to as great a certainty as that of legal estates in the courts of the common law.

Another source of jurisdiction under this head arises upon the construction of *securities* for money lent, which at an early period of our legal history gave employment to the courts of equity. When they held the penalty of a bond to be the form, and that in substance it was only as a pledge to secure the repayment of the sum *bonâ fide* advanced, with a proper compensation for the use, they laid the foundation of a regular series of determinations, which have settled the doctrine of personal pledges or securities, and are equally applicable to mortgages of real property. The mortgagor continues owner of the land, the mortgagee of the money lent upon it; but this ownership is mutually transferred, and the mortgagor is barred from redemption, if, when called upon by the mortgagee, he does not redeem within a time limited by the court; or he may, when out of possession, be barred by length of time, by the statute of limitations. Until *foreclosure*, however, the *equity of redemption* or right which the mortgagor has to redeem his pledge upon payment of his debt, is treated by the courts of equity as a distinct estate; and possesses, in the eyes of equity, all the same properties which a legal estate has in the eye of the law. The mortgagee is thus made to stand in the position of a *trustee*, and as such comes under the jurisdiction of this court.

For equity recognizes not only *express* trusts, such as those which have been mentioned, but also *implied trusts*; which are said either to spring out of the presumed intention of the parties; as in the conveyance of property without any consideration, or any distinct use or trust being declared, where it is consequently presumed that the intention was that it should be held by the grantee for the benefit of the grantor—or, no such presumption of intention being raised, the trust is fixed upon the conscience of the party by operation of law, as where a party having notice of a trust purchases the property from the trustee, in violation thereof; in which case a court of equity will compel the purchaser to carry out the trust.

Trusts of all kinds have thus become the most extensive branch of equity jurisdiction, their administration constituting the chief occupation of these courts; so much so, indeed, that special facilities have been provided by several statutes for obtaining their interference without the necessity of a suit being instituted. Of these perhaps the most important is the Trustee Relief Act, which enables trustees who suppose that there will be difficulty in the administration of the trust funds at once to discharge themselves from all liability by paying the money into court; which thereupon undertakes the administration of it amongst the parties beneficially interested, according to their respective rights and interests.

II. The *concurrent* jurisdiction of the courts of equity extends to all cases of a breach or infringement of legal right, when, under the circumstances, there is not a plain, adequate, and complete remedy at law.

1. The first peculiar remedy obtainable on this ground is the writ of *Injunction*, the most ordinary species of which, is that which operates as a restraint upon the defendant in the exercise of his real or supposed rights; and is, therefore, sometimes called the *remedial* writ of injunction, to distinguish it from the *judicial* writ, which issues after a decree, and is in the nature of a writ of execution. This writ may be had to stay proceedings at law, whatever stage they may have reached; to restrain alienations of property *pendente lite*, and tenants for life and others having limited interest from committing waste. It may be granted to restrain the negotiation of bills of exchange, the sailing of a ship, the transfer of stock, or the alienation of a specific chattel, to prohibit assignees from making a dividend, to prevent parties from removing out of the jurisdiction, or from marrying, or having any intercourse, which the court disapproves of, with a ward. The infringement of a copyright or a patent frequently calls for the exercise of this beneficial process; which may also be had to restrain the fraudulent use of trade marks, or of the names, labels, or other *indiciæ* of the makers or vendors of goods and merchandize, and in a large class of cases, far too numerous to be mentioned here.

2. The second remedy which was long obtainable only in the court of equity, is the *specific performance* of executory agreements. These a court of equity will compel them to be carried into strict

execution, unless where it is improper or impossible. And hence a
fiction is established, that what ought to be done shall, in the courts of
equity, be considered as being actually done, and shall relate back to the
time when it ought to have been done originally; and this fiction is
so closely pursued through all its consequences, that it necessarily
branches out into many rules of jurisprudence, which form a certain
regular system. Courts of equity will, therefore, if necessary, not
only enforce a contract, but award such damages to the injured
party as he may have sustained by the defendant's misconduct.
The most ordinary suit of this kind is for the performance of a contract for the sale of land, which may be brought either by the seller
to compel the other party to complete the purchase to which he has
agreed, or by the buyer to compel the seller to make a conveyance
of the land. But of almost all agreements whatever, specific performance may be had, though the extent to which it can be given
must be in a great degree determined by the circumstance of each
particular case.

3. The powers of obtaining a *discovery*, which the courts of law
now possess in common with the courts of equity, were at one time
the peculiar feature of the latter. This jurisdiction it was, indeed,
which gave them a concurrent jurisdiction with the other tribunals in a large number of cases; and of many this remedy of
a discovery still constitutes the main ground on which a suit is
maintainable.

4. And it was unquestionably for want of this discovery at law,
that the courts of equity early acquired a concurrent jurisdiction
with every other court in all matters of *account*; and, as incident
to accounts, they take cognizance of the *administration of assets*,
consequently of *debts, legacies*, the *distribution of the residue*, and
the *conduct of executors and administrators*. The first application
to the court, in a suit for administration, is often made by the
executor or administrator himself, when he finds the affairs of his
testator or intestate so much involved, that he cannot safely
administer the estate, except under its direction; but an administration suit may be instituted by creditors, or by a single creditor,
on behalf of himself and all other creditors, who shall come in
under the decree.

And in this administration of assets the courts deal not only with
the property of the deceased, which is by law directly liable to the
payment of debts and legacies, but also with all the funds, which
are, in equity, chargeable with the payment of debts or legacies, and
are then called *equitable assets*; because, in obtaining payment out
of them, they can be reached only by the aid of a court of equity.

Thus, if a testator devises land to trustees to sell for the payment of debts, the assets resulting from the execution of the trust are equitable assets upon the plain intent of the testator, notwithstanding the trustees are also made his executors ; for by directing the sale to be for the payment of debts generally, he excludes all preferences ; and the property would not otherwise be primarily liable to the payment of simple contract debts. And the same principle applies, if the testator merely charges his lands with the payment of his debts. The *marshalling of these assets*, as it is termed, in the course of administration, is merely such an arrangement of the different funds, as shall enable all the parties having equities thereon to receive their due proportions, notwithstanding any intervening interests, liens, or other claims of particular persons to prior satisfaction out of a portion of these funds.

As incident to accounts, the courts of equity have also a concurrent jurisdiction with the courts of common law over all dealings in *partnership* ; and this because the remedies furnished by the latter in disputes arising between partners are very inadequate to meet the varied difficulties which ordinarily present themselves in such cases. The courts of law can only award damages for breach of any particular stipulation entered into between the parties. A court of equity can adapt the remedy it affords to the ever-varying exigencies of each particular case. The Court of Chancery has for this reason long possessed an almost exclusive jurisdiction over questions between partners, and has consequently been entrusted with the dissolution and *winding up of joint-stock companies ;* for which purpurpose peculiar powers have been conferred upon it by several statutes.

5. But it would be endless to point out the several avenues in human affairs, and in this commercial age, which lead to or end in accounts ; and I proceed, therefore, to the next head of concurrent jurisdiction, that, namely, which the courts of equity early acquired over almost all matters of *fraud ;* all matters in the private knowledge of the party, which, though concealed, are binding in conscience, and all judgments at law obtained through such fraud or concealment. And this not by impeachment or reversing the judgment itself, but by prohibiting the plaintiff from taking any advantage of a judgment obtained by suppressing the truth ; and which, had the same facts appeared on the trial, as now are discovered, he would never have obtained at all. Such cases are the peculiar care of the courts of equity ; which, to relieve them, have been said to go not only beyond, but even contrary to the rules of law, although the justice of this remark is more than questionable,

as all our courts have judiciously avoided laying down any minute rules as to what shall, or shall not, constitute fraud.

For besides cases of actual and intentional fraud, the courts of equity recognize what are called *constructive frauds*, or such acts or contracts as, although not originating in any evil design to defraud or injure another, yet have a tendency to deceive, or to violate public or private confidence, and are therefore deemed worthy of repression equally with frauds of the more gross and palpable sort. Marriage brokage-bonds, for instance, by which one party engages to compensate another for negotiating an advantageous marriage for him, are considered fraudulent, as being injurious to public policy; and against them equity has relieved the party bound, and even assisted him to recover money already paid. Among constructive frauds, the courts of equity will also class a settlement made secretly by a woman, in contemplation of marriage, of her own property to her separate use, without her intended husband's privity; which will be held void, as in derogation of the marital rights of the husband, and a fraud upon his just expectations. And a secret conveyance made by a woman, under the like circumstances, in favour of a person for whom she is under no moral obligation to provide, will be similarly treated. But if she only reasonably provide for her children by a former marriage, such an arrangement will, in the absence of any deception practised on the intended husband, stand good. Conditions annexed to gifts, legacies, and devises in restraint of marriage, if they be of a general nature, are also looked upon as against public policy, and have been placed by courts of equity among constructive frauds.

Bargains in *restraint of trade* are fraudulent and void, as well in equity as at law, if general and unlimited in their nature; but are not so considered if they only apply to particular places and persons. The former are construed to be a fraud upon the public, as tending to promote monopoly and to discourage enterprise and fair competition. But a contract with another that he shall not carry on a particular trade within a particular limit or for a specified time may be good. All agreements, however, founded upon corrupt considerations and all contracts for buying, selling, or procuring of public offices, are fraudulent and void, as having a tendency to diminish the respectability and purity of officers, and thus to injure the public interest.

Under this branch of jurisdiction may be mentioned two grounds of interference by the Court of Chancery, viz., *accident and mistake*: the former applying in cases of such unforeseen events, acts, or omissions as are not the result of any negligence or misconduct of the party seeking relief; the latter where something has been done or omitted, from ignorance, surprise, imposition, or misplaced confidence. Thus in the case of the loss or destruction of a deed or other instrument, the courts of equity will interfere, on a proper indemnity being given, to prevent the *accident* being taken advantage of by the party liable. So the court will alter and reform a written agreement; when, by *mistake*, it contains either less or more than the parties intended.

6. The last, and a wholly distinct head of concurrent jurisdiction to which I shall refer, is that exercised by the courts of equity in reference to a widow's claim to *dower*: in the *partition of lands* between joint-tenants, tenants in common, or coparceners; and in *settling of the boundaries of estates*, where a confusion of these has taken place.

In the first case, the courts will assist the widow by a discovery of lands or title deeds, and remove impediments to her rendering her legal title available; in the *partition of estates*, the remedy afforded by courts of equity was always so much more effectual than that obtainable under a writ of partition, that the Court of Chancery early obtained, and has long possessed, an almost exclusive jurisdiction: the settling of the boundaries of estates is obviously calculated to prevent a multiplicity of suits, as well as to remedy the mischiefs that must inevitably arise from any confusion arising at the boundaries of property.

III. I now come to what has been called the *auxiliary* jurisdiction of the Court of Chancery, because it comprises those cases in which this court interposes, in order to enable a party to assert his right at common law. This is a very large branch of jurisdiction; for a court of equity will always interfere to prevent a party to any proceeding at law taking an inequitable advantage of some circumstance, which must determine the judgment of the court of law, irrespective of the merits of the cause. A defendant in ejectment, for instance, will be restrained from setting up as a defence an outstanding term of years or other interest in a trustee, lessee, or mortgagee; for the party in possession ought not, in conscience, to use an accidental advantage, to protect his possession against a real right in his adversary.

Under this head, also, may be placed the powers exercised by this court in directing the cancellation of documents, and the remedy it affords to suitors, by the proceedings known as bills *quia timet*, bills of peace, bills for the perpetuation of testimony, and bills of interpleader. Thus,

1. A court of equity will cancel agreements and other instruments, however solemn in their form or operation, which justice or public policy, require to be annulled.

2. It will entertain a bill, *quia timet*, that is, a bill seeking the interference of the court to prevent a wrong or anticipated mischief; the manner in which its aid is given depending on the particular circumstances of the case. Thus it will appoint a receiver to take rents; or will order a fund to be paid into court; will direct securities to be given up, or money to be paid over; or will confine itself to the mere issue of an injunction or other remedial process.

3. A *Bill of Peace* is, to some extent, of the same nature. It is brought to establish and perpetuate a right claimed by the plaintiff, which, from its nature, may be controverted by different persons, at different times, and by different actions: or where separate attempts have been already made unsuccessfully to overthrow the same right, and justice requires that the party should be quieted therein. For,

4. A court of equity will not only interfere in this way, to ascertain a right, but will also do so in order to preserve the evidence of it, whenever it is in danger of being lost. If, for instance, witnesses to a disputable fact are old and infirm, a bill may be filed to *perpetuate the testimony* of those witnesses, although no suit is depending; for, it may be, a man's antagonist only waits for the death of some of them to begin his suit. This is resorted to when lands are devised by will away from the heir-at-law; and the devisee, in order to perpetuate the testimony of the witnesses to such will, exhibits a bill in chancery against the heir, and sets forth the will *verbatim* therein, suggesting that the heir is inclined to dispute its validity: and then, the defendant having answered, they proceed to issue as in other cases, and examine the witnesses to the will; after which the cause is at an end, without proceeding to any decree, no relief being prayed by the bill: but the heir is entitled to his costs, even though he contest the will. This is what is usually meant by proving a will in chancery; and it may be added here, that by statute 5 & 6 Vict. c. 69, a bill in chancery may be filed by any person who would, under the circumstances alleged by him to exist, become entitled, upon the happening of any future event, to any honours, titles, estates, &c., praying the perpetuation of any testimony, which may be material for establishing such claim or right.

5. Finally, the chancery will afford, when necessary, a remedy similar to that now obtainable at law, and which has been already mentioned, under the name of *Interpleader*. This finishes our inquiry as to the matters cognisable in the courts of equity.

CHAPTER XVIII.

OF THE PROCEEDINGS IN COURTS OF EQUITY.

Bill—Its indorsements—Process thereon—Service—Appearance—Demurrer—
Plea—Answer—Oath *ex officio*—Cross-bill—Interrogatories—Disclaimer—
Bill taken *pro confesso*—Proof—Hearing—Decree—Execution—*in personam
in rem*—Re-hearing—Bill of review—Appeal—Order of administration—
Notices—Petitions—Recapitulation.

THE first commencement of a suit in chancery is by preferring a
bill to the Lord Chancellor in the style of a petition, setting forth
the circumstances of the case, as some fraud, trust, or hardship; and
praying relief at the chancellor's hands against the defendant. And,
if it be to quiet the possession of lands, to stay waste, or to stop
proceedings at law, an injunction is also prayed, commanding the
defendant to cease.

This bill must call all necessary parties, as defendants, before the
court, otherwise no decree can be made to bind them; and must be
signed by counsel, as a certificate of its decency and propriety. It
must also state the name and address of the solicitor for the plaintiff;
it bears an indorsement commanding the defendant to appear eight
days after service; and it is then filed with the clerk of records and
writs.

Formerly, upon filing a bill, process of *subpœna* was taken out,
which was a writ commanding the defendant to appear and answer
to the bill, on pain of 100*l.* If the defendant, on service of the
subpœna, did not appear within the time limited by the rules of the
court, and plead, demur, or answer to the bill, he was then said to
be in *contempt*, and successive processes of contempt were awarded
against him; the result being either that the bill was taken *pro
confesso*, or the defendant, if taken, was committed to prison, till he
put in his appearance or answer, or performed whatever else the
process was issued to enforce, and also cleared his contempt by paying the costs which the plaintiff had incurred thereby.

This process to compel appearance and answer has been abolished,
and a simpler and shorter proceeding is now resorted to. Instead of
the subpœna, which merely gave the defendant notice of a bill having
been filed, but afforded him no information of its contents, the bill
itself is now served upon the defendant; or under special circumstances, upon some other person, as, for instance, his solicitor or

agent, as his substitute. If the defendent be a peer, the lord chancellor sends him a *letter missive* to request his appearance, together with a copy of the bill. In default of appearance, the plaintiff may proceed against an *unprivileged* person by attachment; against a privileged person, as a peer or member of parliament, by sequestration of all his personal estate, and the profits of his real; against a corporation, first by *distringas*, and if this fail to produce obedience, by sequestration. Instead, however, of proceeding by way of attachment and sequestration, the plaintiff may *enter an appearance* for any defendant not appearing within the time allowed for so doing.

The suit having been thus instituted by bill, and an appearance having been entered, the defendant must next put in his defence, which he may do either by *demurrer, plea,* or *answer.*

A demurrer in equity is nearly of the same nature as a demurrer in law; being an appeal to the judgment of the court, whether the defendant is bound to answer the bill; as, for want of sufficient matter of equity therein contained; or where the plaintiff, upon his own showing, appears to have no right; or where the bill seeks a discovery of a thing which may cause a forfeiture of any kind, or may convict a man of any criminal misbehaviour. For any of these causes a defendant may demur to the bill. And if, on demurrer, the defendant prevails, the plaintiff's bill, unless he be allowed to amend, is dismissed. If the demurrer be overruled, the cause will proceed.

A plea which is always founded upon matter not apparent in the bill itself, may be either to the *jurisdiction ;* showing that the court has no cognizance of the cause: or to the *person ;* showing some disability of the plaintiff, as by outlawry, excommunication, and the like: or it is in *bar ;* showing some matter wherefore the plaintiff can demand no relief, as an act of parliament, a release, or a former decree. And the truth of this plea the defendant is bound to prove, if put upon it by the plaintiff. But as bills are often of a complicated nature, and contain various matters, a man may plead as to part, demur as to part, and answer to the residue.

An *answer* is the most usual defence that is made to a plaintiff's bill. It is given in upon oath, or the honour of a peer or peeress: but where there are amicable defendants, their answer is usually taken without oath by consent of the plaintiff. This method of proceeding is taken from the ecclesiastical courts, like the rest of the practice in chancery: for there, in almost every case, the plaintiff may demand the oath of his adversary in supply of proof. This oath was made use of in the spiritual courts, as well in criminal

cases of ecclesiastical cognisance, as in matters of civil right: and
it was then usually denominated the oath *ex officio:* whereof the
High Commission Court in particular made a most extravagant and
illegal use; forming a court of inquisition, in which all persons
were obliged to answer in cases of bare suspicion, if the commissioners thought proper to proceed against them *ex officio* for any
supposed ecclesiastical enormities.   When the High Commission
Court was abolished, this oath *ex officio* was abolished with it;
but the enactment of the stat. 13 Car. II. stat. c. 12, which effected
this, does not extend to oaths in a civil suit; and therefore it is
still the practice, both in the spiritual courts and in equity, to
demand the personal answer of the party himself upon oath.

An answer must either deny or confess all the material parts of
the bill; or it may confess and avoid, that is, justify or palliate the
facts.   If one of these is not done, the answer may be excepted to
for insufficiency, and the defendant be compelled to put in a more
sufficient answer.   A defendant cannot pray anything in this his
answer, but to be dismissed the court: if he has any relief to pray
against the plaintiff, he must do it by an original bill of his own,
which is called a *cross-bill,* or by *interrogatories* for the examination of the plaintiff in lieu of a cross-bill, to which there must
be prefixed a concise statement of the subject on which discovery is
sought.

In many cases, when the facts in dispute between the parties
are few, and not of a complicated character, an answer is not now
requisite, and the plaintiff, on the expiration of the time allowed
for answering, but before replication, may move for a decree or
decretal order.   Affidavits may in such cases be filed by the parties,
upon which the court will determine the case unless it be thought
proper, in addition thereto, to examine or cross-examine either party
orally.

A defendant may also disclaim all right or title to the matter in
demand by the plaintiff's bill.   But a *disclaimer* can seldom be put
in alone; for if the defendant has been made a party by mistake,
having at the time no interest in the matter, yet as he may have had
an interest, which he has parted with, the plaintiff may require an
answer sufficient to ascertain whether that is the fact or not; and if
the defendant had had an interest which he has parted with, an
answer may be also necessary to enable the plaintiff to make the
proper person a party instead of the defendant disclaiming.   A disclaimer is therefore usually an answer and disclaimer.

In default of a defendant pleading, answering, or demurring to the
bill, he is in contempt of court, and the plaintiff may proceed against

him; either by attachment, or, if he is privileged, by sequestration; or by having the bill taken *pro confesso*. For when a defendant has allowed all the process of the court to be issued against him without putting in his answer, the court will order that the facts stated in the bill shall be considered as true; and this order may be obtained when the defendant has not been within the jurisdiction for two years, or has absconded without being served, or, after having been served, to avoid subsequent process.

After answer put in, the plaintiff, upon payment of costs, may amend his bill, either by adding new parties, or new matter, or both, upon the new lights given him by the defendant; and the defendant is obliged to answer afresh to such amended bill. But this must be before the plaintiff has replied to the defendant's answer, whereby the cause is at issue; and afterwards, if new matter arises, which did not exist before, he may set it forth by a *supplemental bill*. There may be also a bill of *revivor* when the suit is abated by the death of any of the parties, in order to set the proceedings again in motion, without which they remain at a stand; yet in many cases, bills of *revivor* and *supplement*, and supplemental bills are now unnecessary; for an order of revivor may be obtained on application to the court, and facts which have occurred since the commencement of the suit, may in many cases be stated, by way of amendment, in the original bill.

If the plaintiff finds sufficient matter confessed in the defendant's answer to ground a decree upon, he may proceed to the hearing of the cause upon bill and answer only. But in that case he must take the defendant's answer to be true in every point. Otherwise the course is for the plaintiff to put in a replication to the answer, in which he avers his bill to be true, certain, and sufficient, and the defendant's answer to be directly the reverse; which he is ready to prove as the court shall award; upon which issue is joined upon the facts in dispute. To prove which facts is the next concern.

This was formerly done by taking the *depositions* of witnesses in writing, according to the manner of the civil law. And for that purpose *interrogatories* were framed, or questions in writing, which were to be proposed to, and asked of, the witnesses in the cause, by commissioners who were sworn to take the examinations truly and without partiality, and not to divulge them till published in the court of Chancery.

But this practice having been found, in many respects, insufficient and objectionable, an oral examination has been substituted, which may be had either before one of the examiners of the court, or at the bearing of the cause before the court itself, the witnesses being brought there by *subpœna*, unless the parties verify their respective cases by affidavit.

Either party may be *subpœnaed* to hear judgment on the day fixed for the hearing: and then, if the plaintiff does not attend, his bill is dismissed with costs; or, if the defendant makes default, a decree will be made against him, which will be final, unless he pays the plaintiff's cost of attendance, and shows good cause to the contrary on a day appointed by the court. A plaintiff's bill may also at any time be dismissed for want of prosecution, which is in the nature of a nonsuit at law, if he does not take the steps required by the practice of the court to bring the cause to an end.

The method of hearing causes in court is usually this. The parties on both sides appearing by their counsel, the plaintiff's case is first stated by the senior counsel for the plaintiff, whose junior counsel then reads the evidence, and such parts of the defendant's answer as are thought material to the plaintiff's case. Then the defendant's counsel go through the same process for him; but they are not allowed to read any part of his answer, except in explanation of any part of it that may have been read on the side of the plaintiff. The senior counsel for the plaintiff is then heard in reply.

When all are heard, the court pronounces the *decree*, adjusting every point in debate according to equity and good conscience; which decree being usually very long, the minutes of it are taken down by the registrar. The matter of costs to be given to either party is not here held to be a point of right, but merely discretionary, according to the circumstances of the case, as they appear more or less favourable to the party vanquished.

⁙ The decree is either *interlocutory* or *final*. It very seldom happens that the first decree can be final or conclude the cause. If any matter of fact is strongly controverted, the court is so sensible of the deficiency of trial by written depositions that it will not bind the parties thereto, but direct the matter to be tried by jury; especially such important facts as the validity of a will, or whether A is the heir-at-law to B, or the existence of a *modus decimandi*, or real and immemorial composition for tithes. Such facts were formerly sent for trial to one of the courts of common law; as no jury could, until recently, be summoned to attend this court. But the chancery has now in this respect the same jurisdiction, powers, and authority as any of the superior courts of common law; and issues in fact may accordingly be tried and damages be assessed by the court itself, either with or without the assistance of a jury, in like manner as at the assizes.*

Another thing also may retard the completion of decrees. Frequently long accounts are to be settled, incumbrances and debts to be inquired into, and a hundred little facts to be cleared up, before a decree can do full and sufficient justice. These matters, which were formerly referred to a master in chancery to examine, which examinations frequently lasted for years, are now disposed of at the chambers of the judges, by their chief clerk; who embodies the result of his investigation in the form of a report, which, if approved of by the judge, is adopted and signed by him.

When the preliminary matters have been settled, the cause is again brought to hearing, and a final decree is made; the performance of which is enforced, if necessary, by commitment of the person, or sequestration of the party's estate. The proceeding *in personam* was formerly the only means which a court of equity had of enforcing its decrees; but now, by the interposition of the legislature, it is enabled to proceed *in rem*, the plaintiff being entitled, after decree for delivery of an estate for instance, to a writ of assistance directed to the sheriff of the county in which the lands lie; which writ authorizes him to enter the premises and eject the defendant, and put the plaintiff in possession. Moreover, if a person who has been directed to execute any instrument, or to make a surrender or transfer, refuses or neglects to do so, and will not comply with the order of the court, the court will direct some other person to fulfil the order in the name and in place of the recusant party. And if a person is committed for a contempt in not delivering up books, papers, or other articles, a sequestrator may be authorized to seize them.

Besides these remedies *in rem*, the suitor is also enabled, in order to obtain satisfaction of any pecuniary demand to which he may be entitled, to resort to the process of execution peculiar to the courts of common law; and for this purpose, sue out a writ of *fieri facias*, or writ of *elegit*, which is executed in the same way as such writs are, when issued out of the courts of common law. Decrees of courts of equity are likewise a charge upon real estate, in the same way as the judgments of the courts of common law.

* Formerly also, if a question of mere *law* arose in the course of a cause, it was the practice of this court to refer it to the opinion of the judges of one of the courts of common law, upon a case stated for that purpose; but the chancery must now itself determine any questions of law or *legal right* or *title* which comes before it; for which purpose, however, it may obtain the assistance of any of the common law judges.

U

If by the decree either party thinks himself aggrieved, he may petition for a *rehearing*, whether the cause was heard before the chancellor himself, or the lords justices, or by the master of the rolls, or any of the vice-chancellors. For whoever may have heard the cause, it is the chancellor's decree, and must be signed by him before it is enrolled; which is done of course unless a rehearing be desired. Every petition for a rehearing must be signed by two counsel of character, usually such as have been concerned in the cause, certifying that they apprehend the cause is proper to be re-heard. The rehearing takes place either before the lord chancellor, sitting alone, or before the lords justices of the Court of Appeal; at which time all omissions of either evidence or argument may be supplied. After the decree is once signed and enrolled, it cannot be reheard or rectified, but by bill of review, or by appeal to the House of Lords.

A bill of *review* may be had upon apparent error in judgment, appearing on the face of the decree; or, by special leave of the court, upon oath made of the discovery of new matter or evidence, which could not possibly be had or used at the time when the decree passed. But no new evidence or matter then in the knowledge of the parties, and which might have been used before, shall be a suffi-cient ground for a bill of review. And no bill of review can be brought after twenty years have elapsed from the enrolment of the decree.

An *appeal* to parliament, that is, to the House of Lords, is effected by *petition* to the House of Peers, and not by *writ of error*, as upon judgments at common law. This jurisdiction is said to have begun in 18 Jac. I., and it is certain that the first petition, which appears in the records of parliament, was preferred in that year; and that the first which was heard and determined, though the name of appeal was then a novelty, was presented in a few months after; both levelled against the Lord Chancellor Bacon for corruption and other misbehaviour. It was afterwards warmly controverted by the House of Commons in the reign of Charles II. But this dispute is now at rest; it being obvious to the reason of all man-kind, that when the courts of equity became principal tribunals for deciding causes of property, a revision of their decrees, by way of appeal, became equally necessary as a writ of error from the judg-ment of a court of law. But no new evidence is admitted in the House of Lords upon any account; this being a distinct jurisdiction: which differs very considerably from those instances, wherein the same jurisdiction revises and corrects its own acts, as in rehearings and bills of review. For it is a practice unknown to our law, though constantly followed in the spiritual courts, when a superior court is reviewing the sentence of an inferior, to examine the justice of the former decree by evidence that was never produced below.

Thus much for the general method of proceeding by bill in the courts of equity. It remains only for me to mention shortly a few of the other and less formal proceedings of this court. Thus, instead of filing a bill for administration, a creditor, legatee, or next of kin desiring to have the estate of any deceased person administered in Chancery, may apply directly to a vice-chancellor in chambers, his order having the same force and effect as a decree to the like effect made on the hearing of a cause. But even this course of proceeding is now unusual, for a distribution of the assets may be effected without any interference whatever by the court; as any executor or administrator, after giving such notice to creditors and others to prefer their claims, as would have been directed by the court in an administrative suit, may proceed to distribute the estate of the deceased among the parties entitled thereto, without incurring any liability for the assets so distributed, to any person of whose claim he shall have no notice at the time.

My space will not permit me to do more than allude to a great number of matters which are disposed of by the courts of equity upon *interlocutory applications*. These are simply requests addressed to the court, either orally or in writing, for its interference; and when made *vivâ voce*, are called *motions*: when in writing, *petitions*. Motions are either *of course*, or such as require no previous notice to the other side, and will be granted without any opposition being allowed; or they are *special*, that is, such as the court will exercise its discretion in granting, and which require to be justified by special grounds; although they may be made *ex parte* as well as upon notice. Of the former kind are applications for a writ *ne exeat regno*, or for an injunction to stay waste, matters of urgency, where the danger that threatens the applicant justifies the one-sidedness of the proceeding. But if there is no danger of the object of the motion being defeated by giving notice to the other side, the court will not permit such an application to be made. Petitions are also either *of course* or *not of course*. The latter require to be *answered*, and must therefore be served on the opposite party. A large class of petitions are those which are made under the various acts of parliament which have conferred on the Court of Chancery jurisdiction affecting more or less the rights of property; such as the acts relating to charities; the acts by which the court is authorized to supply the place of defunct, absent, recusant, or incapable trustees; the railway acts; and others of a similar nature, under which purchase or compensation moneys are directed to be paid into the Bank; the statute empowering the Court of Chancery to grant leases of settled estates, or to confer leasing powers upon the trustees of such estates; the Drainage acts; the Unredeemed Stock act; and many others too numerous to mention, and to which the legislature is annually making additions. In these cases, the court may generally exercise the same powers as those which it possesses on a bill being filed; and this short and simple method of obtaining the interference of the court is, accordingly, in all cases which permit of it, that usually resorted to.

In this manner are the several remedies given by the English law for all sorts of injuries, either real or personal, administered by the several courts of justice, and their respective officers. In the course, therefore, of the present volume we have, first, seen and considered the nature of remedies, by the mere act of the parties, or mere operation of law, without any suit in courts. We have next taken a view of remedies by suit or action in courts: and therein have contemplated, first, the nature and species of courts, instituted for the redress of injuries in general; and then have shown in what particular courts application must be made for the redress of particular injuries, or the doctrine of jurisdictions and cognizance. We afterwards proceeded to consider the nature and distribution of wrongs and injuries affecting every species of personal and real rights, with the respective remedies by suit, which the law of the land has afforded for every possible injury. And, lastly, we have deduced and pointed out the method and progress of obtaining such remedies in the courts of justice: proceeding from the first general complaint through all the stages of *process* to compel the defendant's appearance; and of *pleading*, or formal allegation on the one side, and excuse or denial on the other; with the examination of the validity of such complaint or excuse, upon *demurrer*: or the truth of the facts alleged and denied, upon *issue* joined, and its several *trials*: to the *judgment, decree*, or sentence of the law, with respect to the nature and amount of the redress to be specifically given; till, after considering the suspension of that judgment by proceedings in the nature of *appeals*, we have arrived at its final *execution*: which puts the party in specific possession of his right by the intervention of ministerial officers, or else gives him an ample satisfaction, either by equivalent damages, or by the confinement of his body who is guilty of the injury complained of.

BOOK THE FOURTH.

OF PUBLIC WRONGS.

CHAPTER I.

OF THE NATURE OF CRIMES; AND THEIR PUNISHMENT.

General nature of crimes—and punishments—end of punishment—measure of punishment.

WE are now arrived at the fourth and last branch of these commentaries; the consideration of public wrongs, or crimes and misdemeanors; with the means of their prevention and punishment. In the pursuit of which subject I shall consider, in the *first* place, the general nature of crimes and punishments; *secondly*, the persons capable of committing crimes; *thirdly*, their several degrees of guilt, as principals, or accessories; *fourthly*, the several species of crimes, with the punishment annexed to each by the laws of England; *fifthly*, the means of preventing their perpetration; and, *sixthly*, the method of inflicting those punishments which the law has annexed to each several crime and misdemeanor.

First, as to the general nature of crimes and their punishment; or, as it is more usually denominated, the doctrine of the *pleas of the crown;* so called, because the sovereign is supposed by the law to be the person injured by every infraction of the public rights of the community, and is therefore the proper prosecutor for every public offence.

I. A crime is an act committed, or omitted, in violation of a public law, either forbidding or commanding it. This general definition comprehends both crimes and misdemeanors, which, properly speaking, are mere synonymous terms. But in common usage the word "crimes" is made to denote such offences as are of a deeper and more atrocious dye; while smaller faults are comprised under the gentler name of "*misdemeanors*" only; and are so designated, I may add, in contradistinction to *felonies:* the former class comprehending all indictable offences which do not fall within the other, such as assaults, nuisances, non-repair of a highway, and the like.

The distinction of public wrongs from private, of crimes and misdemeanors from civil injuries, seems principally to consist in this: that private wrongs, or civil injuries, are an infringement or privation of the civil rights which belong to individuals, considered merely as individuals: public wrongs, or crimes and misdemeanors, are a breach and violation of the public rights and duties due to the whole community, considered as a community, in its social aggregate capacity. In all cases, therefore, a crime includes an injury; every public offence is also a private wrong, and somewhat more; it affects the individual, and it likewise affects the community. Thus murder is an injury to the life of an individual; but the law of society considers principally the loss which the state sustains by being deprived of a member, and the pernicious example thereby set for others to do the like. Robbery may be considered in the same view: it is an injury to *private* property; were that all, a civil satisfaction in damages might atone for it: the *public* mischief is the thing, for the prevention of which our laws have made it a felony. In these gross and atrocious injuries the private wrong is swallowed up in the public: and we seldom hear any mention made of satisfaction to the individual; the satisfaction to the community being so very great.

There are crimes, however, of an inferior nature, in which the punishment is not so severe but that it affords room for a private compensation also; and herein the distinction of crimes from civil injuries is very apparent. For instance, in the case of an assault, the aggressor may be punished criminally; and the party beaten may also have his private remedy by an action for damages. So, upon the whole, we may observe, that the law has a double view: viz., not only to redress the party injured, but also to secure to the public the benefit of society, by preventing or punishing every breach and violation of those laws, which have been established for the government and tranquillity of the whole.

II. The nature of *crimes and misdemeanors* in general being thus ascertained and distinguished, I proceed, in the next place, to consider the general nature of *punishments*, which are evils or inconveniences consequent upon crimes and misdemeanors; being devised, denounced, and inflicted by human laws, in consequence of disobedience or misbehaviour in those to regulate whose conduct such laws were respectively made. And herein we will briefly consider the *power*, the *end*, and the *measure* of human punishment.

1. It is clear that the right of punishing crimes against the law of nature, as murder and the like, is, in a state of mere nature, vested in every individual. For it must be vested in somebody, otherwise the laws of nature would be vain and fruitless, if none were empowered to put them in execution: and if that power is vested in any *one*, it must also be vested in *all* mankind; since all are by nature equal. In a state of society this right is transferred from individuals to the sovereign power; whereby men are prevented from being judges in their own causes, which is one of the evils that civil government was intended to remedy. Whatever power, therefore, individuals had of punishing offences against the law of nature, that is now vested in the magistrate alone, who bears the sword of justice by the consent of the whole community.

As to offences merely against the laws of society, which are only *mala prohibita*, and not *mala in se*, the temporal magistrate is also empowered to inflict coercive penalties for such transgressions: and this by the consent of individuals, who, in forming societies, invested the sovereign power with the right of making laws, and of enforcing obedience to them when made. The lawfulness, therefore, of punishing such criminals is founded upon this principle, that the law by which they suffer was made by their own consent; it is a part of the original contract into which they entered when first they engaged in society; it was calculated for, and has long contributed to, their own security.

2. The *end* or final cause of human punishments is not by way of atonement or expiation for the crime committed, but as a precaution against future offences of the same kind. This is effected three ways: either by the amendment of the offender himself; for which purpose all corporal punishments, fines, and temporary imprisonments are inflicted: or, by deterring others by the dread of his example from offending in the like way; which gives rise to all ignominious punishments, and to such executions of justice as are open and public: or, lastly, by depriving the party injuring of the power to do future mischief; which is effected by either putting him to death, or condemning him to perpetual confinement or exile. The same one end, of preventing future crimes, is sought by each of these three species of punishment. The public gains equal security, whether the offender himself be amended by wholesome correction, or whether he be disabled from doing any further harm; and if the penalty fails of both these effects, as it may do, still the terror of his example remains as a warning to other citizens.

The *measure* of human punishments, therefore, can never be absolutely determined by any standing invariable rule; but it must be left to the legislature to inflict such penalties as are warranted by the laws of nature and society, and such as appear to be the best calculated to answer the end of precaution against future offences. Yet there are some general principles, drawn from the nature and circumstances of the crime, that may be of some assistance in allotting it an adequate punishment. Thus the greater and more exalted the object of an injury is, the more care should be taken to prevent that injury, and of course under this aggravation the punishment should be more severe. Treason is therefore by the law punished with greater rigour than even actually killing any private subject. Again the violence of passion, or temptation, may sometimes alleviate a crime. Theft, in case of hunger, is more worthy of compassion than when committed through avarice; and to kill a man upon sudden resentment, is less penal than upon cool deliberate malice. The age, education, and character of the offender; the repetition of the offence; the time, the place, the company wherein it was committed; all these, and a thousand other incidents, may aggravate or extenuate the crime. Finally, it may be observed that punishments of unreasonable severity have less effect in preventing crimes, and amending the manners of a people, than such as are more merciful in general, yet properly intermixed with due distinctions of severity. Crimes are more effectually prevented by the *certainty* than by the *severity* of punishment. For the excessive severity of laws hinders their execution; and when the punishment surpasses all measure, the public will frequently out of humanity prefer impunity to it. The laws of the Roman kings, and the twelve tables of the *decemviri*, were full of cruel punishments: the Porcian law, which exempted all citizens from sentence of death, silently abrogated them all. In this period the republic flourished; under the emperors severe punishments were revived, and then the empire fell.

CHAPTER II.

OF THE PERSONS CAPABLE OF COMMITTING CRIMES.

Defect of will—Defect of understanding—Infancy—Lunacy—Drunkenness—Chance—Mistake—Civil subjection—Duress.

WE are next to inquire what persons are, or are not, capable of committing crimes; or, which is all one, who are exempted from the censures of the law upon the commission of those acts which in other persons would be severely punished. In which inquiry, we must have recourse to exceptions; for the general rule is, that no person shall be excused from punishment, excepting such as are expressly exempted.   And thus we shall find that all the excuses, which protect the committer of a forbidden act from punishment, may be reduced to this single consideration—the want or defect of *will*.   An involuntary act, as it has no claim to merit, so neither can it induce any guilt; the concurrence of the will being the only thing that renders human actions either praiseworthy or culpable. Indeed, to make a complete crime cognisable by human laws, there must be both a will and an act.   For though, *in foro conscientiæ*, a fixed design to do an unlawful act is almost as heinous as the commission of it, yet as no temporal tribunal can fathom the intentions of the mind, otherwise than as they are demonstrated by outward actions, it therefore cannot punish for what it cannot know. For which reason in all temporal jurisdictions an *overt* act, or some open evidence of an intended crime, is necessary in order to demonstrate the depravity of the will, before the man is liable to punishment.   And as a vicious will without a vicious act is no civil crime, so, on the other hand, an unwarrantable act without a vicious will is no crime at all.   So that to constitute a crime against human laws, there must be, first, a vicious will; and, secondly, an unlawful act consequent upon such vicious will.

Now there are three cases in which the will does not join with the act: 1. Where there is a defect of understanding.   For where there is no discernment, there is no choice; and where there is no choice, there can be no act of the will, which is nothing else but a determination of one's choice to do or to abstain from a particular action: he, therefore, that has no understanding, can have no will to guide his conduct. 2. Where there is understanding and will sufficient residing in the party, but not called forth and exerted at the time of the action done, which is the case of all offences committed by chance or ignorance.   Here the will sits neuter; and neither concurs with the act, nor disagrees to it. 3. Where the action is constrained by some outward force and violence.   Here the will counteracts the deed; and is so far from concurring with, that it loathes and disagrees to, what the man is obliged to perform.   Infancy, idiocy, lunacy, and intoxication, fall under the first head; misfortune and ignorance may be referred to the second; and compulsion or necessity may properly rank in the third.

I. The law in some cases privileges an infant under twenty-one, as to common misdemeanors: and particularly in cases of omission, as not repairing a bridge or a highway; for, not having the command of his fortune till twenty-one, he wants the capacity to do those things which the law requires.   But where there is any breach of the peace, a riot, battery, or the like, for these an infant is equally liable to suffer as a person of full age.

With regard to felonies, the law is more circumspect, the capacity of doing ill, or contracting guilt, being not so much measured by years and days, as by the strength of the delinquent's understanding and judgment. For one lad of eleven years old may have as much cunning as another of fourteen; and in these cases our maxim is, that *"malitia supplet ætatem."* In all such cases, however, the evidence of that malice which is to supply age, ought to be strong and clear beyond all doubt and contradiction.

II. The second case of a deficiency in will, which excuses from the guilt of crimes, arises also from a defective or vitiated understanding, viz., in an *idiot* or a *lunatic.* For the rule of law as to the latter, which may easily be adapted also to the former, is that *"furiosus furore solum punitur."* In criminal cases, therefore, idiots and lunatics are not punishable for their own acts, if committed when under these incapacities; no, not even for treason itself.

I say not chargeable; for the insanity of a prisoner is ordinarily ascertained before trial; a jury being impanelled on his arraignment to try the question, whether he is capable of understanding and pleading to the charge. If the prisoner be found insane, he is thereafter detained in custody during the pleasure of the crown; for if he recovers, he may be tried for his offence, when his insanity at the time of its commission must be proved, in order to save him from the consequences.

III. Artificial, voluntarily contracted madness, by *drunkenness* or intoxication, our law looks upon as an aggravation of the offence, rather than as an excuse. The use of strong liquors, and the abuse of them by drinking to excess, depend much upon the temperature of the climate in which we live. The same indulgence which may be necessary to make the blood move in Norway, would make an Italian mad. A German, therefore, says Montesquieu, drinks through custom, founded upon constitutional necessity; a Spaniard drinks through choice, or out of the mere wantonness of luxury; and drunkenness, he adds, ought to be more severely punished, where it makes men mischievous and mad, as in Spain and Italy, than where it only renders them stupid and heavy, as in Germany and more northern countries. And accordingly, in the warm climate of Greece, a law of Pittacus enacted, " that he who committed a crime " when drunk, should receive a double punishment;" one for the crime itself, and the other for the inebriety which prompted him to commit it. The Roman law, indeed, made great allowances for this vice: *"per vinum delapsis capitalis pœna remittitur."* But the law of England, considering how easy it is to counterfeit this excuse, and how weak an excuse it is, will not suffer any man thus to privilege one crime by another.

IV. A fourth deficiency of will is where a man commits an unlawful act by *misfortune* or *chance*, and not by design. Of this, when it affects the life of another, we shall find more occasion to speak hereafter; at present only observing, that if any accidental mischief happens to follow from the performance of a *lawful* act in a lawful manner, the party stands excused from all guilt; but if a man be doing anything *unlawful*, and a consequence ensues which he did not foresee or intend, as the death of a man or the like, his want of foresight shall be no excuse; for, being guilty of one offence, in doing antecedently what is in itself unlawful, he is criminally guilty of whatever consequence may follow the first misbehaviour.

V. *Ignorance* or *mistake* is another defect of will; when a man, intending to do a lawful act, does that which is unlawful. For here, the deed and the will acting separately, there is not that conjunction between them which is necessary to form a criminal act.

VI. A sixth species of defect of will is that arising from *compulsion* and inevitable *necessity*. These are a constraint upon the will, whereby a man is urged to do that which his judgment disapproves; and which, it is to be presumed, his will, if left to itself, would reject. Of this nature is the obligation of *civil subjection*, whereby the inferior is constrained by the superior to act contrary to what his own reason would suggest: as when a legislator establishes iniquity by a law, and commands the subject to do an act contrary to morality. The sheriff who burnt Latimer and Ridley was not liable to punishment from Elizabeth, for executing so horrid an office; being justified by the commands of that magistracy, which endeavoured to restore superstition under the holy auspices of its merciless sister, persecution.

As to persons in private relations; the principal case, where constraint of a superior is allowed as an excuse for criminal misconduct, is with regard to the subjection of the wife to her husband; for neither a son or a servant are excused for the commission of any crime by the command or coercion of the parent or master. If a woman commit theft, burglary, or other civil offence by the coercion of her husband—or in his company, which the law construes coercion—she is not guilty of any crime, being considered as acting by compulsion, and not of her own will. But this rule admits of an exception in crimes that are *mala in se*, as murder and the like, because it would be unreasonable to screen an offender from the punishment due to natural crimes, by the refinements of civil society. And in all cases where the wife offends alone, without the company or coercion of her husband, she is responsible for her offence as much as any feme-sole.

Another species of compulsion or necessity is what our law calls *duress per minas:* or threats and menaces, which induce a fear of death or other bodily harm, and which take away, for that reason, the guilt of many crimes and misdemeanors. Therefore, if a man be violently assaulted, and has no other possible means of escaping death, he is permitted to kill the assailant; for here the law of nature, and self-defence its primary canon, have made him his own protector.

There is a third species of *necessity,* viz., when a man has his choice of two evils, and being under a necessity of choosing one, he chooses the least pernicious of the two. Where, for instance, a man, by the commandment of the law, is bound to arrest another for any capital offence, or to disperse a riot, and resistance is made to his authority: it is here justifiable and even necessary to wound or perhaps to kill the offenders, rather than permit the murderer to escape, or the riot to continue. For the preservation of the peace of the kingdom, and the apprehending of notorious malefactors, are of the utmost consequence to the public; and therefore excuse the felony which the killing would otherwise amount to.

There has been much speculation among the writers upon general law, whether a man in extreme want of food or clothing may justify stealing either, to relieve his present necessities? But the law of England admits no such excuse; for by our laws such sufficient provision is made for the poor by the power of the civil magistrate, that it is impossible that the most needy should ever be reduced to the necessity of thieving to support nature.

VII. I need only add one other instance in which the law supposes an incapacity of doing wrong, from the perfection of the person. I mean the case of the sovereign; whom the law will not suppose capable of committing a folly, much less a crime. But of this sufficient was said in the first part of these Commentaries, to which I must refer the reader.

CHAPTER III.

OF PRINCIPALS AND ACCESSORIES.

Principal in the first degree—in the second degree—Accessory before the fact
—after the fact—Punishment.

WE are next to make a few remarks on the different degrees of guilt among persons that are capable of offending; viz., as *principal,* and as *accessory.*

I. A man may be *principal* in an offence in two degrees. A principal in the first degree is he that is the actor, or absolute perpetrator of the crime; and, in the second degree, he is who is present, aiding and abetting the fact to be done. Which *presence* need not always be an actual immediate standing by, within sight or hearing of the fact; but there may be also a constructive presence, as when one commits a robbery or murder, and another keeps watch or guard at some convenient distance. And this rule has also other exceptions: for, in case of murder by poisoning, a man may be a principal felon, by preparing and laying the poison, or persuading another to drink it, who is ignorant of its poisonous quality, or giving it to him for that purpose; and yet not administer it himself, nor be present when the very deed of poisoning is committed.

II. An *accessory* is he who is not the chief actor in the offence, nor present at its performance, but is some way concerned therein, either *before* or *after* the fact committed. In considering the nature of which degree of guilt, we will, first, examine what offences admit of accessories, and what not: secondly, who may be an accessory *before* the fact: thirdly, who may be an accessory *after* it: and, lastly, how accessories, considered merely as such, and distinct from principals, are to be treated.

1. In high treason there are no accessories, but all are principals: the same acts that make a man accessory in felony, making him a principal in high treason, upon account of the heinousness of the crime. In murder and other felonies, there may be accessories: except only in those offences which by judgment of law are sudden and premeditated, as manslaughter and the like; which therefore cannot have any accessories *before* the fact. So too in misdemeanors and in all crimes under the degree of felony, there are no accessories either *before* or *after* the fact; but all persons concerned therein, if guilty at all, are principals: the law not descending to distinguish the different shades of guilt in petty offences.

2. An accessory *before* the fact, is one, who being absent at the time of the crime committed, doth yet procure, counsel, or command another to commit a crime. Herein absence is necessary to make him an accessory; for if such procurer, or the like, be present, he is guilty of the crime as principal. If A then advises B to kill another, and B does it in the absence of A, now B is principal, and A is accessory in the murder. And it is also settled, that whoever procures a felony to be committed, though it be by the intervention of a third person, is an accessory before the fact.

3. An accessory *after* the fact may be where a person, knowing a felony to have been committed, receives, relieves, comforts, or assists

the felon. Therefore, to make an accessory *ex post facto*, it is in the first place requisite that he knows of the felony committed. In the next place, he must receive, relieve, comfort, or assist him. And generally, any assistance whatever given to a felon, to hinder his being apprehended, tried, or suffering punishment, makes the assistor an accessory. To convey instruments to a felon to enable him to break gaol, makes a man an accessory to the felony. But to relieve a felon in gaol with clothes or other necessaries, is no offence; for the crime imputable to this species of accessory is the hindrance of public justice, by assisting the felon to escape the vengeance of the law. To buy or receive stolen goods, knowing them to be stolen, falls under none of these descriptions; it is therefore at common law a mere misdemeanor, and made not the receiver accessory to the theft, because he received the *goods* only, and not the *felon*. But all such receivers are by statute made accessories and felons; and may now be indicted and convicted either as accessories after the fact, or for a substantive felony.

The felony must be complete at the time of the assistance given, else it makes not the assistant an accessory. As if one wounds another mortally, and after the wound given, but before death ensues, a person assists or receives the delinquent, this does not make him accessory to the homicide; for, till death ensues, there is no felony committed. But so strict is the law where a felony is actually complete, in order to do effectual justice, that the nearest relations are not suffered to aid or receive one another. If the parent assists his child, or the child his parent, if the brother receives the brother, the master his servant, or the servant his master, or even if the husband relieves his wife, who have any of them committed a felony, the receivers become accessories *ex post facto*. But a feme-covert cannot become an accessory by the receipt and concealment of her husband; for she is presumed to act under his coercion, and therefore she is not bound, neither ought she, to discover her lord.

4. The general rule of the ancient law was that accessories should suffer the same punishment as their principals. But this is now altered as to accessories *after* the fact, whose offence is obviously of a different species of guilt to that of the principal, as te iding chiefly to evade public justice. Accessories *before* the fact may still, however, be indicted, tried, convicted, and punished in all respects like the principal.

CHAPTER IV.

OF OFFENCES AGAINST GOD AND RELIGION.

Apostacy—Heresy—Reviling the ordinances of the church—Nonconformity—
Protestant dissenters—Papists—Corporation and Test Acts—Blasphemy—
Profane swearing—Witchcraft—Religious impostors—Simony—Profanation
of Lord's Day—Lewdness.

WE are now to enter upon the detail of the several species of crimes and misdemeanors, with the punishment annexed to each by the law of England.

In the very entrance of these Commentaries it was shown, that human laws can have no concern with any but social and relative duties, being intended only to regulate the conduct of man as a member of civil society. All crimes ought, therefore, to be estimated merely . according to the mischiefs which they produce in civil society; and consequently private vices or the breach of mere absolute duties, which man is bound to perform· considered only as an individual, are not, cannot be, the object of any municipal law, any further than as by their evil example, or other pernicious effects, they prejudice the community, and thereby become a species of public crimes. Thus, the vice of drunkenness, if committed privately and alone, is beyond the knowledge, and, of course, beyond the reach of human tribunals; but if committed publicly, in the face of the world, its evil example makes it liable to temporal censures.

On the other hand, there are some misdemeanors, punishable by the municipal law, that have in themselves nothing criminal, but are made unlawful by the positive constitutions of the state, such as poaching, smuggling, and the like. These are naturally no offences at all ; but their whole criminality consists in their disobedience to the supreme power, which has universally assumed the right of making some things unlawful which are in themselves indifferent. Considering, therefore, all offences as deriving their particular guilt, here punishable, from the law of man, I shall distribute the several offences, punishable by the laws of England, under the following general heads : *first*, those which are injurious to religion ; *secondly*, such as violate the laws of nations ; *thirdly*, such as affect the executive power of the state ; *fourthly*, such as infringe the rights of the public or commonwealth , and, lastly, such as derogate from those rights and duties which are owing to particular individuals, and in the preservation and vindication of which the community is interested.

I. Of offences against religion, the first is *apostacy*; or a total renunciation of Christianity, by embracing either a false religion, or no religion at all. This offence was for a long time the object only of the ecclesiastical courts, which corrected the offender *pro salute animæ.* But about the close of the seventeenth century it was thought necessary to enact, by 9 & 10 Will. III., c. 32, that any person educated in, or having made profession of, the Christian religion, denying the Christian religion to be true, or the Holy Scriptures to be of divine authority, should, upon the first offence, be incapable to hold any office; and for the second, be incapable of bringing any action, or being guardian, executor, legatee, or purchaser of lands, and suffer three years' imprisonment without bail. A prosecution under this act is in modern times quite unknown.

II. A second offence is that of *heresy*; which consists not in a total denial of Christianity, but of some of its essential doctrines, publicly and obstinately avowed; what doctrines shall be adjudged heresy being left to the determination of the ecclesiastical judge.

The sanctimonious hypocrisy of the clergy went at first nó farther than enjoining penance, excommunication, and ecclesiastical deprivation, as punishments for this offence; but they soon proceeded to imprisonment by the ordinary, and confiscation of goods *in pios usus.* They next gradually prevailed upon the weakness of bigoted princes, to make the civil power subservient to their purposes, by making heresy not only a temporal, but even a capital offence: the ecclesiastics determining, without appeal, whatever they pleased to be heresy, and shifting off to the secular arm the odium and drudgery of executions, with which they themselves were too tender and delicate to intermeddle. Nay, they pretended to intercede and pray, on behalf of the convicted heretic, *ut citra mortis periculum sententia circa eum moderatur*; well knowing at the same time that they were delivering the unhappy victim to certain death. Hence the capital punishments inflicted on the ancient Donatists and Manichæans by the emperors Theodosius and Justinian; hence also the constitution of the emperor Frederic, mentioned by Lyndewode; adjudging all persons, without distinction, to be burnt with fire, who were convicted of heresy by the ecclesiastical judge. The same emperor, in another constitution, ordained that if any temporal lord, when admonished by the church, should neglect to clear his territories of heretics within a year, it should be lawful to seize and occupy the lands, and utterly to exterminate the heretical possessors. And upon this foundation was built that arbitrary power, so long claimed and so fatally exerted by the pope, of disposing even of the kingdoms of refractory princes to more dutiful sons of the church. The immediate result of this constitution was something singular; and may serve to illustrate at once the gratitude of the holy see, and the just punishment of the royal bigot; for upon the authority of this very constitution, the pope afterwards expelled this very emperor Frederic from his kingdom of Sicily, and gave it to Charles of Anjou.

Christianity being thus deformed by the demon of persecution upon the continent, we cannot expect that our own island should be entirely free from the same scourge. And, therefore, we find among our ancient precedents a writ *de hæretico comburendo*, which is thought by some to be as ancient as the common law itself. A conviction could not be had, however, in any petty ecclesiastical court, but only before the archbishop himself in a provincial synod; till in the reign of Henry IV., the clergy, taking advantage of the king's dubious title to demand an increase of their own power, obtained an act of parliament, which sharpened the edge of persecution by enabling the diocesan alone to convict of heretical tenets; and unless the convict abjured his opinions, the sheriff was bound *ex-officio*, if required by the bishop, to commit the unhappy victim to the flames. The power of the ecclesiastics was afterwards somewhat moderated; for though what heresy *is*, was not then precisely defined, yet we are told in some points what it is *not*: the statute 25 Hen. VIII., c. 14, declaring that offences against the see of Rome are not heresy; and the ordinary being thereby restrained from proceeding in any case upon mere suspicion. And yet the spirit of persecution was not then abated, but only diverted into a lay channel. For in six years afterwards, by statute 31 Hen. VIII., c. 14, the bloody law of the Six Articles was made; and a new and mixed jurisdiction of clergy and laity established for the trial and conviction of heretics.

I shall not perplex the reader with the various repeals and revivals of these sanguinary laws in the two succeeding reigns; contenting myself with remarking that by 1 Eliz., c. 1, all former statutes relating to heresy are repealed, the jurisdiction of heresy being left as it stood at common law, viz., as to the infliction of common censures in the ecclesiastical courts; and in case of burning the heretic, in the provincial synod only. The writ *de hæretico comburendo* consequently remained in force; and we have instances of its being put in execution, upon two Anabaptists, in the 17th of Elizabeth, and upon two Arians in the 9th of James I. But it was totally abolished, and heresy again subjected only to ecclesiastical correction *pro salute animæ*, by the statute 29 Car. II., c. 9. So that in one and the same reign our lands were delivered from the slavery of military tenures, our bodies from arbitrary imprisonment, by the *Habeas-Corpus* Act, and our minds from the tyranny of superstitious bigotry, by demolishing this badge of persecution in the English law.

III. Another species of offences against religion are those affecting the *established church*, which are either positive or negative: positive, by reviling its ordinances; or negative, by non-conformity to its worship.

The offence of *reviling the ordinances* of the church is provided for by the statutes of Edward VI., c. 1, and 1 Eliz. cc. 1 and 2. These acts were passed in the infancy of our present establishment, when the disciples of Rome and Geneva united in inveighing with the utmost bitterness against the English liturgy; but being thought inconsistent with the more tolerant spirit of the present age, have been so far repealed, that they have in effect ceased to be a part of our law. The other, or negative branch of this offence is, 2. *non-conformity*, or the absenting of one's self from divine worship in the established church. Those who did so formerly forfeited one shilling to the poor every Lord's Day they so absented themselves, and 20*l.* to the crown, if they continued such default for a month together.

But the non-conformists, against whom penal laws were directed, were those who offended through a mistaken or perverse zeal. Such were esteemed by statutes since the Reformation to be *papists* and *Protestant dissenters;* both of which were supposed to be equally schismatics in not communicating with the national church; with this difference, that the papists divided from it upon material, though erroneous reasons; but many of the dissenters upon matters of indifference; or, in other words, upon no reason at all. Our ancestors were mistaken in their plans of compulsion and intolerance. The sin of schism, as such, is by no means the object of temporal coercion and punishment. If men differ with the ecclesiastical establishment, the civil magistrate has nothing to do with it, unless their tenets and practice are such as threaten disturbance to the state. He is bound, indeed, to protect the established church; but this point once secured, all *persecution* for diversity of opinions, however ridiculous or absurd they may be, is contrary to every principle of sound policy and civil freedom.

With regard, therefore, to *Protestant dissenters*, although they laboured under several disabilities and restrictions which I shall not undertake to justify, yet the legislature at length interposed, and conditionally suspended the operation of the statutes which imposed these penalties by the *Toleration Act*, 1 Will. and Mary, statute 1, c. 18. But it was not thought fit at that time to extend any indulgence to papists and unitarians; as to whom the disabilities I refer to were not removed till the reign of George III., or finally swept away till our own day. By the acts I allude to, and several statutes of the last and present reign, permitting the marriages of dissenters in their own places of worship, and providing for a civil registration of births, deaths, and marriages, independently of the established church, all persons are now happily left at full liberty to act as their conscience shall direct them, in the matter of religious worship. But some prohibitions still exist which scarcely call for comment. Thus, no mayor or principal magistrate can appear at any dissenting meeting with the ensigns of his office,* on pain of disability to hold that or any other office; and officers of corporations are forbidden to attend with the insignia of office at any place of worship, other than the established church, under a penalty of 100*l*.

As to *papists*, what has been said of the Protestant dissenters holds equally strong for a general toleration of them; nevertheless it was long before the amelioration of the laws accorded to Protestant dissenters was followed by the grant of corresponding privileges to the adherents of the church of Rome. In justification of their treatment, it was urged that the position of the Roman Catholics differed from that of the dissenters, whose separation was founded only upon difference of opinion in religion, and whose principles did not also extend to a subversion of the civil government; and that so long as Roman Catholics acknowledged a foreign power, superior to the sovereignty of the kingdom, they could not complain if the laws of that kingdom did not treat them upon the footing of good subjects. The disabilities under which they so long laboured have, however, been at last removed after a long and arduous struggle; the restrictions which have been retained, being apparently such only as can be justified on the ground either of policy or of justice. Thus, a Roman Catholic cannot vote or advise the crown on ecclesiastical appointments, nor present to a benefice. The establishment of any religious order of males is prohibited; and Jesuits, who have ever been found dangerous, when tolerated, may be banished the kingdom, and if they return, transported for life. Nay, so jealous is the legislature of any attempt at the usurpation of power by foreign ecclesiastics, that a statute was recently passed to prevent English Roman Catholic dignitaries from assuming ecclesiastical titles, in respect of places within the realm; all briefs or letters apostolical for that purpose being declared void, and penalties imposed on persons procuring them from the see of Rome.

Two of the most important statutes which have been repealed in deference to this modern spirit of toleration, were the *Corporation* and *Test* Acts. By the former no person could be legally elected to any

---

* Sir Humphrey Edwin, a lord mayor of London, had the imprudence, soon after the Toleration Act, to go to a Presbyterian meeting-house in his formalities; which is alluded to by Dean Swift in his *Tale of a Tub*, under the allegory of *Jack* getting on a great horse, and eating custard.

office relating to the government of any city or corporation, unless within a twelvemonth before, he had received the sacrament of the Lord's supper according to the rites of the Church of England. The Test Act directed all officers, civil and military, to take the oaths and make a declaration in open court against transubstantiation, within six months after their admission; and also within the same time to receive the sacrament according to the usage of the Church of England, upon forfeiture of 500*l.*, and disability to hold the office. By the repeal of these and the other statutes I have referred to, the offence of non-conformity has practically ceased to exist.

I proceed now to consider some gross impieties and general immoralities which are taken notice of by our municipal law, though rarely, if ever, publicly punished; of this nature is,

IV. *Blasphemy* against the Almighty, by denying his being, or providence; or by contumelious reproaches of our Saviour. Whither also may be referred all profane scoffing at the Holy Scripture, or exposing it to contempt and ridicule, which are offences punishable at common law by fine and imprisonment, for Christianity is part of the law of England. But whatever may be the law on this subject, no attempt has been made in modern times to enforce it. To do so would involve the prosecution of many authors and publishers of works, undoubtedly written with an earnest desire to arrive at the truth; and would not only be an abuse of the law, but would wholly fail in effecting the object in view.

V. Somewhat allied to this, though in an inferior degree, is the offence of profane and common *swearing* and *cursing*, which is punishable in a labourer, sailor, or soldier, by a fine of 1*s.*; in every other person under the degree of a gentleman, of 2*s.*; and in every other gentleman or person of superior rank, of 5*s.*

VI. A sixth species of offences against God and religion, of which our ancient books are full, is a crime of which one knows not well what account to give, the offence, namely, of *witchcraft, conjuration, enchantment,* or *sorcery.* This was prohibited, under severe penalties by several statutes, which continued in force until nearly the middle of the eighteenth century; many poor wretches being sacrificed thereby to the prejudice of their neighbours and their own illusions; not a few having, by some means or other, been led to confess their supposed offence at the gallows. Our legislature at length, in the reign of George II., followed the wise example of Louis XIV., in France, who restrained the tribunals from receiving informations of witchcraft, by enacting that no prosecution should for the future be carried on against any person for any of those charges. But people pretending to tell fortunes, or using any means or device, by palmistry or otherwise, to impose on any person, are deemed rogues and vagabonds, and punishable accordingly.

VII. A seventh species of offenders in this class are all *religious impostors*: such as falsely pretend an extraordinary commission from heaven, or terrify and abuse the people with false denunciations of judgments. These, as tending to subvert all religion, by bringing it into ridicule and contempt, are punishable by the temporal courts with fine and imprisonment.

VIII. *Simony*, or the corrupt presentation of any one to an ecclesiastical benefice for gift or reward, may also be considered an offence against religion; but it is a crime which there are so many methods of avoiding, that simony, however universal a practice, is quite unknown as an offence.

IX. Profanation of the Lord's Day, vulgarly, but improperly, called *sabbath-breaking*, is another offence against religion, punished by our municipal law. But in what the offence consists must be gathered from the various statutes relating to this subject. These, among other things, provide that no fair or market shall be held on the principal festivals, Good Friday, or any Sunday, on pain of forfeiting the goods exposed to sale; that no person shall assemble *out of* their own parishes for any sport whatsoever upon this day, nor use *unlawful* pastimes *in* them; and that no person shall *work* on the Lord's Day, or use any boat or barge, or expose any goods to sale; the selling of meat in public-houses, milk at certain hours, and works of necessity or charity, being excepted. The service of process on Sunday is also illegal; and so is the keeping open of any public-house during the hours of Divine service.

X. *Drunkenness* is punished by statute 21 Jac. I. c. 7, with the forfeiture of 5s., or the sitting six hours in the stocks, if the offender is not able to pay the penalty; by which time the statute presumes the offender will have regained his senses, and not be able to do mischief to his neighbours.

XI. The last offence against religion and morality which I shall mention, as cognisable by the temporal courts and punishable by fine and imprisonment, is that of open and notorious *lewdness*, either by keeping, or indeed, it has been said, in even frequenting, houses of ill fame; or by some grossly scandalous and public indecency. To undress in order to bathe in a place exposed to public view is an offence *contra bonum mores*; so is the exposure for sale of immoral pictures or prints; and generally whatever openly outrages decency, and is injurious to public morals, may be said to be a misdemeanor at common law.

CHAPTER V.

OF OFFENCES AGAINST THE LAW OF NATIONS.

Violation of safe-conducts—of rights of ambassadors—Piracy—Slave trade.

ACCORDING to the method marked out in the preceding chapter, we are next to consider the offences more immediately repugnant to that universal law of society which regulates the mutual intercourse between one state and another and is usually termed the Law of Nations. These are: 1. Violation of safe-conducts; 2. Infringement of the rights of ambassadors; 3. Piracy; and 4. Trading in slaves.

I. As to the first, *violation* of *safe-conducts* or *passports*, expressly granted by the sovereign or his ambassadors to the subjects of a foreign power in time of mutual war; or committing acts of hostilities against such as are in amity, league, or truce with us, who are here under a general implied safe-conduct: these are breaches of the public faith, without the preservation of which there can be no intercourse or commerce between one nation and another; and such offences may, according to the writers upon the law of nations, be a just ground of a national war; since it is not in the power of the foreign prince to cause justice to be done to his subjects by the very individual delinquent, but he must require it of the whole community. And as during the continuance of any safe-conduct, either express or implied, the foreigner is under the protection of the sovereign and the law: and, more especially, as it is one of the articles of *Magna Charta*, that foreign merchants should be entitled to safe-conduct and security throughout the kingdom; there is no question, but that any violation of either the person or property of such foreigner may be punished by indictment in the name of the sovereign, whose honour is more particularly engaged in supporting his own safe-conduct. And it is further expressly enacted by stat. 31 Hen. VI. c. 4, that if any of the king's subjects attempt or offend, upon the sea, or in any port within the king's obeysance, against any stranger in amity, league, or truce, or under safe-conduct; and especially by attacking his person, or spoiling him or robbing him of his goods; the lord chancellor, with any of the justices of either the King's Bench or Common Pleas, may cause full restitution and amends to be made to the party injured.

II. The rights of *ambassadors*, being established by the law of nations, are therefore matter of universal concern, and the common law accordingly recognises them in their full extent, by immediately stopping all legal process sued out through the ignorance or rashness of individuals, which may intrench upon the immunities of a foreign minister or any of his train. And it is further declared by the statute 7 Ann. c. 12, that all persons prosecuting or executing such process, shall be deemed violators of the laws of nations, and disturbers of the public repose; and shall suffer such penalties and corporal punishment as the lord chancellor and the chief justices, or any two of them, shall think fit.

III. *Piracy*, or robbery upon the high seas, is an offence against the universal law of society; a pirate being, according to Sir Edward Coke, *hostis humani generis*.

This offence at common law, consists in committing those acts of robbery and depredation upon the high seas, which, if committed upon land, would have amounted to felony there. But other offences have, by various statutes, been made piracy, and liable to the same penalty. This was formerly death, whether the guilty party were a principal, or merely accessory by setting forth such pirates, or abetting them before the fact, or receiving or concealing them or their goods after it. But modern legislation has modified this severity, and greatly reduced the punishment in the case of accessories after the fact.

The capture of piratical vessels was formerly encouraged by bounties on pirates taken or killed; and seamen wounded in piratical engagements were entitled to the pension of Greenwich Hospital; which no other seamen were, except only such as had served in a ship of war. The statutes as to bounties and rewards for services in piratical engagements are, however, no longer in force; but property captured from pirates is liable to condemnation as *droits of the Admiralty*, to be restored, if private property, to the rightful owners, on payment of one-eighth of the value as salvage; while fitting rewards are assigned for services against pirates.

IV. The carrying on a traffic in slaves may be regarded as another class of offences against the law of nations. Not merely is it an offence against the victims of the trade, but, happily for the interests of humanity, it is now in many instances an offence against express treaties entered into between this country and other states. Any British subject who conveys or removes any person as a slave, is now by statute guilty of piracy, felony, and robbery; for which penal servitude for life may be awarded, so that this crime is now rarely if ever attempted.

These are the principal cases in which the statute law of England interposes to aid and enforce the law of nations, as a part of the common law, by inflicting an adequate punishment upon offences against that universal law, committed by private persons.

CHAPTER VI.

OF HIGH TREASON, AND OTHER OFFENCES AFFECTING THE SUPREME EXECUTIVE POWER.

High treason—compassing death of king—by words—in writing—Violation of queen, &c. &c.—Levying war—Adhering to enemy—Counterfeiting Great Seal—Killing judges——Modern treasons—Punishment of treason—Sedition —Unlawful oaths—Secret societies.

THE crimes affecting the supreme executive power, are: I. Treason; II. Felonies injurious to the royal prerogative; III. *Præmunire*; IV. Other misprisions and contempts. Of which crimes,

I. The first and principal is treason, *proditio*, which in its very name, borrowed from the French, imports a betraying, treachery, or breach of faith; and is the highest civil crime, which, considered as a member of the community, any man can possibly commit. It ought, therefore, to be the most precisely ascertained; and yet by common law, there was a great latitude left in the breast of the judges to determine what was treason, or not so: whereby the creatures of tyrannical princes had opportunity to create abundance of constructive treasons; that is, to raise, by forced and arbitrary constructions, offences into the crime and punishment of treason, which never were suspected to be such. The inconveniences arising from this laxity, were however put an end to by the statute 25 Edw. III. c. 2, which defines what offences only for the future should be held to be treason: in like manner as the *lex Julia majestatis* among the Romans, promulgated by Augustus Cæsar, comprehended all the ancient laws, that had before been enacted to punish transgressors against the state. And we shall find that it comprehends all kinds of high treason then known, under several branches.

1. " When a man doth compass or imagine the death of our lord " the king, of our lady his queen, or of their eldest son and heir." Under this description it is held that a queen regnant, such as Queen Elizabeth, Queen Anne, and Queen Victoria, is within the words of the act; but the husband of such a queen is not. And the king here intended is the king in possession; for it is held that a king *de*

facto and not *de jure*, or in other words, an usurper that has got possession of the throne, js a king within the meaning of the statute; but the most rightful heir of the crown, or king *de jure* and not *de facto*, who has never had plenary possession of the throne, as was the case of the house of York during the three reigns of the line of Lancaster, is not a king within this statute against whom treasons may be committed.

The offence consists in *compassing* or *imagining* the death of the king, &c., which are indeed synonymous terms; the word *compass* signifying the purpose or design of the mind or will, and not, as in common speech, the carrying such design to effect. And, therefore, an accidental stroke, which may mortally wound the sovereign, *per infortuniam*, without any traitorous intent, is no treason: as was the case of Sir Walter Tyrrel, who, by the command of King William Rufus, shooting at a hart, the arrow glanced against a tree, and killed the king upon the spot. But, as this compassing or imagination is an act of the mind, it cannot possibly fall under any judicial cognizance, unless it be demonstrated by some open, or *overt* act. And therefore in this, and the three next species of treason, it is necessary that there appear an open or *overt* act of a more full and explicit nature to convict the traitor upon.

How far mere *words*, spoken by an individual, and not relative to any treasonable act or design, shall amount to treason, was formerly matter of doubt. We have two instances in the reign of Edward IV., of persons executed for treasonable words: the one a citizen of London, who said he would make his son heir of the *Crown*, being the sign of the house in which he lived; the other a gentleman, whose favourite buck the king killed in hunting, whereupon he wished it, horns and all, in the king's belly. These were esteemed hard cases; and the Chief Justice Markham rather chose to leave his place than assent to the latter judgment. But now it seems clearly to be agreed, that by the common law and the statute of Edward III. words spoken amount only to a high misdemeanor, and no treason.

If the words be set down in writing, it argues more deliberate intention: and it has been held that writing is an overt act of treason; for *scribere est agere*. And such writing, though unpublished, has in some arbitrary reigns convicted its author of treason: particularly in the cases of one Peacham, a clergyman, for treasonable passages in a sermon never preached; and of Algernon Sydney, for some papers found in his closet; which, had they been plainly relative to any previously-formed design of dethroning or murdering the king, might doubtless have been properly read in evidence as overt acts of that treason, which was specially laid in the indictment. But being merely speculative, without any intention of making any

x

public use of them, the convicting the authors of treason upon such an insufficient foundation has been universally disapproved. Peacham was therefore pardoned: and though Sydney indeed was executed, yet it was to the general discontent of the nation; and his attainder was afterwards reversed by parliament.

2. The second species of treason is, " if a man do violate the king's " companion, or the king's eldest daughter unmarried, or the wife of " the king's eldest son and heir." By the king's companion is meant his wife; and by violation is understood carnal knowledge, as well without force as with it; and this is high treason in both parties, if both be consenting, as some of the wives of Henry VIII. by fatal experience evinced. The plain intention of this law is to guard the blood royal from any suspicion of bastardy, whereby the succession to the crown might be rendered dubious; and therefore, when this reason ceases, the law ceases with it, for to violate a queen or princess-dowager is held to be no treason: in like manner as by the feudal law, it was a felony and attended with a forfeiture of the fief, if the vassal vitiated the wife or daughter of his lord; but not so, if he only vitiated his widow.

3. The third species of treason is, " if a man do levy war against " our lord the king in his realm." And this may be done by taking arms, not only to dethrone the king, but under pretence to reform religion, or the laws, or to remove evil counsellors, or other grievances whether real or pretended. For the law does not permit any man, or set of men, to interfere forcibly in matters of such high importance, especially as it has established a sufficient power, for these purposes, in the high court of parliament. An insurrection with an avowed design to pull down *all* inclosures, *all* brothels, and the like, is therefore treason ; the universality of the design making it a rebellion against the state, a usurpation of the powers of government, and an insolent invasion of the king's authority. But a tumult, with a view to pull down a particular house, is only a riot.

4. " If a man be adherent to the king's enemies in his realm, " giving to them aid and comfort in the realm, or elsewhere," he is guilty of high treason. This must likewise be proved by some overt act, as by giving them intelligence, by sending them provisions, by selling them arms, by treacherously surrendering a fortress or the like.

5. " If a man counterfeit the king's great or privy seal," this is also high treason. But if a man takes wax bearing the impression of the great seal off from one patent, and fixes it to another, this is held to be only an abuse of the seal, and not a counterfeiting of it :

as was the case of a certain chaplain, who in such manner framed a dispensation for non-residence.

: The next species of treason mentioned in the statute, is " if a man " counterfeit the king's money ; and if a man bring false money into " the realm counterfeit to the money of England, knowing the money " to be false, to merchandise and make payment withal." But this crime is now reduced to felony.

6. The last species of treason ascertained by this statute, is " if a " man slay the chancellor, treasurer, or the king's justices of the one " bench or the other, justices in eyre, or justices of assize, and all " other justices assigned to hear and determine, being in their places " doing their offices." The statute extends only to the actual killing of them, and not to wounding, or a bare attempt to kill them ; and it extends also only to the officers therein specified ; and therefore the barons of the exchequer, as such, are not within the protection of this act.

Thus careful was the legislature, in the reign of Edward III., to specify and reduce to a certainty the vague notions of treason that had formerly prevailed in our courts. But in the unfortunate reign of Richard II., it was extremely liberal in declaring new treasons; the most arbitrary and absurd of all which was the bare purpose and intent of killing or deposing the king, without any overt act to demonstrate it. And yet so little effect have over-violent laws to prevent any crime, that within two years afterwards this very prince was both deposed and murdered ; and in the first year of his successor's reign, an act was passed, which at once swept away the whole load of extravagant treasons which had been recently introduced. But afterwards, between the reigns of Henry IV. and Queen Mary, and particularly in the reign of Henry VIII., the spirit of inventing new and strange treasons was revived ; among which we may reckon the offences of clipping money ; breaking prison or rescue, when the prisoner is committed for treason ; burning houses to extort money ; stealing cattle by Welshmen ; counterfeiting foreign coin ; wilful poisoning ; execrations against the king ; calling him opprobrious names by public writing ; counterfeiting the sign manual or signet ; refusing to abjure the pope ; deflowering or marrying, without the royal licence, any of the king's children, sisters, aunts, nephews, or nieces ; bare solicitation of the chastity of the queen or princess, or advances made by themselves ; marrying with the king, by a woman not a virgin, without previously discovering to him such her unchaste life ; judging or *believing* the king to have been lawfully married to Anne of Cleves ; derogating from the king's royal style and title ; and impugning his supremacy ; and assembling riotously

x 2

to the number of twelve, and not dispersing upon proclamation ; all which new-fangled treasons were totally abrogated by the statute 1 Edw. VI. c. 12, which once more reduced all treasons to the standard of the statute of Edw. III. Since which time the legislature has been more cautious in creating new offences of this kind.

To the treasons already enumerated, must now, however, be added :—

7. Endeavouring to deprive or hinder any person, being the next in succession to the crown, according to the Act of Settlement, from succeeding to the crown, and maliciously and directly attempting the same by any overt act.

8. Maliciously, advisedly, and directly, by writing or printing, maintaining and affirming that any other person hath any right or title to the crown of this realm, otherwise than according to the Act of Settlement ; or that the kings of this realm with the authority of parliament are not able to make laws and statutes, to bind the crown and the descent thereof.

9. In case the crown shall descend on any issue of her Majesty while under the age of eighteen, persons aiding or abetting the marriage of the king or queen without the consent of the regent and parliament, and the person married to such king or queen while under the age of eighteen, are by 3 & 4 Vict. c. 52, s. 4, guilty of high treason.

Under one or other of these *nine* heads the offences now constituting high treason may be ranged. The reader would, however, derive a very incorrect notion of the course of legislation on this important subject, if he were left to suppose that the statutes, to which reference has been made, comprised the whole of the law relating to this offence. But I cannot here enter upon any historical notice of the perturbations which have affected the government of this country, and led to frequent interference by parliament ; and I must content myself therefore with a passing allusion to 1. the treasons which were created in the reign of Elizabeth, relating to *papists* ; and 2. to those created for the security of the protestant succession in the house of Hanover.

The first of the offences which the legislature of Queen Elizabeth thought fit to declare to be treason, was the defending of the pope's alleged jurisdiction ; and the next was the crime committed by any popish priest, born in the dominions of the Crown of England, who came over hither from beyond the seas, unless driven by stress of weather and departing in a reasonable time, and tarried here three days without conforming to the church. In the reign of James I. the parliament went a little further, and declared that if any natural-born subject withdrew from his allegiance, and became reconciled to the pope or see of Rome, or any other prince or state, both he and all such as procured such reconciliation should incur the guilt of high treason.

The other obsolete species of high treason was that created for the security of the *Hanoverian succession*, by the statute 13 & 14 Will. III. c. 3, whereby the pretended Prince of Wales, who was then thirteen years of age, and had assumed the title of King James III., was attainted of high treason; and it was made high treason for any of the king's subjects to hold correspondence with him. A similar penalty was afterwards, in the reign of George II., attached to any recognition of his son, the unfortunate Charles Edward Stuart.

Thus much for the crime of treason, or *læsæ majestatis*, in all its branches; which consists, we may observe, originally, in grossly counteracting that allegiance which is due from the subject; though, in some instances, the zeal of our legislators to stop the progress of some highly pernicious practices has occasioned them a little to depart from this its primitive idea.

The punishment of high treason in general was very solemn and terrible. It was 1. That the offender be drawn to the gallows, and not be carried or walk; though usually, by connivance, at length ripened by humanity into law, a sledge or hurdle was allowed. 2. That he be hanged by the neck, and then cut down alive. 3. That his entrails be taken out, and burned, while he is yet alive. 4. That his head be cut off. 5. That his body be divided into four parts. 6. That his head and quarters be at the king's disposal. But in treasons of every kind the punishment of women was the same, and different from that of men. For, as the decency due to the sex forbade the exposing and publicly mangling their bodies, their sentence was to be drawn to the gallows, and there to be burned alive.*

All this has been altered, however, and the judgment in all cases of high treason now is, that the offender be drawn on a hurdle to the place of execution, and be there hanged by the neck until he be dead, and that afterwards his head be severed from his body, and his body, divided into four quarters, be disposed of as the crown shall think fit.

The consequences of this judgment, attainder, forfeiture, and corruption of blood, must be referred to the latter end of this book,

---

* As an instance of how the Bible may be quoted in support of almost any practice, good, bad, or indifferent, it may be observed that Sir Edward Coke tells us, that this punishment for treason is warranted by divers examples in Scripture; for Joab was drawn, Bithan was hanged, Judas was embowelled, and so on of the rest.

when we shall treat of them altogether, as well in treason as in other offences.

Before closing this chapter, however, it is necessary to refer to a class of offences, which in former times ranked as high treason; but which the humanity of our present laws will not allow of to incur the fatal consequences attached to crimes of that serious nature. These may be classed under the head of 1. Sedition; and 2. Attempts to injure or alarm the sovereign.

The insults publicly offered to the person of king George III., at the period of the French revolution, the ferment then created among the people by numerous publications advocating a change in the institutions of this country, and the frequent assemblies held under the pretext of deliberating on public grievances, and agreeing on petitions, remonstrances, or other addresses to the king or the houses of parliament, led to the passing of two acts of parliament, the one, 36 Geo. III., c. 7, intituled " An Act for the safety and preservation " of his Majesty's Person and Government against treasonable and " seditious practices and attempts;" and the other, 36 Geo. III., c. 8, " An Act for the more effectually preventing seditious meetings and " assemblies."

By the first-named statute, it was made treason to compass the destruction, or bodily harm, deposition, or restraint of the king; while any one using any words to excite the people to hatred and contempt of his Majesty, or of the government and constitution of this realm, thereby incurred the punishment of a high misdemeanor. This act has, however, been partially repealed by 11 & 12 Vict. c. 12; which was passed to meet the mischievous but absurd attempts made shortly before its enactment, to effect a repeal of the legislative union between Great Britain and Ireland. It was felt that to dignify these proceedings with the name of high treason, was only to encourage their continuance or repetition, by endowing the foolish and mis-guided persons who engaged in them with the name of patriots or martyrs; and the statute accordingly reduces their offences to the category of *felony*, and makes them punishable as such.

The other statute, 36 Geo. III. c. 8, was only of a temporary character; but at the same period, and for the same reasons, other provisions still in force were made to repress *mutinous* and *seditious practices*, and the *administration of unlawful oaths*. Secret societies were condemned, and public meetings of more than fifty persons prohibited from assembling in any open place within a mile of Westminster Hall, for the purpose of petition, remonstrance, or ad-dress to the crown or either house of parliament.

The only other statute relating to offences on the verge of high treason is one of the present reign, 5 & 6 Vict. c. 51, passed to prevent a repetition of those annoyances to which the queen was exposed soon after her accession to the throne, by idle and ill-disposed youths discharging fire-arms in her presence if not at her person. As this was done apparently from a morbid love of notoriety, it was considered that a disgraceful punishment would be most appropriate; and the wisdom of this legislation has been happily evinced by the complete cessation of the offence.

CHAPTER VII.

OF OFFENCES AGAINST THE PREROGATIVE.

Definition of *felony*—Offences relating to the coin—Serving in foreign states—
Embezzling stores of war—Desertion.

II. As we are next to consider such *felonies* as more especially affect the supreme executive power, it will not be amiss here to explain briefly the nature and meaning of *felony*.

Felony, then, in the general acceptation of our English law, comprises every species of crime, which occasions at common law the forfeiture of lands or goods. This most frequently happens in those crimes for which a capital punishment either is or was liable to be inflicted. Indeed, treason itself was anciently comprised under the name of felony; and all treasons, therefore, strictly speaking, are felonies; though all felonies are not treason. And to this also we may add, that not only all offences formerly capital, are in some degree or other felony; but that this is likewise the case with some other offences which never were punished with death; as suicide, where the party is already dead; homicide by chance-medley, or in self-defence; and the small thefts formerly termed *petit* larceny or pilfering: all which are, strictly speaking, felonies, as they subject the committers of them to forfeitures. So that upon the whole the only adequate definition of felony seems to be that which is before laid down; viz., an offence which occasions a total forfeiture of either lands or goods, or both, at the common law; and to which capital or other punishment may be superadded, according to the degree of guilt.

The idea of felony was, indeed, until recently, so generally connected with that of capital punishment, that it was hard to separate them; and to this usage the interpretations of the law conformed. And therefore, if a statute made any new offence felony, the law implied that it should be punished with death; viz., by hanging, as well as with forfeiture; but the criminal law has been considerably ameliorated in this respect, every person convicted of a felony, for which *no* punishment is expressly provided, being now punishable with penal servitude or imprisonment. So that felony is reducible to its original signification, a crime to be punished by forfeiture, and to which death may, or may not, be superadded.

This being premised, I proceed to consider such felonies as are more immediately injurious to the royal prerogative; and these are 1. Offences relating to the coin. 2. The offence of serving a foreign prince. 3. The offence of embezzling or destroying stores of war. 4. Desertion from the armies in time of war.

1. Offences relating to the *coin*, under which may be ranked some inferior misdemeanors not amounting to felony, have been the subject of a series of statutes, commencing in the reign of Edward I.; nearly all of which were repealed by the statute 2 Will. IV. c. 34, which consolidated the then laws relating to these crimes. The punishments imposed by that and other statutes relating to the coin were modified, however, by more recent enactments, penal servitude being in all cases substituted for transportation, and imprisonment accompanied, at the discretion of the court, with hard labour, or solitary confinement, or both. And the law on the whole subject has accordingly been again consolidated by the statute 24 & 25 Vict. c. 99. To that statute, therefore, I venture to refer the reader, only pointing out in this place that the law has provided a gradual scale of punishment for offences relating to the coin, the making or counterfeiting of the coin itself being the crime most severely punished.

Tampering with the genuine coin of the realm is almost as penal; but the law deals much more mildly with the *utterer* of base coin, who is often led into the commission of the offence by the more guilty counterfeiter or seller. He is guilty only of a *misdemeanor*, unless he has been previously convicted of a similar offence; in which event the crime amounts to *felony*, involving, of course, severity of punishment.

The statute I have referred to also facilitates the trial and punishment of accessories, and contains other provisions directed against the making, buying or selling, or being in possession of, coining tools, each of which offences is made a *felony*. It is also made a misdemeanor to deface the coin by stamping or defacing it, a practice often resorted to by tradesmen for advertising purposes. The offence of counterfeiting *foreign coin*, and bringing it into this country to circulate, is provided for by the same statute.

2. *Serving* in *foreign states*, which is generally inconsistent with allegiance to one's natural prince, was at one time punished by stat. 3 Jac. I. c. 4; which made it felony for any person to go out of the realm, to serve a foreign prince, without having first taken the oath of allegiance. This statute was extended and amended by subsequent acts, which have since been repealed. The statute now in force is the Foreign Enlistment Act, 59 Geo. III. c. 69, which makes the entering into the aid of a foreign prince or people, in any warlike capacity whatever, or going abroad with that intent, or attempting to get others to do so without the royal licence, a misdemeanor, punishable by fine or imprisonment, or both. The same statute imposes a penalty of 50*l.* on masters of ships and owners assisting in the committal of this offence; while persons fitting out armed vessels to aid the military operations of any foreign powers, without license from the crown, or aiding the warlike equipment of vessels of foreign states, are guilty of a misdemeanor, punishable by fine or imprisonment, or both.

3. *Embezzling* or *destroying* the sovereign's warlike *stores*, was first declared to be felony by 31 Eliz. c. 4. The statute 22 Car. II. c. 5, made the offence capital; but gave power to the judge after sentence to transport the offender for seven years. Both statutes have been virtually repealed, however, by 4 Geo. IV. c. 53; which, nevertheless, leaves this offence still highly penal. Inferior embezzlements and misdemeanors that fall under this denomination, are punishable under other statutes. The annual Mutiny Acts also contain provisions for the trial and punishment by court-martial of persons embezzling military or naval stores. The much more serious offence of setting fire to or destroying any of the sovereign's ships of war,—or any of the royal arsenals, dockyards, or victualling offices, or the materials thereunto belonging,—or military, naval, or victualling stores, or ammunition,—or causing, aiding, procuring, abetting, or assisting in such offence, is still a capital felony.

4. *Desertion* from the sovereign's armies in time of war, whether by land or sea, in England or in parts beyond the sea, is by the standing laws of the land, and particularly by statute 18 Hen. VI. c. 10, and 5 Eliz. c. 5, made felony; but these statutes which also punish other inferior military offences with fines, imprisonment, and other penalties, have become obsolete, the offences at which they strike being usually punished under the Mutiny Acts.

CHAPTER VIII.

OF PRÆMUNIRE.

Statutes of *præmunire*—Wherein the offence consists—What offences now amount to *præmunire*—Punishment.

III. The third species of offence more immediately affecting the sovereign and government, is that of *præmunire*, so called from the words of the writ preparatory to the prosecution thereof: "*præmunire* "*facias A B*," cause A B to be forewarned that he appear before us to answer the contempt wherewith he stands charged: which contempt is particularly recited in the preamble to the writ. It took its origin from the exorbitant power claimed and exercised in England by the pope, which even in the days of blind zeal was too heavy for our ancestors to bear.

The ancient British Church was a stranger to the bishop of Rome, and all his pretended authority. But the pagan Saxon invaders, having driven the professors of Christianity to the remotest corners of our island, their own conversion was afterwards effected by Augustin the monk, and other missionaries from the court of Rome. This naturally introduced some few of the papal corruptions in point of faith and doctrine: but we read of no civil authority claimed by the pope in these kingdoms, till the era of the Norman conquest; when the then reigning pontiff having favoured Duke William in his projected invasion, by blessing his host and consecrating his banners, he took that opportunity also of establishing his spiritual encroachments; which, indeed, he was permitted to do by the policy of the Conqueror. The establishment of the feudal system in most of the governments of Europe, had already suggested a means to the court of Rome for usurping a similar authority over all the preferments of the church; which began first in Italy, and gradually spread itself to England. The pope became a feudal lord; and all ordinary patrons were to hold their right of patronage under this universal superior. Estates held by feudal tenure, being originally gratuitous donations, were at that time denominated *beneficia*: their very name as well as constitution, was borrowed, and the care of the souls of a parish thence came to be denominated a *benefice*. Lay fees were conferred by investiture or delivery of corporal possession; and spiritual benefices, which at first were universally donative, now received in like manner a spiritual investiture, by institution from the bishop, and induction under his authority. As lands escheated to the lord, in defect of a legal tenant, so benefices lapsed to the bishop upon non-presentation by the patron, in the nature of a spiritual escheat. The annual tenths collected from the clergy were equivalent to the feudal render, or rent reserved upon a grant; the oath of canonical obedience was copied from the oath of fealty required from the vassal by his superior; the *primer seisins* of our military tenures, whereby the first profits of an heir's estate were cruelly extorted by his lord, gave birth to as cruel an exaction of first-fruits from the beneficed clergy; and the occasional aids and talliages, levied by the prince on his vassals, gave a handle to the pope to levy, by the means of his legates *à latere*, Peter-pence and other taxations.

At length the Holy Father went a step beyond any example of either emperor or feudal lord. He reserved to himself, by his own apostolical authority, the presentation to all benefices, which became vacant while the incumbent was attending the court of Rome upon any occasion, or on his journey thither, or back again; and moreover such also as became vacant by his promotion to a bishopric or abbey. And this last, the canonists declared, was no detriment at all to the patron, being only like the change of a life in a feudal estate by the lord. Dispensations to avoid these vacancies begat the doctrine of *commendams:* and papal *provisions* were the previous nomination to such benefices by a kind of anticipation, before they became actually void: though afterwards indiscriminately applied to any right of patronage exerted or usurped by the pope. In consequence of which the best livings were filled by Italian and other foreign clergy, equally unskilled in and averse to the laws and constitution of England. The very nomination to bishoprics, that ancient prerogative of the crown, was wrested from King Henry I., and afterwards from his successor King John; and seemingly indeed conferred on the chapters belonging to each see; but by means of the frequent appeals to Rome, through the intricacy of the laws which regulated canonical elections, was eventually vested in the pope. And to sum up this head with a transaction most unparalleled and astonishing in its kind, Pope Innocent III. had at length the effrontery to demand, and King John had the meanness to consent to, a resignation of his crown to the pope, whereby England was to become for ever St. Peter's patrimony; and the dastardly monarch re-accepted his sceptre from the hands of the papal legate, to hold as the vassal of the holy see, at the annual rent of a thousand marks.

Another engine set on foot, or at least greatly improved, by the court of Rome, was a masterpiece of papal policy. Not content with the ample provision of tithes, they endeavoured to grasp at the lands of the kingdom, and, had not the legislature withstood them, would by this time have probably been masters of every foot of ground in the realm. To this end they introduced the monks of the Benedictine and other rules, men of sour and austere religion, separated from the world and its concerns by a vow of perpetual celibacy, yet fascinating the minds of the people by pretences to extraordinary sanctity, while all their aim was to aggrandize the power and extend the influence of their grand superior the pope. And as, in those times of civil tumult, great rapines and violence were daily committed by overgrown lords and their adherents, they were taught to believe, that founding a monastery a little before their deaths would atone for a life of incontinence, disorder, and bloodshed. Hence innumerable abbeys and religious houses were built within a century after the Conquest, and endowed, not only with the tithes of parishes which were ravished from the secular clergy, but also with lands, manors, lordships, and extensive baronies. And the doctrine inculcated was, that whatever was so given to, or purchased by, the monks and friars, was consecrated to God himself; and that to alienate or take it away was no less than the sin of sacrilege.

I might here have enlarged upon other contrivances, which will occur to the recollection of the reader, set on foot by the court of Rome, for effecting an entire exemption of its clergy from any intercourse with the civil magistrate : such as the separation of the ecclesiastical courts from the temporal; the appointment of its judges by merely spiritual authority, without any interposition from the crown; the exclusive jurisdiction it claimed over all ecclesiastical persons and causes ; and the *privilegium clericale*, or benefit of clergy, which delivered all clerks from any trial or punishment except before their own tribunal. I shall only observe at present, that notwithstanding this plan of pontifical power was so deeply laid, and so indefatigably pursued by the unwearied politics of the court of Rome through a long succession of ages ; yet it vanished into nothing, when the eyes of the people were a little enlightened, and they set themselves with vigour to oppose it. So vain and ridiculous is the attempt to live in society, without acknowledging the obligations which it lays us under ; and to effect an entire independence of that civil state, which protects us in all our rights, and gives us every other liberty, that only excepted of despising the laws of the community.

Let us return, however, to the statutes of *præmunire*, which were framed to encounter the attempts of the See of Rome to establish an independent authority in this country. King Edward I., a wise and magnanimous prince, was the first to oppose in earnest these papal usurpations. He would not suffer his bishops to attend a general council, till they had sworn not to receive the papal benediction.

He made light of all papal bulls and processes; attacked Scotland in defiance of one, and seized the temporalities of his clergy, who under pretence of another refused to pay a tax imposed by parliament. He strengthened the statutes of mortmain; thereby closing the great gulf, in which all the lands of the kingdom were in danger of being swallowed. And, one of his subjects having obtained a bull of excommunication against another, he ordered him to be executed as a traitor, according to the ancient law. And in the thirty-fifth year of his reign was made the first statute against papal provisions, the foundation of all the subsequent statutes of *præmunire;* which we rank as an offence immediately against the sovereign, because every encouragement of the papal power is a diminution of the authority of the crown.

In the weak reign of Edward II., the pope again endeavoured to encroach, but the parliament manfully withstood him. Edward III. was of a different temper. To remedy these inconveniences first by gentle means, he wrote an expostulation to the pope; but receiving a menacing and contemptuous answer, withal acquainting him that the emperor, who a few years before at the Diet of Nuremberg, A.D. 1323, had established a law against provisions, and also the king of France had lately submitted to the holy see, the king replied, that if both the emperor and the French king should take the pope's part, he was ready to give battle to them both, in defence of the liberties of the crown. Hereupon more sharp and penal laws were devised against provisors; and when the holy see resented these proceedings, and Pope Urban V. attempted to revive the vassalage and annual rent to which King John had subjected his kingdom, it was unanimously agreed by the estates of the realm, that King John's donation was null and void, being without the concurrence of parliament, and contrary to his coronation oath: and all the temporal nobility and commons engaged, that if the pope should endeavour by process or otherwise to maintain these usurpations, they would resist and withstand him with all their power.

In the reign of Richard II., it was found necessary to strengthen these laws, by prohibiting aliens from being presented to any ecclesiastical preferment, and declaring all liegemen of the king, accepting of a foreign provision, out of the king's protection. Persons bringing citations or excommunications from beyond sea, were also to be imprisoned, forfeit their goods and lands, and suffer pain of life and member. The next statute, however, 16 Rich. II. c. 5, is generally called *the* Statute of *præmunire.* It enacts, that " whoever procures " at Rome, or elsewhere, any translations, processes, excommunica- " tions, bulls, instruments, or other things, which touch the king, " against him, his crown, and realm, and all persons aiding and

" assisting therein, shall be put out of the king's protection, their
" lands and goods forfeited to the king's use, and they shall be
" attached by their bodies to answer to the king and his council : or
" process of *præmunire facias* shall be made out against them as in
" other cases of provisors."

By the statute 2 Hen. IV. c. 3, all persons who accept any provision from the pope, to be exempt from canonical obedience to their
proper ordinary, are also subjected to the penalties of *præmunire*.
And this is the last of our ancient statutes touching this offence ; the
usurped civil power of the bishop of Rome being pretty well broken
down by these statutes, as his usurped religious power was in about
a century afterwards ; the spirit of the nation being so much raised
against foreigners, that about this time, in the reign of Henry V., the
alien priories, or abbeys for foreign monks, were suppressed, and
their lands given to the crown. And no further attempts were
afterwards made in support of these foreign jurisdictions.

This, then, is the original meaning of the offence, which we call
præmunire : viz., introducing a foreign power into this land, and
creating *imperium in imperio,* by paying that obedience to papal
process, which constitutionally belonged to the crown alone, long
before the Reformation in the reign of Henry VIII. : at which time
the penalties of *præmunire* were indeed extended to more papal
abuses than before ; several statutes of that monarch enacting that
to appeal to Rome from any of the king's courts, to sue to Rome for
any licence or dispensation, or to obey any process from thence,
make these parties who do so liable to the pains of *præmunire*. And,
in order to restore to the king in effect the nomination of vacant
bishoprics, and yet keep up the established forms, it is enacted by
statute 25 Hen. VIII. c. 20, that if the dean and chapter refuse to
elect the person named by the king, or any archbishop or bishop to
confirm or consecrate him, they shall fall within the penalties of the
statutes of *præmunire*.

Thus far the penalties of *præmunire* seem to have kept within the
proper bounds of their original institution ; but they being pains of
no inconsiderable consequence, it was thought fit by subsequent acts
of parliament to apply the same penalties to other offences ; some of
which bore more, and some less, relation to this original offence, and
some no relation at all. Most of these statutes having since been
repealed, I content myself with simply referring to them, leaving it
to the student to pursue this subject further if he shall see fit.

I must add, however, that the penalties of *præmunire* may still
be incurred by any one, who asserts, maliciously and advisedly, that
both or either house of parliament have a legislative authority with-

out the king; or that the king and parliament cannot make laws to limit the descent of the crown; or who sends any subject of this realm a prisoner into parts beyond the seas. The like penalty is incurred by any serjeant, counsellor, proctor, attorney, or officer of a court practising without having taken the proper oaths; and by the assembly of peers of Scotland, convened to elect their sixteen representatives in the British parliament, if they presume to treat of any other matter save only the election. Finally, the penalties of *præmunire* attach to all who knowingly and wilfully solemnize, assist, or are present at, any forbidden marriage of such of the descendants of the body of King George II. as are by law prohibited to contract matrimony without the consent of the crown.

What then are these penalties of *præmunire?* They are thus summed up by Sir Edward Coke: " that from the conviction, the " defendant shall be out of the king's protection, and his lands and " tenements, goods and chattels, forfeited to the king; and that his " body shall remain in prison *at the king's pleasure:* or, as other " authorities have it, *during life:*" both which amount to the same thing; as the sovereign by his prerogative may any time remit the whole, or any part, of the punishment, *i.e.*, except in the case of transgressing the statute of *Habeas Corpus,* by sending a subject of the realm a prisoner into parts beyond seas. These forfeitures here inflicted do not, by the way, bring this offence within our former definition of felony; being inflicted by particular statutes, and not by the common law. But so odious was this offence of *præmunire,* that a man that was attainted of the same might have been slain by any other man without danger of law; to obviate which savage notions, the statute 5 Eliz. c. 1, provided, that it should not be lawful to kill any person attainted in a *præmunire,* any law, statute, opinion, or exposition of law to the contrary notwithstanding. This statute has no doubt been repealed by 9 and 10 Vict. c. 59; but it can scarcely be suggested that a man convicted upon a *præmunire* is wholly out of the pale of the law. He can bring no action, however, for any private injury; being so far out of its protection, that it will not guard his civil rights, nor remedy any grievance which he as an individual may suffer. And no man, knowing him to be guilty, can safely give him comfort, aid, or relief.

In conclusion it may be observed, that prosecutions upon a *præmunire* are unheard of in our courts. There is only one instance of such a prosecution in the State Trials, in which case the penalties of a *præmunire* were inflicted upon some persons, for refusing to take the oath of allegiance in the reign of Charles II. Although, therefore, the statutes of *præmunire* have never been formally repealed, the crime may be considered as obsolete. Yet the offence still remains a title in our criminal law; and, therefore, irrespective altogether of its historical value, cannot be passed over.

CHAPTER IX.

OF MISPRISIONS AND CONTEMPTS AFFECTING THE SOVEREIGN AND GOVERNMENT.

Misprision of treason—of felony—concealment of treasure-trove—mal-adminis-tration of offices—embezzling public money—refusal to serve the crown—or join the *posse comitatus*—contempt of the royal person or government—or title—Indemnity Act—Contempt of court—*Striking* in presence of the judges—rescue of a prisoner—threatening jurors or witnesses.

IV. The last species of offences, more immediately against the sovereign and government, are entitled misprisions and contempts.

Misprisions, from the French, *mespris*, a contempt, are all such high offences as are under the degree of capital, but nearly bordering thereon: and it is said that a misprision is contained in every treason and felony whatsoever: and that, if the crown so please, the offender may be proceeded against for the misprision only. Upon this prin-ciple, while the jurisdiction of the Star-chamber subsisted, it was held that the king might remit a prosecution for treason, and cause the delinquent to be censured in that court, merely for a high misde-meanor; as happened in the case of Roger Earl of Rutland, in 43 Eliz., who was concerned in the Earl of Essex's rebellion. Misprisions are either negative, which consist in the concealment of something which ought to be revealed; or positive, which consist in the com-mission of something which ought not to be done.

I. Of the first or negative kind, is what is called *misprision of treason :* consisting in the bare knowledge and concealment of treason, without any degree of assent thereto : for any assent makes the party a traitor. The punishment of this offence is loss of the profits of lands during life, forfeiture of goods, and imprisonment during life.

Misprision of felony is also the concealment of a felony which a man knows, but never assented to; for if he assented, this makes him either principal or accessory. The punishment is imprisonment and fine at the royal pleasure : which pleasure of the sovereign must be observed, once for all, not to signify any extra-judicial will of the sovereign, but such as is declared by his representatives, the judges in his courts of justice; " *voluntas regis in curia, non in camera.*"

The *concealing the treasure-trove* is also a misprision, which was formerly punishable by death, but now only by fine and imprisonment.

II. Misprisions, which are positive, are generally denominated *contempts* or *high misdemeanors*: of which,

1. The first and principal is the *mal-administration* of such high *officers* as are in public trust and employment. This is usually punished by parliamentary impeachment; wherein such penalties, short of death, are inflicted, as to the wisdom of the house of peers shall seem proper. Hitherto also may be referred the offence of *embezzling the public money*, which is, by statute 2 Will. IV. c. 4, a felony and highly penal. Officers concerned in the receipt or management of the revenue, giving in false statements of money in their hands, are guilty of a misdemeanor.

Other misprisons are, in general, such contempts of the executive magistrate as demonstrate themselves by some arrogant and undutiful behaviour towards the crown and government. These are,

2. *Contempts* against the royal *prerogative*: as, by refusing to assist the sovereign in his councils, by advice, if called upon; or in his wars, by personal service against a rebellion or invasion. Under which class may be ranked the neglecting to join the *posse comitatus*, being thereunto duly required; or disobeying an act of parliament, where no particular penalty is assigned; for then it is punishable, like the rest of these contempts, by fine and imprisonment, at the discretion of the courts of justice.

3. *Contempts* and misprisions against the royal *person* and *government* may be by speaking or writing against him, giving out scandalous stories concerning him, or doing anything that may tend to lessen him in the esteem of his subjects. Thus to assert falsely that the sovereign labours under mental derangement is an offence; and so is it an offence to drink to the pious memory of a traitor; or for a clergyman to absolve persons at the gallows, who there persist in the treasons for which they die. For this species of contempt a man may not only be fined and imprisoned, but might, before that punishment was abolished, have suffered the pillory; in like manner, as in the ancient German empire, such persons as endeavoured to sow sedition, were condemned to become the objects of public derision, by carrying a dog upon their shoulders from one great town to another, a punishment which the emperors Otho I. and Frederic Barbarossa inflicted on noblemen of the highest rank.

4. *Contempts* against the sovereign's *title*, not amounting to treason or *præmunire*, are the denial of his right to the crown in common

and unadvised discourse, a heedless species of contempt which is punished by our law with fine and imprisonment. A contempt may also arise from refusing or neglecting to take the oaths, appointed by statute for the better securing the government; and yet acting in a public office, place of trust, or other capacity, for which the said oaths are required to be taken. But an act of indemnity is now passed annually, to relieve all such persons as through ignorance of the law, absence, or unavoidable accident, have omitted to do so.

5. *Contempts* against the royal *palaces* or *courts of justice* have always been looked upon as high misprisions; *striking* in the superior courts of justice, in Westminster-hall, or at the assizes, being still more penal than even in the royal palace. This offence was at one time punishable with the loss of the right hand, imprisonment for life, and forfeiture of goods and chattels, and of the profits of his lands during life; but would not now be so dealt with. A *rescue* of a prisoner comes under this head, being a high contempt, punishable by fine and imprisonment at the discretion of the court.

Not only such as are guilty of an actual violence, but of threatening or reproachful words to any judge sitting in the courts, are guilty of a high misprision, and have been punished with large fines, imprisonment, and corporal punishment. Likewise all such as are guilty of any injurious treatment to those who are immediately under the protection of a court of justice, are punishable by fine and imprisonment: as if a man assaults or threatens his adversary for suing him, a counsellor or attorney for being employed against him, a juror for his verdict, or endeavours to dissuade a witness from giving evidence.

CHAPTER X.

OF OFFENCES AGAINST PUBLIC JUSTICE.

Falsifying records—Obstructing process—Assaulting officers in the performance of their duty—Escape—Breach of prison—Rescue—Returning from transportation—Taking reward to help to return of stolen goods—Receiving stolen goods—Theft-bote—Common barretry—Maintenance—Champerty—Compounding informations—Conspiracy—Threatening letters—Perjury—Subornation—Bribery—Embracery—Negligence in public offices—Oppression of magistrates—Extortion.

THE order of our distribution next leads us to take into consideration such offences as more especially affect the *commonwealth*, or public polity of the kingdom, which may be classed under five heads: viz., offences against public *justice*, against the public *peace*, against public *trade*, against the public *health*, and against the public *police* or *economy*: of each of which we will take a cursory view in their order.

First, then, of offences against public *justice*, some are felonious, others only misdemeanors.

1. Embezzling or vacating *records*, or falsifying certain other proceedings in a court of judicature, is a felonious and highly penal offence; for no man's property would be safe, if records might be suppressed or falsified or persons' names be falsely usurped in courts, or before their public officers. A great variety of statutes have accordingly provided for the punishment of offences of this nature; the earliest of which was in the reign of Richard II. But the law on this subject having been recently consolidated by the statute 24 & 25 Vict. c. 98, it is enough to refer the reader to that act.

2. A second offence against public justice is *obstructing* the execution of lawful *process*. This is at all times an offence of a very high and presumptuous nature; but more particularly so when it is an obstruction of an arrest upon criminal process. Formerly one of the greatest obstructions to public justice was the multitude of privileged places where indigent persons assembled together to shelter themselves from justice, especially in London and Southwark, under the pretext of their having been ancient palaces of the crown, or the like: all of which sanctuaries for iniquity are now demolished. The opposing of any process therein was by several statutes made highly penal; and so is any resistance or obstruction to, or assault committed upon, a peace officer in the execution of his duty. The wilful refusal, indeed, of any person to aid a peace officer in the execution of his duty in preserving the peace, is an indictable misdemeanor at common law.

3. An *escape* of a person arrested upon criminal process, by eluding the vigilance of his keepers before he is put in hold, is also an offence against public justice, punishable by fine or imprisonment. The officer permitting such escape, either by negligence or connivance, is evidently much more culpable than the prisoner; but *private individuals*, who have persons lawfully in their custody, are not less guilty of this offence if they suffer them illegally to depart, for they may at any time protect themselves from liability by delivering over their prisoner to a peace-officer.

4. Breach of prison by the offender himself, when committed for *any* cause, was felony at common law; but this severity was mitigated by the statute *de frangentibus prisonam*, 1 Edw. II. stat. 2.

To break prison and escape, when lawfully committed for any treason
or felony, remains still felony as at the common law; but to break
prison whether it be the county gaol, the stocks, or other usual place
of security, when lawfully confined upon any inferior charge, is
punishable as a misdemeanor by fine and imprisonment.

5. Rescue is the forcibly and knowingly freeing another from an
arrest or imprisonment; and it is generally the same offence in the
stranger so rescuing, as it would have been in a gaoler to have *voluntarily* permitted an escape. Aiding a prisoner to escape from gaol is
equally and in some respects more penal. So strict indeed is the law
with regard to offences of this nature, that to rescue, or attempt to
rescue, the body of the murderer after execution, is itself a felony,
punishable by penal servitude for seven or not less than five years.

6. Another and necessarily highly penal offence against public
justice is the *returning from transportation*, or being at large in
Great Britain, before the expiration of the term for which the offender
was ordered to be transported, or had agreed to transport himself, or
been sentenced to penal servitude.

7. A seventh offence against public justice is *taking a reward*,
under pretence of *helping* the owner to his *stolen goods*. This was a
contrivance carried to a great length of villany in the beginning of
the reign of George I., the confederates of the felons thus disposing of
stolen goods, at a cheap rate, to the owners themselves, and thereby
stifling all further inquiry. The famous Jonathan Wild had under
him a well-disciplined corps of thieves, who brought in all their
spoils to him; and he kept a sort of public office for restoring them
to the owners at half price. To prevent which audacious practice, to
the ruin and in defiance of public justice, the offender was by 4 Geo. I.
c. 11, liable to suffer as the felon who stole them; unless he caused such
principal felon to be apprehended and brought to trial, and also gave
evidence against him. Wild, still continuing in his old practice, was
at last convicted and executed upon this very statute; which has,
however, been superseded by more modern enactments, making the
offence a felony, punishable with penal servitude or with imprisonment, with or without hard labour and solitary confinement.

8. *Receiving of stolen goods, knowing them to be stolen*, is also a
high misdemeanor and affront to public justice. This offence, which
is only a misdemeanor at common law, has been the subject of
several enactments, many of which have been recently consolidated
by statute 24 & 25 Vict. c. 96. The receiver of goods feloniously
stolen, is now guilty of felony; and may be indicted and convicted
either as an accessory after the fact, or for a substantive felony; and
in the latter case, whether the principal felon shall or shall not have

been previously convicted, or shall or shall not be amenable to justice. Where the original stealing or converting of the property is a misdemeanor, the receiver is guilty of a misdemeanor, and where it is punishable on summary conviction, the receiver is liable to the same punishment.

9. Of a nature somewhat similar to the two last species of offences, is *theft-bote*; which is where the party robbed not only knows the felon, but also takes his goods again, or other amends, upon agreement not to prosecute. This is frequently called *compounding of felony;* and formerly was held to make a man an accessory; but is now punished only with fine and imprisonment. To advertise a reward for the return of things stolen, or lost, with no questions asked, or words to the same purport, subjects the advertiser and the printer or publisher to a forfeiture of 50*l.* to any person who will sue for the same, who is entitled also to his full costs of suit.

10. Common *barretry* is the offence of frequently exciting and stirring up suits and quarrels, either at law or otherwise, and was the subject of a prohibitory statute as early as the reign of Edward I. The punishment for this offence, in a common person, is by fine and imprisonment; but if the offender, as is too frequently the case, belongs to the profession of the law, a barretor, who is thus able as well as willing to do mischief, ought also to be disabled from practising for the future. Many such offenders flourish among us, as it seems to be next to impossible to prosecute or convict them. Hereunto may also be referred another offence, of equal malignity and audaciousness; that of suing another in the name of a fictitious plaintiff; either one not in being at all, or one who is ignorant of the suit. This offence, if committed in any of the superior courts, is left, as a high contempt, to be punished at their discretion. But in courts of a lower degree, where the crime is equally pernicious, but the authority of the judges not equally extensive, it is directed by statute 8 Eliz. c. 2, to be punished by six months' imprisonment, and treble damages to the party injured.

11. *Maintenance* is an offence that bears a near relation to the former; being an officious intermeddling in a suit that no way belongs to one, by maintaining or assisting either party with money or otherwise, to prosecute or defend it. A man may however maintain the suit of his near kinsman, servant, or poor neighbour, out of charity and compassion, with impunity. Otherwise the punishment is fine and imprisonment; and by the statute 32 Hen. VIII. c. 9, a forfeiture of ten pounds.

12. *Champerty, campi pár\tditio,* is a species of maintenance, and punished in the same manner: being a bargain with a plaintiff or

defendant *campum partire*, to divide the land or other matter sued
for between them, if they prevail at law; whereupon the champertor
is to carry on the party's suit at his own expense. These last two
offences relate chiefly to the commencement of *civil* suits: but,

13. The *compounding of informations* upon penal statutes are
offences of an equivalent nature in *criminal* causes. Accordingly, to
discourage malicious informers, and to provide that offences, when
once discovered, shall be duly prosecuted, any person making any
composition without leave of the court, or taking any money or
promise from the defendant to excuse him, forfeits 10*l.*, and is liable
to fine and imprisonment. It has not yet occurred to the legislature
apparently, that this and many cognate offences might be prevented,
by assigning the duty of prosecuting the offender to a public officer.

14. A *conspiracy* also to indict an innocent man of felony falsely
and maliciously, is a further abuse and perversion of public justice;
for which the party injured may either have a civil action; or the
conspirators, for there must be at least two to form a conspiracy, may
be indicted at the suit of the crown, and were by the ancient common
law to receive what is called the *villenous* judgment; viz., to lose
their *liberam legem*, whereby they were discredited and disabled as
jurors or witnesses; to forfeit their goods and chattels, and lands for
life; to have those lands wasted, their houses razed, their trees rooted
up, and their own bodies committed to prison. But the villenous
judgment is by long disuse become obsolete; it not having been pronounced for some ages: but instead thereof the delinquents are
sentenced to imprisonment and fine.

To this head may be referred the offence of accusing any person of
a crime, or of an attempt to commit a rape, or infamous crime, with
a view to extort money, an offence of so atrocious a nature that it
may be punished with penal servitude for life.

15. The next offence against public justice is the crime of wilful
and corrupt *perjury*; which is defined by Sir Edward Coke, to be a
crime committed when a *lawful* oath is administered, in some *judicial*
proceeding, to a person who swears *wilfully, absolutely,* and *falsely*, in
a matter *material* to the issue or point in question. The common
law takes no notice of any perjury but such as is committed in some
court of justice, having power to administer an oath; or before some
magistrate or proper officer, invested with a similar authority, in
some proceedings relative to a civil suit or a criminal prosecution:
for it esteems all other oaths unnecessary at least, and therefore will
not punish the breach of them. The statute 5 & 6 Will. IV. c. 62,
however, substituting declarations in lieu of oaths in various cases,
subjects all false declarations to the penalties of perjury; and a great

many statutes, too numerous to be mentioned here, expressly provide that persons making false statements or declarations on oath, relating to the subject matter of these acts, shall be liable to the penalties of perjury, and punished accordingly.

The perjury must be corrupt, that is, committed *malo animo*, wilful, positive, and absolute; not upon surprise, or the like; it also must be in some point material to the question in dispute; for if it only be in some trifling collateral circumstance, to which no regard is paid, it is not penal.

Subornation of perjury is the offence of procuring another to take such a false oath as constitutes perjury in the principal. The punishment of either offence was anciently death; afterwards banishment, or cutting out the tongue; then forfeiture of goods; and now it is fine and imprisonment, with or without hard labour, as the court shall think fit.

16. *Bribery* is an offence against public justice when a judge, or other person concerned in its administration, takes any undue reward to influence his behaviour in his office. This offence is punished, in inferior officers, with fine and imprisonment; and in those who offer a bribe, though not taken, the same. But in judges, especially the superior ones, it has been always looked upon as so heinous an offence, that the chief justice Thorpe was hanged for it in the reign of Edward III. At the present day, however, the species of bribery to which the attention of the public and of the legislature is chiefly directed, is that which destroys the purity of the elections for members of the House of Commons. Professedly to prevent this crime, for in no other light can it be regarded, numerous statutes have been passed, but hitherto without success. Possibly when the offence is made felony, and a public prosecutor appointed, a different result may be attained.

17. *Embracery* is an attempt to influence a juror corruptly to one side by promises, money, entertainments, and the like, the punishment of which is fine and imprisonment. Connected with which was another offence, the *false verdict* of jurors; which, whether occasioned by embracery or not, was anciently considered criminal, and exemplarily punished. A wrong verdict can now, and in civil cases only, be set aside on an application for a new trial; but a corrupt juror may always be proceeded against, and punished as for a misdemeanour.

18. The *negligence of public officers*, intrusted with the administration of justice, is an offence subjecting the offender to fine; and in very notorious cases, to a forfeiture of his office, if it be a beneficial one.

19. There is yet another offence against public justice which is a crime of deep malignity, though happily it has long been unknown in this country, viz., *oppression* on the part of judges, justices, and other *magistrates*, in the administration and under the colour of their office. This is highly punishable, as is,

20. Lastly, *extortion;* which consists in an officer's unlawfully taking, by colour of his office, from any man, any money or thing of value, that is not due to him, or more than is due, or before it is due. The punishment for this offence, which is fortunately equally rare with the former, is fine and imprisonment, and sometimes a forfeiture of the office; the defendant being also made to render double to the party aggrieved, and be punished at the pleasure of the crown, that is to say, at the discretion of the court.

CHAPTER XI.

OFFENCES AGAINST THE PUBLIC PEACE.

Riotous assembly—Riotous destruction of machinery—Proceeding against the hundred—Threatening letters—Threatening to publish a libel—Destroying dock-gates, sea-walls, and public bridges—Destroying turnpikes—Destroying public monuments or works of art—Affrays—Duelling—Affrays in a church—Riots—Duty of *posse comitatus*—Forcible entry—Challenges to fight—Libels—Fox's Act—Liberty of the press.

Of offences against the public peace, some are felonies, and some merely misdemeanors. Of the former class, are,

1. The *riotous assembling of twelve persons*, or more, *and not dispersing upon proclamation*, which was made high treason by 3 & 4 Edw. VI. c. 5, when the king was a minor, and a change in religion to be effected. That statute was repealed by 1 Mar. c. 1, but the prohibition was in substance re-enacted by 1 Mar. st. 2, c. 12, which made the offence a felony; and indemnified the peace officers and their assistants, if they killed any of the mob in endeavouring to suppress such riot. This was thought a necessary security in that sanguinary reign, when popery was intended to be re-established, which was likely to produce great discontents: but at first it was made only for a year, and was afterwards continued for that queen's life. And, by statute 1 Eliz. c. 16, when a reformation in religion was to be once more attempted, it was revived and continued during her life also, and then expired. From the accession of James I. to the death of Queen Anne, it was never once thought expedient to

revive it; but, in the first year of George I., it was judged necessary, in order to support the execution of the Act of Settlement, to renew it, and at one stroke to make it perpetual, with large additions. The capital punishment for these offences has, however, been taken away, but they are still punishable with great severity, if need be.

2. The *riotous destruction* of churches or other buildings, or of machinery, which in the reign of George I. was made a capital felony, is now punishable under the statute 24 & 25 Vict. c. 97, s. 11, which confers on the court a large discretion as to punishment.

In these cases of *felonious* destruction of property the law gives to the parties injured a civil remedy against the *hundred* in which the premises are situated, provided the persons damnified go within seven days before a justice of the peace, state upon oath the names of the offenders, if known, and become bound to prosecute.

3. The offence of *sending* or *delivering a letter demanding with menaces property or money*, is a felonious offence against the public peace, and highly penal. The analogous offence of publishing or threatening to publish a libel upon any person, with intent to extort any money, or obtain some other advantage, is a misdemeanor only. Similar offences were formerly high treason by the statute 8 Hen. V. c. 6.

4. Destroying any *lock, sluice,* or *flood-gate,* erected by authority of parliament on a navigable river, has long been a felony.

Removing any piles or other materials used for securing any sea-bank, &c., or doing any other injury so as to obstruct navigation, is also a felony; the punishment extending to penal servitude, in the former case, for life, and in the latter for seven years. Equally penal is the offence of destroying public bridges, which is likewise a felony.

The remaining offences against the public peace are merely misdemeanors; as,

5. *Maliciously destroying turnpike-gates and toll-bars:* or,

6. *Maliciously destroying or damaging any book, print, statue, or other article,* in any museum, library, or other public repository, or any public picture, statue, or monument.

7. *Affrays;* from *affraier,* to terrify; that is to say, the fighting of two or more persons in some public place; for, if the fighting be in private, it is no *affray,* but an *assault.* Affrays may be suppressed by any private person present, who is justifiable in endeavouring to part the combatants, whatever consequence may ensue. But more especially the constable, or other similar officer, however denominated, is bound to keep the peace. The punishment is by fine and im-

prisonment : the measure of which must be regulated by the circumstances of the case: for, where there is any material aggravation,
the punishment proportionably increases. As where two persons
coolly and deliberately engage in a duel: this being attended with
an apparent intention and danger of murder, and being a high contempt of the justice of the nation, is a strong aggravation of the
affray, though no mischief has actually ensued. Affrays in a church
or churchyard are esteemed very heinous offences. And therefore
by statute 5 & 6 Edw. VI. c. 4, if any clerk in orders shall, by words
only, quarrel, chide, or brawl, in a church or churchyard, the ordinary shall suspend him from the ministration of his office during
pleasure. But if he, in such church or churchyard, proceeds to
smite or lay violent hands upon another person, he shall be excommunicated *ipso facto*. Laymen guilty of riotous, violent, or indecent
behaviour in any church or chapel, churchyard or burying ground,
or who molest, disturb, trouble, or mimic any preacher or any clerk
in holy orders, incur on conviction a penalty of five pounds for each
offence, or an imprisonment not exceeding two months. *Two* persons
may be guilty of an affray : but

8. *Riots, routs,* and *unlawful assemblies* must have *three* persons
at least to constitute them. Unlawfully assembling, if to the number
of twelve, we have just now seen, may constitute a felony; but,
from the number of three to eleven, the offence is a misdemeanor,
punishable by fine and imprisonment only, to which hard labour
may be added. Moreover, any two justices, with the sheriff or under-
sheriff, may come with the *posse comitatus,* and suppress any such
riot, assembly, or rout, arrest the rioters, and record upon the spot
the nature and circumstances of the whole transaction ; which record
alone shall be a sufficient conviction of the offenders. And all
persons, noblemen and others, except women, clergymen, persons
decrepit, and infants under fifteen, are bound to attend the justices
in suppressing a riot, upon pain of fine and imprisonment; any
battery, wounding, or killing of the rioters, that may happen in suppressing the riot being justifiable.*

9. Another offence against the public peace is that of a *forcible
entry* or *detainer* ; which is committed by violently taking or keeping possession of lands and tenements, without the authority of law.
This was formerly allowable to every person disseised, or turned out
of possession, unless his entry was taken away or barred by his own

---

* Nearly related to this head of riots is the offence of tumultuous petitioning which was prohibited by statute 13 Car. II. st. 1, c. 5. But as the Bill
of Rights expressly declares the right of the subject to petition, and all
commitments and prosecutions for such petitioning to be illegal, the statute
of Charles is practically repealed.

neglect, or other circumstances. But this being found very prejudicial to the public peace, it was thought necessary by several statutes
to restrain all persons from the use of such violent methods, even of
doing themselves justice, so that the entry now allowed by law is a
peaceable one only. Two justices may also summarily restore the
possession to the person entitled thereto.

10. Besides actual breaches of the peace, anything that tends to
provoke or excite others to break it, is an offence of the same denomination. Therefore *challenges to fight*, either by word or letter,
or to be the bearer of such challenge, are punishable by fine and
imprisonment, according to the circumstances of the offence.

11. Of a nature very similar to challenges, are *libels, libelli famosi*,
which, taken in their largest and most extensive sense, signify any
writings, pictures, or the like, of an immoral or illegal tendency; but,
in the sense under which we are now to consider them, are malicious
defamations of any person, and especially a magistrate, made public
by either printing, writing, signs, or pictures, in order to provoke him
to wrath, or expose him to public hatred, contempt, or ridicule. The
communication of a libel to any one person is a publication in the
eye of the law: and therefore the sending an abusive private letter
to a man is as much a libel as if it were openly printed, for it equally
tends to a breach of the peace. For the same reason it is immaterial
at common law, with respect to the essence of a libel, whether the
matter of it be true or false; since the provocation, and not the
falsity, is the thing to be punished criminally, though, doubtless, the
falsehood of it may, independently of any statutory provision, aggravate its guilt, and enhance its punishment.

In a civil action, a libel must appear to be false, as well as scandalous; for, if the charge be true, the plaintiff has received no injury.
In a criminal prosecution, on the other hand, the tendency which all
libels have to disturb the public peace, is what the law considers;
and at common law, therefore, the truth of the libel not only constitutes no defence to the charge, but cannot even be given in evidence
in mitigation of punishment. The statute 6 & 7 Vict. c. 96, now,
however, enables a defendant to prove its truth; but this does not
amount to a defence, unless it was for the public benefit that the
facts should be published. And after such a plea, if the defendant
is convicted, the punishment imposed for his offence may be more
severe, if in the opinion of the court his guilt is aggravated by the
defence which he has set up, or the evidence given in support of it.

This statute applies only to libels of a private and personal character, and not to those denominated seditious or blasphemous. In
these, therefore, and in all cases in which there is no plea of justifi-

cation, the only points to be inquired into, are, first, the making or
publishing of the book or writing: and, secondly, whether the matter
be criminal: and if both these points are against the defendant, the
offence against the public is complete.   But upon both points the
jury must exercise their judgment and pronounce their opinion, as a
question of fact, as required by the statute 32 Geo. III. c. 60, which
was passed expressly to remove doubts respecting the functions of
juries in cases of libel.   This celebrated measure, which, from its
still more celebrated author, is usually called Fox's Act, was, it will
be remembered, the result of a lengthened and acrimonious discussion
between Government, backed by the courts of law on the one hand,
and the advocates of popular rights, with whom the juries generally
sympathised, on the other: the courts holding that the jury had no
question to determine but the mere fact of writing, printing or publishing, the latter contending that the guilt or innocence of the defendant was thus taken away entirely from that tribunal, whose
proper constitutional function it was to determine that very
question.

The punishment on conviction for maliciously publishing any de-
famatory libel is fine or imprisonment, or both, as the court may
award, such imprisonment not to exceed the term of one year.   If
however the defendant publish the libel *knowing* it to be *false*, the
imprisonment may be for two years.   And it is to be observed, that the
defendant is entitled, on judgment given for him, to recover costs
from the prosecutor: who on the other hand, if the issue upon a plea
of justification is found for him, is entitled to recover his costs from
the defendant.

In this the *liberty of the press*, properly understood, is by no
means infringed or violated.   The liberty of the press is indeed
essential to the nature of a free state; but this consists in laying no
previous restraints upon publication, and not in freedom from censure
for criminal matter when published.   Every freeman has an undoubted right to lay what sentiments he pleases before the public: to
forbid this, is to destroy the freedom of the press: but if he publishes
what is improper, mischevious or illegal, he must take the consequence of his own temerity.   To subject the press to the restrictive
power of a licenser, as was formerly done, both before and since the
Revolution, is to subject all freedom of sentiment to the prejudices
of one man, and make him the arbitrary and infallible judge of all
controverted points in learning, religion and government.   But to
punish dangerous or offensive writings is necessary for the preservation of peace and good order, of government and religion, the only
solid foundations of civil liberty.   Thus the will of individuals is
still left free; the abuse only of that free will is the object of legal
punishment.   Neither is any restraint hereby laid upon freedom of

thought or inquiry: liberty of private sentiment is still left; the disseminating, or making public, of bad sentiments, destructive of the ends of society, is the crime which society corrects. A man may be allowed to keep poisons in his closet, but not publicly to vend them as cordials. And to this we may add, that the only plausible argument heretofore used for the restraining the just freedom of the press, " that it was necessary to prevent the daily abuse of it," will entirely lose its force, when it is shown that the press cannot be abused to any bad purpose, without incurring a suitable punishment: whereas it never can be used to any good one, when under the control of an inspector. So true will it be found that to censure the licentiousness, is to maintain the liberty of the press.

CHAPTER XII.

OF OFFENCES AGAINST PUBLIC TRADE.

Smuggling—Fraudulent bankruptcy—Destruction of machinery or goods in process of manufacture—Unlawful combinations—Cheating—Obtaining money by false pretences—Giving a false character.

The third class of offences against the commonwealth are those relating to public *trade*, which, like those of the preceding classes, are either felonious or not felonious. Of the first sort are,

1. *Smuggling*, or the importing of goods without paying the duties imposed thereon, an offence which is restrained by several statutes inflicting pecuniary penalties and seizure of the goods for clandestine smuggling; and affixing the guilt of felony, with penal servitude for life, upon more open, daring, and avowed practices. Thus, three persons assembling with fire-arms to assist in the illegal exportation or importation of goods, or in rescuing the same after seizure, or in rescuing offenders in custody for such offences, are guilty of felony, and liable to penal servitude for life. Shooting at, maiming, or dangerously wounding any officer employed in the prevention of smuggling, is equally penal.

Assaulting or obstructing an officer of the revenue in the execution of his duty, is only a misdemeanor; but it is, nevertheless, an offence for which a very severe punishment may be imposed.

2. *Fraudulent bankruptcy*, such as a bankrupt's neglect to surrender, or to discover, all his estate, or concealing his effects to the value of 10*l.*, are, with others which might be mentioned, misdemeanors. Till recently, indeed, they were felonious, all offences

against the policy of the Bankrupt laws being long and justly considered as atrocious species of the *crimen falsi*, which might properly be put upon a level with those of forgery and falsifying the coin.

3. The *malicious destruction of machinery*, or of goods in the process of manufacture, is an offence against public trade as well as against the property of the individual sufferer; the immediate object of the offender being often the destruction of property generally, irrespective altogether of its ownership. This crime, and all those of a like nature are now prosecuted under the statute 24 & 25 Vict. c. 97, consolidating and amending the laws on this subject, and to which it is therefore sufficient to refer.

4. *Unlawful combinations among workmen* have formed the subject of several enactments, all of which were consolidated by the statute 6 Geo. IV. c. 129. The result is, that workmen as well as masters may meet together, for the purpose of determining the wages they will accept, or the hours they will work, and may make any arrangements among themselves for giving effect to their resolutions, which they think fit. But they must carry out their object by lawful means, and not attempt to intimidate or prevent masters from employing, or workmen from taking employment at any wages they may agree for. And especially must they avoid committing any assault in pursuance of any combination to raise the rate of wages; for this is a very serious misdemeanor and highly penal.

5. The last species of offence more immediately against public trade is *cheating*; for trade cannot be carried on without a punctilious regard to common honesty, and faith between man and man. Hither, therefore, may be referred that prodigious multitude of statutes, which were made to restrain and punish deceits in particular trades, but are now either repealed or in desuetude. The obsolete offence also of *breaking the assize* of bread, or the rules laid down by law for ascertaining its price in every given quantity, was reducible to this head of cheating: as is likewise in a peculiar manner the offence of selling by *false scales* or *false weights and measures*.

The punishment of bakers breaking the assize, was anciently to stand in the pillory, and for brewers to stand in the tumbrel or dungcart; which, as we learn from Domesday Book, was the punishment for knavish brewers in the city of Chester so early as the reign of Edward the Confessor. But now the general punishment for all frauds of this kind, if indicted as they may be at common law, is by fine and imprisonment; though the easier and more usual way is by levying on a summary conviction, by distress and sale, the forfeitures imposed by the several acts of Parliament. Under this head, however, is generally ranked the much more serious offence of *obtaining money or goods by false pretences*, which is a misdemeanor punishable, if necessary, by penal servitude for five years. One kind of cheating, and one of frequent occurrence, is the offence of personating a master, and *giving a false character* to a servant, which is punishable by a fine of 20l., and in default imprisonment.

CHAPTER XIII.

OF OFFENCES AGAINST THE PUBLIC HEALTH, AND AGAINST THE PUBLIC POLICE OR ECONOMY.

1. Plague—Small-pox—Quarantine—Selling unwholesome provisions—Nuisances—Noxious trades—Overcrowding common lodging-houses—Employment of children in mines and factories——2. Clandestine marriages—Bigamy Common nuisances—Disorderly houses—Gaming houses—Lotteries—Fireworks—Idle and disorderly persons—Rogues and vagabonds—Incorrigible Rogues—Vagrant Act—Gaming—Private lotteries—Little-goes—Horse-races—Betting-offices—Refusing to serve an office—Furious driving—Cruelty to animals—Taking up dead bodies—Killing Game—Night-poaching.

THE fourth species of offences, more especially affecting the commonwealth, are such as are against the public *health* of the nation; a concern of the highest importance, and for the preservation of which there are in many countries as with us special magistrates or curators appointed.

1. The first statute on this subject deserving of notice, is the 1 Jac. I. c. 31, by which any person infected with the plague, who was commanded by the mayor or constable to keep his house, and ventured to disobey it, might be forced, by the watchman appointed on such melancholy occasions, to obey such necessary command. And if such person went abroad, he was, if he had no plague sore upon him, punishable as a vagabond by whipping; but if he had any infectious sore upon him, uncured, he was then guilty of felony. This statute, happily long obsolete, has, with all the acts continuing it, been repealed. But it is nevertheless a misdemeanor at common law to expose a person labouring under an infectious disorder, such as the small-pox, in the streets or other public places; and it is an offence punishable by imprisonment to produce by *inoculation* or otherwise, the disease of small-pox; the statute 3 & 4 Vict. c. 29,

having conferred powers on the guardians and overseers to contract with the medical officers of parishes for the *vaccination* of the children of all persons there resident; this vaccination being now made compulsory, under penalties summarily recoverable before two justices of the peace.

By the statute 6 Geo. IV., repealing several statutes on the same subject, elaborate provisions have been made for securing the proper performance of quarantine, and obedience to regulations issued by the privy council with respect to vessels suspected of having the plague or other infectious disease on board. Offences against this statute, or disregard of the orders in council, are in ordinary cases punishable by a heavy fine; but the forgery of any of the certificates required by the act, constitutes and is punishable as felony.

2. A second offence coming under this head is the selling of *unwholesome provisions*. To prevent which the statute 51 Hen. III. st. 6, and the ordinance for bakers, c. 7, prohibit the sale of corrupted wine, contagious or unwholesome flesh, or flesh that is bought of a Jew. But an indictment under either statute is quite unknown, the usual mode of proceeding being a prosecution before magistrates under some one of the various statutes, passed to prevent the adulteration of *bread*, *meal*, and other articles of consumption. The sending of diseased meat to market for sale is a serious misdemeanor; the exposure of meat that is unfit for food, for sale, is also highly penal. The sale of adulterated wine in a licensed house, is much less penal, a small fine being imposed for the first offence—a larger penalty and a disqualification from selling any wine by retail for five years being attached to its repetition.

3. The third species of offences, I shall mention, are the result of negligence, rather than of any evil design. They comprise those acts of omission which consist in allowing any premises to remain uncleansed, or permitting any gutter, privy, drain, ashpit, to be so foul, or any animal to be so kept, as to be injurious to health. For summarily abating these *nuisances*, full powers are conferred on the local authorities of towns and populous districts, to whose neglect of duty alone can the repetition of such offences now be attributed.

4. A fourth offence against the public health is the carrying on within the limits of any city, town, or populous district, any noxious trade or manufacture, a kind of nuisance which may also be summarily suppressed on complaint by the local authority to the justices. The only other offences against the public health are,

5. Those connected with the over-crowding of common lodging-houses; or the employment, beyond the times allowed by law, of children under certain ages in mines and factories.

I now come to the last head of offences which more especially
affect the commonwealth, those namely against the public *police* and
economy; by which I mean the due regulation and domestic order
of the kingdom; whereby the individuals of the state, like members
of a well-governed family, are bound to conform their general behaviour to the rules of propriety, good neighbourhood, and good
manners; and to be decent, industrious, and inoffensive in their
respective stations. Of these offences, some are felonies and others
misdemeanors only. Among the former are,

1. *Clandestine marriages*: offences arising from the solemnizing
of marriages in other places, or at other times, or without the publicity required by law, all of them matters of great public concern,
and elaborately provided for by several statutes; to which, however,
it is unnecessary to do more than refer.

Making a false entry in a marriage register; altering it when
made; or forging an entry, or marriage licence; or tampering in
any way almost with these documents, are all offences of a very
penal character.

2. Another felonious offence, with regard to this holy estate of
matrimony, is what is improperly called *bigamy*, which signifies
being twice married; but is more correctly denominated *polygamy*,
or having a plurality of wives at once. Such second marriage,
living the former husband or wife, is simply void, and a mere
nullity, by the ecclesiastical law: and yet the legislature has thought
it just to make it felony, by reason of its being so great a violation
of the public economy and decency of a well-ordered state.

To descend next to offences which are not felonious :—

3. *Common nuisances* are a species of offences against the public
order and economical regimen of the state; being either the doing of
a thing to the annoyance of all the queen's subjects, or the neglecting
to do a thing which the common good requires. The nature of
common nuisances, and their distinction from *private* nuisances,
were explained in the preceding part of these Commentaries. I
shall here only remind the student, that common nuisances are such
inconvenient or troublesome offences, as annoy the whole community
in general, and not merely some particular person; and therefore are
indictable only, and not actionable: as it would be unreasonable to
multiply suits, by giving every man a separate right of action, for
what damnifies him in common only with the rest of his fellow-
subjects. Of this nature are,—1. Annoyances in *highways*, *bridges*,
and public *rivers*, by rendering the same inconvenient or dangerous
to pass, either positively, by actual obstructions; or negatively, by
want of reparations. For both of these, the person so obstructing, or

such individuals as are bound to repair and cleanse them, or in default of these last, the parish at large, may be indicted, distrained to repair and amend them, and in some cases fined. 2. All those kinds of nuisances, which when injurious to a private man are actionable, are, when detrimental to the public, punishable by prosecution, and subject to fine; and it is not necessary that such nuisances should be injurious to health. All disorderly *inns*, or *ale-houses*, *bawdy-houses*, *gaming-houses*, *stage-plays* unlicensed, booths and stages for *rope-dancers*, *mountebanks*, and the like, are public nuisances, and may upon indictment be suppressed and fined. 4. All *lotteries* are also public nuisances. 5. The making and selling of *fireworks* and *squibs*, or throwing them about in any street, which is an offence at common law, is also a common nuisance, punishable by fine. And to this head we may refer the making, keeping, or carriage, of too large a quantity of *gunpowder* at one time, or in one place or vehicle; which is prohibited under heavy penalties and forfeiture. Erecting powder-mills or keeping powder-magazines near a town, is a nuisance at common law.

4. Idleness in any person whatsoever is also a high offence against the public economy. In China it is a maxim, that if there be a man who does not work, or a woman that is idle, in the empire, somebody must suffer cold or hunger: the produce of the lands not being more than sufficient, with culture, to maintain the inhabitants: and therefore, though the idle person may shift off the want from himself, yet it must in the end fall somewhere. The court also of the Areopagus at Athens punished idleness, and exerted a right of examining every citizen in what manner he spent his time; the intention of which was, that the Athenians, knowing they were to give an account of their occupations, should follow only such as were laudable, and that there might be no room left for such as lived by unlawful arts. The civil law expelled all sturdy vagrants from the city; and in our own law, all idle persons or vagabonds, whom our ancient statutes describe to be " such as wake on the night, and sleep on the day, and haunt " customable taverns, and ale-houses, and routs about; and no man " wot from whence they come, ne whither they go;" all these are offenders against the good order, and blemishes in the government, of any kingdom.

Offences of this character formerly amounted, indeed, in some cases to felony. Thus it was felony in idle *soldiers* and *mariners wandering* about the realm, or persons pretending so to be, and abusing the name of that honourable profession. Such a one, not having a testimonial or pass from a justice, limiting the time of his passage; or exceeding the time limited for fourteen days, unless he fell sick; or forging such testimonial, was guilty of a capital felony, a sanguinary law which remained a disgrace to our statute-book till the end of the reign of George III.

Outlandish persons, calling themselves *Egyptians*, or *gypsies*, were long another object of the severity of some of our statutes. These are a strange kind of commonwealth among themselves of wandering impostors and jugglers, who were first taken notice of in Germany about the beginning of the fifteenth century, and have since spread themselves all over Europe. Munster, who is followed and relied upon by Spelman and other writers, fixes the time of their first appearance to the year 1417; under passports, real or pretended, from the Emperor Sigismund, king of Hungary. And Pope Pius II. who died A.D. 1464, mentions them in his history as thieves and vagabonds, then wandering with their families over Europe under the name of Zigari; and whom he supposes to have migrated from the country of the Zigi, which nearly answers to the modern Circassia. In the compass of a few years they gained such a number of idle proselytes, who imitated their language and complexion, and betook themselves to the same arts of chiromancy, begging, and pilfering, that they became troublesome, and even formidable to most of the states of Europe. Hence they were expelled from France in the year 1560, and from Spain in 1591. And the government in England took the alarm much earlier: for in 1530, they are described by statute 22 Hen. VIII. c. 10, as " outlandish people, calling them-
" selves Egyptians, using no craft nor feat of merchandize, who have
" come into this realm and gone from shire to shire and place to
" place in great company, and used great, subtil, and crafty means
" to deceive the people; bearing them in hand, that they by pal-
" mestry could tell men's and women's fortunes; and so many times
" by craft and subtilty have deceived the people of their money, and
" also have committed many heinous felonies and robberies." Where-fore they are directed to avoid the realm, and not to return under pain of imprisonment, and forfeiture of their goods and chattels. Other statutes made Egyptians, who remained one month in the kingdom, or any person, fourteen years old, whether natural-born subject or stranger, who had been seen or found in their fellowship, or who had disguised him or herself like them, who remained in the same one month, at one or several times, guilty of a capital felony. and Sir Matthew Hale informs us, that at one Suffolk assizes no less than thirteen gypsies were executed upon these statutes, a few years before the Restoration.

But, to the honour of our national humanity, there are no instances more modern than this, of carrying these laws into practice; and gypsies are now only punishable as vagrants, in common with other disorderly persons; who are now divided into three classes, *idle* and

disorderly persons, *rogues* and *vagabonds*, and *incorrigible rogues.*
This was first done by the statute 17 Geo. II. c. 5; but this act, and
several others subsequently passed, were repealed, and in great part
re-enacted, by the statute 5 Geo. IV. c. 63, usually called the *Vagrant
Act;* which carefully defines what offenders shall fall within each of
these three classes I have mentioned, and provides a precise scale of
punishment for each offence. Several statutes, however, have since
added to the list. Most of these offenders are punishable summarily by justices of the peace.

Under the head of public economy might formerly have been
ranked the sumptuary laws against *luxury,* and extravagant expenses
in dress, diet, and the like; concerning the general utility of which
to a state, there is much controversy among political writers. Baron
Montesquieu lays it down, that luxury is necessary in monarchies,
but ruinous to democracies. With regard therefore to England,
whose government is compounded of both species, it may still be a
dubious question how far private luxury is a public evil; and as
such cognizable by public laws. And indeed our legislators have
several times changed their sentiments as to this point; for formerly
there were a multitude of penal laws existing, to restrain excess in
apparel; chiefly made in the reigns of Edward III., Edward IV.,
and Henry VIII., against piked shoes, short doublets, and long coats.
While, as to excess in diet, there long remained one ancient statute,
10 Edw. III. st. 3, ordaining that no man should be served, at
dinner or supper, with more than two courses: except upon some
great holidays there specified, in which he might be served with
three.

5. All these statutes have been repealed; but luxury and extravagant expenses in dress, diet, and the like, naturally lead to the
offence of *gaming,* which is generally introduced to supply or retrieve
the expenses occasioned by the former: it being a kind of tacit confession that the company engaged therein do, in general, exceed the
bounds of their respective fortunes; and therefore they cast lots to
determine upon whom the ruin shall at present fall, that the rest
may be saved a little longer.

For the suppression of *gaming-houses,* many statutes have been
passed from time to time; and special provisions are directed by the
statute 9 George IV. c. 61, against any gaming whatever in a public-
house. A licence is also required, under a penalty, to be obtained
annually, by such persons as keep public billiard-tables and baga-
telle boards, or instruments used in any game of a like kind—a provision framed to permit of complaint and refusal of the licence, if
gaming be permitted.

By several statutes of the reign of Geo. II., all private lotteries by tickets, cards, or dice, are prohibited under a penalty of 200*l.* for him that shall erect such lotteries, and 50*l.* a time for the players; and by the statute 42 Geo. III. c. 119, games called *little-goes* are declared to be common and public nuisances, and a penalty of 500*l.* is imposed on persons keeping any office or place for that game, or for any other lottery whatsoever, not authorized by parliament. *Art-unions* have since been excepted by a special act.

The statute 13 Geo. II. c. 19, to prevent the multiplicity of horse-races, another fund of gaming, directed that no plates or matches under 50*l.* value should be run, upon penalty of 200*l.* to be paid by the owner of each horse running, and 100*l.* by such as advertised the plate. But in consequence of a number of vexatious actions having been brought under this statute, it was so far repealed; and all bargains relating to horse-racing placed on the same footing as other contracts.

But particular descriptions will ever be lame and deficient, unless all games of mere chance are at once prohibited; the inventions of sharpers being swifter than the punishment of the law, which only hunts them from one device to another. No sooner were contracts as to horse-racing legalized, than an immense number of petty gaming-houses sprang up, under the name of *betting-offices.* The demoralization, which was found to be the immediate result, called for the interference of the legislature, and a statute was accordingly passed, expressly for the suppression of these haunts of vice; but it is scarcely necessary to say, it is openly disregarded. Our laws against gaming are not so deficient, as ourselves and our magistrates in putting those laws in execution.

6. *Refusing to serve a public office,* without lawful cause, when duly appointed thereto, is a misdemeanor at common law, and as such punishable, if necessary, by fine and imprisonment. A vacancy in the office of sheriff, for instance, may occasion a stop of public justice; and the same principle applies when duties are imposed by statute, as in the case of a common-councilman or an overseer of the poor.

7. An offence against the public police may be committed by any person wantonly and *furiously driving* or riding on the highway, so as to endanger persons passing.

8. Another offence under this head is wanton *cruelty to an animal,* either by over-driving, heating or torturing it, or by carrying it or causing it to be carried in such a manner as to create unnecessary pain or suffering. These offences are by the statute 12 and 13 Vict. c. 92, punishable by a fine of 5*l.* on summary conviction before a magistrate; and any peace-officer, on his own view, or on complaint

of any other person, who shall give his address, is authorized to secure the offender. The same statute contains provisions for the detention of vehicles and animals of which the person having the charge is taken into custody, and for compelling the owners of public vehicles to produce their servants. It prohibits, under penalties, the fighting or baiting of any bull, bear, badger, dog, cock, or other animal; and makes various regulations as to slaughterhouses for horses and other animals not intended for food.

9. *Taking up dead bodies* is also a misdemeanor at common law, unless done by lawful authority. This offence was sometimes committed in order to obtain subjects for dissection in the schools of anatomy; but is now quite unknown, regulations having been made for this purpose by the statute 2 & 3 Will. IV. c. 75. It is also an offence in those whose duty it is to bury the dead, to refuse to do so, and one cognizable by the temporal courts as well as by the courts-Christian.

10. Lastly, there is another offence of so questionable a nature, that I shall not detain the reader with many observations thereupon. And yet it is an offence which the sportsmen of England seem to think of the highest importance; and a matter, perhaps the only one, of general and national concern; I mean the offence of destroying such beasts and fowls as are ranked under the denomination of *g ime:* which, we may remember, was formerly observed to be an offence in all persons alike, who had not authority from the crown to kill game, by the grant of either a free warren, or at least a manor of their own. But the laws, called the game-laws, also inflicted additional punishments on persons guilty of this general offence, unless they were people of such rank or fortune as were therein particularly specified. All persons, therefore, of what property or distinction soever, that killed game out of their own territories, or even upon their own estates, without the king's licence expressed by the grant of a franchise, were guilty of the first original offence, of encroaching on the royal prerogative. And those indigent persons who did so, without having such rank or fortune as was generally called a *qualification*, were guilty not only of the original offence, but of the aggravations also, created by the statutes for preserving the game; which aggravations were so severely punished, and those punishments so implacably inflicted, that the offence against the sovereign was seldom thought of, provided the miserable delinquent could make his peace with the lord of the manor. The offence, thus aggravated, I have ranked under the present head, because the only rational footing, upon which we can consider it as a crime, is, that in low and indigent persons it promotes idleness, and takes them away from their proper employments and callings; which is

an offence against the public police and economy of the common-wealth.

The statutes for preserving the game are many and various, and not a little obscure and intricate; it being remarked that in one statute only, 5 Ann. c. 14, there is false grammar in no fewer than six places, besides other mistakes; the occasion of which, or what denomination of persons were probably the penners of the statutes, I shall not at present inquire. Neither shall I attempt to trace the legislation on this subject, but content myself with remarking that the possession of any *qualification* to kill game is now unnecessary; the right to do so depending simply on the payment of a tax, usually called a game *certificate*.

The offence of trespassing by night in pursuit of game, or in other words the crime of *night-poaching*, is, however, highly penal, and will probably remain so, until the game-laws have, by the advancing intelligence of the people, been entirely swept away.

CHAPTER XIV.

OF HOMICIDE.

1. Justifiable homicide—from necessity—for advancement of justice—for prevention of crime——2. Excusable homicide—from misadventure—in self-defence——3. Felonious homicide—*Felo de se*—Manslaughter—Murder Malice—punishment.

WE are now, lastly, to consider those offences which in a more peculiar manner affect and injure *individuals* or private subjects; which are principally of three kinds—against their *person*, their *habitations*, and their *property*.

Of crimes injurious to the *persons* of private subjects, the most important is the offence of taking away life. The subject, therefore, of the present chapter will be the offence of *homicide*, in its several stages of guilt.

Now homicide is of three kinds; *justifiable*, *excusable*, and *felonious*. The first has no share of guilt at all; the second very little; but the third is the highest crime against the law of nature that man is capable of committing

I. Justifiable homicide is of divers kinds.

1. Such as is owing to some unavoidable *necessity*, without any will, intention, or desire, and without any inadvertence or negligence

in the party killing, and therefore without any shadow of blame. As, for instance, by virtue of such an office as obliges one, in the execution of public justice, to put to death a malefactor, who has forfeited his life by the laws and verdict of his country. This is an act of necessity, and even of civil duty; and, therefore, not only justifiable, but commendable where the law requires it. But the law must *require* it, otherwise it is not justifiable: therefore, wantonly to kill the greatest of malefactors, a felon or a traitor, attainted or outlawed, deliberately, uncompelled, and extra-judicially, is murder.

Again; in some cases homicide is justifiable, rather by the *permission*, than by the absolute *command*, of the law, either for the *advancement* of public *justice*, which without such indemnification would never be carried on with proper vigour: or, in such instances where it is committed for the *prevention* of some atrocious *crime*, which cannot otherwise be avoided.

2. Homicides committed for the *advancement* of public *justice*, are: 1. Where an officer, in the execution of his office, kills a person that assaults and resists him. 2. If an officer, or any private person, attempts to take a man charged with felony, and is resisted; and, in the endeavour to take him, kills him. 3. In case of a riot, or rebellious assembly, as has already been explained. 4. Where the prisoners in a gaol, or going to a gaol, assault the gaoler or officer, and he in his defence kills any of them, it is justifiable for the sake of preventing an escape. But, in all these cases, there must be an apparent necessity on the officer's side, viz., that the party could not be arrested or apprehended, the riot could not be suppressed, the prisoners could not be kept in hold, unless such homicide were committed: otherwise, without such absolute necessity, it is not justifiable.

3. In the next place, such homicide as is committed for the *prevention* of any forcible and atrocious *crime* is justifiable by the law of nature. If any person attempts a robbery or murder of another, or attempts to break open a house *in the night-time*, and shall be killed in such attempt, the slayer shall be acquitted and discharged. As by the Jewish law, " if a thief be found breaking up, and he be " smitten that he die, no blood shall be shed for him: but if the " sun be risen upon him, there shall blood be shed for him; for he " should have made full restitution."

The Roman law justified homicide when committed in defence of the chastity either of one's self or relations; and so, according to Selden, stood the law in the Jewish republic. The English law likewise justifies a woman killing one who attempts to ravish her:

and so too the husband or father may justify killing a man who attempts a rape upon his wife or daughter.

II. Excusable homicide is of two sorts; either *per infortunium*, by misadventure; or *se defendendo*, upon a principle of self-preservation.

1. Homicide *per infortunium* or *misadventure*, is where a man doing a lawful act, without any intention of hurt, unfortunately kills another; as where a man is at work with a hatchet, and the head thereof flies off and kills a stander-by; or where a person is shooting at a mark, and undesignedly kills a man; for the act may be lawful, and the effect merely accidental. So where a parent is moderately correcting his child, a master his apprentice or scholar, or an officer punishing a criminal, and happens to occasion his death, it is only misadventure; for the act of correction is lawful: but if he exceeds the bounds of moderation, either in the manner, the instrument, or the quantity of punishment, and death ensues, it is manslaughter at least; for the act of immoderate correction is unlawful. Likewise, to whip another's horse, whereby he runs over a child and kills him, is held to be accidental in the rider, for he has done nothing unlawful; but manslaughter in the person who whipped him, for the act was a trespass, and at best a piece of idleness, of inevitably dangerous consequence. And in general, if death ensues in consequence of an idle, dangerous, and unlawful sport, as shooting or casting stones in a town, and similar cases, the slayer is guilty of manslaughter, and not misadventure only, for these are unlawful acts.

2. Homicide in *self-defence*, or *se defendendo*, upon a sudden affray is also excusable, and it must be distinguished from that just now mentioned, as calculated to hinder the perpetration of a capital crime, which is not only a matter of excuse, but of justification. The self-defence I now speak of, is that whereby a man may protect himself from an assault, or the like, in the course of a sudden broil or quarrel, by killing him who assaults him. This is what the law expresses by the word *chance-medley*; in which it must appear that the slayer had no other possible, or, at least probable means of escaping from his assailant.

It is frequently difficult to distinguish this species of homicide from manslaughter. The true criterion seems to be this: when both parties are actually combating at the time when the mortal stroke is given, the slayer is then guilty of manslaughter: but if the slayer has not begun to fight, or, having begun, endeavours to decline any further struggle, and afterwards, being closely pressed by his antagonist, kills him to avoid his own destruction, this is homicide by self-defence. And as the *manner* of the defence, so is also the *time* to be considered: for if the person assaulted does not fall upon the aggressor till the fray is over, or when he is running away, this is revenge, and not defence.

There is one species of homicide, *se defendendo*, where the party is equally innocent as he who occasions his death. As in that case mentioned by Lord Bacon, where two persons, being shipwrecked, and getting on the same plank, but finding it not able to save them both, one of them thrust the other from it, whereby he is drowned. He who thus preserves his own life at the expense of another man's is excusable through unavoidable necessity and the principle of self-defence: since their both remaining on the same weak plank is a mutual, though innocent, attempt upon, and endangering of, each other's lives,

III. Felonious homicide is an act of a very different nature from the former, being the killing of a human creature, of any age or sex, without justification or excuse. This may be done either by killing one's self, or another man.

Self-murder, the pretended heroism, but real cowardice of the Stoic philosophers, who destroyed themselves to avoid those ills which they had not the fortitude to endure, was punished by the Athenian law with cutting off the hand which committed the desperate deed. And the law of England ranks this among the highest crimes, making it a peculiar species of felony, a felony committed on one's self. A *felo de se* therefore, is he that deliberately puts an end to his own existence, or commits any unlawful malicious act, the consequence of which is his own death: as if, attempting to kill another, he runs upon his antagonist's sword, or, shooting at another the gun bursts and kills himself. The party must be of years of discretion, and in his senses, else it is no crime. But this excuse ought not to be strained to that length to which our coroner's juries are apt to carry it, *viz.*, that the very act of suicide is an evidence of insanity; as if every man who acts contrary to reason had no reason at all: for the same argument would prove every other criminal *non compos*, as well as the self-murderer. The law very rationally judges that every melancholy or hypochondriac fit does not deprive a man of the capacity of discerning right from wrong, which is necessary, as was observed in a former chapter, to form a legal excuse. And therefore if a real lunatic kills himself in a lucid interval he is a *felo de se* as much as another man.

But now the question follows, what punishment can human laws inflict on one who has withdrawn himself from their reach? They can only act upon what he has left behind him, his reputation and fortune; on the former by an ignominious interment by night, and

without the rights of Christian burial; on the latter by a forfeiture
of all his goods and chattels to the crown, hoping that his care for
either his own reputation, or the welfare of his family, would
be some motive to restrain him from so desperate and wicked
an act.

The other species of criminal homicide is that of killing another
man.   But in this there are also degrees of guilt, which divide the
offence into *manslaughter* and *murder.*   The difference between which
principally consists in this, that manslaughter arises from the sudden
heat of the passions; murder from the wickedness of the heart.

1. *Manslaughter* is the unlawful killing of another without malice
either express or implied : which may be either voluntarily, upon a
sudden heat, or involuntarily, but in the commission of some unlawful act.   And hence it follows that in manslaughter there can
be no accessories before the fact, because it must be done without
premeditation.

As to the first, or *voluntary* branch : if upon a sudden quarrel two
persons fight, and one of them kills the other, this is manslaughter :
and so it is if they upon such an occasion go out and fight in a field,
for this is one continued act of passion : and the law pays that regard to human frailty as not to put a hasty and a deliberate act upon
the same footing with regard to guilt.   But in this, and in every
other case of homicide upon provocation, if there be a sufficient cool-
ing time for passion to subside and reason to interpose, and the person
so provoked afterwards kills the other, this is deliberate revenge, and
not heat of blood, and accordingly amounts to murder.

The second branch, or *involuntary* manslaughter, differs also from
homicide excusable by misadventure, in this, that misadventure
always happens in consequence of a lawful act, but this species of
manslaughter in consequence of an unlawful one.   As when a workman flings down a stone or piece of timber into the street, and kills
a man ; this may be either misadventure, manslaughter, or murder,
according to the circumstances under which the original act was done.
If it were in a country village, where few passengers are, and he calls
out to all people to have a care, it is misadventure only; but if it
were in London, or other populous town, where people are continually passing, it is manslaughter, though he gives loud warning; and
murder, if he knows of their passing, and gives no warning at all, for
then it is malice against all mankind.

The crime of manslaughter amounts to felony, but the law gives
the judge an unbounded discretion as to punishment, that depending
necessarily on the special circumstances of each particular case.

2. We are next to consider the crime of deliberate and wilful

murder; a crime at which human nature starts, and which is, I believe, punished almost universally throughout the world with death. The words of the Mosaic law are very emphatic in prohibiting the pardon of murderers. "Moreover ye shall take no satisfaction for "the life of a murderer, who is guilty of death, but he shall surely "be put to death; for the land cannot be cleansed of the blood that "is shed therein, but by the blood of him that shed it."

Murder is "when a person of sound memory and discretion, un-"lawfully killeth any reasonable creature in being, and under the "king's peace, with malice aforethought, either express or implied." From which definition it will be observed; First, that it must be committed by a *person of sound memory and discretion:* for lunatics or infants, as was formerly observed, are incapable of committing any crime: unless in such cases where they show a consciousness of doing wrong, and of course a discretion, or discernment, between good and evil.

Next, it happens when a person of such sound discretion *unlawfully killeth.* The unlawfulness arises from the killing without warrant or excuse: and there must also be an actual killing to constitute murder; for a bare assault, with intent to kill, is only a great misdemeanor, though formerly it was held to be murder. The killing may be by poisoning,* striking, starving, drowning, and a thousand other forms of death by which human nature may be overcome. If a man, indeed, does an act of which the probable consequence may be, and eventually is, death; such killing may be murder, although no stroke be struck by himself, and no killing may be primarily intended: as was the case of the unnatural son, who exposed his sick father to the air, against his will, by reason whereof he died; of the harlot, who laid her child under leaves in an orchard, where a kite struck it and killed it: and of the parish officers, who shifted a child from parish to parish till it died for want of care and sustenance. And so if a master refuse his apprentice necessary sustenance, or treat him with such continued harshness and severity, that his death is occasioned thereby, the law will imply malice, and the offence will be murder. So if a prisoner die by duress of imprisonment, the person actually offending is guilty of murder. In order also to make the killing murder, it is requisite that the party die within a year and a day after the stroke received, or cause of death administered; in the computation of which the

---

* Of all species of deaths, the most detestable is that of poison; because it can of all others be the least prevented either by manhood or forethought. And therefore by the statute 22 Hen. VIII. c. 9, it was made treason, and a more grievous and lingering kind of death was inflicted on it than the common law allowed; namely, boiling to death.

whole day upon which the hurt was done shall be reckoned the first.

Further: the person killed must be "*a reasonable creature in being, and under the king's peace,*" at the time of the killing. Therefore to kill an alien, a Jew, or an outlaw, who are all under the king's peace and protection, is as much murder as to kill the most regular born Englishman; except he be an alien enemy in time of war.

Lastly, the killing must be committed *with malice aforethought*, to make it the crime of murder. This is the grand criterion which now distinguishes murder from other killing: and this malice prepense, *malitia præcogitata*, is not so properly spite or malevolence to the deceased in particular, as any evil design in general; the dictate of a wicked, depraved, and malignant heart; and it may be either *express* or *implied* in law. Express malice is when one, with a sedate deliberate mind and formed design, doth kill another: which formed design is evidenced by external circumstances discovering that inward intention; as lying in wait, antecedent menaces, former grudges, and concerted schemes to do him some bodily harm. Also, if even upon a sudden provocation one beats another in a cruel and unusual manner, so that he dies, though he did not intend his death, yet he is guilty of murder by express malice; that is by an express evil design, the genuine sense of *malitia*. As when a park-keeper tied a boy, that was stealing wood, to a horse's tail, and dragged him along the park; when a master corrected his servant with an iron bar; and a schoolmaster stamped on his scholar's belly; so that each of the sufferers died; these were justly held to be murders, because the correction being excessive, and such as could not proceed but from a bad heart, it was equivalent to a deliberate act of slaughter. Neither shall he be guilty of a less crime, who kills another in consequence of such a wilful act as shows him to be an enemy to all mankind in general; as coolly discharging a gun among a multitude of people; for this is universal malice.

Also in many cases where no malice is expressed, the law will imply it: as where a man wilfully poisons another; in such a deliberate act the law presumes malice, though no particular enmity can be proved. And if one intends to do another felony, and undesignedly kills a man, this is also murder. Thus if one shoots at A and misses *him*, but kills B, this is murder; because of the previous felonious intent, which the law transfers from one to the other.

It were needless to go through all the cases of homicide, which have been adjudged either expressly, or impliedly malicious: these, therefore, may suffice as a specimen; and we may take it for a general rule that all homicide is malicious, and of course amounts to murder, unless where *justified* by the command or permission of the law; *excused* on the account of accident or self-preservation; or *alleviated* into manslaughter, by being either the involuntary consequence of some act, not strictly lawful, or, if voluntary, occasioned by some sudden and sufficiently violent provocation. And all these circumstances of justification, excuse, or alleviation, it is incumbent upon the prisoner to make out, to the satisfaction of the court and jury: the latter of whom are to decide whether the circumstances alleged are proved to have actually existed; the former, how far they extend to take away or mitigate the guilt. For all homicide is presumed to be malicious, until the contrary appears upon evidence.

The punishment of murder, or of an accessory *before* the fact, is now in all cases, death; accessories *after* the fact may be punished by penal servitude for life.

CHAPTER XV.

OF OFFENCES AGAINST THE PERSONS OF INDIVIDUALS.

Mayhem—Abduction—Rape—evidence therein—Unnatural offences—Assaults —on clergymen—magistrates—aggravated assaults—False-imprisonment— Kidnapping—Deserting seamen.

I PROCEED next to inquire into such other crimes and misdemeanors, as more peculiarly affect the security of the person. And of these, some are felonious, others are simple misdemeanors, and punishable with a lighter animadversion. Of the felonies the first is—

I. Mayhem, *mayhemium*, which has been already considered as a civil injury: but is also looked upon in a criminal light by the law, being an atrocious breach of the peace, and an offence tending to deprive the sovereign of the aid and assistance of his subjects.

By the ancient law of England, he that maimed any man whereby he lost any part of his body, was sentenced to lose the like part; *membrum pro membro*; which was long the law in Sweden. This went afterwards out of use: partly because the law of retaliation is at best an inadequate rule of punishment; and partly because upon a repetition of the offence, the punishment could not be repeated. Several statutes accordingly were passed to put the crime and punishment of mayhem out of doubt, the most severe and effectual of all being the 22 & 23 Car. II. c. 1, called the Coventry Act; passed on the occasion of an assault on Sir John Coventry in the street, and slitting his nose, in revenge for some obnoxious words uttered by him in Parliament.

But this offence has entirely lost its distinctive character in the more general provisions of the law for the protection of persons from acts of violence, which were consolidated by the statute 24 & 25 Vict. c. 100; the leading principle of that act being to make the enormity of the offence, and of course its punishment, to depend, in a great measure, on the intent of the offender; very extensive discretion being conferred on the judges in the infliction of punishment.

II. The second offence, more immediately affecting the personal security of individuals, relates to the female part of the queen's subjects, being that of their *forcible abduction* and *marriage*, which is vulgarly called *stealing an heiress*. This offence was first dealt with by statute 3 Hen. VII. c. 2, which made abduction felony. A subsequent statute, 39 Eliz. c. 9, made it capital; and so it remained till 1 Geo. IV. c. 115, took away the capital punishment. A few years afterwards the act of Henry VII. was repealed by 9 Geo. IV. c. 31, which has been repealed in its turn, the offence being now provided for by the statute I have just referred to, 24 & 25 Vict. c. 100, s. 53, which preserves its felonious nature, and permits the infliction as a punishment of penal servitude for any term not exceeding fourteen years.

An inferior degree of the same kind of offence, but not attended with force, *taking away any woman child unmarried*, was first punished by the statute 4 & 5 Ph. & Mar. c. 8. It is now, by the statute before referred to, a misdemeanor, punishable by fine or imprisonment, or both; and the offence, it is to be observed, is complete, although the girl goes voluntarily.

III. A third offence against the female part also of the queen's subjects, but attended with greater aggravations than that of forcible marriage, is the crime of *rape, raptus mulierum*, or the carnal knowledge of a woman forcibly and against her will.

This crime was punished by the Saxon laws, particularly those of King Athelstan, with death; which was also agreeable to the old Gothic or Scandinavian constitution. But this was afterwards thought too hard, and in its stead another severe, but not capital punishment, was inflicted by William the Conqueror, *viz.*, castration and loss of eyes, which continued till after Bracton wrote, in the reign of Henry the Third.

In the 3 Edw. I., the punishment was much mitigated; but this lenity being productive of the most terrible consequences, it was in 13 Edw. I., found necessary to make the offence felony. And afterwards, by 18 Eliz. c. 7, it was made capital; and so remained till recently, the extreme limit of punishment being now penal servitude for life. To abuse a girl under the age of ten is felony, punishable in the same manner; the same offence committed on a girl above ten, and under twelve, is a misdemeanor, and much less penal; but on what ground this distinction has been made, it is somewhat difficult to perceive.

As to the material facts requisite to be given and proved upon an indictment of rape, and other offences against women, they are not to be publicly discussed, except only in a court of justice. I shall therefore merely add a few remarks from Sir Matthew Hale, with regard to the credibility of the chief witness; for how far she is to be believed, must be left to the jury upon the circumstances of fact that concur in that testimony. Thus: if the witness be of good fame; if she presently discovered the offence, and made search for the offender; if the party accused fled for it; these and the like are concurring circumstances which give greater probability to her evidence. On the other side, if she be of evil fame, and stand unsupported by others; if she concealed the injury for any considerable time after she had opportunity to complain; if the place, where the fact was alleged to be committed was where it was possible she might have been heard, and she made no outcry; these and the like circumstances, if unexplained, carry a strong, but not conclusive, presumption, that her testimony is false or feigned.

A charge of rape can only be sustained when the offence was committed *against the will* of the woman; the law, however, extends its protection to females under the age of twenty-one, not only against the force, but also against the fraud of others. For whoever by false pretences, or other fraudulent means, procures any such female to have illicit connection with a man, is guilty of a misdemeanor, punishable by imprisonment, accompanied with hard labour, for two years.

IV. What has been observed with regard to the proof of *rape*, may be applied to another offence, of a still deeper malignity, the very mention of which is a disgrace to human nature. It will be more eligible to imitate in this respect the delicacy of our English law, which treats it, in its very indictments, as a crime not fit to be named: "*peccatum illud horribile, inter christianos non nominandum.*"

These are all the principal offences more immediately against the personal security of the subject. The inferior offences, or misdemeanors, that fall under this head, are *assaults, batteries, wounding, false imprisonment*, and *kidnapping*.

V. VI. VII. With regard to the nature of the three first of
these offences in general, I have nothing further to add to what has
already been observed, when we considered them as private wrongs,
or civil injuries, for which a satisfaction or remedy is given to the
party aggrieved.   But taken in a public light, as a breach of the
queen's peace, an affront to her government, and a damage done to
her subjects, they are also indictable and punishable at common
law with fine and imprisonment.   Some of these assaults, however,
although unlawful when committed on any person, acquire a higher
degree of guilt when committed on persons in particular situations,
or exercising peculiar duties, and to them consequently the law
affords greater protection.   Thus, by the statute called *articuli
cleri*, 9 Edw. II. c. 3, if any person laid violent hands upon a clergyman, he was subject to three kinds of prosecution, all of which
might be pursued for one and the same offence; an indictment for
the breach of the peace; a civil action, for the damage sustained by
the party injured; and a suit in the ecclesiastical court, first, *pro
correctione et salute animæ*, by *enjoining* penance, and then again
for such sum of money as should be agreed on for *taking off*
the penance enjoined; it being usual in those courts to exchange
their spiritual censures for a round compensation in money; perhaps because poverty is generally esteemed by the moralists the
best medicine *pro salute animæ*.   The statute of Edward II. was,
however, so far repealed by 9 Geo. IV. c. 31; and the only special
protection now given to the clergy consists in its being made a
misdemeanor, to obstruct a clergyman in, or *arrest* him upon civil
process, while he is performing or about to perform, or returning
from the performance of, divine service.

Assaults on magistrates and gamekeepers are in certain prescribed
instances severely punishable, as are likewise assaults on officers of
workhouses, and on relieving and other officers acting under the
poor laws.   So are assaults committed in pursuance of a conspiracy
to raise the rate of wages; assaults by masters on apprentices or
servants, by husbands on their wives, and by parents and others on
children.

The punishment for an assault is usually imprisonment, or fine,
or both; but the court is empowered, in cases of indecent assault,
and assaults occasioning actual bodily harm, to impose hard labour
as part of the sentence.   Common assaults and batteries may and
usually are dealt with by the justices, under the summary jurisdiction conferred on them to commit the offender for two months to
the house of correction, or to impose a fine not exceeding 5*l.*, inclusive of costs.

VIII. The two remaining offences against the persons of indi-

viduals, are infringements of their natural liberty: concerning the
first of which, *false imprisonment*, I must content myself with
referring the student to what has been already observed when we
considered it as a civil injury. The most atrocious degree of this
offence, that of sending any subject of this realm a prisoner into
parts beyond the seas, is punished as a *præmunire*; inferior degrees
of it are punishable, on indictment, if need be, by fine and imprisonment.

IX. The other offence, *kidnapping*, being the forcible abduction
or stealing away of a man, woman, or child, from their own
country, and sending them into another, was capital by the Jewish
law. So likewise in the civil law, *plagium*, was punished with
death. With us it was formerly punished with fine, imprisonment,
and pillory.

The offence of *child-stealing* is now, however, provided for by the
statute 24 & 25 Vict. c. 100, s. 56, which makes it a felony, for
which penal servitude for seven years may be imposed. The cognate offence of forcing a seaman on shore from a vessel, and leaving
him, is punishable summarily under the statute 17 & 18 Vict.
c. 104.

The same statute provides against the wrongful discharge of seamen, whether in British or foreign ports, by requiring masters of
vessels, under the penalty of being guilty of a misdemeanor, to
obtain formal certificates as to the grounds of the discharge from
consular officers, or respectable merchants resident in the place
where the discharge takes place.

And thus much for offences that more immediately affect the
persons of individuals.

CHAPTER XVI.

OF OFFENCES AGAINST THE HABITATIONS OF INDIVIDUALS.

I. Arson—definition—what a burning—punishment.——II. Burglary—definition—time, place, and manner of committing this offence—intent—
punishment—Housebreaking—Sacrilege—Offence of being found by night
armed or disguised, &c. &c.

THE only two offences that more immediately affect the *habitations* of individuals or private subjects, are those of arson and
burglary.

1. Arson *ab ardendo*, is the malicious and wilful burning of the house

or outhouse of another man; for not only the bare dwelling-house, but all outhouses that are parcel thereof, though not contiguous thereto, nor under the same roof, as barns and stables, may be the subject of arson; and this by the common law. This offence is now, however, very clearly defined by the statute 24 & 25 Vict. c. 100, consolidating the law on this subject. Setting fire to a dwelling-house, *any person being therein*, till recently a capital felony, is now punishable, if need be, by penal servitude for life. Setting fire to a church or chapel, office, shop, mill, malthouse, or granary; or to any building used in trade or manufacture; or to farm buildings, or to any station or other building belonging to a railway, dock, or canal, or to any public building, is also felony, punishable in the same manner.

As to what shall be said to be a *burning*, so as to amount to arson, a bare intent, or attempt to do it, by actually setting fire to a house, unless it absolutely *burns*, did not fall within the description of *incendit et combussit;* which were words necessary, in the days of law-Latin, to all indictments of this sort. The burning and consuming of any part was, however, sufficient; though the fire were afterwards extinguished; but under the statute now in force, the offence consists in setting fire to the building, and consequently it is not necessary that it should be burnt or actually consumed.

And it must be a *malicious* burning; otherwise it is only a trespass, and therefore no negligence or mischance amounts to it. But any servant negligently setting fire to a house or outhouses, may be sent to the house of correction for eighteen months; in the same manner as the Roman law directed " *eos, qui negligenter ignes apud " se habuerint, fustibus vel flagellis cœdi.*"

The *punishment* of arson was death by our ancient Saxon laws. And in the reign of Edward I., this sentence was executed by a kind of *lex talionis:* for the incendiaries were burnt to death, as they were also by the Gothic constitutions. The statute 8 Henry VI. c. 6, made the wilful burning of houses, under some special circumstances therein mentioned, amount to the crime of high treason. But it was again reduced to felony by the general acts of Edward VI. and Queen Mary; and for a long period afterwards was subject to the punishment of all capital felonies, namely, hanging. But no offence of this description now subjects the offender to this punishment.

There are some cognate offences, which may be mentioned here, as also highly penal. Thus whoever by gunpowder, or other explosive substance, destroys, or damages the whole or any part of any dwelling-house, *any person being therein;* or by the same means destroys or damages any building, whereby the life of any person is endangered, is guilty of felony, and may be sent to penal servitude for life. The legislature indeed looks upon offences of this nature so seriously, that diverging from the usual rule of law as to attempts, it has made the attempt to blow up buildings, although it fails, also a felony, but not so penal in its consequences.

II. Burglary, or nocturnal housebreaking, *burgi latrocinium*, which by our ancient law was called *ham-socn*, or, as it is in Scotland to this day, *hame-sucken*, has always been looked upon as a very heinous offence; the law of England paying so tender a regard to the immunity of a man's house, that it styles it his castle, and will never suffer it to be violated with impunity. For this reason no outward doors can in general be broken open to execute any civil process; though, in criminal cases, the public safety supersedes the private. A burglar, then, is " he that by night breaketh and " entereth into a mansion-house, with intent to commit a felony."

The *time* must be by night, and not by day; for in the daytime there is no burglary; and *night* is now, by express enactment, to be considered, with reference to this offence, as commencing at nine of the clock in the evening, and concluding at six of the clock in the morning of the next succeeding day.

The *place* must be, according to Sir Edward Coke, a *mansion-house*; and, therefore, to account for the reason why breaking open a church is burglary, as it undoubtedly is, he quaintly observes that it is *domus mansionalis Dei*. No distant barn, warehouse, or the like, are under the same privileges, nor looked upon as a man's castle of defence: nor is a breaking open of houses wherein no man resides, and which, therefore, for the time being, are not mansion-houses, attended with the same circumstances of midnight terror. But a chamber in a college or an inn of court, where each inhabitant has a distinct property, is, to all other purposes as well as this, the mansion-house of the owner.

In the *manner* of committing burglary, there must be both a *breaking* and an *entry* to complete it. And in general it must be an actual breaking, not a mere legal *clausum fregit* by leaping over invisible ideal boundaries, which may constitute a civil trespass, but a substantial and forcible irruption, as by breaking, or taking out the glass of, or otherwise opening, a window: picking a lock, or opening it with a key, lifting the latch of a door, or unloosing any other fastening which the owner has provided. But if a person leaves his doors or windows open, it is his own folly and negligence, and if a man enters therein it is no burglary: yet, if he afterwards unlocks an inner or chamber door, it is so. But to come down a chimney is held a burglarious entry, for that is as much closed as the nature of things will permit. So, if a servant conspires with a robber, and lets him into the house by night, this is burglary in both, for the servant is doing an unlawful act, and the opportunity afforded him of doing it with greater ease rather aggravates than extenuates the guilt. As for the *entry*, any the least degree of it, with any part of the body, or with an instrument held in the hand, is sufficient; as to step over the threshold, or to put a hand or a hook in at a window to draw out goods, are both burglarious entries. The entry may be before the breaking as well as after: for if a person enters a dwelling-house with intent to commit felony, or being in such dwelling-house, commits any felony, and in either case breaks *out* of the dwelling-house in the night time, this by statute is burglary.

As to the *intent*, it is clear that such breaking must be with a felonious intent, otherwise it is only a trespass and entry. And it is the same, whether such intention be actually carried into execution, or only demonstrated by some attempt or overt act, of which the jury is to judge. And therefore such a breach and entry of a house, as has been before described, by night, with intent to commit a robbery, a murder, a rape, or any other felony, is burglary, whether the thing be actually perpetrated or not.

Thus much for burglary, which is a felony at common law, but was not capital till made so by the statute 1 Edw. VI. c. 12. In like manner, the laws of Athens, which punished no simple theft with death, made burglary a capital crime; which it remained with us till quite recently, being now, however, only punishable at the utmost by penal servitude for life.

There are other offences, denominated *housebreaking*, which affect the habitation of individuals, but do not amount to burglary. Such are the breaking and entering a house, warehouse, or shop; or a church or chapel, and stealing therein. These crimes are punishable with great severity; as is likewise the offence of *sacrilege*, or the breaking and entering a church or other place of worship, and committing felony therein.

Somewhat less penal, though of not less dangerous tendency, are several offences created by recent statutes; which make it a misdemeanor in any person to be found *by night* armed with any dangerous or offensive weapon, with intent to break or enter a dwelling-house or other building, and to commit felonly therein; or found *by night* having in his possession, without lawful excuse, any implement of housebreaking; or found *by night* having his face blackened or otherwise disguised, with intent to commit any felony, or found *by night* in any dwelling-house or other building, with intent to commit any felony therein. A repetition of any of these offences is punishable with penal servitude.

CHAPTER XVII.

OF OFFENCES AGAINST PRIVATE PROPERTY.

I. Larceny—definition—taking away the personal goods of another—carrying away—intent—personal goods—things that savour of the realty—bonds, bills, &c.—wreck and treasure trove—game—dogs—punishment of larceny —Compound larceny—larceny from a dwelling-house—larceny from the person — robbery — with wounding — by menaces.——II. Malicious mischief.

THE last species of offences against individuals are such as more immediately affect their property. Of which there are two which are attended with a breach of the peace: *larceny* and *malicious mischief;* and one that is equally injurious to the rights of property, but attended with no act of violence, which is the crime of *forgery.* Of these three in their order :—

I. Larceny, or *theft,* by contraction for latrociny, *latrocinium,* is distinguished by the common law into two sorts: the one called *simple* larceny, or plain theft unaccompanied with any other atrocious circumstance; and *mixed* or *compound* larceny, which also includes in it the aggravation of a taking from one's house or person.

Simple larceny* is " the felonious taking and carrying away of " the personal goods of another."

1. There must be a *taking,* which implies the consent of the owner to be wanting. Therefore no delivery of the goods from the owner to the offender, upon trust, can at common law ground a larceny. As if A lends B a horse, and he rides away with him; or, if I send goods by a carrier, and he carries them away; these are no larcenies at common law. But if the carrier opens a bale or pack of goods, or pierces a vessel of wine, and takes away part thereof, these are larcenies; for here the *animus furandi* is manifest; since he had otherwise no inducement to open the goods. Where, therefore, the possession of goods has been obtained *bonâ fide,* in the first instance, the subsequent conversion is not larceny; but where the original possession is obtained by a trick for the purpose of convert-

* Formerly the stealing of goods above the value of twelve-pence was called *grand* larceny; when of goods to that value, or under, it was *petit* larceny; offences which were considerably distinguished in their punishment. The distinction has been abolished; every larceny being now deemed grand larceny.

ing the goods to the taker's use, it is larceny. The voluntary loan
of a horse to a person who afterwards rides off with it, is not larceny;
but if the possession of the horse was parted with under colour of
a hiring, the intention to steal it existing from the first. it is larceny.*

The *taking* required to constitute larceny may thus be a *taking*
in contemplation of law only. Thus if a servant having, not the possession, but only the care and oversight of the goods, as the butler
of plate, the shepherd of sheep, and the like, steals them, it is felony
at common law. So if a guest robs his inn or tavern of a piece of
plate, it is larceny; for he has not the possession delivered to him,
but merely the use. And it is the same, by statute, if a lodger runs
away with the goods from his ready-furnished lodgings, or steals *a*
fixture therefrom.

And not only in these, but in many other similar cases, has the legislature interfered to remedy a palpable defect in the law. Thus it was
not larceny at common law in a servant to run away with the goods
committed to him by third persons for delivery to his master, and of
which his master never had possession. It was only a breach of
civil trust; and it was necessarily the same in the case of agents,
brokers, bankers, trustees, and others intrusted with property.

The case of a servant misappropriating property delivered to him
for his master, was first dealt with by a statute of Henry VI.; the
statute 7 & 8 Geo. IV. c. 29, was the first which provided in express
terms "for the punishment of embezzlements committed by *agents*
intrusted with property," and was shortly followed by several others
having the same object in view. Of these the most important were
the statute 5 & 6 Vict. c. 39, usually called the *Factor's Act*, and
the statute 20 & 21 Vict. c. 54, which provided for the prosecution
and punishment of *trustees*, fraudulently disposing of trust property,
and of the *directors of public companies*, fraudulently appropriating
the property under their control, keeping fraudulent accounts, or
publishing fraudulent statements, offences unhappily of much too
frequent occurrence. These statutes have been repealed; but their
various provisions were at the same time re-enacted by the statute
24 & 25 Vict. c. 96, which consolidates the statute law relating to
larceny and other similar offences · and to which it may therefore be
sufficient to refer the reader.

2. There must not only be a taking, but a *carrying away; cepit*

* The subtle distinction, above pointed out, between larceny and fraud,
gave rise to the statutes by which the obtaining any property, money, or
valuable security by *false pretence*, with intent to defraud, is made an indictable misdemeanor.

et asportavit was the old law-Latin. A bare removal from the place is, however, enough. As if a thief, intending to steal plate, takes it out of a chest, and lays it upon the floor, but is surprised before he can make his escape with it; this is larceny.

3. This taking, and carrying away, must also be *felonious;* that is, done *animo furandi:* or, as the civil law expresses it, *lucri causâ,* the ordinary evidence of which is where the party does it clandestinely; or, being charged with the fact, denies it. But this is by no means the only criterion of criminality: for in cases that may amount to larceny, the variety of circumstances is so great, and the complications thereof so mingled, that it is impossible to recount all those which may evidence a felonious intent, or *animum furandi;* wherefore they must be left to the due and attentive consideration of the court and jury.

4. This felonious taking and carrying away must also, at the common law, have been *of the personal goods of another:* for if they were things *real,* or savoured of the realty, larceny could not be committed of them. Lands, tenements, and hereditaments cannot in their nature be taken and carried away. And of things likewise that adhere to the freehold, as corn, grass, trees, and the like, or lead upon a house, no larceny could be committed; and the severance of them was merely a trespass. Yet if the thief severed anything from the freehold at *one* time, whereby it was converted into *a personal chattel,* in the constructive possession of him on whose soil it was left; and came again at *another* time, and took it away; it was larceny. But these refinements have been entirely swept away by the statutes I have referred to; and larceny may now be committed of lead, iron, and other things, fixed to buildings; of trees, shrubs, and underwood; of roots, plants, and vegetables, and of ore from mines, as if they were no part of the freehold whatever.

Upon the same principle, the stealing of writings relating to a real estate is no felony at common law, because they concern the land, or according to our technical language, *savour* of the *realty,* and are considered as a part of it. The legislature has consequently again interfered, and has made this offence a felony, and highly penal.

Bonds, bills, and notes, which concern mere *choses in action,* were also at the common law held not to be such goods whereof larceny might be committed; being of no intrinsic value; and not importing any property in *possession* of the person from whom they are taken. But in the reign of George II. they were put upon the same footing, with respect to larcenies, as the money they were meant to secure.

And in the same reign, another anomaly was removed with reference to *treasure trove* and *wreck,* which at common law could not be the subject of larceny till seized by the sovereign or him who had the franchise, for till such seizure no one has a property therein.

Of animals, *feræ naturæ*, and unreclaimed, such as deer, hares, and conies, in a forest, chase, or warren; fish in an open river or pond; or wild fowls at their natural liberty, no larceny can be committed, no one having any *property* therein, either absolute or qualified. But if they are reclaimed or confined, and may serve for food, it is otherwise; for of deer so enclosed in a park that they may be taken at pleasure, fish in a trunk, and pheasants or partridges in a mew, larceny may be committed; and the statute I have mentioned has accordingly specially provided for the prosecution of offences of this nature. Taking or destroying fish is, in certain cases, an indictable misdemeanor; in other circumstances, punishable by fine on summary conviction. Stealing *oysters* or oyster-brood, from a private oyster-bed is felony, and punishable as larceny.

Stealing hawks, in disobedience to the rules prescribed by the statute 37 Edw. III. c. 19, is also felony. It is also said that, if swans be lawfully marked, it is felony to steal them, though at large in a public river: and that it is likewise felony to steal them, though unmarked, if in any private river or pond; otherwise it is only a trespass. But of all valuable domestic animals, as horses and other beasts of draught, and of all animals *domitæ naturæ*, which serve for food, as neat or other cattle, swine, poultry, and the like, and of their fruit or produce, taken from them while living, as milk or wool, larceny may be committed; and also of the flesh of such as are either *domitæ* or *feræ naturæ*, when killed, the statute law only regulating the punishment.

As to those animals which do not serve for food, and which, therefore, the law holds to have no intrinsic value, as dogs of all sorts, and other creatures kept for whim and pleasure, though a man may have a base property therein, and maintain a civil action for the loss of them, yet they are not of such estimation, as that the crime of stealing them amounts to larceny. But *dog-stealing* has been for many years a misdemeanor; and the statute I have before referred to, which has re-enacted the previous enactments to that effect, also contains provision for the protection of birds and beasts kept for pleasure or merely domestic purposes.

Notwithstanding, however, that no larceny can be committed, unless there be some property in the thing taken, and an owner; yet, if the owner be unknown, provided there be a property, it is larceny to steal it; and an indictment will lie for the goods of a person unknown. This is the case of stealing a shroud out of a grave, which is the property of those, whoever they were, that buried the deceased; but stealing the corpse itself, which has no owner, though a matter of great indecency, is no felony, unless some of the grave-clothes be stolen with it. Very different from the law of the Franks, which seems to have respected both as equal offences, when it directed that a person, who had dug a corpse out of the ground in order to strip it should be banished from society, and no one suffered to relieve his wants, till the relations of the deceased consented to his re-admission.

Having thus considered the general nature of simple larceny, I come next to treat of its *punishment*. Theft, by the Jewish law, was only punished with a pecuniary fine, and satisfaction to the party injured. And in the civil law, till some very late constitutions, we never find the punishment capital. The laws of Draco at Athens punished it with death: but his laws were said to be written in blood; and Solon afterwards changed the penalty to a pecuniary mulct. And so the Attic laws in general continued; except that once, in a time of dearth, it was made capital to break into a garden and steal figs: but this law and the informers against the offence grew so odious, that from them all malicious informers were styled sycophants; a name which we have much perverted from its original meaning. From these examples, as well as the reason of the thing, many learned and scrupulous men long questioned the propriety, if not lawfulness, of inflicting capital punishment for simple theft. But notwithstanding all the remonstrances of speculative politicians and moralists, this offence long continued, throughout the greatest part of Europe, to be capital.

Our ancient Saxon laws nominally punished theft with death, if above the value of twelvepence; but the criminal was permitted to redeem his life by a pecuniary ransom; as, among their ancestors the Germans, by a stated number of cattle. In the ninth year of Henry I., however, this power of redemption was taken away, and all persons guilty of larceny above the value of twelvepence were directed to be hanged. The mercy of jurors accordingly made them often strain a point, and bring in the value of the article stolen to be less than twelvepence, for which the punishment was imprisonment or whipping, when it was really much greater. But in cases in which the jury could not, or did not, adopt this course, the criminal only escaped death by the merciful extension to him of the *benefit of clergy*.* This again could only be for the *first* offence; and in in-

* This was a solemn mockery, which was gone through at the bidding of the gaoler, who directed the convict, when called up for judgment, to kneel down and *pray his clergy*. This the person did by repeating a verse of the New Testament, which he had previously learned for the purpose, which was thence called the "neck verse." As this is a matter of some curiosity, I have thought it right to give some account of it in an appendix.

numerable cases of simple larceny the benefit of clergy was taken away by statute : so that many persons now living can recollect the frequency of executions, for offences which are now punished with a few months' imprisonment.   For it was not till the reign of George 1V., that, through the exertions of Sir Samuel Romily, who was opposed by all the judges, the severity of our penal code was at all materially diminished ; and the attention of the public called to the frightful catalogue of crimes for which death might be inflicted.   The punishment for simple larceny was soon after declared to be imprisonment or transportation beyond seas ; for which, I may add here, penal servitude has been recently substituted.

Thus much for the offence of *simple* larceny.

Mixed or *compound* larceny is such as has all the properties of the former, but is accompanied with either one or both of the aggravations of a taking from one's *house* or *person*.   First, therefore, of larceny from the *house*, and then of larceny from the *person*.

1. Larceny from the *house*, though it seems to have a higher degree of guilt than simple larceny, yet is not at all distinguished from the other at common law ; unless where it is accompanied with the circumstance of breaking the house by night ; and then we have seen that it falls under another description, viz., that of burglary.   But by several acts of parliament the benefit of clergy was taken away from larcenies committed in a house in almost every instance ; and it remained therefore a capital offence till the statutes I have just alluded to substituted an arbitrary punishment.   This offence is now provided for by the 24 & 25 Vict. c. 96, to which I have already referred.

2. Larceny from the *person* is either by *privately* stealing, or by open and violent assault, which is usually called *robbery* ; to constitute which offence, the thing taken must be completely, although it be only momentarily, removed from the person ; a removal from the place where it was, so as to constitute a simple larceny, if it still remain attached by any means to the person, not being sufficient.

The offence of *privately* stealing from a man's *person*, as by picking his pocket or the like, privily without his knowledge, was debarred of the benefit of clergy so early as the statute 8 Eliz. c. 4. But then it must have been such a larceny as stood in need of the benefit of clergy, viz., of above the value of twelvepence ; else the offender should not have judgment of death.   For the statute created no new offence, but only prevented the prisoner from praying the benefit of clergy, and left him to the regular judgment of the ancient law.   This severity seems to have been owing to the ease with which such offences are committed, the difficulty of guarding against them, and the boldness with which they were practised at the time when this statute was made : besides that this is an infringement of property in the manual occupation or corporal possession of the owner, which was an offence even in a state of nature. And therefore the *sacculariï*, or cutpurses, were more severely punished than common thieves by the Roman and Athenian laws. At present, with us, the offence of stealing from the person may be punished by penal servitude for any term not exceeding fourteen years, or by an imprisonment not exceeding two years ; but if confessed by the accused, it may form the subject of a summary conviction : and in that case is punishable by imprisonment not exceeding six months, a very different kind of punishment to that which prevailed from the days of Queen Elizabeth to our own time.

Open and violent larceny from the *person*, or *robbery*, the *rapina* of the civilians, is the felonious and forcible taking, from the person of another, of goods or money to any value, by violence or putting him in fear. 1. There must be a taking, otherwise it is no robbery. If the thief, having once taken a purse, returns it, still it is a robbery ; and so it is whether the taking be strictly from the person of another, or in his presence only ; as, where a robber by menaces and violence puts a man in fear, and drives away his sheep or his cattle before his face. But if the taking be not either directly from his person or in his presence, it is no robbery. 2. It is immaterial of what value the thing taken is : a penny as well as a pound, thus forcibly extorted, makes a robbery. 3. Lastly, the taking must be by force, or a previous putting in fear ; which makes the violation of the person more atrocious than privately stealing. This previous violence, or putting in fear, is the criterion that distinguishes robbery from other larcenies ; for if one privately steals sixpence from the person of another, and afterwards keeps it by putting him in fear, this is no robbery, for the fear is subsequent. Yet if a man be knocked down without previous warning, and stripped of his property while senseless, though strictly he cannot be said to be *put in fear*, yet this is undoubtedly a robbery. Or, if a person with a sword drawn begs an alms, and I give it him through mistrust and apprehension of violence, this is a robbery. So if, under a pretence of sale, a man forcibly extorts money from another, neither shall this subterfuge avail him.

This species of larceny was debarred of the benefit of clergy by 23 Hen. VIII. c. 1, and other subsequent statutes, not indeed in general, but only when committed in a dwelling-house, or in or near the public highway. A robbery, therefore, in a distant field, or footpath, was not punished with death ; till the statute 3 & 4 Will. & Mary,

c. 9, took away clergy from both principals and accessories before the fact, in robbery, wheresoever committed. This crime has, however, ceased to be capital, the punishment of the offender being now made to depend on the circumstances accompanying its commission.

There is one species of crime not attended with any actual or attempted violence, which, at common law, and for some time by statute, constituted robbery, viz., the offence of obtaining property by accusation of unnatural practices. This detestable crime is now provided for by the statute 24 & 25 Vict. c. 96, s. 46, and may involve penal servitude for life. And it is not less penal to accuse or threaten to accuse any person of an infamous crime, with intent to extort money, or to send or deliver, with a similar object, any letter or writing containing menaces.

Before quitting this subject I may observe that in all these cases of mixed or compound larceny, if any part of the charge necessary to bring the offence within the statutory enactment applicable to it, cannot be proved, the accused may, nevertheless, be convicted of the minor offence. Thus, if the force necessary to constitute robbery cannot be proved, the offender may be convicted of stealing from the person, or of the attempt. And so, if the property does not appear to have been taken from the person, he may yet be convicted of simple larceny, or of the attempt to commit that offence.

II. *Malicious mischief*, or damage, is the next species of injury to private property which the law considers as a public crime. This is such as is done, not *animo furandi*, or with an intent of gaining by another's loss; which is some, though a weak, excuse : but either out of a spirit of wanton cruelty, or black and diabolical revenge. In which it bears a near relation to the crime of arson ; for as that affects the habitation, so this does the other property of individuals. And, therefore, any damage arising from this mischievous disposition, though only a trespass at common law, is now highly penal.

Some of the offences which may properly be thus classed have indeed been already noticed in treating of arson and of the offences relating to trade ; so that a concise reference to the others is all that need now be attempted.

By 22 Hen. VIII. c. 11, to destroy the powdike in the fens of Norfolk and Ely, was made felony ; and by 6 Geo. II. c. 37, and 10 Geo. II. c. 32, it was also felony without benefit of clergy, maliciously to cut down any river or sea bank, whereby lands might be overflowed or damaged. These statutes were superseded by more modern enactments, which in their turn have been repealed ; the whole statute law relating to malicious injuries to property being now consolidated by the statute 24 & 25 Vict. c. 97.

By 1 Ann. st. 2, c. 9, captains and mariners destroying ships to the prejudice of the owners, and by 4 Geo. I. c. 12, to the prejudice of insurers also, were declared guilty of felony without benefit of clergy. And by 12 Ann. st. 2, c. 18, making any hole in a ship in distress, or doing anything tending to her immediate loss, was also felony without benefit of clergy. These, and similar offences relating to shipping are provided for in the statute I have just referred to; which also makes it highly penal to injure, remove, sink, or destroy the *buoys* of vessels; or exhibit false signals with intent to lead vessels into danger. These last offences may, indeed, involve penal servitude for life.

By statute 43 Eliz. c. 13, to burn any *barn* or *stack* of *corn* or *grain*; or to imprison or carry away any subject, in order to ransom him, or to make prey or spoil of his person or goods upon deadly feud or otherwise, in the four northern counties of Northumberland, Westmoreland, Cumberland, and Durham; or to give or take *blackmail*, was felony without benefit of clergy. This and a statute of Charles II. relating to the burning of *ricks* or *stacks* of corn or grain; a statute of William & Mary, relating to the burning of goss or fern; a statute of George II., providing for the same offences, and a statute of George I. relating to the burning of underwood or coppice, have all been repealed; the statute 24 & 25 Vict. c. 97, regulating the punishment of all these, and of all similar offences, or attempts to commit them.

By statute 6 Geo. I. c. 23, the wilful and malicious tearing, spoiling, burning or defacing of the garments of any person passing in the streets or highways, was made felony. This was occasioned by the insolence of certain weavers and others; who, upon the introduction of some Indian fashions prejudicial to their own manufactures, made it their practice to deface them; either by open outrage, or by privily cutting, or casting *aqua fortis* in the streets upon such as wore them. This act has been repealed; but such offenders are now punishable under the general provisions of the statute I have just referred to.

By statute 9 Geo. I. c. 22, commonly called the Waltham Black Act, occasioned by the devestations committed near Waltham in Hampshire, by persons in disguise or with their faces blackened, who seem to have resembled the Roberdsmen, or followers of Robert Hood, that in the reign of Richard I. committed great outrages on the borders of England and Scotland; by this Black Act, I say, which has in part been mentioned under the several heads of

riots, menaces, mayhem, and larceny, it was enacted that to set fire
to any house, barn, or outhouse, stack of corn or wood; or unlawfully and maliciously to break down the head of any fish-pond
whereby the fish should be destroyed, were felonies without benefit
of clergy; and the hundred was to be chargeable for the damages,
unless the offender were convicted. In like manner by the Roman
law, to cut down trees, and especially vines, was punished in the
same degree as robbery.

The first of these offences, *wilful fire-raising*, is now provided for
by the statute 24 & 25 Vict. c. 97; and the second offence, the breaking
down of fish-ponds, is no longer a felony, but a misdemeanor, punishable, however, under the same statute.

To kill, maim, or wound any cattle, was felony without benefit of
clergy by the Black Act. It had previously been made felony by
22 and 23 Car. II. c. 7; but these statutes have long been repealed.
The killing, maiming, or wounding of any *cattle* is still felony, however, subjecting the offender to penal servitude or imprisonment.
And the word *cattle*, it may be observed, has been held to include
horses, as well as oxen, &c., pigs, and asses; but does not comprise
dogs or other animals not the subject of larceny at common law, which
are to some extent, however, protected against savage treatment by
other statutes.

The cutting of hop-binds was a capital felony by statutes of
George II.; but is so no longer. The Waltham Black Act, already
mentioned, made the cutting down or destroying of any trees planted
in an avenue, or growing in a garden, orchard, or plantation, for
ornament, shelter, or profit, also a felony without benefit of clergy.
Statutes of George III. next provided against the destroying roots,
shrubs, or plants. These acts have all been repealed; and the
offences they referred to are now punishable simply as injuries to
property.

By several statutes of George II. it was made felony, without
benefit of clergy, to set fire to any mine, pit, or depth of coal. And
afterwards by a statute of George III., to burn or destroy mine
engines. These statutes have also been repealed, but the setting
fire to a mine, the *attempting* to do so, the drowning of a mine,
the obstructing, or damaging of the air or waterway of a mine are all
offences of a highly penal character.

To the crimes above enumerated may be added, the destruction of
any bridge, viaduct, or aqueduct; and the cutting down of tele-
graphic apparatus, which are more or less penal according to the circumstances.

It only remains to be added, that in any case of damage to property not specially provided for by the statute I have mentioned, the offender, when the damage exceeds five pounds, may be convicted of a misdemeanor, for which penal servitude or a term of imprisonment may be awarded, according as the offence is committed by day or by night; when the value of the property injured does not exceed five pounds, the offender may be compelled, on summary conviction, to make compensation, or be imprisoned and kept to hard labour for two months.

These are the principal punishments of malicious mischief.

III. Forgery, or the *crimen falsi*, is an offence which was punished by the civil law with deportation or banishment, and sometimes with death. It may with us be defined at common law to be, " the fraudulent making or alteration of a writing to the prejudice of another man's right;" for which the offender may suffer imprisonment, and formerly might have been set in the pillory. By a variety of statutes, a more severe punishment was inflicted on the offender in many particular cases; and statutes to the same effect have become so multiplied of late as almost to become general.

By statute 5 Eliz. c. 14, the offender, for certain cases of this nature was to stand in the pillory, having both his ears cut off, and his nostrils slit, and seared; for others, the pillory, the loss of one ear only, and a year's imprisonment: a second offence being felony without benefit of clergy. From the Revolution, when paper credit was first established, till the reign of George III., capital punishment was multiplied for forgeries to an extent which is scarcely credible; every act of parliament striking at some newly discovered forgery making it felony without benefit of clergy. So that there was hardly a case possible to be conceived, wherein forgery, that tended to defraud, whether in the name of a real or fictitious person, was not made a capital crime. And so it remained till the reign of William IV., when most of these statutes were repealed; and the punishment of death taken away in all except the more serious and important cases. Offenders, who would otherwise have been liable to suffer death, were subjected to transportation for life, or not less than seven years, or imprisonment not exceeding four, and not less than two years.

The forgery of the great or privy seal, privy signet or sign manual, remained high treason, and punishable accordingly; and the forgery of exchequer bills, India bonds, bank-notes, wills, and bills of exchange, and of transfers of stock were all by special enactment still punishable with death. This punishment was, however, very shortly afterwards confined to the offence of forging a will or power of attorney for the transfer of stock; and, before long, the capital punishment for these as well as for certain other forgeries, which had been introduced by some intermediate statutes, was altogether abolished, transportation for life, or for a less period, or imprisonment being substituted

Not a session of parliament now passes without some document being protected by provisions rendering its fabrication highly penal. But offences of this nature may usually be prosecuted under the general provisions of the recent statute 24 & 25 Vict. c 98, which consolidates the law on this subject; and provides minutely for the punishment of every class of offence which can be placed under this head.

These are the principal infringements of the rights of property: which were the last species of offences against individuals or private subjects, which the method of our distribution has led us to consider.

CHAPTER XVIII.

OF THE MEANS OF PREVENTING OFFENCES.

Sureties for the peace, or for good behaviour—who may demand them—how discharged—Sureties for the peace, when granted—how forfeited—Sureties for good behaviour—how forfeited.

WE are now to consider the means of *preventing* the commission of crimes and misdemeanors. And it is an honour to our laws, that they furnish a title of this sort; since *preventive* justice is, upon every principle of reason, of humanity, and of sound policy, preferable in all respects to *punishing* justice; the execution of which is always attended with many harsh and disagreeable circumstances.

This preventive justice consists in obliging those persons, whom there is a probable ground to suspect of future misbehaviour, to give full assurance to the public, that such offence as is apprehended shall not happen; by finding pledges or securities for keeping the peace, or for their good behaviour. By the Saxon constitution these sureties were always at hand, by means of the decennaries or frank-pledges, wherein the whole neighbourhood of freemen were mutually pledges for each other's good behaviour. But this general security being now fallen into disuse, there hath succeeded to it the method of making suspected persons find special securities for their future conduct: of which we find mention in the laws of King Edward the Confessor: "*tradat fidejussores de pace et legalitate tuendâ.*"

This security consists in being bound, with one or more sureties, in a recognizance or obligation to the crown, entered on record, and taken in some court or by some judicial officer, whereby the parties acknowledge themselves to be indebted to the crown in the sum required, for instance, 100*l.*, with condition to be void, if the party shall appear in court on such a day, and in the meantime shall keep the peace; either generally, towards the sovereign and all his liege people; or particularly also, with regard to the person who craves the security. Or, if it be for the good behaviour, then on condition that he shall demean and behave himself well, either generally or specially, for the time therein limited, as for one or more years, or for life. This recognizance, if taken by a justice of the peace, is certified to the next sessions; and if the condition be broken by any breach of the peace in the one case, or any misbehaviour in the other, the recognizance becomes forfeited or absolute; and being *estreated* or extracted, taken out from among the other records, and sent up to the Exchequer; the party and his sureties, having now become absolute debtors of the crown, are sued for the several sums in which they are respectively bound.

Any justices of the peace, by virtue of their commission, or those who are *ex-officio* conservators of the peace, may demand such security according to their own discretion; or it may be granted at the request of any subject, upon due cause shown, provided such demandant be under the protection of the crown. Wives may demand it against their husbands, or husbands, if necessary, against their wives. But feme-coverts, and infants under age, ought to find security by their friends only, and not to be bound themselves: for they are incapable of engaging themselves to answer any debt; which, as we observed, is the nature of these recognizances or acknowledgments.

A recognizance may be discharged by the death of the principal party bound thereby, if not before forfeited; or by order of the court to which such recognizance is certified; or in case he at whose request it was granted, if granted upon a private account, will release it, or does not make his appearance to pray that it may be continued.

Thus far what has been said is applicable to both species of recognizances, for the *peace*, and for the *good behaviour*. But as these two species of securities are in some respects different, especially as to the cause of granting, or the means of forfeiting them, I shall now consider them separately.

1. Any justice of the peace may, *ex-officio*, bind all those to keep the peace who in his presence make any affray; or threaten to kill or beat another; or contend together with angry words; or are brought before him by the constable for a breach of the peace in his

presence; and all such persons as, having been before bound to the peace, have broken it and forfeited their recognizances. Also, whenever any private man has just cause to fear that another will do him a corporal injury, or procure others so to do; he may demand surety of the peace against such person: and every justice of the peace is bound to grant it, if he who demands it will make oath that he is actually under fear of death or bodily harm. This is called *swearing the peace* against another; and, if the party does not find such sureties as the justice in his discretion shall require, he may immediately be committed till he does, or until the expiration of a year; for persons committed to prison for not entering into recognizances or finding sureties to keep the peace, can in no case be detained for more than twelve months.

Such recognizance, when given, may be forfeited by any actual violence, or menace even, to the person of him who demanded it, if it be a special recognizance; or, if the recognizance be general, by any unlawful action whatsoever, that either is or tends to a breach of the peace. But a bare trespass upon the lands or goods of another, which is a ground for a civil action, unless accompanied with a wilful breach of the peace, is no forfeiture of the recognizance. Neither are mere reproachful words, as calling a man knave or liar, any breach of the peace, so as to forfeit one's recognizance, being looked upon to be merely the effect of unmeaning heat and passion, unless they amount to a challenge to fight.

The other species of recognizance, with sureties, is for *good behaviour*; which includes security for the peace, and somewhat more.

First, then, the justices are empowered by the statute 34 Edw. III. c. 1, to bind over to the good behaviour towards the king and his people, all them *that be not of good fame*, wherever they be found; to the intent that the people be not troubled nor endamaged, nor the peace diminished, nor merchants and others, passing by the highways of the realm, be disturbed nor put in the peril which may happen by such offenders. Under the general words of this expression, *that be not of good fame*, it is held that a man may be bound to his good behaviour for causes of scandal, *contra bonos mores*, as well as *contra pacem*. Thus a justice may bind over all nightwalkers; such as keep suspicious company, or are reported to be pilferers or robbers; common drunkards; cheats; idle vagabonds; and other persons whose misbehaviour may reasonably bring them within the general words of the statute, as persons not of good fame: an expression, it must be owned, of so great a latitude, as leaves much to be determined by the discretion of the magistrate himself.

But, if he commits a man for want of sureties, he must express the cause thereof with convenient certainty; and take care that such cause be a good one.

A recognizance for good behaviour may be forfeited by all the same means as one for the security of the peace may be; and also by some others; especially by committing any of those acts of misbehaviour which the recognizance was intended to prevent. But not by barely giving fresh cause of suspicion of that which perhaps may never actually happen; for, though it is just to compel suspected persons to give security to the public against misbehaviour that is apprehended; yet it would be hard, upon suspicion, without the proof of any actual crime, to punish them by a forfeiture of their recognizance.

CHAPTER XIX.

OF COURTS OF A CRIMINAL JURISDICTION.

I. High Court of Parliament—Court of Lord High Steward—Exchequer Chamber—Queen's Bench—High Court of Admiralty—Assizes—Quarter Sessions: Recorder: Petty Sessions: Stipendiary Magistrates—Coroner— II. Central Criminal Court—Courts of Universities.

THE last object of our inquiries will be the method of *inflicting* those *punishments* which the law has annexed to particular offences; in the discussion of which I shall pursue the same method that I followed in the preceding book, with regard to the redress of civil injuries; by, first, pointing out the several *courts* of criminal jurisdiction; and by, secondly, deducing down, in their natural order, and explaining, the several *proceedings* therein.

And in reckoning up the several *courts* of criminal jurisdiction, I shall begin with an account of such as are of a *public* and *general* jurisdiction throughout the whole realm; and mention afterwards those of a *private* and *special* jurisdiction, which are now confined to London and the two universities.

I must, in one respect, however, pursue a different order from that in which I considered the civil tribunals. For there, as the several courts had a gradual subordination to each other, the superior correcting the errors of the inferior, I thought it best to begin with the lowest, and so ascend gradually to those of the most extensive powers. But as it is contrary to the spirit of the law of England, to suffer any man to be tried twice for the same offence; therefore, these criminal courts may be said to be all independent of each other; at least, so far as that the sentence of the lowest of them can never be reversed by the highest jurisdiction in the kingdom, unless for error in law, though sometimes causes may be removed from one to the other before trial. And, therefore, as in these courts of criminal cognizance there is not the same dependence as in the others, I shall rank them according to their dignity, and begin with the highest of all; viz.:

1. The High Court of *Parliament*, which is the supreme court in the kingdom for the execution of laws; by the trial of great offenders whether lords or commoners, in the method of parliamentary impeachment. As for acts of parliament to attaint particular persons of treason or felony, I speak not of them, as they are to all intents and purposes new laws. But an impeachment before the lords by the commons, in parliament, is a prosecution of the established law, being a presentment to the most high and supreme court of criminal jurisdiction by the most solemn grand inquest of the whole kingdom. A commoner cannot, however, be impeached before the lords for any capital offence, but only for high misdemeanors; a peer may be impeached for any crime.

This is a custom derived to us from the constitution of the ancient Germans, who in their great councils sometimes tried capital accusations relating to the public. And it has a peculiar propriety in the English constitution; which has much improved upon the ancient model imported hither from the Continent. For, though in general the union of the legislative and judicial powers ought to be most carefully avoided, yet it may happen that a subject, intrusted with the administration of public affairs, may infringe the rights of the people, and be guilty of such crimes, as the ordinary magistrate either dares not or cannot punish. Of these the representatives of the people, or house of commons, cannot properly *judge*; because their constituents are the parties injured; and can therefore only *impeach*. But before what court shall this impeachment be tried? Not before the ordinary tribunals, which might possibly be swayed by the authority of so powerful an accuser. Reason therefore will suggest, that this branch of the legislature, which represents the people, must bring its charge before the other branch, which consists of the nobility, who may for this purpose be assumed to have neither the same interests nor the same passions as popular assemblies. It is proper that the nobility should judge, to insure justice to the accused; as it is proper that the people should accuse, to insure justice to the commonwealth. And therefore, among other extraordinary circumstances attending the authority of this court, there is one of a very singular nature, which was insisted on by the house of commons in the case of the earl of Danby in the reign of

Charles II., and is now enacted by the Act of Settlement, that no
pardon under the great seal shall be pleadable to an impeachment by
the commons of Great Britain in Parliament.

2. The court of the *Lord High Steward* of Great Britain is a court
instituted for the trial of peers, indicted for treason or felony, or for
misprision of either.   When such an indictment is found, it is to be
removed by a writ of *certiorari* into the court of the Lord High
Steward, which only has power to determine it; the sovereign in
such a case creating a lord high steward *pro hac vice* by commission
under the great seal; which recites the indictment so found, and
gives his grace power to receive and try it, *secundum legem et con-
suetudinem Angliæ.*   Then, when the indictment is regularly
removed, by *certiorari,* the lord high steward directs a precept to a
serjeant-at-arms, to summon the lords to attend and try the indicted
peer.   This precept was formerly issued to summon only eighteen
or twenty, selected from the body of the peers; then the number
came to be indefinite; and the custom was for the lord high steward
to summon such peers as he thought proper.   And accordingly,
when the Earl of Clarendon fell into disgrace with Charles II.,
there was a design formed to prorogue the parliament, in order to
try him by a select number of peers, it being doubted whether the
whole house could be induced to fall in with the views of the court.
But now, by 7 Will. III. c. 3, all the peers who have a right to sit
and vote in parliament shall be summoned; and every lord appearing, shall vote in the trial of such peer.

3. The court of *Exchequer Chamber* has no original jurisdiction
over crimes or offences, but only upon writs of error, to rectify any
injustice or mistake of the law, committed by,

4. The court of *Queen's Bench,* concerning the nature of which we
partly inquired in the preceding book, and which, we may remember, was divided into a *Crown* side and a *Plea* side.   And on the
crown side, or crown office, it takes cognizance of all criminal causes,
from high treason down to the most trivial misdemeanor or breach
of the peace.   Into this court also indictments from all inferior courts
may be removed by writ of *certiorari,* and tried either at bar, or at
nisi prius, by a jury of the county out of which the indictment is
brought; or by order of the court in the case of certain offenders, at
the Central Criminal Court.   The judges of this court are the supreme
coroners for the kingdom.   And the court itself is the principal court
of criminal jurisdiction known to the laws of England.   For which
reason, by the coming of the court of Queen's Bench into any county,
as it was removed to Oxford on account of the sickness in 1665, all
former commissions of *oyer* and *terminer,* and general gaol delivery,
are at once absorbed and determined *ipso facto,* unless preserved by

special statutes, as in the case of the Central Criminal Court, and the sessions of the peace, held before the justices of Middlesex.

5. The High Court of *Admiralty* is a court not only of civil but also of criminal jurisdiction. It has cognizance of all crimes and offences committed either upon the sea, or on the coasts, out of the body or extent of any English county. But, as this court proceeded without a jury, in a method much conformed to the civil law, the exercise of a criminal jurisdiction there was contrary to the genius of the law of England; inasmuch as a man might be there deprived of his life by the opinion of a single judge, without the judgment of his peers. This was always a great offence to the English nation; and, therefore, in the reign of Henry VI. it was endeavoured to apply a remedy in parliament: which then miscarried for want of the royal assent. However, by a statute of Henry VIII., it was enacted, that these offences should be tried by commissioners of *oyer* and *terminer*, under the great seal; and that the course of proceedings should be according to the law of the land. And this was long the only method of trying marine felonies in the court of Admiralty: the judge of the Admiralty presiding therein, as the lord mayor is the president of the session of *oyer* and *terminer* in London. But this court has now been superseded by others; as all offences formerly triable there are within the jurisdiction of the Central Criminal Court; and the justices of assize have all the powers given to commissioners of *oyer* and *terminer* by the statute of Henry VIII.

These courts may be held in any part of the kingdom, and their jurisdiction extends over crimes that arise throughout the whole of it, from one end to the other.* What follow are also of a general nature, and universally diffused over the nation, but yet are of a local jurisdiction, and confined to particular districts. Of which species are,

6. The courts of *oyer* and *terminer*, and general *gaol delivery*: which are held before the Queen's commissioners twice, and sometimes thrice in every year in every county of the kingdom, except London and Middlesex, wherein they were formerly held eight, and are now held twelve times. I have already observed that what is usually called the *assizes*, the judges sit by virtue of five several authorities: two of which, the commission of *assize* and its attendant jurisdiction of *nisi prius*, are of a civil nature, as was then explained at large; to which I shall now add, that these justices have, by virtue of several statutes, a criminal jurisdiction, also, in certain special cases. The third, which is the commission of the peace, was also treated of in the first book of these commentaries, when we

* The *Court of Chivalry*, before referred to, p. 282, has a criminal as well as a civil jurisdiction; but, as already stated, it is entirely obsolete.

inquired into the office of a justice of the peace. The fourth authority is the commission of *oyer* and *terminer*, to hear and determine all treasons, felonies, and misdemeanors. The words of the commission are, "to inquire, hear, and determine:" so that by virtue of this commission they can only proceed upon an indictment found at the same assizes; for they must first *inquire* by means of the *grand jury* or inquest, before they are empowered to *hear* and *determine* by the help of the petit jury. Therefore they have, besides, fifthly, a commission of general *gaol delivery;* which empowers them to try and deliver every prisoner, who shall be in the gaol when the judges arrive at the circuit town, whenever or before whomsoever indicted, or for whatever crime committed. So that, one way or other, the gaols are in general cleared, and all offenders tried, punished, or delivered, twice, and latterly, in the populous districts, thrice in every year.

7. The court of general *quarter sessions* of the peace is a court that must be held in every county once in every quarter of a year, before two or more justices of the peace, whose jurisdiction by the statute 34 Edw. III. c. 1, extended to the trying and determining all felonies and trespasses whatsoever: though they seldom, if ever, tried any greater offence than small felonies within the benefit of clergy; their commission providing, that if any case of difficulty arises, they shall not proceed to judgment, but in the presence of one of the justices of the courts of King's Bench or Common Pleas, or one of the judges of assize.

The jurisdiction of the Quarter Sessions is now, however, much better defined by the statute 5 & 6 Vict. c. 38, which prohibits the courts from taking cognizance of any charge of treason, murder, blasphemy, or offence against religion; perjury; forgery; wilful fire-raising; bigamy; abduction; concealment of birth; libel; bribery; and other offences of a heinous nature. By other statutes, the quarter sessions have no jurisdiction over the offence of entering into or being in land by night armed, for the purpose of taking game, nor over offences committed by fire, or by explosive or destructive substances.

But there are many offences and particular matters, which by particular statutes belong properly to this jurisdiction, and ought to be prosecuted in this court: as the smaller felonies and misdemeanors against the public or commonwealth, and certain matters rather of a civil than a criminal nature, such as the regulation of weights and measures; questions relating to the settlement of the poor; and appeals against a multitude of orders or convictions, which may be made in petty sessions, within the laws relating to the revenue, the highways, and other matters of a local nature. In

some few of these last-mentioned cases, the parties are entitled to
a jury, but in the great majority of them, whether as appeals or as
applications of an original nature, they are disposed of by the justices; whose orders therein may, for the most part, unless guarded
against by particular statutes, be removed into the court of Queen's
Bench, by writ of *certiorari facias*, and be there either quashed or
confirmed.

The records or rolls of the sessions are committed to the custody
of a special officer denominated the *custos rotulorum*, whose nomination, he being the principal *civil* officer in the county, as the lord
lieutenant is the chief in *military* command, is by the royal sign
manual. To him the nomination of the clerk of the peace belongs;
and this office he is expressly forbidden to sell for money.

In many corporation towns there are quarter sessions kept before
justices of their own, within their respective limits: which have
exactly the same authority as the general quarter sessions of the
county, except in a very few instances: one of the most considerable of which is the matter of appeals for orders of removal of the
poor, which, though they be from the orders of corporation justices,
must be to the sessions of the county, by statute 8 & 9 Will. III.
c. 30. And in all the most important of these towns, this court is
presided over by the *recorder* of the borough, who must be a
barrister of not less than five years' standing, and is immediately
on his appointment *ex-officio* a justice of the peace for the borough.

In both corporations and counties at large there are generally
kept special and *petty sessions*, by a few justices, for despatching
smaller business in the neighbourhood, as for hearing appeals against
poor-rates, licensing alehouses, passing the accounts of the parish
officers, and the like; for which and other objects, counties are
usually divided into districts, under the provisions of various statutes
passed for that purpose. Extensive powers of a similar nature are
vested in the *metropolitan* and other *stipendiary magistrates*; one of
whom may at all times exercise the jurisdiction for which the presence
of two justices is otherwise required. But, from the determination
of all justices in petty sessions an appeal may generally be had to
the next court of quarter sessions; unless, indeed, a special case has
been stated for the opinion of one of the superior courts of common
law; for when this is done an appeal is incompetent.*

8. The court of the *coroner* is also a court of record, to inquire,

* I might mention here as criminal courts, still recognized by the law, the
sheriff's tourn; and also the *court-leet*, or *view of frankpledge*; which were
both courts of record, whose business was to present by jury all crimes whatsoever that happened within their jurisdiction; and not only to present, but
also to punish all trivial misdemeanors, from common nuisances and other

2 A

when any one dies in prison, or comes to a violent or sudden death, by what manner he came to his end. And this he is only entitled to do *super visum corporis;* as we saw in the first book of these commentaries; and I, therefore, only mention his court now, by way of regularity, as among the criminal courts of the nation.*

II. The special courts of criminal jurisdiction are very few in number.†

I speak not here of ecclesiastical courts; which punish spiritual sins, rather than temporal crimes, by penance, contrition, and excommunication, *pro salute animæ;* or, which is looked upon as equivalent to all the rest, by a sum of money to the officers of the courts by way of commutation of penance. I am now speaking of such courts as proceed according to the course of the common law, which is a stranger to such unaccountable barterings of public justice; and of these the most important is,

1. The *Central Criminal Court,* which has jurisdiction to hear and determine all treasons, murders, felonies, and misdemeanors, committed within the city of London and the county of Middlesex, and certain parts of the surrounding counties, and also all offences

---

offences against the peace and public trade, down to eavesdropping, waifs, and irregularities in public commons. But both the tourn and the leet have fallen into total desuetude, and hence it is that their business has for the most part gradually devolved upon the quarter sessions.

* The most inferior criminal court is that of the *clerk of the market*, which is incident to every fair and market in the kingdom, to punish misdemeanors therein, as a court of *pie-poudre* is to determine all disputes relating to private or civil property. The object of this jurisdiction, when in use, was principally the cognizance of weights and measures; but this authority is now vested in the courts of quarter sessions; and the court of the clerk of the market is entirely obsolete.

† A special court of criminal jurisdiction, so long as it existed, was the court of the *lord steward* of the *household*, erected by statute 33 Hen. VIII. c. 12, with jurisdiction over all treasons, murders, bloodshed, and other malicious strikings; whereby blood · was shed within the limits, that is, within two hundred feet from the gate of any of the royal palaces. The form and solemnity of the process, particularly with regard to the execution of the sentence for cutting off the hand, which was formerly part of the punishment for shedding blood in the king's court, are very minutely set forth in the statute, and the several offices of the servants of the household in and about such execution are described; from the serjeant of the wood-yard, who furnishes the chopping-block, to the serjeant farrier, who brings hot irons to sear the stump. But the act of Hen. VIII. having been repealed by 9 Geo. IV. c. 31, so far as relates to the punishment of manslaughter and malicious striking, whereby blood shall be shed, this court, which had long before fallen into entire desuetude, may now be considered to have ceased to exist.

committed within the jurisdiction of the Admiralty. This court has superseded one formerly held for London and Middlesex, under a charter granted by Henry I. to the city of London, and confirmed by many subsequent charters of our early kings.

2. As in the preceding book I mentioned the courts of the two universities, or their chancellors' courts, for the redress of civil injuries, it will not be improper now to add a short word concerning the jurisdiction of their criminal courts. The chancellors' courts have authority to determine all causes of property, wherein a privileged person is one of the parties, except only causes of freehold. They may also try all criminal offences or misdemeanors under the degree of treason, felony, or mayhem; the trial of these crimes being reserved for another court, namely, the court of the *lord high steward* of the university.

When therefore an indictment is found at the assizes, or elsewhere, against any scholar of any university, or other privileged person, the vice-chancellor may claim the cognizance of it; and then it comes to be tried in the high steward's court. But the indictment must first be found by a grand jury, and then the cognizance claimed: for the high steward cannot proceed originally *ad inquirendum*, but only, after inquest in the common law courts, *ad audiendum et determinandum*. When the cognizance is allowed, if the offence be *inter minora crimina*, or a misdemeanor only, it is tried in the chancellor's court by the ordinary judge. But if it be for treason, felony, or mayhem, it is then, and then only, to be determined before the high steward, under a special commission of the crown to try the same. If execution be necessary to be awarded, in consequence of finding the party guilty, the sheriff executes the university process; to which he is annually bound by an oath.

CHAPTER XX.

OF SUMMARY CONVICTIONS.

WE are next to consider the proceedings in our courts of criminal jurisdiction; which are of two kinds; *summary* and *regular:* of the former of which I shall briefly speak, before I describe the latter, which will require a more particular examination.

By a *summary* proceeding I mean principally such as is directed by several acts of parliament, for the common law is a stranger to it, unless in the case of contempts, for the conviction of offenders, and the inflicting of certain penalties created by those acts of parliament. In these there is no intervention of a jury, but the party accused is acquitted or condemned by the suffrage of such person only as the statute has appointed for his judge.

I. Of this summary nature are all trials of offences and frauds contrary to the laws of the *excise*, and other branches of the *revenue :* which are to be inquired into and determined by the commissioners of the respective departments, or by justices of the peace in the country ; officers, who are all of them appointed and removable at the discretion of the crown.

II. Another branch of summary proceedings is that before *justices of the peace*, in order to inflict divers petty pecuniary mulcts, and corporal penalties, denounced by act of parliament for many disorderly offences ; such as petty trespasses, assaults, swearing, drunkenness, vagrancy, and others.

In all these cases, when an *information* is laid before a justice that any person has committed an offence for which he is liable to be punished, or a *complaint* is made, upon which the justice has authority to make any order, a *summons* is to be issued ; which must be *served* on the person to whom it is directed ; the constable or other person by whom such service is effected attending at the return of the summons, to *prove the service* thereof, if necessary. If the person summoned does not appear, a *warrant* may be issued for his apprehension. In the case of an information being laid, and substantiated by proper evidence, a warrant may be issued in the first instance ; and upon this warrant, which may be executed in any other district than that in which it is issued, after being *backed* or indorsed by a justice of that district, the person charged may be taken, and brought before the justices ; who have authority to issue summonses, and to compel the attendance, at the hearing, of *witnesses* for the prosecutor, complainant, or defendant, as the case may be.

The information or complaint must then be *heard* and adjudicated upon by the justices, according to the ordinary course of legal procedure, the complainant *proving his case*, the defendant making his answer, and the complainant examining witnesses in *reply*, if need be ; the room in which all this is transacted being deemed *an open court*, to which the public are, therefore, entitled to have free access.

This is, in general, the method of summary proceedings before justices ; but, in many cases, they must have recourse to the particular statutes which create the offence or inflict the punishment, and which usually chalk out the method by which offenders are to be convicted. Otherwise the offences fall under the general rule, and can only be prosecuted by indictment or information at the common law.

Thus, as regards *juvenile offenders*, that is, persons whose age does not exceed *sixteen years*, the justices may convict summarily in any case where an offence is by law deemed to be *simple larceny ;* and pass a sentence not exceeding three months, or impose a fine not exceeding three pounds. They have power, if they think it not expedient to inflict any punishment, to dismiss the accused, even if the offence be proved. And he, on the other hand, may object to the case being summarily disposed of, and insist on being sent for trial by a jury.

In certain other cases, the justices may, *with the assent of the accused,* hear and determine the charge in a summary way; and pass a sentence of three months' imprisonment, with hard labour. And in another class of cases may *punish,* where the accused *confesses* the charge, by an imprisonment not exceeding *six* months. But as hardened offenders would, in either case, inevitably embrace such an opportunity of escaping with a comparatively light punishment, it is wisely provided, that if it appear that the accused has been previously convicted of felony, the justices shall have no jurisdiction so to dispose of the case; but it must be sent to trial by the ordinary tribunals.

III. To this head of summary proceedings may also be properly referred the method, immemorially used by the superior courts of justice, of punishing contempts by *attachment,* and the subsequent proceedings thereon.

The contempts that are thus punished are either *direct,* which openly insult or resist the powers of the courts, or the persons of the judges who preside there; or else are *consequential,* which, without such gross insolence or direct opposition, plainly tend to create a disregard of their authority. The principal instances, of either sort, that have been usually punishable by attachment, are chiefly of the following kinds :—1. Those committed by inferior judges and magistrates: as by proceeding in a cause after it is put a stop to or removed by writ of prohibition, *certiorari,* or the like. 2. Those committed by sheriffs, bailiffs, gaolers, and other officers of the court: by abusing the process of the law, or deceiving the parties, by any act of oppression, or culpable neglect of duty. 3. Those committed by attorneys, who are officers of the courts: by fraud and corruption, injustice to their clients, or other dishonest practice. 4. Those committed by jurymen in the discharge of their office: as making default, when summoned; refusing to be sworn; and other misbehaviours of a similar kind: but not in the mere exercise of their judicial capacities, as by giving a false or erroneous verdict. 5. Those committed by witnesses: by making default when summoned, refusing to be sworn or examined, or prevaricating in their evidence. 6. Those committed by the parties to a suit: as by disobedience to any rule or order; by non-payment of costs; or by non-observance of awards. 7. Those committed by other persons: as by rude and contumelious behaviour in court; by disobeying the queen's writ, or the rules or process of the court; by speaking or writing contemptuously of the court, or of the judges acting in their judicial capacity; or by printing false accounts, or even true ones, in defiance of the prohibition of the court, of causes then depending in judgment.

The process of attachment, for these and the like contempts, must necessarily be as ancient as the laws themselves. For laws, without a competent authority to secure their administration from disobedience and contempt, would be vain and nugatory. A power therefore in the superior courts of justice to suppress such contempts, by an immediate attachment of the offender, results from the first principles of judicial establishments, and must be an inseparable attendant upon every superior tribunal.

I shall, therefore, only for the present observe, that the process by attachment is as ancient as the law itself; it has in modern times been recognised, approved, and confirmed by the decisions of our courts, and by many acts of parliament, and thus by long and immemorial usage is now become part of the law of the land.

CHAPTER XXI.

OF ARRESTS.

1. By warrant.—2. By an officer without warrant.—3. By private persons without warrant.—By hue and cry

WE come now to the *regular* method of proceeding in the courts of criminal jurisdiction; which may be distributed under eleven general heads; viz., 1. Arrest; 2. Commitment, and bail; 3. Prosecution; 4. Process; 5. Arraignment, and its incidents; 6. Plea, and issue; 7. Trial, and conviction; 8. Judgment, and its consequences; 9. Reversal of judgment; 10. Reprieve, or pardon; 11. Execution;—all which will be discussed in the subsequent part of this book.

First, then, of an *arrest*; which is the apprehending or restraining of the person of an alleged delinquent, in order that he may be forth-coming to answer an alleged or suspected crime; and which may be made four ways: 1. By warrant; 2. By an officer without warrant; 3. By a private person also without warrant; 4. By a hue and cry.

1. A warrant may be granted in extraordinary cases by the privy council, or secretaries of state; but ordinarily by justices of the peace. This they may do in any case where they have a jurisdiction over the offence, in order to compel the person accused to appear before them; for it would be absurd to give them power to ex-amine an offender, unless they had also a power to compel him to attend and submit to such examination. And this extends un-doubtedly to all treasons, felonies, and breaches of the peace; and also to all such offences as they have power to punish by statute.

Upon an *information*, therefore, or a *complaint*, in writing and upon oath, a justice may issue his *warrant* to apprehend the person charged or suspected, and cause him to be brought before him or any other justice or justices, to answer the charge and be dealt with according to law. Instead of a warrant, the justice may, in his dis-cretion, and on a mere charge or complaint, without a written infor-mation or oath, issue a *summons* in the first instance; and if that be disobeyed by the person charged, then a warrant for his apprehen-sion.

This warrant ought to be under the hand and seal of the justice, and should set forth the time and place of making, and the cause for which it is made. A *general* warrant to apprehend all persons sus-pected, without naming or particularly describing any person in special, is illegal and void for its uncertainty; for it is the duty of the magistrate, and ought not to be left to the officer, to judge of the ground of suspicion. And a warrant to apprehend all persons, guilty of a crime therein specified, is no legal warrant: for the point, upon which its authority rests, is a fact to be decided on a subse-quent trial; namely, whether the person apprehended thereupon be really guilty or not. It is therefore, in fact, *no* warrant at all; for it will not justify the officer who acts under it: whereas a warrant, properly penned, even though the magistrate who issues it should exceed his jurisdiction, will indemnify the officer who executes the same ministerially.

When a warrant is received by the officer, he is bound to execute it, as far as the jurisdiction of the magistrate and himself extends. A warrant from the chief or other justice of the court of Queen's Bench extends all over the kingdom; and is *teste'd*, or *dated*, *Eng-land*; not *Oxfordshire*, *Berks*, or other particular county. But the warrant of a justice of the peace in one county, as Yorkshire, must, except in the case of fresh pursuit, be *backed*, that is, signed by a justice of the peace in another, as Middlesex, before it can be executed there.

A warrant may be granted on a Sunday, as well as on any other day; and need not be made returnable at any particular *time*, for it remains in force until it is executed; and the person against whom it is issued may be apprehended in the night as well as the day, and on a Sunday; for though the statute 29 Car. II. c. 7, s. 6, prohibits arrests on Sundays, it excepts the cases of treason, felonies, and breaches of the peace.

2. Arrests by *officers, without warrant*, may be executed, 1. By a justice of peace, who may himself apprehend, or cause to be apprehended, by word only, any person committing a felony or breach of the peace in his presence. 2. The sheriff; and, 3. The coroner, may apprehend any felon within the county without warrant. 4. The constable may, without warrant, arrest any one for a breach of the peace committed in his view, and carry him before a justice; and, in case of felony actually committed, or a dangerous wounding, whereby felony is like to ensue, he may upon probable suspicion arrest the felon; and for that purpose is authorized, as upon a warrant, to break open doors, and even to kill the felon, if he cannot otherwise be taken; and if he be killed in attempting such arrest, it is murder in all concerned. 5. Watchmen, either those appointed by the statute of Winchester, 13 Edw. I. c. 4, to keep watch and ward in all towns from sunsetting to sunrising, or beadles, or such as are mere assistants to the constable, may *virtute officii* arrest all offenders, and particularly night-walkers, and commit them to custody till the morning.

3. Any private person, and *à fortiori* a peace-officer, that is present when any felony is committed, is bound to arrest the felon, on pain of fine and imprisonment, if he escapes through the negligence of the standers-by. And they may justify breaking open doors upon following such felon; and if *they kill him*, provided he cannot be otherwise taken, it is justifiable; though if *they are killed* in endeavouring to make such arrest, it is murder.

Upon probable suspicion also a private person may arrest the felon, or other person so suspected; but he does so at his own peril. A *constable* having reasonable ground to suspect that a felony has been committed, is authorized to detain the party suspected, until inquiry can be made by the proper authorities; in order to justify a *private individual* in causing the imprisonment of any one, he must not only make out a *reasonable* ground of suspicion, but he must prove that a felony has actually been committed. A private individual may, however, apprehend any person found *by night*, *i. e.*, between nine p.m. and six a.m., committing an indictable offence, or armed with an offensive weapon, with intent to break into any dwelling-house, or having in his possession, without lawful excuse, any implement of housebreaking, or having his face blackened or otherwise disguised, or *in* any dwelling-house, in either of these cases with intent to commit felony. And any person to whom any property is offered to be sold, pawned, or delivered, if he has reasonable cause to suspect that it has been *stolen*, is authorized, and if in his power is required, to apprehend, and forthwith to take before a justice the party offering the same, together with such property, to be dealt with according to law. A private person cannot, upon probable suspicion merely, justify breaking open doors to arrest a felon or other suspected person ; and if either party kill the other in the attempt, it is manslaughter, and no more. It is no more, because there is no malicious design to kill; but it amounts to so much, because it would be of most pernicious consequence, if, under pretence of suspecting felony, any private person might break open a house, or kill another ; and also because such arrest upon suspicion is barely *permitted* by the law, and not *enjoined*, as in the case of those who are present when a felony is committed.

4. There is yet another species of arrest, wherein both officers and private men are concerned, and that is, upon a *hue* and *cry* raised upon a felony committed. A hue, from *huer*, to shout, and cry, *hutesium et clamor*, is the old common law process of pursuing, with horn and with voice, all felons, and such as have dangerously wounded another. That it might more effectually be made, the hundred was bound by the statute of Winchester, c. 3, to answer for all robberies therein committed unless they took the felon, which was the foundation of an *action against the hundred*, in case of any loss by robbery; and the whole vill or district is still in strictness liable to be amerced, according to the law of Alfred, if any felony be committed therein and the felon escapes. An institution which has long prevailed in many of the Eastern countries, and was in part introduced even into the Mogul Empire, about the beginning of the seventeenth century; which is said to have effectually delivered that vast territory from the plague of robbers, by making in some places the villages, in others the officers of justice, responsible for all the robberies committed within their respective districts. If, however, a man wantonly or maliciously raises a hue and cry, without cause, he shall be severely punished, as a disturber of the public peace.

CHAPTER XXII.

OF COMMITMENT AND BAIL.

Examination of the accused—the depositions—procedure before committal—Commitment and bail.

WHEN a delinquent is arrested, he ought to be carried before a justice of the peace, who is bound immediately to *examine* the circumstances of the crime alleged : and to this end, before committing the accused person to prison for trial, or admitting him to bail, is in his presence to take the statements on oath, or affirmation, of those who know the facts of the case ; these statements, when signed and authenticated by the justice, constituting what are termed the *depositions*. The person accused has a right to question the witnesses, and is usually allowed legal assistance ; but this is in the discretion of the magistrate, for the place where the examination takes place is not an open court ; and the public may be excluded, if such a course will conduce to the ends of justice.

If, from the absence of witnesses, or other reasonable cause, it becomes necessary or advisable to adjourn the examination, this may be done, the accused person being remanded to prison, or allowed to go at large, upon his recognizance, at the discretion of the magistrate.

After the examination of the witnesses for the prosecution has been completed, the depositions are read over to the accused, and he is then asked whether he wishes to say anything in answer to the charge, being warned that he is not obliged to do so, but that whatever he does say will be taken down in writing, and may be given in evidence against him upon the trial. If it appear that some inducement or threat has previously been held out to him, the magistrate should further give him clearly to understand, that he has nothing to hope from any promise of favour held out, and nothing to fear from any threat made to him, as an inducement to make any admission or confession of his guilt ; but that whatever he shall then say may be given in evidence, notwithstanding any such promise or threat.

Whatever he then says in answer, is to be taken down in writing, and after being read over to him, to be signed by the magistrate, and transmitted with the depositions to the court by which he is to be tried.

If, however, upon this inquiry the justice is of opinion that the evidence is not sufficient to put the accused party upon his trial, he may forthwith, if in custody, be discharged. Otherwise, or if the evidence given raise a strong or probable presumption of his guilt, he must either be committed to prison, or give bail : that is, put in securities for his appearance, to answer the charge against him. This commitment, therefore, being only for safe custody, wherever bail will answer the same intention, as in most of the inferior crimes, it ought to be taken. Indeed, to refuse or delay to bail any person bailable, is an offence against the liberty of the subject, in any magistrate, by the common law, as well as by the *Habeas Corpus* Act. And, lest the intention of the law should be frustrated, by justices requiring bail to a greater amount than the nature of the case demands, it is expressly declared by statute 1 Will. & Mary, st. 2, c. 1, that excessive bail ought not to be required. But in felonies and other offences of a serious nature, no bail can be a security equivalent to the actual custody of the person. For what is there that a man may not be induced to forfeit to save his own life? and what satisfaction or indemnity is it to the public to seize the effects of them who have bailed a murderer, if the murderer himself be suffered to escape with impunity? Yet the court of Queen's Bench, or any judge thereof in vacation, may bail for any crime whatever, be it treason, murder, or any other offence, according to the circumstance of the case. And herein the wisdom of the law is very manifest. To allow bail to be taken commonly for such enormous crimes would greatly tend to elude the public justice : and yet there are cases, though they rarely happen, in which it would be hard and unjust to confine a man in prison, though accused even of the greatest offence. The law therefore provides one court, which has a discretionary power of bailing in any case : except only, even to this high jurisdiction, and of course to all inferior ones, such persons as are committed by either house of parliament, so long as the session lasts : or such as are committed for contempts by any of the superior courts of justice.

If the offence be not bailable, or the party cannot find bail, he is to be committed to gaol, there to abide till delivered by due course of law; but whether held to bail or committed to prison, in order to trial, he is entitled to have furnished to him, on demand, copies of the depositions on which he is held to bail or committed; and in either case the prosecutor and witnesses may be bound over in recognizances to appear at the trial in order to prosecute or give evidence. The original information, if any; the depositions; any recognizances taken by the justices; the statement, if any, made by the accused; and his recognizances, if he has been released on bail, must all be delivered to the proper officer on or before the first day of the assizes or sessions to which the accused is sent for trial.

CHAPTER XXIII.

OF THE SEVERAL MODES OF PROSECUTION.

I. Presentment—Inquest of office.——II. Indictment by a grand jury.——
III. Information, *ex officio*—Criminal information.

THE next step towards the punishment of offenders is their prosecution, or formal accusation; which is either upon a previous finding of the fact by an inquest or grand jury, or without such
previous finding. The former is either by *presentment* or
indictment.

I. A *presentment* is a very comprehensive term; including not
only presentments properly so called, but also inquisitions of office
and indictments by a grand jury. Properly speaking, it is the
notice taken by a grand jury of any offence from their own knowledge or observation, without any indictment laid before them at
the suit of the crown; as the presentment of a nuisance, a libel, and
the like; upon which the officer of the court must afterwards frame
an indictment, before the party presented can be put to answer it.
An *inquisition of office* is the act of a jury summoned by the
proper officer to inquire of matters relating to the crown, upon evidence laid before them. Such inquisitions may be afterwards
traversed and examined; as particularly the coroner's inquisition of
the death of a man, when it finds any one guilty of homicide, for
in such cases the offender so presented must be arraigned upon this
inquisition, and may dispute the truth of it; which brings it to a
kind of indictment, the most usual and effectual means of prosc-
cution, and into which we will therefore inquire a little more
minutely.

II. An *indictment* is a written accusation of one or more persons
of a crime or misdemeanor, preferred to, and presented upon oath
by, a grand jury. To this end the sheriff of every county is bound
to return to every session of the peace, and every commission of
oyer and *terminer*, and of general gaol delivery, twenty-four good
and lawful men of the county, having the qualification required by
the law, to inquire, present, do, and execute all those things which,
on the part of the sovereign, shall then and there be commanded
them. As many as appear upon this panel are sworn upon the
grand jury, to the amount of twelve at the least, and not more than

twenty-three ; that twelve may be a majority.   Which number, as well as the constitution itself, we find exactly described so early as the laws of King Ethelred.

This *grand jury*, having chosen their foreman, are next instructed in the articles of their inquiry by a *charge* from the judge who presides upon the bench.   They then withdraw to receive indictments, which are preferred to them in the name of the sovereign, but at the suit of any private prosecutor ; and they are only to hear evidence on behalf of the prosecution ; for the finding of an indictment is only in the nature of an inquiry or accusation, which is afterwards to be tried and determined ; and the grand jury are only to inquire upon their oaths whether there be sufficient cause to call upon the party to answer it.

When the grand jury have heard the evidence, if they think it a groundless accusation, they used formerly to indorse on the back of the bill, " *ignoramus ;*" or, we know nothing of it ; intimating, that though the facts might possibly be true, that truth did not appear to them : but now they assert in English, more absolutely, " not a true bill ;" or, which is the better way, " not found ;" and then the party is discharged without further answer.   But a fresh bill may afterwards be preferred to a subsequent grand jury.   If they are satisfied of the truth of the accusation, they then indorse upon it, " a true bill ;" anciently, " *billa vera.*"   The indictment is then said to be *found*, and the party stands indicted.   But to find a bill there must at least twelve of the jury agree : for so tender is the law of England of the lives of the subjects, that no man can be convicted, upon an indictment, at the suit of the crown of any offence, unless by the unanimous voice of twenty-four of his equals and neighbours : that is, by twelve at least of the grand jury, in the first place, assenting to the accusation ; and afterwards, by the whole petit jury, of twelve more, finding him guilty, upon his trial. But if twelve of the grand jury assent, it is a good presentment, though some of the rest disagree.   And the indictment, when so found, is publicly delivered into court.

III. The other method of prosecution is, without any previous finding by a jury, to fix the authoritative stamp of verisimilitude upon the accusation.   Such, by the common law, was when a thief was taken *with the mainour*, that is, with the thing stolen upon him *in manu.*   For he might, when so detected *flagrante delicto*, be brought into court, arraigned, and tried, without indictment ; as by the Danish law he might be taken and hanged upon the spot, without accusation or trial.   But this proceeding was taken away by several statutes in the reign of Edward III., so that the only species of proceeding at the suit of the crown, without a previous indictment or presentment by a grand jury, now seems to be that of *information.*

Informations, in criminal cases, are of two kinds: first, those filed *ex officio* by the attorney-general; secondly, those in which, though the crown is the nominal prosecutor, yet it is at the relation of some private person; the latter being filed by the master of the Crown-office, who is for this purpose the standing officer of the public.

The objects of an *ex officio* information are properly such enormous misdemeanors as peculiarly tend to disturb or endanger the government; the law giving to the crown, in such cases, the power of an immediate prosecution, without waiting for any previous application to any other tribunal. The objects of the other species, or *criminal informations* as they are usually called, are any gross and notorious misdemeanors, such as libels, not tending to disturb the government, but which, on account of their pernicious example, deserve public animadversion. Either species of information, when filed, must be tried by a petit jury of the county where the offence arises; after which, if the defendant be found guilty, the court must be resorted to for his punishment.

There can be no doubt but that this mode of prosecution is as ancient as the common law itself.* For as the sovereign was bound to prosecute, or at least to lend the sanction of his name to a prosecutor, whenever a grand jury informed him that there was a sufficient ground for instituting a criminal suit: so, when these his immediate officers were otherwise sufficiently assured that a man had committed a gross misdemeanor, they were at liberty to convey that information to the court of King's Bench, and to carry on the prosecution in the name of the crown. But these informations are confined by the constitutional law to mere misdemeanors only: for wherever any *felonious* offence is charged, the same law requires that the accusation be warranted by the oath of twelve men, before the party shall be put to answer it. And to prevent any oppressive use of this method of proceeding by a private subject, the statute 4 & 5 W. & M. c. 18, expressly enacts that the clerk of the crown shall not file any criminal information without an express direction from the court, which can only be obtained on an application by *counsel,* founded upon affidavit; and that every relator shall give security not only to prosecute the information with effect, but also to pay costs to the defendant in case he be acquitted thereon; and,

* This was the regular mode of prosecuting delinquents in the *Star Chamber;* where, however, there was no jury, the members present and constituting the court being the sole judges alike of the *law,* the *fact,* and the *penalty.*

at all events, to pay costs, unless the information shall be tried within a year after issue joined.

These are the only methods of prosecution, which can now be resorted to for the punishment of offences, of which that by indictment is the most general.* I shall therefore confine my subsequent observations principally to this method of prosecution; remarking by the way the most material variations that may arise from the method of proceeding by information.

CHAPTER XXIV.

OF PROCESS UPON AN INDICTMENT.

Bench Warrant—*Habeas Corpus—Capias*—Outlawry—*Certiorari.*

WE have hitherto supposed the offender to be in custody before the finding of the indictment; in which case he is immediately to be arraigned thereon. But if he has fled, or secretes himself; or has not been bound over to appear at the assizes or sessions, still an indictment may be preferred against him in his absence; since, were he present, he could not be heard before the grand jury against it. And, if it be found, then *process* must issue to bring him into court; for the indictment cannot be tried until he personally appears.

Any court before which an indictment is found may issue a *bench warrant* for arresting the party charged; but the more usual course is to apply to a justice of the peace; who, upon production of a certificate by the clerk of the court of the indictment having been found, is bound to issue his warrant for the apprehension of the alleged delinquent, that he may be brought before him, to be dealt with according to law; that is, to be committed for trial or admitted to bail as in ordinary cases. If the person charged is already in prison for some other offence, the justice issues his warrant for his detention until he is removed for trial by writ of *habeas corpus*, which is then the proper course to be adopted.

If the accused is known to have fled, so that he cannot be arrested, and the prosecutor desires to proceed to outlawry, he must resort to the ancient and regular process of the court. This is, first, a writ of *venire facias*, in the nature of a summons to appear, enforced, if necessary, by a *distress infinite* till he do appear. But

* There was formerly another method of prosecution, at the suit of the subject called an *appeal;* for a short account of which, I must refer the reader to the Appendix.

if he has no lands, then a writ of *capias* issues; and, if need be, a second and third, called an *alias* and a *pluries capias*.

After the several writs of *venire facias, distringas,* and *capias* have issued without any effect, the offender shall be put in the *exigent* in order to his outlawry; that is, he shall be exacted, proclaimed, or required to surrender, at five county courts; and if he be returned *quinto exactus,* and does not appear at the fifth exaction or requisition, then he is adjudged to be *outlawed,* or put out of the protection of the law; so that he is incapable of taking the benefit of it in any respect, either by bringing actions or otherwise. The punishment for outlawries upon indictments for misdemeanors is the same as for outlawries upon civil actions, viz., forfeiture of goods and chattels. But an outlawry in treason or felony amounts to a conviction and attainder of the offence, as if the offender had been found guilty. But such outlawry may be reversed by writ of error; the proceedings therein being, as it is fit they should be, exceedingly nice and circumstantial; and, if any single minute point be omitted or misconducted, the whole outlawry is illegal, and may be reversed :* upon which reversal the party accused is admitted to plead to, and defend himself against, the indictment.

Thus much for process to bring in the offender after indictment found; during which stage of the prosecution it is that writs of *certiorari facias* are usually had, though they may be had at any time before trial, unless taken away by statute, to certify and remove the indictment, with all the proceedings thereon, from any inferior court of criminal jurisdiction into the court of Queen's Bench; which is the sovereign ordinary court of justice in causes criminal. And this is frequently done; either, 1. To determine the validity of the indictment; and to quash or confirm it as there is cause: or, 2. Where it is surmised that a partial or insufficient trial will be had in the court below; or, 3. In order to plead the royal pardon in the Queen's Bench: or, 4. To outlaw the offender in those counties or places where the process of the inferior court will not reach him. Such writ of *certiorari,* when issued, supersedes the jurisdiction of the inferior court, and makes all subsequent proceedings therein entirely erroneous and illegal; unless the court of Queen's Bench remands the record to the court below, to be there tried and determined.

At this stage of prosecution also it is that indictments found by the grand jury against a peer must be certified and transmitted into the court of parliament, or into that of the lord high steward; and

* In *Tynte* v. *Reginam,* 7 Q. B. 216, a judgment of outlawry, pronounced in 1729, was reversed after the lapse of 116 years.

that, in places of exclusive jurisdiction, as the two universities, indictments must be delivered, upon claim of cognizance, to the courts therein established, to be there respectively tried and determined.

CHAPTER XXV.

OF ARRAIGNMENT, AND ITS INCIDENTS.

Arraignment—Its incidents—Standing mute—*Peine forte et dure*—The Rack—Entering plea of " not guilty"—Confession.

WHEN the offender either appears voluntarily to an indictment, or is brought in to answer it in the proper court, he is immediately to be *arraigned* thereon ; which is nothing else but to call the prisoner to the bar of the court, to answer the matter charged upon him in the indictment. When he is brought to the bar, the indictment is to be read to him distinctly in the English tongue, which was law, even while all other proceedings were in Latin, that he may fully understand his charge. After which it is to be demanded of him, whether he be *guilty* of the crime whereof he stands indicted, or *not guilty*.

When thus arraigned, he either *stands mute*, or *confesses* the fact ; which circumstances we may call *incidents* to the arraignment ; or else he *pleads* to the indictment, which is to be considered as the next stage of the proceedings. But, first, let us observe these incidents to the arraignment, of standing mute, or confession.

I. Regularly a prisoner is said to stand mute, when, being arraigned for treason or felony, he either, 1. Makes no answer at all ; or 2. Answers foreign to the purpose, or with such matter as is not allowable ; and will not answer otherwise.

If he says nothing, the court ought *ex officio* to impanel a jury to inquire whether he stands obstinately mute, or whether he be dumb *ex visitatione Dei*. If the latter appears to be the case, the judges of the court, who are to be of counsel for the prisoner, and to see that he has law and justice, shall proceed to the trial, and examine all points as if he had pleaded not guilty.

Formerly, if he were found to be obstinately mute, then, if it were on an indictment of high treason, standing mute was equivalent to a conviction, and he received the same judgment and execution. And as in this the highest crime, so also in the lowest species of felony, viz., in petit larceny, and in all misdemeanors, standing mute was always equivalent to conviction. But upon indictments for other felonies, the prisoner was not, by the ancient law, looked upon as convicted, so as to receive judgment for the felony; but should, for his obstinacy, receive the terrible sentence of *peine forte et dure*. Before this was pronounced, however, the prisoner had not only *trina admonitio*, but also a respite of a few hours, and the sentence was distinctly read to him, that he might know his danger; and, after all, if he continued obstinate, and his offence was clergyable, he had the benefit of his clergy allowed him, even though he was too stubborn to pray it. Thus tender was the law of inflicting this dreadful punishment; but if no other means could prevail, and the prisoner continued stubbornly mute, the judgment was then given against him without any distinction of sex or degree. A judgment, which was purposely ordained to be exquisitely severe, that by that very means it might rarely be put in execution.

The rack, or question, to extort a confession from criminals, is a practice of a different nature; *this* having been only used to compel a man to put himself upon his trial; *that* being a species of trial in itself. And the trial by rack is utterly unknown to the law of England; though once, when the Dukes of Exeter and Suffolk, and other ministers of Henry VI., had laid a design to introduce the civil law into this kingdom as the rule of government, for a beginning thereof they erected a rack for torture; which was called in derision the Duke of Exeter's Daughter, and still remains in the Tower of London; where it was occasionally used as an engine of state, not of law, more than once in the reign of Queen Elizabeth. But when, upon the assassination of Villiers Duke of Buckingham by Felton, it was proposed in the privy council to put the assassin to the rack, in order to discover his accomplices; the judges, being consulted, declared unanimously, to their own honour and the honour of the English law, that no such proceeding was allowable by the laws of England.

To return to the *peine forte et dure*, which was the English judgment for standing mute; it was that the prisoner be remanded to prison, and put in a low, dark chamber, and there be laid on his back on the bare floor, naked, unless where decency forbids: that there be placed upon his body as great a weight of iron as he could bear, and more; that he have no sustenance, save only, on the first day, three morsels of the worst bread; and, on the second day, three draughts of standing water, that should be nearest to the prison-door; and in this situation this should be alternately his daily diet *till he died*, or, as anciently the judgment ran, *till he answered*.

This punishment seems to have been introduced by the statute

3 Edw. I. c. 12, which directs such persons " as will not put them-
" selves upon inquests of felonies before the judges at the suit of
" the king, to be put into hard and strong prison, *soient mys en la
" prisone forte en dure,* as those which refuse to be at the common
" law of the land." And, at first, the form of the judgment appears
to have been only a very strait confinement in prison, with hardly
any degree of sustenance. The practice of loading him with
weights, or *pressing him to death,* whence we have still in Newgate
what is called the *press yard,* seems to have been gradually introduced between 31 Edw. III. and 8 Hen. IV., at which last period
it first appears upon our books; being intended as a species of
mercy to the delinquent, by delivering him the sooner from his
torment: and hence, also, it was that the duration of the penance
was then altered; and instead of continuing *till he answered,* it was
directed to continue *till he died.*

The uncertainty of its origin, the doubts that were conceived of
its legality, and the repugnance of its theory, for it rarely was
carried into practice, to the humanity of the laws of England, all
concurred to require a legislative abolition of this cruel process, and
a restitution of the ancient common law; whereby the standing
mute in felony, as well as in treason and in trespass, amounted to a
confession of the charge. But this change did not take place till
the reign of Geo. III.,* when it was enacted that every person who,

* If the corruption of the blood, and the consequent escheat in felony had
been removed, the judgment of *peine forte et dure* might perhaps have still
innocently remained, as a monument of the savage rapacity with which the
lordly tyrants of feudal antiquity hunted after escheats and forfeitures; since
no one would ever have been tempted to undergo such a horrid alternative.
For the law was, that by standing mute, and suffering this heavy penance,
the judgment, and of course the corruption of the blood and escheat of the
lands, were saved in felony and petit treason, though not the forfeiture of the
goods; and therefore this lingering punishment was probably introduced, in
order to extort a plea: without which it was held that no judgment of death
could be given, and so the lord lost his escheat. We find acco.dingly in our
legal history, numerous instances of persons who have had resolution and
patience to undergo so perilous a death in order to benefit their heirs by preventing a forfeiture of their estates. There is a memorable story of an ancestor of an ancient family in the north of England. In a fit of jealousy he
killed his wife, and put to death his children who were at home, by throwing
them from the battlements of his castle; and proceeding with an intent to
destroy his only remaining child, an infant, nursed at a farm-house at some
distance, he was first stopt by a storm of thunder and lightning. This
awakened in his breast the compunctions of conscience. He desisted from his
purpose, and having surrendered himself to justice, in order to secure his
estates to this child, he had the resolution to die under the dreadful judgment
of *peine forte et dure.*

being arraigned for felony or piracy, should stand mute, should be convicted of the same; and the same judgment and execution be thereupon awarded, as if the person had been convicted by verdict or confession.* The adoption of a more humane rule was reserved for a subsequent generation; for now, by statute 7 & 8 Geo. IV. c. 28, if any person shall stand mute of malice, or will not answer directly to the indictment, the court may order a plea of " not guilty," to be entered, on which the trial may proceed, a course, it may be added, which is now invariably adopted.

II. The other incident to arraignment, exclusive of the plea, is the prisoner's actual *confession* of the indictment. Upon a simple and plain confession, the court has nothing to do but to award judgment: but it is usually very backward in receiving and recording such confession, especially in capital felonies, out of tenderness to the life of the subject, and will generally advise the prisoner to retract it, and plead to the indictment.

CHAPTER XXVI.

OF PLEA AND ISSUE.

Plea to the jurisdiction — Demurrer — Plea in abatement—Special pleas in bar; *auterfois acquit; auterfois convict; auterfois attaint;* and pardon— General issue—Not guilty.

THE plea of the prisoner, if he does not confess or stand mute, is either, 1. A plea to the jurisdiction; 2. A demurrer; 3. A plea in abatement; 4. A special plea in bar; or, 5. The general issue.†

I. A plea to the *jurisdiction* is where an indictment is taken before a court that has no cognizance of the offence. If, for example, a man be indicted for a rape at the quarter-sessions, he may except to the jurisdiction of the court without answering to

* Two instances have occurred of persons who refused to plead being condemned and executed; one at the Old Bailey for *murder*, in 1777; the other for *burglary*, at the summer assizes at Wells, in 1792.

† Anciently there was another plea, that of *sanctuary*, whereby, if a person accused of any crime, except treason, wherein the Crown, and sacrilege, wherein the Church, was too nearly concerned, had fled to any church, or churchyard, and within forty days after confessed his guilt and abjured the realm (see *ante*, page 19), he saved his life; but was nevertheless attainted, and forfeited all his goods and chattels. The privilege of sanctuary was taken away in the reign of James I.

the crime alleged. But this plea is rarely resorted to, as the defendant may take advantage of this under the general issue; or if the objection appear on the record, he may demur, move in arrest of judgment, or bring a writ of error. If the offence was committed within its jurisdiction, but the court has not cognizance of it, the defendant may either demur, or the Queen's Bench, upon the indictment, being removed by *certiorari*, will quash it.

II. A demurrer is incident to criminal cases, as well as civil, when the fact as alleged is allowed to be true, but the prisoner joins issue upon some point of law in the indictment, by which he insists that the fact, as stated, is no felony, or whatever the crime is alleged to be. Thus, if a man be indicted for *feloniously* stealing a cat, he may demur to the indictment; denying it to be felony, though he confesses the act of taking it. And if, on demurrer, the point of law be adjudged *against* him, he shall have judgment and execution, as if convicted by verdict. But the court may, and often does, permit the defendant to plead over after judgment against him on demurrer.

III. A plea in *abatement* may be for a *misnomer*, or a false addition to the prisoner. As, if *James* Allen, *gentleman*, is indicted by the name of *John* Allen, *esquire*, he may plead that he has the name of James, and not of John; and that he is a gentleman, and not an esquire. Formerly, if either fact was found by the jury, the indictment abated; but, in the end, there was little advantage accruing to the prisoner; because a new indictment might be framed. And such pleas are in practice unknown; as the court may now amend all such defects.

Let us therefore next consider a more substantial kind of plea, viz. :—

IV. Special pleas in *bar;* which go to the merits of the indictment, and give a reason why the prisoner ought not to answer it at all, nor put himself upon his trial for the crime alleged. These are of four kinds : a former acquittal, a former conviction, a former attainder, or a pardon.

1. First, the plea of *auterfois acquit*, or a former acquittal, is grounded on this universal maxim of the common law of England, that no man is to be brought into jeopardy more than once for the same offence. And hence it is allowed as a consequence, that when a man is once fairly found not guilty, he may plead such acquittal in bar of any subsequent accusation for the same crime.

2. Secondly, the plea of *auterfois convict*, or a former conviction for the same identical crime, though no judgment was ever given, is a good plea in bar to an indictment. And this depends upon the

same principle as the former, that no man ought to be twice brought in danger for one and the same crime. Accordingly, a conviction of manslaughter is a bar to a subsequent indictment of murder; for the fact prosecuted is the same in both, though the offences differ in colouring and in degree. On the same principle, certificates of conviction or discharge for assaults or batteries, or under the statutes giving magistrates summary jurisdiction in the case of juvenile offenders, and over petty larcenies, are a bar to further proceedings, and are in the nature of pleas of *auterfois convict* or *auterfois acquit*.

3. The plea of *auterfois attaint*, or a former attainder, is a good plea in bar for the same felony; and is in effect the same as *auterfois convict*, for no plea setting forth any attainder can be pleaded in bar, unless the attainder, which is the consequence of conviction, be for the same offence as that charged in the indictment.

4. Lastly, a *pardon* may be pleaded in bar, as at once destroying the end and purpose of the indictment, by remitting that punishment which the prosecution is calculated to inflict. There is one advantage that attends pleading a pardon in bar, or in arrest of judgment, *before* sentence is past, which gives it by much the preference to pleading it *after* sentence or attainder. This is, that by stopping the judgment it stops the attainder, and prevents the corruption of the blood; which, when once corrupted by attainder, cannot afterwards be restored, otherwise than by act of parliament. But as the title of pardons is applicable to other stages of prosecutions; and they have their respective force and efficacy, as well after as before conviction, outlawry, or attainder; I shall therefore reserve consideration of them till I have gone through every other title, except only that of execution.

V. The general issue, or plea of *not guilty*. In case of an indictment of felony or treason, there can be no special justification put in by way of plea. As, on an indictment for murder, a man cannot *plead* that it was in his own defence against a robber on the highway, or a burglar; but he must plead the general issue, not guilty, and give this special matter in evidence. For as the facts in treason are said to be done *proditorie et contra ligeantiæ suæ debitum*, and in felony, that the killing was done *felonice*; these charges, of a traitorous or felonious intent, are the points and very *gist* of the indictment, and must be answered directly, by the general negative, not guilty; and the jury upon the evidence will take notice of any defensive matter, and give their verdict accordingly, as effectually as if it were, or could be, specially pleaded. So that this is, upon all accounts, the most advantageous plea for the prisoner.

When the prisoner has thus pleaded not guilty, *non culpabilia*, the clerk of the assize, or clerk of the arraigns, on behalf of the crown, is supposed to reply that the prisoner is guilty, and that he is ready to prove him so, whereby the crown and the prisoner are at once at issue; for by that plea the prisoner, without further form, is deemed to put himself upon the country for trial, the manner of which will be considered in the next chapter.

CHAPTER XXVII.

OF TRIAL AND CONVICTION.

Trial by ordeal; by the corsned; and by battel—Trial by parliament—Trial by jury—Adjournment of—Copies of indictment, &c., in high treason—Copies of depositions in felony—of indictment and information in other cases—Challenges, peremptory and for cause—Evidence—Number of witnesses—Accomplices—Husband and wife—Depositions—Presumptions —Confessions—Dying declarations—Witnesses to character—Reservation of questions of law—Proceedings at the trial—Verdict—Conviction— Previous conviction of felony—Costs of prosecution—Restitution of stolen property—Speaking with the prosecutor.

THE several methods of trial and conviction of offenders, established by the laws of England, were formerly more numerous than at present, through the superstition of our Saxon ancestors; who, like other northern nations, were extremely addicted to divination, a character which Tacitus observes of the ancient Germans. They therefore invented several methods of purgation or trial, to preserve innocence from the danger of false witnesses, and in consequence of a notion that God would always interpose miraculously to vindicate the guiltless. The most ancient of these was that by *ordeal:* which was either the *fire-ordeal* or the *water-ordeal*; but both were abolished by parliament in 3 Hen. III. Another species of purgation, was the trial by the *corsned*, or morsel of execration; which gradually fell into disuse; though the remembrance of it still subsists in certain phrases of abjuration retained among the common people. The other species of ordeal, the trial by *battel*, owed its introduction among us to the Normans, and was not formally abolished till 1818. There remain now only two species of trial, viz., that by parliament and that by jury.

A trial by the peers of Great Britain and Ireland, in the high court of parliament, or in the court of the lord high steward, is to be had when a peer is *indicted* for treason, misprision of treason,

or felony; for in all other criminal prosecutions a peer shall be
tried by jury. Of this enough has been said in a former chapter;
to which I shall now only add that, in the method of its proceedings, it differs little from the trial by jury, except that no
special verdict can be given; because the lords of parliament are
judges sufficiently competent of the law that may arise from the
fact; and except also that the peers need not all agree in their verdict; but the greater number, consisting of twelve at the least, will
conclude and bind the minority.

The trial by jury, or the country, *per patriam*, is that trial by
the peers of every Englishman, which, as the grand bulwark of his
liberties, is secured to him by the great Charter: " *nullus liber homo
" capiatur, vel imprisonetur, aut exulet, aut aliquo alio modo
" destruatur, nisi per legale judicium parium suorum, vel per legem
" terræ.*"
The antiquity and excellence of this trial for the settling of civil
property has been already explained. And it will hold much
stronger in criminal cases; since in times of difficulty and danger,
more is to be apprehended from the violence and partiality of judges
appointed by the crown, in suits between the sovereign and the
subject, than in disputes between one individual and another, as to
private property. Our law has, therefore, wisely placed this barrier
of a presentment and a trial by jury between the liberties of the
people and the prerogative of the crown. It was necessary, for preserving the balance of our constitution, to vest the executive power
of the laws in the prince: and yet this power might be dangerous
and destructive to that very constitution, if exerted without check
or control, by justices of *oyer* and *terminer* occasionally named by
the crown; who might then imprison, despatch, or exile any man
that was obnoxious to the government, by an instant declaration
that such was their will and pleasure. But the founders of the English law have contrived that no man should be called to answer to
the crown for any serious crime, unless upon the preparatory accusation of twelve or more of his fellow-subjects, the grand jury: and
that the truth of every accusation, whether preferred in the shape
of indictment or information, should afterwards be confirmed by
the unanimous suffrage of twelve of his equals and neighbours, indifferently chosen and superior to all suspicion. So that the liberties of England cannot but subsist so long as this *palladium* remains
sacred and inviolate, not only from all open attacks, but also from
all secret machinations, which may sap and undermine it; by introducing new and arbitrary methods of trial, by justices of the peace,
commissioners of the revenue, and other tribunals similarly consti-

tuted. And, however *convenient* these may appear at first, as
doubtless all arbitrary powers, well executed are the most *convenient*, yet let it be again remembered, that delays and little inconveniences in the forms of justice are the price that all free nations·
must pay for their liberty in more substantial matters ; that these
inroads upon this sacred bulwark of the nation are fundamentally
opposed to the spirit of our constitution ; and that, though begun in
trifles, the precedent may gradually increase and spread, to the
utter disuse of juries in questions of the most momentous concern.

What was said of juries in general, and the trial thereby, in *civil*
cases, will greatly shorten our present remarks with regard to the
trial of *criminal* suits : which trial I shall consider in the same
method that I did the former, by following the order and course of
the proceedings themselves, as the most clear and perspicuous way
of treating it.

When therefore a prisoner on his arraignment has pleaded *not
guilty,* and for his trial has put himself upon the country, which
country the jury are, the sheriff of the county must return a panel
of jurors, *liberos et legales homines, de vicineto;* that is, jurors possessed of the requisite qualification, without just exception, and of
the *visne* or neighbourhood; which is the body of the county where
the fact was committed. This, before commissioners of *oyer* and
terminer and gaol delivery, the sheriff does by virtue of a general
precept directed to him beforehand ; and therefore it is there usual
to try all felons immediately or soon after their arraignment. But
the court may always adjourn the trial upon such terms as to bail or
otherwise as seems meet ; and in cases of high treason some delays
must take place; in order that the prisoner may have a copy of the indictment, and of the panel of jurors, and a list of the witnesses against
him, the better to prepare him to make his challenges and defence.

But no person indicted for felony is, or, as the law stands, ever
can be, entitled to copies of the indictment and lists of witnesses
and jurors, before the time of his trial. Yet any person committed
on trial, or admitted to bail, may require and is entitled to have
copies of the depositions on which he has been committed or bailed.
And in offences not amounting to felony, the defendant is entitled to
a copy of the indictment. In prosecutions for misdemeanors instituted by the attorney-general, the court is bound to order a copy of
the information or indictment to be delivered, after appearance, to
the party prosecuted, free of expense to him.

When the trial is called on, the jurors are to be sworn, as they
appear, to the number of twelve, unless they are challenged by either
party.

2 B

For challenges may be made, either on the part of the crown, or on that of the prisoner; and either to the whole array, or to the separate polls, for the very same reasons that they may be made in civil causes. For it is here at least as necessary as there, that the sheriff be totally indifferent; that where an alien is indicted, the jury should be *de medietate*, or half foreigners, if so many are found in the place; which does not indeed hold in treason, aliens being very improper judges of the breach of allegiance; and that the particular jurors should be *omni exceptione majores*; not liable to objection either *propter honoris respectum, propter defectum, propter affectum*, or *propter delictum*.

Challenges upon any of the foregoing accounts are styled challenges *for cause*; which may be without stint in both criminal and civil trials. But in criminal cases, or at least in capital ones, there is, *in favorem vitœ*, allowed to the prisoner an arbitrary and capricious species of challenge to a certain number of jurors, without showing any cause at all; which is called a *peremptory* challenge: a provision grounded on two reasons. 1. As every one must be sensible what sudden impressions and unaccountable prejudices we are apt to conceive upon the bare looks and gestures of another; and how necessary it is, that a prisoner should have a good opinion of his jury, the want of which might totally disconcert him; the law wills not that he should be tried by any one man against whom he has conceived a prejudice, even without being able to assign a reason for such his dislike. 2. Because, upon challenges for cause shown, if the reason assigned prove insufficient to set aside the juror, perhaps the bare questioning his indifference may sometimes provoke a resentment; to prevent all ill consequences from which the prisoner is still at liberty, if he pleases, peremptorily to set him aside.

This privilege of peremptory challenges, though granted to the prisoner, is denied to the crown, who can challenge no jurors without assigning cause; but the crown need not assign cause till all the panel is gone through, and unless there cannot be a full jury without the person so challenged. And then, and not sooner, the counsel for the crown must show the cause: otherwise the juror shall be sworn.*

The peremptory challenges of the prisoner must, however, have

---

* Where there is a challenge for cause, two persons in court, not of the jury, are sworn to try whether the juryman challenged will try the prisoner indifferently. Evidence is then produced to support the challenge; and according to the verdict of the two tryers, the juryman is admitted or rejected. A juryman was thus set aside in O'Coigly's trial for treason, because, upon looking at the prisoners, he had uttered the words "damned rascals."

some reasonable boundary; which was by the common law thirty-five; that is, one under the number of three full juries: the law considering that he who peremptorily challenged a greater number, could have no intention to be tried at all. But this number has been reduced by modern statutes to *twenty*, and every peremptory challenge beyond it is void, so that the trial then proceeds as if no such challenge had been made.

If, by reason of challenges or the default of the jurors, a sufficient number cannot be had of the original panel, a *tales* may be awarded as in civil causes, till the number of twelve is sworn, " well " and truly to try, and true deliverance make, between our sove- " reign lady the queen, and the prisoner whom they have in charge ; " and a true verdict to give, according to the evidence."

When the jury is sworn, if it be a cause of any consequence, the indictment is usually opened, and the evidence marshalled by the counsel for the crown, or prosecution ; the pursuer or his counsel being permitted to cross-examine the witnesses as in civil cases.[*]

The doctrine of evidence upon pleas of the crown is, in most respects, the same as that upon civil actions. There are, however, a few leading points wherein, by several statutes and resolutions, a difference is made between civil and criminal evidence.

First, in all cases of treason, and misprision of treason, *two* lawful witnesses are required to convict a prisoner ; unless he shall willingly and without violence confess the same. And both wit-nesses must be to the same overt act of treason, or one to one overt act, and the other to another overt act, of the same species of trea-son, and not of distinct heads or kinds : and no evidence shall be admitted to prove any overt act not expressly laid in the indictment. And therefore in Sir John Fenwick's case, in King William's time, where there was but one witness, an act of parliament was made on purpose to attaint him of treason, and he was executed.

Secondly, it has long been usual in criminal courts to admit an accomplice to become a witness, or, as it is generally termed, *queen's evidence*, against his fellows ; upon an implied confidence, which the judges have usually countenanced and adopted, that if such accom-plice makes a full and complete discovery, without prevarication or fraud, he shall not himself be prosecuted for that or any other

* It was only by the statute 6 and 7 Will. IV. c. 14, that prisoners charged with *felony* were permitted the assistance of *counsel*, it being a settled rule at common law that no counsel should be allowed such prisoners, unless some point of law arose proper to be debated, when they were *entitled* to the assistance of counsel. It seems difficult to believe that such ever was the law ; and the change, it may be added, was opposed by nearly all the judges.

previous offence of the same degree. There is no positive rule, I
may add, for distinguishing between the weight to be given to the
evidence of accomplices in comparison with other witnesses; but
juries are always recommended not to convict prisoners on their un-
corroborated testimony.

Thirdly, in criminal proceedings, husbands and wives are not
admitted to give evidence for or against each other; for although in
most civil suits they are now admissible, the legislature has, for
obvious reasons, not extended this admissibility to the criminal
courts. Thus the wife cannot be called to prove her marriage when
the husband is indicted for bigamy, so a husband is not admissible
to prove that his wife and others conspired to procure his marriage.
without the consent of his parents. But on this rule a necessary
exception was engrafted by the common law; in those cases, namely,
where a crime has been committed by the one against the other.
And therefore a wife is a competent witness to prove a forcible
abduction and marriage; or an assault upon her by the husband;
or that he assisted at a rape committed on her person; or in general
for any offence against her liberty or person.

Fourthly, the depositions of witnesses duly taken before the committing justices are admissible in evidence on the trial of the
accused, if it is proved that the person making such deposition is
dead, or is so ill as not to be able to travel, and also that the deposition was taken in the presence of the accused, and that he or his
counsel or attorney had a full opportunity of cross-examining the
witness.

Fifthly, all presumptive evidence of felony should be admitted
cautiously: for the law holds that it is better that ten guilty persons escape, than that one innocent suffer. And Sir Matthew Hale
in particular lays down two rules most prudent and necessary to be
observed: 1. Never to convict a man for stealing the goods of a
person unknown, merely because he will give no account how he
came by them, unless an actual felony be proved of such goods: and,
2. Never to convict any person of murder or manslaughter, till at
least the body be found dead; on account of two instances he mentions, where persons were executed for the murder of others, who
were then alive, but missing.

Sixthly, confessions or acknowledgments of guilt, as distinguished
from admissions in civil transactions, form a distinct head of evidence in criminal trials. The requisite formalities which must be
attended to, in order to render the statements of accused persons
made before the committing justices admissible in evidence against

them on the trial, have been already mentioned. Other statements of the accused, *voluntarily* made to any person at any time and in any place, either before or after his apprehension, and whether verbal or in writing, may be proved against him; although, as a general rule, evidence of oral confessions of guilt ought to be received *with great caution*.

Seventhly, dying declarations form a species of evidence admissible only in the single instance of *homicide*, where the death of the deceased is the subject of the charge, and the circumstances of the death are the subject of the dying declaration. The general principle on which this species of evidence is admitted is, that such declarations made in extremity when the party is at the point of death, and when every hope of this world is gone, when every motive to falsehood is silenced, and the mind is induced by the most powerful considerations to speak the truth, have, although made in the absence of the accused, the weight of testimony given on oath in his presence. And it is accordingly essential to the admissibility of these declarations, first, that at the time they were made the declarant should have been in actual danger of death; secondly, that he should then have had a full apprehension of his danger: and lastly, that death should have ensued. But these declarations are in any case admissible only as to matters to which the accused would have been competent to testify if sworn on the trial.

Lastly, the defendant in criminal cases is allowed to call witnesses to prove that he has previously borne a general good character—for honesty, if the charge be one involving larceny, embezzlement, or fraud, or for peaceable demeanor, if it include an accusation of personal violence. Such testimony is important, as leading to the inference that a man of those previous habits would refrain from any such violation of the law. But it is, from its very nature, evidence to which the jury ought only to attach weight, when that adduced for the prosecution is not of a decisive character; for the crown cannot contradict it by affirmative proof of particular immoral acts, only by calling witnesses to give a general bad character.

It occasionally happens during the trial, and more particularly at the close of the case for the prosecution, that objections are taken on behalf of the prisoner, that the facts proved do not amount to the offence charged; or that the evidence in support of the indictment will not justify a conviction. At an earlier stage of the case, objections are not unfrequently offered to the admissibility or to the rejection of evidence; any one of which may gave rise to questions too difficult for the immediate determination of the court. If so, the question may be reserved for the consideration of the justices of either bench and barons of the Exchequer; who are required to meet during term, and in open court, which thence is termed the *court for the consideration of crown cases reserved,* to deliver their judgment, reversing, affirming, or amending that already given, or where the conviction is affirmed and no judgment has been already given, ordering when and where it shall be given. The reservation of a question in this way does not interfere with the course of the trial, for it is only in the event of a conviction that it becomes necessary to reserve the point. Nor does it clash, on the other hand, with the corrective jurisdiction of the courts of appeal; for the judges who determine these reserved questions merely assist with their opinion, the determination of the court below, in whose discretion is exclusively vested the reservation of the question, and to which the judgment, if the conviction be affirmed, is wholly left.

When the evidence for the prosecution is closed, the counsel for the crown, in the event of the prisoner expressing his intention to adduce evidence, addresses the jury. The case for the defence is then opened, and the evidence adduced, the counsel for the prisoner recapitulating its effect to the jury at the close; and the counsel for the crown then replies. If the prisoner does not intend to adduce evidence, his counsel is heard immediately on the close of the evidence for the prosecution; the counsel for the crown rarely, in such cases, replying. The judge next sums up the whole to the jury; who cannot then be discharged, unless in cases of evident necessity, till they have given in their verdict; but are to consider of it, and deliver it in, with the same forms, as upon civil causes: only they cannot, in a criminal case which touches life or member, give a *privy* verdict. And such verdict may be either general, guilty, or not guilty; or special, setting forth all the circumstances of the case, and praying the judgment of the court, whether, for instance, on the facts stated, it be murder, manslaughter, or no crime at all. This is where they *doubt* the matter of the law, and therefore *choose* to leave it to the determination of the court; though they have an unquestionable right of determining upon all the circumstances, and finding a general verdict, if they think proper so to hazard a breach of their oaths.

Formerly, if the verdict were notoriously wrong, the jurors might have been punished, and the verdict set aside by writ of *attaint* at the suit of the crown, but not at the suit of the prisoner. But the practice, which at one time prevailed, of fining, imprisoning, or otherwise punishing jurors, merely at the discretion of the court, for finding their verdict contrary to the direction of the judge, was arbitrary, unconstitutional, and illegal; and is treated as such by

Sir Thomas Smith, nearly three hundred years ago, who accounted "such doings to be very violent, tyrannical, and contrary to the "liberty and custom of the realm of England."

If the jury therefore find the prisoner not guilty, he is then for ever quit and discharged of the accusation. And upon such his acquittal, or discharge for want of prosecution, he shall be immediately set at large. But if the jury find him guilty, he is then said to be *convicted* of the crime whereof he stands indicted. Which conviction may accrue two ways; either by his confessing the offence and pleading guilty, or by his being found so by the verdict of his country.

If a prisoner, charged with a felony not punishable with death, has been before convicted of felony, the indictment generally charges him with having committed the offence *after having been previously convicted of felony*; the legislature having, in order to secure the more exemplary punishment of such offenders, conferred powers on the courts to pass a sentence of much greater severity than that which may be imposed for the single offence. But although a prisoner is so charged, the jury are only directed to inquire whether he is guilty or not guilty of the particular crime there alleged; and it is only when they have found the prisoner guilty of the subsequent offence, that they are then, if the prisoner disputes it, further informed of, or charged to inquire concerning the previous conviction.

When the offender is convicted, there are two collateral circumstances that immediately arise, the first relating to the *costs of the prosecution*; the second, in cases of larceny, to the *restitution of the stolen property.*

1. On a conviction, or even upon an acquittal where there was a reasonable ground to prosecute, and in fact a *bonâ fide* prosecution, for any larceny or other felony, the reasonable expenses of the prosecutor and witnesses are to be allowed. These include the expenses incurred in their attendance before the magistrate; which latter may be allowed, even if no bill of indictment be preferred. The same rule prevails in prosecutions for those *misdemeanors* which partake of the nature of *crimes.* These costs when allowed are paid, in the first place, by the treasurer of the county, to whom the amount is repaid out of the Consolidated Fund.

2. By the common law there was no restitution of goods upon an indictment, because it is at the suit of the crown only; and therefore it was provided by 21 Hen. VIII. c. 11, which has been reenacted and extended by more modern statutes, that if any person

were convicted of larceny, by the evidence of the party robbed, he should have full restitution of his money, goods, and chattels; or the value of them out of the offender's goods, if he had any, by a writ to be granted by the justices. Upon which it is held that upon indictments of larceny, the writ of restitution reaches the goods so stolen, notwithstanding the property of them is endeavoured to be altered by sale in market overt. And though this may seem somewhat hard upon the buyer, yet the rule of law is, that " *spoliatus* " *debet, ante omnia, restitui;*" especially when he has used all the diligence in his power to convict the felon. And, since the case is reduced to this hard necessity, that either the owner or the buyer must suffer, the law prefers the right of the owner, who has done a meritorious act by pursuing a felon to condign punishment, to the right of the buyer, whose merit is only negative, that he has been guilty of no unfair transaction. Accordingly, it is now usual for the court, upon the conviction of the offender to order, without any writ, the immediate restitution of the stolen property to be made to the several prosecutors. But such restitution cannot be directed in the case of any valuable security *bonâ fide* paid or discharged by any person liable to the payment thereof, or of any negotiable instrument *bonâ fide* taken for a valuable consideration, without notice, or without any reasonable cause to suspect that the same had been stolen or illegally obtained. Without any such writ of restitution, however, the party whose property has been stolen may peaceably retake his goods, wherever he happens to find them; or may bring his action of trover for his goods, and recover a satisfaction in damages. But such action lies not before prosecution; for so felonies would be made up and healed: and also recaption is unlawful, if it be done with intention to smother or compound the larceny; it then becoming the heinous offence of theftbote, as was mentioned in a former chapter.

It is not uncommon, when a person is convicted of a misdemeanor, which principally and more immediately affects some individual, as a battery, imprisonment, or the like, for the court to permit the defendant to *speak with the prosecutor*, before any judgment is pronounced; and if the prosecutor declares himself satisfied, to inflict but a trivial punishment. This is done to reimburse the prosecutor his expenses, and make him some private amends, without the trouble and circuity of a civil action. But it is a dangerous practice: and though it may be intrusted to the discretion of the judges in the superior courts, it ought never to be allowed in local or inferior jurisdictions, such as the quarter-sessions, where prosecutions for assaults are too frequently commenced, rather for private lucre than for the great ends of public justice. Even a voluntary

forgiveness, by the party injured, ought not in true policy to inter-
cept the stroke of justice. "This," says the Marquis Beccaria, who
pleads with equal strength for the *certainty* as for the *lenity* of punishment, "may be an act of good-nature and humanity, but it is
" contrary to the good of the public, For, although a private citi-
" zen may dispense with satisfaction for his private injury, he can-
" not remove the necessity of public example. The right of punish-
" ing belongs not to any one individual in particular, but to the
" society in general, or the sovereign who represents that society:
" and a man may renounce his own portion of this right, but he
" cannot give up that of others."

CHAPTER XXVIII.

OF JUDGMENT AND ITS CONSEQUENCES.

Arrest of judgment—Pardon—Judgments generally—Fines—Consequences of
  judgment.——I. Attainder—forfeiture of lands—in treason—in felony—
  forfeiture of goods.——II. Corruption of blood.

THE next stage of criminal prosecution, after trial and conviction,
is that of *judgment*. For when, upon a charge of *felony*, the jury
have brought in their verdict of guilty, in the presence of the prisoner, he is either immediately, or at a convenient time soon after,
asked by the court, if he has anything to offer why judgment should
not be awarded against him.[*] Where the defendant has been
found guilty of a *misdemeanor*, the trial of which may, and sometimes does, happen in his absence, after he has once appeared, a
capias may be awarded to bring him in to receive judgment; and
if he absconds, he may be prosecuted to outlawry; or if he is under
recognizances to appear, and makes default, the recognizances may
be estreated, and a warrant issued for his apprehension.

But whenever the defendant appears in person, he may at this
period, as well as at his arraignment, offer any exceptions to the
indictment, in *arrest* or stay of judgment. And if his objections be
valid; if, for instance, he has been found guilty of what does not
constitute an offence in point of law, the judgment will be arrested,
and the whole proceedings be set aside. But he may be indicted
again.

[*] It was at this point of the proceedings that the prisoner was entitled to
pray his clergy; the nature of which privilege has been already referred to
(*ante p.* 514), and will be found fully explained in the Appendix.

A *pardon* also, as has been before said, may be pleaded in arrest of judgment, and it has the same advantage when pleaded here, as when pleaded upon arraignment ; viz., the saving the attainder, and of course the corruption of blood.

If all these resources fail, the court must pronounce that judgment which the law has annexed to the crime. Of these some are capital, which extend to the life of the offender, and consist generally in being hanged by the neck till dead; though in very atrocious crimes other circumstances of terror, pain, or disgrace, are superadded : as in high treason, being drawn or dragged to the place of execution; beheading and quartering; and in murder, burial within the precincts of the prison. Some punishments consist in loss of liberty, by perpetual or temporary *penal servitude* or *imprisonment.* Some extend to confiscation, by forfeiture of lands, or movables, or both, or of the profits or lands for life : others induce a disability of holding offices or employments, being heirs, executors, and the like. Some are merely pecuniary, by stated or discretionary *fines :* and lastly, there are others, that consist principally in their ignominy, though most of them are mixed with some degree of corporal pain; such as *whipping* and *hard labour.* The latter for almost all offences now accompanies a sentence of imprisonment. *Solitary confinement* may also be ordered in almost every case of felony, and in many of the more aggravated misdemeanors; but can in no case exceed in duration one month at a time, or three months in the space of one year. There were formerly some offences, which occasioned a mutilation or dismembering, by cutting off the hand or ears: and others which fixed a lasting stigma on the offender, by slitting the nostrils, or branding in the hand or cheek; but all these are now unknown to the law. The pillory has long ceased to be a punishment; fine and imprisonment, or both, having been substituted for it in cases where it was the only punishment to be inflicted. The stocks and the ducking-stool have long been disused.

It is a special feature of our law, however, and deserving of notice, that the species, though not always the quantity or degree, of punishment is *ascertained* for every offence. If judgments were to be the private opinions of the judge, men would then be slaves to their magistrates ; and would live in society, without knowing exactly the conditions and obligations which it lays them under. Where an established penalty is annexed to crimes, the criminal may read their certain consequence in that law; which ought to be the unvaried rule, as it is the inflexible judge, of his actions.

The discretionary fines and discretionary length of imprisonment, which our courts are enabled to impose, may seem an exception to this rule. But the general nature of the punishment, viz., by fine or imprisonment, is, in these cases, fixed and determinate : though the duration and quantity of each must frequently vary, from the aggravations or otherwise of the offence, the quality and condition of the parties, and from innumerable other circumstances. The *quantum*, in particular, of pecuniary fines neither can, nor ought to, be ascertained by any invariable law, for the value of money itself changes from a thousand causes; and, at all events, what is ruin to one man's fortune may be matter of indifference to another's. Our statute law has not therefore often ascertained the quantity of fines, nor the common law ever; it directing such an offence to be punished by fine in general, without specifying the certain sum; which is fully sufficient, when we consider, that however unlimited the power of the court may seem, it is far from being wholly arbitrary; but its discretion is regulated by law. For the Bill of Rights has particularly declared, that excessive fines ought not to be imposed, nor cruel and unusual punishments inflicted : which had a retrospect to some unprecedented proceedings in the court of King's Bench, in the reign of King James II.: and the same statute further declares, that all grants and promises of fines and forfeitures of particular persons before conviction, are illegal and void. The reasonableness of fines in criminal cases has also been usually regulated by the determination of *Magna Charta*, c. 14, concerning amercements for misbehaviour by the suitors in matters of civil right. " *Liber homo non amercietur pro parvo delicto, nisi secun-* " *dum modum ipsius delicti; et pro magno delicto, secundum mag-* " *nitudinem delicti, salvo contenemento suo: et mercator eodem* " *modo, salva mercandisa sua: et villanus eodem modo amercietur,* " *salvo wanagio suo.*" A rule that obtained even in Henry II.'s time, and means only, that no man shall have a larger amercement imposed upon him than his circumstances or personal estate will bear; saving to the landholder his contenement, or land; to the trader his merchandize; and to the countryman his wainage, or team and instruments of husbandry.

When sentence of death is pronounced, the immediate inseparable consequence by the common law is *attainder*. He is then called attaint, *attinctus*, stained, or blackened. He is no longer of any credit or reputation; for, by an anticipation of his punishment, he is already dead in law. This is after *judgment*: for there is great difference between a man *convicted* and *attainted*; though they are frequently through inaccuracy confounded together. After conviction only, a man is liable to none of these disabilities; for there is still in contemplation of law a possibility of his innocence. Something may be offered in arrest of judgment: the indictment may be erroneous, which will render his guilt uncertain, and thereupon the present conviction may be quashed: he may obtain a pardon, which sup-

poses some latent sparks of merit, which plead in extenuation of his
fault. But when judgment is once pronounced, both law and fact
conspire to prove him completely guilty; and there is not the remotest possibility left of anything to be said in his favour. And
therefore, either upon judgment of outlawry, or of death, for treason
or felony, a man shall be said to be attainted.

The consequences of attainder are forfeiture and, at common law,
corruption of blood.

I. Forfeiture is twofold; of real and personal estates.

By attainder in high treason a man forfeits to the crown all his
lands and tenements of inheritance; and the profits of all lands
and tenements, which he had in his own right for life or years, so
long as such interest shall subsist. This forfeiture relates backwards to the time of the treason committed: so as to avoid all
intermediate sales and incumbrances, but not those before the fact:
and therefore a wife's jointure is not forfeitable for the treason of
her husband, because settled upon her previous to the treason committed. The natural justice of this confiscation of property, for
treason, is founded on this consideration, that he who has thus violated the fundamental principles of government, has abandoned his
connexions with society; and has no longer any right to those advantages which before belonged to him as a member of the community; among which *social* advantages, the right of transferring
or transmitting property to others is one of the chief.

And this forfeiture, it may be added, is by no means derived
from the feudal policy, as has been already observed, but was antecedent to the establishment of that system in this island; being
transmitted from our Saxon ancestors, and forming a part of the
ancient Scandinavian constitution.

By attainder for felony, the offender also forfeits all his chattel
interests absolutely, and the profits of all estates of freehold during
life; and by attainder for *murder* he forfeits after his death, all
his lands and tenements in fee simple, but not those in tail, to the
crown, for a very short period of time: for the king shall have them
for a year and a day, and may commit therein what waste he
pleases; which is called the king's *year, day,* and *waste.* This year,
day, and waste, it has long been the practice to compound for: but
otherwise they regularly belong to the crown: and, after their expiration, the land would naturally have descended to the heir, as in
gavelkind tenure, it still does, did not its feudal quality interrupt
such descent, and give it by way of escheat to the lord.

This forfeiture for felony arises only upon attainder; and, therefore, a *felo de se* forfeits no lands of inheritance or freehold, for he
never is attainted as a felon. It likewise relates back to the time of

the offence committed, as well as forfeitures for treason ; so as to avoid all intermediate charges and conveyances. This may be hard upon such as have unwarily engaged with the offender : but the cruelty and reproach must lie on the part, not of the law, but of the criminal, who has thus knowingly and dishonestly involved others in his own calamities.

These are all the forfeitures of real estates created by the common law as consequential upon attainders by judgment of death or outlawry. I here omit the particular forfeitures created by the statutes of *præmunire* and others, because I look upon them rather as a *part* of the judgment and penalty, inflicted by the respective statutes, than as *consequences* of such judgments ; as in treason and the few felonies above mentioned they are. But I shall just mention, as a part of the forfeiture of real estates, the forfeiture of the profits of lands during life : which extends to two other instances, besides those already spoken of ; misprision of treason, and striking in Westminster Hall, or drawing a weapon upon a judge there sitting in the courts of justice.

The forfeiture of goods and chattels accrues in every one of the higher kinds of offence : in treason or misprision thereof, felonies of all sorts, self-murder or felony *de se*, larceny, and the above-mentioned offence of striking, &c., in Westminster Hall ; and the property vests in the crown *without office found*.

There is a remarkable difference or two between the forfeiture of lands and of goods and chattels. 1. Lands are forfeited upon *attainder*, and not before : goods and chattels are forfeited by *conviction*. 2. The forfeiture of lands has relation to the time of the fact committed, so as to avoid all subsequent sales and incumbrances ; but the forfeiture of goods and chattels has no relation backwards ; so that those only which a man has at the time of conviction shall be forfeited. Therefore a traitor or felon may *bonâ fide* sell any of his chattels, real or personal, for the sustenance of himself and family between the fact and conviction ; for personal property is of so fluctuating a nature, that it passes through many hands in a short time ; and no buyer could be safe, if he were liable to return the goods which he had fairly bought, provided any of the prior vendors had committed a treason or felony. Yet if they be collusively and not *bonâ fide* parted with, merely to defraud the crown, the law will reach them ; for they are all the while truly and substantially the goods of the offender ; and as he, if acquitted, might recover them himself, as not parted with for a good consideration, so, in case he happens to be convicted, the law will recover them for the crown.

II. Another consequence, which at common law results from

attainder, is the *corruption of blood*, both upwards and downwards; so that, until comparatively recently, an attainted person could neither inherit lands from his ancestors, nor retain those he was already in possession of, nor transmit them by descent to any heir; but the same escheated to the lord of the fee, subject to the sovereign's superior right of forfeiture: and the person attainted also obstructed all descents to his posterity, wherever they were obliged to derive a title through him to a remoter ancestor.

This was one of those notions which our laws adopted from the feudal constitutions, at the time of the Norman Conquest; as appears from its being unknown in those tenures which are indisputably Saxon. When almost every other oppressive mark of feudal tenure had been happily worn away in these kingdoms, it was high time that this *corruption of blood*, with all its connected consequences, not only of present escheat, but of future incapacities of inheritance even to the twentieth generation, should likewise be abolished. Nevertheless, it was only by the statute 3 & 4 Will. IV. c. 106, that this object was effected; so that the attainder of any relation, who dies before the descent takes place, no longer prevents any person from inheriting, who would otherwise have been capable of doing so.

CHAPTER XXIX.

ON REVERSAL OF JUDGMENT.

I. By avoiding the judgment—*without* writ of error—*by* writ of error—by act of parliament.——II. By avoiding its execution—by reprieve—by pardon.

WE are next to consider how judgments may be set aside; which may be effected either, 1. By falsifying or reversing the judgment; or, 2. By reprieve or pardon.

1. A judgment may be falsified, reversed, or avoided, either *without* or *by* a writ of error. It may be reversed or avoided *without a writ of error*, for matters foreign to or *dehors* the record, that is, not apparent upon the face of it; so that they cannot be assigned for error. Thus, if any judgment whatever be given by persons who had no good commission to proceed against the person condemned, it is void; and may be falsified by showing the special matter without writ of error. As, where a commission issues to A and B, and twelve others, or any two of them, of which A or B shall be one, to take and try indictments; and any of the other twelve proceed without the interposition or presence of either A or B; in this case all

proceedings, trials, convictions, and judgments are void for want of a proper authority in the commissioners, and may be falsified upon bare inspection without the trouble of a writ of error.

2. Judgment may be reversed *by writ of error:* which lies from all inferior criminal jurisdictions to the court of Queen's Bench, and from the Queen's Bench to the court of Exchequer Chamber, and thence to the House of Peers; and may be brought for notorious mistakes in the indictment, as when the offence is improperly or insufficiently described therein, or in the judgment or other parts of the record; as where a man is found guilty of perjury and receives the judgment of felony. These writs of error, to reverse judgments in cases of *misdemeanor,* are not to be allowed of course, but on sufficient probable cause shown to the attorney-general; and then they are understood to be grantable of common right, and *ex debito justitiæ.* But writs of error to reverse attainders in cases of felony are only allowed *ex gratiâ;* and not without express warrant under the royal sign manual, or at least by the consent of the attorney-general. These, therefore, can rarely be brought by the party himself, especially where he is attainted for an offence against the state; but they may be brought by his heir, or executor, after his death, in more favourable times; which may be some consolation to his family.

3. An attainder may be reversed by act of parliament; which may be and has been frequently done, without examining too closely into the truth or validity of the errors assigned. And sometimes, though the crime be universally acknowledged and confessed, yet the merits of the criminal's family shall after his death obtain a restitution in blood, honours, and estate, or some, or one of them, by act of parliament; which, so far as it extends, has all the effect of reversing the attainder, without casting any reflections upon the justice of the preceding sentence.

The effect of falsifying, or reversing an *outlawry,* is that the party shall be in the same plight as if he had appeared; and, if it be before plea pleaded, he shall be put to plead; if after conviction, he shall receive sentence. But when judgment pronounced upon conviction, is falsified or reversed, all former proceedings are absolutely set aside, and the party stands as if he had never been at all accused; restored in his credit, his capacity, and his estates; with regard to which last, though they be granted away by the crown, yet the owner may enter upon the grantee, and turn him out without ceremony. But he still remains liable to another prosecution for the same offence; for the first being erroneous, he never was in jeopardy thereby.

II. The execution of the judgment may be avoided by a reprieve, or a pardon; whereof the former is temporary only, the latter permanent.

1. A reprieve, from *reprendre*, to take back, is the withdrawing of a sentence for an interval of time; whereby the execution is suspended. This may be, first, *ex arbitrio judicis*; either before or after judgment; as, where the judge is not satisfied with the verdict, or the evidence is suspicious, or the indictment is insufficient; or sometimes if it be a small felony, or any favourable circumstances appear in the criminal's character, in order to give room to apply to the crown for either an absolute or conditional pardon. Or, secondly, *ex mandato regis*, from the mere pleasure of the crown, expressed in any way to the court by whom the execution is to be awarded. This is the mode in which reprieves are generally granted, through the intervention of one of the secretaries of state.

Reprieves may also be *ex necessitate legis*: as, where a woman is capitally convicted, and pleads her pregnancy; though this is no cause to stay the judgment, yet it is to respite the execution till she be delivered. This is a mercy dictated by the law of nature, *in favorem prolis*; and therefore no part of the bloody proceedings in the reign of Queen Mary, has been more justly detested than the cruelty, that was exercised in the Island of Guernsey, of burning a woman big with child; and when, through the violence of the flames, the infant sprang forth at the stake, and was preserved by the bystanders, after some deliberation of the priests who assisted at the sacrifice, they cast it again into the fire as a young heretic. In case this plea be made in stay of execution, the judge must direct a jury of twelve matrons to inquire the fact; and if they bring in their verdict *quick with child*, execution shall be stayed generally till the next session; and so from session to session, till either she is delivered, or proves by the course of nature not to have been with child at all.

Another cause of regular reprieve is, if the offender become *non compos* between the judgment and the award of execution; for regularly, as was formerly observed, though a man be *compos* when he commits a capital crime, yet if he becomes *non compos* after, he shall not be indicted; if after indictment, he shall not be convicted; if after conviction, he shall not receive judgment; if after judgment, he shall not be ordered for execution; for "*furiosus solo furore punitur*," and the law knows not but he might have offered some reason, if in his senses, to have stayed these respective proceedings. It is therefore an invariable rule, when any time interves between the attainder and the award of execution, to demand of the prisoner what he has to allege, why execution should not be awarded against him; and if he appears to be insane, the judge in his discretion may and ought to reprieve him.

2. The last and surest resort is in the sovereign's most gracious *pardon;* the granting of which is the most amiable prerogative of the crown. Law, indeed, cannot be framed on principles of compassion to guilt; yet justice, by the constitution of England, is bound to be administered in mercy, as is promised by the sovereign in the coronation oath. And the queen, therefore, may pardon all offences that are merely against the crown or the public. I say against the crown or the public, because, 1. The committing any man to prison out of the realm is, by the *Habeas Corpus* Act, a *præmunire* and *unpardonable.* 2. The crown cannot pardon where private justice is principally concerned in the prosecution; therefore the queen cannot pardon a common nuisance, while it remains unredressed, or so as to prevent an abatement of it, though afterwards she may remit the fine. Neither, lastly, can the crown pardon an offence against a popular or penal statute, after information brought: for thereby the informer has acquired a private property in his part of the penalty.

There is also a restriction, of a peculiar nature, that affects the prerogative of pardoning in the case of parliamentary impeachments; viz., that the royal pardon cannot be *pleaded* to any such impeachment, so as to stop the prosecution of great offenders. Therefore when, in the reign of Charles II., the Earl of Danby was impeached by the House of Commons of high treason, and other misdemeanors, and pleaded the king's pardon in bar of the same, the commons alleged, "that the pardon so pleaded was illegal and void." Soon after the revolution, the commons renewed the same claim, and voted, "that a pardon is not *pleadable in bar* of an impeachment;" and at length, it was enacted by the Act of Settlement, "that no pardon "under the Great Seal of England shall be *pleadable* to an impeach-"ment by the commons in parliament." But, after the impeachment has been determined, it is not understood that the royal grace is further restrained or abridged: for, after the attainder of the six rebel lords in 1715, three of them were from time to time reprieved by the crown, and at length received a pardon.

A pardon must, until recently, have been issued under the great seal; but is now simply granted by warrant under the royal sign manual, countersigned by one of the principal secretaries of state. It may be *absolute* or *conditional*: that is, the sovereign may extend his mercy upon what terms he pleases; and may annex to his bounty a condition either precedent or subsequent, on the performance whereof the validity of the pardon will depend; and this by the common law. Which prerogative is usually exerted in the pardon of felons, on condition of being confined to hard labour for a stated time, or of transportation to some foreign country for life, or for a term of years; such transportation or banishment being allowable and warranted by the *Habeas Corpus* Act, 31 Car. II. c. 2, s. 14. When once granted, it may either be pleaded upon arraignment, or in arrest of judgment, or in bar of execution; and the *effect* of it is to make the offender a new man; to acquit him of all corporal penalties and forfeitures annexed to that offence for which he obtains his pardon; and to give him a new credit and capacity.

CHAPTER XXX.

OF EXECUTION.

THERE now remains nothing to speak of but *execution*, the completion of human punishment. And this, in all cases, as well capital as otherwise, must be performed by the legal officer, the sheriff or his deputy; whose warrant for so doing was anciently by precept under the hand and seal of the judge, as it is still practised in the court of the lord high steward, upon the execution of a peer, though in the court of the peers in parliament, it is done by writ from the crown. Afterwards it was established, that in case of life, the judge may command execution to be done without any writ. And now the usage is, for the judge to sign the calendar, or list of all the prisoners' names, with their separate judgments in the margin, which is left with the sheriff. As for a capital felony, it is written opposite to the prisoner's name, "let him be hanged by the neck;" formerly, in the days of Latin and abbreviation, *sus. per coll.* for "*suspendatur per collum.*" And this is the only warrant that the sheriff has for so material an act as taking away the life of another.

The sheriff is to do execution within a convenient time; the time and place of execution being by law no part of the judgment, whether for murder or any other offence. It has been well observed, that it is of great importance that the punishment should follow the crime as early as possible; that the prospect of gratification or advantage, which tempts a man to commit the crime, should instantly awake the attendant idea of punishment. Delay of execution serves only to separate these ideas; and then the execution itself affects the minds of the spectators rather as a terrible sight than the necessary consequence of transgression.

The sheriff cannot alter the manner of the execution by substituting one death for another, without being guilty of felony himself, as has been formerly said. It is held also by Sir Edward Coke and Sir Matthew Hale, that even the king cannot change the punishment of the law, by altering the hanging into beheading; though when beheading is part of the sentence, the king may remit the rest.

But others have thought, and more justly, that this prerogative is part of the common law. When Lord Stafford was executed for the popish plot in the reign of Charles II., the then sheriffs of London, having received the king's writ for beheading him, petitioned the House of Lords for a command or order from their lordships how the said judgment should be executed; for, he being prosecuted by impeachment, they entertained a notion, which is said to have been countenanced by Lord Russell, that the king could not pardon any part of the sentence. The lords resolved that the scruples of the sheriffs were unnecessary, and declared that the king's writ ought to be obeyed. Disappointed of raising a flame in that assembly, they immediately signified to the House of Commons by one of the members, that they were not satisfied as to the power of the said writ. That house took two days to consider of it; and then sullenly resolved that the house was *content* that the sheriff do execute Lord Stafford by severing his head from his body. It is further related, that when afterwards the said Lord Russell was condemned for high treason upon indictment, the king, while he remitted the ignominious part of the sentence, observed, "that his lordship would now "find he was possessed of that prerogative which, in the case of Lord "Stafford he had denied him." One can hardly determine which most to disapprove of, the indecent and sanguinary zeal of the subject, or the cool and cruel sarcasm of the sovereign.

To conclude: it is clear that if, upon judgment to be hanged by the neck till he is dead, the criminal be not thoroughly killed, but revives, the sheriff must hang him again. For the former hanging was no execution of the sentence; and if a false tenderness were to be indulged in such cases, a multitude of collusions might ensue. Nay, even while abjurations were in force, such a criminal so reviving was not allowed to take sanctuary and abjure the realm; but his fleeing to sanctuary was held an escape in the officer.

We have thus arrived at the *last* stage of criminal proceedings, or execution, the end and completion of human *punishment*, which was the sixth and last head to be considered under the division of *public wrongs*, the fourth and last object of the laws of England.

[APPENDIX.

APPENDIX.

---◦◦◦---

WAGER OF BATTEL. [*Ante*, p. 381.]

TRIAL by *wager of battel, vadiatio duelli*, seems to have owed its origin to the military spirit of our ancestors, joined to a superstitious frame of mind; as it was in the nature of an appeal to Providence, under an apprehension and hope, however presumptuous and unwarrantable, that heaven would give the victory to him who had the right. The decision of suits by this appeal to the God of battles, is by some said to have been invented by the Burgundi, one of the northern or German clans that planted themselves in Gaul. And it is true, that the first written injunction of judiciary combats that we meet with, is in the laws of Gundebald, A.D. 501, which are preserved in the Burgundian code. Yet it does not seem to have been merely a local custom of this or that particular tribe, but to have been the common usage of all those warlike people from the earliest times. And it may also seem from a passage in Velleius Paterculus, that the Germans, when first they became known to the Romans, were wont to decide all contests of right by the sword: for when Quintilius Varus endeavoured to introduce among them the Roman laws and method of trial, it was looked upon, says the historian, as a "*novitas incognitæ disciplinæ, ut solita armis decerni jure terminarentur.*" And among the ancient Goths in Sweden we find the practice of judiciary duels established upon much the same footing as they formerly were in our own country.

· This trial was introduced into England, among other Norman customs, by William the Conqueror; but was only used in three cases, one military, one criminal, and the third civil. The first in the court of chivalry and honour; the second in appeals of felony; and the third upon issue joined in a writ of right, formerly the last and most solemn decision of real property. For in writs of right the *jus proprietatis,* which is frequently a matter of difficulty, was in question; but other real actions being merely questions of the *jus possessionis,* which are usually more plain and obvious, our ancestors did not in them appeal to the decision of Providence. Another pretext for allowing it, upon these final writs of right, was also for the sake of such claimants as might have the true right, but yet by the death of witnesses, or other defect of evidence, be unable to prove it to a jury. But the most curious reason of all is given in the *Mirror*, that it is allowable upon warrant of the combat between David for the people of Israel of the one party, and Goliah for the Philistines of the other party: a reason which Pope Nicholas I. very seriously decides to be inconclusive.

The last trial by battel that was waged in the court of common pleas at Westminster (though there was afterwards one in the court of chivalry in 1631, and another in the county palatine of Durham in 1638) was in the thirteenth year of Queen Elizabeth, A.D. 1571, as reported by Sir James Dyer, and was held in Tothill Fields, Westminster, "*non sine magna juris consultorum perturbatione*," saith Sir Henry Spelman, who was himself a witness of the ceremony. The form, as appears from the authors before cited, is as follows :

When the tenant in a writ of right pleads the general issue, viz., that he hath more right to hold than the demandant hath to recover, and offers to prove it by the body of his champion, which tender is accepted by the demandant; the tenant in the first place must produce his champion, who, by throwing down his glove as a gage or pledge, thus *wages* or stipulates battel with the champion of the demandant, who, by taking up the gage or glove, stipulates on his part to accept the challenge. The reason why it is waged by champions, and not by the parties themselves, in civil actions, is because, if any party to the suit dies, the suit must abate and be at an end for the present, and therefore no judgment could be given for the lands in question if either of the parties were slain in battel, and also that no person might claim an exemption from this trial, as was allowed in criminal cases, where the battel was waged in person.

A piece of ground is then in due time set out, of sixty feet square, enclosed with lists, and on one side a court erected for the judges of the court of common pleas, who attend there in their scarlet robes ; and also a bar is prepared for the learned serjeants at law. When the court sits, which ought to be by sunrising, proclamation is made for the parties and their champions, who are introduced by two knights, and are dressed in a coat of armour, with red sandals, bare-legged from the knee downwards, bareheaded, and with bare arms to the elbows. The weapons allowed them are only batons, or staves of an ell long, and a fore-cornered leather target ; so that death very seldom ensued this civil combat. In the court military, indeed, they fought with sword and lance, according to Spelman and Rushworth ; as likewise in France, only villeins fought with the buckler and baton, gentlemen armed at all points. And upon this and other circumstances, the president Montesquieu hath, with great ingenuity, not only deduced the impious custom of private duels upon imaginary points of honour, but hath also traced the heroic madness of knight-errantry, from the same original of judicial combats. But to proceed.

When the champions, thus armed with batons, arrive within the lists or place of combat, the champion of the tenant takes his adver-

sary by the hand, and makes oath that the tenements in dispute are
not the right of the demandant, and the champion of the demandant,
then taking the other by the hand, swears in the same manner that
they are; so that each champion is, or ought to be, thoroughly persuaded of the truth of the cause he fights for. Next an oath against
sorcery and enchantment is to be taken by both the champions, in
this or a similar form : "Hear this, ye justices, that I have this day
"neither eat, drank, nor have upon me, neither bone, stone, nor grass,
"nor any enchantment, sorcery, or witchcraft, whereby the law of
"God may be abased, or the law of the devil exalted. So help me
"God and his saints."*

The battel is thus begun, and the combatants are bound to fight till
the stars appear in the evening; and, if the champion of the tenant
can defend himself till the stars appear, the tenant shall prevail in
his cause, for it is sufficient for him to maintain his ground, and
make it a drawn battel, he being already in possession; but if victory
declares itself for either party, for him is judgment finally given.
This victory may arise from the death of either of the champions,
which indeed hath rarely happened; the whole ceremony, to say the
truth, being a near resemblance to certain rural athletic diversions,
which are probably derived from this original. Or victory is obtained if either champion proves *recreant*, that is, yields, and pronounces that horrible word of *craven*, a word of disgrace and obloquy
rather than of any determinate meaning. But a horrible word it,
indeed, is to the vanquished champion, since as a punishment to him
for forfeiting the land of his principal by pronouncing that shameful
word, he is condemned, as a recreant, *amittere liberam legem*, that is,
to become infamous, and not be accounted *liber et legalis homo*,
being supposed by the event to be proved foresworn, and therefore
never to be put upon a jury, or admitted as a witness in any cause.

This is the form of a trial by battel, which was the only decision
of a writ of right after the conquest till Henry II., by consent of
parliament, introduced the *grand assize*, a peculiar species of trial by
jury, in concurrence therewith, giving the tenant his choice of either
the one or the other. Which example of discountenancing these
judicial combats was imitated about a century afterwards in France,
by an edict of Louis the Pious, A.D. 1260, and soon after by the rest
of Europe. The establishment of this alternative, Glanvil, chief-
justice to Henry II., and probably his adviser herein, considers as a
most noble improvement, as in fact it was, of the law.

* In order to prevent any unfairness in the arms, or the use of any enchant-
ments, the champions appear to have been compelled sometimes to strip themselves of their accoutrements, and leave them under the care of an officer of
the palace, for the inspection of the judges; and that this was not always unnecessary, we may easily believe, as in the Year-book, 29 E. 3, p. 12, where
this was done in a suit between the bishop and earl of Salisbury, for Salisbury
Castle, the reporter says, "and it was said that the justices had found in the
coat of Shawel, who was the bishop's champion, several rolls of 'orisons and
sortileges.' "

WAGER OF LAW. [*Ante*, p. 381.]

The wager of law, *vadiatio legis*, is so called, because, as in the wager of battel, the defendent gave a pledge, gage, or *vadium*, to try the cause by battel, so here he was to put in sureties, or *vadios*, that at such a day he will make his law, that is, take the benefit the law has allowed him. For our ancestors considered that there were many cases where an innocent man, of good credit, might be overborne by a multitude of false witnesses, and therefore established this species of trial, by the oath of the defendant himself; for if he will absolutely swear himself not chargeable, and appears to be a person of reputation, he shall go free and for ever acquitted of the debt or other cause of action.

This method of trial is not only to be found in the codes of almost all the northern nations that broke in upon the Roman empire, and established petty kingdoms upon its ruins; but its original may also be traced as far back as the Mosaical. law. "If a man deliver unto "his neighbour an ass, or an ox, or a sheep, or any beast to keep, "and it die, or be hurt, or driven away, no man seeing it, then shall "an oath of the Lord be between them both, that he hath not put his "hand unto his neighbour's goods, and the owner of it shall accept "thereof, and he shall not make it good."

We shall likewise be able to discern a manifest resemblance between this species of trial and the canonical purgation of the popish clergy, when accused of any capital crime. The defendant, or person accused, was in both cases to make oath of his own innocence, and to produce a certain number of compurgators, who swore they believed his oath. Somewhat similar also to this is the *sacramentum decisionis*, or the voluntary and decisive oath of the civil law, where one of the parties to the suit, not being able to prove his charge, offers to refer the decision of the cause to the oath of his adversary, which the adversary was bound to accept, or tender the same proposal back again, otherwise the whole was taken as confessed by him. But though a custom somewhat similar to this prevailed formerly in the city of London,* yet in general the English law does not thus, like the civil, reduce the defendant, in case he is in the wrong, to the dilemma of either confession or perjury; but is indeed so tender of permitting the oath to be taken, even upon the defendent's own request, that it allows it only in a very few cases; and in those it has also devised other collateral remedies for the party injured, in which the defendant is excluded from his wager of law.

The manner of waging law is this. He that has waged, or given

* Sir W. Blackstone refers to the ancient customs of the Sheriffs' Court of London, an account of which will be found in the Liber Albus. A similar custom prevailed in some of the local courts of the more ancient towns in the kingdom, among which the Cinque Ports may be mentioned. A *reference to the oath of the defendant* is the law and daily practice of Scotland.

security, to make his law, brings with him into court eleven of his neighbours: a custom, which we find particularly described so early as in the league between Alfred and Guthrun the Dane; for by the old Saxon constitution every man's credit in courts of law depended upon the opinion which his neighbours had of his veracity. The defendant, then standing at the end of the bar, is admonished by the judges of the nature and danger of a false oath. And if he still persists, he is to repeat this or the like oath: " Hear this, ye " justices, that I do not owe unto Richard Jones the sum of ten pounds, " nor any penny thereof, in manner and form as the said Richard " hath declared against me, so help me God." And thereupon his eleven neighbours, or compurgators, shall avow upon their oaths, that they believe in their consciences, that he saith the truth; so that himself must be sworn *de fidelitate*, and the eleven *de creduli-tate*. It is held indeed by later authorities, that fewer than eleven compurgators will do: but Sir Edward Coke is positive that there must be this number; and his opinion not only seems founded upon better authority, but also upon better reason; for, as wager of law is equivalent to a verdict in the defendant's favour, it ought to be established by the same or equal testimony, namely, by the oath of *twelve* men.

In the old Swedish or Gothic constitution, wager of law was abso-lutely required in many *civil* cases; which Stiernhook, an author of their own, very justly charges as being the source of frequent perjury. This, he tells us, was owing to the popish ecclesiastics, who intro-duced this method of purgation from their canon law; and having sown a plentiful crop of oaths in all judicial proceedings, reaped afterwards an ample harvest of perjuries: for perjuries were punished in part by pecuniary fines, payable to the coffers of the church. But with us in England wager of law was never *required*; and was only *admitted*, where an action was brought upon such matters as might be supposed to be privately transacted between the parties; and wherein the defendant might be presumed to have made satisfaction without being able to prove it. Therefore it was only in actions of debt upon simple contract, actions of detinue, and of account, where the debt might have been paid, the goods restored, or the account balanced, without any evidence of either: it was only in these actions, I say, that the defendant was admitted to wage his law: so that wager of law did not lie when there was any speciality (as a bond or deed), to charge the defendant, for that would be cancelled, if satisfied, but when the debt grew by word only: nor did it lie in an action of debt, for arrears of an account, settled by auditors in a former action. And by such wager of law (when admitted) the plaintiff was perpetually barred; for the law, in the simplicity of ancient times, presumed that no one would forswear himself for any worldly thing.

A man outlawed, attainted for false verdict, or for conspiracy or perjury, or otherwise become infamous, as by pronouncing the horrible word in a trial by battel, was not permitted to wage his.

law. Neither was an infant under the age of twenty-one; and therefore, on the other hand, the defendant, where an infant was plaintiff, could not wage his law. But a feme-covert, when joined with her husband, might be admitted to wage her law; and an alien might do it in his own language. .

It was moreover a rule, that when a man was compellable by law to do anything, whereby he became creditor to another, the defendant in that case should not be permitted to wage his law; for then it would be in the power of any bad man to run in debt first, against the inclinations of his creditor, and afterwards to swear it away. But where the plaintiff had given voluntary credit to the defendant, there he might wage his law; for, by giving him such credit, the plaintiff had himself borne testimony that he was one whose character might be trusted. Upon this principle it was that in an action of debt against a prisoner by a gaoler for his victuals, the defendant could not wage his law; for the gaoler could not refuse the prisoner, and ought not to suffer him to perish for want of sustenance. But otherwise it would for the board or diet of a man at liberty. In an action of debt brought by an attorney for his fees, the defendant could not wage his law, because the plaintiff was compellable to be his attorney. And so, if a servant was retained according to the statute of labourers, 5 Eliz. c. 4, which obliged all single persons of a certain age, and not having other visible means of livelihood, to go out to service: in an action of debt for the wages of such a servant, the master could not wage his law, because the plaintiff was compellable to serve. But it had been otherwise had the hiring been by special contract, and not according to the statute.

In no case where a contempt, trespass, deceit, or any injury *with force*, was alleged against the defendant, was he permitted to wage his law; for it was impossible to presume he had satisfied the plaintiff his demand in such cases, where damages were uncertain, and left to be assessed by a jury. Nor would the law trust the defendant with an oath to discharge himself, where the private injury was coupled as it were with a public crime, that of force and violence; which would be equivalent to the purgation oath of the civil law, which ours has so justly rejected.

Executors and administrators, when charged for the debt of the deceased, were not admitted to wage their law; for no man could with a safe conscience wage law of another man's contract, that is, swear that he never entered into it, or at least that he privately discharged it. The king also had his prerogative; for, as all wager of law imported a reflection on the plaintiff for dishonesty, therefore there should be no such wager on actions brought by him. And this prerogative extended and was communicated to his debtor and accomptant; for, on a writ of quo minus, in the exchequer for a debt on simple contract, the defendant was not allowed to wager his law.

Thus the wager of law was never permitted, but where the defendant bore a fair and irreproachable character; and it also was confined to cases where a debt might be supposed to be discharged, or satisfaction made in private without any witnesses to attest it: and many other prudential restrictions accompanied this indulgence. But at length it was considered, that (even under all its restrictions) it threw too great a temptation in the way of indigent or profligate men; and therefore by degrees new remedies were devised, and new forms of action were introduced, wherein no defendant was at liberty to wage his law. So that ultimately no plaintiff need have apprehended any danger from the hardiness of his debtor's conscience, unless he voluntarily chose to rely on his adversary's veracity, by bringing his action in an obsolete instead of a modern form. Therefore it was, that, so long as wager of law subsisted, an action of debt was not brought upon a simple contract, that being supplied by an action of *trespass on the case* for the breach of a promise or *assumpsit*; wherein, though the specific debt cannot be recovered, yet damages may, equivalent to the specific debt. And, this being an action of trespass, no law could be waged therein. So, instead of an action of *detinue* to recover the very thing detained, an action of trespass on the case, in *trover* and *conversion* was brought, wherein, though the horse or other specific chattel cannot be had, yet the defendant shall pay damages for the conversion equal to the value of the chattel; and for this trespass also no wager of law was allowed. In the room of actions of *account*, a bill in equity was usually filed, wherein, though the defendant answers upon his oath, yet such oath is not conclusive to the plaintiff, but he may prove every article by other evidence, in contradiction to what the defendant has sworn. So that wager of law fell quite out of use, being avoided by the mode of bringing the action, long before it was abolished by the statute 3 & 4 Will. IV. c. 42, s. 13.

APPEAL.　[*Ante*, p. 543.]

An *appeal* was a prosecution at the suit of the subject, and not, as in ordinary cases, at the suit of the sovereign, as representing the public. In this sense, an appeal did not signify any complaint to a superior court of injustice done by an inferior one, which is the general use of the word; but an accusation by a private subject against another for some heinous crime, demanding punishment on account of the particular injury suffered, rather than for the offence against the public. This method of prosecution probably had its origin in those times when a private pecuniary satisfaction, called a *weregild*, was constantly paid to the party injured, or his relations, to expiate enormous offences. It was a custom derived to us, in common with other northern nations, from our ancestors, the ancient Germans; among whom, according to Tacitus, "*luitur homicidium* "*certo armentorum ac pecorum numero; recipitque satisfactionem* "*universa domus.*" In the same manner, by the Irish Brehon law, in case of murder, the Brehon or judge was used to compound between the murderer and the friends of the deceased who prosecuted him, by causing the malefactor to give unto them, or to the child or wife of him that was slain, a recompense, which they called an *eriach*. And thus we find in our Saxon laws (particularly those of King Athelstan) the several weregilds for homicide established in progressive order, from the death of the ceorl or peasant, up to that of the king himself. And in the laws of King Henry I., we have an account of what other offences were then redeemable by weregild, and what were not so. As therefore during the continuance of this custom a process was certainly given, for recovering the weregild by the party to whom it was due; it seems that when these offences by degrees grew no longer redeemable, the private process was still continued, in order to insure the infliction of punishment upon the offender, though the party injured was allowed no pecuniary compensation for the offence.

But though appeals were thus in the nature of prosecutions for some atrocious injury committed more immediately against an individual, yet it also was anciently permitted, that any subject might appeal another subject of high treason, either in the courts of common law, or in parliament, or (for treasons committed beyond the seas) in the court of the high constable and marshal. And so late as 1631 there was a trial by battel awarded in the Court of Chivalry on such an appeal of treason; but that in the first was *virtually* abolished by the statutes 5 Edw. III. c. 9, and 25 Edw. III. c. 24, and in the second *expressly* by statute 1 Hen. IV. c. 14. So that the only appeals continuing in force after these statutes, for things done within the realm, were appeals of felony and mayhem.

An appeal of *felony* might have been brought for crimes committed either against the parties themselves or their relations. The crimes against the parties themselves were *larceny, rape,* and *arson.* And for these, as well as for mayhem, the persons robbed, ravished, maimed, or whose houses were burnt, might institute this private process. The only crime against one's relation for which an appeal could be brought was that of *killing* him, by either murder or manslaughter. But this could not be brought by every relation, but only by the wife for the death of her husband, or by the heir male for the death of his ancestor; which heirship was also confined, by an ordinance of King Henry I., to the four nearest degrees of blood. It was given to the wife on account of the loss of her husband; therefore, if she married again, before or pending her appeal, it was lost and gone; or, if she married after judgment, she could not demand execution. The heir, as was said, must also have been heir male, and such a one as was the next heir by the course of the common law at the time of the killing of the ancestor. But this rule had three exceptions:—1. If the person killed left an innocent wife, she only, and not the heir, had the appeal; 2. If there were no wife, and the heir were accused of the murder, the person who next to him would have been heir male, must have brought the appeal;

2 o 2

3. If the wife killed her husband, the heir might appeal her of the death. And, by the statute of Gloucester, 6 Edw. 1. c. 9, all appeals of death must have been sued within a year and a day after the completion of the felony by the death of the party, which seems to be only declaratory of the old common law; for in the Gothic constitutions we find the same, " *præscriptio annalis, quæ currit* " *adversus actorem, si de homicidâ ei non constat intra annum a* " *cæde factâ, nec quenquam interea arguat et accuset.*"

These appeals might be brought previous to any indictment; and if the appellee were acquitted thereon, he could not be afterwards indicted for the same offence. In like manner as by the old Gothic constitution, if any offender gained a verdict in his favour, when prosecuted by the party injured, he was also understood to be acquitted of any crown prosecution for the same offence; but, on the contrary, if he made his peace with the king, still he might be prosecuted at the suit of the party. And so, with us, if a man were acquitted on an indictment of murder, or found guilty, and pardoned by the king, still he ought not (in strictness) to go at large, but be imprisoned or let to bail till the year and day were passed, by virtue of the statute 3 Hen. VII. c. 1, in order to be forthcoming to answer any appeal for the same felony, not having as yet been punished for it, though if he had been found guilty of manslaughter on an indictment, and had had the benefit of clergy, and suffered the judgment of the law, he could not afterwards be appealed; for it is a maxim in law, that " *nemo bis punitur pro eodem delicto.*" Before this statute was made, it was not usual to indict a man for homicide within the time limited for appeals, which produced very great inconvenience, of which more hereafter.

If the appellee were acquitted, the appellor (by virtue of the statute of Westm. 2, 13 Edw. I. c. 12) suffered one year's imprisonment and paid a fine to the king, besides restitution of damages to the party for the imprisonment and infamy which he had sustained; and if the appellor were incapable to make restitution, the abettors did it for him, and were also liable to imprisonment. This provision, as was foreseen by the author of Fleta, proved a great discouragement to appeals; so that henceforward they ceased to be in common use.

If the appellee were found guilty, he suffered the same judgment as if he had been convicted by indictment; but with this remarkable difference, that on an indictment, which is at the suit of the king, the king might pardon and remit the execution: on an appeal, which was at the suit of a private subject, to make an atonement for the private wrong, the king could no more pardon it than he could remit the damages recovered on an action of battery. In like manner as, while the weregild continued to be paid as a fine for homicide, it could not be remitted by the king's authority. And the ancient usage was, so late as Henry IV.'s time, that all the relations of the slain should drag the appellee to the place of execution—a custom founded upon that savage spirit of family resentment which prevailed universally through Europe after the irruption of the northern nations, and is peculiarly attended to in their several codes of law, and which prevails even now among the wild and untutored inhabitants of America, as if the finger of nature had pointed it out to mankind, in their rude and uncultivated state. However, the punishment of the offender might be remitted and discharged by the concurrence of all parties interested; and as the king by his pardon might frustrate an indictment, so the appellant by his release might discharge an appeal; "*nam quilibet potest renunciare juri, "pro se introducto.*"

After having become entirely obsolete, an *appeal* of murder was brought in the year 1818. To add if possible to the astonishment of the public at this resuscitation of a mode of proceeding, which had not been resorted to for nearly two centuries, the appellee waged his battel; his right to do so in the circumstances being solemnly argued and determined in his favour. The appellor, however, proceeded no further; and the legislature immediately afterwards abolished this species of prosecution altogether.

The reader will find the case *Ashford* v. *Thornton* fully reported in the first volume of the Reports of Barnwell and Alderson, p. 405.

TRIAL BY ORDEAL. [*Ante*, p. 551.]

This was the most ancient species of trial, and was peculiarly distinguished by the appellation of *judicium Dei*; and sometimes *vulgaris purgatio*, to distinguish it from the canonical purgation, which was by the oath of the party. It was of two sorts, either *fire*-ordeal, or *water*-ordeal; the former being confined to persons of higher rank, the latter to the common people. Both these might be performed by deputy: but the principal was to answer for the success of the trial; the deputy only venturing some corporal pain, for hire, or perhaps for friendship. Hence, perhaps, the common form of speech "of going through fire and water to serve another." Fire-ordeal was performed either by taking up in the hand, unhurt, a piece of red-hot iron, of one, two, or three pounds' weight; or else by walking, barefoot and blindfold, over nine red-hot ploughshares, laid lengthwise at unequal distances: and if the party escaped being hurt, he was adjudged innocent; but if it happened otherwise, as without collusion it usually did, he was then condemned as guilty. However, by this latter method, Queen Emma, the mother of Edward the Confessor, is mentioned to have cleared her character, when suspected of familiarity with Alwyn, Bishop of Winchester.

Water-ordeal was performed either by plunging the bare arm up to the elbow in boiling water, and escaping unhurt thereby, or by casting the person suspected into a river or pond of cold water, and if he floated therein without any action of swimming, it was deemed an evidence of his guilt, but if he sunk he was acquitted. It is easy to trace out the traditional relics of this water-ordeal in the ignorant barbarity practised in many countries to discover witches by casting them into a pool of water, and drowning them to prove their innocence. And in the Eastern Empire, the fire-ordeal was used to the same purpose by the Emperor Theodore Lascaris, who, attributing his sickness to magic, caused all those whom he suspected to handle the hot iron: thus joining (as has been well remarked) to the most dubious crime in the world the most dubious proof of innocence.

And indeed this purgation by ordeal seems to have been very ancient and very universal in the times of superstitious barbarity. It was known to the ancient Greeks: for in the " Antigone " of Sophocles, a person suspected by Creon of a misdemeanor declares himself ready " to handle hot iron, and to walk over fire," in order to manifest his innocence: which, the scholiast tells us, was then a very usual purgation. And Grotius gives us many instances of water-ordeal in Bithynia, Sardinia, and other places. There is also a very peculiar species of water-ordeal said to prevail among the Indians on the coast of Malabar, where a person accused of any enormous crime is obliged to swim over a large river abounding with crocodiles, and if he escapes unhurt he is reputed innocent. As in Siam, besides the usual methods of fire and water ordeal, both parties are sometimes exposed to the fury of a tiger let loose for that purpose, and if the beast spares either, that person is accounted innocent; if neither, both are held to be guilty; but if he spares both, the trial is incomplete, and they proceed to a more certain criterion.

One cannot but be astonished at the folly and impiety of pronouncing a man guilty unless he was cleared by a miracle, and of expecting that all the powers of nature should be suspended by an immediate interposition of Providence to save the innocent, whenever it was presumptuously required. And yet in England, so late as King John's time, we find grants to the bishops and clergy to use the *judicium ferri, aquæ, et ignis.* And, both in England and Sweden, the clergy presided at this trial, and it was only performed in the churches or in other consecrated ground : for which Stiernhook gives the reason : " *non defuit illis operæ et laboris pretium ; semper enim* " *ab ejusmodi judicio aliquid lucri sacerdotibus obveniebat.*" But to give it its due praise, we find the canon law very early declaring against trial by ordeal, or *vulgaris purgatio,* as being the fabric of the devil, " *cum sit contra præceptum Domini, non tentabis Dominum* " *Deum tuum.*" Upon this authority, though the canons themselves were of no validity in England, it was thought proper (as had been done in Denmark above a century before) to disuse and abolish this trial entirely in our courts of justice by an act of parliament in 3 Henry III., according to Sir Edward Coke, or rather by an order of the king in council.

TRIAL BY THE CORSNED. [*Ante*, p. 551.]

Another species of purgation, somewhat similar to the former, but probably sprung from a presumptuous abuse of revelation in the ages of dark superstition, was the trial by the *corsned*, or morsel of execration : being a piece of cheese or bread, of about an ounce in weight, which was consecrated with a form of exorcism, desiring of the Almighty that it might cause convulsions and paleness, and find no passage, if the man was really guilty, but might turn to health and nourishment if he was innocent ; as the water of jealousy among the Jews was, by God's special appointment, to cause the belly to swell, and the thigh to rot, if the woman was guilty of adultery. This corsned was then given to the suspected person, who at the same time also received the holy sacrament ;[*] if indeed the corsned was not, as some have suspected, the sacramental bread itself, till the subsequent invention of transubstantiation preserved it from profane uses with a more profound respect than formerly. Our historians assure us that Godwin, Earl of Kent, in the reign of King Edward the Confessor, abjuring the death of the king's brother, at last appealed to his corsned, "*per buccellam deglutiendam abjuravit,*" which stuck in his throat and killed him. This custom has been long since gradually abolished, though the remembrance of it still subsists in certain phrases of abjuration retained among the common people.

However, we cannot but remark, that though in European countries this custom most probably arose from an abuse of revealed religion, yet credulity and superstition will, in all ages and in all climates, produce the same or similar effects. And therefore we shall not be surprised to find, that in the kingdom of Pegu there subsisted a trial by the corsned, very similar to that of our ancestors, only substituting raw rice instead of bread. And, in the kingdom of Monomotapa, they have a method of deciding law suits equally whimsical and uncertain. The witness for the plaintiff chews the bark of a tree endued with an emetic quality, which, being sufficiently masticated, is then infused in water, which is given the defendant to drink. If his stomach rejects it, he is condemned ; if it stays with him, he is absolved, unless the plaintiff will drink some of the same water ; and if it stays with him also, the suit is left undetermined.

[*] " If a friendless servant of the altar be charged with an accusation, who has no support to his oath, let him go to the corsned, and then thereat fare as God will, unless he may clear himself on the housel." (LL. Canut. c. 6 ; 1 Thorpe, 363.)

TRIAL BY BATTEL. [*Ante*, p. 551.]

The nature of the trial by battel, in cases of civil injury, that is, upon issue joined in a writ of right, has just been explained. And it might be had, as we have seen, in an appeal of felony. I have here, therefore, only to add, that it might be demanded at the election of the appellee, and that it was carried on with equal solemnity as that on a writ of right; but with this difference, that there each party might hire a champion, but here they must have fought in their proper persons. And therefore if the appellant were a woman, a priest, an infant, or of the age of sixty, or lame or blind, he or she might counterplead and refuse the wager of battel, and compel the appellee to put himself upon the country. Also peers of the realm, bringing an appeal, could not be challenged to wage battel, on account of the dignity of their persons; nor the citizens of London, by special charter. So likewise if the crime were notorious, as if the thief were taken with the *mainour*, or the murderer in a room with a bloody knife, the appellant might refuse the tender of battel from the appellee; for it was unreasonable that an innocent man should stake his life against one who was already half-convicted.

The form and manner of waging battel upon appeals were much the same as upon a writ of right; only the oaths of the two combatants were vastly more striking and solemn. The appellee, when appealed of felony, pleaded *not guilty*, and threw down his glove, and declared he would defend the same by his body; the appellant took up the glove, and replied that he was ready to make good the appeal, body for body. And thereupon the appellee, taking the book in his right hand, and in his left the right hand of his antagonist, swore to this effect : " *Hoc audi, homo, quem per manum teneo*," &c. " Hear this, O man, whom I hold by the hand, who callest thyself " John by the name of baptism, that I, who call myself Thomas by " the name of baptism, did not feloniously murder thy father, William " by name, nor am any way guilty of the said felony. So help me " God, and the saints; and this I will defend against thee by my body, " as this court shall award." To which the appellant replied, holding the Bible and his antagonist's hand in the same manner as the other: " Hear this, O man, whom I hold by the hand, who callest thyself " Thomas by the name of baptism, that thou art perjured; and there- " fore perjured, because that thou feloniously didst murder my father, " William by name. So help me God, and the saints; and this I will " prove against thee by my body, as this court shall award."* The battel was then to be fought with the same weapons, viz., batons,

---

* There is a striking resemblance between this process and that of the court of Areopagus, at Athens, for murder, wherein the prosecutor and prisoner were both sworn in the most solemn manner; the prosecutor, that he was related to the deceased (for none but near relations were permitted to prosecute in that court), and that the prisoner was the cause of his death; the prisoner, that he was innocent of the charge against him. (Pott. Antiq. b. 1, c. 19.)

the same solemnity, and the same oath against amulets and sorcery, that were used in the civil combat ; and if the appellee were so far vanquished, that he could not or would not fight any longer, he was adjudged to be hanged immediately ; and then, as well as if he were killed in battel, Providence was deemed to have determined in favour of the truth, and his blood was attainted. But if he killed the appellant, or could maintain the fight from sunrising till the stars appeared in the evening, he was acquitted. So also if the appellant became recreant, and pronounced the horrible word of *craven*, he lost his *liberam legem*, and became infamous ; and the appellee recovered his damages, and also was for ever quit, not only of the appeal, but of all indictments likewise for the same offence. Trial by battel was abolished in 1819 by the statute 59 Geo. III. c. 46.*

BENEFIT OF CLERGY. [*Ante*, pp. 514, 561.]

Clergy, the *privilegium clericale*, or, in common speech, *the benefit of clergy*, had its origin from the pious regard paid by Christian princes to the church in its infant state, and the ill use which the popish ecclesiastics soon made of that pious regard. The exemptions which they granted to the church were principally of two kinds : 1. Exemption of *places* consecrated to religious duties from criminal arrests, which was the foundation of sanctuaries ; 2. Exemption of the *persons* of clergymen from criminal process before the secular judge in a few particular cases, which was the true origin and meaning of the *privilegium clericale*.

But the clergy, increasing in wealth, power, honour, number, and interest, began soon to set up for themselves ; and that which they obtained by the favour of the civil government, they now claimed as their inherent right, and as a right of the highest nature, indefeasible, and *jure divino*. By their canons, therefore, and constitutions, they endeavoured at, and where they met with easy princes obtained, a vast extension of these exemptions, as well in regard to the crimes themselves, of which the list became quite universal, as in regard to the persons exempted, among whom were at length comprehended not only every little subordinate officer belonging to the church or clergy, but even many that were totally laymen.

In England, however, although the usurpations of the pope were

* The last time, previously to the case of *Ashford v. Thornton*, before referred to, that the trial by battel was awarded in this country was in the case of Lord Rao and Mr. Ramsay, in the 7 Car. I. The king, by his commission, appointed a constable of England to preside at the trial, who proclaimed a day for the duel, on which the combatants were to appear with a spear, a long sword, a short sword, and a dagger ; but the combat was prorogued to a further day, before which the king revoked the commission. An account of the proceedings will be found in vol. 11 Harg. St. Tr. p. 124.

very many and grievous, till Henry VIII. entirely exterminated his supremacy, yet a total exemption of the clergy from secular jurisdiction could never be thoroughly effected, though often endeavoured by the clergy; and therefore, though the ancient *privilegium clericale* was in *some* capital cases, yet it was not *universally*, allowed. And in those particular cases, the use was for the bishop or ordinary to demand his clerks to be remitted out of the king's courts as soon as they were indicted: concerning the allowance of which demand there was for many years a great uncertainty, till at length it was finally settled in the reign of Henry VI., that the prisoner should first be arraigned, and might either *then* claim his benefit of clergy, by way of declinatory plea, or *after conviction* by way of arresting judgment. This latter way was most usually practised, as it was more to the satisfaction of the court to have the crime previously ascertained by confession or the verdict of a jury; and also it was more advantageous to the prisoner himself, who might possibly be acquitted, and so need not the benefit of his clergy at all.

Originally the law held, that no man should be admitted to the privilege of clergy but such as had the *habitum et tonsuram clericalem*. But in process of time a much wider and more comprehensive criterion was established: every one that could read, a mark of great learning in those days of ignorance and her sister superstition, being accounted a clerk or *clericus*, and allowed the benefit of clerkship, though neither initiated in holy orders, nor trimmed with the clerical tonsure. But when learning, by means of the invention of printing, and other concurrent causes, began to be more generally disseminated than formerly, and reading was no longer a competent proof of clerkship, or being in holy orders, it was found that as many laymen as divines were admitted to the *privilegium clericale*, and therefore, by statute 4 Hen. VII. c. 13, a distinction was once more drawn between mere lay scholars and clerks that were really in orders. And though it was thought reasonable still to mitigate the severity of the law with regard to the former, yet they were not put upon the same footing with actual clergy: being subjected to a slight degree of punishment, and not allowed to claim the clerical privilege more than once. Accordingly, the statute directed that no person once admitted to the benefit of clergy should be admitted thereto a second time unless he produced his orders: and in order to distinguish their persons, all laymen who were allowed this privilege were to be burnt with a hot iron in the brawn of the left thumb. This distinction, between learned laymen and real clerks in orders, was abolished for a time by the statutes 28 Hen. VIII. c. 1, and 32 Hen. VIII. c. 3, but it is held to have been virtually restored by statute 1 Ed. VI. c. 12; which statute also enacts, that lords of parliament and peers of the realm, having place and voice in parliament, may have the benefit of their peerage, equivalent to that of clergy, for the first offence (although they cannot read, and without being burnt in the hand), for all offences then clergyable to commoners, and also for the crimes of housebreaking, highway robbery, horse-stealing, and robbing of churches.

After this, burning, the laity, and before it the real clergy, were discharged from the sentence of the law in the king's courts, and delivered over to the ordinary, to be dealt with according to the ecclesiastical canons. Whereupon the ordinary, not satisfied with the proofs adduced in the profane secular court, set himself formally to work to make a purgation of the offender by a new canonical trial, although he had been previously convicted by his country, or perhaps by his own confession. This trial was held before the bishop in person, or his deputy, and by a jury of twelve clerks: and there, first, the party himself was required to make oath of his own inno- cence; next there was to be oath of twelve compurgators, who swore they believed he spoke the truth; then witnesses were to be ex- amined upon oath, but on behalf of the prisoner only; and, lastly, the jury were to bring in their verdict upon oath, which usually acquitted the prisoner, otherwise, if a clerk, he was degraded or put to penance. Mr. Justice Hobart remarks with much indignation the vast complication of perjury and subornation of perjury in this solemn farce of a mock trial; the witnesses, the compurgators, and the jury being all of them partakers in the guilt; the delinquent party also, though convicted before on the clearest evidence, and conscious of his own offence, yet was permitted and almost compelled to swear himself not guilty; nor was the good bishop himself, under whose countenance this scene of wickedness was daily transacted, by any means exempt from a share of it. And yet, by this purgation, the party was restored to his credit, his liberty, his lands, and his capacity of purchasing afresh, and was entirely made a new and an innocent man.

This scandalous prostitution of oaths, and the forms of justice, in the almost constant acquittal of felonious clerks by purgation, was the occasion that, upon very heinous and notorious circumstances of guilt, the temporal courts would not trust the ordinary with the trial of the offender, but delivered over to him the convicted clerk, *absque purgatione facienda;* in which situation the clerk convict could not make purgation; but was to continue in prison during life, and was incapable of acquiring any personal property, or re- ceiving the profits of his lands, unless the king should please to pardon him. Both these courses were in some degree exceptionable; the latter being perhaps too rigid, as the former was productive of the most abandoned perjury. As therefore these mock trials took their rise from factious and popish tenets, tending to exempt one part of the nation from the general municipal law; it became high time, when the reformation was thoroughly established, to abolish so vain and impious a ceremony.

Accordingly the statute 18 Eliz. c. 7, enacted, that, for the avoid- ing of such perjuries and abuses after the offender had been allowed his clergy, he should not be delivered to the ordinary as formerly; but, upon such allowance and burning in the hand, he should forth- with be enlarged and delivered out of prison; with proviso, that the judge might if he thought fit, continue the offender in gaol for any

time not exceeding a year. And thus the law continued, for above
a century, unaltered, except only that the statute 21 Jac. I. c. 6,
allowed that women convicted of simple larcenies under the value
of ten shillings should (not properly have the benefit of clergy, for
they were not called upon to read; but) be burned in the hand, and
whipped, stocked, or imprisoned, for any time not exceeding a year.
And a similar indulgence, by the statutes 3 & 4 W. & M. c. 9, and
4 & 5 W. & M. c. 24, was extended to women, guilty of any clergyable felony whatsoever; who were allowed once to claim the benefit
of *the statute*, in like manner as men might claim the benefit of
clergy, and to be discharged upon being burned in the hand, and
imprisoned for any time not exceeding a year. The punishment of
burning in the *hand* being found ineffectual, was also changed by
statute 10 & 11 Will. III. c. 23, into burning in the most visible
part of the left *cheek*, nearest the nose: but such an indelible stigma
being found by experience to render offenders desperate, this provision was repealed about seven years afterwards, by statute 5 Ann.
c. 6; and till that period all women, all peers of parliament and
peeresses, and all male commoners who could read, were discharged
in all clergyable felonies; the males absolutely, if clerks in orders;
and other commoners, both male and female, upon branding; and
peers and peeresses without branding, for the first offence: yet all
liable (excepting peers and peeresses), if the judge saw occasion, to
imprisonment not exceeding a year. And those men who could not
read, if under the degree of peerage, were hanged.

Afterwards, indeed, it was considered that education and learning
were no extenuations of guilt, but quite the reverse; and that, if
the punishment of death for simple felony was too severe for those
who had been liberally instructed, it was, *à fortiori*, too severe for
the ignorant also. And thereupon, by the same statute 5 Ann. c. 6,
it was enacted that the benefit of clergy should be granted to all
those who were entitled to ask it, without requiring them to read
by way of conditional merit. And experience having shown that so
very universal a lenity was frequently inconvenient, and an encouragement to commit the lower degrees of felony; and that,
though capital punishments were too rigorous for these inferior
offences, yet no punishment at all (or next to none) was as much
too gentle; it was further enacted by the same statute, that when
any person was convicted of any theft, or larceny, and burnt in the
hand for the same according to the ancient law, he should also, at
the discretion of the judge, be committed to the house of correction
or public workhouse, to be there kept to hard labour, for any time
not less than six months, and not exceeding two years; with a power
of inflicting a double confinement in case of the party's escape from
the first. And it was also enacted by the statutes 4 Geo. I. c. 11,
and 6 Geo. I. c. 28, that when any persons should be convicted of
any larceny, either grand or petit, or any felonious stealing or taking
of money or goods and chattels either from the person or the house
of any other, or in any other manner, and who by the law should
be entitled to the benefit of clergy, and liable only to the penalties

of burning in the hand or whipping, the court in their discretion, instead of such burning in the hand or whipping, might direct such offenders to be transported to America (or, by statute 19 Geo. III. c. 74, to any other parts beyond the seas) for seven years : and if they returned or were seen at large in this kingdom within that time, it should be felony without benefit of clergy. By the subsequent statutes 16 Geo. II. c. 15, and 8 Geo. III. c. 15, provisions were made for the more speedy and effectual execution of the laws relating to transportation, and the conviction of such as transgress them. But by the statute 19 Geo. III. c. 72, all offenders liable to transportation might in lieu thereof, at the discretion of the judges, be employed, if males (except in the case of petty larceny), in hard labour for the benefit of some public navigation ; or, whether males or females, might in all cases be confined to hard labour in certain penitentiary houses, erected by virtue of the said act, for the several terms therein specified, but in no case exceeding seven years, with a power of subsequent mitigation, and even of reward, in case of their good behaviour. But if they escaped and were retaken, for the first time an addition of three years was made to the term of their confinement, and a second escape was felony without benefit of clergy.

In forming the plan of these penitentiary houses, the principal objects were, by sobriety, cleanliness, and medical assistance, by a regular series of labour, by solitary confinement during the intervals of work, and by due religious instruction, to preserve and amend the health of the unhappy offenders, to inure them to habits of industry, to guard them from pernicious company, to accustom them to serious reflection, and to teach them both the principles and practice of every Christian and moral duty. And if the whole of this plan had been properly executed, and its defects timely supplied, such a reformation might have been effected in the lower classes of mankind, and such a gradual scale of punishment been affixed to all gradations of guilt, as in time to supersede the necessity of capital punishment, except for very atrocious crimes.

It was also enacted by the statute 19 Geo. III. c. 74, that, instead of burning in the hand (which was sometimes too slight and sometimes too disgraceful a punishment), the court in all clergyable felonies might impose a pecuniary fine ; or (except in the case of manslaughter) might order the offender to be once or oftener, but not more than thrice, either publicly or privately whipped ; such private whipping (to prevent collusion or abuse) to be inflicted in the presence of two witnesses, and in case of female offenders in the presence of females only: which fine or whipping had the same consequence as burning in the hand : and the offender so fined or whipped was equally liable to a subsequent detainer or imprisonment.

In this state did the benefit of clergy stand at the period of its abolition, very considerably different from its original institution : the wisdom of the English legislature having, in the course of a long and laborious process, extracted by a noble alchemy rich medicines out of poisonous ingredients; and converted, by gradual mutations, what was at first an unreasonable exemption of particular popish ecclesiastics, into a merciful mitigation of the general law, with respect to capital punishment.

From the whole of this detail we may collect that, however in times of ignorance and superstition that monster in true policy may for a while subsist, of a body of men residing in the bowels of a state, and yet independent of its laws; yet, when learning and rational religion have a little enlightened men's minds, society can no longer endure an absurdity so gross as must destroy its very fundamentals. For by the original contract of government, the price of protection by the united force of individuals is that of obedience to the united will of the community. This united will is declared in the laws of the land: and that united force is exerted in their due and universal execution.

Let us now see to what *persons* the benefit of clergy was allowed; and this must be chiefly collected from what has been observed in the preceding article. For, upon the whole, we may pronounce that all clerks in orders were without any branding, and of course without any transportation, fine, or whipping (for those were only substituted in lieu of the other), to be admitted to this privilege, and immediately discharged, and this as often as they offended. Again, all lords of parliament, and peers of the realm having place and voice in parliament, by the statute 1 Ed. VI. c. 12 (which was likewise held to extend to peeresses: *Duchess of Kingston's* case in parliament, April 22, 1776), were discharged in all clergyable and other felonies provided for by the act, without any burning in the hand, or imprisonment, or other punishment substituted in its stead, in the same manner as real clerks convict: but this was only for the first offence. Lastly, all the commons of the realms, not in orders, whether male or female, were for the first offence to be discharged of the capital punishment of felonies within the benefit of clergy, upon being burnt in the hand, whipped, or fined, or suffering a discretionary imprisonment in the common goal, the house of correction, one of the penitentiary houses, or in the places of labour for the benefit of some navigation; or, in case of larceny, upon being transported for seven years, if the court thought proper. It has been said that Jews and other infidels and heretics were not capable of the benefit of clergy till after the statute 5 Ann. c. 6, as being under a legal incapacity for orders. But I much question whether this was ever ruled for law, since the reintroduction of the Jews into England, in the time of Oliver Cromwell; the statute of Queen Anne having certainly made no alteration in this respect: it only dispensing with the necessity of reading in those persons who, in case they could read, were before the act entitled to the benefit of their clergy.

For what *crimes* let us next inquire was the *privilegium clericale,* or benefit of clergy, to be allowed? And it is to be observed that, neither in high treason, nor in petty larceny, nor in any mere misdemeanors, was it indulged at the common law; and therefore we may lay it down for a rule that it was allowable only in petit treason and capital felonies: which for the most part became legally entitled to this indulgence by the statute *de clero*, 25 Edw. III. st. 3, c. 4, which provided that clerks convict for treasons or felonies, touching other persons than the king himself or his royal majesty, should have the privilege of holy church. But yet it was not allowable in all felonies whatsoever: for in some it was denied even by the common law, viz., *insidiatio viarum*, or lying in wait for one on the highway; *depopulatio agrorum*, or destroying and ravaging a county; and *combustio domorum*, or arson, that is, the burning of houses; all of which are a kind of hostile acts, and in some degree border upon treason. And farther, all these identical crimes, together with petit treason, and very many acts of felony, were ousted of clergy by particular acts of parliament. Upon all which statutes for excluding clergy I shall only observe, that they were nothing else but the restoring of the law to the same rigour of capital punishment in the first offence that was exerted before the *privilegium clericale* was at all indulged, and which was still exerted upon a second offence in almost all kinds of felonies, unless committed by clerks actually in orders. But so tender was the law of inflicting capital punishment in the first instance for any inferior felony, that notwithstanding by the marine law, as declared in statute 28 Hen. VIII. c. 15, the benefit of clergy was not allowed in any case whatsoever; yet, when offences were committed within the admiralty jurisdiction, which would be clergyable if committed by land, the constant course was to acquit and discharge the prisoner. And to conclude this head of inquiry, we may observe the following rules: 1. That in all felonies, whether created by statute or by common law, clergy was allowable, unless taken away by express words of an act of parliament. 2. That where clergy was taken away from the principal, it was not of course taken away from the accessory, unless he were also particularly included in the words of the statute. 3. That when the benefit of clergy was taken away from the *offence* (as in case of murder, robbery, rape, and burglary), a principal in the second degree being present, aiding and abetting the crime, was as well excluded from his clergy as he that was principal in the first degree. But, 4. That where it was only taken away from the *person committing* the offence (as in the case of stabbing, or committing larceny in a dwelling-house, or privately from the person), his aiders and abettors were not excluded, through the tenderness of the law, which determined that such statutes should be taken literally.

Lastly, let us observe what the consequences were to the party of allowing him this benefit of clergy. I speak not of the branding, fine, whipping, imprisonment, or transportation: which were rather concomitant conditions than consequences of receiving this indulgence. The consequences were such as affected his present interest, and future credit, and capacity: as having been once a felon, but now purged from that guilt by the privilege of clergy, which operated as a kind of statute pardon.

And we may observe, 1. That by his conviction he forfeited all his goods to the king, which being once vested in the crown, should not afterwards be restored to the offender. 2. That, after conviction, and till he received the judgment of the law, by branding, or some of its substitutes, or else was pardoned by the king, he was to all intents and purposes a felon, and subject to all the disabilities and other incidents of a felon. 3. That after burning, or its substitute, or pardon, he was discharged for ever of that and all other felonies before committed, within the benefit of clergy; but not of felonies from which such benefit was excluded, and this by statutes 8 Eliz. c. 4, and 18 Eliz. c. 7. 4. That by the burning, or its substitute, or the pardon of it, he was restored to all capacities and credits, and the possession of his lands, as if he had never been convicted. 5. That what has been said with regard to the advantages of commoners and laymen, subsequent to the burning in the hand, was equally applicable to all peers and clergymen, although never branded at all, or subjected to other punishment in its stead. For they had the same privileges, without any burning, or any substitute for it, which others were entitled to after it.

Notwithstanding, however, the various legislative provisions by which it was thus from time to time attempted to modify the operation of the *privilegium clericale*, so as to allow it to remain a part of the complicated system of punishment which formerly prevailed, its total abolition necessarily formed a part of those measures for consolidating and amending the criminal law, which were adopted by the legislature in the reign of George IV. The various acts of parliament I have referred to were accordingly repealed by the statute 7 & 8 Geo. IV. c. 27; and the privilege itself at the same time entirely abolished by the statute 7 & 8 Geo. IV. c. 28. But as the effect of this would have been to leave no punishment for any felony but death, it was at the same time enacted that no person convicted of felony should thereafter suffer capitally.

A doubt having been started whether the act 1 Edw. VI. c. 2, retaining the benefit of clergy to lords of parliament and peers of the realm, might not be in force notwithstanding the statute 7 & 8 Geo. IV. c. 28, it was specially repealed by 4 & 5 Vict. c. 22; and every lord of parliament or peer of the realm having place or voice in parliament, against whom any indictment for felony may be found, must now plead to such indictment, and upon conviction is liable to the same punishment as any other of the queen's subjects.

GENERAL INDEX.

Persons of ill fame, 523.
Petit jury, 541, 542.
Petit serjeanty, 140.
Petition of Right, 312, 353, 354.
  proceedings by, in Chancery, 354.
Petitioning, right of, 22.
  tumultuous, 482, n.
Petty-Bag Office, 354.
Petty constables, 80.
Petty larceny, 510, n.
Petty sessions, 529.
Piepoudre, court of, 278, 530, n.
Pictures, immoral, 453.
Piracy, 455.
Piscary, 129.
Placemen excluded from the House of
  Commons, 33.
Plague, 487.
Plea, in abatement or in bar, 371.
Pleas in abatement, in civil actions, 371.
  to indictment, 543.
  in bar, in civil actions, requisites of, 372.
  in equity, 429.
  to an indictment, 545, 549.
  to the jurisdiction, in civil cases, 371.
  in criminal cases, 548.
Pleadings, formerly viva voce, now in
  writing, 368.
Pleas of the Crown, 283, 437.
Pledge, 246.
Plough-bote, 343.
Poaching, 495.
Pocket-sheriffs, 77.
Police, 80, 489.
Police, public, offences against, 487, 489, 493.
Policy, 249.
Political liberty, 17.
Polls, challenge to the, 386.
Poor, 81.
  Law Amendment Act, 82.
  laws, history of, 81.
  settlement of the, 81.
Popish priests, laws against, 451.
Ports and havens, 63.
Posse comitatus, 77, 409.
Possession, estate in, 159.
  right of, 167.
Possibility, tenant in tail, after possibility
  of issue extinct, 150.
Post fine, 211.
Post-office duties, 73.
Postea, 397.
Poundage, 272.
Pound-breach, what, and remedy for, 317.
Power of attorney, forgery of, 520.
Powder-magazines, 499.
Præcipe, 328.
Prebendary, 88.
Precedents, authority of, 9.
Pre-emption, 68.
Premises in a deed, 194.
Prerogative, different kinds of, 56.
  contempts of, 473.
  offences against, 463.
  titles to chattels by, 232.
Prerogative Court of Canterbury, 291, n.
Prescription, title by, 181.
  distinguished from custom, 182.
Presentation, 91.
Presentment, prosecution by, 540
President of the Council, 53.

Presumptions, 392.
Presumptive evidence, 392.
Prevention of crime, homicide for, 496.
Previous conviction, effect of, 533.
Primer fine, 211.
Primer seisin, 136.
Prince of Wales, 51.
Princes of the blood royal, 51.
Principal, in crimes, 444.
Prints, copyright in, 230.
Prison, breach of, 475.
Private Act of Parliament, 209.
Private property, offences against, 510.
Privilege of Parliament, 26.
Privileged communications, 309.
Privy Council, 53.
  Judicial Committee of, 291.
  jurisdiction in lunacy, 54.
  in ecclesiastical causes, 291.
Privy purse, 75.
Privy seal and signet, 458, 520.
Prize Court, 292.
Prizes, Admiralty jurisdiction as to, 301.
Probate, Court of, 292.
  jurisdiction of, 300.
Probate, 263.
Procedendo, writ of, 301.
  writ of, for refusal or neglect of justice,
  301.
Process, ancient, to compel appearance in,
  in the courts of law, 360.
  modern, by writ of summons, 360.
  ancient, in the Court of Chancery, 358.
  modern, to compel an appearance, 361,
  363.
  upon an indictment, 543.
  obstructing, offence of, 475.
  obstructing, 475.
Prochein amy, 110.
Præmunire, 466, 569.
  how incurred, 470.
  punishment of, 471.
  statutes of, 469, 470.
Profanation of Sunday, 453.
Prohibition, writ of, 303.
  in what cases it issues, 303.
  proceeding upon, 303.
Promise, what it is, 321.
  remedy for breach of, 322.
Promissory note, 252.
Property, origin of, 121.
  injuries to, personal, 316.
  right to private, 21.
  cheating purchaser of, 317.
Property-tax, 73.
Prorogation of Parliament, 38.
Prosecution of offenders, 540.
Protection of children, 107.
  of ambassadors, 364.
Protest of bill of exchange, 252.
Protestant Dissenters, 450.
Protestant Succession, 48.
Provincial constitutions, 12.
Proving will in Chancery, 427.
Provisions, papal, 467.
Provisions, selling when bad, offence of,
  488.
Proviso, trial by, 385.
Provisors, statutes against, 469.
Proxies in the House of Lords, 29.
Public Act of Parliament, 13.

CPSIA information can be obtained
at www.ICGtesting.com
Printed in the USA
LVHW080334230120
644400LV00008B/319